Rick Steves's

GREECE
ATHENS & THE
PELOPONNESE

Rick Steves with Cameron Hewitt and Gene Openshaw

D0428429

Jun 2018

CONTENTS

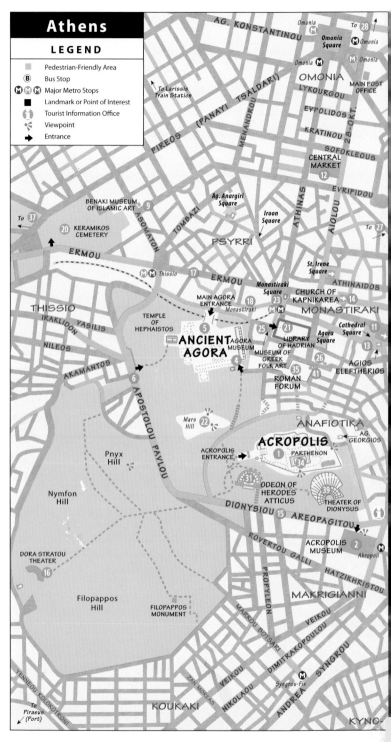

SIGHTS

1. Acropolis
2. Acropolis Museum
3. Adrianou Street
4. Agora Museum
5. Ancient Agora
6. Apostolou Pavlou Street
7. Arch of Hadrian
8. Benaki Museum of Greek History & Culture
9. Benaki Mus. of Islamic Art
10. Byzantine & Christian Mus.
11. Cathedral (Mitropolis)
12. Central Market
13. Church of Agios Eleftherios
14. Church of Kapnikarea
15. Dionysiou Areopagitou St.
16. Dora Stratou Theater
17. Ermou Street
18. Flea Market
19. Jewish Museum
20. Keramikos Cemetery
21. Library of Hadrian
22. Mars Hill (Areopagus)
23. Monastiraki Square
24. Museum of Cycladic Art
25. Museum of Greek Folk Art (opens in 2019)
26. Museum of Greek Popular Instruments
27. To Mus. of the City of Athens
28. To National Archaeological Museum & Exarchia District
29. National Garden
30. National War Museum
31. Odeon of Herodes Atticus
32. Panathenaic (Olympic) Stadium
33. Parliament
34. Parthenon
35. Roman Forum
36. Syntagma Square
37. To Technopolis & Gazi District
38. Temple of Olympian Zeus
39. Theater of Dionysus
40. Tomb of the Unknown Soldier & Evzone Guards
41. Tower of the Winds
42. Zappeion

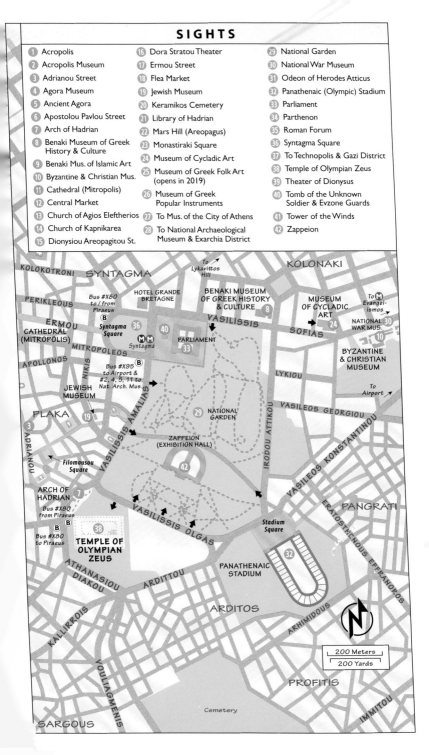

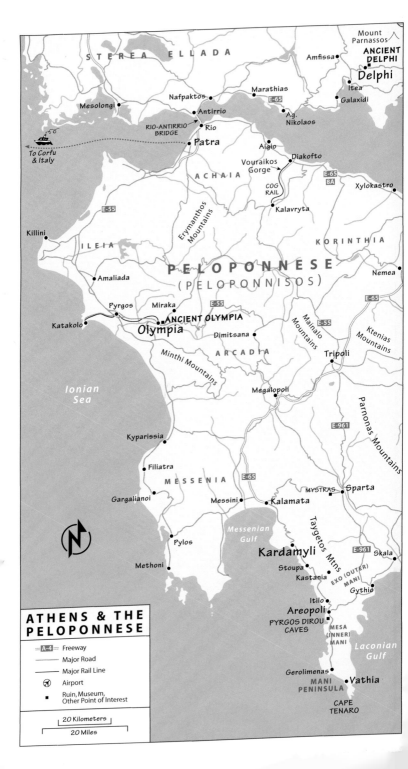

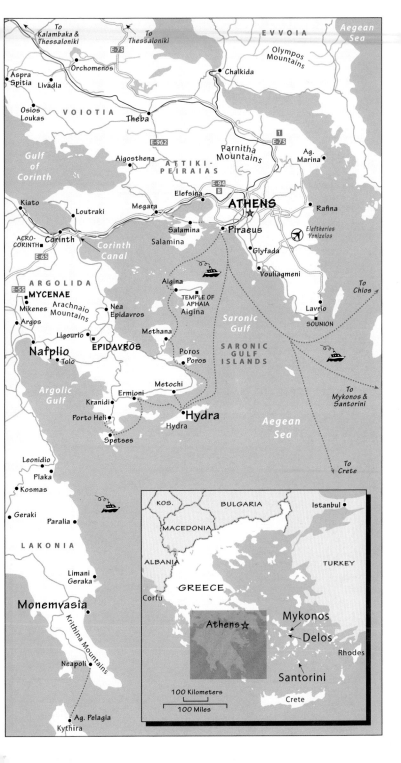

GREECE
ATHENS & THE
PELOPONNESE

Welcome to Rick Steves' Europe

Travel is intensified living—maximum thrills per minute and one of the last great sources of legal adventure. Travel is freedom. It's recess, and we need it.

I discovered a passion for European travel as a teen and have been sharing it ever since—through my tours, public

television and radio shows, and travel guidebooks. Over the years, I've taught thousands of travelers how to best enjoy Europe's blockbuster sights—and experience "Back Door" discoveries that most tourists miss.

This book offers you a balanced mix of Greek cities and villages, ancient sites and Byzantine churches, great museums and relaxing beaches. And it's selective—rather than listing dozens of historic attractions, I recommend only the best ones. My self-guided museum tours and city walks give insight into Greece's vibrant history and today's living, breathing culture.

I advocate traveling simply and smartly. Take advantage of my money- and time-saving tips on sightseeing, transportation, and more. Try local, characteristic alternatives to expensive hotels and restaurants. In many ways, spending more money only builds a thicker wall between you and what you traveled so far to see.

We visit Greece to experience it—to become temporary locals. Thoughtful travel engages us with the world, as we learn to appreciate other cultures and new ways to measure quality of life.

Judging from the positive feedback I receive from readers, this book will help you enjoy a fun, affordable, and rewarding vacation—whether it's your first trip or your tenth.

Kalo taxidi! Happy travels!

Rick Steves

INTRODUCTION

Democracy and mathematics. Medicine and literature. Theater and astronomy. Mythology and philosophy. All of these, and more, were first thought up by a bunch of tunic-clad Greeks in a small village huddled at the base of the Acropolis. The ancient Greeks—who reached their apex in the city of Athens—have had an unmatched impact on European and American culture. For many North American travelers, coming to Greece is like a pilgrimage to the cradle of our civilization.

A century and a half ago, Athens was a humble, forgotten city of about 20,000 people. Today it's the teeming home of three million Greeks—nearly half of the 11 million people in all of Greece. Athens is famous for its sprawl, noise, graffiti, and pollution. The best advice to tourists has long been to see the big sights, then get out. But over the last decade or so, the city has made a concerted effort to curb pollution, clean up and pedestrianize the streets, spiff up the museums, and invest in one of Europe's better public transit systems. All of these urban upgrades reached a peak as Athens hosted the 2004 Olympic Games.

And yet, the conventional wisdom still holds true: Athens is a great city to see...but not to linger in. This book also includes the best Greek destinations outside the capital, including the highlights of the Peloponnese—Greece's heartland peninsula, the site of the ancient oracle at Delphi, and the castaway islands of Hydra, Mykonos, and Santorini.

In this book, I'll give you all the information and opinions necessary to wring the maximum value out of your limited time and money. If you plan two weeks or less in this part of Greece and have a normal appetite for information, this book is all you need. Destinations include the predictable biggies (such as the Acropolis and ancient Olympia), but I've also mixed in a healthy dose of Back

Greece at a Glance

These attractions are listed (as in this book) starting with Athens, moving to the Peloponnese, and then covering other regions.

▲▲▲**Athens** Greece's capital, featuring the ancient world's most magnificent sight—the Acropolis—a pair of world-class museums, an atmospheric Old Town, and funky neighborhoods bursting with avant-garde nightlife.

▲▲▲**Nafplio** Greece's first capital and finest midsized town, with a cozy port, an elegant Old Town, a cliff-topping fortress, and energetic street life; handy to nearby ancient sites (Mycenae and Epidavros).

▲**Epidavros** Best-preserved theater of the ancient world, with unbelievable acoustics.

▲**Mycenae** Legendary mountaintop palace/fortress with iconic Lion Gate, massive beehive tomb, and mythic links to the Trojan War.

▲▲**Olympia** Birthplace of the Olympic Games, with impressive temple ruins, a still-functional stadium, and an intimate museum of ancient masterpieces.

▲**Kardamyli** Cozy, unspoiled beach town, providing a handy jumping-off point for the Mani Peninsula.

Door intimacy (workaday towns such as Kardamyli, rustic seaside viewpoints, and neighborhood tavernas where you'll enjoy a warm welcome).

The best is, of course, only my opinion. But after spending much of my life exploring and researching Europe, I've developed a sixth sense for what travelers enjoy. The places featured in this book will make anyone want to shout, *"Opa!"*

ABOUT THIS BOOK

Rick Steves Greece: Athens & the Peloponnese is a personal tour guide in your pocket. This book is organized by destinations. Each is a minivacation on its own, filled with exciting sights, strollable neighborhoods, affordable places to stay, and memorable places to eat.

The first half of this book focuses on Athens and contains the following chapters:

Greece offers an introduction to this mesmerizing land, including a crash course in the Greek alphabet.

▲**Mani Peninsula** Remote, rustic region with dramatic hill towns, spectacular caves (Pyrgos Dirou), and breathtaking, jagged coastlines.

▲▲**Monemvasia** Greece's Gibraltar-like fortress on an imposing rock peninsula jutting out into the sea, blending Venetian and Byzantine charm, traffic-free cobbled lanes, and million-dollar views.

▲▲**Delphi** Mountainside draped with the Sanctuary of Apollo and other once-grandiose structures, where ancients came to consult the oracle.

▲▲▲**Hydra** Idyllic island getaway, convenient to Athens and the Peloponnese, with picturesque harbor, casual beaches, enticing coastal hikes, and no cars (but plenty of donkeys).

▲▲**Mykonos** Quintessential (and very popular) Greek isle with postcard-perfect whitewashed village, old-fashioned windmills, and pulsating nightlife; ruins on nearby Delos mark the birthplace of Apollo and a once-mighty shipping center.

▲▲**Santorini** Romantic island destination built on the remains of a volcano crater, renowned for cliff-clinging white villages punctuated by blue-domed churches, volcanic black-sand beaches, and spectacular sunsets.

Orientation to Athens has specifics on public transportation, helpful hints, local tour options, easy-to-read maps, and tourist information. The "Planning Your Time" section suggests a schedule for how to best use your limited time.

Sights in Athens describes the top attractions and includes their cost and hours.

Self-Guided Walks and **Tours** take you through interesting neighborhoods, pointing out sights and fun stops. In Athens these include a city walk, the Ancient Agora, the Acropolis, the Acropolis Museum, the National Archaeological Museum, and a walk through Psyrri and the Central Market.

Sleeping in Athens describes my favorite hotels, from good-value deals to cushy splurges.

Eating in Athens serves up a buffet of options, from inexpensive tavernas to fancy restaurants.

Shopping & Nightlife in Athens gives you tips for shopping painlessly and enjoyably, and guides you to music, folk dances, outdoor movies, and bustling nighttime neighborhoods.

Athens Connections outlines your options for traveling to destinations by car or bus, and includes information on getting to and from Athens' airport.

The **Peloponnese** section includes in-depth chapters on the historic peninsula's top sights: **Nafplio, Epidavros, Mycenae, Olympia, Kardamyli** and the **Mani Peninsula,** and **Monemvasia.**

The **Beyond Athens & the Peloponnese** section covers the ancient oracle site at **Delphi** and the idyllic islands of **Hydra, Mykonos,** and **Santorini.**

The **Greek History & Mythology** chapter gives you a quick overview of the country's past.

The **Practicalities** chapter near the end of this book is a traveler's tool kit, with my best advice about money, sightseeing, sleeping, eating, staying connected, and transportation (buses, boats, car rentals, driving, and flights).

The **appendix** has the nuts and bolts: useful phone numbers and websites, a holiday and festival list, books and films, a climate chart, a handy packing checklist, and Greek survival phrases.

Throughout this book, you'll find money- and time-saving tips for sightseeing, transportation, and more. Some businesses—especially hotels and walking-tour companies—offer special discounts to my readers, indicated in their listings.

Browse through this book, choose your favorite destinations, and link them up. Then have a great trip! Traveling like a temporary local, you'll get the absolute most of every mile, minute, and dollar. And, as you visit places I know and love, I'm happy that you'll be meeting some of my favorite Greeks.

Planning

This section will help you get started planning your trip—with advice on trip costs, when to go, and what you should know before you take off.

TRIP COSTS

Five components make up your trip costs: airfare, surface transportation, room and board, sightseeing and entertainment, and shopping and miscellany.

Airfare to Europe: A basic round-trip flight from the US to Athens can cost, on average, about $1,000-2,000 total, depending on where you fly from and when (cheaper in winter). If your trip extends beyond Greece, consider saving time and money by flying into one city and out of another; for instance, into Paris and out of Athens. Overall, Kayak.com is the best place to start searching for flights on a combination of mainstream and budget carriers. Note

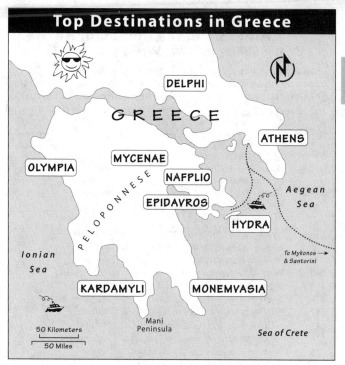

Top Destinations in Greece

that if you're visiting only Greece, the airport at Athens is your most convenient way in and out of the country.

Transportation in Europe: If you're just touring Athens, you can get around easily on foot and on the Metro (plan on $30 for three full days in Athens and a round-trip ticket to/from the airport). If you're venturing beyond the capital—say, doing a two-week loop of this book's destinations—figure per-person costs of $150 by public transit (boat to Hydra, bus to everything else) or $450 by car (not including tolls, gas, and supplemental insurance). If you need a car for three weeks or more, leasing can save you money on insurance and taxes.

Room and Board: You can thrive in Greece on $105 a day per person for room and board (less on the Peloponnese). This allows $15 for lunch, $20 for dinner, and $70 for lodging (based on two people splitting the cost of a $140 double room that includes breakfast). Students and tightwads can enjoy Greece for as little as $60 a day ($30 for a bed, $30 for meals and snacks).

Sightseeing and Entertainment: In Athens, figure $12-24 per major sight (Acropolis, National Archaeological Museum), $10 for minor ones (Benaki Museum of Greek History and Culture, Byzantine and Christian Museum), and $40-90 for splurge

Athens and the Peloponnese in Two Weeks

Outside of Athens, this region is best visited by car. If you'd rather get around by bus, you'll see less in virtually the same amount of time (or you can add more days to your itinerary to see it all).

Best Trip by Car

Day	Plan	Sleep
1	Arrive Athens	Athens
2	Athens	Athens
3	Athens	Athens
4	Boat to Hydra	Hydra
5	Hydra	Hydra
6	Boat back to Athens, pick up rental car, drive to Delphi	Delphi
7	Sightsee Delphi, drive to Olympia	Olympia
8	Sightsee Olympia, drive to Kardamyli	Kardamyli
9	Relax in Kardamyli	Kardamyli
10	Mani Peninsula loop drive, on to Monemvasia	Monemvasia
11	Monemvasia	Monemvasia
12	See Mycenae en route to Nafplio	Nafplio
13	Nafplio, side-trip to Epidavros	Nafplio
14	Return to Athens, drop off rental car	Athens
15	Fly home, or continue to Mykonos and/or Santorini by plane or boat	

Best Trip by Public Transportation

Day	Plan	Sleep
1	Arrive Athens	Athens
2	Athens	Athens
3	Athens	Athens
4	Morning in Athens, afternoon bus to Delphi	Delphi
5	Sightsee Delphi	Delphi
6	Morning bus to Athens, then boat to Hydra	Hydra
7	Hydra	Hydra
8	Morning boat back to Athens, then bus to Olympia	Olympia
9	Sightsee Olympia	Olympia
10	Morning bus to Nafplio	Nafplio
11	Day trip to Mycenae	Nafplio
12	Day trip to Epidavros	Nafplio
13	Bus to Athens	Athens
14	Fly home, or continue to Mykonos and/or Santorini by plane or boat	

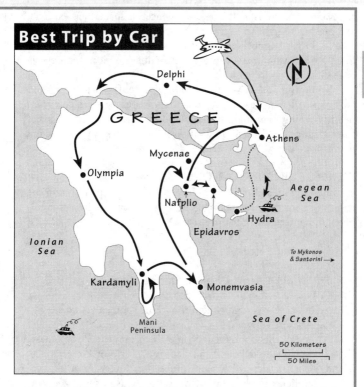

Bus Notes: Research and consider your bus connections carefully (usually easier to do on site than online); these can be limited and complicated, especially on the Peloponnese.

Two nights in Delphi offer a fine escape from big-city Athens, but if you have limited time, you can see Delphi either as a day trip on Day 4 (return to Athens to spend the night) or as a single overnight (bus from Athens to Delphi on the morning of Day 4, afternoon sightseeing and overnight in Delphi, then bus to Athens and boat to Hydra on Day 5).

The bus itinerary leaves out the hardest-to-reach destinations: Kardamyli/Mani Peninsula (best by car or with a hired local driver) and Monemvasia.

If you've seen enough ancient sites, you could skip Olympia (which is time-consuming to reach by bus), and instead visit Monemvasia (reachable by bus, but involves more travel time than Olympia) or enjoy more beach time on Hydra.

Without a car, the easiest connection from Hydra to the Peloponnese is via Athens, but adventurous travelers might want to tackle the cheaper and shorter—though more complicated—boat-taxi-bus connection to Nafplio instead; for tips, see page 243.

With an extra week and a bunch of patience, you could include all of the recommended destinations.

INTRODUCTION

experiences (such as walking tours, concerts, special art exhibits, and big-bus tours). An overall average of $30 a day works for most people. Don't skimp here. After all, this category is the driving force behind your trip—you came to sightsee, enjoy, and experience Greece.

Shopping and Miscellany: Figure 50 cents per postcard and $3-4 per coffee or ice-cream cone. Shopping can vary in cost from nearly nothing to a small fortune. Good budget travelers find that this category has little to do with assembling a trip full of lifelong memories.

SIGHTSEEING PRIORITIES

So much to see, so little time. How to choose? Depending on the length of your trip, and taking geographic proximity into account, here are my recommended priorities.

2-3 days:	Athens
5 days, add:	Hydra
7 days, add:	Delphi
10 days, add:	Nafplio, Epidavros, Mycenae
12 days, add:	Olympia, Monemvasia
14 days, add:	Kardamyli and the Mani Peninsula, and slow down

Although this book focuses on Athens and the Peloponnese, I've also included Mykonos and Santorini—two of Greece's best islands—for travelers with more time. The "Greece at a Glance" sidebar (earlier) can help you decide where to go. A suggested itinerary is on page 6.

WHEN TO GO

The "summer" and "winter" seasons can vary, but summer is roughly Easter through October, when Athens can be crowded.

Peak Season: In summer, Athens is packed with tourists, and hotel prices can be correspondingly high. July and August are the hottest months.

Shoulder Season: Late spring and fall are pleasant, with comfortable weather, no rain, and lighter crowds (except during holiday weekends).

Winter Season: Weather from late October through mid-March is colder. Though rain is rare in Athens, this is the time for it. Some sights close for lunch, TI offices keep shorter hours, and some tourist activities vanish altogether. Hotel rates are soft; look for bargains.

∩ Rick Steves Audio Europe ∩

My free Rick Steves Audio Europe app makes it easy for you to download my audio tours of many of Europe's top attractions and listen to them offline during your travels. For Greece, these include major sights and neighborhoods in Athens. Sights covered by audio tours are marked in this book with this symbol: ∩. The app also offers insightful travel interviews from my public radio show with experts from Greece and around the globe. It's all free! You can download the app via Apple's App Store, Google Play, or Amazon's Appstore. For more info, see www.ricksteves.com/audioeurope.

Before You Go

You'll have a smoother trip if you tackle a few things ahead of time. For more information on these topics, see the Practicalities chapter (and www.ricksteves.com, which has helpful travel tips and talks).

Make sure your passport is valid. If it's due to expire within six months of your ticketed date of return, you need to renew it. Allow up to six weeks to renew or get a passport (www.travel.state.gov).

Arrange your transportation. Book your international flights. Figure out your main form of transportation within Greece: It's worth thinking about renting a car, buying boat tickets online in advance, or booking cheap European flights. (You can wing it once you're there, but it may cost more or sell out.) Drivers: Consider bringing an International Driving Permit (sold at AAA offices in the US, www.aaa.com) along with your license.

Book rooms well in advance, especially if your trip falls during peak season or any major holidays or festivals, or if you're hoping to land a particular hotel on Mykonos or Santorini, where perennial visitors often book their favorite rooms months ahead.

Consider travel insurance. Compare the cost of the insurance to the cost of your potential loss. Check whether your existing insurance (health, homeowners, or renters) covers you and your possessions overseas.

Call your bank. Alert your bank that you'll be using your debit and credit cards in Europe. Ask about transaction fees, and get the PIN number for your credit card. You don't need to bring euros for your trip; you can withdraw euros from cash machines in Europe.

Use your smartphone smartly. Sign up for an international service plan to reduce your costs, or rely on Wi-Fi in Europe instead. Download any apps you'll want on the road, such as maps, translation, transit schedules, and Rick Steves Audio Europe (see sidebar).

Rip up this book! Turn chapters into mini guidebooks: Break the book's spine and use a utility knife to slice apart chapters, keeping gummy edges intact. Reinforce the chapter spines with clear wide tape; use a heavy-duty stapler; or make or buy a cheap cover (see Travel Store at www.ricksteves.com), swapping out chapters as you travel.

Pack light. You'll walk with your luggage more than you think. Bring a single carry-on bag and a daypack. Use the packing checklist in the appendix as a guide.

Travel Smart

If you have a positive attitude, equip yourself with good information (this book), and expect to travel smart, you will.

Read—and reread—this book. To have an "A" trip, be an "A" student. Note opening hours of sights, closed days, crowd-beating tips, and whether reservations are required or advisable. Check the latest at www.ricksteves.com/update.

Be your own tour guide. As you travel, get up-to-date info on sights, reserve tickets and tours, reconfirm hotels and travel arrangements, and check transit connections. Visit local tourist information offices (TIs). Upon arrival in a new town, lay the groundwork for a smooth departure; confirm the boat, bus, or road you'll take when you leave.

Outsmart thieves. Pickpockets abound in crowded places where tourists congregate. Treat commotions as smokescreens for theft. Keep your cash, credit cards, and passport secure in a money belt tucked under your clothes; carry only a day's spending money in your front pocket. Don't set valuable items down on counters or café tabletops, where they can be quickly stolen or easily forgotten.

Minimize potential loss. Keep expensive gear to a minimum. Bring photocopies or take photos of important documents (passport and cards) to aid in replacement if they're lost or stolen.

Beat the summer heat. If you wilt easily, choose a hotel with air-conditioning, start your day early, take a midday siesta at your hotel, and resume your sightseeing later. Churches offer a cool haven (wearing shorts inside is discouraged, but usually tolerated). Take frequent ice cream breaks.

Guard your time and energy. Taking a taxi can be a good value if it saves you a long wait for a cheap bus or an exhausting walk across town. To avoid long lines, follow my crowd-beating tips, such as making advance reservations, or sightseeing early or late.

Be flexible. Even if you have a well-planned itinerary, expect changes, strikes, closures, sore feet, bad weather, and so on. Your Plan B could turn out to be even better.

Attempt the language. Many Greeks—especially in the tourist trade and in cities—speak English, but if you learn some Greek, even just a few phrases, you'll get more smiles and make more friends. Practice the survival phrases near the end of this book, and even better, bring a phrase book.

Connect with the culture. Interacting with locals carbonates your experience. Enjoy the friendliness of the Greek people. Ask questions; most locals are happy to point you in their idea of the right direction. Set up your own quest for the best baklava, Byzantine church, or secluded beach. When an opportunity pops up, make it a habit to say "yes."

Greece...here you come!

GREECE

Hellas / Ελλάς

Slip a coaster under that rickety table leg, take a sip of wine, and watch the sun extinguish itself in the sea. You've arrived in Greece.

Greece offers sunshine, seafood, whitewashed houses with bright-blue shutters, and a relaxed, Zorba-the-Greek lifestyle. As the cradle of Western civilization, it has some of the world's greatest ancient monuments. While it's a late bloomer in the modern age and retains echoes of a simpler time-passed world, contemporary Greece has one of Europe's fastest-changing cultural landscapes. With its classical past, hang-loose present, and edgy future, Greece offers something for every traveler.

Start in Athens, a microcosm of the country. By day, tour the Acropolis, the Agora, and the history-packed museums. Light a candle alongside black-clad widows at an icon-filled church. Haggle with a sandal maker at the busy market stalls, or have coffee with the locals in a Plaka café. At night, Athens becomes a pan-European party of eating, drinking, and dancing in open-air tavernas. In the colorful Thissio or rickety-chic Psyrri neighborhoods, rub elbows with trendy Athenians to get a taste of today's urban Greece.

With its central location, Athens is the perfect launch pad for farther-flung Greek destinations. Commune with ancient spir-its at the center of the world: the oracle near the picturesque mountain hamlet of Delphi. Take a vacation from your busy vacation on one of the best and easiest-to-reach Greek isles, traffic-free Hydra. For longer island getaways, the picture-perfect, whitewashed village

of Mykonos and the dramatically situated towns overlooking the flooded volcano crater at Santorini are tops.

An hour's drive west of Athens, the Peloponnese is the large peninsula that hangs from the rest of the Greek mainland by the narrow Isthmus of Corinth. Its name, which means "the Island of Pelops," derives from the mythical hero Pelops. This wild, mountainous landscape is dotted with the ruins of Mycenaean palaces, ancient temples, frescoed churches, and countless medieval hilltop castles built by the Crusaders and the Venetians. At Mycenae, visit the hub of a civilization that dominated Greece from 1600 to 1200 B.C. Hike up the stone rows of the world's best-preserved ancient theater, at Epidavros. Run a lap at Olympia, site of the first Olympic Games. To round things out, enjoy the stunning landscapes of the wild Mani Peninsula and the charming old Venetian towns of Monemvasia (a fortified, village-topped giant rock hovering just offshore) and Nafplio (the first capital of independent Greece). As you hop from town to town, compare Greek salads and mountains-and-olive-grove views.

Greece possesses a huge hunk of human history. It's the place that birthed the Olympics; the mischievous gods (Zeus, Hermes, Dionysius); the tall tales of Achilles, Odysseus, and the Trojan

War; the rational philosophies of Socrates, Plato, and Aristotle; democracy, theater, mathematics...and the gyro sandwich.

Besides viewing impressive remnants of its Golden Age (450-400 B.C.), you'll see Byzantine churches, Ottoman mosques, and Neoclassical buildings marking the War of Independence—all part of Greece's 3,000-year history.

Greece is easy on travelers. Tourism makes up 18 percent of the gross domestic product, and the people are welcoming and accommodating. Greeks pride themselves on a concept called *filotimo* ("love of honor"), roughly translated as openness, friendliness, and hospitality. Social faux pas by unwary foreigners are easily overlooked by Greeks. The food is uncomplicated, the weather is good, and the transportation infrastructure is sufficient.

Greece's geography of mountains, peninsulas, and 3,000 islands divides the Greek people into many regions, each with its distinct cultural differences. "Where are you from?" is a common conversation-starter among Greeks.

Greece is also divided by a severe generation gap. Up until late 1974 (when the military junta was ousted), Greek society was traditional, economically backward, and politically repressed. Then the floodgates opened, and Greece has gone overboard trying to catch up with the modern world.

You'll find two Greeces: the traditional/old/rural Greece and the modern/young/urban one. In the countryside, you'll still see men on donkeys, women at the well, and people whose career choice was to herd goats across a busy highway. In the bigger cities, it's a concrete world of honking horns and buzzing mobile phones. Well-dressed, educated Greeks listen to hip-hop music and Instagram their exotic vacations. As the rural exodus continues, the urban environment is now home to a majority of Greeks. Young Greeks seem to overcompensate for their country's conservative past with excessive consumerism, trendiness, and antiauthoritarianism.

Still, Greece is unified by language and religion. The Greek Orthodox Church—a rallying point for Greeks during centuries of foreign occupation—remains part of everyday life. Ninety-five percent of all Greeks declare themselves Orthodox, even if they rarely go to church. The constitution gives the Orthodox Church special privileges, blurring church-state separation.

Orthodox elements appear everywhere. Icon shrines dot the highways. Orthodox priests—with their Old Testament beards, black robes, necklaces, cake-shaped hats, and families in tow—mingle with parishioners on street corners and chat on their mobile phones. During the course of the day, Greeks routinely pop into churches to light a candle, asking for favors. Even the young celebrate feast days with their families and make the sign of the cross when passing a church. Greek lives are marked by the age-old rituals of baptism, marriage, and funeral.

It seems like every man in Greece shares the same few names: Georgios, Kostas, Nikos, Vassilis, Dimitris, Constantinos, and Yiannis. That's because many still follow the custom of naming boys after their grandfathers, using the names of Orthodox saints. Most surnames seem to have the same endings: -polous, -aikis, or -idis; all mean "son of." Names ending in -ous or -os are usually male; -ou names are female.

Despite modern changes, men and women still live in somewhat different spheres. Women rule the home and socialize at open-air marketplaces. Fewer women join the workforce than in other European countries.

Men rule the public arena. You'll see them hanging out endlessly at coffee shops, playing backgammon, watching soccer games on TV (basketball is also popular), and arguing politics with loud voices and dramatic gestures.

Greeks are family-oriented, with large extended families. Kids live at home until they're married, and then they might just move into a flat upstairs in the same apartment building. The "family" extends to the large diaspora of emigrants. Three million Greek-Americans (including George Stephanopoulos, Pete Sampras, and Tina Fey) keep ties to the home country through their Orthodox faith and their Big Fat Greek Weddings.

The pace of life in Greece remains relaxed. People work in the mornings, then take a midafternoon siesta, when they gather with their families to eat the main meal of the day. On warm summer nights, even the kids stay up very late. Families spill into the streets to greet their

Greece Almanac

Official Name: It's the Hellenic Republic (*Elliniki Dhimokratia* in Greek). In shorthand, that's Hellas—or Greece in English.

Population: Greece is home to 10.8 million people (similar to the state of Ohio). About 93 percent are Greek citizens, and 7 percent are citizens of other countries—mainly Albania, Bulgaria, and Romania. Greece does not collect ethnic data. More than 95 percent are Greek Orthodox, the state religion. A little more than 1 percent are Muslim. The dominant language is Greek.

Latitude and Longitude: 39°N and 22°E. The latitude is the same as Maryland.

Area: With 51,485 square miles, Greece is a bit smaller than Alabama.

Geography: Greece is a mountainous peninsula that extends into the Mediterranean Sea between Albania and Turkey in southern Europe. It includes the Peloponnesian Peninsula—separated from the mainland by a canal—and 3,000 rugged islands (227 are inhabited). Nearly four-fifths of the country's landscape is covered by mountains, the highest of which is Mount Olympus (9,570 feet). About 30 percent of the land is forested. Flat, arable plains are centered in Macedonia, Thrace, and Thessaly. Greece's coastline is the 10th longest in the world at 9,246 miles.

Biggest Cities: One in three Greeks lives in the capital of Athens (about 664,000 in the city, 3.1 million including the greater metropolitan area). Thessaloniki has 315,000 (790,000 in its urban area).

Economy: Greece has a GDP of $286 billion, with a GDP per capita of $26,000. A European Union member, Greece has used the euro as its currency since 2002. At first, its economy—based

neighbors on the evening stroll. For entertainment, they go out to eat (even poor people), where they order large amounts and share it family-style.

Later, they might gather to hear folk songs sung to a bouzouki, a long-necked mandolin. These days the music is often amplified, fleshed out with a synthesizer, and tinged with pop influences. People still form a circle to dance the traditional dances, with arms outstretched or thrown across one another's shoulders. A few might get carried away, "applaud" by throwing plates, napkins, or flowers, and dance on the tables into the wee hours.

While pollution is still problematic for traffic-choked cities and dirty beaches, things have improved following the 2004 Olympics, a source of pride for the Greeks. The country's capital has traffic-free pedestrian zones, modern public transport, a state-of-the-art airport, a fledgling recycling program, and the stunning Acropolis Museum.

heavily on tourism, shipping, and agriculture—benefited from an infusion of EU cash. But by the end of the decade the country was in a severe recession. In 2010, 2012, and again in 2015, Greece accepted huge bailout packages from the EU and was forced to adopt severe (and controversial) spending cuts and tax increases.

Government: Greece is a parliamentary republic, headed by a largely ceremonial president elected by the parliament. Power resides with the prime minister, chosen from the majority political party. Left-wing coalition leader Alexis Tsipras became prime minister in September 2015.

Flag: A blue square bears a white cross (the symbol of Greek Orthodoxy) in the upper-left corner, against a field of horizontal blue-and-white stripes. The blue is said to stand for the sky and seas, while the white represents the purity of the push for Greek independence. Each of the nine stripes is said to symbolize a syllable in the Greek motto, *Eleutheria e Thanatos,* which translates as "Freedom or Death."

The Average Zorba: The average Greek is 43 years old, will live to be 80, and has 1.4 children. About 80 percent of Greeks have mobile phones. A typical local eats over 60 pounds of cheese a year (mostly feta)—the highest per capita cheese consumption in the world.

It's easy to surrender to the Greek way of living. With its long history and simple lifestyle, Greece has a timeless appeal.

GREECE'S ECONOMIC AND OTHER CHALLENGES

In the early 2010s, Greece became infamous as one of the world's most troubled economies. Embarrassingly high national debt figures prompted foreign investors to abandon Greek bonds; but, after several hefty EU/International Monetary Fund bailouts, the country is putting its economy back together.

In the view of many observers (and many Greeks), the problems started because Greeks had lived beyond their means, worked too little, retired too early, consumed too much, produced too little, enjoyed too much job security, created a real-estate bubble with overvalued properties, and funded too much on a growing deficit. The black market thrived, and many Greeks practiced tax evasion as if it were a fine art (limiting tax revenue).

Also, the government itself was notoriously corrupt and nepotistic. Government employees—with cushy jobs, 100 percent job security, and great benefits—were seen as luxuriating away their work lives in worry-free comfort. Stories of fiscal scandal and fraud filled the news almost daily, sparking public anger and driving Greece's young people into the streets in constant demonstrations challenging every public institution.

The Greek government scrambled to salvage the economy by raising taxes, cutting back staff, selling off public agencies, and getting more serious about tax collection. As a result, everything people consumed cost more, with a significant chunk of their income going to the government to rescue the economy. Many businesses went bankrupt during the crisis, resulting in less competition—and higher consumer prices.

While Greece's economy gets back on track, the country is also grappling with other issues. Young, well-educated, multilingual Greeks feel that they're overqualified for what their country has to offer and are tempted to go abroad for employment. This "brain drain" of bright young people is a threat to Greece's future.

At the same time, Greece's once-homogeneous populace feels threatened by immigrants happy to take low-paying jobs—the person cleaning your hotel room is likely an immigrant. The culture that gave us the word "xenophobic" is suspicious of threats from abroad. Like other European countries, Greece must figure out how to keep its own cultural identity even as it becomes more of a melting pot. Beyond the cultural issues, Greece is concerned about the financial costs involved. The country bore the brunt of the huge wave of immigrants and refugees who recently fled the Middle East and North Africa, for whom Greece was the most logical stepping stone into the rest of Europe. Meanwhile, the country's inefficient, underfunded bureaucracy has done a poor job of accommodating the basic needs of the new arrivals.

Still, Greeks are optimistic by nature. They're quick to point out that, regardless of the challenges, the olives remain just as tasty, the water just as blue, and the sun—like the Greek people—just as warm.

GREEK LANGUAGE

Even though the Greek alphabet presents challenges to foreign visitors, communication is not hard. You'll find that most people in the tourist industry—and almost all young people—speak fine English. Many signs and menus (especially in Athens and major tourist spots) use both the Greek and our more familiar Latin alphabet. Greeks realize that it's unreasonable to expect visitors to learn Greek (which has only 14 million speakers worldwide). It's essential for them to find a common language with the rest of the world—especially their European neighbors to the west—so they learn English early and well.

Of course, not everyone speaks English. You'll run into the most substantial language barrier when traveling in rural areas and/or dealing with folks over 60, who are more likely to have learned French as a second language. Because signs and maps aren't always transliterated into our alphabet (i.e., spelled out using a Latin-letter equivalent), a passing familiarity with the basics of the Greek alphabet is helpful for navigating—especially for drivers (see "Greek Alphabet," below).

There are certain universal English words all Greeks know: hello, please, thank you, OK, pardon, stop, menu, problem, and no problem. While Greeks don't expect you to be fluent in their tongue, they definitely appreciate it when they can tell you're making an effort to pronounce Greek words correctly and use the local pleasantries.

It's nice to learn "Hello" (*"Gia sas,"* pronounced "yah sahs"), "Please" (*"Parakalo,"* "pah-rah-kah-LOH"), and "Thank you" (*"Efharisto,"* "ehf-hah-ree-STOH"). Watch out for this tricky point: The Greek word for "yes" is *ne* (pronounced "neh"), which sounds a lot like "no" to us. What's more, the word for "no" is *ohi* (pronounced "OH-hee"), which sounds enough like "OK" to be potentially confusing. For more Greek words, see the "Greek Survival Phrases" in the Appendix.

Don't be afraid to interact with locals. You'll find that doors open a little more quickly when you know a few words of the language. Give it your best shot.

Greek Alphabet

Most visitors find the Greek alphabet daunting, if not indecipherable. At first, all the signs look

like...well, Greek to us. However, Greek has more in common with English than may be immediately apparent. Technically the world's oldest complete alphabet (Phoenician, its predecessor, had no vowel symbols), Greek is the parent of our own Latin alphabet—itself named for the first two Greek letters

Greek from A to Ω

Transliterating Greek to English is an inexact science, but here is the Greek alphabet, with the most common English counterparts for the Greek letters and letter combinations.

Greek	English Name	Common Transliteration	Pronounced
A α	alpha	a	A as in father
B β	beta	b or v	V as in volt
Γ γ	gamma	y or g	Y as in yes or G as in go*
Δ δ	delta	d or dh	TH as in then
E ε	epsilon	e	E as in get
Z ζ	zeta	z	Z as in zoo
H η	eta	i	I as in ski
Θ θ	theta	th	TH as in theme
I ι	iota	i	I as in ski
K κ	kappa	k	K as in king
Λ λ	lambda	l	L as in lime
M μ	mu	m	M as in mom
N ν	nu	n	N as in net
Ξ ξ	xi	x	X as in ox
O o	omicron	o	O as in ocean
Π π	pi	p	P as in pie
P ρ	rho	r	R as in rich (slightly rolled)
Σ σ, ς	sigma	s or c	S as in sun
T τ	tau	t	T as in tip
Υ υ	upsilon	y	Y as in happy
Φ φ	phi	f or ph	F as in file
X χ	chi	ch, h, or kh	CH as in loch (gutturally)
Ψ ψ	psi	ps	PS as in lapse
Ω ω	omega	o or w	O as in ocean

*Gamma is pronounced, roughly speaking, like the English "hard" G only when it comes before consonants, or before the letters a, o, and ou.

(alpha and beta). Because it's used worldwide among mathematicians and scientists (not to mention frats and sororities), you may recognize some letters from your student days—but that doesn't help much when you're trying to read a map or a menu.

Fortunately, with a little effort the alphabet becomes a lot less baffling. Many uppercase Greek letters look just like their Latin counterparts (such as A, B, and M), and a few more look similar with a little imagination (Δ, Ξ, and Σ look a little like D, X, and S, if you squint). A few look nothing like anything in our alphabet, and a couple are particularly confusing (Greek's P is our R, and Greek's H is our I).

Getting comfortable with the lowercase letters is more challenging. Just like in our alphabet, most lowercase letters are similar to their uppercase versions, but a few bear no resemblance at all.

Once you're familiar with the letters, it's less of a challenge to learn how each is said. Nearly every letter (except P and H) is pronounced roughly like the Latin letter it most resembles. As for the handful of utterly unfamiliar characters, you'll just have to memorize those.

Most Greek words have one acute accent that marks the stressed vowel (such as ά rather than α, έ rather than ε, ί rather than ι, ό rather than ο, and ύ rather than υ). These accents are worth paying attention to, as a change in emphasis can bring a change in meaning. Also, note the list of letter combinations below—pairs of letters that, when together, sound a little different than expected (similar to our own "th" or "ch" combinations).

Learn to recognize and pronounce each letter, and you'll be able to sound out the words you see around you: Μάνη = M-a-n-i, Mani (the peninsula, pronounced MAH-nee). Greek is phonetic—it has rules of pronunciation, and it sticks to them. As you stroll the streets, practice reading aloud—you may be surprised how quickly you'll be able to sound out words.

Certain Greek letter combinations create specific sounds. These include:

Greek		Transliteration	Pronounced
ΑΙ	αι	e	E as in get
ΑΥ	αυ	av/af	AV as in have, or AF as in after
ΕΙ	ει	i	I as in ski
ΕΥ	ευ	ev/ef	EV as in never, or EF as in left
ΟΙ	οι	i	I as in ski
ΟΥ	ου	ou/u	OU as in you
ΓΓ	γγ	ng	NG as in angle
ΓΚ	γκ	ng/g	NG as in angle, or G as in go (at start of word)
ΜΠ	μπ	mb/b	MB as in amber, or B as in bet (at start of word)
ΝΔ	νδ	nd/nt/d	ND as in land, or D as in dog (at start of word)
ΤΣ	τσ	ts	TS as in hats
ΤΖ	τζ	dz	DS as in lands, or DG as in judge

Greek Place Names

One Greek word can be transliterated into English in many different ways. For example, the town of Nafplio may appear on a map or road sign as Navplio, Naufplio, or Nauvplio. Even more confusing, there are actually two different versions of Greek: proper Greek, which was used until the 1950s (and now sounds affected to most Greeks); and popular Greek, a simplified version that is the norm today. This means that even Greeks might use different names for the same thing (for example, the city names Nafplio and Patra are popular Greek, while Nafplion and Patras are formal Greek).

The following list includes the most common English spelling and pronunciation for Greek places. If the Greeks use their own differently spelled transliteration, it's noted in parentheses.

English	Pronounced	Greek Transliteration
Greece (Ellada or Hellas)	eh-LAH-thah, eh-LAHS	Ελλάδα or Ελλάς
Athens (Athina)	ah-THEE-nah	Αθήνα
Delphi	thell-FEE (or dell-FEE)	Δελφοί
Epidavros	eh-PEE-dah-vrohs	Επίδαυρος
Hydra	EE-drah	Ύδρα
Kardamyli	kar-dah-MEE-lee	Καρδαμύλη
Mani	MAH-nee	Μάνη
Monemvasia	moh-nehm-vah-SEE-ah	Μονεμβασία
Mycenae (Mikenes)	my-SEE-nee (mee-KEE-nehs)	Μυκήνες
Mykonos	MEE-koh-nohs	Μύκονοσ
Nafplio	NAF-plee-oh	Ναύπλιο
Olympia	oh-leem-PEE-ah	Ολυμπία
Peloponnese (Peloponnisos)	PEL-oh-poh-neez (pel-oh-POH-nee-sohs)	Πελοπόννησος
Piraeus	pee-reh-AHS	Πειραιάς
Santorini (Thira)	sahn-toh-REE-nee (THEE-rah)	Θήρα

Note that these are the pronunciations most commonly used in English. Greeks might put the emphasis on a different syllable—for example, English-speakers call the Olympics birthplace oh-LEEM-pee-ah, while Greeks say oh-leem-PEE-ah.

ATHENS
ΑΘΉΝΑ / Αθήνα

ORIENTATION TO ATHENS

Though sprawling and congested, Athens has a compact, enjoyable core capped by the famous Acropolis—the world's top ancient site. In this historic town, you'll walk in the footsteps of the great minds that created democracy, philosophy, theater, and more...even as you're dodging motorcycles on "pedestrianized" streets. Romantics can't help but get goose bumps as they kick around the same pebbles that once stuck in Socrates' sandals, with the floodlit Parthenon forever floating ethereally overhead.

Many tourists visit Athens without ever venturing beyond the Plaka (Old Town) and the ancient zone. With limited time, this is not a bad plan, as greater Athens offers few sights (other than the excellent National Archaeological Museum). But for a more authentic taste of the city, check out the trendy Psyrri district—right next door to the Plaka—with its dilapidated-chic hipster dining and nightlife scene. Other thriving and fun-to-explore districts near the center are Thissio and Gazi.

Because of its prominent position on the tourist trail—and the irrepressible Greek spirit of hospitality—the city is user-friendly. It seems that virtually all Athenians speak English, major landmarks are well-signed, and most street signs are in both Greek and English.

ATHENS: A VERBAL MAP

Ninety-five percent of Athens is noisy, polluted modern sprawl: characterless, poorly planned, and hastily erected concrete suburbs that house the area's rapidly expanding population. The

Athens Landmarks

Area	Description	Pronounced (Greek Name)
Syntagma	Main square	SEEN-dag-mah
Plaka	Old town	PLAH-kah
Adrianou	Old town's main street	ah-dree-ah-NOO
Akropoli	Acropolis	ah-KROH-poh-lee
Dionysiou Areopagitou / Apostolou Pavlou	Pedestrian walkways near Acropolis	dee-oo-nee-SEE-oo ah-reh-oh-pah-GEE-too / ah-poh-STOH-loo PAW-loo
Archaea Agora	Ancient market	ar-HEH-ah ah-goh-RAH
Monastiraki	Market district	moh-nah-stee-RAH-kee
Psyrri	Nightlife district	psee-REE
Thissio	Western dining district	thee-SEE-oh
Gazi	Artsy district	GAH-zee
Makrigianni / Koukaki	Southern residential and hotel districts	mah-kree-YAH-nee / koo-KAH-kee
Kolonaki	Wealthy museum and residential area	koh-loh-NAH-kee
Exarchia	Edgy student district	ex-AR-hee-yah
Piraeus	Athens' port	pee-reh-AHS

ORIENTATION

construction of the Metro and other infrastructure for the 2004 Olympics was, in many ways, the first time urban planners had ever attempted to tie the city together and treat it as a united entity.

But most visitors barely see that part of Athens. Almost everything of importance to tourists is within a few blocks of the Acropolis, in the Plaka, Monastiraki, Syntagma, and Psyrri neighborhoods. As you explore this city-within-a-city on foot, you'll realize just how small it is.

A good map is a necessity for enjoying Athens on foot. The fine map the TI gives out works great. Get a good map and use it.

Athens by Neighborhood

The Athens you'll be spending your time in includes the following districts:

The Plaka (PLAH-kah, Πλάκα): This neighborhood at the foot of the Acropolis is the core of the tourist's Athens. One of the only parts of town that's atmospheric and Old World-feeling, it's also the most crassly touristic. Its streets are lined with souvenir shops, tourist-oriented tavernas, a smattering of small museums, ancient Greek and Roman ruins, and pooped tourists. The Plaka's narrow, winding streets can be confusing at first, but you can't get too lost with a monument the size of the Acropolis looming overhead to keep you oriented. Think of the Plaka as Athens with training wheels for tourists. While some visitors are mesmerized by the Plaka, others find it obnoxious and enjoy venturing outside it for a change of scenery.

Monastiraki (moh-nah-stee-RAH-kee, Μοναστηρακι): This area ("Little Monastery") borders the Plaka to the northwest, surrounding the square of the same name. It's known for its handy Metro stop (where line 1/green meets line 3/blue), seedy flea market, and souvlaki stands. The Ancient Agora is nearby (roughly between Monastiraki and Thissio).

Psyrri (psee-REE, Ψυρή): Formerly a dumpy ghetto just north of Monastiraki, Psyrri is now a thriving nightlife and dining district. Along its northern edge is the bustling Central Market. Don't be put off by the crumbling, graffiti-slathered buildings of Psyrri...this is one of central Athens' most appealing areas to explore after dark, and for now, locals still outnumber tourists here.

Syntagma (SEEN-dag-mah, Σύνταγμα): Centered on Athens' main square, Syntagma ("Constitution") Square, this urban-feeling zone melts into the Plaka to the south. While the Plaka is dominated by tourist shops, Syntagma is where local urbanites do their shopping. Syntagma is bounded to the east by the Parliament building and the vast National Garden.

Thissio (thee-SEE-oh, Θησείο): West of the Ancient Agora, Thissio is an upscale, local-feeling residential neighborhood with piles of outdoor cafés and restaurants. It's easily accessible thanks to the handy "Acropolis Loop" pedestrian walkway bordering the base of the Acropolis.

Gazi (GAH-zee, Γκάζι): At the western edge of the tourist's Athens (just beyond Thissio and Psyrri), Gazi is trendy and artsy, with lots of nightclubs and younger-skewing eateries. Its centerpiece is a former gas-works-turned-events center called Technopolis.

Makrigianni (mah-kree-YAH-nee, Μακρυγιάννη) and **Koukaki** (koo-KAH-kee, Κουκάκι): Tucked just behind (south of) the Acropolis, these overlapping urban neighborhoods with characterless apartment blocks are so nondescript that many locals just call Makrigianni the "south Plaka." If you want to escape the crowds of the Plaka, this area—with hotels and restaurants within easy walking distance of the ancient sites—makes a good home base.

Kolonaki (koh-loh-NAH-kee, Κολωνάκι): Just north and

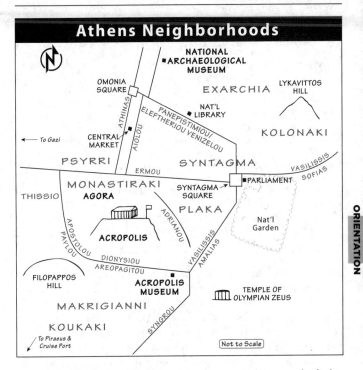

Athens Neighborhoods

NATIONAL ARCHAEOLOGICAL MUSEUM

OMONIA SQUARE

LYKAVITTOS HILL

EXARCHIA

NAT'L LIBRARY

KOLONAKI

ATHINAS

AIOLOU

PANEPISTIMIOU/ ELEFTHERIOU VENIZELOU

← To Gazi

CENTRAL MARKET

PSYRRI

SYNTAGMA

VASILISSIS SOFIAS

ERMOU

MONASTIRAKI

SYNTAGMA SQUARE

PARLIAMENT

THISSIO

AGORA

PLAKA

Nat'l Garden

ADRIANOU

ACROPOLIS

APOSTOLOU PAVLOU

DIONYSIOU AREOPAGITOU

VASILISSIS AMALIAS

FILOPAPPOS HILL

ACROPOLIS MUSEUM

TEMPLE OF OLYMPIAN ZEUS

MAKRIGIANNI

SYNGROU

KOUKAKI

To Piraeus & Cruise Port

Not to Scale

ORIENTATION

east of the Parliament/Syntagma Square area, this upscale diplomatic quarter is home to several good museums and a yuppie dining zone. It's huddled under the tall, pointy Lykavittos Hill, which challenges the Acropolis for domination of the skyline.

Exarchia (ex-AR-hee-yah, Εξάρχεια): Just beyond Kolonaki is this rough-and-funky student zone. The home of many protesters grabbing Greek headlines, it's a fascinating but not-for-everyone glimpse into an Athens that few tourists experience.

Major Streets: Various major streets define the tourist's Athens. The base of the Acropolis is partially encircled by a broad traffic-free walkway, named **Dionysiou Areopagitou** (Διονυσίου Αρεοπαγίτου) to the south and **Apostolou Pavlou** (Αποστόλου Παύλου) to the west; for simplicity, I call these the **"Acropolis Loop."** Touristy **Adrianou** street (Αδριανού) curves through the Plaka a few blocks away from the Acropolis' base. Partly pedestrianized **Ermou** street (Ερμού) runs west from Syntagma Square, defining the Plaka, Monastiraki, and Thissio to the south and Psyrri to the north. Where Ermou meets Monastiraki, **Athinas** street (Αθηνάς) heads north to Omonia Square. Running parallel to Athinas, heading north to the Central Market area, **Aiolou** street (Αιόλου) is mostly traffic-free and lined with shops and

ORIENTATION

Greek Words and English Spellings

Any given Greek name—for streets, sights, businesses, and more—can be transliterated many different ways in English. Throughout this book, I've used the English spelling you're most likely to see locally, but you will definitely notice variations. If you see a name that looks (or sounds) similar to one in this book, it's likely the same place. For example, the Ψυρρή district might appear as Psyrri, Psyrrí, Psyri, Psirri, Psiri, and so on.

Most major streets in Athens are labeled in Greek in signs and on maps, followed by the transliteration in English. The word ΟΔΟΣ *(odos)* means "street," ΛΕΩΦΌΡΟΣ *(leoforos)* is "avenue," and ΠΛΑΤΕΙΑ *(plateia)* is "square."

If a name used in this book appears locally only in Greek, I've included that spelling to aid your navigation.

affordable eateries; the trendy **St. Irene/Agia Irini Square** (Άγια Ειρήνη) marks its southern end.

The tourist zone is hemmed in to the east by a series of major highways: The north–south **Vasilissis Amalias** avenue (Βασιλίσσης Αμαλίας) runs between the National Garden and the Plaka/Syntagma area. To the south, it jogs around the Temple of Olympian Zeus and becomes **Syngrou** avenue (Συγγρού). To the north, at the Parliament, it forks: The eastward branch, **Vasilissis Sofias** (Βασιλίσσης Σοφίας), heads past some fine museums to Kolonaki; the northbound branch, **Panepistimiou** (usually signed by its official name, **Eleftheriou Venizelou,** Ελευθερίου Βενιζέλου), angles northwest past the library and university buildings to Omonia Square.

PLANNING YOUR TIME

Although Athens is a massive city, its main sights can be seen quickly. The top sights—the Acropolis, Ancient Agora, Acropolis Museum, and National Archaeological Museum—deserve about two hours apiece. Two days total is plenty of time for the casual tourist to see the city's main attractions and have a little time left over for exploring (or to add more museums).

Day 1: In the morning, follow my Athens City Walk, then grab a souvlaki at Monastiraki. After lunch, as the crowds subside, visit the ancient biggies: First tour the Ancient Agora, then hike up to the Acropolis (confirm how late it's open). Be the last person off the Acropolis. Stroll down the Dionysiou Areopagitou pedestrian boulevard, then promenade to dinner—in Thissio, Monastiraki, Psyrri, or the Plaka.

Day 2: Spend the morning visiting the Acropolis Museum

Daily Reminder

Sunday: Most sights are open, but the Central Market is closed. The Monastiraki flea market is best to visit today. An elaborate changing of the guard—including a marching band—usually takes place at 11:00 in front of the Parliament building. State-run sights and museums, including the Acropolis, are free on the first Sunday of the month during off-season (Nov-March).

Monday: Many museums and galleries are closed, including the Benaki Museum of Greek History and Culture, Benaki Museum of Islamic Art, Byzantine and Christian Museum, and the Museum of Greek Popular Instruments. The Keramikos Cemetery Museum is closed on Mondays off-season (Nov-March).

Tuesday: These sights are closed today: Benaki Museum of Greek History and Culture, Benaki Museum of Islamic Art, Museum of Cycladic Art, and Museum of the City of Athens.

Wednesday: The Benaki Museum of Islamic Art is closed.

Thursday: All major sights are open.

Friday: All major sights are open.

Saturday: The Jewish Museum of Greece is closed.

Evening Sightseeing: Many sights are open late in summer, often until 20:00. Year-round, the Museum of Cycladic Art is open until 20:00 on Thursday, the Acropolis Museum is open until 22:00 on Friday, and the Benaki Museum of Greek History and Culture is open Thursday and Saturday until 24:00.

ORIENTATION

and exploring the Plaka. For lunch, graze your way through my "Psyrri & Central Market Walk." Then head to the National Archaeological Museum.

Day 3: Museum lovers will want more time to visit other archaeological sites (especially those included with your Acropolis combo-ticket), museums, and galleries. The city has many "also-ran" museums that reward patient sightseers. I'd suggest heading out toward Kolonaki to take in the Benaki Museum of Greek History and Culture, Museum of Cycladic Art, and Byzantine and Christian Museum.

Note that a third (or fourth) day could also be used for the long but satisfying side-trip by bus to Delphi or a quick getaway by boat to the isle of Hydra—each more interesting than a third or fourth day in Athens. But these sights—and many others—are better as an overnight stop.

ORIENTATION

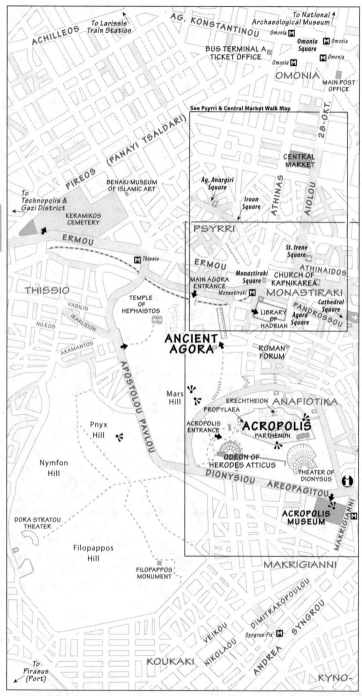

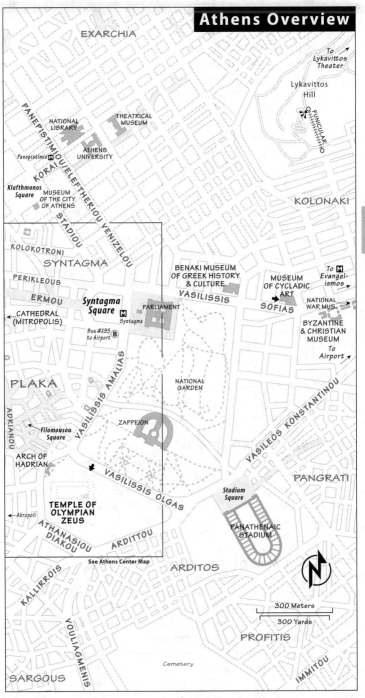

Athens Overview

EXARCHIA

To Lykavittos Theater

Lykavittos Hill

FUNICULAR

PANEPISTIMIOU/ELEFTHERIOU VENIZELOU

NATIONAL LIBRARY

THEATRICAL MUSEUM

KORAI

Panepistimio Ⓜ

ATHENS UNIVERSITY

KOLONAKI

Klafthmonos Square

MUSEUM OF THE CITY OF ATHENS

STADIOU

KOLOKOTRONI

SYNTAGMA

PERIKLEOUS

ERMOU

BENAKI MUSEUM OF GREEK HISTORY & CULTURE

MUSEUM OF CYCLADIC ART

To Ⓜ Evangel-ismos

VASILISSIS

NATIONAL WAR MUS.

Syntagma Square Ⓜ Syntagma

PARLIAMENT

SOFIAS

BYZANTINE & CHRISTIAN MUSEUM

CATHEDRAL (MITROPOLIS)

Bus #X95 to Airport Ⓑ

To Airport

PLAKA

VASILISSIS AMALIAS

NATIONAL GARDEN

ADRIANOU

Filomousou Square

ZAPPEION

VASILEOS KONSTANTINOU

ARCH OF HADRIAN

PANGRATI

Akropoli

VASILISSIS OLGAS

Stadium Square

TEMPLE OF OLYMPIAN ZEUS

ATHANASIOU DIAKOU

ARDITTOU

PANATHENAIC STADIUM

See Athens Center Map

ARDITOS

KALLIRROIS

ORIENTATION

300 Meters

300 Yards

PROFITIS

VOULIAGMENIS

Cemetery

IMMITOU

SARGOUS

N

Overview

TOURIST INFORMATION

The Greek National Tourist Organization (EOT), with its main branch near the Acropolis Museum, covers Athens and the rest of the country. Although their advice can be hit-or-miss, it's worth a stop to pick up their free city map, *Athens Live* booklet, and their slick, glossy book on Athens. They also have information on museums and hours, entertainment options, and bus and train connections (Mon-Fri 8:00-20:00, Sat-Sun 10:00-16:00, shorter hours off-season; on pedestrian street leading to Acropolis Museum at Dionysiou Areopagitou 18, Metro: Akropoli; tel. 210-331-0392, www.visitgreece.gr, info@gnto.gr).

Helpful Websites: A great resource for anyone visiting Greece is **Matt Barrett's Athens Survival Guide** (www.athensguide.com). Matt, who splits his time between North Carolina and Greece, splashes through his adopted hometown like a kid in a wading pool, enthusiastically sharing his discoveries and observations on his generous website. While his practical information isn't always the most up-to-date, his perspectives and advice are top-notch. Matt covers emerging neighborhoods that few visitors venture into, and offers offbeat angles on the city and recommendations for untouristy restaurants. He also blogs about his latest impressions of the city.

ARRIVAL IN ATHENS

For information on arriving in (or departing from) Athens by plane, boat, bus, train, or car, see the Athens Connections chapter.

GETTING AROUND ATHENS

The tourist core of Athens is surprisingly walkable. Many travelers—on a short visit and sleeping in the Plaka—find they don't need to take any public transit at all, once they're settled into their hotel. But for a longer visit, it's smart to get comfortable with public transportation, which is useful for reaching the National Archaeological Museum, the port of Piraeus, or the airport.

By Public Transportation

Athens' buses, trams, and Metro use the same ticketing system. Note that the city is gradually transitioning from paper tickets to a smart card that's reusable and rechargeable. Be prepared for either system to be in place. Also note that the tickets described next—except for the tourist ticket—do *not* cover journeys to the airport (see the Athens Connections chapter for information on getting to and from the airport).

ORIENTATION

A **basic ticket** (€1.40, or just €0.60 if over 65 or under 18) is good for 90 minutes on all public transit and covers transfers.

If planning more than three rides in a day, consider the **24-hour ticket** (€4.50).

For a longer visit using lots of public transit, you might get your money's worth with a **five-day ticket** (€9).

If starting and finishing at the airport, consider the **three-day tourist ticket** (€22), which includes a round-trip airport transfer on the Metro or Express bus #X95 as well as unlimited in-city travel on all Metro lines, the suburban railway *(Proastiakos)*, the tram, and bus.

You can buy tickets at machines, staffed ticket windows (located at some Metro stations), and some of the newsstands that dot Athens' streets. On the Metro, be sure to stamp your ticket in a validation machine before you board (look for one near the ticket booth, or at the top of the entrance escalator). For buses, validate your ticket in the orange machine as you board. Tickets only need to be stamped the first time. Those riding without a ticket (or with an unstamped ticket) are subject to stiff fines. If you have a multi-ride paper ticket, you only need to validate it the first time.

For information on all of Athens' public transportation, see www.oasa.gr. Beware of pickpockets when taking public transit.

Metro

The Metro is the most straightforward way to get around Athens. Just look for signs with a blue M in a green circle. The Metro—

mostly built, renovated, or expanded for the 2004 Olympics—is slick and user-friendly. Signs are in both Greek and English, as are announcements inside subway cars. Trains run every few minutes on weekdays, and slightly less frequently on weekends (5:00-24:00, later on Fri-Sat, www.stasy.gr).

The Metro lines are color-coded and numbered. Use the end-of-the-line stops to figure out which direction you need to go.

Line 1 (green) runs from the port of Piraeus in the southwest to Kifissia in the northern suburbs. Because this is an older line—officially called ISAP (Η.Σ.Α.Π.) or electrical train *(elektrikos)* rather than "Metro"—it is slower than the other two lines. Key stops include **Piraeus** (boats to the islands), **Thissio** (enjoyable neighborhood with good restaurants and nightlife), **Monastiraki** (city center), **Omonia** (15-minute walk from National Archaeological Museum), and **Victoria** (10-minute walk from National

Archaeological Museum). You can transfer to line 2 at Omonia and to line 3 at Monastiraki (sometimes labeled "Monastirion").

Line 2 (red) runs from Anthoupoli in the northwest to Helliniko (Elliniko) in the southeast. Important stops include **Larissa Station** (train station), **Omonia** (National Archaeological Museum), **Syntagma** (city center), **Akropoli** (Acropolis and Makrigianni/Koukaki hotel neighborhood), and **Syngrou-Fix** (Makrigianni/Koukaki hotels). Transfer to line 1 at Omonia and to line 3 at Syntagma.

Line 3 (blue)—probably the most useful for tourists—runs from Aghia Marina in the west to the airport in the east. Important stops are **Keramikos** (near Keramikos Cemetery and the lively Gazi district), **Monastiraki** (city center), **Syntagma** (city center), **Evangelismos** (Kolonaki neighborhood, with Byzantine and Christian Museum and National War Museum), and the **Airport** (requires a separate ticket). Transfer to line 1 at Monastiraki and to line 2 at Syntagma. Line 3 is being extended past Aghia Marina, into Piraeus (the new Piraeus station will open right next to the original one).

Bus

Public buses can help connect the dots between Metro stops, though the city center is so walkable that most visitors never ride one. In general, I'd avoid Athens' slow and overcrowded buses (taxis and Uber are cheap and easy), but there are a few exceptions: Buses #2, #4, #5, and #11 run from Syntagma north up the busy Eleftheriou Venizelou corridor, bearing right on 28 Oktovriou and stopping near the National Archaeological Museum (at the Polytechneio stop). From near Monastiraki (on Athinas street), bus #035 also gets you to the National Archaeological Museum. Express bus #X80 links the cruise terminals to Dionysiou Areopagitou (near the Acropolis Museum). Three special airport buses (€6 each) are also helpful: express bus #X95 to Syntagma Square, express bus #X96 to Piraeus, and express bus #X93 to both bus terminals (bus info: www.oasa.gr).

Tram

The **Athens Coastal Tram**—essentially worthless to tourists—starts at Syntagma and runs 18 miles through the neighborhoods of Neos Kosmos and Nea Smyrni, emerging at the sea near Paleo Faliro. From there it splits: One branch heads north, to the modern stadium and Olympic coastal complex in Neo Faliro (SEF/Σ.Ε.Φ.); the other runs south, past the marinas and beaches to the Voula neighborhood (www.stasy.gr).

The city also has various **suburban rail lines,** but you're unlikely to need them. For details, talk to the TI or your hotelier.

By Taxi

Despite the vulgar penchant some cabbies here have for ripping off tourists (especially at the cruise terminals), Athens is a great taxi town. Its yellow taxis are cheap and handy (€3.50 minimum charge covers most short rides in town; after that it's €0.74/km—tariff 1 on the meter, plus surcharges: €1.20 from Piraeus ports and train and bus stations, €4 from the airport—already included in airport flat rate). Between midnight and 5:00 in the morning or outside the city limits, prices are about 50 percent higher (tariff 2). Outside the city limits, you're better off negotiating a rate with your driver rather than using the meter, and you are responsible for any tolls. Baggage costs €0.45 for each large suitcase (generally items over 10 kilograms—about 22 pounds). To avoid rip-offs, make sure the meter is on (unless traveling out of the city) and set to tariff 1 (unless it's the middle of the night). Find out in advance roughly how much the fare should be (ask at hotel or restaurant).

Hotels and restaurants can call to order a taxi ("radio-taxi"), but there's a €2-4 surcharge. Warning: Cabbies may try to cheat you with a higher surcharge. Hold firm.

Uber works in Athens just as it does at home and is generally cheaper than a taxi (often even half the cost), though there is a €3 minimum charge.

By Private Car with Driver

These companies offer excursions from the cruise terminal for individuals and small groups, as well as transfers and tours from Athens: **George's Taxi,** run by George Kokkotos and his sons, has a solid reputation (for 4 people or fewer, call Nikolas at 693-220-5887; for larger groups, call Billy at 697-443-0678; www.taxigreece.com, taxigreece@yahoo.com). **Olympic Traveller** car service, run by Christos Dorzioti, has cars and minivans in Athens and Olympia (tel. 262-402-3908, mobile 697-320-1213, www.olympictraveller.com, info@olympictraveller.com).

HELPFUL HINTS

Theft Alert: Be wary of pickpockets, especially in crowds. Avoid carrying a wallet in your back pocket, and hold purses or small day bags in front, particularly at the following locations: Monastiraki flea market, Central Market, changing of the guard at the Tomb of the Unknown Soldier, major public transit routes (such as the Metro between the city and Piraeus or the airport), at the port, and on the main streets through the Plaka, such as Adrianou and Pandrossou.

Emergency Help: The Tourist Police have a 24-hour help line in English and other languages for emergencies (tel. 171 or 1571). Their office, south of the Acropolis in the Makrigianni/Koukaki district, is open 24 hours daily (Veikou 43, tel. 210-920-0724).

Traffic Alert: Streets that appear to be "traffic-free" often are shared by motorcycles or moped drivers weaving their vehicles through the crowds. Keep your wits about you, and don't step into a street—even those that feel pedestrian-friendly—without looking both ways.

Slippery Streets Alert: Athens (and other Greek towns) have some marble-like streets and red pavement tiles that become very slick when it rains. Watch your step.

Check Sight Hours Locally: The hours for sights in Greece have been known to change without much notice. I've listed the posted hours, but it's smart to check locally for the most up-to-date information.

Free Sights: The Museum of Greek Popular Instruments, National Garden, and all of Athens' churches have no entry fee.

Sights and museums run by the state, including the Acropolis, are free on all national holidays and on the first Sunday of the month during off-season (Nov-March).

Laundry: A full-service launderette in the heart of the Plaka will wash, dry, and fold your clothes (same-day service if you drop off by noon; Mon and Wed 8:00-17:00, Tue and Thu-Fri until 20:00, closed Sat-Sun; Apollonos 17, tel. 210-323-2226). **Athens Studios,** one of my recommended accommodations near the Acropolis Museum, operates a self-service launderette (daily 7:00-24:00, Veikou 3A—see map on page 178, tel. 210-922-4044).

Tours in Athens

♫ To sightsee on your own, download my series of free audio tours that illuminate some of Athens' top sights and neighborhoods, including the Acropolis, the Agora, the National Archaeological Museum, and my Athens City Walk (see sidebar on page 9).

ON WHEELS
Bus Tours

Various companies offer half-day, bus-plus-walking tours of Athens that include a guided visit to the Acropolis (about €55). Longer tours also include a guided tour of the Acropolis Museum (€70).

Some companies also offer a night city tour that finishes with dinner and folk dancing at a taverna (€65) and a 90-mile round-trip afternoon drive down the coast to Cape Sounion and the Temple of Poseidon (€50, not worth the time if visiting ancient sites elsewhere in Greece). These buses pick up passengers at various points around town and near most hotels.

The most established operations include the well-regarded **Hop In** (modern comfy buses, narration usually English only, tel. 210-428-5500, www.hopin.com), **CHAT Tours** (tel. 210-323-0827, www.chatours.gr), **Key Tours** (tel. 210-923-3166, www.keytours.gr), and **GO Tours** (tel. 210-921-9555, www.gotours.com.gr). It's convenient to book tours through your hotel; most act as a booking agent for at least one tour company. While hotels do snare a commission, some offer discounts to their guests.

Athens and Beyond: Some of these companies also offer day-long tours to Delphi and to Mycenae, Nafplio, and Epidavros (either tour around €100 with lunch, €85 without), two-day tours to the monasteries of Meteora (from €200), and more. **Greek Travelling** offers day trips from Athens to the Peloponnese and mainland, as well as airport transfers and customized private tours of Athens (English-speaking drivers, reasonable rates, mobile 697-

320-1213, www.greektravelling.com, info@greektravelling.com; charming guides Christos and Niki).

Hop-On, Hop-Off Bus Tours

Several hop-on, hop-off bus tour companies offer 1.5-hour loops and 24-hour tickets for €16-20, including **CitySightseeing Athens** (red buses, www.citysightseeing.gr), **Athens Open Tour** (yellow buses, www.athensopentour.com), and the cheaper **Open Top Bus** (blue buses, www.sightsofathens.gr). The main stop is on Syntagma Square, though you can hop on and buy your ticket at any stop—look for signs around town. Because most of the major sights in Athens are within easy walking distance of the Plaka, I'd use this only if I wanted an overview of the city or had extra time to get to the outlying sights.

Tourist Trains

Two different trains do a sightseeing circuit through Athens' tourist zone. As these goofy little trains can go where big buses can't, they can be useful for people with limited mobility. You can catch the **Sunshine Express** train on Aiolou street along the Hadrian's Library fence at Agora Square, or near the entrance to the Acropolis Museum (€5, hourly 11:00-22:00, Oct-April Sat-Sun only, 50-minute loop, tel. 211-405-5373, www.athensbytrain.gr, info@athensbytrain.com). The **Athens Happy Train** is similar, but offers hop-on, hop-off privileges at a few strategic stops (€5, 2/hour 9:00-24:00, 40-minute loop; catch it at the bottom of Syntagma Square or at Monastiraki Square; tel. 213-039-0888, www.athenshappytrain.com).

ON FOOT

Walking Tours

Athens Walking Tours offers several walks, including just the Acropolis (€29, daily at 11:15, 1.5 hours), the Acropolis and City Tour (€39 plus entry fees, daily at 9:30, 3.5 hours), and their combo Acropolis, City Tour, and Acropolis Museum Tour (€56 plus entry fees, daily at 9:30, 5.5 hours, reserve in advance, tel. 210-884-7269, mobile 694-585-9662, www.athenswalkingtours.gr, Despina). They also offer a food tour, wine tasting tour, and cooking lesson with dinner.

Context Athens' "intellectual by design" walking tours are geared for serious learners and led by "docents" (historians, architects, and academics) rather than by guides. They cover ancient sites and museums and offer themed walks with topics ranging from food to architecture to the Byzantine era (details on their website, US tel. 800-691-6036, www.contexttravel.com/city/athens).

Alternative Athens delves into the Greek capital's contemporary side, with a less strict focus on weighty history. They run excellent food tours, as well as walks focusing on street art, Greek designers, Athens' neighborhoods, and Greek mythology (mobile 694-840-5242, www.alternativeathens.com).

Food Tours

A good way to experience Greek culture is through its cuisine. Several companies offer culinary walking tours around Athens (see page 190 for a rundown).

Local Guides

A good private guide can bring Athens' sights to life. While there's some variation, most charge around €50 per hour. I've enjoyed working with each of these guides: **Effie Perperi** (mobile 697-739-6659, effieperperi@gmail.com); **Angelos Kokkaliaris** (mobile 697-412-7127, www.athenswalkingguide.com, angelo@athenswalkingguide.com); **Dora Mavrommati** (mobile 694-689-9300, mavrom.dor@gmail.com); **Faye Georgiou** (mobile 697-768-5503, fayegeorgiou@yahoo.gr); **Anastasia Gaitanou** (mobile 694-446-3109, anastasia2570@yahoo.com); and **Danae Kousouri** (mobile 697-353-3219, danaekousouri@gmail.com). **Apostolos Douras** doesn't lead tours of the ancient sites, but enjoys showing visitors the modern side of Athens, especially street art (mobile 697-854-4912, adouras@gmail.com).

ORIENTATION

SIGHTS IN ATHENS

The sights listed in this chapter are arranged by neighborhood for handy sightseeing. When you see a 📖 in a listing, it means the sight is covered in much more depth in one of my self-guided walks or tours. A 🎧 means the walk or tour is available as a free audio tour (via my Rick Steves Audio Europe app—see page 9). Some walks and tours are available in both formats—take your pick.

This is why Athens' most important attractions get less coverage in this chapter—we'll explore them later in the book, where you'll also find info on avoiding lines, saving money, and finding a decent bite to eat nearby.

For general tips on sightseeing, see page 503. Be aware that open hours at some sights may vary from those printed in this book. Check locally before planning your day. Also, be sure to check www.ricksteves.com/update for any significant changes that may have occurred since this book was printed.

ACROPOLIS AND NEARBY

A broad pedestrian boulevard that I call the "Acropolis Loop" strings together the Acropolis, Mars Hill, Theater of Dionysus, Acropolis Museum, and the Ancient Agora.

▲▲▲Acropolis

The most important ancient site in the Western world, the Acropolis (which means "high city" in Greek) rises gleaming like a beacon above the gray concrete drudgery of modern Athens. This is where, circa 450 B.C., the Athenian ruler Pericles

Acropolis Tickets

A **basic Acropolis ticket** costs €20 (€10 Nov-March) and covers entry to the Acropolis, as well as access to sights on the north and south slopes, including the Theater of Dionysus. If buying this ticket, you can save time by purchasing it at the Theater of Dionysus ticket office rather than the often-crowded Acropolis ticket office.

If you plan to visit Athens' other major ancient sites, the €30 **Acropolis combo-ticket** is the better deal, as it covers not only the Acropolis and Theater of Dionysus, but also the Ancient Agora (€8), Roman Forum (€6), Temple of Olympian Zeus (€6), Library of Hadrian (€4), and Keramikos Cemetery (€8; individual entry prices are cut in half for all of these sights in winter; no winter discount on combo-ticket). The combo-ticket is valid for five days, and since you can buy it at any participating sight, it allows you to skip the ticket-buying line at the Acropolis. Note that the Acropolis combo-ticket has one designated stub for the Acropolis, but all the others are interchangeable, so you can visit each covered sight once, or the same one several times.

These sights are always free for those 18 and under. They're also free on national holidays, and on the first Sunday of the month from November through March.

spared no expense in transforming a site laid waste by an earlier war with Persia into a complex of lavishly decorated temples to honor the city's patron goddess, Athena. The mighty Parthenon, the most famous temple on the planet, and three other major monuments built during this Golden Age—the Erechtheion, Propylaea, and Temple of Athena Nike—survive in remarkably good condition given the battering they've taken over the centuries. Ongoing restoration work means that you'll likely see some scaffolding—but even that can't detract from the greatness of this sight.

Cost and Hours: €20, €10 off-season (Nov-March), covered by Acropolis combo-ticket; daily 8:00-20:00, Oct until 18:00, Nov-March until 17:00; main entrance at western end of the Acropolis—if you're at the Ancient Agora in the Plaka, signs point uphill; tel. 210-321-4172, www.culture.gr.

See the 📖 Acropolis Tour chapter or download my free 🎧 audio tour.

▲▲"Acropolis Loop"
(a.k.a. Dionysiou Areopagitou and Apostolou Pavlou)

One of Athens' best attractions, this wide, well-manicured, delightfully traffic-free pedestrian boulevard borders the Acropolis to the south and east. It's composed of two streets with tongue-twisting names—Dionysiou Areopagitou and Apostolou Pavlou (think

SIGHTS

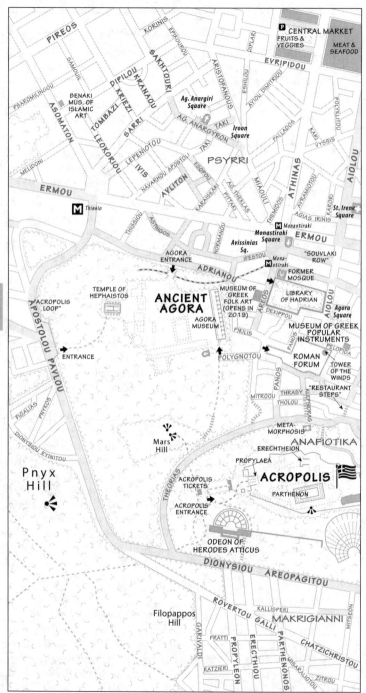

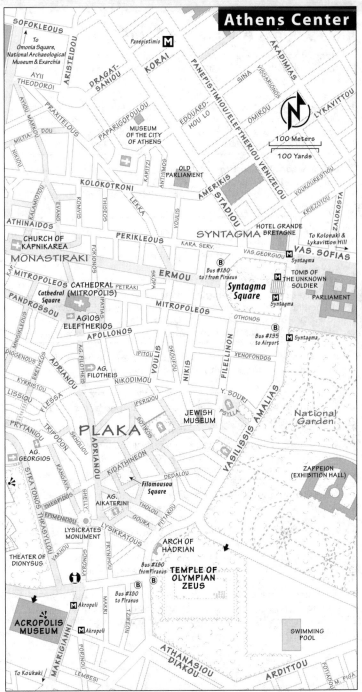

Athens at a Glance

Sights generally keep consistent morning opening hours but can close earlier than listed in the afternoon. Many closing times depend on the sunset. Check locally.

▲▲▲**Acropolis** The most important ancient site in the Western world, where Athenians built their architectural masterpiece, the Parthenon. **Hours:** Daily 8:00-20:00, Oct until 18:00, Nov-March until 17:00. See page 40.

▲▲▲**Acropolis Museum** Modern temple for ancient art. **Hours:** Daily 8:00-20:00 except Mon until 16:00, Fri until 22:00; Nov-March Mon-Thu 9:00-17:00, Fri until 22:00, Sat-Sun until 20:00. See page 48.

▲▲▲**Ancient Agora** Social and commercial center of ancient Athens, with a well-preserved temple and an intimate museum. **Hours:** Daily 8:00-20:00, Oct until 18:00, Nov-March until 15:00. See page 48.

▲▲▲**National Archaeological Museum** World's best collection of ancient Greek art, displayed chronologically from 7000 B.C. to A.D. 500. **Hours:** Daily 8:00-20:00; Nov-March Mon 12:00-17:00, Tue-Sun 8:00-15:00. See page 57.

▲▲**"Acropolis Loop"** Traffic-free pedestrian walkways ringing much of the Acropolis with vendors, cafés, and special events. See page 41.

▲▲**Anafiotika** Delightful neighborhood draped across the hillside north of the Acropolis. See page 50.

▲▲**Temple of Olympian Zeus** Remains of the largest temple in ancient Greece. **Hours:** Daily 8:00-20:00, Oct until 18:00, Nov-March until 15:00. See page 54.

▲▲**Psyrri** Vibrant neighborhood near the center, great for eating, exploring, and escaping other tourists. See page 56.

▲▲**Benaki Museum of Greek History and Culture** Exquisite collection of artifacts from the ancient, Byzantine, Ottoman, and modern eras. **Hours:** Wed and Fri 10:00-18:00, Thu and Sat until 24:00, Sun until 16:00, closed Mon-Tue. See page 58.

▲▲**Museum of Cycladic Art** World's largest compilation of Cycladic art, from 4,000 years ago. **Hours:** Wed-Mon 10:00-17:00 except Thu until 20:00 and Sun from 11:00, closed Tue. See page 59.

▲▲**Byzantine and Christian Museum** Fascinating look at the Byzantines, who put their own stamp on Greek and Roman culture. **Hours:** Daily 8:00-20:00. See page 60.

▲**Mars Hill** Historic spot—with a classic view of the Acropolis—where the Apostle Paul preached to the Athenians. See page 46.

▲**Thissio** Good neighborhood for food and drink, often accompanied by fine views of the Acropolis. See page 49.

▲**Gazi** Former industrial zone, now a young, colorful eating and nightlife spot. See page 50.

▲**Roman Forum and Tower of the Winds** Ancient Roman marketplace with wondrously intact tower. **Hours:** Daily 8:00-17:00, shorter hours off-season. See page 50.

▲**Museum of Greek Popular Instruments** Musical instruments from the 18th century to today. **Hours:** Tue-Sun 8:00-15:00, closed Mon. See page 51.

▲**Syntagma Square** Famous public space with a popular changing-of-the-guard ceremony five minutes before the top of each hour. See page 52.

▲**Ermou Street** Pleasant traffic-free pedestrian street brimming with international chain stores and fun people-watching. See page 53.

▲**Church of Kapnikarea** Small 11th-century Byzantine church with symbols of Greek Orthodox faith. **Hours:** Likely open daily 8:30-13:30 plus Tue and Thu-Fri 17:00-19:30. See page 53.

▲**Church of Agios Eleftherios** Tiny Byzantine church decorated with a millennia of Christian bric-a-brac. **Hours:** Likely open daily 8:30-13:30 & 17:00-19:30. See page 53.

▲**Panathenaic (a.k.a. "Olympic") Stadium** Gleaming marble stadium restored to its second-century A.D. condition. **Hours:** Daily 8:00-19:00, Nov-Feb until 17:00. See page 55.

▲**Central Market** A fun and aromatic sensory adventure, with a mind-boggling assortment of food and local color. **Hours:** Mon-Sat 7:00-15:00, closed Sun. See page 56.

▲**Museum of the City of Athens** Exhibits about Athenian history, housed in a former royal residence. **Hours:** Mon and Wed-Fri 9:00-16:00, Sat-Sun 10:00-15:00, closed Tue. See page 62.

SIGHTS

of them as Dionysus Street and Apostle Paul's Street); for simplicity, I refer to them collectively as the "Acropolis Loop." One of the city's many big upgrades from its 2004 Olympics-hosting bid, this walkway immediately became a favorite local hangout, with vendors, al fresco cafés, and frequent special events enlivening its cobbles.

Dionysiou Areopagitou, wide and touristy, runs along the southern base of the Acropolis. It was named for Dionysus the Areopagite, first bishop and patron saint of Athens and a member of the ancient Roman-era senate that met atop Mars Hill (described next). The other section, **Apostolou Pavlou**—quieter, narrower, and tree-lined—curls around the western end of the Acropolis and the Ancient Agora. It feels more local and has the best concentration of outdoor eateries. This section was named for the Apostle Paul, who presented himself before Dionysus the Areopagite at Mars Hill.

Where Apostolou Pavlou meets the Thissio Metro stop, you can head west on Ermou—a similarly enjoyable pedestrianized boulevard—to reach the Gazi district's Technopolis and the Keramikos Cemetery. If you head east on Ermou (with traffic), you'll come to Syntagma Square. Or, if you want to encircle the base of the Acropolis, head east on Adrianou, the pedestrian street you'll hit just before the Thissio Metro stop, and stroll through the Plaka on your way back to Dionysiou Areopagitou.

▲Mars Hill (Areopagus)

The knobby, windswept hill crawling with tourists in front of the Acropolis is Mars Hill, also known as Areopagus (from *Areios Pagos,* "Ares Hill," refer-

ring to the Greek version of Mars). While the views from the Acropolis are more striking, rugged Mars Hill (near the Acropolis' main entrance, at the western end) makes a pleasant perch. As you're climbing Mars Hill, be warned: The stone stairs (and the top of the rock) have been polished to a slippery shine by history, and can be treacherous even when dry. Watch your step and use the metal staircase.

This hill has an interesting history. After Rome conquered Athens in 86 B.C., the Roman overlords wisely decided to extend citizenship to any free man born here. (The feisty Greeks were less likely to rise up against a state that had made them citizens.) Whereas Rome called the shots on major issues, minor matters of local governance were determined on this hill by a gathering of leaders. During this time, the Apostle Paul—the first great Christian missionary and author of about half of the New Testament—preached to the Athenians here on Mars Hill. Paul looked out over the Agora and started talking about an altar he'd seen—presumably in the Agora (though archaeologists can't confirm)—to the "Unknown God." (A plaque embedded in the rock near the stairs contains the Greek text of Paul's speech.) Although the Athenians were famously open-minded, Paul encountered a skeptical audience and only netted a couple of converts (including Dionysus the Areopagite—the namesake of the pedestrian drag behind the Acropolis). Paul moved on to Corinth, where he enjoyed a better reception.

Theater of Dionysus

The scant remains of this theater are scattered southeast of the Acropolis, just above the Dionysiou Areopagitou walkway. During Roman times, the theater was connected to the Odeon of Herodes Atticus (described in the Acropolis Tour chapter) by a long, covered stoa, creating an ensemble of inviting venues. But its illustrious history dates back well before that: It's fair to say that this is where

our culture's great tradition of theater was born. During Athens' Golden Age, Sophocles and others watched their plays performed here. Originally just grass, with a circular dirt area as the stage, the theater was eventually expanded, and stone seating added, to accommodate 17,000 patrons in about 330 B.C., during the time of Alexander the Great. Later the Romans added a raised stage. Because the theater is included in any Acropolis ticket, consider a stroll through its rubble. Plans are afoot to restore the theater to its former greatness.

Cost and Hours: €2, covered by either Acropolis ticket or Acropolis combo-ticket, same hours as the Acropolis, main gate across from Acropolis Museum, tel. 210-322-4625.

▲▲▲Acropolis Museum

This museum is a modern-day temple to the Acropolis. Located at the foot of Athens' famous ancient hill, it contains relics from

the Acropolis, including statues of young men and women, gods and goddesses, reliefs that once adorned the hilltop temples, and five of the six original Caryatids (lady-columns) that once held up the roof of the Erechtheion temple. But the highlight is a life-size re-creation of the frieze that once wound all the way around the outside of the Parthenon, blending original pieces with copies of panels housed in the British Museum and other collections. Completed in 2009, the stunning glass building is a work of art in itself. The top floor sits slightly askew, like a graduation cap, mimicking the orientation of the Parthenon. The glass walls are designed not only to flood the place with natural light, but also to disappear into the background so that the architecture plays second fiddle to the real stars: the statuary and the views of the Acropolis.

Cost and Hours: €5; daily 8:00-20:00 except Mon until 16:00, Fri until 22:00; Nov-March Mon-Thu 9:00-17:00, Fri until 22:00, Sat-Sun until 20:00. The museum faces the south side of the Acropolis from across the broad Dionysiou Areopagitou pedestrian drag, and is right at the Akropoli Metro stop; tel. 210-900-0900, www.theacropolismuseum.gr.

📖 See the Acropolis Museum Tour chapter.

ANCIENT AGORA AND BEYOND

These sights are listed in geographic order, starting with the Agora and fanning out from there (mostly to the west—see the map on page 31). You can walk to the cemetery and the Gazi district via the wide, pedestrianized Ermou street.

▲▲▲Ancient Agora: Athens' Market

If the Acropolis was Golden Age Athens' "uptown," then the Ancient Agora was "downtown." Although literally and figuratively overshadowed by the impressive Acropolis, the Agora was for eight centuries the true meeting place of the city—a hive of commerce, politics, and everyday bustle. Everybody who was anybody in ancient Athens spent time here, from Socrates and Plato to a visiting missionary named Paul. Built upon, forgotten, and ignored for centuries, the Agora was excavated in the 1930s. Now it's a center of archaeological study and one of the city's top tourist attractions. A visit here lets you ponder its sparse remains, wander through a modest museum in a rebuilt stoa (the Agora Museum), admire its beautifully preserved Temple of Hephaistos, and imagine sharing this hallowed  space with the great minds of the ancient world.

Cost and Hours: €8, covered by Acropolis combo-ticket; daily 8:00-20:00, Oct until 18:00, Nov-March until 15:00; Agora Museum has the same hours (except on Mon off-season, when it opens at 11:00); main entrance on Adrianou—from the Monastiraki Metro stop, walk a block south (uphill, toward the Acropolis); tel. 210-321-0180, www.culture.gr.

See the 📖 Ancient Agora Tour chapter or download my free 🎧 audio tour.

SIGHTS

▲Thissio

This trendy zone, around the far side of the Acropolis (just follow the main pedestrian drag), has a hipster vibe and a thriving passel of cafés and restaurants with Acropolis views, plus an appealing open-air cinema (see Shopping & Nightlife in Athens). If you stroll around the "Acropolis Loop," you'll wander right past it. Consider stopping off for a meal, a drink, or just to poke around.

Benaki Museum of Islamic Art

Sometimes it seems the Greeks would rather just forget the Ottoman chapter of their past...but when you're talking about nearly 400 years, that's difficult to do. If you're intrigued by what Greeks consider a low point in their history, pay a visit to this branch of the Benaki Museum (listing for main branch, Benaki Museum of Greek History and Culture, appears later). The 8,000-piece collection, displayed in two renovated Neoclassical buildings, includes beautifully painted ceramics, a rare 14th-century astrolabe, and an entire marble room from a 17th-century Cairo mansion.

Cost and Hours: €9; Thu-Sun 10:00-18:00, closed Mon-Wed; northeast of Keramikos Cemetery at Agion Asomaton 22, at the corner with Dipilou, Metro: Thissio, tel. 210-325-1311, www.benaki.gr.

Keramikos Cemetery

Named for the ceramics workshops that used to surround it, this is a vast place to wander among marble tombstones from the seventh century B.C. onward. While the sprawling cemetery provides more exercise than excitement—and requires a good imagination to take on much meaning—the small, modern museum is a delight. With a wealth of artifacts found right here, it explains the evolution of ancient burial rituals one age at a time.

Cost and Hours: €8, covered by Acropolis combo-ticket; daily 8:00-20:00, Oct until 18:00, Nov-March until 15:00 and closed Mon; air-con, Ermou 148, Metro stops: Thissio or Keramikos, tel. 210-346-3552.

▲Gazi

Just beyond Keramikos Cemetery, this former industrial zone is now super-trendy, gentrified, and colorful—with lots of great restaurants (see recommendations in Eating in Athens chapter) and hopping nightclubs.

Gazi huddles around the **Technopolis** events center complex, built in the remains of a 19th-century gas works. Technopolis hosts an eclectic assortment of cultural happenings, including art exhibits, rock concerts, and experimental theater. After dark, the still-standing smokestacks are illuminated in red, giving an eerie impression of its former industrial activity (Pireos 100, Metro: Keramikos—as you exit, walk to the square brick smokestacks, tel. 210-346-1589, www.technopolis-athens.com).

IN THE PLAKA AND MONASTIRAKI

These sights are scattered around the super-central Plaka neighborhood. The first three sights are covered in more detail in the 📖 Athens City Walk chapter and my free 🎧 audio tour.

▲▲Anafiotika

Clinging to the northern slope of the Acropolis (just above the Plaka), this improbable Greek-island-on-a-hillside feels a world apart from the endless sprawl of concrete and moped-choked streets that stretch from its base. For a break from the big city, escape here for an enjoyable stroll.

▲Roman Forum
(a.k.a. "Roman Agora")
and Tower of the Winds

After the Romans conquered Athens in 86 B.C., they built their version of an agora—the forum—on this spot. Today it's a pile of ruins, watched over by the marvelously intact Tower of the Winds. Panels circling the top of the tower depict the eight winds that shape Athenian weather. The ticket office and entry gate are near the tallest standing colonnade, and the tower is explained on a plaque.

Cost and Hours: €6, covered by Acropolis combo-ticket; daily 8:00-17:00, shorter hours off-season; corner of Pelopida and Aiolou streets, Metro: Monastiraki, tel. 210-324-5220.

Library of Hadrian

About a block from the Roman Forum, down Aiolou street, is an area of Roman ruins containing what's left of the Library of Hadrian (erected A.D. 131-132), along with a few remains of various churches that were built in later periods, including a fifth-century tetraconch church (with four semicircular apses) and a simple 12th-century church. Tucked away in a corner building is a 10-foot statue of Nike stepping on a globe, uncovered in 1988.

Cost and Hours: €4, covered by Acropolis combo-ticket; daily 8:00-15:00, possibly open later in summer; across from Agora Square, Metro: Monastiraki, tel. 210-324-5220.

▲Museum of Greek Popular Instruments

Small but well-presented, this charming collection is one of the most entertaining museums in Athens. On its three floors, you can wander around listening (on headphones) to different instruments and styles of music. Examine instruments dating from the 18th century to today. The main floor shows off drums, flutes, and bagpipes. Upstairs are stringed instruments—fiddles, violins, mandolins, and so on. And downstairs are bells, the boards hammered by Orthodox priests to announce worship services, and other percussion instruments. Throughout, photos, video clips, and paintings illustrate the instruments being played, and everything is described in English. This easily digestible collection is an enjoyable change of pace from more of the same old artifacts.

Cost and Hours: Free; Tue-Sun 8:00-15:00, closed Mon; near Roman Forum at Diogenous 1, Metro: Monastiraki, tel. 210-325-0198.

Jewish Museum of Greece

Many Jewish communities trace their roots back to medieval Spain's Sephardic diaspora and, before that, to classical Greece. (Before the Nazis invaded, Greece had 78,000 Jews; more than 85 percent of them perished in the Holocaust.) This collection of more than 8,000 Jewish artifacts—thoughtfully displayed on four

SIGHTS

floors of a modern building—traces the history of Greek Jews since the second century B.C. Downstairs from the entry, you can visit a replica synagogue with worship items. Then spiral up through the split-level space (borrowing English descriptions in each room) to see exhibits on Jewish holidays, history, Zionism, the Nazi occupation and Holocaust, traditional dress, and the everyday lives of Greek Jews.

Cost and Hours: €6; Mon-Fri 9:00-14:30, Sun 10:00-14:00, closed Sat; Nikis 39, at the corner with Kidathineon—ring bell to get inside; Metro: Syntagma, tel. 210-322-5582, www.jewishmuseum.gr.

Museum of Greek Folk Art

This museum, scheduled to reopen in 2019 in a new location near Monastiraki Square, displays four centuries (17th-20th) of items relating to Greek life. The collection includes traditional artwork and folk costumes, plus a look at religion, food, and where and how Greeks lived in earlier times. They may also reopen a ceramics collection in the nearby former mosque that overlooks Monastiraki Square.

Cost and Hours: Closed for renovation—check their website or call ahead for updates, tel. 210-322-9031, www.melt.gr.

IN SYNTAGMA

The Syntagma area borders the Plaka to the north and east. All of these sights are covered in detail in the ▢ Athens City Walk chapter and my free ⌂ audio tour. I've listed only the essentials here.

▲Syntagma Square (Plateia Syntagmatos)

The "Times Square" of Athens is named for Greece's historic 1843 constitution, prompted by demonstrations right on this square. A major transit hub, the square is watched over by Neoclassical masterpieces such as the Hotel Grande Bretagne and the parliament building.

Parliament

The former palace of King Otto is now a house of democracy. In front, colorfully costumed evzone guards stand at attention at the

Tomb of the Unknown Soldier and periodically do a ceremonial changing of the guard to the delight of tourists (guards change five minutes before the top of each hour, less elaborate crossing of the guard around :25 after, full ceremony with marching band Sundays at 11:00—get there early as they may start a bit before 11:00).

▲Ermou Street

This pedestrianized thoroughfare, connecting Syntagma Square with Monastiraki (and on to Thissio and Keramikos Cemetery), is packed with international chain stores. It's enjoyable for people-watching and is refreshingly traffic-free in an otherwise congested area.

CHURCHES IN THE PLAKA AND SYNTAGMA AREA

All of these sights are covered in detail in the 📖 Athens City Walk chapter and my free 🎧 audio tour. Only the basics are listed here.

▲Church of Kapnikarea

Sitting unassumingly in the middle of Ermou street, this small 11th-century Byzantine church offers a convenient look at the Greek Orthodox faith.

Cost and Hours: Free, likely open daily 8:30-13:30 plus Tue and Thu-Fri 17:00-19:30.

Cathedral (Mitropolis)

Dating from the mid-19th century, this is the big head church of Athens—and therefore of all of Greece. The cathedral, with a beautifully restored interior, is the centerpiece of a reverent neighborhood, with a pair of statues out front honoring great heroes of the Church; surrounding streets lined with religious paraphernalia shops (and black-cloaked, long-bearded priests); and the cute little Church of Agios Eleftherios (described next).

Cost and Hours: Free, likely open daily 8:00-19:00, closed 13:00-16:30 off-season, Plateia Mitropoleos.

▲Church of Agios Eleftherios

This tiny church, huddled in the shadow of the cathedral, has a delightful hodgepodge of ancient and early Christian monuments embedded in its facade. Like so many Byzantine churches, it was partly built (in the late 12th century) with frag-

SIGHTS

ments of earlier buildings, monuments, and even tombstones...a hodgepodge of millennia-old bits and pieces.

Cost and Hours: Free, likely open daily 8:30-13:30 & 17:00-19:30, Plateia Mitropoleos.

EAST OF THE PLAKA

These two sights, dating from Athens' Roman period, overlook a busy highway at the edge of the tourist zone (just a few steps up Dionysiou Areopagitou from the Acropolis Museum and Akropoli Metro stop, or a 10-minute walk south of Syntagma Square). Both are described in greater detail in the 📖 Athens City Walk chapter and my free 🎧 audio tour.

▲Arch of Hadrian

This stoic triumphal arch stands at the edge of the new suburb of ancient Athens built by the Roman Emperor Hadrian in the second century A.D. (always viewable).

▲▲Temple of Olympian Zeus

Started by an overambitious tyrant in the sixth century B.C., this giant temple was not completed until Hadrian took over seven cen-

turies later. Now 15 of the original 104 Corinthian columns stand evocatively over a ruined base in a field. You can get a good view of the temple ruins through the fence by the Arch of Hadrian, but if you have the Acropolis combo-ticket, consider dropping in for a closer look.

Cost and Hours: €6, covered by Acropolis combo-ticket; daily 8:00-20:00, Oct until 18:00, Nov-March until 15:00; Vasilissis Olgas 1, Metro: Akropoli; tel. 210-922-6330, www.culture.gr.

SOUTH AND EAST OF PARLIAMENT AND SYNTAGMA SQUARE

The busy avenue called Vasilissis Amalias rumbles south of Syntagma Square, where you'll find the following sights. Note that the Arch of Hadrian and the Temple of Olympian Zeus (both described earlier) are just south of the National Garden and Zappeion.

National Garden

Extending south from the parliament, the National Garden is a wonderfully cool retreat from the traffic-clogged streets of central Athens. Covering an area of around 40 acres, it was planted in

1839 as the palace garden, created for the pleasure of Queen Amalia. Opened to the public in 1923, the garden has many pleasant paths, a café, WCs, scattered picturesque ancient columns, a playground, and several zoo-type exhibits of animals.

Cost and Hours: Free, open daily from dawn to dusk.

Zappeion

At the southern end of the National Garden stands the grand mansion called the Zappeion, surrounded by formal gardens of its own. To most Athenians, the Zappeion is best known as the site of the Aigli Village outdoor cinema in summer (behind the building, on the right as you face the colonnaded main entry; for details, see the Shopping & Nightlife in Athens chapter). But the building is more than just a backdrop. During Ottoman rule, much of the Greek elite, intelligentsia, and aristocracy fled the country. They returned after independence and built grand mansions such as this. Finished in 1888, it was designed by the Danish architect Theophilus Hansen, who was known (along with his brother Christian) for his Neoclassical designs. The financing was provided by the Zappas brothers, Evangelos and Konstantinos, two of the prime movers in the campaign to revive the Olympic Games. This mansion housed the International Olympic Committee during the first modern Olympics in 1896 and served as a media center during the 2004 Olympics. Today the Zappeion is a conference and exhibition center.

Cost and Hours: Gardens free and always open, building only open during exhibitions for a fee, Vasilissis Amalias, Metro: Akropoli or Evangelismos.

▲Panathenaic (a.k.a. "Olympic") Stadium

In your travels through Greece, you'll see some ruined ancient stadiums (including the ones in Olympia and Delphi). Here's your chance to see one intact. This gleaming marble stadium has many names. Officially it's the Panathenaic Stadium, built in the fourth century B.C. to host the Panathenaic

Games. Sometimes it's referred to as the Roman Stadium, because it was rebuilt by the great Roman benefactor Herodes Atticus in the second century A.D., using the same prized Pentelic marble that was used in the Parthenon. This magnificent material gives the place its most popular name: Kalimarmaro ("Beautiful Marble") Stadium. It was restored to its Roman condition in preparation for the first modern Olympics in 1896. It saw Olympic action again in 2004, when it provided a grand finish for the marathon and a wonderful backdrop for the Paralympics opening ceremony. Today, it's occasionally used for ceremonies and concerts. In ancient times, around 50,000 spectators filled the stadium; today, 45,000 people can pack the stands.

Cost and Hours: €5, includes good audioguide; daily 8:00-19:00, Nov-Feb until 17:00; southeast of the Zappeion off Vasileos Konstantinou, Metro: Akropoli or Evangelismos, tel. 210-752-2985, www.panathenaicstadium.gr.

NORTH OF MONASTIRAKI

Athinas street leads north from Monastiraki Square to Omonia Square (see map on page 31). Walking this grand street offers a great chance to feel the pulse of modern workaday Athens, with shops tumbling onto broad sidewalks, striking squares, nine-to-fivers out having a smoke, and lots of urban energy. Psyrri begins just across the street from Monastiraki, and just beyond is the Central Market (for more on both of these, see the 🕮 Psyrri & Central Market Walk chapter). Farther up Athinas street, past Omonia Square, is the superb National Archaeological Museum.

▲▲Psyrri

This funky district, just north of the Ancient Agora, offers a real-world alternative to the tourist-clogged, artificial-feeling Plaka. While it's outwardly grungy and run-down, Psyrri has blossomed with a fun range of eateries, cafés, and clubs, with everything from dives to exclusive dance halls to crank-'em-out chain restaurants (for recommendations on where to eat, see the Eating in Athens chapter).

▲Central Market

Take a vibrant, fragrant stroll through the modern-day version of the Ancient Agora. It's a living, breathing, and smelly barrage on all the senses. You'll see dripping-fresh meat, livestock in all stages of dismemberment, still-wriggling fish, exotic nuts, and sticky figs. It may not be Europe's most charming market, but it offers a lively contrast to Athens' ancient sites. The entire market square is a delight to explore, with a dizzying variety of great street food and a carnival of people-watching (open Mon-Sat 7:00-15:00, closed

Sun, on Athinas between Sofokleous and Evripidou, between Metro stops Omonia and Monastiraki).

▲▲▲National Archaeological Museum

This museum is the single best place on earth to see ancient Greek artifacts. Strolling through the chronologically displayed collection—from 7000 B.C. to A.D. 500—is like watching a time-lapse movie of the evolution of art. You'll go from the stylized figurines of the Cycladic Islands, to the golden artifacts of the Mycenaeans (including the so-called Mask of Agamemnon), to the stiff, stoic kouros statues of the Archaic age. Then, with the arrival of the Severe style (epitomized by the *Artemision Bronze*), the art loosens up and comes to life. As Greece enters the Classical Period, the *Bronze Statue of a Youth* is balanced and lifelike. The dramatic *Artemision Jockey* hints at the unbridled exuberance of Hellenism, which is taken to its extreme in the *Statue of a Fighting Gaul*. Rounding out the collection are Roman statuary, colorful wall paintings from Thira (today's Santorini), and room upon room of ceramics.

Cost and Hours: €10, €5 off-season; daily 8:00-20:00; Nov-March Mon 12:00-17:00, Tue-Sun 8:00-15:00; live guides available for hire in lobby; 28 Oktovriou (a.k.a. Patission) #44—see page 32 for transit options; tel. 213-214-4800, www.namuseum.gr.

See the 📖 National Archaeological Museum Tour chapter or download my free 🎧 audio tour.

Exarchia

For an edgier taste of Athens, wander into Exarchia, just a short walk behind the National Archaeological Museum. Wedged between the National Technical University, Omonia Square, and Lykavittos Hill, Exarchia is populated mostly by students, immigrants, and counterculture idealists. The neighborhood is defiant, artsy, coated in graffiti, and full of life. According to locals, many of the anarchists who have been the firepower behind Athens' violent protests call this area home.

Exarchia can be intimidating—even dangerous—and is a bit

farther afield than other areas described in this book. For some people, this is the seedy underbelly of Athens they came to see; others can't wait to get back to the predictable souvlaki stands and leather salesmen of the Plaka. If you do venture here, exercise caution and, unless you're street-smart and comfortable in gritty urban neighborhoods, think twice before wandering around after dark.

From the small Exarchia Square, side streets spin off into grungy neighborhoods. Mainstream businesses tend to steer clear of this area; instead, streets are lined with alternative boutiques, record stores, and cafés.

About two blocks south of the square—at the corner of Mesolongiou and Tzabella streets—is a memorial to Alexandros Grigoropoulos, a local teen who was shot and killed here in December 2008 when police fired into a crowd of protestors. The incident sparked an attention-grabbing wave of riots across Greece, and ever since, frustrated neighbors keep the cops out and do their own policing. The juxtaposition between Exarchia and the adjacent, very ritzy Kolonaki district makes the tragedy even more poignant. (You might notice that Exarchia's border with Kolonaki is marked by police vans.)

THE KOLONAKI MUSEUM STRIP, EAST OF SYNTAGMA SQUARE

The district called Kolonaki, once the terrain of high-society bigwigs eager to live close to the Royal Palace (now the parliament), is today's diplomatic quarter. Lining the major boulevard called Vasilissis Sofias are many embassies, a thriving local yuppie scene, and some of Athens' top museums outside the old center. These are listed in the order you'd reach them, heading east from the parliament (see map on page 31).

▲▲Benaki Museum of Greek History and Culture

This exquisite collection takes you on a fascinating walk through the ages. And, as it's housed in a gorgeous Neoclassical mansion, it gives a peek at how Athens' upper crust lived back in the 19th century. The mind-boggling array of artifacts—which could keep a museum lover busy for hours—is crammed into 36 galleries on four floors, covering seemingly every era of history: antiquity, Byzantine, Ottoman, and modern. The private collection nicely complements the many state-run museums in town. Each item is labeled in English, and it's all air-conditioned. The Benaki gift shop is a fine place to buy jewelry (replicas of museum pieces).

Cost and Hours: €9; Wed and Fri 10:00-18:00, Thu and Sat until 24:00, Sun until 16:00, closed Mon-Tue; classy rooftop café where some of today's high society hang out, across from back corner of National Garden at Koumbari 1, Metro: Syntagma, tel. 210-367-1000, www.benaki.gr.

Visiting the Museum: The first exhibit kicks things off by saying, "Around 7000 B.C., the greatest 'revolution' in human experience took place: the change from the hunting-and-gathering economy of the Paleolithic Age to the farming economy of the Neolithic Age..." You'll see fine painted vases, gold wreaths of myrtle leaves worn on heads 2,300 years ago, and evocative Byzantine icons and jewelry. Look for Byzantine icon art, including two pieces by Domenikos Theotokopoulos before he became El Greco (glass case in center of room).

Upstairs, the first floor picks up where most Athens museums leave off: the period of Ottoman and Venetian occupation. Here you'll find traditional costumes, furniture, household items, farm implements, musical instruments, and entire rooms finely carved from wood and lovingly transplanted from Northern Greece. In Rooms 22 and 23, a fascinating exhibit shows Greece through the eyes of foreign visitors, who came here in the 18th and 19th centuries (back when Athens was still a village, spiny with Ottoman minarets) to see the same ruins you're enjoying today.

Climb up through smaller rooms to the café and exhibit hall (which has good temporary exhibits). On the top floor, Romantic art depicts Greece's stirring and successful 19th-century struggle for independence. Finally, one long hall brings you into the 20th century.

▲▲Museum of Cycladic Art

This modern, cozy, enjoyable, and manageable museum shows off the largest exhibit of Cycladic art anywhere, collected by one of Greece's richest shipping families (the Goulandris clan). While you can see Cycladic art elsewhere in Athens (such as in the National Archaeological Museum), it's displayed and described most invitingly here. While the first floor is all Cycladic, there are four floors—each with a fine exhibit. Note that the museum's entrance is a few steps up the side street (Neophytou Douka); the more prominent corner building, fronting Vasilissis Sofias, is their larger annex (or "New Wing"), hosting special exhibits. A pleasant café is near the gift shop on the ground floor.

Cost and Hours: €7, half-price on Mon and off-season; Wed-Mon 10:00-17:00 except Thu until 20:00 and Sun from 11:00,

SIGHTS

closed Tue; Neophytou Douka 4, Metro: Evangelismos, tel. 210-722-8321, www.cycladic.gr.

Visiting the Museum: The **first floor** up focuses on art from the Cycladic Islands, which surround the isle of Delos, off the coast southeast of Athens. The Aegean city-states here—predating Athens' Golden Age by 2,000 years—were populated by a mysterious people who left no written record. But they did leave behind an ample collection of fertility figurines. These come in different sizes but follow the same general pattern: skinny, standing ramrod-straight, with large alien-like heads. Some have exaggerated breasts and hips, giving them a violin-like silhouette. Others (likely symbolizing pregnancy) appear to be clutching their midsections with both arms. These items give an insight into the matriarchal cultures of the Cycladic Islands. With their astonishing simplicity, the figurines appear almost abstract, as if Modigliani or Picasso had sculpted them.

While that first floor is the headliner, don't miss three more floors of exhibits upstairs: ancient Greek art, Cypriot antiquities, and scenes from daily life in antiquity. The highlight—for some, even better than the Cycladic art itself—is the engrossing **top-floor exhibit** that explains ancient Greek lifestyles. Artifacts, engaging illustrations, and vivid English descriptions resurrect a fun cross-section of the fascinating and sometimes bizarre practices of the ancients: weddings, athletics, agora culture, warfare, and various female- and male-only activities (such as the male-bonding/dining ritual called the symposium). Listen for the music that accompanies the exhibit—historians' best guess at what the ancients listened to. One movie uses actors and colorful sets to dramatize events in the life of "Leon," a fictional young man of ancient Greece. Another movie demonstrates burial rituals (for the dearly departed Leon), many of which are still practiced by Orthodox Christians in Greece today.

▲▲Byzantine and Christian Museum

This excellent museum displays key artifacts from the Byzantine Empire, covering the chapters of the Greek story that come after its famed Golden Age. It traces the era from Emperor Constantine's move from Rome to Byzantium (which he renamed Constantinople, now known as Istanbul) in A.D. 330 until the fall of Constantinople to the Ottomans in 1453. While the rest of Europe fell into the Dark Ages, Byzantium shone brightly. And, as its dominant language and education were

Greek, today's Greeks proudly consider the Byzantine Empire "theirs." Outside of the Golden Age of antiquity, the Byzantine era is considered the high-water mark for Greek culture.

Cost and Hours: €8, daily 8:00-20:00, excellent café/restaurant, Vasilissis Sofias 22, Metro: Evangelismos, tel. 210-213-9501, www.byzantinemuseum.gr.

Visiting the Museum: The museum consists of two buildings around an entry courtyard. The building in the center sells tickets and hosts temporary exhibits, while the one on the left features the permanent collection, which sprawls underground through the complex and is thoughtfully described in English.

The permanent exhibit—organized both chronologically and thematically—traces the story of the Byzantine Empire, from the waning days of antiquity through the fledgling days of early Christianity and on to the glory days of Byzantium. It's divided into two sections.

The **first section,** "From the Ancient World to Byzantium," explains how the earliest Byzantine Christians borrowed artistic forms from the Greek and Roman past and adapted them to fit their emerging beliefs. For example, the classical Greek motif of the calf bearer became the "good shepherd" of Byzantine Christianity, while early depictions of Jesus are strikingly similar to the Greek "philosopher" prototype. You'll also view mosaics and capitals from the earliest "temples" of Christianity and see how existing ancient temples were "Christianized" for new use. Other topics include Coptic art (from Egyptian Christians) and graves and burial customs.

The **second section,** "The Byzantine World," delves into various facets of Byzantium—the administration of a vast empire, the use of art in early Christian worship, wall paintings transplanted from a Byzantine church, the role of Athens (and the surrounding region of Attica) in the Byzantine Empire, the introduction of Western European artistic elements by Frankish and Latin Crusaders during the 13th century, everyday countryside lifestyles (to balance out all that stuffy ecclesiastical art), the final artistic flourishing of the 13th and 14th centuries, and the fall of Constantinople (and the Byzantine emperor) to Ottoman Sultan Mehmet the Conqueror. Altogether, it's a fascinating place to learn about a rich and often-overlooked chapter of Greek history.

National War Museum

This imposing three-story museum documents the history of Greek warfare, from Alexander the Great to today. The overtly patriotic exhibit, staffed by members of the armed forces, stirs the Greek soul. Start by riding the elevator upstairs to the first

floor. Here you'll get a quick chronological review of Greek military history, including replicas of ancient artifacts you'll see for real in other museums—fine history lessons in early war technology. The mezzanine level focuses on the Greek experience in the 20th century, including World War I (with amazing video clips) and World War II (Nazi occupation, resistance, and liberation). Back on the ground floor you'll parade past military uniforms, browse an armory of old weapons, and (outside) ogle modern military machines—tanks, fighter jets, and more (visible from the street, even when the museum is closed).

Cost and Hours: €4; daily 9:00-19:00, Nov-March until 17:00; Rizari 2 at Vasilissis Sofias, Metro: Evangelismos, tel. 210-725-2975, www.warmuseum.gr.

NORTH OF SYNTAGMA SQUARE

A few blocks up from Syntagma Square and the traffic-free Ermou street thoroughfare are more museums, including the impressive National History Museum, the Numismatic Museum (coins), and this place:

▲Museum of the City of Athens

Housed in the former residence of King Otto and Queen Amalia (where they lived from 1836 to 1843), this museum combines an elegant interior with a charming overview of the 19th- and early-20th-century history of Athens.

Cost and Hours: €5; Mon and Wed-Fri 9:00-16:00, Sat-Sun 10:00-15:00, closed Tue; outdoor café, Paparigopoulou 5, Metro: Panepistimio, tel. 210-323-1397, www.athenscitymuseum.gr.

Visiting the Museum: The ground floor has two highlights. In the first room is a giant panoramic late-17th-century painting of Louis XIV's ambassador and his party, with Athens in the background. The work shows a small village occupied by Ottomans (with prickly minarets rising from the rooftops), before the Parthenon was partially destroyed (it's the only painting depicting an intact Athens and Parthenon).

In the next room, a large model shows Athens circa 1842, just as it was emerging as the capital of Greece. A touchscreen computer lets you choose various locations on the model, read more about those sights, virtually circle around them, and watch videos.

Upstairs are lavishly decorated rooms and exhibits that emphasize King Otto's role in the fledgling Greek state following the Ottoman defeat. Throughout the place you'll see idyllic paintings of Athens as it was a century and a half ago: a red-roofed village at the foot of the Acropolis populated by Greek shepherds in traditional costume. Stepping back outside into the smog and noise after your visit, you'll wish you had a time machine.

SIGHTS

ATHENS CITY WALK

From Syntagma Square to Monastiraki Square

Athens is a bustling metropolis of nearly four million people, home to one out of every three Greeks. Much of the city is unappealing, cheaply built, poorly zoned 20th-century sprawl. But the heart and soul of Athens is engaging and refreshingly compact. This walk takes you through the striking contrasts of the city center—from chaotic, traffic-clogged urban zones, to sleepy streets packed with bearded priests shopping for a new robe or chalice, to peaceful, barely-wide-enough-for-a-donkey back lanes that twist their way up toward the Acropolis. Along the way, we'll learn about Athens' rich history, the intriguing tapestry of Orthodox churches that dot the city, and the way that locals live and shop.

The walk begins at Syntagma Square, meanders through the fascinating old Plaka district, and finishes at lively Monastiraki Square (near the Ancient Agora, markets, good restaurants, and a handy Metro stop). This sightseeing spine will help you get a once-over-lightly look at Athens, which you can use as a springboard for diving into the city's various colorful sights and neighborhoods.

Orientation

Length of This Walk: Allow plenty of time. This three-part walk takes two hours without stops or detours. But if you explore and dip into sights here and there—pausing to ponder a dimly lit Orthodox church, or doing some window (or actual) shopping—it can enjoyably eat up a half-day or more. This walk is also easy to break up—stop after Part 2 and return for Part 3 later.

When to Go: Do this walk early in your visit, as it can help you get your bearings in this potentially confusing city. Morning is best, since many churches close for an afternoon break, and other sights—including the Acropolis—are too crowded to enjoy by midmorning.

Getting There: The walk begins at Syntagma Square, just northeast of the Plaka tourist zone. It's a short walk from the recommended Plaka hotels; if you're staying away from the city center, get here by Metro (stop: Syntagma).

Churches: Athens' churches are free but keep irregular hours—generally open daily 8:30-13:30 and some evenings (17:00-19:30). If you want to buy candles at churches (as the locals do), be sure to have a few small coins.

Cathedral: Free, likely open daily 8:00-19:00 (closed 13:00-16:30 off-season).

Temple of Olympian Zeus: €6, covered by Acropolis combo-ticket (see page 41); daily 8:00-20:00, Oct until 18:00, Nov-March until 15:00.

Roman Forum: €6, covered by Acropolis combo-ticket, daily 8:00-17:00, shorter hours off-season.

Library of Hadrian: €4, covered by Acropolis combo-ticket, daily 8:00-15:00, possibly open later in summer.

Tours: ∩ Download my free Athens City Walk **audio tour.**

Dress Code: Wearing shorts inside churches is frowned upon, though usually tolerated.

Starring: Athens' top squares, churches, and Roman ruins, connected by bustling urban streets that are alternately choked with cars and mopeds, or thronged by pedestrians, vendors... and fellow tourists.

The Walk Begins

This lengthy walk is thematically divided into three parts: The first part focuses on modern Athens, centered on Syntagma Square and the Ermou shopping street. The second part focuses on Athens' Greek Orthodox faith, with visits to three different but equally interesting churches. And the third part is a wander through the charming old core of Athens, including the  touristy Plaka and the mellow Greek-village-on-a-hillside of Anafiotika.

PART 1: MODERN ATHENS

This part of our walk lets you feel the pulse of a European capital.

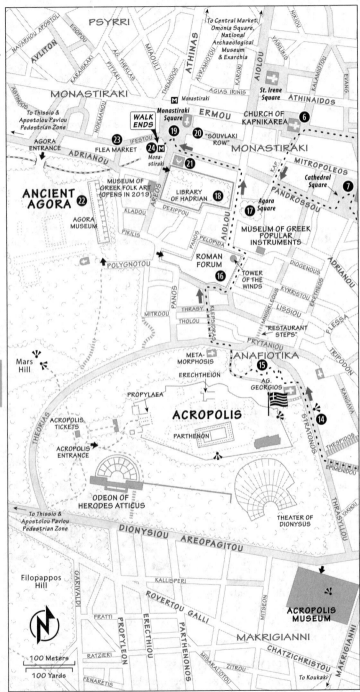

CITY WALK

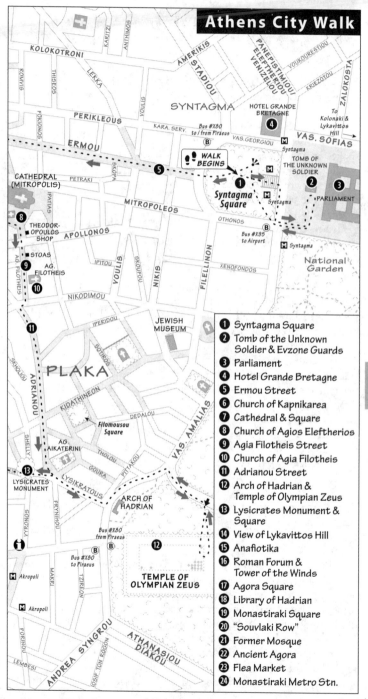

Athens City Walk

1. Syntagma Square
2. Tomb of the Unknown Soldier & Evzone Guards
3. Parliament
4. Hotel Grande Bretagne
5. Ermou Street
6. Church of Kapnikarea
7. Cathedral & Square
8. Church of Agios Eleftherios
9. Agia Filotheis Street
10. Church of Agia Filotheis
11. Adrianou Street
12. Arch of Hadrian & Temple of Olympian Zeus
13. Lysicrates Monument & Square
14. View of Lykavittos Hill
15. Anafiotika
16. Roman Forum & Tower of the Winds
17. Agora Square
18. Library of Hadrian
19. Monastiraki Square
20. "Souvlaki Row"
21. Former Mosque
22. Ancient Agora
23. Flea Market
24. Monastiraki Metro Stn.

CITY WALK

• *Start at Syntagma Square. From the leafy park at the center of the square, climb to the top of the stairs (in the middle of the square) and stand across the street from the big, Neoclassical Greek Parliament building.*

❶ Syntagma Square (Plateia Syntagmatos)

Facing the Parliament building (east), get oriented to the square named for Greece's constitution (*syntagma;* SEEN-dag-mah).

From this point, sightseeing options spin off through the city like spokes on a wheel.

Fronting the square on the left (north) side are high-end hotels, including the opulent Hotel Grande Bretagne (with its swanky rooftop garden restaurant).

Directly to the left of the Parliament building is the head of Vasilissis Sofias avenue, lined with embassies and museums, including the Benaki Museum of Greek History and Culture, Museum of Cycladic Art, Byzantine and Christian Museum, and National War Museum. This boulevard leads to the ritzy Kolonaki quarter, with its funicular up to the top of Lykavittos Hill.

Extending to the right of the Parliament building is the National Garden, Athens' "Central Park." Here you'll find the Zappeion mansion-turned-conference-hall (with a fine summer outdoor cinema nearby) and, beyond the greenery, the evocative, ancient Panathenaic Stadium.

On your right (south) is one of Athens' prime transit hubs, with stops for bus #X95 to the airport, and the Athens Coastal Tram. Beneath your feet is the Syntagma Metro station, the city's busiest.

Behind you, at the west end of the square, stretches the traffic-free shopping street called Ermou, which heads to the Plaka neighborhood and Monastiraki Square. (We'll be heading that way soon.) Nearby is the terminus for one of Athens' two tourist trains.

Take in the square and modern Athens: People buzz about on their way to work, handing out leaflets, feeding pigeons, or just enjoying a park bench shaded by a variety of trees. Plane trees, cypress, and laurel make Syntagma a breezy and restful spot. Breathe deeply and ponder the fact that until 1990, Athens was the most polluted city in Europe. People advertising facial creams would put a mannequin outside on the street for three hours and film it turning black. The message: You need our cream.

But over the last few decades, green policies have systematically

cleaned up the air. Traffic, though still pretty extreme, is limited:
Even- and odd-numbered license plates are prohibited in the center
on alternate days (though downtown residents are exempt). Check
the license plates of passing cars (not taxis or motorcycles): On any
given day, the majority end with either an even or an odd number—depending on the day of the week. While car traffic is down,
motorcycle usage is up (since bikes are exempt). Central-heating
fuel is more expensive and much cleaner these days (as required by
European Union regulations), more of the city center is pedestrianized, and the city's public transport is top-notch.

• *Using the crosswalk (one on either side of Syntagma Square), cross the
busy street. Directly in front of the Parliament you'll see the...*

❷ Tomb of the Unknown Soldier and the Evzone Guards

Standing amid pigeons and tourists in front of the imposing Parliament building overlooking Syntagma Square, you're at the center
of Athens' modern history. Above the simple marble-slab tomb—
marked only with a cross—is a carved image of the Unknown Soldier, a heavily armed dying Greek, inspired by the statue of a dying
nude from the ancient Aphaia temple on the island of Aigina, very
close to Athens. Etched into the stone on each side of the tomb are
the names of great battles in Greek military history from 1821 forward (practice your Greek alphabet by trying to read them: Cyprus,
Korea, Rimini, Crete, and so on).

The tomb is guarded by the much-photographed evzone, an
elite infantry unit of the Greek army. The guard changes five min-

utes before the top of each hour, with a
less elaborate crossing of the guard at :25
after. They march with a slow-motion,
high-stepping march to their new positions, then stand ramrod straight, where
you can pose alongside them. A full
changing-of-the-guard ceremony, complete with marching band, takes place
every Sunday at 11:00 (arrive a bit early).

These colorful characters are clad in
traditional pleated kilts *(fustanella),* white
britches, and pom-pom shoes. (The outfits
may look a little goofy to a non-Greek, but
their mothers are very proud.) The uniforms, worn everywhere in Greece, were
made famous by the Klephts, ragtag bands of mountain guerrilla
fighters. After nearly four centuries under the thumb of the Ottoman Empire (from today's Turkey, starting in 1453), the Greeks
rose up. The Greek War of Independence (1821-1829) pitted the

powerful Ottoman army against the lowly but wily Klephts. The soldiers' skirts have 400 pleats...one for each year of Ottoman occupation (and don't you forget it). Although considered heroes today for their courage, outrageous guerrilla tactics, and contribution to the Liberation Army in the 19th century, the Klephts were once regarded as warlike bandits (their name shares a root with the English word "kleptomania").

As the Klephts and other Greeks fought for their independence, a number of farsighted Europeans (including the English poet Lord Byron)—inspired by the French Revolution and their own love of ancient Greek culture—came to their aid. In 1829, the rebels finally succeeded in driving their Ottoman rulers out of central Greece, and there was a movement to establish a modern democracy. However, the Greeks were unprepared to rule themselves, and so, after the Ottomans came...Otto.

• *For the rest of the story, take a step back for a view of the...*

❸ Parliament

The origins of this "palace of democracy" couldn't have been less democratic. The first independent Greek government, which had its capital in Nafplio, was too weak to be viable. As was standard operating procedure at that time, the great European powers forced Greece to accept a king from established European royalty.

In 1832, Prince Otto of Bavaria became King Otto of Greece. A decade later, after the capital shifted to Athens, this royal palace was built to house King Otto and his wife, Queen Amalia. The atmosphere was tense. After fighting so fiercely for its independence from the Ottomans, the Greeks now chafed under royal rule from a dictatorial Bavarian monarch. The palace's over-the-top luxury only angered impoverished locals.

On September 3, 1843, angry rioters gathered in the square to protest, demanding a democratic constitution. King Otto stepped onto the balcony of this building, quieted the mob, and gave them what they wanted. The square was dubbed Syntagma (Constitution), and modern Athens was born. The former royal palace has been the home of the Greek parliament since 1935. Today this is where 300 Greek parliamentarians (elected to four-year terms) tend to the business of the state—or, as more cynical locals would say, become corrupt and busily get themselves set up for their cushy, post-political lives.

The Story of Modern Athens

By the time of the Greek War of Independence (1821-1829), Athens had declined, becoming little more than a rural backwater on the fringes of the Ottoman Empire. Its population had shrunk to about 2,000 people occupying a cluster of red-tiled Turkish houses on the northern side of the Acropolis (the area now known as the Plaka).

When it came to choosing a capital for the new nation, Athens wasn't even considered. The first choice was Nafplio on the Peloponnese, which the Ottomans had also favored as a seat of government. It would probably have stayed that way, if it weren't for the assassination of Greece's first president, Ioannis Kapodistrias, in 1831. His death led to international pressure to install an outsider, 17-year-old Prince Otto of Bavaria, as the first king of Greece.

Otto was as wet behind the ears as any teenager, and was heavily influenced by his forceful father, King Ludwig I of Bavaria (grandfather of "Mad" King Ludwig, of Neuschwanstein Castle fame). These Bavarians—great admirers of classical Athens—insisted that the city become the capital in 1834. They also were responsible for the shape of the new Athens, ferrying in teams of Bavarian architects to create a plan of broad avenues and grand Neoclassical buildings—much as they had done in Munich.

The character of Athens changed once more after 1922, when the defeat of the occupying Greek army in Turkey resulted in a forced population exchange between the two rivals. Athens' population doubled almost overnight, and any thought of town planning went out the window as authorities scrambled to build cheap apartment blocks to house the newcomers.

Greece's belated industrialization in the 1950s, coupled with the hard times of the Nazi occupation and civil war (when villagers, who could no longer afford to feed themselves, flocked to the city), sparked a wave of migration from rural areas. It's amazing to think that the city with less than a million inhabitants in 1950 now has about four million. The trend continues to this day: More than a third of Greece's population now lives in greater Athens.

When they hosted the Olympic Games in 2004, the Greeks turned over a new leaf and discovered a passion for city planning. Improvements in infrastructure, public transportation, and an overall beautification program quickly pulled the city up to snuff, making it an increasingly attractive tourist destination.

• *Cross back to the heart of Syntagma Square, and focus on the grand building fronting its north side.*

❹ Hotel Grande Bretagne and Neoclassical Syntagma

Imagine the original Syntagma Square (which was on the outskirts of town in the early 19th century): a big front yard for the new royal palace, with the country's influential families building mansions around it. Surviv-

ing examples of 19th-century architecture—as well as more modern buildings renovated in a neo-Neoclassical style so they'd fit in—include Hotel Grande Bretagne, the adjacent Hotel King George Palace, the Zappeion in the National Garden (not visible from here), and the stately architecture lining Vasilissis Sofias avenue behind the palace (now embassies and museums).

Many of these grand buildings date from Athens' Otto-driven Neoclassical makeover. Eager to create a worthy capital for Greece, Otto imported teams of Bavarian architects to draft a plan of broad avenues and grand buildings in what they imagined to be the classical style. This "Neoclassical" look is symmetrical and geometrical, with pastel-colored buildings highlighted in white trim. The windows are rectangular, flanked by white Greek half-columns (pilasters), fronted by balconies, and topped with cornices. Many of the buildings are also framed at the top with cornices. As you continue on this walk, notice not only the many Neoclassical buildings, but also the more modern buildings that try to match the same geometric lines.

Syntagma Square is also worth a footnote in American Cold War history. In December 1944, Greek communists demonstrated here, inducing the US to come to the aid of the Greek government. This became the basis (in 1947) for the Truman Doctrine, which pledged US aid to countries fighting communism and helped shape American foreign policy for the next 50 years.

• *Head down to the bottom of Syntagma (directly across from the Parliament). Stroll down the traffic-free street near the McDonald's.*

❺ Ermou Street

The pedestrian mall called Ermou (air-MOO) leads from Syntagma down through the Plaka to Monastiraki, then continues westward to the ancient Keramikos Cemetery and the Gazi district. Not long ago, this street epitomized all that was terrible about Ath-

ens: lousy building codes, tacky neon signs, double-parked trucks, and noisy traffic. When Ermou was first pedestrianized in 2000, merchants were upset. Now they love the ambience created as countless locals stroll through what has become a people-friendly shopping zone.

This has traditionally been the street of women's shops. However, these days Ermou is dominated by international chain stores, which appeal to young Athenians but turn off older natives, who lament the lack of local flavor. For authentic, hole-in-the-wall shopping, many Athenians prefer the streets just to the north, such as Perikleous, Lekka, and Kolokotroni.

Even so, this people-crammed boulevard is a pleasant place for a wander. Do just that, proceeding gradually downhill and straight ahead for eight short blocks. As you window-shop, notice that some of Ermou's department stores are housed in impressive Neoclassical mansions. Talented street performers provide an entertaining soundtrack. All of Athens walks along here: businesspeople, teenagers texting on iPhones, Orthodox priests stroking their beards, activists gathering signatures, illegal vendors who sweep up their wares and scurry when they see police, and, of course, tourists. Keep an eye out for vendors selling various snacks—including pretzel-like sesame rings called *koulouri* and slices of fresh coconut.

After seven blocks, on the right (in front of Forever 21), look for the little **book wagon** selling cheap lit. You'll likely see colorful, old-fashioned alphabet books (labeled αλφαbhtαpιo, *alphabetario*), which have been reprinted for nostalgic older Greeks. The English word "alphabet" comes from the first two Greek letters (alpha, beta).

• *Continue one more block down Ermou to begin...*

PART 2: THE GREEK ORTHODOX CHURCH

This part of our walk introduces you to the Orthodox faith of Greece, including stops at three different churches. The Greek faith is one denomination of Eastern Orthodox Christianity; for more information on its history and rituals, see the sidebar later in this chapter.

• *Stranded in the middle of both Ermou street and the commercial bustle of the 21st century is a little medieval church.*

❻ Church of Kapnikarea

After the ancient Golden Age, but before Otto and the Ottomans, Athens was part of the Byzantine Empire (A.D. 323-1453). In the 11th and 12th centuries, Athens boomed, and several Eastern Or-

The Eastern Orthodox Church

In the fourth century A.D., the Roman Empire split in half, dividing Eastern Europe and the Balkan Peninsula down the middle. Seven centuries later, with the Great Schism, the Christian faith diverged along similar lines, into two separate branches: Roman Catholicism in the west (based in Rome and including most of Western and Central Europe), and Eastern or Byzantine Orthodoxy in the east (based in Constantinople—today's Istanbul—and prevalent in far-eastern Europe, Russia, the eastern half of the Balkan Peninsula, and Greece). The root *orthos* is Greek for "right," and *dogma* is "faith," making orthodoxy the "right belief." And it seems logical that if you've already got it right, you're more conservative and resistant to change.

Over the centuries the Catholic Church shed old traditions and developed new ones. Meanwhile, the Eastern Orthodox Church—which remained consolidated under the stable and wealthy Byzantine Empire—stayed true to the earliest traditions of the Christian faith. Today, rather than having one centralized headquarters (such as the Vatican for Catholicism), the Eastern Orthodox Church is divided into about a dozen regional branches that remain administratively independent but share the same rituals. Some branches include the Russian Orthodox Church, the Serbian Orthodox Church, the Bulgarian Orthodox Church, and the Greek Orthodox Church, which is based at Athens' cathedral. The Greek constitution recognizes Orthodox Christianity as the "prevailing" religion of Greece. The Archbishop of Athens is Greece's "pope."

The doctrine of Catholic and Orthodox churches remains very similar, but many of the rituals are different. As you enter any Greek Orthodox church, you can join in the standard routine: Drop a coin in the wooden box, pick up a candle, say a prayer, light the candle, and place it in the candelabra. Make the sign of the cross and kiss the icon.

Where's the altar? Orthodox churches come with an altar screen covered with curtains and icons (the "iconostasis"). The standard design of the iconostasis calls for four icons flanking the central door, with Jesus to the right, John the Baptist to Jesus' right, Mary and the Baby Jesus on the left, and an icon featuring the saint or event that the church is dedicated to on the far left.

This iconostasis divides the lay community from the priests—the material world from the spiritual one. Following Old Testament Judeo-Christian tradition, the Bible is kept on the altar behind the iconostasis. The spiritual heavy lifting takes place behind the iconostasis, where the priests symbolically turn bread and wine into the body and blood of Jesus. Then they open the doors or curtains and serve the Eucharist to their faithful flock—spooning the wine from a chalice while holding a cloth under each chin so as not to drop any on the floor.

Notice that there are few (if any) pews. Worshippers stand through the service as a sign of respect (though some older parishioners sit on the seats along the walls). Traditionally, women stand on the left side, men on the right (equal distance from the altar, to represent that all are equal before God).

The Orthodox faith tends to use a Greek cross, with four equal arms (like a plus sign, sometimes inside a circle), which focuses on God's perfection. The longer Latin cross, more typically used by Catholics, more literally evokes the Crucifixion, emphasizing Jesus' death and sacrifice. This also extends to the floor plans of church buildings: Many Orthodox churches have Greek-cross floor plans rather than the elongated nave-and-transept designs that are common in Western Europe.

Unlike many Catholic church decorations, Orthodox icons (golden paintings of saints) are not intended to be lifelike. Packed with intricate symbolism and often cast against a shimmering golden background, they're meant to remind viewers of the metaphysical nature of Jesus and the saints rather than their physical form, which is considered irrelevant. You'll almost never see statues, which are thought to overemphasize the physical world—and, to Orthodox people, feel a little too close to the forbidden worship of graven images.

Most Eastern Orthodox churches have at least one mosaic or painting of Christ in a standard pose—as *Pantocrator,* a Greek word meaning "Ruler of All." The image, so familiar to Orthodox Christians, shows Christ as King of the Universe, facing directly out, with penetrating eyes. Behind him is a halo divided by a cross, with the bottom arm of the cross hidden behind Christ—an Orthodox symbol for the Crucifixion, hinting of the Resurrection and salvation that follow.

Orthodox services generally involve chanting (a dialogue that goes back and forth between the priest and the congregation), and the church is filled with the evocative aroma of incense, combining to heighten the experience for the worshippers. While many Catholic and Protestant services tend to be more of a theoretical and rote covering of basic religious tenets (come on—don't tell me you understand every phrase in the Nicene Creed), Orthodox services are about creating a religious experience. Each of these elements does its part to help the worshipper transcend the physical world and enter into communion with the spiritual one.

thodox churches like this one were constructed.

The Church of Kapnikarea is a classic 11th-century Byzantine church. Notice that it's square and topped with a central dome. Telltale signs of a Byzantine church include tall arches over the windows, stones surrounded by a frame of brick and mortar, and a domed cupola with a cross on top. The large white blocks are scavenged from other, earlier monuments (also typical of Byzantine churches from this era). Over the door is a mosaic of glass and gold leaf, which, though modern, is made in the traditional Byzantine style.

Inside the Church: Notice the Greek-cross floor plan and the early 20th-century, modern-yet-still-medieval art. It's decorated with standing candelabras, hanging lamps, tall arches, a wooden pulpit, and a few chairs. If you wish, you can do as the Greeks do and follow the standard candle-buying, icon-kissing ritual. The icon displayed closest to the door gets changed with the church calendar. You may notice lipstick smudges on the protective glass and a candle-recycling box behind the candelabra.

Look up into the central dome, lit with windows, which symbolizes heaven. Looking back down is the face of Jesus, the omnipotent *Pantocrator* God blessing us on Earth. He holds a Bible in one hand and blesses us with the other. On the walls are iconic murals of saints. Notice the focus on the eyes, which are considered a mirror of the soul and a symbol of its purity.

• *From here, head toward the Acropolis, downhill on Kapnikareas street (straight ahead as you leave the church, or to the left as you come down Ermou street). Go two blocks to the traffic-free Pandrossou shopping street. Turn left and walk up the pedestrian street to the cathedral.*

❼ Cathedral (Mitropolis) and Cathedral Square (Plateia Mitropoleos)

Built from 1842 to 1862, this "metropolitan church" (as the Greek Orthodox call their cathedrals) is the most important in Athens, which makes it the head church of the Greek Orthodox faith. The cathedral was under scaffolding for many years after sustaining damage in a 1999 earthquake, but now it's all spiffed up and gleaming.

Inside the Cathedral: The cathedral is vast, dimly lit, and carries a mysterious majesty. You'll notice many of the same features you saw in the little church up the street. Candles and lipstick-smudged icons. No pews. Ethereal depictions of saints. And a big, white-marble iconostasis, with elaborate golden doors, separating the spiritual world from our material world.

Stand back and observe the ritual: Locals enter and buy candles at the self-service kiosks just inside the door. They light them in nearby bronze candelabras, and kiss their choice of icons. The pieces of paper (by the wooden icon frame on the right side of the main aisle) are written prayers, left by the faithful.

Head up the right aisle as far as you can. Looking high up at the underside of the dome, you'll see a depiction of Christ *Pantocrator*—a much bigger version of the theme we saw in the last church. As you pan back down, notice the balconies lining the nave. Traditionally, women worshipped apart from men in the balconies upstairs. But after women got the vote in Greece in 1952, they've been able to worship in the prime, ground-floor real estate alongside the men.

On the Square: Back outside, find the statue facing the cathedral. This was erected by Athens' Jewish community as thanks to **Archbishop Damaskinos** (1891-1949), the

rare Christian leader who stood up to the Nazis during the occupation of Greece. At great personal risk, Damaskinos formally spoke out against the Nazi occupiers on behalf of the Greek Jews he saw being deported to concentration camps. When a Nazi commander threatened to put Damaskinos before a firing squad, the archbishop defiantly countered that he should be hanged instead, in good Orthodox tradition. After the occupation, Damaskinos served as regent and then prime minister of Greece until the king returned from exile.

Here Damaskinos is depicted wearing the distinctive hat of an archbishop (a kind of fez with cloth hanging down the sides). He carries a staff and blesses with his right hand, making a traditional Orthodox sign of the cross, touching his thumb to his ring finger. This gesture forms the letters ICXC, the first and last letters of the Greek name for Jesus Christ (ΙΗΣΟΥΣ ΧΡΙΣΤΟΣ—traditionally C was substituted for Σ). Make the gesture yourself with your right hand. Touch the tip of your thumb to the tip of your ring finger and check it out: Your pinkie forms the I, your slightly crossed index and middle fingers are the X, and your thumb and ring finger make a double-C. Jesus Christ, that's clever. If you were a priest, you'd make the sign of the cross three times, to symbolize the Father, the Son, and the Holy Spirit.

The double-headed eagle that hangs around Damaskinos' neck is an important symbol of the Orthodox faith. It evokes the Byzantine Empire, during which Orthodox Christianity was at its peak as the state religion. Appropriately, the eagle's twin heads have a double meaning: The Byzantine Emperor was both the secular and spiritual leader of his realm, which exerted its influence over both East and West. (Historically, any power that wanted to be considered the successor of the ancient Roman Emperor—including the Holy Roman Empire and the Austro-Hungarian Empire—has appropriated this symbol.)

Hiding against the back wall, behind Damaskinos' right shoulder, is another statue—one of a warrior holding a sword. This is **Emperor Constantine XI Palaeologus** (1404-1453), the final ruler of the Byzantine Empire. He was killed defending Constantinople from the invading Ottomans, led by Mehmet the Conqueror. Considered the "last Greek king" and an unofficial saint, Constantine XI's death marked the ascension of the Ottomans as overlords of the Greeks for nearly four centuries. On his boots and above his head, you'll see the double-headed eagle again.

• *The small church tucked behind the right side of the cathedral is the...*

❽ Church of Agios Eleftherios

A favorite of local church connoisseurs, the late-12th-century Church of Agios Eleftherios (St. Eleutherius) is also known as

Panaghia Ghorghoepikoos ("Virgin Mary, quick to answer prayers") and is sometimes referred to as "the old cathedral." It was used by the archbishops of Athens after the Ottomans evicted them from the church within the Parthenon. It's a jigsaw-puzzle hodgepodge of B.C. and A.D. adornments (and even tombstones) from earlier buildings. For example, the carved marble reliefs above the door were scavenged from the Ancient Agora in the 12th century. They are part of a calendar of ancient Athenian festivals, thought to have been carved in the second century A.D. The frieze running along the top of the building depicts a B.C. procession.

Later, Christians added their own symbols to the same panels, making the church a treasure trove of medieval symbolism. There are different kinds of crosses (Maltese, Latin, double) as well as carved rosettes, stars, flowers, and griffins feeding on plants and snakes. Walk around the entire exterior. Then step inside to sample unadorned 12th-century Orthodox simplicity.

• *Exit the church, go up to the main sidewalk level, and walk around to the back side of the church where you'll find a religious gear shop and the start of...*

❾ Agia Filotheis Street

This neighborhood is a hive of activity for Orthodox clerics. The priests dress all in black, wear beards, and don those fez-like hats. Despite their hermetic look, most priests are husbands, fathers, and well-educated pillars of the community, serving as counselors and spiritual guides to Athens' cosmopolitan populace.

Notice the stores. Just behind and facing the little church is the shop of the **Theodoropoulos** family—whose name manages to use nearly every Greek character available (ΘΕΟΔΩΡΟΠΟΥΛΟΣ). They've been tailoring priestly robes since 1907.

This is the first of many **religious objects stores** that line the street. Facing this, turn right, cross Apollonos street, and continue exploring the shops of Agia Filotheis street. The Orthodox religion comes with ample paraphernalia: icons, gold candelabras, hanging lamps, incense burners, oil lamps, chalices, various crosses, and gold objects worked in elaborate repoussé design.

Pop into the **stoa** (arcades) at #17 (on the left) to see workshops of the artisans who make these objects—painters creating or restoring icons in the traditional style, tailors making bishops' hats and robes, and carvers making little devotional statuettes.

A few more steps up on the left, the ❿ **Church of Agia Filotheis** (named, like the street, for a patron of Athens—St. Philothei) is adjacent to an office building (at #19) that serves as the headquarters for the Greek Orthodox Church. Athenians come here to file the paperwork to make their marriages (and divorces) official.

• *Just a few steps up the street from here begins...*

PART 3: ATHENS' "OLD TOWN" (THE PLAKA AND ANAFIOTIKA)

This part of our walk explores the atmospheric twisty lanes of old Athens. Remember, back before Athens became Greece's capital in the early 1800s, the city was a small town, consisting of little more than what we'll see here.

• *Continue up Agia Filotheis street until you reach a tight five-way intersection. The street that runs ahead and to your right (labeled ΑΔΡΙΑΝΟΥ)—choked with souvenir stands and tourists—is our next destination. Look uphill and downhill along...*

⓫ Adrianou Street

This intersection may be the geographical (if not atmospheric) center of the neighborhood called the Plaka. Touristy Adrianou street is a main pedestrian drag that cuts through the Plaka, running roughly east–west from Monastiraki to here. Adrianou offers the full gauntlet of Greek souvenirs: worry beads, sea sponges, olive products, icons, carpets, jewelry, sandals, knock-off vases and Greek statues, profane and tacky T-shirts, and on and on. It also has plenty of cafés for tourists seeking a place to sit and rest their weary feet.

• *Bear left onto Adrianou and window-shop your way gently uphill for several short blocks. Finally, the street dead-ends at a T-intersection with Lysikratous street. (There's a small square ahead on the left, with palm trees, the Byzantine church of Agia Aikaterini, and an excavated area showing the street level 2,000 years ago.)*

From here you can turn right and take a few steps uphill to the Lysicrates Monument and Square (and skip ahead to the section on the Lysicrates Monument). But if you've got more time and stamina, it's worth a two-block walk to the left down Lysikratous street to reach the remains of the Arch of Hadrian (which you can already see from this intersection).

⓬ Arch of Hadrian and Temple of Olympian Zeus

After the Romans conquered the Greeks, Roman emperor Hadrian (or Adrianos) became a major benefactor of the city of Athens. He built a triumphal arch, completed a temple beyond it (now ruined), and founded a library we'll see later. He also created a "new Athens" in the area beyond the arch (sometimes known as Hadrianopolis). The grand archway overlooks the bustling modern Vasilissis Amalias avenue, facing the Plaka and Acropolis. (If you turned left and followed this road for 10 minutes, you'd end up back on Syntagma Square—where we began this walk.)

Arch of Hadrian

The arch's once-brilliant white Pentelic marble is topped with Corinthian columns, the Greek style preferred by the Romans. Hadrian built it in A.D. 131 to celebrate the completion of the Temple of Olympian Zeus (which lies just beyond—described next). Like a big gate marking the entrance to a modern Chinatown, this arch represented the dividing line between the ancient city and Hadrian's new "Roman" city. An inscription on the west side informs the reader that "This is Athens, ancient city of Theseus," while the opposite frieze carries the message, "This is the city of Hadrian, and not of Theseus."

• *Look past the arch to see the huge (and I mean huge) Corinthian columns remaining from what was once a temple dedicated to Zeus. For a closer look, cross the busy boulevard (crosswalk to the right). You can pretty much get the gist by looking through the fence. But to get close to those giant columns and wander the ruins, you can enter the site (covered by the Acropolis combo-ticket). To reach the entrance (a five-minute walk), curl around the left side of the arch, then turn right (following the fence) up the intersecting street called Vasilissis Olgas. The entrance to the temple is a few minutes' walk up, on the right-hand side.*

Temple of Olympian Zeus (Olympieion)

This largest ancient temple in mainland Greece took almost 700 years to finish. It was begun late in the sixth century B.C. during

the rule of the tyrant Peisistratos. He died before the temple was completed, and his successors were expelled from Athens. The temple lay abandoned, half-built, for centuries until the Roman emperor Hadrian arrived to finish the job in A.D. 131. This must have been a big deal for Hadrian, as he came here in person to celebrate its inauguration. Romans did things big. When completed, the temple was 360 feet by 145 feet, consisting of two rows of 20 columns on each of the long sides and three rows of eight columns along each end (counting the corners twice). Although only 15 of the original 104 Corinthian columns remain standing, their sheer size (a towering 56 feet high) is enough to create a powerful impression of the temple's scale. The fallen column—which resembles a tipped-over stack of bottle caps—was toppled by a storm in 1852. The temple once housed a suitably oversized statue of Zeus, head of the Greek gods who lived on Mount Olympus, and an equally colossal statue of Hadrian.

• *Return to Lysikratous street and backtrack two blocks, continuing past the small square with the church you passed earlier. After another block, you'll run into another small, leafy square with the Acropolis rising behind it. In the square is a round, white, columned monument.*

⓭ Lysicrates Monument and Square

This elegant marble monument has Corinthian columns that support a dome that once held an ornamental vase on top. A frieze

runs along the top, representing Dionysus turning pirates into dolphins. This is the sole survivor of many such monuments that once lined this ancient "Street of the Tripods." It was so called because the monuments came with bronze tripods that displayed cauldrons (like those you'll see in the museums) as trophies. These ancient "Oscars" were awarded to winners of choral and theatrical competitions staged at the Theater of Dionysus on the southern side of the Acropolis. This

now-lonely monument was erected in 334 B.C. by "Lysicrates of Kykyna, son of Lysitheides"—proud sponsor of the winning choral team that year. Excavations in the surrounding area have uncovered the foundations of other monuments, which are now reburied under a layer of red sand and awaiting further study.

The square itself, shaded by trees, is a pleasant place to take a break before climbing the hill. Have a frappé or coffee at the café tables, grab a cheap cold drink from the cooler in the hole-in-the-wall grocery store to the left, or just sit for free on the benches under the trees.

• From here you're only two blocks from the TI (on the pedestrianized street leading to the Acropolis Museum, at Dionysiou Areopagitou 18), so it's handy for a visit. Otherwise, circle around the left side of the Lysicrates Monument, then head uphill toward the Acropolis, climbing the staircase called Epimenidou. At the top of the stairs, turn right onto Stratonos street, which leads around the base of the Acropolis. As you walk along, the Acropolis and a row of olive trees are on your left. For Athenians, the sound of the crickets here evokes the black-and-white movies that were filmed in this area in the 1960s. To your right you'll catch glimpses of another hill off in the distance.

⓮ View of Lykavittos Hill

This cone-shaped hill (sometimes spelled "Lycabettus") topped with a tiny white church is the highest in Athens, at just over 900 feet above sea level. The hill can be reached by a funicular, which

leads up from the Kolonaki neighborhood to a restaurant, café, and view terrace at the top. Although it looms high over the cityscape, Lykavittos Hill will always be overshadowed by the hill you're climbing now.

• *At the small Church of St. George of the Rock (Agios Georgios), go uphill, along the left fork. As you immerse yourself in a maze of tiny, whitewashed houses, follow signs that point to the Acropolis (even if the path seems impossibly narrow). This charming "village" is a neighborhood called...*

⓯ Anafiotika

These lanes and homes were built by people from the tiny Cycladic island of Anafi, who came to Athens looking for work after Greece gained its independence from the Ottomans. (Many stoneworkers and builders hired to construct the modern city of Athens built these higgledy-piggledy residences after-hours.) In this delightful spot, nestled beneath the walls of the Acropolis, the big city seems miles away. Keep following the *Acropolis* signs as you weave

through narrow paths lined with flowers and dotted with cats dozing peacefully in the sunshine (or slithering luxuriously past your legs). Though descendants of the original islanders still live here, Anafiotika (literally "little Anafi") is slowly becoming a place for wealthy locals to keep an "island cottage" in the city. As you wander through the oleanders, notice the male fig trees—no fruit—that keep flies and mosquitoes away. Smell the chicken-manure fertilizer (and cat

poop), peek into delicate little yards, and enjoy the blue doors and maroon shutters...it's a transplanted Cycladic world. Posters of Anafi hang here and there, evoking the sandy beaches of the ancestral home island.

• *Follow the narrow walkway until you emerge from the maze of houses and hit a wider, cobbled lane. Turn right (downhill) and continue down the steep incline. When you hit a wider road (Theorias), turn left and walk toward the small, Byzantine-style Church of the Metamorphosis. (Note: To reach the Acropolis entry from here, you would continue along this road as it bends left around the hill. For now, though, let's continue our walk.)*

Just before the church, turn right and go down the steep, narrow

staircase (a lane called Klepsidras, with the sign for the Athens Univer-
sity History Museum). You'll pass the first university of Athens (with a
free little museum) on the right. Cross the street called Tholou and con-
tinue down Klepsidras as it narrows. Enjoy the graffiti. You'll pass a
charming, recommended little café a block before you emerge at a railing
overlooking some ruins.

⑯ Roman Forum and Tower of the Winds

The rows of columns framing this rectangular former piazza were
built by the Romans, who conquered Greece around 150 B.C. and

stayed for centuries. This square—
sometimes called the "Roman
Agora"—was the commercial center,
or forum, of Roman Athens, with a
colonnade providing shade for shoppers browsing the many stores that
fronted it. Centuries later, the Ottomans made this their grand bazaar.
The mosque was built upon a church
that was built upon a Roman temple.
The mosque, one of the oldest and best-preserved Ottoman structures, survives (although its minaret, like all minarets in town, was
torn down by the Greeks when they won their independence from
the Ottomans in the 19th century).

Take a few steps to the right to see the octagonal, domed
Tower of the Winds. The carved reliefs depict winds as winged

humans who fly in, bringing the
weather. Built in the first century
B.C., this building was an ingenious
combination of clock, weathervane, and guide to the planets. The
beautifully carved reliefs represent
male personifications of the eight
winds of Athens, with their names
inscribed. As you walk down the
hill (curving right, then left around
the fence, always going downhill),
you'll see reliefs depicting Lips, the
southwest wind, holding a ship's
steering rudder; Zephyros, the mild west wind, holding a basket
of flowers; Skiron, scattering glowing coal from an inverted bronze
brazier, indicating the warmer winter winds; and Boreas, the howling winter wind from the north, blowing a conch shell. The tower
was once capped with a weathervane in the form of a bronze Triton
(half-man, half-fish) that spun to indicate which wind was blessing or cursing the city at the moment. Bronze rods (no longer vis-

ible) protruded from the walls and acted as sundials to indicate the time. And when the sun wasn't shining, people told time using the tower's sophisticated water clock, powered by water piped in from springs on the Acropolis. Much later, under Ottoman rule, dervishes used the tower as a place for their whirling worship and prayer.

• *It's possible but unnecessary to enter the ruins: You've seen just about everything from this vantage point. Don't confuse the Roman Forum with the older, more interesting Ancient Agora, which is near the end of this walk. From just below the Tower of the Winds, head to the right down Aiolou street one block to...*

⓱ Agora Square (Plateia Agoras)

This leafy, restaurant-filled square is the touristy epicenter of the Plaka.

On the left side of the square you'll see the second-century A.D. ruins of the ⓲ **Library of Hadrian** (open to the public). The four lone columns that sit atop the apse-like foundations are the remains of a fifth-century church. The ruins around it are all that's left of a big rectangular complex that once boasted 100 marble columns. Destroyed in the third century A.D., it was a cultural center (library, lecture halls, garden, and art gallery), built by the Greek-loving Roman emperor for the Athenian citizens. Notice how the excavated stones rest neatly in stacks awaiting funding for reconstruction.

• *Continue downhill alongside the ruins to the next block, where Aiolou intersects with the claustrophobic Pandrossou market street (which we walked along earlier). Remember that this crowded lane is worked by expert pickpockets—be careful. Look to the right up Pandrossou: You may see merchants sitting in folding chairs with their backs to one another, competition having soured their personal relationships. Turn left on Pandrossou and wade through the knee-deep tacky tourist souvenirs. Several shops here (including one we just passed on Aiolou, and two more on Pandrossou) supply fans of the "Round Goddess"—a.k.a. soccer (each team has its own store). Continue until you spill out into Monastiraki Square.*

⓳ Monastiraki Square Spin-Tour

We've made it from Syntagma Square—the center of urban Athens—to the city's *other* main square, Monastiraki Square, the gateway to the touristy Old Town. To get oriented to Monastiraki Square, stand in the center, face the small church with the cross on top (which is north), and pan clockwise.

The name Monastiraki ("Little Monastery") refers to this square, the surrounding neighborhood, the flea-market action nearby...and the cute **Church of the Virgin** in the square's center (12th-century Byzantine, mostly restored with a much more modern bell tower).

Beyond the church (straight ahead from the end of the square), **Athinas street** heads north to the Central Market, Omonia Square, and (after about a mile) the National Archaeological Museum.

Just to the right (behind the little church) is the head of **Ermou street**—the bustling shopping drag we walked down earlier (though no longer traffic-free here). If you turned right and walked straight up Ermou, you'd be back at Syntagma Square in 10 minutes.

Next (on the right, in front of the little church) comes Mitropoleos street—Athens' ⑳ **"Souvlaki Row."** Clogged with outdoor tables, this atmospheric lane is home to a string of restaurants that serve sausage-shaped, skewered meat—grilled up spicy and tasty. The place on the corner—Bairaktaris (ΜΠΑΪΡΑΚΤΑΡΗΣ)—is the best known, its walls lined with photos of famous politicians and artists who come here for souvlaki and pose with the owner. But the other two joints along here—Thanasis and Savas—have a better reputation for their souvlaki. You can sit at the tables, or, for a really cheap meal, order a souvlaki to go. (For details, see the Eating in Athens chapter.) A few blocks farther down Mitropoleos is the cathedral we visited earlier.

Continue spinning clockwise. Just past Pandrossou street (where you entered the square), you'll see a ㉑ **former mosque** (look for the Arabic script under the portico and over the wooden door). Known as the Tzami (from the Turkish word for "mosque"), this was a place of worship from the 15th to 19th century.

To the right of the mosque, behind the fence along Areos street, you might glimpse some huge Corinthian columns. This is the opposite end of the **Library of Hadrian** complex we saw earlier. Areos street stretches up toward the Acropolis. If you were to walk a block up this street, then turn right on Adrianou, you'd reach the ㉒ **Ancient Agora**—one of Athens' top ancient attractions (for more, see the 🕮 Ancient Agora Tour chapter or download my free

🎧 audio tour). Beyond the Agora are the delightful Thissio neighborhood, ancient Keramikos Cemetery, and Gazi district.

As you continue panning clockwise, next comes the pretty yellow building that houses the **Monastiraki Metro station.** This was Athens' original, 19th-century train station—Neoclassical with a dash of Byzantium. This bustling Metro stop is the intersection of two lines: the old line 1 (green, with connections to the port of Piraeus, the Thissio neighborhood, and Victoria—near the National Archaeological Museum) and the modern line 3 (blue, with connections to Syntagma Square and the airport). The stands in front of the station sell seasonal fruit and are popular with commuters.

Just right of the station, Ifestou street leads downhill into the ❷❸ **flea market** (antiques, jewelry, cheap clothing, and so on—described in the Shopping & Nightlife in Athens chapter). If locals need a screw for an old lamp, they know they'll find it here.

Keep panning clockwise. Just beyond busy Ermou street (to the left of Athinas street, behind the A for Athens hotel—which has a rooftop bar popular for its views) is the happening **Psyrri** district. For years a run-down slum, this zone is being gentrified by twentysomethings with a grungy sense of style. Packed with cutting-edge bars, restaurants, cafés, and nightclubs, it may seem foreboding and ramshackle, but it is actually fun to explore. (Wander through by day to get your bearings, then head back at night when it's buzzing with activity.)

❷❹ Monastiraki Metro Station

Excavations for the Monastiraki Metro station revealed an ancient aqueduct, which confined Athens' Eridanos River to a canal. The river had been a main axis of the town since the eighth century B.C. In the second century A.D., Hadrian and his engineers put a roof over it, turning it into a more efficient sewer. If you have a transit ticket (required to enter the turnstile), ride the escalator down to see an exposed bit of ancient Athens—Roman brick and classic Roman engineering. A cool mural shows the treasure trove archaeologists uncovered with the excavations.

This walk has taken us from ancient ruins to the Roman era, from medieval churches and mosques to the guerrilla fighters of Greek Independence, through the bustling bric-a-brac of the modern city, and finally to a place where Athens' infrastructure—both ancient and modern—mingles.

• *Our walk is over. If you've worked up an appetite, savor a spicy souvlaki on "Souvlaki Row" or eat your way through the local and colorful Psyrri neighborhood (see the* 📖 *Psyrri & Central Market Walk chapter—the walk begins right here).*

ANCIENT AGORA TOUR

Αρχαία Αγορά

While the Acropolis was the ceremonial showpiece, the Agora was the real heart of ancient Athens. Although used as a residential and burial area since 3000 B.C., it became a public space around 600 B.C. For some 800 years, until its destruction by barbarians in A.D. 267, it was the hub of all commercial, political, and social life in Athens, as well as home to much of its religious life.

Agora means "gathering place," but you could call this space by any of the names we typically give to the busiest part of a city—downtown, main square, forum, piazza, marketplace, commons, and so on. It was a lively place where the pace never let up—much like modern Athens.

Little survives from the classical Agora. Other than one very well-preserved temple and a rebuilt stoa, it's a field of humble ruins. But that makes it a quiet, uncrowded spot to wander and get a feel for the ancients. Nestled in the shadow of the Acropolis, it's an ideal prelude to your visit there.

Orientation

Cost: €8, covered by €30 Acropolis combo-ticket (which you can buy here; see sidebar on page 41).

Hours: Daily 8:00-20:00, Oct until 18:00, Nov-March until 15:00. The Agora Museum inside has the same hours (except on Mon off-season, when it opens at 11:00).

Information: Tel. 210-321-0180, www.culture.gr.

Getting There: From the Monastiraki Metro stop, walk a block south (uphill, toward the Acropolis). Turn right on Adrianou street, and follow the pedestrian-only, café-lined street along the railroad tracks for about 200 yards. The Agora entrance is on your left, across from a small, yellow church. The entrance can be hard to spot: It's where a path crosses over the railroad tracks (look for a small, pale-yellow sign that says *Ministry of Culture—Ancient Agora*).

Compass Points: The Agora's main entrance is north; the Acropolis is south.

Visitor Information: Panels with printed descriptions of the ruins are scattered helpfully throughout the site.

Tours: ⌒ Download my free Ancient Agora audio tour.

Services: Machines behind the ticket booths sell cheap bottled water. The only WCs on the site are inside the Stoa of Attalos, at its northernmost end.

Eating: Picnicking is not allowed in the Agora. Loads of cafés and tavernas line busy Adrianou street near the entrance, and more good eateries front the Apostolou Pavlou pedestrian walkway that hems in the western edge of the Agora, in the district called Thissio.

Starring: A well-preserved temple, a rebuilt stoa, three monumental statues, and the ruins of the civilization that built the Western world.

The Tour Begins

Entering the site from Adrianou street, belly up to the illustration at the top of the ramp that shows the Athenian Agora at the peak

of its size. Face the Acropolis (to the south), look out over the expanse of ruins and trees, and get oriented.

The long column-lined building to the left is the reconstructed Stoa of Attalos (#13 on the illustration). To your right, atop a hill (the view is likely blocked by trees) is the well-preserved Temple of Hephaistos (#20). The pathway called the Panathenaic Way (#21) runs from the Agora's entrance up to the Acropolis. Directly ahead of you are three tall statue-columns (also probably obscured by trees)—part of what was once the Odeon of Agrippa (#12).

In the distance, the Agora's far end is bordered by hills. From left to right are the Acropolis (#1), the Areopagus ("Hill of Ares," or Mars Hill, #2), and Pnyx Hill (#3).

Although the illustration implies that you're standing somewhere behind the Stoa Poikile ("Painted Stoa," #28), in fact you are located in front of it, closer to the heart of the Agora, to the left of the Altar of the Twelve Gods (#26). In ancient times, that altar

AGORA

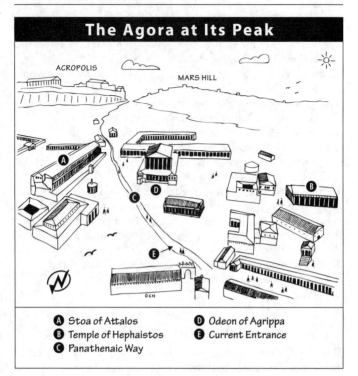

The Agora at Its Peak

A Stoa of Attalos   **D** Odeon of Agrippa
B Temple of Hephaistos   **E** Current Entrance
C Panathenaic Way

was considered the geographical center of Athens, from which distances were measured. Today, the area north of the altar (and north of today's illustration) remains largely unexcavated and inaccessible to tourists, taken over by the railroad tracks and Adrianou street.

This self-guided tour starts at the Stoa of Attalos (with its museum), then crosses the Agora to the Temple of Hephaistos, returning to the Panathenaic Way via three giant statues. Finally, we'll head up the Panathenaic Way toward the Acropolis.

• *Walk to the bottom of the ramp at your left for a better view. Find a shady spot to ponder...*

❶ The Agora

What lies before you now is a maze of ruins—the remains of many centuries of buildings.

A millennium before the time of Socrates, during the Mycenaean Period (around 1600-1200 B.C.), this area held the oldest cemetery in Athens. Later, the Agora was developed into a political forum—the center for speeches, political announcements, and demonstrations. The rectangular area (about 100 yards by 200 yards, bordered by hills) naturally evolved into a marketplace, with sellers lured by the crowds. Over time, that central square became

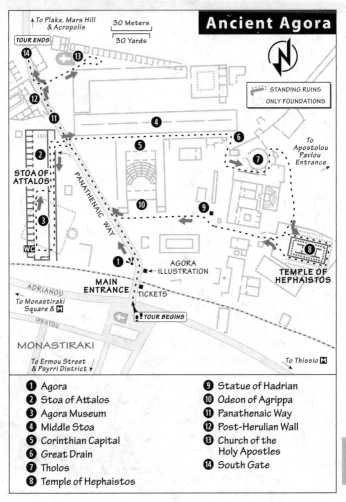

Ancient Agora

To Plaka, Mars Hill & Acropolis

TOUR ENDS

30 Meters
30 Yards

STANDING RUINS
ONLY FOUNDATIONS

To Apostolou Pavlou Entrance

STOA OF ATTALOS

PANATHENAIC WAY

WC

AGORA
←ILLUSTRATION

MAIN ENTRANCE
TICKETS

TEMPLE OF HEPHAISTOS

ADRIANOU
To Monastiraki Square & Ⓜ

IFESTOU

TOUR BEGINS

MONASTIRAKI

To Ermou Street & Psyrri District

To Thissio Ⓜ

❶ Agora
❷ Stoa of Attalos
❸ Agora Museum
❹ Middle Stoa
❺ Corinthian Capital
❻ Great Drain
❼ Tholos
❽ Temple of Hephaistos
❾ Statue of Hadrian
❿ Odeon of Agrippa
⓫ Panathenaic Way
⓬ Post-Herulian Wall
⓭ Church of the Holy Apostles
⓮ South Gate

AGORA

surrounded by buildings, then filled in with more buildings. There were stoas like the (reconstructed) Stoa of Attalos (above on the left), used for shops and offices; temples such as the Temple of Hephaistos; and government buildings. Imagine the square framed by these buildings—decorated with painted statues and friezes, fronted with columns of gleaming white marble, topped with red-tile roofs. The square itself was studded with trees and dotted with statues, fountains, and altars. Merchants sold goods from wooden market stalls.

The square buzzed with people—mostly men and lower-class working women, as the place was considered a bit vulgar for genteel matrons. Both men and women would be dressed in simple tunics (men's were knee-length, women's to the ankle). The Agora was the place to shop—to buy clothes, dishes, or to get your wagon wheel fixed. When a perishable product was available—for example, a catch of fresh fish—a certain bell was rung to announce its arrival. If you needed a zoning permit for your business, you came to the courthouse. You could make an offering to the gods at a number of temples and altars. At night people attended plays and concerts, and nearby tavernas hummed with excited drinkers. Many people passed through here on their way to somewhere else, as this was the main intersection in town (and ancient Athens probably had a population of at least 100,000). On holidays, the procession ran down main street, the Panathenaic Way. At any time, this was the place to come to run into your friends, to engage in high-minded discussion with philosophers such as Socrates or Diogenes, or just to chat and hang out.

• *Now go to the long, intact, colonnaded building on your left (entrance at the south/far end), which is the…*

❷ Stoa of Attalos

This stoa—an ancient shopping mall—was originally built by the Greek-loving King Attalos II of Pergamon (in modern-day Turkey, 159-138 B.C.) as a thank-you gift for the education he'd received in Athens. That structure is long gone, and the building we see today is a faithful reconstruction built in the 1950s by the American School of Classical Studies.

This is a typical two-story stoa. Like many of the Agora's buildings, it's made of white Pentelic and gray-blue Hymettus marble from the quarries northeast of the city. The portico is supported on the ground floor by 45 Doric columns (outer layer) and 22 Ionic columns (inner layer). The upper story uses Ionic columns. This mix of Doric and Ionic was typical of buildings from the period.

Stoas, with their covered walkways, provided protection from sun and rain for shoppers and merchants. This one likely served as a commercial mall. The ground floor was divided by walls into 21 rooms that served as shops (it's now the museum). Upstairs were offices (which today house more of the Agora Museum and research facilities of the American School of Classical Studies).

Like malls of today, the Agora's stoas were social magnets. Imagine ancient Greeks (their hard labor being done by slaves and servants) lounging here, enjoying the shade of the portico.

AGORA

The design of the pillars encourages people to lean against them (just as you may be doing right now), with fluting starting only above six feet for the comfort of philosophers. (These smooth-bottomed columns were typical for

public buildings, whereas temple columns—which the hoi polloi didn't loiter around—always had fluting all the way to the base.)

• *Inside, the Stoa of Attalos houses the...*

❸ Agora Museum

The Agora is mostly ruins, but the excellent little museum displays some choice rubble that helps bring the place to life. Before entering, enjoy the arcade. On the wall facing the fifth column, find the impressive sculpted head of a bearded man with a full head of hair. This **Head of a Triton** (c. A.D. 150) comes from one of the statues that decorated the Odeon of Agrippa. Three of his fellow statues are still standing (we'll see them soon).

Walk halfway down the arcade and step inside the museum (included with your Agora ticket). Its modest but engaging collection fills a single long hall and part of the next level up. Look in the corner by the desk for the 1952 photo showing this spot before the reconstruction.

This well-described chronological stroll through art from 3200 B.C. gives you a glimpse of life in ancient Athens. Along the hall on the left, big panels show the Agora and Acropolis during each age, allowing you to follow their physical evolution. It's hard to believe that everything on display was found right here at the grounds of the Agora.

One of the oldest pieces here is the fragment of a reclining female figure, displayed in the glass case in the center (from the fourth millennium B.C.). The first few cases show off **jars** from various eras, including Neolithic (when the Agora was first inhabited) and Geometric (1050-700 B.C.). Much of this exhibit shows how Greek pottery evolved over time. Pottery was a popular export product for the seafaring Greeks, and by tracing local styles of pottery manufacture and decoration, archaeologists have learned about their trading habits. The earliest pottery featured geometric patterns, then came floral and animal motifs, and finally painted human silhouettes—first showing black figures on the natural orange clay, then red figures on a black background. Also in this display is what the Greeks received in return for their pots: ivory and gold, both likely from Egypt.

AGORA

In case 26 (on the right), look for the cute little baby's **commode,** with a photo showing how it was used. Case 24 has a comb—notable as one of the very rare surviving wooden items found here. Nearby (case 69, on left) are Archaic-era statue heads with smiling faces.

Cases 30-32 (on right), with items from **early democracy,** are especially interesting. The "voting machine" (*klerote-rion,* case 31) was used to choose judges. Citizens put their name in the slots, then black and white balls went into the tube to randomly select who would serve (much like your turn in jury duty). Below the machine are bronze ballots from the fourth century. The pottery shards with names painted on them (*ostrakan,* case 30) were used as ballots in voting to ostracize someone accused of corruption or tyranny. Find the ones marked ΘΕΜΙΣΘΟΚΛΕΣ NEOKLEOS (item #37) and ARISSTEIΔES (item #17, see photo). During the Golden Age, Themistocles and Aristides were rivals (in both politics and romance) who served Athens honorably, but were exiled in political power struggles.

In case 32, see the *klepsydra* ("water thief")—a water clock used to time speeches at Council meetings. It took six minutes for the 1.7 gallons to drain out. A gifted orator truly was good to the last drop...but not a second longer.

Across the hall (under the banner, between cases 68 and 67) is the so-called **"Stele of Democracy"** (c. 336 B.C.). This stone

monument is inscribed with a decree outlawing tyranny. Above, a relief carving shows Lady Democracy crowning a man representing the Athenian people.

Next to that (in case 67) is a **bronze shield** captured from defeated Spartans in the tide-turning Battle of Sphacteria, which gave Athens the

AGORA

upper hand in the first phase of the Peloponnesian War. The next case over (case 66) displays herm heads. With news and directions attached, these functioned as signposts along roads.

A bit farther along, in the middle of the room, find the case of **coins.** These drachms and tetradrachms feature Athena with her helmet. In Golden Age times, a drachm was roughly a day's wage. The ancients put coins like these in the mouth of a deceased person as payment for the underworld ferryman Charon to carry the soul safely across the River Styx. Coin #7, with the owl, was a four-drachm piece; that same owl is on Greece's €1 coin today.

For a reminder that the ancients weren't so different from us, look for the two **barbecue grills** (case 61, left; and case 42, right).

The exhibit winds up with **Roman sculptural heads** (cases 58 and 56, left), which show how the Romans were more honest than the Greeks when it came to portraying people with less-than-ideal features, and even more pottery items—including various toys (case 48, right).

• *Exit this room at the far end and turn right into the stoa, passing a WC and water fountain. At the very end of the stoa, find the stairway leading up to the second level.*

The best part of this open-air upper floor is the nice **views** it affords down into the Agora and across to the Temple of Hephaistos. While you're up here, study the models of the Agora from various eras, which are helpful for mentally resurrecting the rubble. The statues displayed here aren't much different from those you'll see at the Acropolis Museum and the National Archaeological Museum, but their well-written English descriptions and striking setting make them worth at least a quick visit. Before heading downstairs, peer into the storage cases along the back of the stoa: Shelf upon shelf hold pottery shards, all of them dug up right here in the Agora.

• *You can exit the upper level at the far end, returning to where we began our visit to the stoa. Leave the stoa through its southern end (where you entered), then cross the main road and continue straight (west) along the lane, across the middle of the Agora. You're walking alongside the vast ruins (on your left) of what once was the...*

❹ Middle Stoa

Stretching clear across the Agora, this was part of a large complex of what were likely shops and office buildings. It was a long, narrow rectangle (about 500 by 60 feet), similar to the reconstructed Stoa of Attalos you just left. You can still see the two lines of stubby column fragments that once supported the roof, a few stone steps, and (at the far end) some of the reddish foundation blocks. Constructed around 180 B.C., this stoa occupied what had been open space in the center of the Agora.

• *Midway down the lane (near the wooden ramp), you'll come across a huge and frilly upper cap, or capital, of a column.*

❺ Corinthian Capital

This capital (dating from the fourth century B.C.) once stood here atop a colossal column, one of a dozen columns that lined the monumental entrance to the Odeon of Agrippa, a theater that extended northward from the Middle Stoa. (We'll learn more about the Odeon later on this tour.) The capital's elaborate acanthus-leaf decoration is a nice example of the late Corinthian style. Rarely used in Greek buildings, the Corinthian style became wildly popular with the Romans.

From here look back toward the entrance, overlooking what was once the vacant expanse at the center of the Agora. In 400 B.C., there was no Middle Stoa and no Odeon—this was all open space. As Athens grew, the space was increasingly filled in with shops and monuments. Now imagine the place in its heyday (see "The Agora in Action" sidebar).

• *Continue westward across the Agora. Near the end of the Middle Stoa, you'll see a gray wellhead—still in its original spot and worn by the grooves of ropes. From here look up at the Acropolis, where the towering but now-empty pedestal once sported the Monument of Agrippa, a grand statue with four horses. Just to the right, Mars Hill—likely topped with tourists today—is where the Apostle Paul famously preached the Gospel. Below the Erechtheion are broken columns shoring up the side of the hill. These were rubble from temples destroyed by the Persians.*

Just beyond the well to the right is a big drain and a round foundation—the tholos. Backtrack from the well a few steps to cross the wooden ramp, and go left to find the ditch that was once part of the...

❻ Great Drain

Dug in the fifth century B.C. and still functioning today, these ditches channel rainwater runoff from the southern hills through the Agora. Here at the southwest corner of the Agora, two main collection ditches meet and join. You can see exposed parts of the stone-lined ditch. The well we just passed was also part of this system.

• *Passing across the ditch and through the line of shrubbery, take the left fork toward a 60-foot-across round footprint with a stubby column in its center. This is the...*

❼ Tholos

This rotunda-shaped building was an assembly place for the administrators of Athens' City Council. Built around 465 B.C., it originally had six inner Ionic columns that held up a conical roof. In the middle was an altar (marked today by the broken column).

The fundamental unit of Athenian democracy was the Assembly, made up of the thousands of adult male citizens who could vote. Athenian citizens were organized into 10 tribes; in order to prevent the people living in any one geographical area from becoming dominant, each tribe was composed of citizens from city, coastal, and inland areas. Each man in the Assembly was considered to be from one of these tribes.

All of Athens' governing bodies met in the Agora. Though some Assembly meetings were held in the Agora's main square, the main assemblies took place just uphill, on the slope of Pnyx Hill. The City Council also met in the Agora. The Council consisted of 500 men (50 from each of the 10 tribes) who were chosen from the Assembly by lottery to serve a one-year term. The Council proposed and debated legislation, but because Athens practiced direct (not representational) democracy, all laws eventually had to be approved by the whole Assembly. The Council chose 50 ministers who ran the day-to-day affairs.

As part of the civic center complex, the *tholos* served several functions. It was the headquarters, offices, and meeting hall for the 50 administrators. Many lived and ate here, since the law required that at least a third of these ministers be on the premises at all times (they served for terms of only 36 days). The *tholos* also housed the city's official weights and measures. Any shopper in the Agora could use these to check whether a butcher or tailor was shortchanging them. As the center of government, the *tholos* of any ancient Greek city was also a kind of temple. The altar in the middle held an eternal flame, representing the hearth of the extended "family" that was Athens.

• *Beyond and above the* tholos *is the hill-capping Temple of Hephaistos. To reach it, climb the stairs to the left and go through the trees, pausing along the way at a viewpoint with a chart. Enjoy the ideal views of the entire Agora and Acropolis from here. Then continue to the...*

❽ Temple of Hephaistos

One of the best-preserved and most typical of all Greek temples, this is textbook Golden Age architecture. Started in 450 B.C.—just before the Parthenon—it was built at Athens' peak as part of the massive reconstruction of the Agora after invading Persians destroyed the city (480 B.C.). But the temple wasn't completed and dedicated until 415 B.C., as work stalled when the Greeks started erecting the great buildings of the Acropolis. Notice how the frieze

AGORA

The Agora in Action

Think of thousands of angry Athenian citizens assembled here, listening to speeches as they voted to ostracize a corrupt or tyrannical leader. Other than ostracisms, general assemblies usually were not held here, but on Pnyx Hill, which rises southwest of the Agora.

The roving philosopher **Socrates** (469-399 B.C.) spent much of his life simply hanging out in the Agora, questioning passersby, and urging people to "know thyself." Socrates discussed the meaning of piety, as recorded by Plato in the dialogue called the Euthyphro. "The lover of inquiry," said Socrates, "must follow his beloved wherever it may lead him." Shortly after, Socrates was tried and condemned to death here for "corrupting the youth"...by encouraging them to question Athenian piety.

Plato, Socrates' disciple and chronicler of his words, spent time teaching in the Agora, as did Plato's disciple **Aristotle.** (Their schools—Plato's Academy and Aristotle's Lyceum—were located elsewhere in Athens.)

The great statesman **Pericles**—whose Funeral Oration over the Greek dead from the first year of the Peloponnesian War is a famous expression of Athenian ideals—must have spent time here, since he oversaw the rebuilding program after the Persian invasion.

around the outside of the building was only decorated on the side facing the Agora (it's blank on the other three sides, as were most temples of this kind—the Parthenon is unusual for its continuous, wrap-around frieze).

This is a classic peristyle temple (like the Parthenon), meaning that the building is surrounded by columns—six on each end, 13 on the long sides (counting the corners twice). Also like the Parthenon, it's made of Pentelic marble in the Doric style, part of Pericles' vision of harking back to Athens' austere, solid roots. But the Temple of Hephaistos is only about half the size of the grand Parthenon and with fewer refinements (compared to the Parthenon's elaborate carvings and fancy math).

When Athens triumphed over Sparta in one battle during the Peloponnesian War (425 B.C.), **General Cleon** displayed the shields of captured prisoners in the Agora. This action mocked the Spartans for their surrender, since brave Spartans were always supposed to die with their shields on.

Diogenes the Cynic lived as a homeless person in the Agora and shocked the Athenians with his anti-materialist and free lifestyle. He lived in a wooden tub (in disregard for material comfort), masturbated openly (to prove how simply one's desires could be satisfied), and wandered the Agora with a lighted lamp in daylight (looking for one honest man in the corrupt city). According to legend, Alexander the Great was intrigued by this humble philosopher who shunned materialism. One day he stood before him and said, "Diogenes, I will give you whatever you want. What would you like?" History's first hippie looked at the most powerful man on earth and replied, "Please get out of my sunshine."

The earliest Greek plays and concerts were performed here in the open air and, later, in theaters (including the Odeon of Agrippa). The playwright **Aristophanes** set scenes in the Agora, and the tragedian **Sophocles** spent time here.

Imagine the buzz in the Agora at key points in Athens' history—as Athenians awaited the onslaught of the Persians and debated what to do, or as they greeted the coming of Alexander the Great, the conquering Romans, and the invasions of the Herulians and Slavs.

The **Apostle Paul** likely talked religion here in the Agora on his way to Corinth in A.D. 49 (Acts 17:17). He would have seen the various altars dedicated to pagan gods, which he decried from Mars Hill, overlooking the Agora.

The temple's entrance was on the east end, facing the Agora. Priests would enter through the six columns here, crossing through a covered portico (note the coffered ceiling) and an alcove ringed by three walls, called the *pronaos* or "pre-temple," before reaching the central hall *(cella)*. Large bronze statues of Hephaistos, the blacksmith god, and Athena, patroness of Athens and of arts and crafts, once stood in this central hall. In ancient times, metalworking and pottery shops surrounded the temple, but in the third century B.C. some were replaced with gardens, similar to today's. Behind the *cella* (the west end) is another three-sided alcove, matching the *pronaos*.

The carved reliefs (frieze and metopes) that run around the upper part of the building are only partly done; some panels may have been left unfinished.

At the end overlooking the Agora, look between the six columns and up at the frieze above the *pronaos* to find scenes of the mythical hero Theseus battling his enemies, trying to unite Athens. Theseus would go on to free Athens from the dominance of Crete by slaying the bull-headed Minotaur. The frieze decorations led Athenians to mistakenly believe that the temple once held the remains of Theseus—and to this day, they call it the Theseion.

Walk around behind the temple, to the far (west) end. The frieze above the three-sided alcove depicts the mythological battle between the Lapith tribe and centaurs during a wedding feast. Other scenes you'll see around the building (there are many interpretations) include Hercules (his labors and deification) and the birth of Erichthonios (one of Athens' first kings, who was born when spurned Hephaistos tried to rape Athena, spilled semen, and instead impregnated Gaia, the earth).

In the seventh century A.D., the temple was converted into the Church of Agios Georgios, and given the vaulted ceiling that survives today. During the Ottoman occupation, the Turks kept the church open but permitted services to be held only once each year (on St. George's Day). Because it was continually in use, the temple-turned-church is remarkably well preserved—but notice the bullet holes, damage sustained mostly in the 1820s, when the Greeks resisted the Turks.

• *Note that there's a "back door" exit nearby for those wanting to take the smooth, paved walkway up to the Acropolis, rather than the rough climb above the Agora. To find the exit, face the back of the temple, turn right, and follow the path to the green gate, which deposits you on the inviting, café-lined Apostolou Pavlou pedestrian drag. From here you could turn left and walk up toward the Acropolis.*

But there's still more to see in the Agora. Wind your way down the hill (northeast) to the middle of the Agora and find the headless...

❾ Statue of Hadrian

The first Roman emperor to wear a beard (previously a Greek fashion), Hadrian (r. A.D. 117-138) was a Grecophile and benefactor of Athens. Get close to this second-century A.D. statue and notice the insignia on the breastplate. There's Romulus and Remus, being suckled by the she-wolf who supports Athena on her back. This was Hadrian's vision—that by conquering Greece, Rome actually saved it.

Hadrian was nicknamed Graecula ("The Little Greek") for his love of Greek philosophy, literature, and a handsome Greek teenager named Antinous. Hadrian personally visited Athens, where he financed a comprehensive building program, including the Arch of Hadrian, Library of Hadrian, Temple of Olympian Zeus (which had been started by the Greeks), and a whole new master-planned neighborhood. (For more on these sights, see the 📖 Athens City Walk chapter or download my free 🎧 audio tour.) Hadrian's legacy endures. The main street through the Plaka is now called Adrianou—"Hadrian's" street.

• *Continuing on, head straight down the lane (to the left of Hadrian) and you'll pass three giants on four pedestals, which once guarded the...*

⓾ Odeon of Agrippa

This theater/concert hall (a.k.a. the "Palace of the Giants"), once fronted by a line of six fierce Triton and Giant statues, was the centerpiece of the Agora during the Roman era.

A plaque explains the history of this building: During the Golden Age, this site was simply open space in the very center of the Agora. The *odeon* (a venue designed mainly for musical performances) was built by the Roman general and governor Marcus Agrippa in the time of Caesar Augustus (around 15 B.C.), when Greece was a Roman-controlled province. For the theater-loving Greeks and their Greek-culture-loving masters, the *odeon* was a popular place. Two stories tall and built into the natural slope of the hill, it could seat more than a thousand people.

Back then, the entrance was on the south side (near the Middle Stoa), and these Triton and Giant statues didn't yet exist. Patrons entered from the south, walking through two rows of monumental columns, topped by Corinthian capitals. After the lobby, they emerged at the top row of a 20-tier, bowl-shaped auditorium, looking down on an orchestra and stage paved with multicolored marble and decorated with statues. The sightlines were great because the roof, spanning 82 feet, had no internal support columns. One can only assume that, in its heyday, the *odeon* hosted concerts, poetry readings, and more lowbrow Roman-oriented entertainment.

Around A.D. 150, the famously unsupported roof collapsed. By then Athens had a bigger, better performance venue (the Odeon of Herodes Atticus, on the other side of the Acropolis), so the Odeon of Agrippa was rebuilt at half the size as a 500-seat lecture hall. The new entrance was here on the north side, fronted by six colossal statues serving as pillars. Only two Tritons (with fish tails), a Giant (with a snake's tail), and an empty pedestal remain.

The building was burned to the ground in the Herulian invasion of A.D. 267 (explained later, under "Post-Herulian Wall"). Around A.D. 400, a large palace was built here, which also served as the university (or "gymnasium," which comes from the Greek word for "naked"—young men exercised in the buff during PE here). It lasted until the Constantinople-based Emperor Justinian closed all the pagan schools in A.D. 529.

• *Continue to the main road, where you'll see we've made a loop. Now turn right and start up toward the Acropolis on the...*

⓫ Panathenaic Way

The Panathenaic Way was Athens' main street. It started at the main city gate (the Dipylon Gate, near the Keramikos Cemetery), cut diagonally through the Agora's main square, and wound its way up to the Acropolis—two-thirds of a mile in all. The Panathenaic Way was the primary north-south road, and here in the Agora it intersected with the main east-west road to the port of Piraeus. Though some stretches were paved, most of it (then as now) was just packed gravel. It was lined with important temples, businesses, and legal buildings.

During the Panathenaic Festival held in the summer, this was the main parade route. Every four years on Athena's birthday, Greeks celebrated by giving her statue a new dress, called a *peplos*. A wheeled float carrying the *peplos* was pushed up this street. Thousands participated—some on horseback, others just walking—while spectators watched from wooden grandstands erected along the way. When the parade reached the Acropolis, the new dress was ceremonially presented to Athena and used to adorn her life-size statue at the Erechtheion. Today's tourists use the same path to connect the Agora and the Acropolis.

• *Continue up the Panathenaic Way, past the Stoa of Attalos. Along the left-hand side of the Panathenaic Way are several crude walls and column fragments.*

⓬ Post-Herulian Wall

This wall marks the beginning of the end of Roman Athens.

In A.D. 267, the barbarian Herulians sailed down from the Black Sea and utterly devastated Athens. (The crumbling Roman

Empire was helpless to protect its provinces.) The Herulians burned most of the Agora's buildings to the ground, leaving it in ashes.

As soon as the Herulians left, the surviving Athenians began hastily throwing up this wall—cobbled together from rubble—to

keep future invaders at bay. They used anything they could find: rocks, broken columns, statues, frieze fragments, all thrown together without mortar to make a wall 30 feet high and 10 feet thick. Archaeologists recognize pieces scavenged from destroyed buildings, such as the Stoa of Attalos and the Odeon of Agrippa.

Up until this point, the Agora had always been rebuilt after invasions (including the Persians in 480 B.C. and Romans in 89 B.C.); but after the Herulians, the Agora never recovered as a public space. What remained suffered through a Slavic invasion in A.D. 580. By A.D. 700, it was a virtual ghost town, located outside the city walls, exposed to bandits and invaders. Only the hardiest of souls used it as a residence. Considering how accessible the Agora was over the centuries as a quarry for pre-cut stones, it's no wonder that so little of it survives today.

• *Next came the Christians. On the right is the...*

⓭ Church of the Holy Apostles

This charming little church with the lantern-like dome marks the Agora's revival. Built around A.D. 1000, it commemorates

St. Paul's teaching in the Agora. Under protection from the Christian rulers of Byzantium (in Constantinople, modern-day Istanbul), Athens—and the Agora—slowly recovered from centuries of invasions and neglect. The church was built on the ruins of an ancient nymphaeum, or temple atop a sacred spring, and became one of many Christian churches that served the booming populace of Byzantine Athens.

This church was the prototype for later Athenian churches: a Greek-cross floor plan with four equal arms, topped by a dome and featuring windows with tall horseshoe-shaped arches. (The narthex, or entrance, was added later, spoiling the four equal arms.)

The church was built of large, rectangular, finished stone blocks rather than small bricks. Ringing the eaves is a decorative pattern of bricks shaped into calligraphic Kufic script (developed in the city of Kufa).

Enter (if the church is open) around the far side. It contains some interesting 17th-century Byzantine-style frescoes. The windows are in flower and diamond shapes. From the center, look up at Jesus as *Pantocrator* ("ruler over all") at the top of the dome, and see the icon on the altar and the faded frescoes on the walls. Notice the remains of the marble altar screen with wide-open spaces—frames that once held icons.

• *End your tour by continuing up the Panathenaic Way to the south exit gates and looking back over the Agora and modern Athens.*

Legacy of the Agora

By the 18th century, the Agora had become a flourishing Turkish residential district. The Church of the Holy Apostles was only one

of many churches serving the populace. In the early 20th century, outdoor movies were shown in the Agora. In the 1930s, the American School of Classical Studies purchased and demolished buildings that had stood for centuries, forcing everyone from their houses and businesses—all so they could dig here. The Church of the Holy Apostles was the only structure left standing, and it was heavily renovated by the American School to return it to its original state. Excavation in the Agora has continued nearly without pause for the past 70-some years.

Now that the ancient Agora has become a museum, the role of city center has shifted to Athens' many modern neighborhoods. Produce is bought and sold at the Central Market. The government center is at Syntagma Square. Multiple neighborhoods—the Plaka, Psyrri, Thissio, and Gazi—harbor nightlife. Monastiraki and a dozen other squares have become the new social-center "agoras." And the Metro has replaced the Panathenaic Way as the city's main artery.

• *Your tour is finished. There are three exits from the Agora: the gate through which you entered, at Adrianou street; the "back door" gate behind the Temple of Hephaistos; and the* ⓮ ***south gate*** *next to the Church of the Holy Apostles (where you are now).*

To head to the Acropolis (to complete your own Panathenaic Festival), exit through the gate by the church. You may be able to continue straight up the hill, through the rubble. However, the gate here may be closed. If so, exit the gate, turn left, then turn right in front of the yellow building, and take the first street on your right (Dioskouron). Hike up this street, climb the stairs by the restaurant, and keep going all the way up to the Acropolis. See the 📖 *Acropolis Tour chapter or download my free* 🎧 *audio tour.*

ACROPOLIS TOUR

Ακρόπολη

Even in this age of superlatives, it's hard to overstate the historic and artistic importance of the Acropolis. Crowned by the mighty Parthenon, the Acropolis ("high city") rises above the sprawl of modern Athens, a lasting testament to ancient Athens' glorious Golden Age in the fifth century B.C.

On this tour we'll hike up through the Propylaea gate, gaze up at the Temple of Athena Nike, ogle the famous Caryatid statues at the Erechtheion, and—of course—spend some time at the Parthenon. Climbing Acropolis Hill and rambling its ruins, you'll feel like you've journeyed back in time to the birthplace of Western civilization. And it all comes with breathtaking, far-as-the-eye-can-see views over the rooftops of Athens—one of Europe's most sprawling cities.

Orientation

Cost: €20 for Acropolis-only ticket; €30 for Acropolis combo-ticket, which covers Athens' other major ancient sites (see page 41). In the off-season (Nov-March), it's €10 for the Acropolis-only ticket and free the first Sun of each month. If you buy your Acropolis ticket elsewhere, you can bypass the ticket booth here.

Hours: Daily 8:00-20:00, Oct until 18:00, Nov-March until 17:00. Be aware that hours are subject to change; check locally before planning your day.

Information: Tel. 210-321-4172, www.culture.gr.

Crowd-Beating Tips: The place is miserably packed with tour groups from 10:00 to about 12:30 (when you might have to wait up to 45 minutes to get a ticket). On some days, as many as 6,000 cruise passengers converge on the Acropolis in a single morning. Buying a ticket at another sight may save ticket-buying time, but doesn't ensure a speedy entry: The worst lines are caused by the bottleneck of people trying to squeeze into the site through the Propylaea gate.

You have two good options: To avoid both crowds and heat, come in the cool morning hours, right when it opens. You'll be leaving just as everyone else is pouring in. Otherwise, I like to visit late in the day—as the sun goes down, the white Parthenon stone gleams a creamy golden brown, and what had been a tourist war zone is suddenly peaceful. Once I showed up late and had the place to myself in the cool of early evening. But be aware that it can still be quite hot in the late afternoon.

Getting There: There's no way to reach the Acropolis without a lot of climbing (though wheelchair users can take an elevator—see below). Figure a 10- to 20-minute hike from the base of the Acropolis up to the hilltop archaeological site. There are multiple paths up, but the only ticket office and site entrance are at the western end of the hill (to the right as you face the Acropolis from the Plaka).

If you're touring the Ancient Agora, you can hike up to the Acropolis entrance directly from there (see instructions at the end of the previous chapter). The approach from the Dionysiou Areopagitou pedestrian zone behind (south of) the Acropolis is slightly steeper. From this walkway, various well-marked paths funnel visitors up to the entrance; the least steep one climbs up from the parking lot at the western end of the pedestrian zone. You can reach this path either by taxi or by tourist train (the Athens Happy Train—see page 38), but it still involves quite a bit of uphill hiking.

If you use a **wheelchair,** you can take the elevator that ascends the Acropolis (from the ticket booth, go around the left side of the hilltop). However, once you are up top, the site is not particularly level or well-paved, so you may need help navigating the steep inclines and uneven terrain.

Visitor Information: Supplement the tour in this chapter with the free information brochure (you may have to ask for it when you buy your ticket) and info plaques posted throughout.

Tours: If you'd like a live **guide,** consider making advance arrangements with one of my recommended local guides (see page 39). You can hire your own tour guide at the entrance, but I wouldn't—the guides here tend to be rude, overpriced, and underqualified.

Download my free Acropolis **audio tour.** This sight is particularly suited to an audio tour, as it allows your eyes to enjoy the wonders of the Acropolis while your ears learn its story.

Length of This Tour: Allow two hours. Visitors with more time can precede this tour with the Ancient Agora Tour (see the previous chapter).

Baggage Check: Backpacks are allowed; baby strollers are not. There's a checkroom just below the ticket booth near Mars Hill.

Services: There are WCs at the Acropolis ticket booth and more WCs and drinking fountains atop the Acropolis in the former museum building (behind the Parthenon). Also inside the turnstiles are machines selling cheap, cold bottles of water. Near the ticket booth are a juice/snack stand (which sells over-priced sparkling water but not plain bottled water), a drinking fountain, a post office, and a museum shop. Note that picnicking is not allowed on the premises.

Plan Ahead: Wear sensible shoes—Acropolis paths are steep and uneven. In summer, it gets very hot on top, so take a hat, sunscreen, sunglasses, and a bottle of water.

Starring: The Parthenon and other monuments from the Golden Age, plus great views of Athens and beyond.

BACKGROUND

The Acropolis has been the heart of Athens since the beginning of recorded time. This limestone plateau, faced with sheer, 100-foot cliffs and fed by permanent springs, was a natural fortress. The Mycenaeans (c. 1400 B.C.) ruled the area from their palace on this hilltop, and Athena— the patron goddess of the city—was worshipped here from around 800 B.C. on.

But everything changed in 480 B.C. when Persia invaded Greece for the second time. As the Persians approached, the Athenians evacuated the city, abandoning it to be looted and vandalized. All the temples atop the Acropolis were burned to the ground. The Athenians fought back at sea, winning an improbable naval victory at the Battle of Salamis. The Persians were driven out of Greece, and Athens found itself suddenly victorious. Cash poured into Athens from the other Greek city-states, which were eager to be allied with the winning side.

By 450 B.C., Athens was at the peak of its power and the treasury was flush with money...but in the city center, the Acropolis still lay empty, a vast blank canvas. Athens' leader at the time, Peri-

Acropolis Overview

- - - - STANDING RUINS
- - - - ORIGINAL FOOTPRINT

To Ancient Agora
To Monastiraki

ANAFIOTIKA

Mars Hill

THEORIAS

ELEVATOR
ERECHTHEION

To Plaka

BEULÉ GATE
PROPYLAEA

ACROPOLIS FLAG

TICKETS

ACROPOLIS ENTRANCE

TEMPLE OF ATHENA NIKE

STRATONOS

To Plaka

WC

THESPIDOS

EPIMENIDOU

PARTHENON

To Apostolou Pavlou & Thissio

ODEON OF HERODES ATTICUS

THEATER OF DIONYSUS

THRASSILOU

DIONYSIOU AREOPAGITOU

BUS PARKING LOT

Filopappos Hill

GARIVALDI

PROPYLEON

EREGHTHIOU

PARTHENONOS

ROVERTOU GALLI

MAKRIGIANNI

KALLISPERI

ACROPOLIS MUSEUM

100 Meters
100 Yards

Akropoli M

cles, was ambitious and farsighted. He funneled Athens' newfound wealth into a massive rebuilding program. Led by the visionary architect/sculptor Pheidias (490-430 B.C.), the Athenians transformed the Acropolis into a complex of supersized, ornate temples worthy of the city's protector, Athena.

The four major monuments—the Parthenon, Erechtheion, Propylaea, and Temple of Athena Nike—were built as a coherent ensemble (c. 450-400 B.C.). Unlike most ancient sites, which have layer upon layer of ruins from different periods, the Acropolis we see today was started and finished within two generations—a snapshot of the Golden Age set in stone.

The Tour Begins

• *Climb up to the Acropolis ticket booth and the site entrance, located at the west end of the hill.*

Near this entrance (below and toward the Ancient Agora) is the huge, craggy boulder of **Mars Hill** (a.k.a. Areopagus). Consider

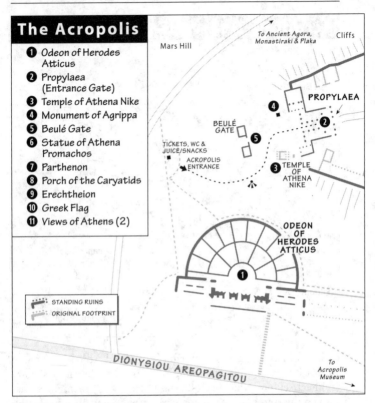

The Acropolis

1. Odeon of Herodes Atticus
2. Propylaea (Entrance Gate)
3. Temple of Athena Nike
4. Monument of Agrippa
5. Beulé Gate
6. Statue of Athena Promachos
7. Parthenon
8. Porch of the Caryatids
9. Erechtheion
10. Greek Flag
11. Views of Athens (2)

Mars Hill

To Ancient Agora, Monastiraki & Plaka   Cliffs

PROPYLAEA

BEULÉ GATE

TICKETS, WC & JUICE/SNACKS

ACROPOLIS ENTRANCE

TEMPLE OF ATHENA NIKE

ODEON OF HERODES ATTICUS

STANDING RUINS
ORIGINAL FOOTPRINT

DIONYSIOU AREOPAGITOU

To Acropolis Museum

climbing this rock for great views of the Acropolis' ancient entry gate, the Propylaea, and the Ancient Agora. Mars Hill's bare, polished rock is extremely slippery—a metal staircase to the left helps somewhat. (For more on Mars Hill and its role in Christian history, see page 46.) If you choose not to climb it, you'll at least get great views of it from the front steps of the Acropolis.

Before you show your ticket and enter the Acropolis site, make sure you have everything you'll need for your visit. Remember, after you enter the site, there are no services except WCs and water fountains.

• *Enter the site and start climbing the paths that switchback up the hill, following signs on this one-way tourist route (bearing to the right). Before you reach the summit, peel off to the right for a bird's-eye view of the...*

❶ Odeon of Herodes Atticus

The grand Odeon huddles under the majestic Propylaea. Tourists call it a "theater," but Greeks know it's technically an *odeon*, as it was mainly used for musical rather than theatrical performances.

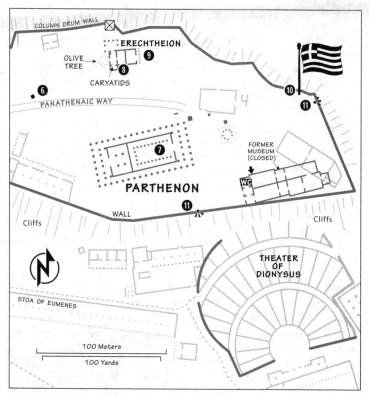

(*Odeon*—like the English word "ode"—comes from the Greek word for "song.")

A large 5,000-seat **amphitheater** built during Roman times, it's still used for performances. From this perch you get a good

look at the stage setup: a three-quarter-circle orchestra (where musicians and actors performed in Greek-style theater), the overgrown remnants of a raised stage (for actors in the Roman tradition), and an intact stage wall for the backdrop. Originally it had a wood-and-tile roof as well.

The Odeon is sometimes called the Herodion, after Herodes Atticus, a wealthy landowner who had the building erected in A.D. 161 in memory of his wife. Herodes Atticus was a Greek with Roman citizenship, a legendary orator, and a friend of Emperor Hadrian. This amphitheater is the most famous of the many impressive buildings he financed around the country.

ACROPOLIS

Destroyed by the invading Herulians a century after it was built, the Odeon was reconstructed in the 1950s to the spectacular state it's in today. It's open to the public only during performances, such as the annual Athens & Epidavros Festival, when an international lineup of dance, music, and theater is performed beneath the stars. If there's something on tonight, you may see a rehearsal from here.

• *After climbing a few more steps, you'll see two gates: On the right, steps lead down to the Theater of Dionysus (described on page 47); on the left is the actual entry uphill into the Acropolis. Stay left and continue up to reach the grand entrance gate of the Acropolis: the Propylaea. Stand at the foot of the (very) steep marble staircase, facing up toward the big Doric columns.*

As you face the Propylaea, to your left is a tall, grayish stone pedestal with nothing on it: the Monument of Agrippa. On your right, atop the wall, is the Temple of Athena Nike. Behind you stands a doorway in a wall, known as the Beulé Gate.

❷ Propylaea

The entrance to the Acropolis couldn't be through just any old gate; it had to be the grandest gate ever built. Ancient visitors would stand here, catching their breath before the final push to the summit, and admire these gleaming columns and steep steps that almost fill your field of vision. Imagine the psychological impact this awe-inspiring, colonnaded entryway to the sacred rock must have had on ancient Athenians. The odd mix of **stairs**

here shows how the way up looked in different eras. The original ascent, a ramp that allowed sacrificial animals to make the climb, was replaced with a grand marble staircase in Hellenistic times, and then with a zigzag road (partly still intact) in the Middle Ages. (A few original stairs survive under the wooden ramp.)

The Propylaea (pro-PEE-leh-ah) is U-shaped, with a large central hallway (the six Doric columns), flanked by side wings that reach out to embrace the visitor. The central building looked like a mini-Parthenon, with Doric columns topped by a triangular pediment. Originally, the Propylaea was painted bright colors.

The left wing of the Propylaea was the **Pinakotheke,** or "painting gallery." In ancient times this space contained artwork and housed visiting dignitaries and VIPs.

The buildings of the Acropolis were all built to complement one another. The Propylaea was constructed in five short years

(437-432 B.C.), just after the Parthenon was finished. Its design (by Mnesicles) was meant to give the visitor a hint of the Parthenon to come. Both buildings are Doric (with Ionic touches) and are aligned east-west, with columns of similar width-to-height ratios.

• *Before ascending, notice the monuments flanking the entryway. To the right of the Propylaea, look up high atop the block wall to find the...*

❸ Temple of Athena Nike

The Temple of Athena Nike (Greeks pronounce it "NEEK-ee") was started as the Propylaea was being finished (c. 427-421/415 B.C.). It was designed by Callicrates, one of the architects of the Parthenon. This little temple—nearly square, 11 feet tall, with four columns at both ends—had delightful proportions. Where the Parthenon and Propylaea are sturdy Doric, this temple pioneered the Ionic style in Athens, with elegant scroll-topped columns.

The Acropolis was mainly dedicated to the **goddess Athena,** patron of the city. At this temple, she was worshipped for bringing the Athenians victory ("Nike"). A statue of Athena inside the temple celebrated the turning-point victory over the Persians at the Battle of Plataea in 479 B.C. It was also meant to help ensure future victory over the Spartans in the ongoing Peloponnesian War. The statue was never given wings because Athenians wanted Athena to stay and protect their city—hence the place became known as the Temple of Wingless Athena.

The Temple of Athena Nike has undergone **extensive restoration.** From 2001 to 2010, it was completely disassembled, then cleaned, shored up, and pieced back together. This was the third time in its 2,500-year history that the temple had been entirely taken apart. The Ottomans pulled it down at the end of the 17th century and used the stone elsewhere, but Greeks reassembled the temple after regaining their independence. In 1935 it was taken apart for renovation and put back together in 1939. Unfortunately, that shoddy work did more harm than good—prompting the most recent restoration. Now it's been done the right way and should hold for another 2,500 years.

• *To the left (as you face the Propylaea) is the...*

❹ Monument of Agrippa

This 25-foot-high pedestal, made of big blocks of gray marble with

ACROPOLIS

yellow veins, reaches as high up as the Temple of Athena Nike. The (now-empty) pedestal once held a bronze statue of the **four-horse chariot** owned by Eumenes II, king of Pergamon—the winner of the race at the 178 B.C. Panathenaic Games.

Over the centuries, each ruler of Athens wanted to put his mark on the mighty Acropolis. When Rome occupied the city, Marc Antony placed a statue of himself and his girlfriend Cleopatra atop the pedestal. After their defeat, the Roman general Agrippa (son-in-law of Augustus) replaced it with a statue of himself (in 27 B.C.).

• *Before entering, look downhill. Behind you is the...*

⑤ Beulé Gate

This **ceremonial doorway** was built by the Romans, who used the rubble from buildings that had recently been destroyed in the barbarian Herulian invasion of A.D. 267. (The gate's French name comes from the archaeologist who discovered it in 1852.) During Roman times, this gate was the official entrance to the Acropolis, making the Propylaea entry even grander.

• *Climb the steps (or today's switchback ramps for tourists). Partway up, try to pull off to one side—out of the way of the steady torrent of tourists—to take a closer look...*

Inside the Propylaea

Imagine being part of the grand parade of the Panathenaic Festival, held every four years. The procession started at Athens' city gate

(near the Keramikos Cemetery), passed through the Agora, then went around Mars Hill, through the central hall of the Propylaea, and up to the glorious buildings atop the summit of the Acropolis. Ancient Greeks approached the

Propylaea by proceeding straight up a ramp in the middle, which narrowed as they ascended, funneling them into the central passageway. There were five doorways into the Propylaea, one between each of the six columns.

The Propylaea's **central hall** was once a roofed passageway. The marble-tile ceiling, now partially restored, was painted sky blue and studded with stars. Floral designs decorated other parts of the building. The interior columns are Ionic, a bit thinner than the Doric columns of the exterior. You'll pass by some big column drums with square holes in the center, where iron pins once held the drums in place. (Greek columns were not usually made from a single piece of stone, but

from sections—"column drums"—stacked on top of one another.)

• *Pass through the Propylaea. As you emerge out the other end, you're on top of the Acropolis. There it is—the Parthenon! Just like in the books (except for the scaffolding). Stand and take it all in.*

The Acropolis

The "Acropolis rock" is a mostly flat limestone ridge covering seven acres, scattered with ruins. There's the Parthenon ahead to the right. To the left of that, with the six lady pillars (Caryatids), is the Erechtheion. The Panathenaic Way ran between them. The processional street and the buildings were aligned east–west, like the hill.

Ancient visitors here would have come face-to-face with a welcoming 30-foot ❻ **Statue of Athena Promachos,** which stood

between the Propylaea and the Erechtheion. (Today there's just a field of rubble; the statue's former location is marked on the left by three stones forming a low wall.) This was one of three statues of Athena on the Acropolis. The patron of the city was worshipped for her wisdom, purity, and strength; here she appeared in her role as "Frontline Soldier" *(promachos),* carrying a shield and spear. The statue was cast by Pheidias, the visionary sculptor/architect most responsible for the design of the Acropolis complex. The bronze statue was so tall that the shining tip of Athena's spear was visible from ships at sea. The statue disappeared in ancient times, and no one knows its fate.

Two important buildings, now entirely gone, flanked this statue and the Panathenaic Way. On the right was the **Chalkotheke,** a practical storage area for the most precious gifts brought to the temple—those made of copper and bronze. On the left stood the **Arrephorion,** a house where young virgins called *ergastinai* worked at looms to weave the *peplos,* the sacred dress given to Athena on her birthday.

• *Move a little closer for the classic view of the world's most famous temple. If you're tired, I've installed a handy white marble bench for you to take a load off while you take in the...*

❼ Parthenon
West End

The Parthenon is the hill's showstopper—the finest temple in the ancient world, standing on the highest point of the Acropolis, 490 feet above sea level. It's now largely in ruins, partly from the ravages of time, but mostly from a direct mortar-shell hit sustained in 1687 (launched by a Venetian army aiming for the gunpowder stored inside by the Ottomans).

It's impressive enough today, but imagine how awesome the Parthenon must have looked when it was completed nearly 2,500 years ago (if the west end is behind scaffolding during your visit, circle around to the east side). This is Greece's largest **Doric temple:** 228 feet long and 101 feet wide. At each end were 8 outer and 6 inner fluted Doric columns, with 17 columns along each side, plus 23 inner columns in the Doric and 4 in the Ionic style. The outer columns are 34 feet high and 6 feet in diameter. In its heyday, the temple was decorated with statues and carved reliefs, all painted in vivid colors. It's considered Greece's greatest Doric temple—but not its purest example because it incorporates Ionic columns and sculpture.

The Parthenon served the **cult of Virgin Athena.** It functioned as both a temple (with a cult statue inside) and as the treasury of Athens (safeguarding the city's funds, which included the treasury of the Athenian League).

This large temple was completed in less than a decade (447-438 B.C.), though the sculptural decoration took a few years more (finished c. 432). The project's overall look was supervised by the master sculptor-architect Pheidias, built by well-known architects Ictinus and Callicrates, and decorated with carved scenes from Greek mythology by sculptors Agoracritos and Alcamenes.

It's big, sure. But what makes the Parthenon truly exceptional is that the architects used a whole bagful of **optical illusions** to give the building an ever-so-subtle feeling of balance, strength, and

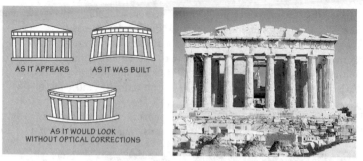

AS IT APPEARS   AS IT WAS BUILT

AS IT WOULD LOOK
WITHOUT OPTICAL CORRECTIONS

harmonious beauty. Architects know that a long, flat baseline on a building looks to the human eye like it's sagging, and that parallel columns appear to bend away from each other. To create a building that looked harmonious, the Parthenon's ancient architects calculated bends in the construction. The base of the Parthenon actually arches several inches upward in the middle to counteract the "sagging" illusion. Its columns tilt ever so slightly inward (one of the reasons why the Parthenon has withstood earthquakes so well). If you extended all the columns upward several miles, they'd eventually touch. The corner columns are thicker to make them appear the same size as the rest; they're also spaced more closely. And the columns bulge imperceptibly halfway up (an effect called "entasis"), giving the subconscious impression of stout, barrel-chested men bearing the weight of the roof. For a building that seems at first to be all about right angles, the Parthenon is amazingly short on straight, structural lines.

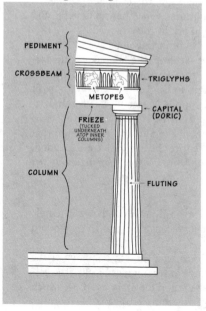

PEDIMENT

CROSSBEAM

TRIGLYPHS

METOPES

CAPITAL
(DORIC)

FRIEZE
(TUCKED
UNDERNEATH
ATOP INNER
COLUMNS)

COLUMN

FLUTING

All these clever refinements form a powerful subconscious impression on the viewer that brings an otherwise boring architectural box to life. It's amazing to think that all this was planned and implemented in stone so long ago.

The statues and carved reliefs that once decorated the outside of the Parthenon are now mostly faded or missing, but a few remain. Look up at the crossbeam atop the eight columns, decorated with panels of relief carvings called **metopes,** depicting

Athenians battling Amazons. Originally there were 92 Doric-style metopes in high relief, mostly designed by Pheidias himself.

The crossbeams once supported a triangular pediment (now gone). This area was once filled in with statues, showing Athena with her olive tree competing with Poseidon and his trident to be Athens' patron god. Today just one statue remains (and it's a reconstruction).

Approach closer and look between the eight columns. Inside, there's another row of eight columns, supporting a covered

entrance porch. Look up above the inner eight columns. Decorating those crossbeams are more relief carvings—the "frieze." Originally, a 525-foot-long **frieze** of panels circled the entire building. It showed the Panathenaic parade—women, men on horseback, musicians, sacrificial animals being led to the slaughter—while the gods looked on. All of the sculptures—metopes, pediment, and frieze—were originally painted in bright colors.

Today, most of the originals are in museums across Europe. In the early 1800s, the cream of the crop, the famous Elgin Marbles (but you'd better call them the "Parthenon Marbles" here in Greece), were taken by Lord Elgin to England, where they now sit in the British Museum. The Acropolis Museum (which stands at the base of the hill—you'll see it from a distance later on this tour) was built to house the fragments of the Parthenon sculpture that Athens still owns...and to try to entice the rest back from London.

• *Continue along the Panathenaic Way, walking along the long left (north) side of the Parthenon.*

North Side

This view of the Parthenon gives you a glimpse into how the temple was constructed and how it is being reconstructed today by modern archaeologists.

Looking between the columns, you can see remnants of the interior walls, built with thousands of rectangular blocks. The columns formed an **open-air porch** around the main building, which had an entry hall and *cella* (inner sanctum). Large marble roof tiles were fitted together atop wooden beams. These tiles were carved so thin that the interior glowed with the light that shone through it.

The Parthenon's columns are in the Doric style—stout, lightly fluted, with no base. The simple capital on top consists of a convex plate topped with a square slab. The capitals alone weigh eight to nine tons. The crossbeams consist of a lower half ("architrave") and an upper half, its metopes interspersed with a pattern of grooves (called triglyphs).

The Parthenon (along with the other Acropolis buildings) was constructed from the very finest materials, including high-quality, white Pentelic marble from Penteliko Mountain, 16 miles away. Unlike the grand structures of the Egyptians (pyramids) and the Romans (Colosseum), the Parthenon was built not by slaves but by free men who drew a salary (though it's possible that slaves worked at the quarries).

Imagine the engineering problems of quarrying and transporting more than 100,000 tons of marble. Most likely the **column drums** (5-10 tons each) were cut at the quarry and rolled here. To hoist the drums in place, the builders used four-poster cranes (and Greek mathematics), centering the drums with a cedar peg in the middle. The drums were held together by metal pins that were coated in lead to prevent corrosion, then fitted into a square hole cut in the center of the drum. (The Ottomans scavenged much of this lead to make bullets, contributing to the destruction of the temple over the ages.) Because the Parthenon's dimensions are not mathematically precise (intentionally so), each piece had to be individually cut and sized to fit its exact place. The Parthenon's stones are so well-crafted that they fit together within a thousandth of an inch. The total cost to build the Parthenon (in today's dollars) has been estimated at over a billion dollars.

• *Continue on to the...*

East End and Entrance

This end was the original entrance to the temple. Over the doorway, the triangular pediment depicted the central event in Athe-

nian history—the **birth of Athena,** their patron goddess. Today, the pediment barely survives, and the original statues of the gods are partly in the British Museum. Originally, the gods were gathered at a banquet (see a copy of the reclining Dionysus at the far left—looking so drunk he's afraid to come down). Zeus got a headache and asked Hephaistos to relieve it. As the other gods looked on in astonishment, Hephaistos split Zeus' head open, and—at the peak of the pediment—out rose Athena. The now-missing statues were surprisingly realistic and three-dimensional, with perfect anatomy and bulging muscles showing through transparent robes.

Imagine this spot during the age of Pericles and Socrates. Stand back far enough to take it all in, imagine the huge statue of Athena that once stood inside (see next page), and picture the place in all its glory on the day of the **Panathenaic parade.** The procession would have traveled through the Agora, ascended the Acropolis, passed through the Propylaea, and arrived here at the altar of Athena in front of the entrance of the Parthenon. People gathered on the surrounding grass (the hard stone you see today was once covered with plants). Musicians played flutes and harps, young women carried gifts, and men on horseback reined in their restless animals. On open-air altars, the priests offered a sacrifice of 100 oxen (a hecatomb—the ultimate sacrificial gift) to the goddess Athena.

Here at the Parthenon entrance, a select few celebrants were chosen to go inside. They proceeded up the steps, passed through the majestic columns into the foyer *(pronaos),* and entered the main hall, the *cella*—100 feet long, 60 feet wide, and 4 stories tall. At the far end of the room stood an enormous, 40-foot-tall statue of **Athena Parthenos** (Athena the Virgin). This was a chryselephantine statue, meaning "of gold and ivory"—from the Greek *chrysos,* "gold," and *elephantinos,* "ivory." Its wooden core was plated with ivory to represent her skin and pure gold to define her garments. Dressed as a warrior, she wore a helmet and rested her shield at her side. Her image was reflected in a pool in the center of the room. (The pool also served a practical purpose: The humidity helped preserve the ivory treasures.) In Athena's left hand was a spear propped on the ground. In her upturned right hand was a statuette of Nike—she literally held Victory in the palm of her hand.

The statue—the work of the master Pheidias—was either carried off in A.D. 426 to Constantinople, where it subsequently vanished, or was burned by the Herulians in A.D. 267. (A small-scale Roman copy is on display in Athens' National Archaeological Museum.) Another famous chryselephantine statue by Pheidias—of a seated Zeus—was located in Olympia and considered one of the Seven Wonders of the Ancient World.

The culmination of the Great Panathenaic parade every four years was the presentation of a newly woven *peplos* to Athena. The dress was intended for the life-size wooden statue of Athena kept at the Erechtheion (described later).

• *The modern brown-brick building behind you once housed the **former Acropolis museum**—its collection has been painstakingly moved into*

*the modern Acropolis Museum down the hill. WCs and a drinking foun-
tain are located alongside the old museum building.*

*Across the street from the Parthenon stands the Erechtheion, where
the Panathenaic parade ended. Start by enjoying its famous...*

❽ Porch of the Caryatids

An inspired piece of architecture, this balcony has six beautiful maidens functioning as columns that support the roof. Each

of the **lady-columns** has a base
beneath her feet, pleated robes
as the fluting, and a fruit-basket
hat as the capital. Both feminine
and functional, they pose gracefully, exposing a hint of leg—a
combination of architectural elements and sculpture.

These are faithful copies of
the originals, five of which are on
display in the Acropolis Museum. The sixth was removed (c. 1805)
by the sticky-fingered Lord Elgin, who shipped it to London. The
Caryatids were supposedly modeled on *Karyatides*—women from
Karyai (modern Karyes, near Sparta on the Peloponnese), famous
for their upright posture and noble character.

The Erechtheion (c. 421-406 B.C.) is sometimes ascribed to
Mnesicles, the man who designed the Propylaea. Whereas the
Propylaea and Parthenon are both sturdy Doric, the Erechtheion is
elegant Ionic. In its day, it was a stunning white building (of Pentelic marble) with painted capitals and a frieze of white relief on a
darker blue-gray background.

Near the porch (below, to the left) is an **olive tree**, a replacement for the one Athena planted here in her face-off with Poseidon. Olive trees are called "the gift of Athena to Athens" (we'll
learn the story behind this soon). Greece has more than 140 million of these trees.

• *Walk around to the right and view the Erechtheion from the east end,
with its six Ionic columns in a row.*

❾ Erechtheion

Though overshadowed by the
more impressive Parthenon, the
Erechtheion (a.k.a. Erechtheum)
was perhaps more prestigious. It
stood on one of the oldest sites
on the hill, where the Mycenaeans had built their palace. (It lay
mainly on the south side, facing

Acropolis Now: The Renovation Project

The scaffolding, cranes, and modern construction materials you see here are part of an ongoing renovation project. The challenge is to save what's left of the Parthenon from the modern menaces of acid rain and pollution, which have al-

ready caused irreversible damage. Funded by Greece and the EU, the project began in 1976, which means that they've been at it more than four times as long as it took to build the Parthenon in the first place.

The project first involves cataloging every single stone of the Parthenon—blocks, drums, capitals, bits of rock, and pieces lying on the ground or in museums around the world. Next, archaeologists hope to put it back together, like a giant 70,000-piece jig-saw puzzle. Along the way, they're fixing previous restorations that were either inaccurate or problematic. For example, earlier restorers used uncoated iron and steel rods to hold things together. As weather fluctuations caused the metal to expand, the stone was damaged. This time around, restorers are using titanium rods.

Whenever possible, the restorers use original materials. But you'll also see big blocks of new marble lying on the

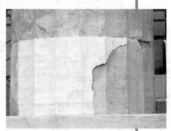

ground—freshly cut from the same Pentelic quarries that supplied the original stone. The new marble is being used to replace damaged and missing pieces. Many of the columns have light-colored "patches" where the restorers have installed the new stone, cut to fit exactly. Though it looks much whiter, in time the newly cut marble will age to match the rest of the Parthenon.

When complete, the renovated Parthenon won't look like a fully restored building—just a shored-up version of the ruin we see today. If you want to see what the Parthenon temple looked like in its heyday, there's a full-scale replica open to visitors...in Nashville, Tennessee.

the Parthenon, under the huge scattered stones—all that's left of the seventh-century Athena Temple.) Inside the Erechtheion was a life-size, olive-wood statue of Athena in her role of **Athena Polias** ("Protector of the City"). Pericles took the statue with him when the Athenians evacuated their city to avoid the invading Persians. Dating from about 900 B.C., this statue, much older and more venerable than either of Pheidias' colossal statues, supposedly dropped from the sky as a gift from Athena.

This unique, two-story structure fits nicely into the slope of the hill. The east end (with the six Ionic columns) was the upper-

level entrance. The lower entrance was on the north side (on the right), 10 feet lower, where you see six more Ionic columns. (These columns are the "face of the Acropolis" that Athenians see from the Plaka.) The **Porch of the Caryatids** is attached to the south side of the building. Looking inside the temple, you can make out that the inner worship hall, the *cella*, is divided in two by walls.

This complex layout accommodated the worship of various gods who had been venerated here since the beginning of time. Legend says this was the spot where Athena and Poseidon fought for naming rights to the city. Poseidon threw his trident, which opened a gash in the earth to bring forth water. It left a diagonal crack that you can still see in the pavement of the entrance farthest from the Parthenon (although lightning is a more likely culprit). But Athena won the contest by stabbing a rock with her spear, sprouting an olive tree near the Porch of the Caryatids. The twin *cella*s of the Erechtheion allowed the worship of both gods—Athena and Poseidon—side by side to show that they were still friends.

• *Look to the right (beyond the Plaka-facing porch). The modern **elevator** carries people with limited mobility up to the Acropolis. The north wall of the Acropolis has a retaining wall built from **column drums**. This is about all that remains of an earlier half-finished Parthenon that was destroyed after the Persian invasion of 480 B.C. The Persians razed the entire Acropolis, including an unfinished temple then under construction. The Athenians rebuilt as fast as they could with the scattered material to fortify the city against Sparta.*

Turn 180 degrees and walk to the far end of the Acropolis. There you'll find an observation platform with a giant...

⓾ Greek Flag

The blue-and-white Greek flag's nine stripes symbolize the nine syllables of the Greek phrase for "Freedom or Death." That phrase

After the Golden Age:
The Acropolis Through History

Classical: The Parthenon and the rest of the Acropolis buildings survived through classical times largely intact, despite Herulian looting (A.D. 267). As the Roman Empire declined, precious items were carried off, including the 40-foot Athena statue from the Parthenon.

Christian: The Christian emperor Theodosius II (Theodosius the

Great) labored to outlaw pagan worship and to close temples and other religious sites. After nearly a thousand years as Athena's temple, the Parthenon became a Christian church (fifth century A.D.). It remained Christian for the next thousand years, first as the Byzantine Orthodox Church of Holy Wisdom, then as Mother Mary of Athens (11th century), and at the end as a Roman Catholic cathedral of Notre Dame (dedicated to Mary in 1205 by Frankish Crusaders). Throughout medieval times it was an important stop on the pilgrimage circuit.

The Parthenon's exterior was preserved after its conversion to a church, but pagan sculptures and decorations were removed (or renamed), and the interior was decorated with colorful Christian frescoes. The west end of the building became the main entrance, and the interior was reconfigured with an apse at the east end.

Muslim: In 1456, the Turks arrived and converted the Parthenon into a mosque, adding a minaret. The Propylaea gateway was used as a palace for the Turkish ruler of Athens. The Turks had no respect for the sacred history of the Acropolis—they even tore down stones just to get the lead clamps that held them in place in order to make bullets. (The exasperated Greeks even offered them bullets to stop destroying the temple.) The Turks also used

ACROPOLIS

took on new meaning when the Nazis entered Athens in April 1941. According to an oft-repeated (but unverified) story, the evzone (member of a select infantry unit) guarding the flag flying here was ordered by the Nazis to remove it. He calmly took it down, wrapped himself in it—and jumped to his death.

About a month later, two heroic teenagers, Manolis Glezos and

the Parthenon to store gunpowder, unfortunately leading to the greatest catastrophe in the Acropolis' long history. It happened in…

1687: A Venetian army laid siege to the Acropolis. The Venetians didn't care about ancient architecture. As far as they were concerned, it was a lucky hit of mortar fire that triggered the massive explosion that ripped the center out of the Parthenon, rattled the Propylaea and the other buildings, and wiped out the Turkish defenders. Pieces of the Parthenon lay scattered on the ground, many of them gathered up as souvenirs by soldiers.

Lord Elgin: In 1801, Lord Elgin, the British ambassador to the Ot-tomans in Constantinople, got "permission" from the sultan to gather sculptures from the Parthenon, buy them from locals, and even saw them off the building (Greeks scoff at the idea that "permission" granted by an occupying power should carry any weight). He carted half of them to London, where the "Elgin Marbles" are displayed in the British Museum to this day, despite repeated requests for their return. Although a few original frieze, metope, and pediment carvings still adorn the Parthenon, most of the sculptures are on display in museums, including the Acropolis Museum.

From Independence to the Present: In the 19th century, newly independent Greece tore down the Parthenon's minaret and the other post-Classical buildings atop the Acropolis, turning it into an archaeological zone. Since then the site has been excavated and has undergone several renovations. Today, the Acropolis strikes wonder in the hearts of visitors, just as it has for centuries.

Apostolis Santas, scaled the wall, took down the Nazi flag and raised the Greek flag. This was one of the first well-known acts of resistance against the Nazis, and the boys' bravery is honored by a plaque near the base of the steps. To this day, Greeks can see this flag from just about anywhere in Athens and think of their hard-won independence.

• *Walk out to the end of the rectangular promontory to see the…*

⓫ View of Athens

The Ancient Agora spreads below the Acropolis, and the sprawl of modern Athens whitewashes the surrounding hills. In 1830, the population of Athens' core was about 5,000. By 1900, it was 600,000, and during the 1920s, with the influx of Greeks from Turkey, the population surged to 1.5 million. The city's expansion could barely keep up with its exploding population. With the boom times in the 1950s and 1980s, the city grew to nearly four million. Pan around. From this perch you're looking at the homes of one out of every three Greeks.

Looking down on the **Plaka,** find (looking left to right) the Ancient Agora, with the Temple of Hephaistos. Next comes the Roman Forum (the four columns and palm trees) with its round, white, domed Temple of the Winds monument. The **Anafiotika** neighborhood clings to the Acropolis hillside directly below us. About eight blocks beyond that, find the dome of the cathedral.

Lykavittos Hill, Athens' highest point, is crowned with the Chapel of St. George (and an expensive view restaurant; cable car

up the hill). Looking farther in the distance, you'll see lighter-colored bits on the mountains behind—these are **Pentelic quarries,** the source of the marble used to build (and now restore) the monuments of the Acropolis.

As you continue panning to the right, you'll spot the beige Neoclassical **Parliament** building, marking Syntagma Square; the **National Garden** is behind and to the right of it. In the garden is the yellow **Zappeion,** an exhibition hall. The green area in the far distance contains the 60,000-seat, marble **Panathenaic Stadium**—an ancient venue (on the site where Golden Age Athens held its games), which was rehabbed in 1896 to help revive the modern Olympics.

• *Complete your visual tour of Athens at the south edge of the Acropolis. To reach the viewpoint, walk back toward the Parthenon, then circle along its left side, by the cliff-top wall. Belly up to that wall for...*

More Views of Athens

Look to the left. In the near distance are the huge columns of the **Temple of Olympian Zeus.** Begun in the sixth century B.C., it wasn't finished until the time of the Roman emperor Hadrian, 700 years later. It was the biggest temple in all of Greece, with 104 Corinthian

pillars housing a 40-foot seated statue of Zeus, a replica of the famous one created by Pheidias in Olympia. This area was part of Hadrian's "new Athens," a planned community in his day, complete with the triumphal **Arch of Hadrian** near the temple.

The **Theater of Dionysus**—which hosted great productions (including works by Sophocles) during the Golden Age—lies in ruins at your feet (a visit to these ruins is covered by your Acropolis ticket).

Beyond the theater is the wonderful **Acropolis Museum**, a black-and-gray modern glass building, with three rectangular floors stacked at irregular angles atop each other. The top floor, which houses replicas and some originals of the Parthenon's art, is angled to match the orientation of that great temple.

Looking right, you see **Filopappos Hill**—the green, tree-dotted hill topped with a marble funerary monument to a popular Roman senator, Philopappos, who died in the early second century. This hill is where the Venetians launched the infamous mortar attack of 1687 that destroyed the Parthenon. Today, a theater here hosts popular folk-dancing performances (described in the Shopping & Nightlife in Athens chapter).

Farther in the distance, you get a glimpse of the turquoise waters of the **Aegean** (the only island visible is Aegina). While the Persians were burning the Acropolis to the ground, the Athenians watched from their ships as they prepared to defeat their foes in the history-changing Battle of Salamis. In the distance, far to the right, is the port of Piraeus (the main departure point for boats to the islands).

• *Our tour is finished. Enjoy a few final moments with the Acropolis before you leave. If you're not yet ready to return to modern Athens, you can continue your sightseeing at several nearby sights.*

*To reach the Theater of Dionysus ruins and the Acropolis Museum: Head left when you exit the Acropolis site, and walk down to the Dionysiou Areopagitou pedestrian boulevard. Turn left and follow this walkway along the base of the Acropolis. You'll pass (on the left) the **Theater of Dionysus** ruins, and (on the right) the **Acropolis Museum.** ▢ See the Acropolis Museum Tour chapter.*

*To reach the Ancient Agora: Turn right as you exit the Acropolis site, pass Mars Hill, and follow the Panathenaic Way down to the **Ancient Agora** (possible to enter through the "back door," facing the Acropolis; walk straight through the Agora to the main entrance). To begin my tour see the ▢ Ancient Agora Tour chapter or download my free 🎧 audio tour.*

ACROPOLIS MUSEUM TOUR

Μουσείο Ακρόπολης

Athens' Acropolis Museum is a custom-built showcase for artifacts from the Acropolis, complemented by modern exhibits. The state-of-the-art building—housing the Parthenon sculptures still in Greek hands, the original Caryatids from the Erechtheion, and much more—is the boldest symbol yet of today's Athens.

The museum also serves as a sort of 21st-century Trojan horse, intended to lure away the "Elgin Marbles" (as the Brits call the Parthenon sculptures taken to London in the 1800s) from the British Museum and back to Athens. For years the Greeks have asked for the marbles back, and for years the Brits have claimed that Greece can't give them a suitable home. Even now, with this ultramodern facility ready and waiting, Britain is reluctant to give in, for fear of setting a precedent...and getting "me, too" notices from Italy, Egypt, Iran, Iraq, and all the other nations who'd like to reclaim the missing pieces of their cultural heritage.

With or without the Elgin Marbles, the Acropolis Museum has trumped the National Archaeological Museum as the most exciting exhibit in town, and is definitely worth your time.

Orientation

Cost: €5.

Hours: Daily 8:00-20:00 except Mon until 16:00, Fri until 22:00; Nov-March Mon-Thu 9:00-17:00, Fri until 22:00, Sat-Sun until 20:00.

Information: Tel. 210-900-0900, www.theacropolismuseum.gr.

Getting There: It's the gigantic, can't-miss-it modern building facing the south side of the Acropolis from across the broad Dionysiou Areopagitou pedestrian drag. The museum is next to the Akropoli Metro stop on Makrigianni, a street lined with restaurants.

Visitor Information: Museum guards (with red badges) can answer questions, and a 13-minute video plays continuously in the upper atrium (level 3).

Baggage Check: There's a free bag check at the counter near the turnstiles at the base of the ramp (required for big bags). If you're dining at the museum's restaurant after your visit, note that the bag check closes when the museum does.

Length of This Tour: Allow 1.5 hours.

Services: Wheelchairs and strollers are available. A gift shop is on the ground floor and level 2 has a bookstore.

Eating: Choose from the ground-floor **café** or the **restaurant** on level 2. Since the **$$$** menu is the same in both places (overpriced and unimaginative, but good enough), you might as well enjoy the smashing Acropolis views from the restaurant upstairs. You can even visit the restaurant without a museum ticket, but you'll need to get a guest pass at the ticket desk.

Starring: Greek national pride, a helpful overview of the Acropolis' history, marble masterpieces from one of the most influential archaeological sites in human history—and high hopes that more will eventually join the collection.

OVERVIEW

Even as it echoes the ancient history all around it, the Acropolis Museum's striking, glassy building—designed by Swiss-born, New York-based architect Bernard Tschumi—gives a postmodern jolt to Athens' otherwise staid concrete cityscape. Its two lower  levels are aligned with the foundations of ancient ruins discovered beneath the building (which are exposed and still being excavated). The top floor sits askew, imitating the orientation of the Parthenon. A long terrace extends over the main entry, with café tables stretching toward panoramic views of the Acropolis. The museum's glass walls maximize the natural light inside the building and also "disappear," focusing attention on the statuary and views of the Acropolis itself.

ACROPOLIS MUSEUM

Visitors enter into a grand lobby. The ground floor (level 0) has the ticket office, WCs, museum shop, and temporary exhibits. To proceed chronologically through the exhibits, you'd start with the Archaic collection on level 1, then go upstairs (to the top floor—level 3) for the Parthenon section, then back down to level 1 for Hellenistic and Roman sculpture. But for this tour, we'll do the small Hellenistic and Roman section as an out-of-chronological-sequence side-trip from the Archaic and Classical sections, and let the top-floor Parthenon sculptures be our finale.

The Tour Begins

• *Near the big video screen just past the ticket desk, start by getting a good look at the models that show the Acropolis as it evolved from 1200 B.C. to A.D. 1500. Then, after going through the turnstiles, head up the long, glass...*

RAMP

Pause to look through the glass floor at the ancient ruins being excavated beneath the museum. The major buildings of ancient Athens were at the Acropolis and Agora—this was a neighborhood of everyday houses and shops. Appropriately, the ramp is lined with artifacts that were found in the sanctuaries and houses on the slopes leading up to the Parthenon. Many of these artifacts, dating from the fourth millennium B.C. to the fifth century A.D., owe their well-preserved state to having been buried with their owners.

Among the ramp's highlights is case #5 (on the left), which takes you step-by-step through marriage rituals in ancient Athens. Case #6 gives insight into the similarities between ancient Greek pagan worship rituals and later Christian styles. Notice the Christian-looking votives thanking the gods for prayers answered. On the right, just before the stairs, is an offering box (like you see in churches today); this one stood at the Sanctuary of Aphrodite. To assure a good marriage, you'd have been wise to pop in a silver drachma.

LEVEL 1

• *Climb the stairs at the top of the ramp. Straight ahead is a collection of statues in a triangular frame.*

Acropolis Museum—Level 1

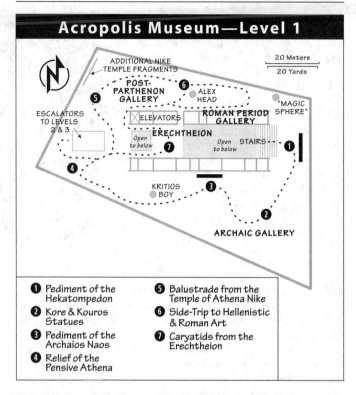

20 Meters
20 Yards

ADDITIONAL NIKE TEMPLE FRAGMENTS

POST-PARTHENON GALLERY

⑤

⑥ ALEX HEAD

"MAGIC SPHERE"

ESCALATORS TO LEVELS 2 & 3

ELEVATORS

ROMAN PERIOD GALLERY

ERECHTHEION

Open to below

⑦

Open to below

STAIRS

①

④

KRITIOS BOY

③

②

ARCHAIC GALLERY

① Pediment of the Hekatompedon

② Kore & Kouros Statues

③ Pediment of the Archaios Naos

④ Relief of the Pensive Athena

⑤ Balustrade from the Temple of Athena Nike

⑥ Side-Trip to Hellenistic & Roman Art

⑦ Caryatids from the Erechtheion

① Pediment of the Hekatompedon

Throughout the centuries, three temples of Athena have occupied the spot where the Parthenon stands today. The fragments assembled here, from 570 B.C., once adorned the Hekatompedon ("100 feet"), the first of those temples. The still-under-construction building was leveled by invading Persians in 480 B.C., paving the way for the Parthenon to be built. On the left, Hercules fights the sea monster Triton. In the center are the scant remains of two lions killing a bull. To the right is a three-headed demon with a snake tail. Each figure holds an object in its hand, representing the elements of wind, water, and fire. While their expressions are more goofy than demonic, they illustrate the struggle of man versus nature. Traces of the original paint are still apparent.

• *Turn right and enter a gallery flooded with daylight.*

② Archaic Gallery: Kore and Kouros Statues

In this column-lined gallery stand several kore (female) and kouros (male) statues. They sport the characteristic stiff poses, braided hair, generic faces, and mysterious smiles of the Archaic era (c. 700-480 B.C.). For more on Archaic statues, see page 145.

The men are generally naked, showing off buff and toned bodies. The bearded dudes are adults, and boys are beardless. The women are modestly clothed, but pull their robes to the side. Before the coming-of-Golden-Age realism and the "wet drapery" technique that enabled sculptors to portray the bodies beneath robes, this was a crude way to lend some motion and to show a little of their figures. The kore statues are almost always holding something: The Greeks believed women shouldn't approach the gods without a gift of some kind. The equestrian statues represent the upper class—those wealthy elites who owned horses and liked to show them off.

• *Halfway down the gallery, on the right against the interior wall, is the...*

❸ Pediment of the Archaios Naos

These sculptures once decorated the temple to Athena that stood next to the Hekatompedon. The temple, damaged after the Persian Wars, was used until the new Parthenon was completed. In the center, Athena, dressed in an ankle-length cloak, strides forward, brandishing a snake as she attacks a giant, who sprawls backward onto his bum. The figures were part of a scene depicting the "Gods Versus Giants" battle atop the temple. The pesky Persians invaded Greece several times over a 50-year period (c. 499-449 B.C.). On the plus side, the wars forced Greeks to band together, and Athens emerged as a dominant naval power. Athenians rebuilt the Acropolis as a symbol of rebirth, with the Parthenon as its centerpiece. In just a few short decades, Greek society—and art—evolved rapidly and remarkably.

Enjoying the statuary in this hall, you can trace the evolution of Greek art from the static Archaic period to the mastery of the body as a living thing, free and full of movement, in the Golden Age. In the Classical style of fifth-century B.C. Greece, the spine moves realistically with the hips. This is nicely illustrated by the nearby **Kritios Boy,** 20 steps past the pediment statues. Look up at, and then circle, the Kritios Boy as he gracefully seems to step into Greece's Golden Age.

• *Continue down the gallery. By the windows near the up escalator, look for a small, well-preserved marble relief.*

❹ Relief of the Pensive Athena

The goddess, dressed in a helmet and belted *peplos*, rests her forehead thoughtfully on her spear (460 B.C.). Although she was called "pensive," some think she was actually meant to be mourning the deaths of her citizens in the Persian War.

• *Backtrack a tad, then veer left past a bank of elevators. Continue past an open gallery with some statuesque women (we'll visit them in a minute). After the second bank of elevators, look for a U-shaped series of squarish marble slabs on your left.*

❺ Balustrade from the Temple of Athena Nike

This set of reliefs (c. 410 B.C.) originally decorated the balustrade of the Temple of Athena Nike—which

perches above and to the right, as you hike up the steep steps at the entrance to the Acropolis. Nike figures had a better chance of survival through the ages than other statues because anti-pagan Christian vandals mistook the winged Nikes for angels. Take a moment to examine the various Nike activities depicted here: adjusting her sandal, leading a bull to sacrifice, ascending a staircase, and so on.

Nearby, displayed along the outer wall, are more chunks of the Temple of Athena Nike. You'll see toes gripping rocks, windblown robes, and realistically twisted bodies—exuberant, life-filled carvings signaling Athens' emergence from the Persian War.

• *Turn right and go up the long gallery for a...*

❻ Side-Trip to Hellenistic and Roman Art

Before heading upstairs for the highlight of the collection, continue around on this floor to the small stretch of statues from the Hellenistic and Roman period.

The life-size **head of Alexander the Great,** on a square pillar in the center of the gallery, is a rare original, likely sculpted from life (336 B.C.). Alexander's upper lip curls, and his thick hair sprouts from the center of his forehead, immediately identifying this remarkable man.

When he died, in 323 B.C., this Macedonian had conquered the rest of Greece—and spread Greek culture throughout the Mediterranean world and as far east as India.

Farther back, near the window, find the spooky **"magic sphere"** that resembles a dirty soccer ball covered with graffiti. It's actually a marble orb etched with mysterious symbols (Roman, second or third century A.D.). Archaeologists believe that this was a good-luck charm taken to competitions at the Theater of Dionysus, which sits just below the Acropolis.

• *Now turn around, retracing your steps, and turn left at the bank of elevators. Around the corner, on their own, as if starring in their own revue on a beautifully lit stage, are the...*

❼ Caryatids from the Erechtheion

Here stand five of the original six lady-columns that once supported the roof of the prestigious Erechtheion temple. (The six on the Acropolis today are copies; another original is in London's British Museum.) Despite their graceful appearance, these sculptures were structurally functional. Each has a fluted column for a leg, a capital-like hat, and buttressing locks of hair in the back. The Caryatids were modeled on and named after the famously upright women of Karyai, near Sparta.

Time and the elements have ravaged these maidens. As recently as the 17th century (see the engravings), they had fragile arms holding ritual bowls for libations. Until the 1950s (before modern smog), their worn-down faces had crisp noses and mouths. In a half-century of Industrial Age pollution, they experienced more destruction than in the previous 2,000 years. But their future looks brighter now that they've been brought indoors out of the acidic air, cleaned up with a laser, and safely preserved for future generations. (For more on the Caryatids in their original location, see page 121.)

• *From the Caryatid gallery, walk back to the Relief of the Pensive Athena, and ride the escalators up. Pause at level 2 to enjoy the view—under the escalator—-of the Archaic statues we just visited (the second level also has a restaurant and terrace with grand Acropolis views). Then head for the top floor.*

LEVEL 3

• *The escalator deposits you at the* "cella"—*symbolizing, in actual size, the inner sanctum of the Parthenon. Two models show how the west and east pediment statues (which are mostly fragments today) would have looked in their prime.*

Parthenon Models

The **east pediment** (the model on the right) features Nike crowning newly born Athena with a wreath of olive branches. Zeus allowed Athena, the goddess of wisdom, to rise from his brain fully grown and fully armed, to inaugurate the Golden Age of Athens. The other gods at this Olympian banquet—naked men and clothed women—are astounded by the amazing event. At the far left, Helios' four horses are doing their morning chore, dragging the sun out of the sea. And on the far right, Selene, the moon goddess, follows the horses back as she sets into the sea.

The **west pediment** (on the left) shows Athena and Poseidon competing for Athens' favor by giving gifts to the city. Poseidon spurts water (beneath him) and Athena presents an olive tree (behind the two of them). A big, heavenly audience looks on. Had Poseidon bested Athena, you'd be in Poseidonia today instead of Athens.

• *Before entering the Parthenon Gallery, enjoy the* **video** *at the far end of the atrium, which covers the Parthenon's 2,500-year history—including a not-so-subtle jab at how Lord Elgin got the marbles and made off with them to England. (For more on Lord Elgin, see the sidebar on page 124).*

Finally, leave this central zone and enter the huge outer gallery that rings the cella.

The Parthenon Frieze

This top floor re-creates the exact dimensions of the Parthenon—with the frieze (mounted lower for easier viewing), the metopes (up above), and the east and west pediments, all in their proper

positions. The stainless-steel columns mark the location of each marble column.

Study the museum's highlight—a life-size replica of the 525-foot frieze that once wrapped all the way around the outside of the Parthenon. The relief panels depict the

Great Panathenaic, the procession held every four years in which citizens climbed up to the Parthenon to celebrate the birth of their city. Feel the impetus to stroll. Go with the flow, watching the parade unfold as it processes to the east.

Men on horseback, gods, chariots, musicians, priests, riders, officers, warriors, and sacrificial animals are all part of the grand parade, all heading in the same direction—uphill. At the heart of the procession are maidens dressed in pleated robes. They shuffle along, carrying gifts for the gods, including incense burners, along with jugs of wine and bowls to pour out offerings. The procession culminates in the presentation of a new *peplos* to Athena, as the gods look on.

Notice the details—for example, the muscles and veins in the horses' legs and the intricate folds in the cloaks and dresses. Some

panels have holes drilled in them, where accessories such as gleaming bronze reins were fitted to heighten the festive look. Of course, all these panels were originally painted in realistic colors. As you move along, notice that, despite the bustle of figures posed every which way, the frieze has one unifying element—most of the people's heads are at the same level, creating a single ribbon around the Parthenon.

Of the original marble frieze, the museum owns only 32 feet. These panels were already so acid-worn in 1801 that Lord Elgin didn't bother taking them. Filling in the gaps in this jigsaw puzzle are white plaster replicas of panels still in London's British Museum (marked BM), in Paris' Louvre, and in Copenhagen. Blank spaces represent panels that are forever lost. Small 17th-century engravings show how the frieze looked before the 1687 explosion that devastated the Parthenon.

Take some time to enjoy not just the frieze, but also the metopes (at the tops of the columns) and the pediment sculptures at either end. (If you've been up to the Parthenon, these will be familiar; if not, now's a good time to skim the 🕮 Acropolis Tour chapter for the complete story.) Everything we know about the statues that adorned that great temple has been re-created in this one perfect space.

• *Now stroll through the gallery and look out the windows. Take a moment to...*

Ponder the Parthenon

There's the Parthenon itself, perched on the adjacent hilltop. Let the museum disappear around you, leaving you to enjoy the art  and the temple it once decorated. The Parthenon is one of the most influential works humankind has ever created. For 2,500 years it's inspired generations of architects, sculptors, painters, engineers, and visitors from around the globe. Here in the Acropolis Museum, you can experience the power of this cultural landmark. The people of Athens relish the Acropolis Museum. Local guides grow taller with every visit, knowing that Greece finally has a suitable place to preserve and share the best of its artistic heritage.

• *On your way down, stop by the restaurant on level 2 for its exterior terrace and the awesome view of the Acropolis.*

NATIONAL ARCHAEOLOGICAL MUSEUM TOUR

Εθνικό Αρχαιολογικό Μουσείο

The National Archaeological Museum is far and away the top ancient Greek art collection anywhere. Ancient Greece set the tone for all Western art that followed, and this museum lets you trace its evolution—taking you in air-conditioned comfort from 7000 B.C. to A.D. 500 through beautifully displayed and described exhibits on one floor. You'll see the rise and fall of Greece's various civilizations: the Minoans, the Mycenaeans, those of Archaic Greece, the Classical Age and Alexander the Great, and the Romans who came from the west. You can also watch Greek sculpture evolve, from prehistoric Barbie dolls, to stiff Egyptian-style, to the *David*-like balance of the Golden Age, to wet T-shirt, buckin'-bronco Hellenistic, and finally, to the influence of the Romans. Walk once around fast for a time-lapse effect, then go around again for a closer look.

This museum is a great way to either start or finish off your sightseeing through Greece. It's especially worth visiting if you're traveling beyond Athens, because it displays artifacts found all around Greece, including Mycenae, Epidavros, Santorini, and Olympia— and the treasures displayed here are generally better than those remaining at the sites themselves. The sheer beauty of the statues, vases, and paintings helps bring the country's dusty ruins to life.

Orientation

Cost: €10, €5 off-season.

Hours: Daily 8:00-20:00; Nov-March Mon 12:00-17:00, Tue-Sun 8:00-15:00.

Information: Tel. 213-214-4800, www.namuseum.gr.

Getting There: The only major Athens sight outside the city center, the museum is a mile north of the Plaka at 28 Oktovriou (a.k.a. Patission) #44. Your best bet is to take a **taxi,** which costs about €6 from the Plaka (or less by Uber). By **Metro,** use the Omonia stop (as you exit, follow signs to *28 Oktovriou/28 October street,* and walk seven blocks to the museum—about 15 minutes) or the Victoria stop (about a 10-minute walk). You can also hop a **bus:** A short walk north of Monastiraki is the Voreu (ΒΟΡΕΟΥ, "North") stop, where you can catch bus #035; ride it to the Patesion (ΠΑΤΗΣΙΩΝ) stop, a block in front of the museum. Or, from Syntagma Square (near the corner of the National Garden), catch bus #2, #4, #5, or #11 to Polytechneio (ΠΟΛΥΤΕΧΝΕΙΟ).

Tours: There are no audioguides, but live **guides** hang out in the lobby waiting to give you a €50, hour-long tour of hit-or-miss quality.

🎧 Download my free National Archaeological Museum audio tour.

Length of This Tour: Allow, at the very least, two hours for this tour; more if you want to dig deeper into this world-class museum.

Baggage Check: Free and required, except for small purses.

Services: A museum shop, WCs, and an inviting café surround a shady and restful courtyard in the lower level (to access from the main entrance lobby, take the stairs down behind ticket desk); these are easiest to access at the beginning or end of your museum tour.

No-no's: Goofy poses in front of statues are not allowed. The Greek museum board considers this disrespectful of the ancient culture and is very serious about it—you'll hear, "No posing!" from stern guards if someone stands in front of the Zeus/Poseidon statue and tries to match his thunderbolt-/trident-throwing pose.

Eating: The **$$$ Museum Garden** café in the park in front of the building is pricey, but the generous portions are shareable, and it stays open after the museum closes (nice outdoor tables, or spacious indoor seating).

Starring: The gold Mask of Agamemnon, stately kouros and kore statues, the perfectly posed *Artemision Bronze,* the horse and jockey of Artemision, and the whole range of Greek art.

The Tour Begins

The collection is delightfully chronological. To sweep through Greek history, simply visit the numbered rooms in order. From the entrance lobby (Rooms 1-2), start with the rooms directly in front of you (Rooms 3-6), containing prehistoric and Mycenaean artifacts. Then circle clockwise around the building's perimeter on the ground floor (Rooms 7-33) to see the evolution of classical Greek statuary. Breeze through the rooms at the back of the building, then go upstairs to see several more exhibits. Keep track of your ticket—you'll need to scan it again to enter some of the exhibits.

The following self-guided tour zeroes in on a few choice pieces (out of many) that give an overview of the collection. See these items, then browse to your heart's content. Note that my descriptions here are brief—for more detail, read the excellent posted English information in each room.

• *From the entrance lobby, go straight ahead into the large central hall (Room 4). This first area—Rooms 3-6—is dedicated to prehistory (7000-1050 B.C., including the treasures of the Mycenaeans. Start in the small side room to the right, Room 6. In several of this room's cases—including the one directly to the right as you enter—you'll find stiff marble figures with large heads. Look closely into that first case, filled with...*

❶ Cycladic Figurines

Goddess, corpse, fertility figure, good-luck amulet, spirit guide, beloved ancestor, or Neolithic porn? No one knows for sure the

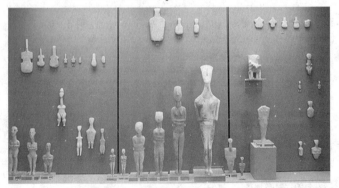

purpose of these female figurines, which are older than the Egyptian pyramids. Although these statuettes were made only in the Cycladic Islands, well-traveled ones have been found all over Greece. The earliest Greeks may have worshipped a Great Mother earth goddess long before Zeus and company (variously called Gaia, Ge, and other names), but it's not clear what connection she had, if any, with these statuettes. The ladies are always naked, usually with

National Archaeological Museum

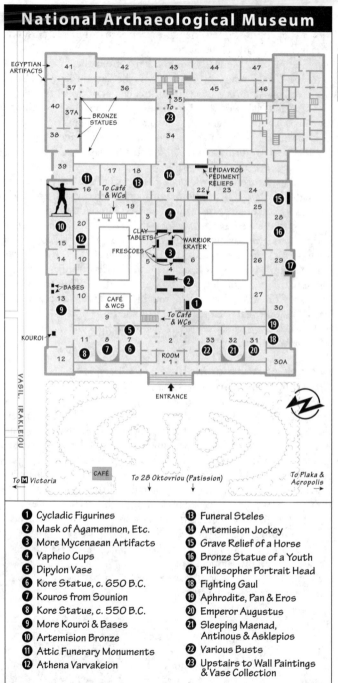

1 Cycladic Figurines
2 Mask of Agamemnon, Etc.
3 More Mycenaean Artifacts
4 Vapheio Cups
5 Dipylon Vase
6 Kore Statue, c. 650 B.C.
7 Kouros from Sounion
8 Kore Statue, c. 550 B.C.
9 More Kouroi & Bases
10 Artemision Bronze
11 Attic Funerary Monuments
12 Athena Varvakeion

13 Funeral Steles
14 Artemision Jockey
15 Grave Relief of a Horse
16 Bronze Statue of a Youth
17 Philosopher Portrait Head
18 Fighting Gaul
19 Aphrodite, Pan & Eros
20 Emperor Augustus
21 Sleeping Maenad, Antinous & Asklepios
22 Various Busts
23 Upstairs to Wall Paintings & Vase Collection

folded arms. The figures evolved over the years from flat-chested, to violin-shaped, to skinny. There is evidence that the eyes, lips, and ears were originally painted on.

The map on the wall (straight across from the entry) demarcates the Cycladic region, showing how the sacred island of Delos, near Mykonos, marks the center of the circle, or cycle, formed by the Cycladic Islands. As these islands were in close proximity, there was plenty of trade and contact between them. In the glass case to the right of the map are two interesting figurines: one playing the harp, the other a flute—proof that humans have been making music for at least 5,000 years.

Before returning to the main room, stroll the long, dead-end Cycladic Hall. You'll see more figurines, painted vases, and tools such as knives and spears made of worked obsidian. Obsidian objects like these were probably exportable treasures, as the Cycladic society was a relatively peaceful culture with an artistic sense of style. Notice the finely painted bathtub on the left. And you'll see carved marble bowls so thin and delicate that light shines through, along with bronze blades, tweezers, and needles. All of these artifacts are from around 2500 b.c., roughly 1,000 years before Mycenae and 2,000 years before Greece's Golden Age.

• *Return to the long central hall (Room 4), divided into four sections. Here you'll find the...*

❷ Mask of Agamemnon and Other Mycenaean Treasures

Room 4 displays artifacts found in the ruins of the ancient fortress-city of Mycenae, 80 miles west of Athens. You'll see finely decorated swords, daggers, body armor, and jewelry, all found buried alongside bodies in Mycenaean graves. Many items were discovered in the cemetery that archaeologists call "Grave Circle A." (For more on the history of this site, see the Mycenae chapter.) The objects' intricately hammered detail and the elaborate funeral arrangements point to the sophistication of this early culture.

In the glass case facing the entry door is the so-called **Mask of Agamemnon** (c. 1550 b.c.). Made of beaten gold and showing a man's bearded face, this famous mask was tied over the face of a dead man—note the tiny ear-holes for the string.

The Mycenaeans dominated southern Greece a thousand years before the Golden Age (1600-1200 b.c.). Their (real) history was lost in the misty era of Homer's (fanciful) legends of the Trojan War. Then Mycenae was unearthed in the 19th century by the German businessman Heinrich Schliemann (the Indiana Johann of his era). Schliemann, fascinated by the works of Homer, had recently discovered the real-life ruins of Troy (in western Turkey), and he was convinced that Mycenae was the city of the Greeks who'd conquered Troy. That much, at least, may be historically true. Schliemann went on to declare this funeral mask to be that of the legendary King Agamemnon, which *isn't* true, because the mask predates the fall of Troy (c. 1300 B.C.).

You're surrounded by 30 pounds of gold pounded into decorative funerary objects, excavated from the graves of 19 bodies found in a circular tomb. In the second case on the left wall, find the two babies whose bodies were completely covered in a blanket of gold leaf.

On the back side of the Mask of Agamemnon case, look closely at the knife and sheath with a warrior-versus-lions scene. Compared with the Minoan and Cycladic civilizations, Mycenaean society was warlike, and their weapons were artfully rendered.

• In the next section of Room 4, you'll find...

❸ More Mycenaean Artifacts

A **model of the Acropolis of Mycenae** (left side) shows the dramatic hilltop citadel where many of these objects were unearthed. Find the famous Lion Gate entrance (#1 on the model), the round cemetery known as Grave Circle A (#2), and the king's royal palace crowning the hill (#8). Also in Room 4 are **frescoes** from the royal palace, done in bright colors in the Minoan style. At the end of this area, on the left, **clay tablets** show the Mycenaean written language known as Linear B, whose syllabic script (in which marks stand for syllables) was cracked only in the 1950s.

Back near where you entered, other colorful wall frescoes (from nearby Tiryns) show a Minoan influence and feature scenes such as men with dogs hunting wild boar and men ritually leaping over bulls.

• Look at the back side of the display case in the center of this section.

The painted, two-handled vase known as the **House of the Warrior Krater** (#1426) was Schliemann's favorite find. A woman (far left) waves goodbye to a line of warriors heading off to war, with their fancy armor and duffle bags hanging from their spears. Although this provided the world with its first glimpse of a Mycenaean soldier, it's a timeless scene with countless echoes across the generations.

• In the center of the last section of Room 4 is a glass case displaying the...

❹ Vapheio Cups

These gold cups (c. 1600-1550 B.C.), found with other precious items in a Mycenaean tomb, are metalwork masterpieces. The intricate

worked detail on #1 shows a charging bull sending a guy head over heels. On #2 you'll see a bull and a cow making eyes at each other, while the hind leg of another bull gets tied up by one good-looking cowboy. These realistic, joyous scenes are the product of the two civilizations that made 15th-century B.C. Greece the wonder of Europe—the Mycenaeans and the Minoan culture of Crete.

Near where you entered this room, note the light and flexible bone helmet (14th-13th century B.C.). Made from many pieces of boar tusk, a helmet such as this was a prized possession.

Between roughly 1450 and 1150 B.C., the Minoan society collapsed, and Minoan artisans had to find work painting frescoes and making cups for the rising Mycenaean culture. Then, around 1100 B.C., the Mycenaeans disappeared from history's radar screen. Whether from invasion, famine, internal strife, or natural disaster, these sudden disappearances plunged Greece into 500 years of Dark Ages (c. 1200-700 B.C.). Little survives from that chaotic time, so let's pick up the thread of history as Greece began to recover a few centuries later.

• Backtrack to the entrance lobby, then turn right, and begin circling clockwise around the perimeter of the building, starting in Room 7. After scanning your ticket again to enter this room, look for the tall vase on your right.

❺ Dipylon Vase

This monumental ocher-and-black vase (c. 750 B.C.), as tall as a person, is painted with a funeral scene. Vases such as this marked the graves of well-off Greeks; the belly-handled shape of this one tells us it likely honored a woman (men's graves were typically marked by pedestalled vases).

In the center, the deceased lies on a funeral bier, flanked by a line of mourners who pull their hair in grief. It's far from realistic.

The triangular torsos, square arms, circular heads, and bands of geometric patterns epitomize the style of what's known as the Geometric Period (9th-8th century B.C.). A few realistic notes pop through, such as the raw emotions of the mourners and some grazing antelope and ibex (on the neck of the vase). Note the one little child in attendance. Discovered in Athens' Keramikos Cemetery, the vase gets its name from the nearby Dipylon Gate, the ancient city's renowned main entrance.

After four centuries of Dark Ages and war, the Greeks of the eighth century B.C. were finally settling down, establishing cities, and expanding abroad (as seen on the map near the big vase), with colonies in western Turkey (Ionia), southern Italy (Magna Graecia), and Sicily. They were developing a written language and achieving the social stability that could afford to generate art. This vase is a baby step in that progression. Next, large-scale statues in stone were developed.

• *In Rooms 7-14 you'll get a look at some of these giant statues, including the early Greek statues called...*

Kore and Kouros

Some of the earliest surviving examples of post-Mycenaean Greek art (c. 700-480 B.C.) are these life-size and larger-than-life statues of clothed young women (kore/korai) and naked young men (kouros/kouroi). Influenced by ancient statues of Egyptian pharaohs, the earliest of these are big and stiff, with triangular faces and arms at their sides. As you walk through the next few rooms, you'll see the statues become more realistic and natural in their movements, with more personality than we see in these earlier rigid shells.

• *Take a closer look at a few particular statues. First, facing the vase in the middle of Room 7 is a...*

❻ **Kore** (c. 650 B.C.): With hands at her sides, a skinny figure, a rectangular shape, and dressed in a full-length robe (called a chiton), this kore looks as much like a plank of wood as a woman. Her triangular lion-mane hairstyle resembles an Egyptian headdress. The writing down her left leg says she's dedicated to Apollo. Stroll around. The Egyptian influence is clear.

• *In the next room (Room 8), your eyes go right to a very nice pair of knees that belong to a...*

❼ **Kouros from Sounion** (c. 600 B.C.): A typical kouros from the Archaic period, this young naked man has braided dreadlocks and a stable forward-facing pose, and is stepping forward slightly with his left leg. His fists are clenched at his sides, and his scarred face obscures an Archaic smile—a placid smile that suggests the inner secret of happiness. His anatomy is strongly geometrical and stylized, with almond-shaped eyes, oval pecs, an arched rib cage, cylindrical thighs, and a too-perfect symmetry. While less plank-like than earlier statues, he's still much flatter than an actual person. The overdeveloped muscles (look at those quads!) and his narrow waist resemble those of an athletic teenager.

Rather than strict realism, kouros statues capture a geometric ideal. The proportions of the body parts follow strict rules—for example, most later kouros statues are precisely seven "heads" tall. Although this kouros steps forward slightly, his hips remain even (think about it—the hips of a real person would shift forward on one side). The Greeks were obsessed with the human body—remember, these statues were of (idealized) humans, not gods. Standing naked and alone, these statues represented a microcosm of the rational order of nature.

Statues were painted in vivid, lifelike colors. Notice that the rough surface of the marble lacks the translucent sheen of Classical Age statues. (Archaic chisels were not yet strong or efficient enough to avoid shattering the crystalline marble.)

Kouros statues were everywhere, presented as gifts to a god at a sanctuary or to honor the dead in a cemetery. This one was dedicated to Poseidon at the entrance to the temple at Sounion. As a funeral figure, a kouros symbolized the deceased in his prime of youth and happiness, forever young.

• *Continue into the next room (Room 11). On the left, holding a flower, is a...*

❽ **Kore** (c. 550 B.C.): Where a male kouros was naked and either life-size or larger than life (emphasizing masculine power), a female kore was often slightly smaller than life and modestly clothed, capturing feminine grace (males were commonly naked in public, but women never were). This petite kore stands with feet together, wearing a pleated chiton belted at the waist. Her hair is braided and held in place with a diadem (a wreath-like headdress), and she wears a necklace. Her right hand tugs at her dress, indicating motion (a nice trick if the artist lacks the skill to actually show it), while her left hand holds a flower. Like most ancient statues, she was painted in lifelike colors, including her skin. Her dress was red—you can still see traces

The Four Stages of Greek Sculpture

Archaic (c. 700-480 B.C.): Rigid statues with stylized anatomy, facing forward, with braided hair and mysterious smiles (see photo).

Severe (c. 480-460 B.C.): More realistic and balanced statues (with no smiles), capturing a serious nobility. Works from this transitional period are sometimes described as Early Classical.

Classical (c. 460-323 B.C.): Realistic statues of idealized beauty with poses that strike a balance between movement and stillness, with understated emotion. (Within this period, the Golden Age was roughly 450-400 B.C.)

Hellenistic (c. 323-30 B.C.): Photorealistic (even ugly) humans engaged in dramatic, emotional struggles, captured in snapshot poses that can be wildly unbalanced.

of the paint—adorned with flower designs and a band of swastikas down the front. (In ancient times—before German archaeologist Schliemann's writings popularized it and Hitler appropriated it—the swastika was a harmless good-luck symbol representing the rays of the sun.) This kore, like all the statues in the room, has that distinct Archaic smile (or smirk, as the Greeks describe it). Browse around. Study the body types—the graceful, *Avatar*-like builds, those mysterious smirks, and the rigid hairdos.

• *The next room—a long hall labeled Room 13—has...*

❾ More Kouroi and Bases for Funerary Kouroi: These statues, from the late Archaic period (around 500 B.C.), once decorated the tombs of hero athletes—perhaps famous Olympians. (The map just inside the door shows the continued expansion of Greek civilization in the sixth century B.C.) Notice that these young men are slightly more relaxed and realistic, with better-formed thighs and bent elbows. Some kouros statues stood on pedestals, like the two square marble bases located farther down Room 13 (left side). The indentations atop each base held a kouros statue that represented an idealized version of the deceased. On the first base, the carved relief shows wrestlers and other athletes. Perhaps this was an excuse for the artist to show off a new ability to depict the body in a

twisting pose. Around the right side, notice the cute dog-and-cat fight. The second base features a field hockey-like game, each scene reflecting the vigor of the deceased man in his prime.

During the Archaic period, Greece was prospering, growing, expanding, trading, and colonizing the Mediterranean. The smiles on the statues capture the bliss of a people settling down and living at peace. But in 480 B.C., Persia invaded, and those smiles soon vanished.

• *Pass through Room 14 and into Room 15, which is dominated by one of the jewels of the collection, the...*

⑩ *Artemision Bronze*

This statue was discovered amid a shipwreck off Cape Artemision (north of Athens) in 1928. The weapon was never found, so no one

knows for sure if this is Zeus or Poseidon. The god steps forward, raises his arm, sights along his other arm at the distant target, and prepares to hurl his thunderbolt (if it's Zeus) or his trident (if it's Poseidon).

The god stands 6'10" and has a physique like mine. His hair is curly and tied at the back, and his now-hollow eyes once shone white with inset bone. He plants his left foot and pushes off with the right. Even though every limb moves in a different direction, the whole effect is one of balance. The statue's dimensions are a study in Greek geometry. His head is one Greek foot high, and he's six heads tall (or one Greek fathom). The whole figure has an "X" shape that would fit into a perfect circle, with his navel at the center and his fingertips touching the rim. Although the bronze statue—cast with the "lost wax" technique (explained later, under *"Artemesion Jockey")*—is fully three-dimensional, it's most impressive from the front. (Later Greek statues, from the Hellenistic era, seem fully alive from every angle, including the three-quarter view.)

This Zeus/Poseidon, from c. 460 B.C., is an example of the transition into the Classical style, as sculpture evolved beyond the so-called Severe style (480-460 B.C.). (The famous charioteer of Delphi, pictured on page 365, is textbook Severe: far more lifelike than a kouros, but still frontal and unmoving.) Historically, the Severe/Early Classical Period covers the time when Greece battled the Persians and emerged victorious—the era when ordinary men had also just shaken off tyrants and taken control of their own destiny through democracy. The Greeks were entering the dawn of the

Golden Age. During this time of horrific war, the Greeks made art that was serious (no more Archaic smiles), unadorned, and expressed the noble strength and heroism of the individuals who had carried them through tough times. The statues are anatomically realistic, celebrating the human form.

With his movements frozen, as if Zeus/Poseidon were posing for a painting, we can examine the wonder of the physical body. He's natural yet ideal, twisting yet balanced, moving while at rest. (Later Greek sculptures would improve upon this, with figures that look almost as if they've been caught mid-motion with the click of a camera.) With his geometrical perfection and godlike air, the figure sums up all that is best about the art of the ancient world.

Browse the rest of the art in this room from this generation, including a mini-Zeus in the early Severe style with a thunderbolt and a sacred eagle (just to the right of Zeus/Poseidon), painted vases, and funeral monuments.

Next we enter the Golden Age. Room 16 is filled with big, tall vases made of marble, labeled ⓫ **Attic Funerary Monuments.** These grave markers take the shape of the ceramic urns used for the ashes of cremated bodies in ancient times. One of these vases (#4485) is particularly touching: A grieving family looks on as Hermes (with his winged sandals) leads a young woman to the underworld.

• *Continue through Room 16 and into Room 17, then turn right into Room 19. The WCs and café are out the door and downstairs, in the courtyard. For the next star attraction, continue through Room 19 and hook left into Room 20. At the far end of this room is item #129, the...*

⓬ *Athena Varvakeion*

This marble statue, known as the *Athena Varvakeion* (c. A.D. 250), is considered the most faithful copy of the great *Athena Parthenos* (438 B.C.) by Pheidias. It's essentially a one-twelfth-size replica of the 40-foot statue that once stood in the Parthenon. Although a miniature copy of the glorious original, it provides a good look at Greek art at its Golden Age pinnacle. Athena stands dressed in flowing robes, holding a small figure of Nike (goddess of victory) in her right hand and a shield in her left. Athena's helmet sprouts plumes with winged horses and a sphinx. To give a sense of scale of the original, the tiny Nike in Athena's hand was six feet tall in the Parthenon statue.

Athena is covered in snakes. She wears a snake belt and bracelet; coiled snakes decorate her breastplate and one is curled up inside her shield, representing the goddess' connection to her half-snake son, who was born out of the earth and considered to be one of the ancestors of the Athenians. The snake-headed Medusa (whom Athena helped Perseus slay) adorns the center of her chest.

• *Backtrack to Room 17, turn right, and continue circling the museum clockwise into Room 18, which has...*

⓭ Funeral *Steles*

The tombstones that fill this room, all from the fifth century B.C., are more good examples of Golden Age Greek art. With a mastery of the body, artists show poignant scenes of farewell, as loved ones bid a sad goodbye to the dead, who are seated. While the dead are often just shaking hands, there's usually a personal meaning with each scene. For example, on the tombstone on the left wall, a woman who died in childbirth looks at her baby, held by a servant as it reaches for its dead mother. Other scenes include a beautiful young woman, who died in her prime, narcissistically gazing into a mirror. Servants are shown taking part in the sad event, as if considered part of the family. In the center of the room, a rich and powerful woman ponders which treasure from her jewel box to take with her into eternity. Though shallow reliefs, these works are effectively three-dimensional. There's a timeless melancholy in the room, a sense that no matter who you are—or how powerful or affluent your family is—when you go, you go alone...and shrouds have no pockets.

• *Pass into Room 21, a large central hall. We'll take a temporary break from the chronological sequence to see statues dating from the second century B.C., when Greece was ruled by Rome. The hall is dominated by the...*

⓮ *Artemision Jockey*

In this bronze statue (c. 140 B.C.), the horse is in full stride, and the young jockey looks over his shoulder to see if anyone's gaining on them. The statue was recovered in pieces from the seafloor off Cape Artemision. Missing were the reins the jockey once held in his left hand and the whip he used with his right to spur the horse to go even faster—maybe too fast, judging by the look on his face.

Greeks loved their horse races, and this statue may celebrate a victory at one of the Panhellenic Games. The jockey is dressed in a traditional short tunic, has inlaid eyes, and his features indicate that he was probably ethnically part Ethiopian.

The statue, like other ancient bronzes created by Greeks in Roman times, was made not by hammering sheets of metal, but with the classic "lost wax" technique. The artist would first make a rough version of the statue from clay, cover it with a layer of wax, and then cover that with another layer of clay to make a form-fitting mold. When heated in a furnace to harden the mold, the wax would melt—or be "lost"—leaving a narrow space between the clay model and the mold. The artist would then pour molten bronze into the space, let it cool, break the mold, and—*voilà!*—end up with a hollow bronze statue. This particular statue was cast in pieces, which were then welded together. After the cast was removed, the artist added a few surface details and polished it smooth. Notice the delightful detail on the rider's spurs, which were lashed to his bare feet.

Stylistically, we've gone from stiff Archaic, to restrained Severe, to balanced Classical...to this wonderful example of the unbridled emotion of Hellenism. Like other Hellenistic sculptures, this one doesn't sit primly, as the poised Classical statues did, but dominates its space.

The other statues in the room are second-century B.C. Roman copies of fifth-century B.C. Greek originals. The Romans were great warriors, engineers, and administrators, but they had an inferiority complex when it came to art and high culture. For high-class Romans, Greek culture was the ideal, which created a huge demand for Greek statues. As demand exceeded supply, making copies of Greek originals became a big industry, and the Romans excelled at it. In fact, throughout Europe today, when you see a "Greek" statue, it's likely a Roman copy of a Greek original. Thanks to excellent copies like the ones in this room, we know what many (otherwise lost) Golden Age Greek masterpieces looked like.

While the Greeks could cast a freestanding bronze statue with no problem, when the Romans tried to re-create it in marble, the statue needed extra support. Here's a tip: When you see a tree trunk buttressing some statue, it's a Roman copy.

• *To return to our chronological tour (picking up back before the Romans arrived), head straight past the jockey into Room 22, with pediment reliefs (Sack of Troy on the right, Greeks vs. Amazons on the left) that once decorated the Temple of Asklepios at Epidavros. Then pass through a couple of rooms displaying funeral monuments with progressively higher relief and more monumental scale until you reach the long Room 28, where you'll come face-to-face with a large...*

ARCH. MUSEUM

⓯ Grave Relief of a Horse

The spirited horse steps lively and whinnies while an Ethiopian boy struggles with the bridle and tries to calm him with food. The realistic detail of the horse's muscles and veins is astonishing, offset by the panther-skin blanket. The horse's head pops out of the relief, becoming fully three-dimensional. The boy's pose is slightly off-balance, anticipating the "unposed poses" of later Hellenism (this relief is from the late fourth century B.C.). We sense the emotions of both the overmatched boy and the nervous horse. We also see a balance between the horse and boy, with the two figures creating a natural scene together rather than standing alone.

To the left, the *stele* labeled #738 is the last masterpiece of this style—in such deep relief that it's barely attached to the stone behind it.

• *Farther down Room 28 stands the impressive, slightly-larger-than-life-size...*

⓰ Bronze Statue of a Youth

Scholars can't decide whether this statue (c. 340-330 B.C.) is reaching out to give someone an apple or demonstrating a split-finger fastball. He may be Perseus, holding up the head of Medusa, but he's most likely the mythical Paris, awarding a golden apple to the winner of a beauty contest between goddesses (sparking jealousies that started the Trojan War). Imagine how striking this statue would have been in its original full shine, before the bronze darkened with age.

The figure is caught in midstep as he reaches out, gazing intently at the person he's giving the object to. Split this youth vertically down the middle to see the *contrapposto* (or "counter-poise") stance of so many Classical statues. His left foot is stable, while the right moves slightly, causing his hips to shift. Meanwhile, his right arm is tense while the left hangs loose. These subtle, contrary motions are in perfect balance around the statue's vertical axis.

In the Classical Age, statues reached their peak of natural realism and balanced grace. During the following Hellenistic Period, sculptors added to that realism, injecting motion and drama. Statues are fully three-dimensional (and Hellenistic statues even more so, as they have no "front": You have to walk around them to see the whole picture). Their poses are less rigid than those in the Archaic period and less overtly heroic than those of the Severe. The beauty of the face, the perfection of the muscles, the balance of elegant grace and brute power—these represent the full ripeness of the art of this age.

• *Continue into the small Room 29. To the left of the following door, find a black bronze head in a glass case. Look into the wild and cynical inlaid eyes of this...*

⓲ Head from a Statue of a Philosopher

This philosopher was a Cynic, part of a movement of nonmaterialist nonconformists founded in the fourth century B.C. by

Diogenes. The term "cynic" aptly describes these dislikable, arrogant guys with unkempt hair. The statue's aged, bearded face captures the personality of a distinct individual and is considered a portrait likeness. From c. 240 B.C., it's typical of the Hellenistic Period, the time after the Macedonian Alexander the Great conquered the rest of Greece and proceeded to spread Greek values across much of the Mediterranean and beyond. Hellenistic Greek society promoted a Me-Generation individualism, and artists celebrated everyday people like this. Rather than Photoshop out their eccentricities, they presented their subjects warts and all. For the first time in history, we see human beings in all their gritty human glory: with wrinkles, male-pattern baldness, saggy boobs, and middle-age spread, all captured in less-than-noble poses.

The glass case to the left shows other parts of his body. The statue was likely shipped in pieces (like an Ikea self-assembly kit) for practical purposes.

This statue, like a number of the museum's statues, was found by archaeologists on the seabed off the coast of Greece. Two separate shipwrecks in ancient times have yielded treasures now in this museum: At the wreck off Cape Artemision, Zeus/Poseidon and the bronze horse and jockey were found. Another wreck, off the tiny island of Antikythira (near the southern tip of the Peloponnesian Peninsula), is the source of this statue, as well as the bronze statue of a youth (the one that's either Paris or Perseus).

• *Continue into the long Room 30 and head to the far end to find the...*

⑱ Statue of a Fighting Gaul

Having been wounded in the thigh (note the hole), this soldier has fallen to one knee and reaches up to fend off the next blow. The style of his helmet indicates that he's not a Greek, but a Gaul (from ancient France). The artist catches the exact moment when the tide of battle is about to turn. The face of this Fighting Gaul says he's afraid he may become the Dying Gaul.

The statue (c. 100 B.C.) sums up many of the features of Hellenistic art: He's frozen in motion in a wild, unbalanced pose that dramatizes his inner thoughts. The diagonal pose runs up his left leg and out his head and outstretched arm. Rather than a noble, idealized god, this is an ordinary soldier caught in an extreme moment. His arms flail, his muscles strain, his eyes bulge, and he cries out in pain. This statue may have been paired with others in a theatrical mini-drama that heightened emotion. Hellenism shows us the thrill of victory, and—in this case—the agony of defeat.

• *To the right, on the other side of a doorway, is a...*

⑲ Statue of Aphrodite, Pan, and Eros

In this playful marble ensemble (c. 100 B.C.) from the sacred island of Delos, Aphrodite is about to whack Pan with her sandal. Strik-

ing a classic *contrapposto* pose (with most of her weight on one foot), Aphrodite is more revealing than modest, her voluptuous body polished smooth. There's a bit of whimsy here, as Aphrodite seems to be saying, "Don't! Stop!"...but may instead be saying, "Don't stop." The actions of the (literally) horny Pan can also be interpreted in two ways: His left arm is forceful, but his right is gentle—holding her more like a dance partner. Eros, like an omnipresent Tinkerbell, comes to Aphrodite's aid—or does he? He has the power to save her if she wants help, but with a hand on Pan's horn and a wink, Eros seems to say, "OK,

Pan, this is your chance. Come on, man, go for it." Pan can't believe his luck. This marble is finer than those used in earlier statues, and it has been polished to a sheen with an emery stone. As you walk around this delightful statue, enjoy the detail, from the pudgy baby feet and the remnants of red paint on the sandal to the way the figures all work together in a cohesive vignette.

Across the room, another sculpture shows the ability of the artists of this age to capture action and tell a story. Find the carved relief showing two hairy men stomping grapes in big stone bins. Between them, like wrestlers dancing, two other brutes are toting a giant two-handled vase (krater) filled with grape juice, hauling it off to the next step in the process of becoming wine.

• *Now, enter Room 31 to see a...*

⓴ Statue of the Emperor Augustus

This statue of Augustus, founder of the Roman Empire and its first emperor (c. 12-10 B.C.), is the only known statue of him on horse-back, although it is missing its lower half.

He holds the (missing) reins in his left hand and raises his right hand in a gesture of blessing or of oration—an expression of the emperor's power. Although Greece was conquered by the Romans (146 B.C.), Greek culture ultimately "conquered" the Romans, as the Grecophile Romans imported Greek statues to Italy to beautify their villas. They preserved Greece's monuments and cranked out high-quality copies of Greek art. When the Roman Emperor Augustus began remaking the city of Rome, he used Greek-style Corinthian columns—a veneer of sophistication on buildings erected with no-nonsense, brick-and-concrete Roman-arch engineering. It's largely thanks to the Romans and their respect for Greek culture that so much of this ancient art survives today.

• *Step into Room 32 and find a portrait of a beautiful woman asleep on a rock.*

⓵ Sleeping Maenad (and Friends)

In the center of the room is a marble statue (c. A.D. 120) featuring a sleeping Maenad, a female follower of the god Dionysus. This Roman copy was made during the reign of Emperor Hadrian. Like a sleeping beauty, this slumbering Maenad lies exposed atop a rock on a soft skin of a panther. As if being mooned by the Maenad, a bust of the emperor himself stands on the nearby wall. (He politely averts his eyes.)

Hadrian was a Grecophile in two senses—he not only loved Greek culture, but he also had a hunky young Greek boyfriend named Antinous. Just to Hadrian's left is a fine portrait bust of **Antinous** (or is it Channing Tatum?). Look into his disarmingly beautiful eyes. After the young man drowned in the Nile in A.D. 130, the depressed Hadrian had him deified and commissioned statues of him throughout the empire.

At the (missing) feet of the Maenad stands a statue of the Greek god of medicine, **Asklepios,** from the renowned ancient Sanctuary of Epidavros. Asklepios is portrayed with his snake and stick—back then, snakes were involved in healing procedures in the sanctuaries of the god. This statue is a Roman copy (A.D. 160) of a fourth-century Greek original.

• *Continue into Room 33 to see...*

㉒ Busts from the Late Roman Empire

These busts (A.D. 300-500) capture the generic features and somber expressions of the late Roman Empire. As Rome decayed and fell to barbarians, the empire shifted its capital eastward to Constanti-

nople (modern Istanbul). For the next thousand years, the Byzantine Empire, which included Greece, lived on as an enlightened, Christian, Greek-speaking enclave, while Western Europe fell into poverty and ignorance. During that time, Greek culture was mostly lost to the West and lay hidden until it was rediscovered during Europe's Renaissance (c. 1500). Gradually, Greek sites were unearthed, its statues cleaned up and repaired, and Greek culture once again was revived in all its inspirational glory.

• *Exit into the entrance lobby and take a breath. You've seen the core of this museum and its highlights. If you have an appetite for more, stay on the ground level, return to the boy on the horse, and walk straight to the back-left corner of the building (passing through Rooms 4, 21, and 34). You'll find bronze statues in Rooms 36-39 and devotional offerings—statuettes and intricate artifacts—from the Sanctuary of Olympia. Egyptian artifacts are in Rooms 40 and 41.*

The museum's upper level holds one more major set of works that deserves a look: prehistoric wall paintings. Find the grand ❷❸ staircase in Room 35 (behind the jockey). At the top of the stairs, continue straight into Room 48, and go to the far end of the room to see the best of Santorini...

Cycladic Wall Paintings

These magnificent paintings were uncovered on the walls of homes at the ancient settlement of Akrotiri on the island of Thira (better known today as Santorini). When the island's volcano blew in a massive, bigger-than-Krakatoa eruption (c. 1630 B.C.), it preserved these frescoes in a thick blanket of ash. (Luckily, the town's inhabitants escaped, probably having been encouraged by a large earthquake and previous minor eruption to pack up their more-portable treasures and find a less-cranky island.)

Akrotiri's people shared an artistic tradition with the Minoans (centered on the isle of Crete), but gave it their own twist. Unlike most early peoples, the Thirans were not fighters but traders, and their work made them prosperous. Their unfortified homes and palaces housed elaborate furniture (in the next room, see the bed, cast in plaster from a hole in the ash) and were decorated with colorful frescoes like these, which celebrate life in rolling springtime landscapes and everyday scenes. Flirting swallows soar over hillsides of lilies. An antelope buck turns to make eyes at a doe. Two boys, perhaps a prince and his servant, box (notice their mostly shaved heads). The frescoes are  vivid, featuring primary colors of red, yellow, and blue, with thick black outlines. These are probably "secco" frescoes, started while the plaster wall was wet but continued even after it had dried. Those pigments absorbed by the plaster create the glowing translucent effect that distinguishes these paintings. Remember that most early cultures used art only as propaganda for a king, to commemorate a famous battle, or to represent a god. But the Aegeans were among the first to love beauty for its own sake. That love of beauty became part of the legacy of ancient Greece.

• *As long as you're upstairs, you might as well enter Room 49 (turn left as you exit) to browse a world-class...*

Vase Collection

Starting in this room, you can walk clockwise through eight rooms showing the evolution of pottery from the Bronze Age, to Geometric/Archaic, to Severe, to Classical. In the sixth century B.C., artists painted black figures on a red background. During the Classical Age, the trend was red-on-black (with the occasional red-and-black on white). It's amazing to see how these ancient potters mastered the art of creating three-dimensional scenes on a two-dimensional surface, and a curvy one at that. Along the way you can also see two well-preserved skeletons from the Keramikos Cemetery.

• *Whew! Our tour is over. It's time to leave the ancients and make your way back to central Athens and the modern world.*

PSYRRI & CENTRAL MARKET WALK

Until recently, the Psyrri neighborhood was a grimy area of workshops and cottage industries—famous locally as a onetime hotbed of poets, musicians, revolutionaries, and troublemakers. Now it's one of central Athens' trendiest areas. Cosmetically, this isn't Athens' prettiest area—it's filled with pungent odors, crumbling buildings, and graffiti. But if you take some time to explore, you'll find Psyrri is a great place to simply hang out—with excellent restaurants, creative boutiques, and a welcoming atmosphere. When people call Athens "the new Berlin"...they're thinking of Psyrri.

This two-part walk guides you from Athens' central square, Monastiraki, through the Psyrri district, and around its vivid market zone. It's light on history, but heavy on local life and full of opportunities to sample some Athenian treats. It's a nice change of pace from this book's heavy-hitting historical walks.

Orientation

Length of This Walk: Allow just over an hour—more if you stop for snacks and meals.

When to Go: Ideally, do the walk on an empty stomach, around lunchtime, when the market is thriving and you have plenty of room to fill up on snacks. Note that the Central Market shuts down around 15:00 and is closed all day Sunday, and a couple of the coffee shops and bakeries mentioned in this walk close around 17:00. The walk can also be interesting in the early evening, just as the nightlife scene is livening up.

Getting There: The walk begins at Monastiraki Square, with its own Metro stop (and at the end of my "Athens City Walk").

Starring: Funky graffiti, fragrant market stalls, and delectable Athenian snacks.

The Walk Begins

PSYRRI

Begin on Monastiraki Square. While this is a hub both for transit and sightseeing, we're going to turn our back on those and take a stroll through the adjacent Psyrri area.

· *With the Acropolis and the yellow Metro station behind you, cross busy Ermou street, and head up the lane on the left side of the A for Athens hotel (the street is labeled* ΜΙΑΟΥΛΗ/Miaouli*). Walk one short block up this street, to the stairs on your right (leading to another entrance to the Monastiraki Metro station). You've plunged into a world of wild graffiti. Turn around and look up at the mural on the side of the building you just walked past for a prime example of Athenian...*

❶ Street Art

Let's be honest: Athens is not the most architecturally stimulating city, and many buildings are in a state of disrepair. For this rea-

son, many Athenians welcome tasteful street art as urban beautification. In the run-up to the 2004 Olympics, the city commissioned street artists to help dress up the city. Years later, the economic crisis drove underemployed artists to use blank walls as a canvas to express their frustrations—often with an edge of social criticism.

This mural—titled *Colorful Warrior*—was done by one of Athens' most respected street artists, Vangelis Choursoglou (who goes by the street name "Woozy"). Woozy's portfolio includes murals in London, Nicaragua, and Shenzhen, China. In Athens, city authorities grant permits to certain artists, like Woozy. Unauthorized graffiti is officially illegal, but artists are rarely arrested, and most do their work clandestinely, late at night.

This walk passes lots of street art—everything from basic tags (green "Gate 13" and red "Gate 7" graffiti is the work of rival soccer fans) to beautiful murals. Much of it was created by alumni of the Athens School of Fine Arts.

· *Head back the way you came to busy Ermou street. Turn right, walk one block, then angle right up the seedy-feeling Agias Theklas street. Just a few steps up the street, look for the* Melissinos Poet Sandal Maker sign.

❷ Melissinos Art Sandal Shop

Humble Psyrri has always been the home of hardworking crafts-

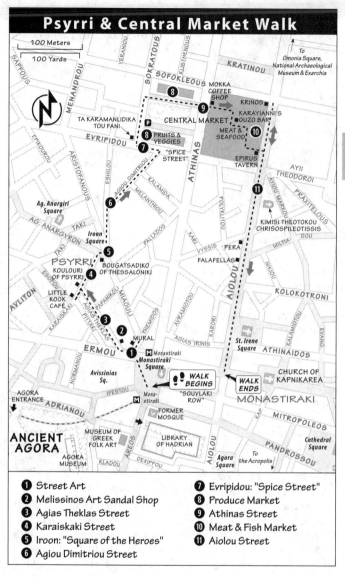

Psyrri & Central Market Walk

100 Meters

100 Yards

To Omonia Square, National Archaeological Museum & Exarchia

N

MOKKA COFFEE SHOP

TA KARAMANLIDIKA TOU FANI

CENTRAL MARKET

KRINOS

KARAYIANNI'S OUZO BAR

MEAT & SEAFOOD

P

FRUITS & VEGGIES

"SPICE STREET"

EPIRUS TAVERN

AYII THEODOROI

Ag. Anargiri Square

KIMISI THEOTOKOU CHRISOSPILEOTISSIS

Iroon Square

PERA

FALAFELLAS

PSYRRI

KOULOURI OF PSYRRI

BOUGATSADIKO OF THESSALONIKI

LITTLE KOOK CAFÉ

MURAL

St. Irene Square

CHURCH OF KAPNIKAREA

WALK BEGINS

"SOUVLAKI ROW"

WALK ENDS

MONASTIRAKI

Avissinias Sq.

Monastiraki Square

Monastiraki

FORMER MOSQUE

Cathedral Square

ANCIENT AGORA

AGORA ENTRANCE

MUSEUM OF GREEK FOLK ART

LIBRARY OF HADRIAN

AGORA MUSEUM

To the Acropolis

Agora Square

1 Street Art
2 Melissinos Art Sandal Shop
3 Agias Theklas Street
4 Karaiskaki Street
5 Iroon: "Square of the Heroes"
6 Agiou Dimitriou Street

7 Evripidou: "Spice Street"
8 Produce Market
9 Athinas Street
10 Meat & Fish Market
11 Aiolou Street

people and small factories (in contrast to central business hub Syntagma and the touristy Plaka). And this shop has been a neighborhood landmark since 1920, as you can tell by the windows displaying celebrities who have worn Melissinos sandals over the decades, from Jackie O to Anthony Quinn to John Lennon.

Sandal maker Pantelis Melissinos, who's also a poet, painter, and playwright, is third-generation in his craft. His father, Stavros,

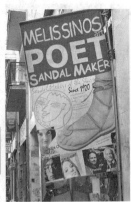

was also a master sandal maker. The story goes that when the Beatles came to the shop in 1968, they asked Stavros why he didn't ask for their autographs. He replied, "Why did they not ask for mine? I will be around long after the Beatles." He was right. If you're in the market for locally made sandals, peruse their catalog; they can even customize a pair for you (for details, see page 198 of the Shopping & Nightlife in Athens chapter).

• *Continue along this street called...*

❸ Agias Theklas

As you stroll into the heart of Psyrri, notice the architectural mix: once-attractive historic buildings that are dilapidated; historic buildings that have been lovingly restored; and eyesore midcentury concrete for which there's little hope. You can see why graffiti might be considered, by some, an improvement.

Continuing along this street, look for slices of local life: crammed little hardware stores overflowing into the streets, neighborhood grocery stores, and so on. With its hip cachet, proximity to downtown sightseeing, and ample residential buildings, Psyrri is becoming a hotspot for Airbnb rentals. Many locals worry that, as has happened in other newly trendy neighborhoods of big, touristy cities, it's only a matter of time before

long-time residents are priced out. Stay tuned.

At the first intersection with Papanikoli street, you'll reach the location of an apartment (now long gone) where English poet Lord Byron stayed in 1810. He resided at the home of the Makri family, where he became infatuated with their 12-year-old daughter—who inspired him to pen the poem, "Maid of Athens, ere we part / Give, oh give me back my heart!"

• *Soon you reach the intersection with Karaiskaki street. Turn left and take a little detour down this popular little patch of Psyrri.*

❹ Karaiskaki Street

A half-block down is the **Little Kook** café (can't miss it, at #17), which captures the creative spirit of Psyrri. This fairy tale-themed coffee and tea house sprawls through several buildings on either side of the street and down the alley called Pittaki. Ogle the café's wildly creative window displays, which change with the seasons: During autumn, they have Halloween-themed displays; in December, it's Christmas; in summers past they've had

a circus theme. A giant dragon perches on top of the main building with rearing stallions below. Pittaki lane is strung with dozens of mismatched light fixtures. You could pause here for a break in the wildly fanciful interior, with elaborate, multitiered cakes to match...but we'll soon encounter lots of other tempting (and more authentically Athenian) snacks. Pace yourself.

Head back up the way you came on Karaiskaki. At the intersection with Agias Theklas, on the left, is the recommended

Koulouri of Psyrri (marked *ΚΟΥΛΟΥΡΙ ΤΟΥ ΨΥΡΡΗ*). *Koulouri* are those little sesame-encrusted dough rings sold cheaply at carts all over Athens. This is the bakery that supplies most of those carts (notice the row of delivery scooters parked just across the street). Step into the shop and buy one—you won't find one fresher.

Athenians eat *koulouri* a variety of ways: plain, as a sandwich, or dipped in honey (adding sweetness to all that sesame tastes a bit like peanut butter). The name comes from the Greek word for "zero" (inspired by its shape). *Koulouri* date back to early Christian times, but were introduced here in Athens only in the 1920s, following the Greco-Turkish War, which saw massive population exchanges. About one million ethnic Greeks living in Asia Minor (today's Turkey) moved to the Athens area, bringing with them an influx of culinary influences—many of which we'll savor as we nibble our way through this part of town.

• *Continue up Karaiskaki street. Soon you'll turn a bend into the main square of Psyrri.*

❺ Iroon: "Square of the Heroes"

This lively square—filled with al fresco café tables—is entertaining day and night. The space is called "Square of the Heroes" for the Greek freedom fighters who settled here following independence from the Ottomans. Many Psyrri streets are named for Greek heroes. And the name Psyrri itself comes from an early resident named Psiris, who built a church here, in what's now the epicenter of the neighborhood named for him.

Notice how Psyrri's streets spin off from this central hub at all angles, like wings on a pinwheel. The higgledy-piggledy street plan is evidence that Psyrri dates from the Ottoman period (pre-1820s)—a stark contrast to the basic grid of nearby Syntagma, which was built later, after independence. Early on, Psyrri was settled primarily by islanders from Naxos, but its central location also attracted diplomats, aristocrats, scholars from the nearby university, and, after the War of Independence, those "heroes" honored by this square's name.

But by the late 19th century, the local mafia began to exert its influence. Athens lacked an organized police force, so people seeking protection turned to a strongarm group called the Koutsavakides, who wore long moustaches, pointed boots, and walked with an exaggerated limp. Over time, the Koutsavakides essentially took over Psyrri and made it their own city-within-a-city. Those who could afford to fled to other parts of town (such as the on-the-rise Kolonaki district). In the 1890s, the government cracked down on the Koutsavakides, but by that time Psyrri had already fallen into a slum. It remained that way—the humble residence of sandal makers and factory workers—until the late 1990s.

That's when artists, designers, and alternative lifestyle enthusiasts discovered Psyrri, taking advantage of its cheap rents and marvelous location. Then, as Athens prepared to host the Olympics, Psyrri was targeted for redevelopment, with rezoning laws designed to lure restaurants and nightclubs. Gentrification quickly followed, and now Psyrri is one of the city's most in-demand areas.

Look up, to where a giant **mural** laughs down over this leafy square. This is the work of Alexandros Vasmoulakis, another respected Athenian street artist.

Ready for another snack? Just to the right from where you entered the square is the recommended **Bougatsadiko of Thessaloniki** (labeled *ΜΠΟΥΓΑΤΣΑΔΙΚΟ*), which specializes in a delicate and delicious pastry called *bougatsa*. Step inside to see if the baker is at work: He rolls out a sheet of super-elastic dough, then pulls, prods, and tosses it like an oversized pizza crust until it's as thin as the skin of a balloon. Then he folds it over several times, fills it with custard, and pops it in the oven. Ask for a portion at the counter—it's especially good when it's hot. *Bougatsa* is more common in the northern city of Thessaloniki than it is here—so the nod to that city in the shop's name is a mark of quality.

To continue our walk, wade through the tables and take the street that angles off to the right of the big mural, passing sev-

eral touristy tavernas. Many of these look-alikes are part of a local chain and can be aggressive about luring in diners. Still, it's a fun scene and worth considering later for dinner (see my recommendations on page 186).

• *Pass under the ivy canopy. At the fork just after that, bear right, up...*

❻ Agiou Dimitriou Street

Enjoy this quieter, more local-feeling part of Psyrri. As you approach the market area, you'll notice the painfully hip atmosphere slowly mellow to workaday.

On the left, at #12, is a row of interesting businesses: First, a giant, well-stocked store selling all manner of baskets, buckets, and containers. Then, a little hole-in-the-wall shop selling distractions for Greek men: worry beads, pocketknives, shaving gear, pipes, and dice and backgammon boards. Right next to that is the easy-to-miss door (marked αυλή) to one of my recommended restaurants—hidden in a courtyard and called, simply, "Courtyard" (this is a good, untouristy alternative to many Psyrri tavernas).

Farther along, humble storefronts sell textiles and fake flowers, and a few little "everything" shops spill out into the street. This is a sign that your transition from trendy Psyrri to the real-world market is nearly complete. Carry on.

• *At the end of Agiou Dimitriou street is the back of the market.*

CENTRAL MARKET

Athens' Central Market (Varvakios Agora/ Βαρβάκειος Αγορά) isn't cute or idyllic, like a small-town French *halles*, and it's not a tourist trap, like Barcelona's La Boqueria.

But the Central Market is refreshingly real: a thriving market-place where workaday Athenians stock up on ingredients. A walk through the market is a treat for all the senses—sights, smells, and sounds. This walk will help you navigate and appreciate its many parts. And in case you're a fan of Greek food (and who isn't?), I'll point out some distinctively local restaurants and treats to enjoy while you're here.

• *Approaching the market from Psyrri on Agiou Dimitriou street, you'll run right into…*

❼ Evripidou: "Spice Street"

Different streets in the Central Market area specialize in different products. And, as you can tell from the first whiff, Evripidou is all about spices.

The lingering impact of ethnic-Greek refugees from Turkey, who moved to Athens in the 1920s, is pungently evident on this street, where exotic spice shops were opened reminiscent of Istanbul bazaars. Turning left on Evripidou, you'll pass three spice shops in row. Step into one (the first one, Χατζηγεωργίου, has a nice selection) and inhale. Intoxicating!

Spice shops here sell a variety of products. You'll see bushels of rice, grains, nuts, and dried fruits. Keep an eye out for bunches of partially dried flowering herbs tied up with string—this is Greek mountain tea, an herbal mixture revered for its healing properties. You'll also see classic Greek oregano, thyme, basil, and the precious Greek red saffron.

Tucked among the spice shops are some butchers, including the venerable Miran, where display cases and café tables sit

under hanging salamis and other meats. The big slabs coated in bright-red spices are *pastourma,* a salted-and-dried meat with a powerful rub of paprika, cumin, fenugreek, garlic, and other spices. You might already know it by its English name—pastrami. (Though at these shops, the most commonly used meat is camel—another aspect of Middle Eastern cuisine that caught on here in the 1920s.)

You'll also see a few Asian grocers and spice markets along here—a reminder that Athens remains, as it always has been, a cultural melting pot of more than just the Eastern Mediterranean world.

At the next corner, across the street, is the deli called **Ta**

Karamanlidika tou Fani, with a menu that includes some explosively flavorful *pastourma* dishes. It's also a full-service restaurant— one of my recommended (and favorite) places for lunch or dinner near the market.

• *Take a right here, on Sokratous (in front of the deli/restaurant), and head up the street. Soon, on the right, you'll see the first part of this area's...*

❽ Produce Market

Known as Anoikti Agora ("Open Market"), this is the largest open-air market in Greece (when combined with the nearby Varvakeios market)—though it's unceremoniously wedged on either

side of a big parking garage. I'd skip the first row of vendors—with olives, eggs, dried fish, and other semi-perishable goods—and continue past the parking-garage entrance to the more-interesting second row. This strip explodes with fresh fruits and veggies—whatever's in season.

You'll also encounter pet shops, pots and pans, heaps of nuts and dried fruits, and a dozen different kinds of olives and feta sold from the barrel. And you'll see bushels of legumes—lentils, chickpeas, beans, and so on. Legumes are a staple of Greek cooking, and sold in abundance here. Traditionally legumes were a precious source of vegetable protein in a hardscrabble land. In fact, Greek's national dish is not souvlaki, *horiatiki* salad (what we call "Greek salad"), or baklava, but a bean soup called *fasolada*.

• *Reaching the end of the produce market, you'll run into busy...*

❾ Athinas Street

One of the main thoroughfares of central Athens, this street connects Monastiraki (a 10-minute walk to your right) with the transportation hub called Omonia (about 10 minutes to your left). Directly across the street is the yellow, Neoclassical meat and fish market. We'll head inside soon, but first...I need a coffee. If you'd like to join me, cross the street and walk a couple of steps left (next to the market entrance) to the recommended **Mokka Coffee Shop.**

Regarded as one of Athens' best, this coffee house offers both espresso-style lattes and macchiatos, and more traditional Greek coffee—an unfiltered preparation that's similar to Turkish coffee (but milder, as the beans are roasted at a lower temperature). This is listed on the menu as "*ibrik* single" or "*ibrik* double"—named for the little copper pitcher they use to prepare it (while *ibrik* is the old Arabic word, modern Greeks call this a *briki*). Tell them how much sugar you want when you order. First, they put the very fine grounds, cold water, and sugar into the *briki*. Then they nestle the *briki* into a tray of hot sand to heat it. Greeks know a quality coffee by

the rich, velvety, light-brown foam that forms at the top. When you get your coffee, drink it slowly to avoid getting a mouthful of the highly caffeinated "mud" at the bottom of the cup. Greeks claim that because it's unfiltered, more healthy nutrients stay in your brew, compared to filtered coffee.

While you sip, think of the way that simple rituals—like drinking coffee—can become cultural cornerstones. Traditionally the coffee house was where Greek men would gather to gossip and grouse, while clacking their worry beads and playing backgammon. Meanwhile, women would invite each other over for coffee in their homes. After finishing the drink, one of the women would swirl the grounds around inside the empty cup and read fortunes. Some traditional and/or nostalgic Greeks worry about the loss of these one-time sacred cultural institutions, as Starbucks and its imitators bully Greece into the modern world.

• *Now that you can't sit still, you might as well explore the adjacent...*

❿ Meat and Fish Market

Opened in 1886, the Central Market's meat and fish hall is a vivid parade of proteins. Vegetarians might want to skip this part.

Let's head into the gut of the market. Walk up the main corridor of the **meat market** (just next to Mokka, directly across the street from where we came through the produce market). Tables are piled high with beef, pork, chicken, lamb, and goat. Notice the livestock proudly pictured on the signs above some of the stalls. Little delivery scooters nudge their way past pedestrians.

About half way up this main drag, watch carefully on the right (high up) for the sign to

ΔΗΜΟΤΙΚΗ Ψαραγορά ("Municipal Fish Market"). Turn right up this lane. On your left is the recommended **Karayiannis Ouzo Bar**—a great spot to sample another Greek specialty, the anise-flavored liquor ouzo. (It's marked by the sign ΜΠΥΡΑ-ΟΥΖΟ-ΤΣΙΠΟΥΡΟ, advertising the holy triumvirate of cheap Greek booze: beer, ouzo, and grappa-like *tsipouro* brandy.) Kostas sells cheap glasses of ouzo and little plates of bar snacks to enjoy while observing the market bustle.

Just beyond is the **fish market.** Watch your step here—the floors are wet and slippery. Turn left and make your way past the

display tables, piled high with big fish (red mullet, sea bream, sea bass), small fish (sardines, anchovies, smelt), fish steaks (mostly from swordfish, tuna, or bonito), mussels, shrimp, Mediterranean lobster (clawless), squid (calamari), the similar cuttlefish, and octopus.

While Greece is a maritime country, the waters of the Aegean are overfished, and supply struggles to meet demand—especially in the tourist season. Much of the fish and seafood served in Greek restaurants is frozen and imported...especially in landlocked places, like Athens. If you see *kat* or just a *k* next to a menu item, it's identifying ingredients that are frozen *(katepsygmenos)*. When Athenians want fresh fish and seafood, they head to tavernas in the seafront suburbs, such as Piraeus (and, farther out, Anavyssos). Also look for planks of dried and salted cod, stacked like firewood. These are rehydrated and rinsed before cooking. The smaller dried fish are smoked herring.

At the end of the first stretch of fish, keep going straight (jogging right a bit) to return to the meat market. In the passage, you'll pass displays showcasing the **"fifth quarter"** of hard-to-sell meat: hooves, tripe, liver, and other organs. You may also see barrels of snails—a cheap source of protein during times of hardship, when locals developed a taste for the little critters that persists today.

When you pop out at the meat market, turn right. A few steps beyond, on the left, is the recommended **Epirus Tavern,** another lowbrow market eatery (look for the big *Η. ΗΠΕΙΡΟΣ* sign). This simple, cafeteria-style spot slings Greek classics, including some of the tripe we just saw.

• *Turn left up the little passage just before Epirus Tavern. This leads to the pleasant, pedestrian-friendly...*

⓫ Aiolou Street

Quieter than the parallel Athinas drag, Aiolou is emerging as one of downtown Athens' most appealing streets. From here, you could turn right and enjoy strolling about 10 minutes gently downhill toward Monastiraki Square.

But first...a final treat. Turn left and head 50 yards up Aiolou street to **Krinos** (Κρίνος, on the left), a recommended pastry shop where locals have been indulging their sweet tooth since 1923. Step into the time-warp interior for a big plate of *loukoumades*—piping-hot doughnuts, fresh out of the industrial fryer. The English menus at the tables explain your options—drizzled with syrup, walnuts, ice cream, Nutella, or a combination; order at the counter in back.

• *From here, the National Archaeological Museum is relatively close—about a 15-minute walk, or a quick taxi ride north. Or, if you want to head back down to the city center, continue down Aiolou street.*

Aiolou to Monastiraki: Turn right as you leave Krinos, walking toward the Acropolis, which floats dreamily on the horizon.

This mostly pedestrianized urban street has sprung to life in recent years, with interesting stores, designer coffee shops, and lots of lunch-focused restaurants for busy urbanites. A block down is the gorgeously restored **Kimisi Theotokou Chrisospileotissis church,** with icon and candle kiosks out front. Step into the beautiful, serene interior.

Farther along, you'll pass the Sgourda dishware company (outfitting Athenian homes since 1870), then cross the streets that fan out at odd angles, continuing straight downhill. This block has some quick-and-cheap lunch spots, including Pera (with Asian street food including *lachmatzoun*—a flatbread sometimes called "Turkish pizza") and the very popular Falafellas. Street musicians often perform along here.

Farther downhill are more trendy eateries and the little **square of St. Irene**—the epicenter of hip, young locals, day or night. The recommended Kosta souvlaki stand is on this square, which used to be known as the square of the flower vendors; these days only one remains open, and it's still loyally frequented by Athenians.

The next block downhill is dense with even more cheap eats. You'll see everything from *loukoumades* to healthy drinks to sandwiches on *koulouri* bread rings.

• *Hitting Ermou street, you're back in the heart of Athens. Monastiraki, where we began our walk, is a block to the right. The cathedral is a couple of blocks to the left. And the Acropolis is straight up. Enjoy!*

SLEEPING IN ATHENS

Athens has a fine array of accommodations. The Plaka and Syntagma have some big, fancy, business-class hotels, but small, inexpensive guesthouses are relatively scarce and overbooked. For more options, expand your search beyond the old center. I've found a few gems in the Makrigianni and Koukaki neighborhoods, behind the Acropolis and a short walk from the Plaka action. These offer a more neighborhoody, less touristy experience, and slightly lower prices.

The accommodations listed here cluster around the €95-150 range, but include everything from €25 bunks to deluxe €350 doubles. In general, temper your expectations. Athenian buildings are often cheaply constructed, with well-worn public spaces and temperamental plumbing and elevators. A welcoming front-desk staff can help compensate, but be ready for hiccups. Any hotel charging less than about €100 may include a few quirks. Spending just €20-30 extra is enough to buy you a much higher degree of comfort. If you're even a little high maintenance (be honest), consider splurging here. If you want an Acropolis-view room, you'll usually pay a higher rate. Budget travelers: Don't be sucked in by *very* cheap, too-good-to-be-true deals (most of those hotels are located in sleazy districts around Omonia Square, or down in the coastal suburbs of Glyfada and Voula).

Athens is a noisy city, and Athenians like to stay out late. This, combined with an epidemic of flimsy construction and the abundance of heavy traffic on city streets, can make things challenging

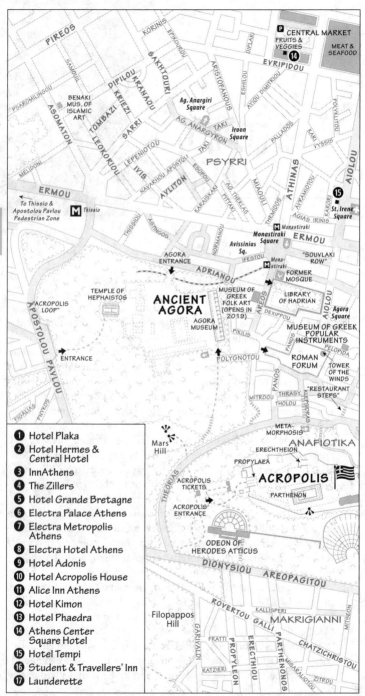

1. Hotel Plaka
2. Hotel Hermes & Central Hotel
3. InnAthens
4. The Zillers
5. Hotel Grande Bretagne
6. Electra Palace Athens
7. Electra Metropolis Athens
8. Electra Hotel Athens
9. Hotel Adonis
10. Hotel Acropolis House
11. Alice Inn Athens
12. Hotel Kimon
13. Hotel Phaedra
14. Athens Center Square Hotel
15. Hotel Tempi
16. Student & Travellers' Inn
17. Launderette

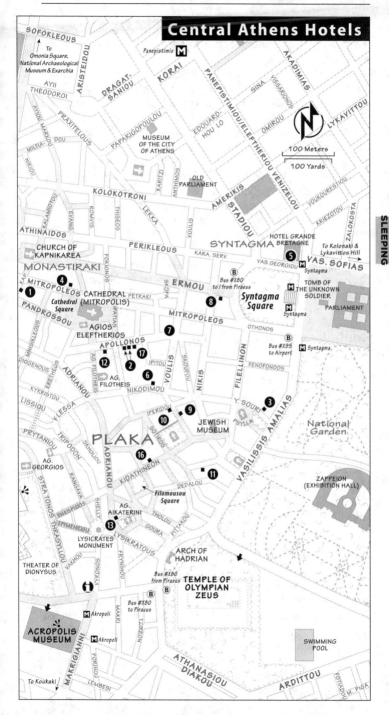

Central Athens Hotels

for light sleepers. I've tried to recommend places in quieter areas, but finding a peaceful corner isn't always possible (be ready to use earplugs).

Short-term rentals (such as Airbnb) can be a good option in Athens. You can often find a well-equipped, spacious, centrally located apartment for less than the cost of a midrange hotel room. Given the hit-or-miss quality of Athenian hotels, a carefully chosen apartment can be an excellent value; search for places in my recommended hotel neighborhoods.

Wherever you sleep, book accommodations well in advance, especially if you'll be traveling during peak season or if your trip coincides with a major holiday or festival (see page 545).

For information and tips on pricing, getting deals, making reservations, and finding a short-term rental, see page 506.

HOTELS IN THE CENTER

Sleeping in the Plaka and Syntagma area offers close proximity to the sights (you'll rarely need public transportation). It can be more congested and more touristy than outlying neighborhoods, but in general, the pluses of sleeping in this zone outweigh the minuses.

Boutique and Business-Class

$$$ Hotel Plaka, buried on an urban street in the busy heart of town, has a rooftop bar/terrace and 67 modern rooms (some with Acropolis views) with updated bathrooms. Its classy management adds some nice touches, such as a staff member on hand at breakfast to answer travel questions (RS%, elevator, at the corner of Mitropoleos and Kapnikarea, reservation tel. 210-322-2706, reception tel. 210-322-2096, www.plakahotel.gr, plaka@athenshotelsgroup.com).

$$$ Hermes Hotel, professionally run by the folks at Hotel Plaka, has lower rates and a slightly more appealing location on a less-trafficked street closer to Syntagma. Many of its 45 rooms have balconies, and guests share an inviting lobby, a pleasant lounge, a kids' activity room, and a rooftop patio with a peek at the Acropolis (RS%, possible to add child's cot, elevator, Apollonos 19, reservation tel. 210-322-2706, reception tel. 210-323-5514, www.hermeshotel.gr, hermes@athenshotelsgroup.com).

$$$ InnAthens feels urban and urbane. It sits at the edge of the Plaka—a bit less convenient than the others I list here—with 20 industrial-mod rooms ringing an atrium, and a recommended wine bar on the premises (elevator, Souri 3 at intersection with busy Filellinon, tel. 210-325-8555, www.innathens.com, info@innathens.com).

$$$ The Zillers is a conveniently located boutique hotel that fills an old townhouse facing the cathedral. It feels posh—with marble, hardwood, and a classic spiral staircase—but still friendly. Six of the 10 rooms have Acropolis views, as does the roof garden's restaurant and cocktail bar; streetside rooms are more expensive and come with some traffic and church-bell noise (Mitropoleos 54, tel. 210-322-2278, www.thezillersathenshotel.com, info@ thezillersathens.com).

$$$ Central Hotel has 84 cookie-cutter rooms, sleek public spaces, and an anonymous business-class vibe. There are several classes of rooms with prices based on whether they have balconies and/or views. If you stick with the cheaper rooms, it's a good value (elevator, swanky rooftop terrace with café and Jacuzzi, Apollonos 21, tel. 210-323-4357, www.centralhotel.gr, reservation@ centralhotel.gr).

Splurges

$$$$ Hotel Grande Bretagne, a five-star splurge with 320 sprawling and elegantly furnished rooms, is considered the best hotel in Greece and ranks among the grand hotels of the world. It's *the* place to stay if you have royal blood—or wish you did and feel like being treated like royalty for a few days. Built in 1862 to accommodate visiting heads of state, it became a hotel in 1874 and still retains its 19th-century elegance. No other hotel in Athens can boast such a rich history (breakfast extra, elevator, overlooking Syntagma Square at Vassileos Georgiou 1, tel. 210-333-0000, www.grandebretagne.gr, info.gb@starwoodhotels.com). If you'd rather just eat here, consider their recommended rooftop restaurant.

$$$$ Electra Palace Athens is a luxury five-star hotel with 155 rooms in a quiet corner of the Plaka, not far from Syntagma. It's pricey but plush, if a bit snooty, with top-notch service and elegance (elevator, garden patio, indoor pool, Acropolis-view outdoor pool in summer, Nikodimou 18, tel. 210-337-0000, www. electrahotels.gr, salesepath@electrahotels.gr). Nearby, the same company operates two similarly equipped hotels: **$$$$ Electra Metropolis Athens,** with 216 rooms in the busy heart of Syntagma near the cathedral (Acropolis-view roof garden, Mitropoleos 15, tel. 214-100-6200) and **$$$$ Electra Hotel Athens,** at #5 on the busy pedestrian Ermou street (tel. 210-337-8000).

DOWNTOWN BUDGET SLEEPS

$$ Hotel Adonis, with 26 retro-simple but thoughtfully managed rooms, stands on the quiet, traffic-free upper reaches of Kodrou, right in the heart of the Plaka. A couple of rooms on the fourth floor have good views of the Acropolis, as does the rooftop bar (reserve with credit card but pay in cash; includes breakfast on roof terrace—which is also open at night for drinks and snacks, elevator, public areas can be smoky, Kodrou 3, tel. 210-324-9737, www.hotel-adonis.gr, info@hotel-adonis.gr, owner Spiros, assisted by Nikos).

$$ Hotel Acropolis House was once a wealthy lawyer's villa, and it still feels homey. While it has more "personality" than amenities, you'll find antiques scattered amid the dark-wood furnishings in its lobby and 23 tight, old-fashioned rooms, offered at what its owners call "realistic prices." Many rooms have balconies—ask when you reserve (cheaper rooms with private bathroom across the hall, reserve with credit card but pay in cash, no elevator, Kodrou 6, tel. 210-322-2344, www.acropolishouse.gr, hotel@acropolishouse.gr, run by Emmanuella with help of charmingly gregarious Jasmine, Andreas, and others).

$$ Alice Inn Athens, with four rooms filling a classic townhouse tucked on an untouristed street deep in the Plaka, feels more like an Irish B&B than an Athenian hotel. Irish-Greek owner John provides hospitality and funky charm; each room is different and well-described on their website (breakfast extra, Tsatsou 9, tel. 210-323-7139, www.aliceinnathens.com, stay@aliceinnathens.com).

$$ Hotel Kimon rents 15 well-worn but perfectly fine rooms over a jolly, suitcase-themed lobby. Its location—in the Plaka, near the cathedral—is handy, and the price is right (cheaper "economy" rooms are simpler and very affordable, breakfast extra, no elevator, top-floor terrace with a corner that looks up at the Acropolis, Apollonos 27, tel. 210-331-4658, www.kimonhotelathens.com).

$$ Hotel Phaedra is simple but nicely located, overlooking a peaceful Plaka square with ancient ruins and a Byzantine church. The institutional hallways lead to 21 plain rooms—most with balconies and views. Six rooms have private bathrooms across the hall (breakfast extra, Acropolis-view rooftop terrace, elevator, 2 blocks from Hadrian's Arch at Herefondos 16, at intersection with Adrianou, tel. 210-323-8461, www.hotelphaedra.com, info@hotelphaedra.com; Marianna and Periklis).

At Central Market: Part of the Plaka and Hermes Hotel group, **$$ Athens Center Square Hotel** is less expensive than its sister properties—mostly because it's farther away from the main sightseeing action. It overlooks the seedy market square, but it's close to the Central Market and Psyrri dining areas. Its 54 rooms are functional, minimalist, and colorfully painted, and the roof garden has Acropolis views (RS%, elevator, just off Athinas street overlooking the produce market at Aristogitonos 15, reservation tel. 210-322-2706, reception tel. 210-321-1770, www.athenscentersquarehotel.gr, acs@athenshotelsgroup.com).

On St. Irene Square: Expect old-fashioned hospitality at old-fashioned prices at **$ Hotel Tempi,** run by friendly Yiannis and Katerina. The 24 rooms are spartan, and the bathrooms are cramped and minimal (especially the shared ones)—but the rates are just right. It's well-situated on lively St. Irene Square (Agia Irini), which is filled with trendy cafés, bars, and cheap eats. Rooms in front come with balconies overlooking the square, with views of the Acropolis and nighttime noise (cheaper rooms with shared bathroom, breakfast extra, lots of stairs, elevator is for luggage only, kitchen, Aiolou 29, tel. 210-321-3175, www.tempihotel. gr, info@tempihotel.gr).

Hostel: A classic backpacker place in the Plaka, ¢ **Student & Travellers' Inn** is the perfect spot to meet up with young travelers, with renovated rooms and an in-house travel agency specializing in trips to the Greek islands (elevator, pay laundry service, courtyard bar, kitchen, Kidathineon 16, tel. 210-324-4808, www. studenttravellersinn.com, info@studenttravellersinn.com; managed by Pericles, a.k.a. Perry).

MAKRIGIANNI AND KOUKAKI, BEHIND THE ACROPOLIS

With the Acropolis Museum standing boldly as their gateway, the adjoining residential areas of Makrigianni and Koukaki, just south of the Acropolis, feel typically Athenian urban. (Some locals call Makrigianni the "south Plaka" instead.) Full of six-story concrete apartment buildings, hole-in-the-wall grocery stores, and corner cafés, these neighborhoods let you feel like a temporary Athenian while still providing relatively easy access to major sights. Most can be reached by a longish walk—figure 5-10 minutes to the edge of the Plaka (which involves passing a gauntlet of aggressively touristy eateries near the Acropolis Museum), then another 10 minutes to Monastiraki. These hotels are all located between the Akropoli and Syngrou-Fix Metro stops. Be aware that to reach most points of interest from these stops, you'll change Metro lines at Syntagma.

$$$ Hotel Hera is a tempting splurge, with 38 plush rooms above a classy lobby. With helpful service, lots of thoughtful little touches, an air of elegance, and a handy location near the Acropolis end of this neighborhood, it's a fine value (elevator, rooftop Acropolis-view restaurant, Falirou 9, tel. 210-923-6682, www.herahotel. gr, info@herahotel.gr).

$$ Art Gallery Hotel is a comfy, well-run small hotel with 21 faded but affordable rooms in a quieter part of this neighborhood, sitting above the busier main thoroughfares. The original artwork in the halls and rooms adds charm (breakfast extra, elevator, fourth-floor bar open at night, look for ΞΕΝΟΔΟΧΕΙΟ sign at Erechthiou 5, tel. 210-923-8376, www.artgalleryhotel.gr, artgalleryhotel@gmail.com). Say hello to Artie, the hotel's cat.

$$ Athens Studios, run by the gang at Athens Backpackers (described later), rents 37 nicely appointed, good-value apartments

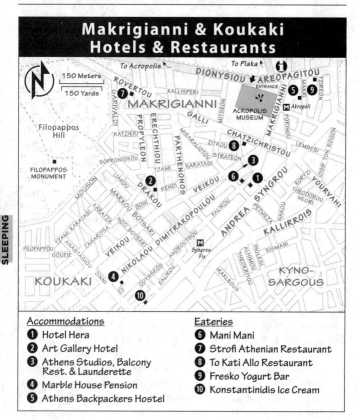

Makrigianni & Koukaki Hotels & Restaurants

Accommodations
1. Hotel Hera
2. Art Gallery Hotel
3. Athens Studios, Balcony Rest. & Launderette
4. Marble House Pension
5. Athens Backpackers Hostel

Eateries
6. Mani Mani
7. Strofi Athenian Restaurant
8. To Kati Allo Restaurant
9. Fresko Yogurt Bar
10. Konstantinidis Ice Cream

with retro-mod decor, kitchens, a rooftop bar with a Thai restaurant, and other nice touches (elevator; sports bar, fish café, and public launderette on ground floor; pay long-term luggage storage available, Veikou 3A, tel. 210-923-5811, www.athensstudios.gr, info@athensstudios.gr, Daniel).

$ Marble House Pension is a small, family-run place hiding at the end of a little cul-de-sac, a few minutes' walk past my other listings in this area. The 16 cozy rooms—most with small balconies—are simple but well cared for, and (true to its name) it's decorated with real marble. If you don't mind the more remote location, it's an excellent deal (cheaper rooms with shared bath, reserve with credit card but pay in cash, breakfast extra, air-con extra, 3 floors with no elevator, closed Jan-Feb; 5-minute walk from Syngrou-Fix Metro at Zini 35a—from Zini street take the alley to the left of the tidy Catholic church, tel. 210-923-4058, www.marblehouse. gr, info@marblehouse.gr; Christos with mom Nancy and dad Thanos). They also rent a beautifully appointed modern apartment next door.

Hostel: The best place in town for backpacker bonding, ¢ **Athens Backpackers** is youthful and fun-loving with two bars, including one on the rooftop. Well-run by gregarious Aussies, it offers good bunks and an opportunity to meet up with other travelers (big communal kitchen, public launderette at Athens Studios; cheap city walking tours offered daily in summer, less frequent off-season; Makri 12, tel. 210-922-4044, www.backpackers.gr, info@ backpackers.gr).

EATING IN ATHENS

Greek food is just plain good. And Athens, the melting pot of Greece (and the Balkans), is one of the best places to experience the cuisine, thanks to a stunning variety of tasty and affordable eateries.

I've listed these restaurants by neighborhood. You probably won't be able to resist dining in the touristy Plaka at least once—it's fun, folkloric, and full of clichés (beware the tourist traps). But don't be afraid to venture elsewhere. For a trendy and youthful local scene, target Psyrri and Gazi—just beyond the tourist zone. For those staying near the Acropolis Museum in Makrigianni or Koukaki, I've listed a couple of convenient options (including my two favorite elegant restaurants in all of Athens).

EATING TIPS

For advice on eating in Greece, including details on ordering, dining, and tipping in restaurants, types of eateries, and Greek cuisine and beverage descriptions, see the Practicalities chapter.

Restaurants: Locals and tourists alike fill tavernas, *mezedopolio*s (eateries selling small plates called *mezedes*), *ouzeries* (bars selling ouzo liquor and pub grub), and other traditional eateries dishing up the basics. Greeks like to eat late—around 21:00 or later. Restaurants in Athens tend to stay open until midnight or even past that.

Smoking: Though smoking is not allowed in indoor spaces, don't be surprised to find that some restaurants and bars don't enforce it.

Budget Snacks: To save money and time, try one of Greece's street-food specialties. Options include souvlaki (meat-on-a-skewer meal), savory pie (filled with meat, cheese, or vegetables), *koulouri* (bread rings), *loukoumades* (Greek doughnuts), and more (in this chapter I recommend places to try all of these).

Food Tours: To learn about local eating traditions and sample lots of Greek cuisine, join a food tour; for recommendations, see the sidebar later in this chapter. For a do-it-yourself approach, follow my self-guided walk through the Psyrri neighborhood, which hits several fun eating spots and leads you through the Central Market action. ◫ See the Psyrri & Central Market Walk chapter.

TOURISTY MEALS IN THE PLAKA

Diners—Greeks and tourists alike—flock to the Plaka. In this neighborhood, the ambience is better than the food. I've avoided the obvious, touristy joints on the main pedestrian drag—with shards of broken plates in the cobbles and obnoxious touts out front luring diners with a desperate spiel—in favor of more authentic-feeling eateries huddled on the quieter hillside just above. Eat at one of my recommendations, or simply choose the place with your favorite view of an ancient monument, on a square that appeals to you, or with live music. Prices are pretty consistent and painless, and the quality is acceptable.

At the top of the Plaka, the stepped lane called Mnisikleous (stretching up toward the Acropolis) is lined with eateries featuring interchangeable food and delightful outdoor seating. Many of these places have live music and/or rooftop gardens.

$$ Geros tou Moria Tavern is a sprawling and venerable place with three eating areas. The tour-group-friendly, powerfully air-conditioned indoor dining hall features a more formal menu and live Greek music and dance (no cover, nightly in summer from 20:15). The more intimate Palio Tetradio ("Old Notebook") has a terrace, cozy-in-the-winter indoor seating, and more *mezedes*. Maybe best of all are the tables along the steps under grapevines (daily 9:00-24:00, Mnisikleous 27, tel. 210-322-1753, www.gerostoumoria-restaurant.com).

$$ Scholarhio Ouzeri Kouklis, at the intersection of Tripodon and Epicharmou streets, serves only small plates. While jammed with tourists, it's fun, inexpensive, and ideal for small

groups wanting to try a variety of traditional *mezedes* and drink good, homemade booze on an airy perch at the top of the Plaka. Since 1935, the Kouklis family has been making ouzo liquor and feeding people here—maintaining a 1930s atmosphere. Waiters present a big platter of dishes, and you choose. Drinks are cheap, and the stress-free €15 meal deals (including dessert) are worth considering. Many wait for a spot to open up on the lively front terrace, but you can instead climb to the upstairs dining room with its romantic balconies for two (daily 11:00-24:00, Tripodon 14, tel. 210-324-7605, www.scholarhio.gr). Show Vasilis and his gang this book and they'll welcome you with free homemade ouzo—if you ask.

$$$ Xenios Zeus (ΞΕΝΙΟΣ ΖΕΥΣ) sits proudly at the top of the Mnisikleous steps, offering good, traditional, home-cooking Greek food inside or out on a terrace overlooking Athens' rooftops (daily 11:00-24:00, closed Nov-March, Mnisikleous 37, tel. 210-324-9514, http://xenioszeus.com.gr). They promise a free bottle of ouzo to diners with this book (be sure to ask).

$$ Klepsidra Café is parked on a characteristic corner high in the Plaka with an island ambience and a somewhat younger and more local crowd. With tiny tables littering the ramshackle steps, they serve light bites, good desserts, traditional coffee, and booze (daily 9:00-24:00, Thrasivoulou 9, tel. 210-321-2493).

$$$ Palia Taverna tou Psara ("Old Fisherman's Tavern") is a big, slick, impersonal, pricey eatery that enjoys bragging about the many illustrious guests they've hosted since opening in 1898. It's the kind of place where a rowdy, rollicking group of a hundred can slam down a dish-'em-up Greek meal. While often dominated by tour groups, it can be enjoyable. There's live folk music (generally

Fri-Sat from 20:00) in the lower building and, kitty-corner across the way, a grand rooftop terrace (daily 12:00-24:00, Eretheos 16, tel. 210-321-8734, www.psaras-taverna.gr).

NEAR SYNTAGMA SQUARE

These options are in the gritty urban streets near Syntagma Square and the Plaka—an area that's more residential and pleasantly less touristic.

$$$$ 2MAZI Restaurant Wine Bar—a play on the Greek word for "together"—began as the collaboration of two well-known local chefs. Filling a tranquil, leafy courtyard, it's a well-established place to enjoy modern Greek gourmet cooking in a stylish setting with equally stylish locals (daily 13:00-24:00, Nikis 48, tel. 210-322-2839, reservations smart, www.2mazi.gr).

$$$ Tzitzikas and Mermigas ("The Ant and the Cricket") serves modern, regional Greek cuisine. Choose between two levels of indoor seating in a fun, mod atmosphere—surrounded by vintage grocery ads—or grab a sidewalk table in a bustling urban zone. It's named for the folktale about a hardworking ant and the lazy cricket who goofs off...only to come asking for help when winter arrives (daily 13:00-24:00, Mitropoleos 12, tel. 210-324-7607).

$$$ Avocado Vegetarian Café is a good bet if you need a yoga-friendly eatery with a passion for organic farming, and nothing with eyeballs. The menu includes pastas, pizzas, veggie burgers, and sandwiches, as well as lots of energy juices (Mon-Sat 11:00-22:00, Sun 12:00-19:00, Nikis 30, tel. 210-323-7878).

$$ Kimolia (Κιμωλία) **Art Café** is a cute little pastel place at the edge of the Plaka. They have light café fare at reasonable prices, a relaxing vibe, and friendly service. It's a nice place to take a break (daily 10:00-24:00, Ypereidou 5, tel. 211-184-8446).

$$$ Athinaikon Restaurant, with a heritage going back to the 1930s, is a venerable businessman's favorite, serving a variety of traditional *mezes* and Greek, Italian, and other Mediterranean recipes. You'll dine in a no-nonsense art-deco/modern interior with professional service and a local crowd. It feels polished and international, but still affordable (Mon-Sat 12:00-24:00, Sun until 19:00, a block from the cathedral at Mitropoleos 34, tel. 210-325-2688).

$$$$ Hotel Grande Bretagne's Roof Garden Restaurant is posh as can be. Perhaps the most venerable place in town to dine on Greek and Mediterranean cuisine, it's pure fancy-hotel-restaurant elegance—in a rooftop garden with spectacular Acropolis views. If you're looking to splurge on grand panoramas and fine dining, this is a good choice (daily 13:00-24:00, reservations required for dinner, "smart casual" dress code, on Syntagma Square, tel. 210-333-0766, www.grandebretagne.gr). If you don't want such an expensive meal, drop by their swanky bar for a pricey beer or cocktail.

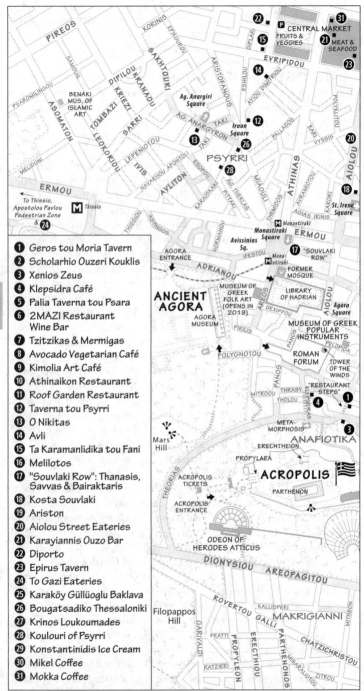

EATING

1   Geros tou Moria Tavern
2   Scholarhio Ouzeri Kouklis
3   Xenios Zeus
4   Klepsidra Café
5   Palia Taverna tou Psara
6   2MAZI Restaurant Wine Bar
7   Tzitzikas & Mermigas
8   Avocado Vegetarian Café
9   Kimolia Art Café
10 Athinaikon Restaurant
11 Roof Garden Restaurant
12 Taverna tou Psyrri
13 O Nikitas
14 Avli
15 Ta Karamanlidika tou Fani
16 Melilotos
17 "Souvlaki Row": Thanasis, Savvas & Bairaktaris
18 Kosta Souvlaki
19 Ariston
20 Aiolou Street Eateries
21 Karayiannis Ouzo Bar
22 Diporto
23 Epirus Tavern
24 To Gazi Eateries
25 Karaköy Güllüoglu Baklava
26 Bougatsadiko Thessaloniki
27 Krinos Loukoumades
28 Koulouri of Psyrri
29 Konstantinidis Ice Cream
30 Mikel Coffee
31 Mokka Coffee

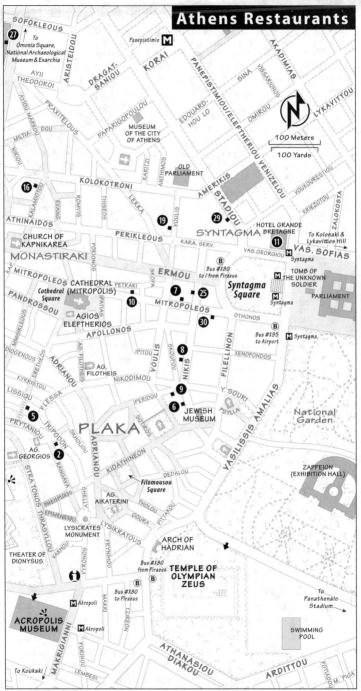

Athens Restaurants

EATING

Souvlaki: A Quick and Cheap Meal

My favorite fast-food meal in Greece is souvlaki—it's quick, cheap, filling, and oh so Greek. As international fast-food places have moved in, the traditional souvlaki stand is a little less ubiquitous than before... but more worthwhile than ever.

Souvlaki is meat—usually pork or lamb—grilled on a little skewer (as its name means) and served on a plate or wrapped in pita bread to make a sandwich. When you get it "to go," the meat is tucked into a wonderful greasy pita pocket with lettuce, tomato, onions, and *tzatziki* (cucumber-yogurt-garlic sauce). If you like yours spicy, grab the shaker and sprinkle on some red pepper (or ask the vendor to season it for you). A souvlaki is often bulked up with doughy French fries (which you can opt out of if you speak up). If you order souvlaki in a restaurant, insist on a "souvlaki sandwich" or you'll generally get a big meaty plate...at an equally meaty price.

The **gyro** *(yee-roh)* is a virtually identical type of sandwich made with meat cooked on a spinning vertical rotisserie (also called a gyro, meaning "turn"). The meat—usually pork, chicken, or a combination—is shaved into a steamy, tasty pile and then tucked into a pita with the usual accompaniments.

The **kebab**—your third "meat on a spindle" option—is also sold at many souvlaki stands. This is basically a long, skinny, uncased sausage made of minced meat, pierced by a souvlaki spindle, and grilled. It's served the same way as a souvlaki or a gyro: wrapped in pita with tomatoes, onions, and *tzatziki*.

(This sidebar was written with the help of Matt Barrett, whose GreeceTravel.com website is a wonderful resource.)

PSYRRI

The mix of trendy and crusty gives this fun area just north of Monastiraki a unique charm. Your options include slick, touristy tavernas with live traditional music (many are painted in the same Greek saloon style—these places are fresh, formulaic, and part of a chain), highly conceptual café/bars catering to cool young Athenians, and clubs with DJs or live music for partying the night away. While I've listed a few restaurants to consider, the scene is ever-changing and the vibe is different each night—you might just wander and see what feels best.

Iroon Square is the lively hub of the action. From there the streets called Agiou Dimitriou and Agion Anargyron are lined with the most accessible and fun places. The third street, Miaouli, which extends from Iroon Square toward Monastiraki, is a younger, university scene—packed with the outdoor tables of unpretentious, local-feeling pubs and tavernas. Lepeniotou and Esopou streets have the most creatively themed café/bars—most of them mellow and colorful—great spots to relax with a drink and appreciate the decor. Each one has its own personality and idiosyncratic style (from Lebanese to Argentinian).

$$ Taverna tou Psyrri is right in the heart of the restaurant action, with checkerboard tablecloths, a garden terrace hidden in the back, a straightforward menu, and good prices (daily 12:00-24:00, Eschilou 12, tel. 210-321-4923).

$$ O Nikitas (Ο Νικήτας) sits on a peaceful square, serving mainly *mezedes* and good food to a local crowd (Wed-Sat 12:00-23:00, Sun-Tue until 18:00, across from church at Agion Anargyron 19, tel. 210-325-2591).

$$ Avli (αυλή; "Courtyard") is for the adventurous. Stepping through its speakeasy door you'll find a long, skinny, and thriving courtyard with a jumble of tiny tables and Greeks wondering, "How did that tourist find this place?" They have no menu, instead serving a daily *meze* plate (daily 12:00-24:00, Agiou Dimitriou 12—look for the small doorway labeled αυλή).

Near Central Market: $$ Ta Karamanlidika tou Fani (Τα Καραμανλίδικα του Φάνη) is my favorite in the area, offering a nice change of pace from the typical Psyrri tavernas. It's a quality meat-and-cheese shop that doubles as a restaurant. With its mix of authentic Byzantine and Cappadocian flavors, aged cheese, and

cured meats, it's a tasty reminder that many Greek Turks settled here in Athens in the 1920s—bringing their Anatolian cuisine with them. Several dishes include *pastourma*—meat coated in delicious herbs and spices, similar to pastrami. You'll enjoy a variety of tasty small plates and the friendly service of Maria and her gang (Mon-Sat 12:00-23:00, closed Sun, a block off Athinas at Evripidou 52, tel. 210-325-4184).

Near St. Irene Square: This area, surrounding the Church of St. Irene (Agia Irini) immediately east of Psyrri, has emerged as one of Athens' top dining and nightlife areas. Simply exploring the fast-changing scene around here is a delight. For a memorable meal, head a block behind the church and turn left to find **$$$ Melilotos** (ΜΕΛΙΛΩΤΟΣ), a chic but accessible spot with indoor and outdoor seating on a lively lane. The food, melding Greek ingredients and traditions with international influences, is delicious (daily 12:00-24:00, Kalamiotou 19, tel. 210-322-2458, www.melilotos.gr).

CHEAP AND CASUAL EATS IN THE CENTER
Street Food

$ "Souvlaki Row" near Monastiraki: Monastiraki Square (where it meets Mitropoleos street) is souvlaki heaven, with three frantic restaurants—**Thanasis** (Θανάσης), **Savvas** (Σάββας), and **Bairaktaris** (ΜΠΑΪΡΑΚΤΑΡΗΣ)—spilling into the street and keeping hordes of hungry eaters happy. The dominant operation, Bairaktaris, while not necessarily the best eating value, has a boisterous, fun-loving interior. These places also sell meat shaved from gyros, kebabs, hearty Greek salads, a few other standard Greek dishes, wine, beer, and ouzo. They're all open daily until very late. A gyro or souvlaki sandwich **to go** costs about €2—just head inside, order and pay at the cashier, then take your receipt to the counter to claim your moveable meal. It can be tricky to find a comfortable bench or other suitable perch in this crowded neighborhood—plan to munch as you walk. All three places also have **table seating,** with higher prices and much bigger portions. The ambience is lively, especially at the outdoor tables. A big plate of four souvlaki (plus pita bread, onions, and tomatoes) costs €9-10 and can easily be shared by two or three people; a smaller helping of two souvlaki—plenty for a filling meal (and shareable for light eaters)—runs about €5-6.

Souvlaki on St. Irene Square: $ Kosta (ΚΩΣΤΑ) is a beloved hole-in-the-wall that's been serving up good souvlaki pitas since the 1940s. This is a classic place: no gyro slices or kebabs...just traditional €2 skewer-roasted souvlaki. You can get it to go or grab a stool on the tiny square facing St. Irene's Church to enjoy the almost Parisian ambience (Mon-Fri 9:00-17:00, closed Sat-Sun, off Aiolou Street a block north of Ermou).

Savory Pies near Syntagma Square: In business for more than a century, **$ Ariston** (ΑΡΙΣΤΟΝ) is one of Athens' top spots for savory and sweet pastries. Choose between *spanakopita* (spinach pie), *tiropita* (cheese pie), *kreatopita* (minced pork meat pie), *meletzanitopita* (eggplant pie), and lots more (leek, shrimp, olives and feta, and so on...all labeled in English). They also have lovely sweet desserts made with flaky phyllo (Mon-Sat 7:30-18:00, Tue and Thu-Fri until 21:00, closed Sun; 2 blocks from Syntagma toward the Plaka at Voulis 10, tel. 210-322-7626).

$ Eateries on Aiolou Street: The pedestrianized lane called

EATING

Aiolou, which runs north from near Monastiraki, offers plenty of fast and affordable options. At the base of Aiolou, **Oven Sesame** (#17, at intersection with Ermou) makes sandwiches on *koulouri* (bread rings). A few doors up, **Tylixto** (#19) rolls up tasty Greek wraps while **Lukumades** (#21) sells Greek-style doughnuts. Additional options are a few more blocks up, toward the Central Market: **Falafellas** (#51) is a popular hole-in-the-wall selling falafel sandwiches; **Pera** (#57) specializes in *lachmatzoun*—a Middle Eastern flatbread sometimes called "Turkish pizza." The Central Market area, with many more options, lies just beyond (see next).

Home-Style Cooking Near Central Market

These places are packed with locals and in-the-know travelers who've done their homework to find basic but good, authentic grub. These are great finds for adventurous diners, or those looking to do as the Athenians do. For more on the market, see the Psyrri & Central Market Walk chapter.

$ Karayiannis Ouzo Bar, in the thick of the Central Market and run by Kostas, is great for a drink and snack. Pay about €3-4 for an ouzo and little plate of *mezes* to enjoy while you observe the action (on a side aisle, midway down the fish section in the Central Market, Mon-Sat 7:30-15:00—sometimes later, closed Sun). It's easy to miss—just look for the sign advertising *ΜΠΥΡΑ-ΟΥΖΟ-ΤΣΙΠΟΥΡΟ*—beer, ouzo, *tsipouro* (grappa-like brandy).

$$ Diporto, which has been in business since 1887, feels like a time warp. It's difficult to find—true to its name, it has "two doors" (both painted a drab brown and below ground level) leading to its unfinished-cellar space. On any given day, they have just a few dishes—all simmering in pots on the rustic stove. Service and ambience are basically nonexistent, but local old-timers—who crowd around a few rickety, shared tables—appreciate the cooking (lunch only, closed Sun, Sokratous 9, across from the parking garage entrance of the produce market).

$$ Epirus Tavern (ΟΙΝΟΜΑΓΕΙΡΕΙΟ Η. ΗΠΕΙΡΟΣ), in the meat section of the Central Market, is the place for a low-brow, stick-to-your-ribs meal (though, unfortunately, priced for tourists). This place is known for its meat soups, particularly those made with tripe (Mon-Sat 6:00-19:30, closed Sun, 4 Filopimenos, tel. 210-324-0773).

GAZI

Residents here must be dizzy at the rapid change sweeping through what was recently a depressed industrial zone. Towering overhead are the square, brick smokestacks of Technopolis, a complex of warehouses, old gasworks, and brick factory buildings that now host galleries and theaters with a world of cutting-edge culture.

Food Tours

Food tours are a great way to get to know Greeks, who love to cook and love to eat. With a good tour, you'll learn a lot about Greek history and culture through food, plus you'll get to sample classic dishes. Here are a few good choices:

Alternative Athens offers a shorter tour that includes a Greek coffee, a walk through the Central Market, Greek sweets, a meat-and-cheese shop, a specialty grocery store, and a chance to sample some typical *mezedes* (€50/person, Mon-Sat at 10:00, none on Sun, 3.5 hours, mobile 694-840-5242, www.alternativeathens.com; they also offer home-cooked meal experiences).

Culinary Backstreets' longer tours are for people who love to eat. They offer three tours (each one 5.5 hours): Backstreet Plaka, Downtown Athens, and a "Moveable Sunday Feast." The groups are smaller, and you'll stop at more places (from family-run holes-in-the-wall to trendier eateries), linger longer at stops, and eat more unique food—a lot more of it. You won't want to eat for the rest of the day ($135/person, all run 9:30-15:00 but on different days—check their schedule, 2-7 people, www.culinarybackstreets.com).

Simply ride the Metro to Keramikos. Exiting the station, you'll emerge at the top of the main square—a delightful park surrounded by streets lined with super-stylish restaurants, clubs, bars, and cafés. While wild-and-alternative places to eat and drink dot the back lanes, the main square is busy with options accessible to any tourist. Stand looking downhill, with the gasworks smokestacks to your back. On the right is a line of clubs and cocktail bars. On the left is a line of happening restaurants. I've listed my favorite three (starting just steps away and working downhill).

$$$ A Little Taste of Home serves an eclectic mix of Greek, Middle Eastern, and other international dishes, collected during the travels of owner Ahmad (who's from Syria). If you're homesick, they brag that they can prepare just about any recipe you request (with some advance notice). It's tucked a few steps down the main Gazi restaurant drag, with a clean, cozy, contemporary interior and a few outdoor tables (Tue-Fri 18:30-24:00, Sat-Sun from 13:00, closed Mon, Dekeleon 3, tel. 210-341-0013).

$ Kandavlos Souvlaki, a thriving student hangout with white tables and a clubby crowd, serves the best cheap souvlaki in Gazi. You can choose between takeout or table service (daily 11:00-24:00, Persefonis 47, tel. 210-342-4725).

$$ Gazi College Eatery is a fresh, modern, and inviting place for a light meal or drink in the company of a student crowd that's typical of the area. It offers a fun menu of international comfort foods—pizzas, pastas, salads, burgers, sandwiches—in a bold interior with a big wall of old books (daily 8:00-24:00, Persefonis 53, tel. 210-342-2112).

MAKRIGIANNI AND KOUKAKI

The area around the Acropolis Museum—where this neighborhood meets the Plaka—is home to a trendy and touristy row of restaurants, cafés, and ice-cream shops along pedestrian Makrigianni street. The other pedestrian street, Dionysiou Areopagitou, also has plenty of tourist-friendly options between the museum and the Arch of Hadrian. While there are countless hardworking eateries along these streets, the following restaurants are worth serious consideration. For locations, see the map on page 178.

$$$ Mani Mani offers a touch of class for reasonable prices, with cuisine and ingredients from the Mani Peninsula. The dining is indoors only, and the food, like the decor, is thoughtfully updated Greek. Chef Alex cooks, Yolanda (his wife) greets you, and their staff provides solid service. As this is justifiably popular, reservations are smart (daily 14:00-23:00 in summer, shorter hours off-season, go upstairs at Falirou 10, tel. 210-921-8180, www.manimani.com.gr).

$$$$ Strofi Athenian Restaurant is my choice in Athens for white-tablecloth, elegantly modern, rooftop-Acropolis-view dining. Niko Bletsos and his staff offer attentive service, gorgeously presented plates, and classic Greek cuisine—especially lamb. And though they have a fine air-conditioned interior, the rooftop is comfortable regardless of how hot or cool the evening. For a flood-lit Acropolis view, you'll be glad you made reservations (Tue-Sun 12:00-24:00, closed Mon, about 100 yards down Propyleon street off Dionysiou Areopagitou at Rovertou Galli 25, tel. 210-921-4130, www.strofi.gr).

$$$ Balcony is an upscale but unpretentious restaurant and bar in the heart of the neighborhood. They serve contemporary Greek cuisine accompanied by a good wine list in either the high-ceilinged dining room or up in the roof garden with apartment-building views (daily 12:00-24:00, Veikou 1, tel. 211-411-8437, www.balconyathens.com).

$$ To Kati Allo Restaurant, immediately under the far side of the Acropolis Museum, is the quintessential neighborhood hole-in-the-wall. Run by English-speaking Kostas Bakatselos and his family (including Jennifer, the American daughter-in-law), this place offers both sidewalk seating and fan-cooled inside tables. The blackboard menu features a short list of cheap, fresh, and tasty local options—many of them prepared on the big rotisserie that spins just inside the window (daily 11:00-24:00, just off Makrigianni street at Chatzichristou 12, tel. 210-922-3071).

EATING

SUGAR, CAFFEINE, AND OTHER DRUGS
Snacks and Sweets

Baklava: Various bakeries around town sell takeaway portions of this classic Greek treat, but connoisseurs swear by one that started in Istanbul (sorry, Greek patriots). **Karaköy Güllüoglu** is a nondescript shop on an urban Syntagma street with tempting display cases featuring various types of baklava—both traditional walnut and pistachio, as well as some interesting variations (long hours daily, Nikis 10, tel. 210-321-3959).

Bougatsa, Loukoumades, and *Koulouri:* These three local specialties are all worth a try. **Bougatsadiko Thessaloniki** makes some of the best *bougatsa*—thin pastry with cream inside (if not on display just ask for it; open long hours daily, 1 Iroon Square, tel. 210-322-2088). **Krinos** (Κρίνος) is famed for its *loukoumades*—fried Greek doughnuts (Mon-Sat 7:00-17:00, Tue and Thu-Fri until 20:30, closed Sun, 87 Aiolou, tel. 210-321-6852). *Koulouri*—sesame bread rings, sold at corner carts throughout the city—are a popular Athenian on-the-run snack, especially in the morning. For the best, visit **Koulouri of Psyrri** (ΚΟΥΛΟΥΡΙ ΤΟΥ ΨΥΡΡΗ), which supplies most of the street vendors in the city and where you can try one fresh out of the oven (long hours daily, Karaiskaki 23, tel. 210-321-5962). For more on these bakeries and their specialties, see the Psyrri & Central Market Walk chapter.

Yogurt Bars: These shops invite you to create a build-your-own Greek-yogurt dream. The best places source high-quality (unfrozen) Greek yogurt, then offer a variety of mix-ins—from fresh fruit to honey and nuts to "spoon sweets" (preserves in a variety of exotic flavors). They can also blend in ice and milk to make smoothies. These places are popping up all over the city, so be choosy; one good spot is **Fresko Yogurt Bar** near the Acropolis Museum (Dionysiou Areopagitou 3). The city also has an abundance of frozen yogurt places (self-service, add mix-ins, pay by weight), but most of these are no different from what you get back home.

Ice Cream: Konstantinidis is a local favorite for ice cream and, after my discerning taste test, I enthusiastically agree. While a chain, they do a good job of embracing their "good old days" heritage (they also have a variety of pastries). You'll find two branches downtown: Stadiou 3 (3 blocks northwest of Syntagma) and Syngrou Ave 98 (the biggest and best, just beyond the Syngrou-Fix Metro station; see map on page 185).

Coffee

If you want good local coffee for half the price of Starbucks—and want your money to stay in Greece—you'll find handy branches of the local chain **Gregory's** (Γρηγόρης) all over town. They have all

the typical coffee drinks you'd find at home, plus light bites, pastries, and trendy ambience. The **Mikel Coffee** chain is a bit pricier and more posh (one handy location is near Syntagma Square at Mitropoleos 3).

For Greek coffee made the traditional way (heated in a tray of hot sand), visit **Mokka,** near Central Market (daily 6:00-17:00, 44 Athinas, tel. 210-321-6892, see page 167 for a full description).

Wine and Booze Tasting

$$$ By the Glass wine bar is a jazz-cool, relaxed place where you can enjoy a quiet table out on a breezy arcade, or sit at the bar and learn from the server about

Greek wines. Their menu includes countless wines by the tiny glass for a euro or two each; the staff can help you assemble a flight. They also serve plates of mixed Greek cheeses and meats, salads, and other upscale nibbles (daily 10:00-24:00, between the Plaka and the National Garden at Y. Souri 3, inside the InnAthens hotel, tel. 210-323-2560).

$$ Heteroclito is a sophisticated-but-unpretentious, urban-feeling wine bar buried in the tight streets near Syntagma Square (facing the cathedral). They serve several carefully curated Greek wines by the glass, along with a short list of accompanying plates (Mon-Sat 12:30-24:00, Sun from 18:00, Fokionos 2 at corner with Petraki, tel. 201-323-9406).

Brettos—the oldest distillery in Athens, dating from 1909—is a popular stop for tourists and locals wanting to taste various shots and wines by the glass. While buried in the Plaka kitsch, it seems a world apart once you step inside and grab a stool under huge old casks and lit-up bottles of colorful liquors (daily 10:00-24:00, just off Adrianou at Kydathineon 41, tel. 210-323-2100).

SHOPPING & NIGHTLIFE IN ATHENS

Athens may not be a top shopping destination, but it does offer plenty of options for visitors who want to pick up good Greek souvenirs. On the other hand, Athens *is* known for its lively after-hours scene. In this chapter, you'll find tips for shopping and for enjoying the city after dark.

Shopping in Athens

Most shops catering to tourists are open long hours daily (souvenir stores in the Plaka can be open past midnight). Those serving locals are open roughly 9:00 to 20:00 on weekdays, have shorter hours on Saturday, and are closed on Sunday. Afternoon breaks are common, and some places close early a few nights a week.

For details on getting a VAT (Value-Added Tax) refund on your purchases, see the Practicalities chapter.

Shopping Areas: The main streets of the Plaka—especially **Adrianou** and **Pandrossou**—are crammed with crass tourist-trap shops selling cheap plaster replicas of ancient artifacts, along with calendars, magnets, playing cards, postcards, and profane T-shirts. Competition is fierce, so there's room to bargain, especially if you're buying several items. **Forget Me Not** is one of the more tasteful shops along here, with a thoughtfully curated selection of artsy souvenirs, including ceramics, housewares, fun T-shirts, and locally produced clothing and beachwear (Adrianou 100, tel. 210-325-3740, www.forgetmenotathens.gr).

For midrange shopping at mostly international chain stores, stroll the pedestrianized **Ermou street** between Syntagma Square and Monastiraki. You'll find more local flavor at Greek shops such as **Kem** (handbags; Kornarou 1, just off Ermou) and the clothing stores **Regalinas** (Ermou 37) and **Bill Cost** (Ermou 14).

While tourists and big-money Athenians strut their stuff on Ermou, many locals prefer the more authentic shops on the streets just to the north, such as **Perikleous, Lekka,** and **Kolokotroni.**

For top-end international boutiques (like Prada and Louis Vuitton), head for the swanky **Kolonaki** neighborhood, just north of Syntagma Square—particularly posh Voukourestiou street.

Monastiraki Flea Market: This famous flea market stretches west of Monastiraki Square, along Ifestou street and its side streets.

You'll see plenty of souvenir shops, but the heart of the market is Avissinias Square, filled with antique shops selling furniture, household items, jewelry, dusty books, knickknacks, and stuff that might raise eyebrows at the airport. It's a fun place for tourists and pickpockets to browse, but isn't ideal for buying gifts for friends back home. There's something going on every day, but the market is best and most crowded on Sundays, when store owners lay out the stuff they've been scouting for all week. If buying here, make sure to bargain (Sun flea market open 8:00-15:00, packed with locals by 10:00, Metro: Monastiraki or Thissio).

Department Store: The largest department store in Athens is **Attica,** which feels pretty much like a US department store and has a cafeteria on the top floor but no views (Mon-Fri 10:00-21:00, Sat until 20:00, closed Sun, near Syntagma Square at 9 Panepistimiou, tel. 211-180-2600).

Jewelry

Serious buyers say that Athens is the best place in Greece to purchase jewelry, particularly at the **shops along Adrianou.** The choices are much better than you'll find elsewhere, and—if you know how to haggle—so are the prices. The best advice is to take your time, and don't be afraid to walk away. The sales staff gets paid on commission, and they hate to lose a potential customer. Most stores have similar selections, which they buy from factory wholesalers. If feeling shy about bargaining, ask "Do you have any discounts?" to start the conversation.

For something a bit more specialized (with high prices), visit **Byzantino,** which made the jewelry worn by Greek dancers in the closing ceremonies of the 2000 Sydney Olympics. They create pricey handmade replicas of museum pieces, along with some original designs (daily 10:00-21:00, Adrianou 120, tel. 210-324-6605, www.byzantino.com, run by Kosta).

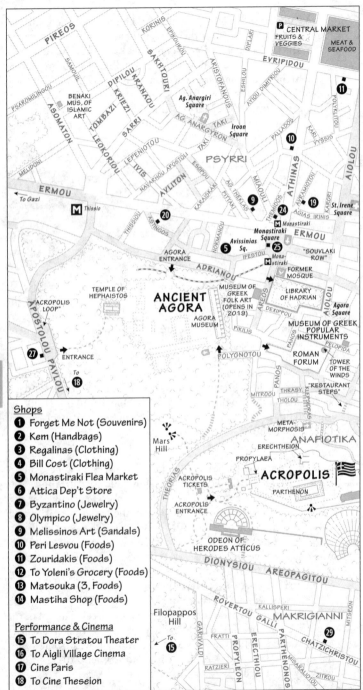

SHOPPING & NIGHTLIFE

Shops
1. Forget Me Not (Souvenirs)
2. Kem (Handbags)
3. Regalinas (Clothing)
4. Bill Cost (Clothing)
5. Monastiraki Flea Market
6. Attica Dep't Store
7. Byzantino (Jewelry)
8. Olympico (Jewelry)
9. Melissinos Art (Sandals)
10. Peri Lesvou (Foods)
11. Zouridakis (Foods)
12. To Yoleni's Grocery (Foods)
13. Matsouka (3, Foods)
14. Mastiha Shop (Foods)

Performance & Cinema
15. To Dora Stratou Theater
16. To Aigli Village Cinema
17. Cine Paris
18. To Cine Theseion

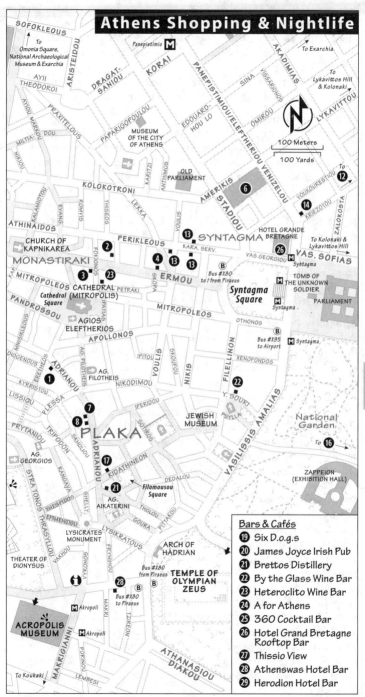

Athens Shopping & Nightlife

Bars & Cafés
19 Six D.o.g.s
20 James Joyce Irish Pub
21 Brettos Distillery
22 By the Glass Wine Bar
23 Heteroclito Wine Bar
24 A for Athens
25 360 Cocktail Bar
26 Hotel Grand Bretagne Rooftop Bar
27 Thissio View
28 Athenswas Hotel Bar
29 Herodion Hotel Bar

Olympico creates their own modern pieces in the Greek style, along with museum copies. They also sell pieces made by artisans from all over Greece (daily 10:00-21:00, Adrianou 122, tel. 210-324-8697, George).

The gift shop at the **Benaki Museum of Greek History and Culture** (described on page 58) is also popular for its jewelry.

Handmade Sandals

The best place to buy real leather sandals is **Melissinos Art,** the famous "poet sandal maker" of Athens. You'll find an assortment of styles in basic shades of tan for about €40-50 per pair. The price goes up if you want to customize a pair with leather or beading in various colors, and you'll have to wait a day or two (daily 10:00-20:00, off-season until 18:00, just off Monastiraki Square at the edge of Psyrri, Agias Theklas 2, tel. 210-321-9247, www.melissinos-art.com). For more on this shop, see page 160.

Religious Items

Icons and other Greek Orthodox objects can make good souvenirs. For the best selection, visit the shops near the cathedral, along Agia Filotheis street (most are closed Sat-Sun, described on page 79).

Specialty Foods

All over Athens you'll see specialty food stores selling locally produced goods, such as olive oil, wine and liqueurs, mustards, and sweets like boxed baklava, *loukoumi* (a.k.a. Greek delight), and jars of "spoon sweets" (jam-like spreads).

The best place to shop for these is where the locals do—near the Central Market. Specialty grocers and spice shops cluster around Athinas and Evripidou streets, including **Peri Lesvou,** which sells items produced on the island of Lesbos (closed Sun, Athinas 27, tel. 210-323-3227) and **Zouridakis,** featuring products from Crete (closed Sun, Evripidou 25, tel. 210-321-1109).

Yoleni's is a top-end, all-purpose Greek grocery store in the posh Kolonaki area, about a 10-minute walk from Syntagma Square. Its shelves are stocked with high-end wine, olive oil, liqueur, honey, and other temptations. They also have a café (with sandwiches and salads), wine bar, steak house, and venue for cooking classes (long hours daily, Stolonos 9, tel. 212-222-3622, www.yolenis.com).

For chocolate and other Greek goods, check out **Matsouka** (ΜΑΤΣΟΥΚΑ) and its offshoots, dominating a block of Karageorgi Servias, around the corner from Syntagma Square (with other branches around the city; all open long hours daily). Their main branch (at #10) sells nuts, candies, dried fruit, honey, olive oil, and other food items. Across the street is their spice shop; nearby (at #3) is their coffee-roasting operation; and a half-block away

Worry Beads

As you travel through Greece, you may notice Greek men spinning, stroking, and generally fidgeting with their worry beads.

Greeks use these beaded strings to soothe themselves and get focused—especially during hard times. Loosely based on prayer beads, but today a secular hobby, worry beads make for a fun Greek souvenir. You'll see them sold all over central Athens.

Many major faiths employ some version of stringed beads as a worship aid, typically to help keep track of prayers while calming and focusing the mind. Think of the Catholic rosary, Muslim prayer beads, and the long, knotted rope belts worn by medieval monks. Hindus and Buddhists also make use of beads. Greeks—likely inspired by Muslims during the nearly 400 years of Ottoman rule—adopted the habit, but it no longer carries any religious connotations.

The most typical type of worry bead is the *komboloï*, a loop with an odd number of beads (it can be any number, as long as it's odd). The top of the loop may have a fixed "main bead" (or two), also called the "priest." The newer *begleri*—popular only since the 1950s—is a single string with an even number of beads (so it can be comfortably balanced in the hand).

The beads are made from a variety of materials. The basic tourist version is a cheap "starter set" made from synthetic materials, similar to marbles. You'll pay more for organic materials, which are considered more pleasant to touch: precious stones, bones, horn, wood, coral, mother-of-pearl, seeds, and more. The most prized worry beads are made of amber. Most valuable are the hand-cut amber beads, which are very soft and fragile; machine-cut amber is processed to be stronger.

When buying, go ahead and try several different strings to find one that fits well in your hand; tune in to the smoothness of the beads and the sound they make when clacking together.

There is no "right" or "wrong" way to use your worry beads—everyone finds a routine that works for them. Some flip or spin the beads in their hands, while others sit quietly and count the beads over and over. There are as many ways to use worry beads as there are Greeks. Their seemingly nervous habit appears to have the opposite effect—defusing stress and calming the nerves.

(at the corner with Voulis) is their top-end chocolate shop, selling pricey Greek, French, and Belgian pralines. Even if not buying, step inside and take a deep whiff. Notice the case of fancy desserts. Greeks bring these to a home when they're invited for a visit instead of, say, a bottle of wine.

Also near Syntagma Square, **Mastiha Shop** specializes in (and is named for) a unique Greek treat—a sweet resin produced only by trees on a particular part of Chios island. *Mastica* has been revered since ancient times for its medicinal properties in treating stomach ailments. These days, this shop uses the distinctively flavorful substance for a number of products—from cookies and liqueurs to essential oils and preserves. *Mastica* is also commonly used in chewing gum (look for the EΛMA brand, sold at newsstands all over Greece) and as a sweet treat for kids, who dip a spoon in a jar of *mastica* syrup and eat it like a lollipop. Drop in for some free samples (closed Sun, a block above Syntagma Square at Panepistimiou 6, tel. 210-363-2750).

Nightlife in Athens

Athens is a thriving city...and the Athenians know how to have a good time after hours. I've provided some ideas for how to spend an evening, from folk performances to outdoor movies, enjoying rooftop cocktails, or simply strolling around and finding a scene that appeals to you.

Athens is most inviting from May through October (aside from miserably hot August), when al fresco activities such as outdoor cinema, festivals (including the Athens & Epidavros Festival), folk-dancing shows at Dora Stratou Theater, and outdoor sidewalk cafés and bars are in full swing.

In the heat of summer, some clubs close down to relocate to outdoor venues on the coast. In the winter, your options are limited to indoor venues (concerts and other performances). But folk musicians, who tend to spend their summers in small towns and islands, hibernate in Athens in winter—offering ample opportunities to hear traditional music. A number of tavernas feature live music and dancing locals year-round, providing a wonderful setting for a late dinner.

Events Listings: Athens has a constantly rotating schedule of cultural activities, such as concerts to suit every audience. For local events, look for publications such as the English-language version of the daily newspaper *Kathimerini* (www.ekathimerini.com).

Festivals

Athens' biggest party is the **Athens & Epidavros Festival,** held every June and July. The festival's highlights are its world-class per-

formances of dance, music, and theater at the ancient Odeon of Herodes Atticus, nestled spectacularly below the flood-lit Acropolis. Outdoor perfor-mances at other venues enliven the already hopping city. Per-formances also take place at the famous Theater of Epidavros on the Peloponnese (these extend into August). Tickets go on sale in early May. You can buy them online, over the phone, and at the fes-tival box office (closed Sun, in the arcade at Panepistimiou 39, op-posite the National Library, tel. 210-327-2000, www.greekfestival.gr). Same-day tickets are also sold at the theater box office.

Folk Dancing

The **Dora Stratou Theater** on Filopappos Hill is the place to go to see authentic folk dancing. The theater company—the best in Greece—was originally formed to record and preserve the coun-try's many traditional dances. Their repertoire includes such favor-ites as the graceful *kalamatianos* circle dance, the *syrtaki* (famously immortalized by Anthony Quinn in *Zorba the Greek*), and the dra-matic solo *zimbetikos* (€15, 1.5-hour performances run late May-late Sept, generally Wed-Fri at 21:30, Sat-Sun at 20:30, no shows Mon-Tue, morning tel. 210-324-4395, evening tel. 210-921-4650, www.grdance.org). The theater is on the south side of Filopappos Hill. If you're taking the Metro, get off at Petralona (10-minute walk) rather than the farther Akropoli stop (20-minute walk). To walk to the theater from below the Acropolis, figure at least 20 minutes (entirely around the base of Filopappos Hill, signposted from western end of Dionysiou Areopagitou).

Other Outdoor Venues

The rebuilt ancient theater at the foot of the Acropolis, the **Odeon of Herodes Atticus,** occasionally hosts concerts under the stars. The theater atop **Lykavittos Hill** is another outdoor favorite. Both of these are used in summer for the Athens & Epidavros Festival.

Outdoor Cinema

Athens has a wonderful tradition of outdoor movies. Screenings take place most nights in summer (around €10, roughly June-Sept, sometimes in May and Oct depending on weather; shows start around 20:00 or 21:00, depending on when the sun sets; many offer a second, later showing). Drinks are served at these "theaters," which are actually compact open-air courtyards with folding chairs. Movies typically are shown in their original language, with Greek subtitles (though children's movies might be dubbed in Greek). Of

Athens' many outdoor cinema venues, these are particularly well known, convenient, and atmospheric. Call or check online to see what's playing.

Aigli Village Cinema is a cool, classic outdoor theater in the National Garden (at the Zappeion), playing the latest blockbusters with a great sound system (tel. 210-336-9369, www.aeglizappiou.gr).

Cine Paris, in the Plaka, shows movies on the roof with Acropolis views (overlooking Filomousou Square of Kidathineon 22, tel. 210-322-2071, www.cineparis.gr).

Cine Theseion, along the Apostolou Pavlou pedestrian drag in the Thissio neighborhood, enjoys grand floodlit Acropolis views from some of its seats—one of the reasons it was voted the "best outdoor cinema in the world." It shows both classic and current movies (Apostolou Pavlou 7, tel. 210-347-0980 or 210-342-0864, www.cine-thisio.gr).

Apostolou Pavlou Promenade and Thissio

A peaceful pedestrian lane circles the Acropolis, providing locals and visitors alike a delightful place for an evening stroll. This promenade is what I call the "Acropolis Loop" (consisting of Dionysiou Areopagitou to the south and Apostolou Pavlou to the west). As the sun goes down, it's busy with locals (lovers, families, seniors, children at play) and visitors alike.

The promenade cuts through the Thissio district, just beyond the Agora, where the tables and couches of clubs and cocktail bars clog the pedestrian lanes under the Acropolis. More upscale than the Plaka, Thissio gives you an easy escape from the tired tourism of that zone. Thissio is basically composed of three or four streets running into Apostolou Pavlou (part of the "Acropolis Loop"). Iraklidon street is a tight lane with people socializing furiously at café tables squeezed under trees. Akamantos street, while still colorful, is a bit more sedate. Backgammon boards chatter, TVs blare the latest sporting events, and young Athenians sip their iced coffees en masse. As the sun sets and the floodlit temples of the Acropolis ornament the horizon, you understand why this quiet and breezy corner is such a hit with locals enjoying an evening out.

Come here just to stroll through a fine café scene, enjoy a drink and some great people-watching, or see a movie under the stars (at Cine Theseion, listed earlier).

To reach Thissio, walk the pedestrian lane around the Acropolis from either end. It makes a wonderful destination after the more peaceful stretch from the Acropolis Museum (Metro: Akropoli). Or ride the Metro to Thissio, then follow the crowds uphill along the broad Apostolou Pavlou walkway toward the Acropolis. For more details about this main drag, see page 41.

Other Fun Nightlife Spots

Athens abounds with bar/cafés serving drinks in lively and atmospheric settings (including on rooftops boasting grand views). I've listed a few good areas to explore. Note that although bars are supposed to be nonsmoking, many places don't adhere to this rule. Expect to leave most bars smelling of smoke.

Psyrri: Immediately north of Thissio, this area is downscale and more cutting-edge than its neighbor...seedy-chic. The center of this district is Iroon Square, with several cute bar/cafés spilling into the square under a jolly mural. Nearby Lepeniotou and Esopou streets are good to explore for their creatively decorated places. You can get your bearings by doing my self-guided walk of

Psyrri (□ see the Psyrri & Central Market Walk chapter); for dining recommendations, see the Eating in Athens chapter.

St. Irene (Agia Irini) Square and Nearby: The square surrounding the Church of St. Irene, a short walk east of Psyrri (across busy Athinas street), offers one of the most delightful wine-and-coffee scenes in the center. Day or night you'll find the place filled with locals enjoying the stylish, modern bar/cafés and classy ambience. The streets that peel off from the square are largely traffic-free and lined with places that invite you to explore and come in for a drink. The best of these is **Six D.o.g.s** bar, hiding down some stairs in a nondescript alley between the square and Psyrri. This sunken open-air courtyard with high stone walls, leafy trees overhead, and seating on multilevel terraces serves up tropical cocktails and plenty of atmosphere (6 Avramioutou, tel. 210-321-0510).

Monastiraki Square and Nearby: Right on Monastiraki Square, several rooftop bars offer some of the best views of the city (described later). Nearby Adrianou street has a line of inviting restaurants and cafés with outdoor seating—some with spectacular Acropolis views. For something completely un-Greek, head a few blocks away to **James Joyce Irish Pub** to drink a pint of your favorite Irish brew (Astiggos 12, tel. 210-323-5055).

Near the Old Parliament: Several bars are scattered along the streets surrounding the Old Parliament building and Kolokotronis Square (just off Stadiou). This area offers a quieter, darker feel than the neighborhoods described earlier, and serves a more professional-feeling clientele. Just wander the streets—Anthimou Gazi, Christou Lada, and Kolokotroni—to find a spot that suits your tastes.

Plaka/Syntagma: Although the Plaka is jammed full of tourists and few locals, it couldn't be more central or user-friendly, with live traditional music spilling out of seemingly every other taverna. One particularly pleasant area to explore is the stepped lane called Mnisikleous. For drinks, I enjoy **Brettos** distillery (with a casual atmosphere surrounded by large casks), **By the Glass** (a sophisticated wine bar serving good food), and **Heteroclito** (another good wine bar with food; near the cathedral, closer to Syntagma Square). All of these are described at the end of the Eating in Athens chapter.

Gazi: This neighborhood, west of Keramikos Cemetery, feels more local and authentically lively—but young. You'll find clubs, bars, and restaurants on the streets spiraling out from its main square (which, conveniently, surrounds the Keramikos Metro stop). For an orientation to this area, including some recommended restaurants, see the Eating in Athens chapter.

Kolonaki: This upscale and stylish district, at the foot of Lykavittos Hill, is Athens' top area for yuppie nightlife.

Exarchia: The very grungy student/anarchist zone that stretches north of Kolonaki is rougher around the edges than the other places I describe here. But adventurous travelers might enjoy exploring the area...with caution. (First, read the description on page 57.)

Rooftop Bars

A touristy-yet-appealing way to spend an evening is at one of Athens' many rooftop bars, all with views of floodlit monuments.

The rooftop of the **A for Athens** hotel hosts both locals and tourists who come to gawk at its views. Thanks to its prime spot on Monastiraki Square, it offers dramatic views of the Acropolis looming above the city. If this place is too crowded, try the **360 Cocktail Bar** on the same square (but with less impressive panoramas).

For a similarly great view and overpriced cocktails, visit the recommended rooftop restaurant and bar of the **Hotel Grande Bretagne,** across the street from Syntagma Square. If strolling the pedestrian promenade through Thissio, consider a stop at the **Thissio View** restaurant and bar (Apostolou Pavlou 25).

There are also several rooftop bars at hotels near the Acropolis Museum, including the Modern Restaurant, on top of the **Athenswas Hotel** (5 Dionysiou Areopagitou), and the Point α Bar at the **Herodion Hotel** (4 Rovertou Galli). You'll be in the company of other tourists, and views are less impressive, as you're looking at the backside of the Acropolis, but these spots are convenient to some of my recommended accommodations in Makrigianni and Koukaki.

SHOPPING & NIGHTLIFE

ATHENS CONNECTIONS

Athens is the transportation hub for all of Greece. Because the tourist core of Athens is so compact, with good public transportation, don't rent a car until you are ready to leave the city—you absolutely do *not* want to drive in Athens traffic. If you're venturing to landlocked destinations beyond Athens, the best option for the rest of your trip is to travel by car. Buses can get you just about anywhere for a reasonable fare, but connections to remote areas can be long and complicated, and straightforward schedule information is hard to come by (note that most of my recommended sights beyond Athens do not have train service). Boats and planes work well for reaching the islands. For specifics on transportation beyond Athens, see the "Connections" sections in each of the following chapters. For general information on transportation by plane, boat, bus, and car, see the Practicalities chapter.

By Plane

ELEFTHERIOS VENIZELOS INTERNATIONAL AIRPORT

Athens' airport is at Spata, 17 miles east of downtown (airport code: ATH, tel. 210-353-0000—press 2 for English, www.aia.gr). This slick, user-friendly airport has two sections: B gates (serving European/Schengen countries—no passport control) and A gates (serving other destinations, including the US). Both sections feed into the same main terminal building (with a common baggage claim, ATMs, shops, car-rental counters, information desks, and additional services). On the top floor (above entrance/exit #3) is a mini museum of Greek artifacts dug up from the area around the airport.

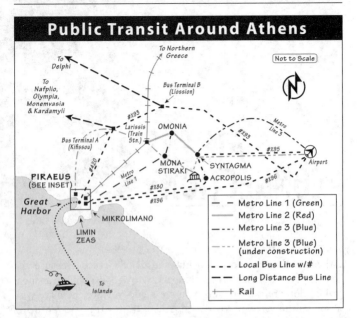

Getting from the Airport to Downtown

Your best route into the city depends on where you want to go: If you're headed to Syntagma Square, the bus is generally better (cheapest, very frequent, and scenic—but slow). For Monastiraki, Psyrri, or the Makrigianni area south of the Plaka, the Metro is more direct—and isn't susceptible to traffic jams. Electronic boards in the baggage and arrivals halls show when the next buses and trains are leaving.

By Bus: Buses wait outside exit #5. Express bus #X95 costs €6 and operates 24 hours daily between the airport and Syntagma Square (3-5/hour, roughly 1 hour depending on traffic; tel. 185, www.oasa.gr). The downtown bus stop is on Othonos street, along the side of Syntagma Square; get off after the bus takes a 180-degree turn around a big square filled with palm trees.

By Metro: Line 3/blue zips you downtown in 45 minutes for €10 (2/hour, direction: Aghia Marina, daily 6:30-23:30; €18 for 2 people, €24 for 3, half-price for people under 18 or over 65, ticket good for 90 minutes on other Athens transit; consider the €22 three-day tourist ticket, which includes round-trip airport transfer by Metro or bus as well as unlimited in-city travel on all public transit).

To reach the Metro from the airport arrivals hall, go through exit #3, cross the street, go up the escalator, and cross the skybridge to the rail terminal. Buy tickets at the machines or ticket window, and follow signs down to the platforms. In downtown Athens, this train stops at Syntagma (where you can transfer to line 2/red) and Monastiraki (transfer to line 1/green).

To return to the airport by Metro, you can catch a train from Syntagma (2/hour, 5:30-24:00). Keep in mind that some Metro trains terminate at Doukissis Plakentias. If so, just hop off and wait—another train that continues to the airport should come along soon.

By Taxi or Uber: A well-marked taxi stand outside exit #3 offers fixed-price transfers that include all fees and tolls (€38 to central Athens, covers up to 4 people, fare increases to €50 or more between 24:00 and 5:00). If you are comfortable using Uber back home, you can also use it in Athens to get to and from the airport—often cheaper than a taxi.

By Car Service: A variety of private services offer airport transfers for approximately the same cost as a taxi, but often with a nicer car and a more personal and professional approach. Most hotels have a service they like to work with, or you can book on your own (reserve at least a day before). Consider **George's Taxi** or **Olympic Traveller** (contact info for both services on page 36). Or try **Athens Tour Taxi** (mobile 693-229-5395, www.athenstourtaxi. com, atsathens@gmail.com, Panagiotis and Konstantinos Tyrlis) or any number of other services (check reviews online and take your pick).

Getting from the Airport to Other Transit Points

To reach the **port of Piraeus,** you can take express bus #X96 (€6, runs 24 hours daily, 2-4/hour, 1-1.5 hours depending on traffic; leaves from outside airport exit #5, stops at Piraeus' Karaiskaki Square, then at the Metro station; tel. 185, www.oasa.gr). A taxi from the airport to the port costs about €45.

Express bus #X93 goes directly to **bus terminals A and B** (same price and frequency as #X96, above).

By Boat

ATHENS' PORT: PIRAEUS

Piraeus, a city six miles south-west of central Athens, has been the port of Athens since ancient times. Today it's also the main port for services to the Greek islands, making it the busiest passenger port in the Mediter-

ranean. While the port is vast, most of it is used for ferry traffic; all cruise ships moor at one end.

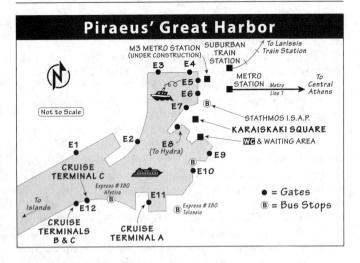

Orientation to Piraeus

All ferries, hydrofoils, catamarans, and cruise ships use Piraeus' Great Harbor (Megas Limin). To the east are two smaller harbors used for private yachts: Limin Zeas and the picturesque Mikrolimano, or "Small Harbor."

The vast Great Harbor area is ringed by busy streets. At the northeast corner is the hub of most activity: the Metro station, housed inside a big yellow Neoclassical building with white trim (sometimes labeled "Electric Railway Station" on maps). Trainspotters with time to kill can visit the free and good little electric-railway museum inside. Next door to the Metro station is the suburban train station, and nearby (toward the port), you'll notice construction for the extension of Metro line 3. Just south of the Metro station is Karaiskaki Square, which juts out into the harbor. Cheap eateries, flophouse hotels, and dozens of travel agencies round out the dreary scene. The port does have several air-conditioned waiting areas and WCs (between gates E8 and E9) and big electronic display boards showing gate numbers and times for upcoming departures.

Gates: Twelve "gates" (docks) wrap around the harbor for about three miles, numbered in clockwise order. Gate assignments depend on both the destination and the company operating the line, but you can generally expect the following:

    E1: Dodecanese Islands

    E2: Crete; North Aegean Islands (Samos, Ikaria, Chios, Mytilene)

    E3: Crete and Kithira (vehicle entrance)

    E4: Kithira (vehicle exit)

    E5: Bus Terminal

E6: Cyclades (including **Mykonos** and **Santorini**), pedestrian walkway to Metro

E7: Cyclades (including high-speed boats to **Mykonos** and **Santorini**)

E8: Saronic Gulf Islands (Argosaronikos in Greek, including **Hydra,** Spetses, Paros, and Ermioni)

E9: Cyclades (including **Mykonos** and **Santorini**), Samos, Ikaria

E10: Vehicle exit from E9

E11: Cruise Terminal A

E12: Cruise Terminals B and C

These departure gates could change—carefully check your ticket for the gate number, and ask a local if you're unsure.

Information: Official tourist information is in short supply here, although temporary TI kiosks may pop up near the cruise terminals when ships arrive. Your best sources of information are the many travel agencies scattered around the area; all have a line on current boats, where they leave from, and how to get tickets. The port police, with several offices clearly marked in English, can be helpful (tel. 210-414-7800). You can also call the Piraeus Port Authority ship-schedule line at toll tel. 14541. The port authority website is www.olp.gr.

Baggage Storage: A bag storage/Internet access shop is near the Metro station. Go under the pedestrian bridge; it's about 50 yards down on the main street (daily 7:00-22:00).

Getting from Piraeus to the Islands

For tips on buying tickets and the lowdown on Greece's ferry network, see page 532 of the Practicalities chapter. Know ahead of time which gate your ferry leaves from (see earlier).

Arriving at the Piraeus Metro station (end of the line), you'll step out into a chaotic little square. Circle around the construction zone to the crosswalk, then cross the busy road to enter the port area. Straight ahead are gates E6 and E7. Gates with higher numbers are to your left; those with lower numbers are to your right. (For example, Hydra-bound boats usually depart from gate E8, to your left on the far side of the tree-filled park.) If your boat leaves from gates E1 or E2 on the north side of the port, look for a free shuttle bus just inside the port gate.

From Piraeus by Boat to: Hydra (6-8/day June-Sept, 4/day Oct-May, 1.5-2 hours), **Mykonos** (3/day in high season—1 fast boat, 3 hours; 2 slow boats, 5.5 hours; off-season likely 1 slow boat daily), **Santorini** (3/day in high season—2 fast boats, 5 hours; 1 slow boat, 8 hours; off-season likely 1 slow boat daily). The frequency and durations listed here are approximate; schedules can change from season to season, and sailings can be canceled on short notice—confirm everything locally.

Getting from Piraeus Ferry Terminals to Athens

By Train: Metro line 1/green conveniently links Piraeus with downtown Athens (€1.40, good for 90 minutes including transfers, departs about every 10-15 minutes between 6:00 and 24:00). The Metro station is in a big, yellow Neoclassical building near gate E6 (hiding behind the sprawling construction zone for a new Metro station). Buy your ticket from a machine, validate it, and hop on the train. In about 20 minutes, the Metro reaches the city-center Monastiraki stop, near the Plaka and many recommended hotels and sights. (For Syntagma, Akropoli, and Syngrou-Fix Metro stops, ride one more stop to Omonia to transfer to line 2/red.) Warning: The Metro line between Piraeus and downtown Athens teems with pickpockets—watch your valuables and wear a money belt.

A **suburban train** also connects Piraeus' train station with Athens, but there's no reason to take it (less frequent, more transfers).

By Taxi: A taxi between Piraeus and downtown Athens should cost about €25, and can take anywhere from 20-40 minutes, depending on traffic and on your starting/ending point at Piraeus. Uber works well, and is often cheaper.

By Bus to Bus Terminal A (Kifissou): For long-distance buses to the Peloponnese, you'll need to connect through Athens. To reach Athens' Bus Terminal A (Kifissou), take bus #420 (1-2/hour, catch bus at stop across the street from Gate E6).

Getting from Piraeus Cruise Terminals to Athens

Piraeus has three cruise terminals at two different docks. The main terminal—Terminal A ("Miaoulis")—is at dock E11. Farther out, dock E12 has two terminal buildings: Terminal B ("Themistocles") and Terminal C ("Alkimos"). For more details, see my *Rick Steves Mediterranean Cruise Ports* guidebook.

Getting to Athens: You can either hire a **taxi** (these wait outside the cruise terminals; €25 is a fair fare to downtown), summon an **Uber,** or arrange in advance for a **private car and driver** to pick you up from Piraeus and take you on an excursion around town (try one of my recommended drivers listed on page 36).

If you don't want to hire a taxi or driver, the easiest option is to pay for an all-day **hop-on, hop-off bus tour,** which stops at all the major sights in Athens (€16-20; for more info on the various hop-on, hop-off companies, see page 38). Catch these from outside each cruise terminal.

For a cheaper, public-transit option, **express bus #X80** is most direct. This designed-for-cruisers route takes you from outside the cruise terminals into Athens, stopping at Dionysiou Areopagitou (near the Acropolis Museum) and Syntagma Square (2/hour when cruise ships are in town, 1 hour). Or you can do a bus-plus-Metro combo: Ride local **bus #843** to the Piraeus Metro station (bus stop: Stathmos ISAP/ΣΤΑΘΜΟΣ Η.Σ.Α.Π.), then hop the **Metro** into downtown Athens. For any bus, you'll need to buy a ticket before you board—either at a newsstand kiosk or at a small ticket kiosk (usually located near a stop). For Terminal A, use bus stop Teloneio (ΤΕΛΩΝΕΙΟ); for Terminals B and C, it's Afetira (ΑΦΕΤΗΡΙΑ).

Getting from Piraeus to the Airport

From Piraeus, you can reach the airport by taxi (around €50) or by bus #X96, which goes directly to the airport (€6, runs 24 hours daily, 2-4/hour depending on time of day, 1-1.5 hours depending on traffic). In Piraeus, bus #X96 stops directly in front of the Metro station (Stathmos ISAP/ΣΤΑΘΜΟΣ Η.Σ.Α.Π. stop), and also along the top of Karaiskaki Square (Plateia Karaiskaki/ΠΛ. ΚΑΡΑΙΣΚΑΚΗ stop, between gates E7 and E8).

By Bus

Athens has two major intercity bus stations—both far from downtown, and neither conveniently reached by Metro. Buses serving the south, including the Peloponnese, use the bus station called Kifissou, or "Terminal A." Most buses serving the north, including Delphi, use the station called Liossion, or "Terminal B."

Although most destinations in this book are served by at least one daily direct bus from Athens, connecting between destinations outside Athens can involve several changes. Even though all Greek buses are operated by ΚΤΕΛ (KTEL), there's no useful general website or phone number (each region has its own website for its own schedules; some are better than others). There is a list of local phone numbers and websites at www.ktelbus.com, but you'll need to know the name of the province where you are traveling. You can get details for buses originating in Athens by phoning 14505.

TERMINAL A (KIFISSOU)

This bus station is about three miles northwest of the city center. Getting here on public transit is a pain involving a Metro-plus-bus connection (Metro to Omonia then bus #051) or a bus-plus-longish-walk (bus #12 from Syntagma Square to the Papathanasiou/ΠΑΠΑΘΑΝΑΣΙΟΥ stop, then 10 minutes by foot). It's easier to take a taxi (pay no more than €15 from central Athens). Buses from here head to southwest Greece.

In the station's vast ticket hall (follow signs to ΕΚΔΟΤΗΡΙΑ), the counters are divided by which region they serve; if you aren't sure which one you need, ask at the information desk near the main door. Beyond the ticket hall are a cafeteria, a restaurant, and a supermarket, and the door out to the buses. This immense bus barn is crammed with well-labeled bus stalls, which are organized—like the ticket windows—by region. Taxis wait out in front of the ticket hall, as well as under the canopy between the ticket hall and the bus stalls (Terminal A info tel. 210-512-4910).

There's also a ticket office for Terminal A a couple of blocks from Omonia Square at 59 Sokratous street—much closer to the city center (see map on page 31, look for ΕΚΔΟΤΗΡΙΑ sign; Mon-Fri 7:00-17:15, Sat 7:30-15:30, closed Sun, tel. 210-523-7889).

By Bus from Terminal A to: Nafplio (roughly hourly direct, 2.5 hours), **Epidavros** (2-3/day, 2.5 hours), **Mycenae** (go to Nafplio first, then 2-3/day, none on Sun, 45 minutes), **Olympia** (8/day, 5.5 hours, transfer in Pyrgos), **Monemvasia** (4-5/day, 6 hours), **Kardamyli** (1/day, transfer in Kalamata, 6 hours).

TERMINAL B (LIOSSION)

Smaller, more manageable, and a bit closer to the city center, Liossion (lee-oh-SEE-yohn) is in northwest Athens, a 15-minute, €8 taxi ride from the Plaka. You can also take the Metro to Attiki and then take any bus going north on Liossion street about a mile to Praktoria. Buses from here head northwest (Terminal B info tel. 210-831-7186).

By Bus from Terminal B to: Delphi (4-5/day, 3 hours).

By Train

Greek trains are of limited usefulness to travelers sticking to the destinations described in this book, as many routes were cut during financially difficult times (especially on the Peloponnese). That may change, as the Greek train system has been privatized (it was sold to Italian railway operator FS in 2017); however, it will take some time before it is up to Western European standards.

Though essentially useless if connecting south, the train does serve areas north of Athens well (such as Thessaloniki). If you do take the train from Athens, you'll most likely use **Larissa Station,** just north of downtown (on Metro line 2/red). For now, surviving trains are operated by Greek Railways (www.trainose.gr, or call customer service, which has English-speaking staff—open 24 hours, tel. 14511). For more extensive travels beyond Greece, you can study your options at www.ricksteves.com/rail.

By Car

RENTING A CAR

Syngrou avenue is Athens' "rental car lane," with all the established, predictable big companies (and piles of little ones) competing for your business. Syngrou is an easy walk from the Plaka and recommended hotels in Makrigianni and Koukaki. Budget travelers can often negotiate deals by checking with a few rental places and haggling. Or consider local company **Swift/Escape,** run by Elias and Salvador, who can help you drive out of central Athens to avoid the stress of city-center driving (1-day rental: €40-60 depending on size of car; 3-day rental: from €118 for compact; extra charge to drop car outside of Athens; open Mon-Sat 9:00-19:00, until 17:00 in winter, open Sun and after hours by request; at 43 Syngrou avenue, tel. 210-923-3919, www.greektravel.com/swift, elimano95@gmail.com).

ROUTE TIPS FOR DRIVERS

Avoid driving in Athens as much as possible—traffic is stressful, and parking is a headache. Before you leave Athens, get detailed directions from your rental agency on how to get back to their office and drop off your car.

Here's your strategy for getting out of the city: If you're heading north, such as to **Delphi,** aim for expressway 1 northbound (toward Lamia; see specific directions on page 369). To head for the **Peloponnese,** go westbound on expressway 6, which feeds into expressway 8 to Corinth (the gateway to the Peloponnese). The handy E-75 expressway (a.k.a. Kifissou avenue), which runs north-south just west of downtown Athens, offers an easy connection to either of these.

Assuming you pick up your car on or near Syngrou avenue, and traffic isn't that heavy, the best bet (with the fewest traffic lights and turns) is usually to simply head south on Syngrou. As you approach the water, the road forks; follow signs toward *Piraeus* on the left. After the merge, get into the right lane and be ready to hop on E-75 northbound. Then watch for your exit: for the Peloponnese, exit for expressway 6 (which merges into expressway 8 to Corinth); for Delphi, continue straight north to expressway 1.

CONNECTIONS

THE
PELOPONNESE
ΠΕΛΟΠΟΝΝΗΣΟΣ /
Πελοπόννησος

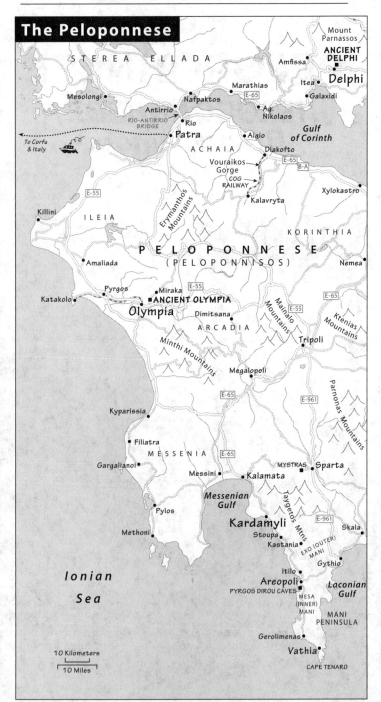

The Peloponnese

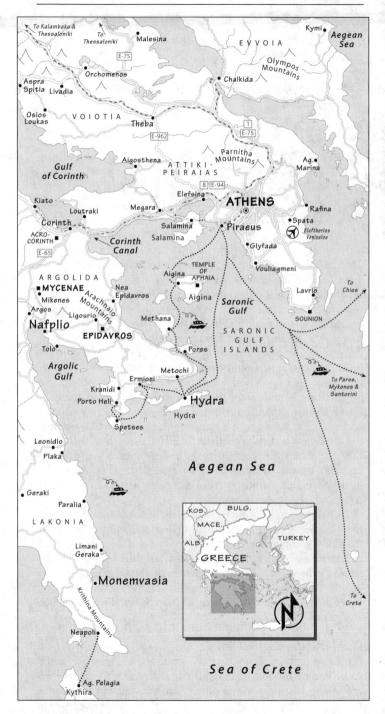

NAFPLIO

ΝΑΎΠΛΙΟ / Ναύπλιο

The charming Peloponnesian port town of Nafplio is small, cozy, and strollable. Though it has plenty of tourism, Nafplio is both elegant and proud. It's a must-see on any Greek visit because of its historical importance, its accessibility from Athens (an easy 2.5-hour drive or bus ride), and its handy location as a home base for touring the ancient sites of Epidavros and Mycenae (each a short drive away and described in the next two chapters). Nafplio has great pensions, appealing restaurants, fine beaches, a thriving evening scene, and a good balance of real life and tourist convenience.

Nafplio is understandably proud of its special footnotes in Greek history. Thanks to its highly strategic position—nestled under cliffs at the apex of a vast bay—it changed hands between the Ottomans and the Venetians time and again. But Nafplio ultimately distinguished itself in the 1820s by becoming the first capital of a newly independent Greece, headed by President Ioannis Kapodistrias. Although those glory days have faded, the town retains a certain genteel panache.

Owing to its prestigious past, Nafplio's harbor is guarded by three castles: one on a small island (Bourtzi), another just above the Old Town (ancient Akronafplia), and a third capping a tall cliff above the city (Palamidi Fortress). All three are wonderfully floodlit at night. If you're not up for the climb to Palamidi, explore Nafplio's narrow and atmospheric back streets, lined with elegant Venetian houses and Neoclassical mansions, and dip into its likeable museums.

PLANNING YOUR TIME

Nafplio is light on sightseeing opportunities, but heavy on ambience. Two nights and one day is more than enough time to enjoy everything the town has to offer. With one full day in Nafplio,

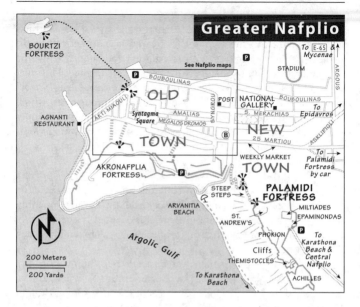

consider the arduous hike up to the Palamidi Fortress first thing in the morning, before the worst heat of the day (bring water and wear good shoes; to save time and sweat, you can also drive or taxi there). Then get your bearings in the Old Town by following my self-guided walk, and visit any museums that appeal to you. In the afternoon, hit the beach. (If you get a late start, do the hike in the early evening.)

Nafplio also serves as an ideal launch pad for visiting two of the Peloponnese's best ancient sites (each about a 30-minute drive and covered in the next two chapters): the best-preserved ancient theater anywhere, at **Epidavros;** and the older-than-old hilltop fortress of **Mycenae.** It's worth adding a day to your Nafplio stay to fit these in. If you have a **car,** you can see both of these (and drive up to the Palamidi Fortress) in a full day; for an even more efficient plan, consider squeezing them in on your way into or out of town (for example, notice that Mycenae is between Nafplio and the major E-65 expressway to the north). These sites are also reachable by **bus.** While it's possible to do them both by bus on the same day, for a more relaxed approach consider two full days in Nafplio, spending a half-day at each site, and two half-days in the town.

Orientation to Nafplio

Because everything of interest is concentrated in the peninsular Old Town, Nafplio feels smaller than its population of 15,000. The mostly traffic-free Old Town is squeezed between the hilltop Akronafplia fortress and the broad seafront walkways of Bouboulinas and Akti Miaouli; the core of this area has atmospherically tight pedestrian lanes, bursting with restaurants and shops. Syntagma Square (Plateia Syntagmatos) is the centerpiece of the Old Town. From here traffic-free Vasileos Konstantinou—called "Big Street" (Megalos Dromos) by locals—runs east to Syngrou street, which separates the Old Town from the New Town. The tranquil upper part of the Old Town, with some of my favorite accommodations, is connected by stepped lanes.

TOURIST INFORMATION

Nafplio's TI is just inside Town Hall, on Town Hall Square (daily 9:00-20:00, tel. 27520-24444). Check locally to confirm opening hours for sights and museums given in this chapter. If side-tripping out to Epidavros or Mycenae in the off-season, call to double-check opening times.

Note that the town's name can be spelled in a number of ways in English: Nafplio, Nauplio, Navplio, Naufplio, Nauvplio, and so on—and all these variations may also appear with an "n" at the end (Nafplion, etc.).

ARRIVAL IN NAFPLIO

By Car: Parking is free, easy, and central along the port, which runs in front of the Old Town (look for the big lots). If you're staying higher up, ask your hotel about more convenient parking (for example, near the old, abandoned Hotel Xenia on the road up to the Akronafplia fortress).

By Bus: The bus station is conveniently located half a block off Syngrou street, right where the Old Town meets the New; from here all my recommended accommodations are within a 10-minute walk.

HELPFUL HINTS

Market Days: A market featuring local products like honey, wine, and olives takes over Martiou street on Wednesdays and Saturdays until 14:00.

Festivals: Nafplio hosts a classical music festival in late June. It features a mix of Greek and international performers playing at such venues as the Palamidi and Bourtzi fortresses (details at TI). The town is also a good base for seeing drama and music performances at the famous Theater of Epidavros during the Athens & Epidavros Festival (weekends in July-Aug; see page 200). The local bus company operates special buses to the festival.

Post Office: The post office is at the corner of Syngrou and Sidiras Merarchias (Mon-Fri 7:30-20:00, Sat 7:30-14:00, closed Sun).

Bookstores: Odyssey sells international newspapers, maps, local guidebooks, and paperbacks in English (long hours daily, on Syntagma Square next to the National Bank building, tel. 27520-23430).

Travel Agency and Car Rental: Stavropoulos Tours, conveniently located near the bus station, can help you book flights and boat tickets anywhere in Greece (handy for trips you may be planning within the Aegean Islands or to Hydra), and provides bus information (Mon-Fri 9:30-14:30 & 18:00-21:00, Sat 9:30-14:30, closed Sun, also closed Mon in winter, credit cards accepted with small fee, 24 Plapouta street, tel. 27520-25915, mobile 694-777-9162, www.stavropoulostours.gr, helpful Theodore). Several **car rental** places are nearby (across from the Land Gate on Syngrou street).

Local Guide: Patty Staikou is a charming Nafplio native who enjoys sharing her town and nearby ancient sites with visitors (about €50/hour, she'll meet you at Epidavros or Mycenae, mobile 697-778-3315, staipatt@yahoo.gr).

Nafplio Walk

This self-guided walk, which takes about 1.5 hours, will give you a feel for Nafplio's pleasant Old Town.

• *We'll begin on the harborfront square opposite the fortified island, marked by a sturdy obelisk.*

❶ Square of the Friends of the Greeks (Plateia Filellinon)

This space is named for the French soldiers who fell while fighting for Greek independence in 1821. On the memorial ❷ **obelisk,**

a classical-style medallion shows brothers in arms: Hellas and Gallia (Greeks and French). On the other side is the French inscription.

You might see a cruise ship docked here on the **waterfront.** The port was deepened a few years back to accommodate a busy cruise industry (bigger ships, however, still drop anchor around the bend).

Plenty of Nafplio bars, cafés, restaurants, and tavernas face the harbor. The embankment called ❸ **Akti Miaouli** promenades to the left with a long line of sedate al fresco tables. (These places are worth an extra euro or two for the view.) The promenade becomes a scenic shoreline path that continues all the way around the point to Ar-

NAFPLIO

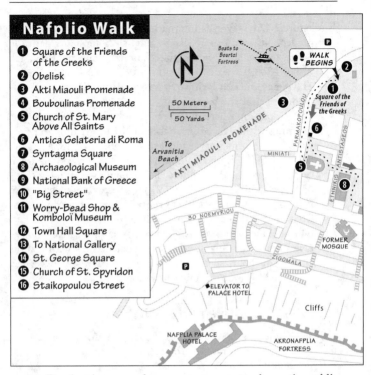

Nafplio Walk

1. Square of the Friends of the Greeks
2. Obelisk
3. Akti Miaouli Promenade
4. Bouboulinas Promenade
5. Church of St. Mary Above All Saints
6. Antica Gelateria di Roma
7. Syntagma Square
8. Archaeological Museum
9. National Bank of Greece
10. "Big Street"
11. Worry-Bead Shop & Komboloï Museum
12. Town Hall Square
13. To National Gallery
14. St. George Square
15. Church of St. Spyridon
16. Staikopoulou Street

vanitia Beach, where a road returns to town up and over the saddle between the two fortresses.

The ❹ **Bouboulinas** promenade heads in the other direction (to the right, as you face the water)—first passing fine and recommended fish tavernas and then a string of bars.

From the harbor, you can also see the three Venetian forts of Nafplio (and another across the bay). The mighty little for-

tress island just offshore, called **Bourtzi,** was built during the first Venetian occupation (15th century) to protect the harbor. Most of what you see today is an 18th-century reconstruction from the second Venetian occupation. A shuttle boat departs from here to visit the island. It's

a fun little trip, but there's little to see beyond a pleasant city view (described later, under "Nafplio's Three Venetian Fortresses").

Capping the hill high above is the **Palamidi Fortress** (highest, to the left). Locals claim that the Palamidi Fortress, built in just three years (1711-1714), is the best-preserved Venetian fort in the Mediterranean. It can be reached by climbing nearly a thousand

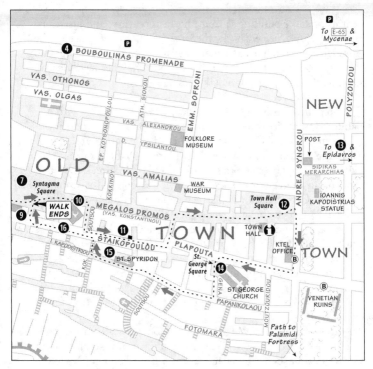

stone stairs...or by paying around €7 for a taxi. (I taxi up and walk down.) The view is rewarding, but the building itself is a bulky, impressive, empty shell. Below the Palamidi Fortress and to the right is Nafplio's ancient acropolis, the **Akronafplia fortress,** built upon the remains of an ancient fort. The big stones at the base of its wall date from the third century B.C.

Across the bay and in the distance beyond the island fort of Bourtzi is a **fourth Venetian fort,** dramatically capping a hill. This 300-year-old fort is built upon the ancient Acropolis of Argos (which dates from the Mycenaean Age, about 1500 B.C.).

With all this defensive investment, you can imagine how much Venice valued this strategic city as a trade and naval station. Today, locals still call the bay "Porto Catena." That's Italian for "Chain Port," as chains once were strung from the island fort to the mainland in order to control ship traffic.

• *With your back to the water, walk up the street to the right of Hotel Grande Bretagne (Farmakopoulou). After a block, on the first corner (left), is a popular gelateria. Resist temptation for just a minute and first head across the small square to the...*

❺ Church of St. Mary Above All Saints

This church has a proud history: It originally dates from the 15th century; today's building is from the 18th century; and just a few years ago, they peeled back, then reapplied, all the plaster. The priest at this church is particularly active, keeping it open late into the evening (long after many other Nafplio churches have closed). Outside the door he posts a daily message—a thought to ponder or a suggested prayer.

Step inside—it's generally open. The flat ceiling with the painted Trinity in three circular panels shows a Venetian influence—most Greek Orthodox churches of this period are domed. The more typical iconostasis, a wall of Greek Orthodox icons, separates worshippers from priests. As is standard in Greek churches, the icon in the center changes with the season. In the front left corner are Q-tips and little plastic baggies for taking home priest-blessed oil. ("If you believe, then it heals.") A glass case in the same corner shows off relics (mostly bones of saints) and little treasures (such as the Ostrich Egg, painted in Russia and symbolic of the Resurrection). There are a few more museum cases on the right. If you're so moved, drop in a coin for a candle (near the entry) and light up a prayer. Notice the heavy-duty venting for the busy candle trays and the icon above the candles featuring the saint-protected city of Nafplio.

The mural just outside the church (on the wall, to the right of the door as you leave) is something of a nationalistic history of Greece in a nutshell. Follow it, starting with Adam and Eve to the Golden Age of ancient Greece (featuring Socrates, Plato, Aristotle, and others), the founding of Christianity and the Greek church, the building of the monasteries at Meteora, the Ottoman occupation (see the Greek priest being hanged by a Turk), independence (with a banner that says "democracy" in Greek), World Wars I and II (find the Nazi with a gun and a Greek resistance hero mightily perched on a rock), and finally, the Greek version of heaven, which looks like Meteora.

• *Now dip into...*

❻ Antica Gelateria di Roma

Greece has great honey-dripping desserts, but nobody does ice cream like the Italians. This popular, fun-loving, air-conditioned ice-cream parlor is run by Marcello and family, who offer a taste of Italy: gelato, fruit-based *sorbetto*, as well as other treats such as biscotti, *limoncello*, and cappuccino. This is one holdover from the Venetian occupation that no local will complain about. (For more details on this *gelateria*, see "Eating in Nafplio," later).

• *Gelato in hand, exit Marcello's; go left behind the church and into the big square.*

❼ Syntagma Square (Plateia Syntagmatos)

Like the main square in Athens, Nafplio's central plaza is dubbed "Constitution Square," celebrating the 1843 document that estab-

lished a constitutional monarchy for Greece. Nafplio was one of the first towns liberated from the Ottoman Turks (1822), and became the new country's first capital. The square is a delightful mix of architectural styles, revealing the many layers of local history.

Survey this scene in a counterclockwise spin-tour, starting on your immediate right. The big building flying the Greek flag was originally the Venetian arsenal. Of course, wherever Venice ruled, you'll find its symbol: the winged lion of its patron saint, Mark (over the door). The building is stout with heavily barred windows because it once stored gunpowder and weapons. Today it houses the town's ❽ **Archaeological Museum** (described later, under "Sights in Nafplio").

Just to the left of the museum is a domed former **mosque.** In 1825, with the Muslim Ottomans expelled, this building was taken over and renovated to house independent Greece's first parliament. (Now it serves as a conference center.)

The big ❾ **National Bank of Greece** harkens back to the very earliest Greek civilizations, with its dark-red columns that taper

toward the base, as if they were tree trunks stood on their heads (shaped and painted just like the ones in the circa-1500 b.c. Minoan palaces on Crete). In front of the bank stands another Venetian winged lion from the old fortress. The second former

mosque fronting this square (see red tile domes at the far end) was converted after independence into Greece's first primary school; today it's a gallery and theater. To the left, look up past the popular cafés and restaurants to appreciate the square's series of stately Neoclassical buildings. The square is a popular hangout for parents enjoying coffee while their kids run wild—future soccer stars-in-training.

• *Head across the square and walk down the pedestrian street (opposite the side you entered).*

⓾ The "Big Street" (Megalos Dromos)

Nafplio's main drag, connecting the main square with Town Hall Square, is named for King Constantine (Vasileos Konstantinou). Locals know it as Megalos Dromos ("Big Street").

The town is something of a shoppers' paradise—many streets are crammed with shops selling everything from the usual tacky tourist trinkets to expensive jewelry, all aimed at the fat wallets of Athenian weekenders. This is a fine scene in the early evening when everyone's out strolling.

• *Turn right at the first corner up the narrow alley (Soutsou), then turn left onto touristy Staikopoulou. After about a block, on the left (at #25), is a...*

⓫ Worry-Bead Shop

This shop features a remarkable selection of worry beads—the cheapest, synthetic sets cost about €8; the priciest, which can cost hundreds of euros, are antique or made of amber (for more information on worry beads, see page 199). The **Komboloï Museum** upstairs shows off a few small rooms of the owner's vast collection, while a handful of English labels explain how variations on worry beads are used by many different faiths (€2, generally open 9:30-20:00). A few doors farther down you'll find the shops of an olive-tree woodcarver and a sandal maker.

• *At the next intersection, turn left and walk one block back down to the "Big Street." Turn right onto the "Big Street" and follow it until you emerge into...*

⓬ Town Hall Square

A statue marks the one-time location of the palace of **King Otto** (ΟΘΩΝ), the first head of state of post-Ottoman Greece. (The great powers—England, France, and Russia—insisted that the newly independent Greeks have a monarchy, so Otto was imported from Bavaria.) He wasn't here for long, though: An enthusiastic student of classical history, Otto was

NAFPLIO

charmed by the idea of reviving the greatness of ancient Athens, and moved the capital to Athens after just one year. (The palace that stood here burned down in 1929.)

Otto, looking plenty regal, gazes toward the New Town. Fifty yards in front of Otto (on the right) is the Neoclassical "first high school of Greece"—today's Town Hall, and home to the TI. The monument in front celebrates a local hero from the war against the Ottomans. Until recently this square was named "Three Admirals Square"—remembering those three great European powers that helped the Greeks overthrow their Ottoman rulers in the 1820s.

• *At the far end of Town Hall Square, you hit the busy...*

Syngrou Street and the New Town

This thoroughfare separates the Old Town from the New. Out of respect for the three-story-tall Old Town, no new building is allowed to exceed that height—even in the New Town.

In the square across the street, a statue honors **Ioannis Kapodistrias,** the president of Greece's short-lived republic (back when Nafplio was the capital). He faces the Old Town...and Otto, who stepped in when the president's reign was cut tragically short. (We'll get the whole story later.)

Just behind Kapodistrias is a family-friendly **park.** If you want a cheap and fast meal, consider grabbing a bite at one of the family-filled gyros and souvlaki eateries surrounding the park (order and pay at the bar, then find a bench in the park). Goody's (on the left, by the post office) is the local kids' favorite hamburger joint, found all over Greece.

A few minutes' walk straight ahead, past the end of the park, is the ⓭ **National Gallery,** which shows off evocative artwork from the Greek War of Independence (described later, under "Sights in Nafplio").

Facing Ioannis, head south (right) on Syngrou street. The commotion at the end of the block surrounds Nafplio's tiny but busy **bus station.** KTEL (or KTEΛ in Greek) is the national bus company; in its office, you can try buying tickets from the counter, or get friendlier customer service buying directly from the driver or the ticket machine out front (if it's working, cash only).

At the next corner we'll turn right. But first, just behind the row of buses, you'll see the ruined remains of Nafplio's **Land Gate,** part of the city's 18th-century Venetian fortifications. Take a little loop from here through the gate and study the amazing Venetian stone defensive work around and above you.

• *Return to the corner, and head back into the Old Town on Plapouta street. Walk to...*

❿ St. George Square

The focal point of the square, Nafplio's *mitropolis* (equivalent to a Catholic cathedral), is dedicated to St. George and was the neighborhood church for King Otto (whose palace was once on Town Hall Square, which we walked through earlier). Step into the church's dark interior (noticing the clever system that prevents the doors from slamming) to see a gigantic chandelier hovering overhead.

Back outside, surveying St. George Square, you get a feel for an old Nafplio neighborhood. Like most of the Old Town, well-worn Neoclassical buildings date from the boom that followed the city's rise to prominence when it was Greece's first capital. During the 1820s and 1830s, Nafplio became a haven to refugees from other lands still threatened by the Ottomans.

• *Walk a block slightly uphill (toward the fortress) and turn right on Papanikolaou street.*

Upper Streets of the Old Town

Strolling this quiet lane, note that the Neoclassical grid-planned town is to your right, while the higgledy-piggledy Ottoman town climbs the hillside (with winding and evocative lanes and stepped alleys) on your left. Consider as you walk how Greece's struggling economy leaves so many buildings with such potential in abandoned shambles.

Straight ahead (100 yards away) stands the white bell tower marking the ⓯ **Church of St. Spyridon** and its square. Facing the square (on the left, hiding in a niche in the wall, near the steps) is the first of several 18th-century Turkish fountains you'll see. When the Ottomans controlled Greece, they still used the Arabic script you see here, rather than the Latin alphabet used for modern Turkish. This panel names the guy who paid for the fountain, tells

when he had it built (1734-1735), and why (to provide water for his horses). Other fountains have similar tributes, verses from the Quran, or
jaunty greetings.

Continue straight along the side of the church to another **Ottoman fountain** (on the left)—with its characteristic cypress-tree-and-flowers decor.

Between here and the door of the church (on the right) is the spot marking the rough equivalent—to the Greeks—of Ford's Theater (where Lincoln was assassinated). Ioannis Kapodistrias was elected the first president of independent Greece in 1828. But just three years later, in 1831, he was shot and stabbed in this spot by Mani landowners who feared his promises of land reform. This led to chaos, less democratic idealism, and the arrival of Greece's imported Bavarian royalty (King Otto, whom we met earlier).

Pop into the church if it's open. Across from the church is a collapsing *hamam*, a Turkish bath from the 18th century.

• *At the next corner (Kokkinou street), turn right and climb down the slippery marble steps to Staikopoulou street (where we saw the worry bead shop, earlier). This time we'll take it left, back to Syntagma Square.*

⑯ Staikopoulou Street

This bustling pedestrian drag is lined with grill restaurants (the harborfront is better for fish) and their happy hustlers, and another fine Ottoman fountain (on the right after a block).

A couple of blocks down, head right and back into Syntagma Square. Find the tiny black cube in the center and sit on it. Apart from being a handy meeting point for the town's kids and a stand for the community Christmas tree, it means absolutely nothing.

• *Your walk is over. From here you can enjoy the rest of the city. In addition to the museums we've already passed (which you can circle back to now), a few more sights—including a folklore museum and a war museum—are within a few blocks. Adventurers may want to head to any of Nafplio's Venetian forts. Or, if you're ready to relax, hit the beach (all described under "Sights and Activities in Nafplio," next).*

Sights and Activities in Nafplio

MUSEUMS

▲▲Nafplio Archaeological Museum

Nafplio's top museum gives a concise overview of prehistoric Greece and the Mycenaean civilization. Visit here for a great warm-up before you go to Mycenae.

Cost and Hours: €6, includes lengthy audioguide; generally Tue-Sun 8:00-15:00, closed Mon; at the bottom of Syntagma Square, tel. 27520-27502, www.culture.gr.

Visiting the Museum: The museum occupies the top two floors of the grand Venetian arsenal on the main square.

The delightful little collection (starting on the ground floor, well-described in English) was excavated from nearby tombs. While nothing here is from Mycenae itself, many of the artifacts date from the same late Bronze Age (c. 1500 B.C.)—a reminder that the region is rich in late Bronze Age sites. The display runs in chronological order, with Stone Age tools suddenly giving way to dolphin frescoes inspired by the Minoan civilization on Crete. Eye-catching jewelry includes a bull-shaped crystal bead (look for the magnifying glass inside a glass case) and strings of gold beads.

The star of the museum stands in the center: the "Dendra Panoply," a 15th-century B.C. suit of bronze armor that was discovered in a Mycenaean chamber tomb. Also found at the site (and displayed here) is a helmet made from boar tusks. Experts consider this the oldest surviving suit of armor in all of Europe.

The second floor displays artifacts from the Age of Homer to the Roman occupation. Particularly striking are the ceremonial

terra-cotta masks along one wall. Dating from the seventh century B.C., these likely were designed to scare off evil spirits. Check out the display of rare glasswork from the first century A.D.—somehow these pieces have survived two millennia without getting smashed.

NAFPLIO

▲National Gallery
(Alexandros Soutzos Museum, Nafplio Annex)

Housed in a grandly restored Neoclassical mansion, this museum features both temporary and permanent exhibits. The permanent collection, displayed upstairs, is de-voted to Romantic artwork (mostly paintings) stemming from the in-spirational Greek War of Independence (1821-1829), which led to Nafplio's status as the first capital of independent Greece. The small, manageable collection is arranged thematically. The English descriptions here are worth reading, as they explain the historical underpinnings for the art, illuminating common themes such as the dying hero, naval battles, and the hardships of

war. The art itself might not be technically masterful, but the patriotism shimmering beneath it is stirring even to non-Greeks.

Cost and Hours: €3, free on Mon; open Mon and Wed-Sat 10:00-15:00, Wed and Fri also 17:00-20:00, Sun 10:00-14:00, closed Tue; a 5-minute walk into the New Town from the post office along a major road called Sidiras Merarchias, at #23, tel. 27520-21915, www.culture.gr.

Peloponnese Folklore Foundation Museum

Dedicated to Peloponnesian culture, this modern exhibit fills two floors with clothing, furniture, and jewelry that trace the cultural history of Nafplio and the surrounding region. While not explained in a particularly engaging way, the interesting collection—which ranges from colorful and traditional costumes, to stiff urban suits, to formal gowns, to looms and spinning wheels—is at least well-displayed.

Cost and Hours: €2; Mon-Sat 9:00-14:30, Sun 9:30-15:00, fun gift shop with Greek crafts, Vasileos Alexandrou 1, tel. 27520-28379, www.pli.gr.

War Museum (Nafplio Branch)

This small exhibit, operated and staffed by the Greek armed forces, is best left to ardent Greek patriots and military buffs; for most others it's not worth the small admission fee. It displays old illustrations and photos of various conflicts (some providing a peek into Nafplio's past cityscape), plus weapons and uniforms (with some English descriptions). The top floor, dedicated to the modern era, displays some interesting WWII-era political cartoons from the Greek perspective.

Cost and Hours: €3; Tue-Sun 9:00-19:00, off-season until 17:00, closed Mon, on Amalias, tel. 27520-25591, www.warmuseum.gr.

NAFPLIO'S THREE VENETIAN FORTRESSES

In the days when Venice was the economic ruler of Europe (15th-18th centuries), the Venetians fortified Nafplio with a trio of

stout fortresses. These attempted—but ultimately failed—to fend off Ottoman invasion. Conquered by the Ottomans in 1715, Nafplio remained in Turkish hands until the Greeks retook the city in 1822. Today all three parts of the Venetian fortifications are open to visitors (with nothing to see but stones and views). These are listed in order from lowest to highest.

Bourtzi

While this heavily fortified island—just offshore from Nafplio's waterfront—looks striking, there's not much to do here (pictured above). Still, it's a pleasant vantage point, offering fine views back on the city.

Cost and Hours: Boats depart regularly from the bottom of the square called Friends of the Greeks/Plateia Filellinon, €4.50 round-trip, won't run with fewer than 4 people, check sign on promenade for next departure, once on island it's free to enter the fortress, tel. 69777-16998.

Akronafplia

Nafplio's ancient acropolis, capping the low hill just behind the Old Town, is fairly easy to reach (a manageable but sometimes-steep

10- to 15-minute uphill hike—from the Old Town, just find your way up on any of a number of narrow stepped lanes, then bear left to reach the main road that leads up into the eastern end of the fortress). The earliest surviving parts of this fortress date back to the third century B.C., but the Venetians brought it up to then-modern standards in the 15th century. Up top, there's little to see aside from a few ruins (free to enter and explore anytime). The top of the parklike hill is flanked by two modern hotels: At the east end (toward

Palamidi), stands the deserted and decaying Hotel Xenia; and at the west end (below a little heliport at the end of the road), the top-of-the-top Nafplia Palace hotel entices you to enjoy a drink from its terrace café. You can avoid the hike up by riding the elevator from the top of the Old Town to this hotel (see "Nafplio Walk" map).

▲▲Palamidi Fortress

This imposing hilltop fortress, built by the Venetians between 1711 and 1714, is the best-preserved of its kind in Greece. Palamidi tow-

ers over the Old Town, protected to the west by steep cliffs that plunge 650 feet to the sea. From its highest ramparts, you can spot several Aegean islands and look deep into the mountainous interior of the Peloponnesian Peninsula.

Cost and Hours: €8, €4 off-season, daily 8:30-sunset (or earlier), tel. 27520-28036. If you plan to go in the afternoon, call first to confirm the closing time.

Getting There: You can reach the fortress the old-fashioned way: by **climbing** the loooong flight of 999 steps that leads up from

the road to Akronafplia fortress (near the top end of Polyzoidou street and the bus stop, just outside the Old Town). The toughest part of the climb is the heat: Bring water, and either get an early start or go later in the day.

Alternatively, you can catch a **taxi** to the top for about €7 one-way (and perhaps take the steps down). If you have a car, you can **drive** to the top and park for free: Follow signs east of town for the beach at *Karathona*/Καραθώνα, and after ascending the hill, watch for the turnoff on the right up to *Palamidi*/Παλαμηδη.

Services: WCs are just outside the St. Andrew's Bastion, near the ticket kiosk for hill climbers, and in the parking lot.

Visiting the Fortress: The fortress is actually a collection of fortresses or bastions within its exterior walls. Notice how the various bastions could defend themselves against each other if attackers breached the outer walls or one of the bastions was taken. You can navigate with the pamphlet included with your ticket and by following the handy signs and info posts you'll see throughout. St. Andrew's Bastion is the main bastion to visit. I'd study this one and then just explore the other bastions with a sense of fun and wonder.

St. Andrew's Bastion (Agios Andreas) is the best preserved and offers great views over the rooftops of old Nafplio. Inside,

find the small church. Behind it, under the first archway, is a tiny entrance leading to the cell of the miserable little Kolokotronis Prison (you'll need to crouch and scramble to get inside). While untrue, Greeks love the legend that the Greek hero, Theodoros Kolokotronis, was imprisoned here by his political opponents after playing a key role in liberating Greece from Ottoman rule. Back outside, scamper up the giant vaults, which form an angled approach up to the ramparts. Imagine that the entire vault structure functioned as a cistern. Enjoy the views.

ACTIVITIES
Beaches
When ready for some beach time or a swim you have three good choices in and near Nafplio (all free, with easy parking and showers): Arvanitia (in town), Karathona (1.5 miles away via a lovely walk), and Tolo (6 miles away, with good bus connections).

Arvanitia Beach, on the backside of the peninsula, is a 10-minute walk from the Old Town (walk over the saddle between the two forts or along the pedes-

trian path leading from the Old Town and around the peninsula). It's a small, pebbly beach with clear, deep water. Crowded in summer, it's popular with the young crowd and has a bar and a free open-air gym workout zone in the parking lot.

Karathona Beach is for more serious beach-going. This half-mile-long sandy beach with shallow water is popular with families, dotted with beachfront tavernas, and lined with palm trees. From Nafplio's Arvanitia Beach you can walk there in 30 minutes along the delightful seafront lane.

Tolo Beach, the best beach of all with nice sand and shallow water, is farther away (6 miles from Nafplio, hourly buses from bus station). You'll find plenty of services (hotels, restaurants, rental paddle boats, and a small town of shops and cafés).

Walking

One of the great delights of a Nafplio visit is to take a stroll along the waterfront. Locals are understandably proud of their tree-lined, peaceful, and scenic walking and jogging lane that circles the peninsula from the town center to Arvanitia Beach and Karathona Beach. Start on the promenade nearest the island fort and walk out onto the spit, and then continue around the peninsula to Arvanitia Beach. For a longer walk, continue another 1.5 miles from Arvanitia to Karathona Beach, passing beneath the Palamidi Fortress on the way. While you can circle back to the town center from Karathona Beach via the New Town, most people prefer to retrace their steps along the waterfront.

Wine Tasting at the Karonis Wine Shop

Dimitri Karonis specializes in Greek wines and ouzo, and gives serious wine shoppers an informative wine tasting (Mon-Sat 8:30-14:00 & 18:00-21:30, closed Sun, near Syntagma Square at Amalias 5, call or email ahead to set up more in-depth tasting for €5-8, tel. 27520-24446, info@karoniswineshop.gr).

SIGHTS NEAR NAFPLIO

Both of these ancient attractions are within a half-hour drive of Nafplio (in different directions) and covered in the next two chapters.

▲▲▲Epidavros

This ancient site, 23 miles (by car) east of Nafplio, has an underwhelming museum, forgettable ruins...and the most magnificent theater of the ancient world. It was built nearly 2,500 years ago to seat 15,000. Today it's kept busy reviving the greatest plays of antiquity. You can catch musical and dramatic performances from July through August. Try to see Epidavros either early or late in the day; the theater's marvelous acoustics are best enjoyed in near-solitude.

▲▲▲Mycenae

This was the capital of the Mycenaeans, who won the Trojan War and dominated Greece 1,000 years before the Acropolis and other Golden Age Greek sights. The classical Greeks marveled at the huge stones and workmanship of the Mycenaean ruins. Visitors today can still gape at the Lion's Gate; peer into a cool, ancient cistern; and explore the giant *tholos* tomb called the Treasury of Atreus. The tomb, built in the 15th century B.C., is like a huge underground igloo, with a vast subterranean dome of cleverly arranged stones.

Nightlife in Nafplio

Nafplio enjoys a thriving after-hours scene with several nightlife microclimates—the age of the clientele varies every few blocks. I enjoy simply joining the evening strolling scene at all these places. For the best sunset stroll, head down the promenade Akti Miaouli and then out on the spit to the tiny lighthouse. Poke around to find the café or bar that appeals to you most for a pre- or post-dinner drink. Note that there are no true dance clubs in Nafplio, which has a strict noise ordinance: No loud music in the Old Town after 23:00. (Instead, huge seasonal outdoor clubs sprout along the roads leading out of town.) A few zones to consider:

Akti Miaouli Promenade: The upper crust enjoys the cafés lining the promenade Akti Miaouli. Prices are higher, but the water views (with the illuminated island fortress) might be worth the expense. At its farthest southern end is a lively playground and a fun, youthful place for drinks. This promenade leads to the break-water spit and then to the path leading both romantically and sce-nically around the peninsula.

Bouboulinas Promenade and Beyond: Beyond the fish restaurants are several café/bars—once *the* place to be seen, they now provide a peaceful setting for a drink. A block beyond the Bouboulinas promenade is a stretch of teen-friendly fast-food plac-es (Trendy Grill, pizza, bakery), described later under "Eating in Nafplio."

Syntagma Square and Nearby: People of all ages seem to enjoy the floodlit marble drawing-room vibe of Syntagma Square.

Cafés and restaurants with ample, atmospheric al fresco seating surround a relaxed open area with people at play. Kids hap-pily run free in the square, playing soccer into the wee hours. From Syn-tagma, the street called

NAFPLIO

Konstantinou is home to several popular café/bars. To find them, just follow the noise.

Arvanitia Beach: BluBlanc Beach Bar comes out of hibernation every summer at Arvanitia Beach, transforming it from a popular swimming spot by day into a dance party at night (May-Sept, tel. 27520-96031).

Cinema: The local cinema (at Kolokotronis Park) plays movies in their original languages with Greek subtitles. In summer, the theater moves nearby into the open air.

Sleeping in Nafplio

Nafplio enjoys an abundance of excellent accommodations. Because this is a chic getaway for wealthy Athenians, many of the best beds are in well-run, boutique-ish little pensions. (Some of the smaller pensions are run by skeleton staffs, so don't expect 24-hour reception; let them know what time you'll arrive so they can greet you.) The many options allow hotel seekers to be picky.

It's boom or bust in Nafplio. At the busiest times (June, July, especially Aug, and weekends year-round), hotels are full and prices go up; outside these times, hoteliers are lean and hungry, and rates become soft. Don't be afraid to ask for a deal, especially if you're staying more than a couple of nights. If your hotel doesn't include breakfast, most cafés in town sell a basic breakfast for €5-6.

Most of these accommodations are uphill from the heart of the Old Town. The good news: They provide fresh breezes, have almost no mosquitoes, and offer a quiet retreat from the bustling old center. The bad news: You'll climb a few flights of stairs to reach your room.

$$$ Ippoliti Hotel (ΙΠΠΟΛΥΤΗ) is a classy business-hotel splurge, with 19 elegantly decorated, hardwood-floor rooms with antique touches. In summer, breakfast is served on the patio beside the small swimming pool (elevator, small gym, near waterfront at Ilia Miniati 9, at corner with Aristidou, tel. 27520-96088, www.ippoliti.gr, info@ippoliti.gr).

$$ Amfitriti Palazzo's seven plush rooms, highest up, have balconies with sweeping views and fun classy-mod decor, with some rooms built right into the rock (family room, top of the hill—just under the old wall, tel. 27520-96250, www.amfitriti-pension.gr, info@amfitriti-pension.gr, Aggeliki and family).

$$ Amymone Pension (Αμυμώνη) and **Adiandi Hotel** (Αδιάντη) are a pair of super-stylish, trendy boutique hotels that share an owner and are a few doors apart along one of Nafplio's most inviting restaurant lanes. The anything-but-cookie-cutter rooms all have different color schemes, decor, and boldly painted headboards made from recycled materials, such as doors. Their ju-

NAFPLIO

Accommodations
1. Ippoliti Hotel
2. Amfitriti Palazzo Hotel
3. Amymone Pension & Adiandi Hotel
4. Pension Marianna
5. Byron Hotel
6. Hotel Leto Nuevo
7. Chroma Design Hotel & Suites
8. Aetoma Hotel
9. Pension Rigas
10. Pension Filyra
11. Pension Anapli

Eateries & Other
12. Mezedopoleio O Noulis
13. Taverna Paleo Arhontiko
14. I Gonia tou Kavalari
15. Kastro Karima
16. Alaloum Restaurant
17. Aiolos Taverna
18. To Omorfo Tavernaki
19. Arapakos Restaurant
20. Agnanti
21. Trattoria La Gratella
22. Mitato Souvlaki
23. Gyro Grill & Pizza Alpha
24. Trendy Grill Strip
25. Supermarket
26. Antica Gelateria di Roma
27. Karonis Wine Shop
28. Odyssey Bookshop
29. Travel Agency

nior suites have balconies, sitting areas, and computers. The very central location can come with more noise than my other listings, and both hotels have lots of stairs with no elevator. The Amymone has eight rooms (Othonos 39, tel. 27520-99477 or 27520-22073, www.amymone.gr, info@amymone.gr), while the Adiandi has seven rooms (Othonos 31, same telephone as above, www.hotel-adiandi.com, info@hotel-adiandi.com).

$$ Pension Marianna is my choice for the most welcoming place in town. The friendly Zotos brothers—Petros, Panos, and Takis—offer genuine hospitality, fair rates, and comfortable rooms in their stony little paradise. It's scenically situated just under the lower Akronafplia wall, well worth the steep climb up the stairs from the Old Town. The 26 rooms—some with views and/or little balconies—are scattered throughout several levels. Atop it all is an airy terrace where you can enjoy a breakfast made up of organic products from their nearby farm (RS%, family rooms, breakfast extra, no elevator, Potamianou 9, tel. 27520-24256, www.hotelmarianna.gr, info@hotelmarianna.gr). Park above town at the giant, abandoned Hotel Xenia at the Akronafplia fortress and walk a few steps down.

NAFPLIO

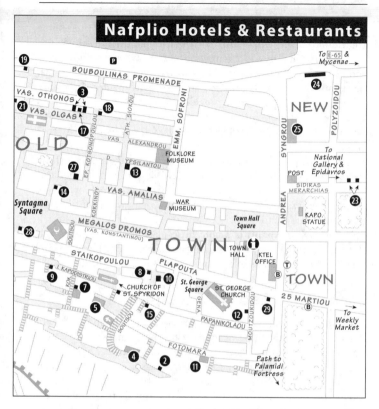

Nafplio Hotels & Restaurants

$$ Byron Hotel is a traditional, family-run standby with 18 simple, older-feeling rooms in a scenic setting up some stairs above the Old Town (Platonos 2, tel. 27520-22351, www.byronhotel.gr, byronhotel@otenet.gr, Aris).

$$ Hotel Leto Nuevo is partway up the slopes of the Akronafplia fortress. Its 18 boutiquish rooms all have sea views and either a bathtub or rain shower; ask about elusive and popular room #121, which is higher up (discount without breakfast, Zigomala 28, tel. 27520-28093, www.letohotelnafplio.gr, info@letohotelnafplio.gr, Sofia and her son Vasilis).

$$ Chroma Design Hotel and Suites has seven colorful, trendy rooms in a renovated old mansion, higher up along some stairs (lovely garden area, rooftop view terrace, corner of Zigomala and Kokkinou, tel. 27520-27686, www.thehouseprojecthotels.com, info@thehouseprojecthotels.com, Aggeliki and Ioanna).

$$ Aetoma Hotel is a family-run gem offering five individually styled rooms with high ceilings, balconies, and lots of natural light in the house where owner Panagiota was born. She and her

NAFPLIO

son, Akis, now invite travelers to share in the history of their home (Spiridonos 2, tel. 27520-27373, www.aetoma.gr, stay@aetoma.gr).

$ Pension Rigas is a gem with seven cozy, charmingly rustic rooms in a refurbished old building with exposed stone and beams, hardwood floors, high ceilings, and lots of character. Its comfy lobby and small patio area provide a convivial space for guests to share travel stories (Kapodistriou 8, tel. 27520-23611, www.pension-rigas.gr, rigaspension@hotmail.com, run by friendly Australian Lena).

$ Pension Filyra (Φιλύρα) has six tastefully and colorfully decorated rooms at a nice price in a few buildings in the heart of the Old Town (room stocked with basic continental breakfast, Aggelou Terzaki 29, tel. 27520-96096, www.pensionfilyra.gr, pensionfilyra@gmail.com).

$ Pension Anapli is a cute little place with seven colorful, dressed-up rooms with iron-frame beds (Fotomara 21, tel. 27520-24585, www.pensionanapli.gr, info@pensionanapli.gr).

Eating in Nafplio

Nafplio is bursting with tempting eateries. Because most of them cater to Athenians on a weekend break, they aim to please repeat customers. This also means that prices can be a bit high. In two high-profile restaurant zones—the tavernas along Staikopoulou street (just above Syntagma Square) and the fish restaurants on Bouboulinas street (along the waterfront)—waiters compete desperately for the passing tourist trade. While I'd avoid the places on Staikopoulou, if you want seafood, the Bouboulinas fish joints are the best in town. I've focused most of my coverage on the tight pedestrian lanes between these two areas, toward the water from Syntagma Square, where values are good and ambience is excellent. Several places offer live traditional Greek music (generally weekends in summer after 20:30 or 21:00; get details from your hotel).

RESTAURANTS

$$$ Mezedopoleio O Noulis—run by Noulis, the man with the mighty moustache shown on the sign—serves up an inviting range of *mezedes* (appetizers). Three or four *mezedes* constitute a tasty meal for two people. This authentic-feeling place offers a rare chance to sample *saganaki flambé* (fried cheese flambéed with Metaxa brandy). As Noulis likes to do it all himself, don't come here if you're in a hurry (mid-May-Sept Mon-Sat 13:00-15:00 & 19:00-23:00, closed Sun; Oct-mid-May Tue-Sun 13:00-16:00, closed Mon; no reservations, Moutzouridou 21, tel. 27520-25541).

$$$ Taverna Paleo Arhontiko ("Old Mansion") is a favorite town hangout for its classic homestyle Greek dishes, reasonable prices, lovely ambience, and live music (nightly from 21:00 in summer). It gets packed on weekends, when reservations are recommended (12:00-24:00, at corner of Ypsilandou and Siokou, tel. 69818-68914, Anja and Tassos).

$$ I Gonia tou Kavalari ("Kavalari's Corner"), nestled behind Syntagma Square, is an easygoing rustic eatery with live music twice a week and a tempting menu of inexpensive *mezedes* (Tue-Sun 12:00-24:00, closed Mon, Amalias 2, tel. 25725-00180).

$$$ Kastro Karima, on a quiet street near the Church of St. Spyridon, serves simple but tasty dishes at reasonable prices, including a variety of traditional spreads. Choose between sidewalk tables or the stony-chic interior (daily 12:00-24:00, Papanikolaou 32, tel. 27520-25279).

$$ Alaloum Restaurant serves inventive Greek and Mediterranean dishes and a famous "mother-in-law's salad." The portions are huge, and sharing is encouraged (sit inside or out, Wed-Mon 13:00-24:00, closed Tue and for two weeks in June, D. Ipsilantou 3, tel. 27520-29883). Michalis organizes live music most weekends in summer at around 21:00.

Tavernas on Olgas Street: The lane called Olgas, tucked away in a grid of streets just two blocks up from the waterfront, is filled with charming, family-run tavernas serving Greek classics to happy tourists. At any of these, you can choose between a cozy, rustic interior or outdoor tables. Window-shop along here and consider these two good options: **$$ Aiolos** (good mixed-grill platters, drunken  chicken, *saganaki,* and *sousamotiro*—fried cheese with sesame seeds, Olgas 30, tel. 27520-26828) or **$$ To Omorfo Tavernaki,** literally "The Beautiful Little Tavern" (traditional home-style Greek dishes, Kotsonopoulou 1, tel. 27520-25944, Tsioli family).

$$$ Fish Restaurants on Bouboulinas: As you stroll the harborfront, you'll soon come upon the fishy aromas and aggressive come-ons of the town's best seafood eateries (all open daily, roughly 12:00-24:00). Wherever you choose to dine, part of the fun is the strolling scene. Seafood here is typically priced by the kilogram or half-kilogram (figure about 250-300 grams for a typical portion—around €10-20 for a seafood entrée, or about €6-15 for a meat dish). **Arapakos Restaurant,** more elegant than the others with a dressy interior and great outdoor tables, is understandably favored by the town's big shots (Bouboulinas 81, tel. 27520-27675, www.arapakos.gr).

Peaceful and on the Water: $$$ Agnanti is worth considering if you want to be alone with the sea and great views. Just beyond the breakwater spit at Nafplio's "Sea Gate," offering only outside tables, it's like eating on a dock (seafood pasta is a favorite, open daily for lunch and dinner, closed Nov-Feb, walk a few minutes down Akti Miaouli Promenade and look for stone building on the right side just after the path veers left, mobile 693-290-6593, Andrew).

Italian: $$$ Trattoria La Gratella is your best bet if you crave Italian. They serve tasty and reasonably priced pizza, pasta, and *secondi* with a bright and modern interior and nice outdoor tables (June-Nov Mon-Fri 17:00-24:00, Sat-Sun 12:00-24:00; Dec-May daily 17:00-24:00; Olgas 44, tel. 27520-28350).

CHEAP GYRO PITA AND SOUVLAKI JOINTS

Each of these places serves souvlaki and gyro pita sandwiches and more for a quick, inexpensive meal. You can sit inside or out on the sidewalk, or get takeaway.

$$ Mitato Souvlaki is an inviting little joint just steps off the main square (daily 11:30-24:00, off Syntagma Square behind National Bank building at Staikopoulou 14, tel. 27520-21159).

Dining in Kolokotronis Park: Several cheap, family- and student-style diners line the park (along Sidiras Merarchias street, just beyond Town Hall Square), all with noisy indoor seating and peaceful options in the park. **$ Gyro Grill** offers perhaps the cheapest hot dinner in town. **$$ Pizza Alpha** is a few doors down.

Trendy Grill Strip: This thriving strip of eateries is where high-school kids take their dates (facing the harbor and parking, just east of the Bouboulinas promenade). Along with **$$ Trendy**—the busiest souvlaki joint in town—you'll find **$$ Pizza Scuola** and the **$ Mesali Bakery** (with classic Greek sweets and baklava).

Picnics: The **supermarket** near the park is the most convenient of several supermarkets in town (Mon-Sat 8:00-21:00, closed Sun, 50 yards behind the post office at corner of Syngrou and Flessa).

DESSERT

Antica Gelateria di Roma is *the* place to go for a mouthwatering array of *gelati* (dairy-based ice cream) and *sorbetti* (fruit-based sorbet) made fresh on the premises daily by Italian gelato master Marcello Raffo, his wife Monica, and his sister Claudia. The Raffos also offer other Italian snacks and drinks (daily 8:00-24:00, free Wi-Fi, Farmakopoulou 3, at corner with Kominou, tel. 27520-23520).

Nafplio Connections

BY BUS

The tiny bus station is convenient and central, and has a printed schedule in English. Their website has an English option and sells tickets (www.ktelargolida.gr). While the ticket agent can give information, confirm your plans (and transfers) with your driver or other passengers.

Direct buses go to **Athens** (nearly hourly, 2.5 hours), **Epidavros** (3-4/day, 1/day late on Sun, 45 minutes), and **Mycenae** (2-3/day, none Sun, 45 minutes).

Journeys to other Peloponnesian destinations require multiple transfers; get an early start, and be prepared for frustrations and delays: **Tripoli** (2/day, 1.5 hours—transfer point for many other destinations), **Monemvasia** (1/day, 4.5 hours, change in Tripoli and Sparta), **Olympia** (2/day, 5 hours, change in Tripoli). For these destinations, KTEL, the national bus system, has a minimal website (www.ktelbus.com).

BY TAXI

To cut some time off the trip to the ancient sites, you can take a taxi to **Mycenae** or **Epidavros** (€50-70 round-trip for either one, with one-hour wait, bargain hard for the best price).

BY BOAT

To reach long-distance boats connecting to **Hydra** and the other islands in the nearby Saronic Gulf, you'll first need to get to the ports of Tolo, Ermioni, or Metochi. For specifics on ferry connections from these ports to Hydra, see page 399.

Getting to the Ports: Infrequent excursion boats (2-3/week April-Oct) to Hydra operated by Pegasus Tours leave from the port at **Tolo,** a short drive or bus ride (20 minutes) from Nafplio. These boats usually leave fairly early in the morning, so stop by the bus station in Nafplio to check morning bus times and to get your ticket.

Hellenic Seaways ferries leave from farther away in **Ermioni** (a.k.a. Hermioni), about 1.5 hours southeast of Nafplio. Buses that are supposedly going to Ermioni usually go instead to Kranidi, a larger town about six miles from Ermioni's port (3/day Mon-Sat, 1/day Sun, 2 hours; this Nafplio-Kranidi bus connection may require a transfer at the town of Ligourio—pay careful attention so as not to miss the change). From Kranidi, it's about a €15-20 taxi ride to the dock at Ermioni (try to split the fare with other Ermioni-bound travelers).

Passenger ferries (either the Freedom Boat or Metoxi Express) leave from even farther away in **Metochi,** which is best reached by car (allow 2 hours).

ROUTE TIPS FOR DRIVERS

Nafplio is a quick and easy drive from Athens—about 2 hours, much of it on toll highways. (When asked about the poor little road connecting the city to the toll highway, locals explain it's intentional...to keep the Athenians out.) To reach **Monemvasia** from Nafplio (3-4 hours), consider taking the scenic route described on page 339.

EPIDAVROS

ΕΠΙΔΑΥΡΟΣ / Επίδαυρος

Nestled in a leafy valley some 20 miles east of Nafplio, Epidavros was once the most famous healing center in the ancient Greek world. It was like an ancient Lourdes, a place of hope where the sick came to be treated by doctor-priests acting on behalf of Asklepios, the god of medicine.

The site began as a temple to Apollo, god of light, who was worshipped here in Mycenaean times. By the fourth century B.C., Apollo had been replaced by his son, Asklepios (who was said to have been born here). Because pilgrims prayed to Asklepios for health, a sanctuary was needed, with a temple, altars, and statues to the gods. The sanctuary reached the height of its popularity in the fourth and third centuries B.C., when it boasted medical facilities, housing for the sick, mineral baths, a stadium for athletic competitions, and a theater.

These days the famous theater is Epidavros' star attraction. It's the finest and best-preserved of all of Greece's ancient theaters—and that's saying something in a country with 132 of them. Epidavros also has some (far) less interesting sights. The once-great sanctuary is now little more than a lonely field of rubble. The small Archaeological Museum displays a few crumbled fragments of statuary. But the theater alone makes Epidavros worth the side-trip.

GETTING THERE

By Car: From **Nafplio** it's a 30-minute **drive** to the east, along winding roads. There's plenty of free parking at the site.

Head east out of Nafplio and follow the signs. If you're connecting Epidavros and Mycenae (see next chapter; allow 60 minutes), you can avoid driving all the way back into Nafplio by watching carefully for signs to either site, which direct you to a roundabout outside central Nafplio.

Be aware that names on signs can vary. Epidavros can be spelled "Epidaurus" in English. Confusingly, many locations in this area carry the name Epidavros/Επιδαυρος. Don't be distracted by signs to Nea ("New") Epidavros/Νεα Επιδαυρος, or Palea ("Old") Epidavros/Παλαιά Επιδαυρος, which will route you to a modern coastal town far from the theater. Instead, continue following signs pointing to the *Ancient Theater*.

By Bus: From **Nafplio,** buses run to Epidavros (Mon-Sat 3-4/day—buses usually leave Nafplio at 10:30, 12:30 or 14:30, and 17:30; 1/day late on Sun; possibly fewer buses Oct-April, 45 minutes). Return buses from Epidavros to Nafplio typically leave in the afternoon (Mon-Sat 2-3/day, last bus usually around 18:00; 1/day late on Sun). Confirm bus schedules locally.

It's possible to see both Epidavros and Mycenae in one long day from Nafplio by bus (in summer): If the schedule hasn't changed, you could take the 10:00 bus from Nafplio to Mycenae, spend about 2 hours at the site, and return to Nafplio on the 13:00 bus; then catch the 14:30 bus to Epidavros, tour the site, and return to Nafplio on the last bus, arriving back in the city about 19:00. (This wouldn't work on Sun, when there are no buses to Mycenae). Taking the bus to Epidavros first and then to Mycenae doesn't work (giving you only 30 minutes at Epidavros and only 15 at Mycenae).

From **Athens,** buses head to Nafplio, then continue on to Epidavros (2-3/day, 2.5 hours, may require transfer in Nafplio—ask when you buy your ticket).

By Taxi: You can get to Epidavros by **taxi** from Nafplio (€50-70 round-trip with one-hour wait).

ORIENTATION TO EPIDAVROS

Cost: €12 (€6 off-season) includes the theater, Archaeological Museum, and the rest of the Sanctuary of Epidavros archaeological site.

Hours: Daily April-Oct 8:00-20:00 (in theory), off-season until 17:00. Tel. 27530-22009, www.culture.gr. Off-season and during holidays, sights can close suddenly: Check locally before planning your day.

Length of This Tour: Unfortunately, Epidavros is not really "on the way" to anything else. Budget two to three hours for the round-trip excursion from Nafplio. You can see the entire site in an hour, but it's delightful to linger at the theater.

Services: There's not much here. A simple café/restaurant is along the lane between the parking and ticket office, and a food shack in the parking lot sells slushies and snacks. WCs are near the parking lot, and more are near the museum.

EPIDAVROS

Performances: The theater is still used today for performances on summer weekends during the annual Athens & Epidavros Festival (generally July-Aug Fri-Sat at around 21:00; ideally buy tickets the day before, schedule at www.greekfestival.gr). Special buses run from Athens and Nafplio on performance nights.

Starring: The most intact (and most spectacularly situated) theater from ancient Greece.

●SELF-GUIDED TOUR

From the parking lot, follow signs up the lane to the ticket desk. Buy your ticket and enter. The theater, sanctuary, and museum are all a couple minutes' walk from one another. The stunning theater is 90 percent of the experience: Climb the seats, take some photos, try out the acoustics—and that's it. Then zip through the little museum and wander the grounds beyond.

• *From the entry gate, go straight and climb the stairs on the right up to the theater. Enter the theater, stand in the center of the circular "orchestra" and take it all in. (I've marked your spot with a weathered marble stump, where fellow theatergoers might be posing, singing, or speaking.)*

Theater of Epidavros (c. 300 B.C.)

This magnificent sight is built into the side of a tree-covered hill. The perfect symmetry of its two tiers of seating stands as a tribute

to Greek mathematics. It's easy to locate the main elements of a typical Greek theater: the round **orchestra,** the smaller **stage** area *(skene),* and the **seating** *(kavea).*

The audience sat in the bleacher-like seats (made of limestone blocks) that were set into the hillside, wrapping partially around the performers. Together, the lower rows and 21 upper rows (added by the Romans, c. 50 B.C.) seated up to 15,000. The spectators looked down on the orchestra, a circular area 70 feet across where the group of actors known as the chorus sang and danced. Behind the orchestra are the rectangular foundations of the *skene* (which is often covered with a modern stage). The *skene* had a raised stage where actors performed, a back wall for scenery, dressing rooms in the back, and various doorways and ramps where actors could make dramatic entrances and exits. The *skene* was not very tall, so spectators in the upper seats could look over it during the performance, taking in the view of the valley below.

The ancient acoustical engineering is remarkable. The acous-

Greek Theater

The Greeks invented modern theater, and many plays written 2,500 years ago are still performed today.

In prehistoric times, songs, poems, and rituals were performed to honor Dionysus, the god of wine and revelry. By the sixth century B.C., these fertility rites developed into song competitions between choruses of men who sang hymns about Dionysus, heroes, and gods. The contests were held at religious festivals as a form of worship.

Later, Athenian playwrights (such as Thespis, the first "thespian") introduced spoken monologues that alternated with the chorus' songs. Over time, these monologues became dialogues between several actors that became as important as the chorus. Plays evolved from Dionysian hymns to stories of Dionysus to stories of all sorts—myths of gods and heroes, and comedies about contemporary events. By the Golden Age (c. 450-400 B.C.), Athens was the center of a golden age of theater, premiering plays by Sophocles, Euripides, and Aristophanes.

Greek plays fall into three categories. Tragedies, the oldest and most prestigious, feature gods and legends—and usually ended with the hero dying. Comedies are satires about contemporary people and events. "Satyr plays" spoof the seriousness of tragedies—for example, Oedipus with a massive strap-on phallus.

Greek drama, like Greek art and philosophy, put human beings at center stage. The theaters were built into hillsides, giving the audience a glimpse of human emotions against the awesome backdrop of nature. The plays showed mortals wrestling with how to find their place in a cosmos ruled by the gods and Fate.

tics are superb—from the orchestra, whisper to your partner on the top row. (The center stone marks where an altar to Dionysus, the god of wine and theater, once stood.)

Picture a typical performance of a Greek tragedy here at this theater. Before the show began, spectators filed in the same way tourists do today, through the passageway between the seating and the *skene*. The performance began with a sober monologue by a lone actor, setting the scene. Next, the chorus members entered in a solemn parade, singing as they took their place in the orchestra circle. Then the story unfolded through dialogue on the stage, interspersed with songs by the chorus members. At play's end, the chorus sang a song summing up the moral of the play, then paraded out the way they came.

The chorus—a group of three to fifty singers—was a key part of Greek plays. They commented on the action through songs, accompanied by flute or lyre (small harp), and danced around in the orchestra (literally, "dancing space").

For about seven centuries (c. 300 B.C.-A.D. 400), the theater at Epidavros hosted song contests and plays, until the Christian Em-

peror Theodosius II closed the sanctuary in the fifth century. Over time, the theater became buried in dirt, preserving it until it was unearthed in almost original condition in 1881. Today it is once again a working theater.

Even if you're not here for one of the theater's official performances, you can still enjoy the show: Tourists often take turns performing monologues, reciting poems, or just clapping to try out the acoustics. If there's an actor inside you, speak up. Try reciting any of the ancient Greek passages presented in the sidebar.

When you've finished your turn on stage, climb the stairs to the seats to join the spectators. From up here can you fully appreciate the incredible acoustics—not to mention the remarkable scale and intactness of the place. No matter how high you climb, you can hear every word of the naturally amplified performances down below...all while enjoying the backdrop of sweeping mountains and olive groves.

• *Walk down the stairs across from the theater to find the...*

Archaeological Museum

The exhibits in this dusty little old-school museum come with English descriptions. The first room (of three) displays various *steles* (inscribed stone tablets). Some of these document successful cases where patients were healed here by the god Asklepios. Others are rules governing the hospital. The only people to be excluded from the sanctuary were the terminally ill and pregnant women (both were considered too high-risk—their deaths would sully the sanctuary's reputation). The room also holds a case displaying some medical instruments that'll make you glad you were born after the

Greek Monologues

To get you into the theatrical mood, here are a few (condensed) passages from some famous Greek plays.

Oedipus Rex (or Oedipus Tyrannus), by Sophocles

A man unwittingly kills his father, sleeps with his mother, and watches his wife commit suicide. When he learns the truth, he blinds himself in shame and sorrow:

> "With what eyes could I ever behold again my honored
>   father or my unhappy mother, both destroyed by me?
> This punishment is worse than death, and so it should be.
> I wish I could be deaf as well as blind, to shut out all sorrow.
> My friends, come bury me, hide me from every eye,
> cast me into the deepest ocean and let me die.
> Anything so I can shake off this hated life.
> Come friends, do not be afraid to touch me, polluted as I am.
> For no one will suffer for my sins—no one but me."

Antigone, by Sophocles

The heroine Antigone defies the king in order to give her brother a proper burial. Here she faces her punishment:

> "O tomb, my bridal chamber, where I go most miserably,
> before my time on earth is spent!
> What law of heaven have I broken?!
> Why should I ever beseech the gods again,

invention of anesthetics. (You can see small pots for measuring dosages.)

The second room has many (headless) statues of gods who were invoked in the healing process—most of them textbook examples of that wonderfully relaxed *contrapposto* (S-shaped) stance that was revived centuries later by Renaissance sculptors (find the statue striking an especially sassy pose). The columns and cornice on display were part of the sanctuary's impressive entryway (propylaea).

The star of the final room is an extremely well-preserved capital from a Corinthian column. The builders of the temple buried it on the site, perhaps as an offering to the gods. Archaeologists who dug it up in the 19th century were astonished at its condition; it may have been the proto-

if I am to be punished for doing nothing but good.
If I am guilty, I accept my sin.
But if it is my accusers that are wrong,
I pray that they do not suffer any more than the evils they
have inflicted upon me."

Plutus, by Aristophanes

In this comedy, a man befriends a blind beggar who is actually Plutus, the god of wealth, in disguise. He helps Plutus regain his sight by bringing him to Epidavros. (If the monologue lacks some of Aristophanes' famed side-splitting humor, maybe it's because I left out the bit about cutting a huge fart in the presence of the god Asklepios.)

"Having arrived at the Temple of Asklepios, we first led our patient to the sea to purify him. Back at the temple, we gave offerings of bread and wheat cake, then bedded down. During the night, the god Asklepios appeared, sitting on the bed. He took a clean rag and wiped Plutus' eyelids. He then whistled, and two huge snakes came rushing from the temple and licked the patient's eyelids. As quick as you could drain 10 shots of wine, Plutus stood up—he could see! Asklepios disappeared with the snakes, and, as dawn broke, we clapped our hands with joy and gave praise and thanks to the mighty god."

type for all the capitals in the temple complex. The room also displays two replicas of small, square reliefs (left wall) showing the god Asklepios on his throne. Asklepios is often depicted as a kindly, bearded man, carrying a staff with a snake wound around it, the forerunner of today's medical symbol.

• *Outside, follow the stone-lined path to the left as you leave the museum (and only WC within the site) to the sprawling field of ruins called the...*

Sanctuary of Epidavros

While Epidavros' theater is stunning, the ruins of the sanctuary itself (in a huge open field between the theater and parking lot) are a distant also-ran compared with those at other great ancient sites, such as Delphi and Olympia. The various ruins are well-described in English, but precious little survives—orient yourself using one of the numerous maps and wander. Walking from the museum to the far end of the site, you'll first pass the hotel overlooking the ruins (up the short staircase on your

right). Next are the baths, dining hall, stadium, circular temple *(tholos)*, dormitory (stoa of Abaton), and foundations of the Temple of Asklepios—in that order.

Considering that the sanctuary was a kind of healing resort with a mix of doctors and priests to serve the visitors or patients, it needed a hotel. Only the footprint of a 160-room, luxury two-floor-tall spa hotel survives. You can see the stone foundations (the wood-and-tile superstructure is long gone) and thresholds with hinge holes.

Logically there would be a bathhouse and restaurant for so many important guests. And the scant remains of those are

seen next. Beyond them stretches a fine stadium. Every four years, Epidavros' 6,000-seat stadium was used for the Festival of Asklepios (similar to other ancient Greek athletic competitions).

Archaeologists are reconstructing one important building beyond the stadium—the circular building, or *tholos,* had a labyrinth in its basement. Some believe the sick would go here to meditate with snakes. Exactly why and what happened is still a mystery.

The sick would then spend the night in the stoa of Abaton (the large dormitory building just beyond the *tholos*). Here they would likely pray for a miracle while meditating on the experience they had with the snakes. Perhaps they hoped to be visited in a dream by Asklepios, who could give them the secret to their cure. Stories of the miracles people experienced here spread far and wide, making Epidavros very popular.

Like a square memorial, just to the right is the covered foundation of the Temple of Asklepios—the center of this sacred complex.

MYCENAE

MYKHNEΣ / Μυκήνες

Mycenae—a fortress city atop a hill—was the hub of a mighty civilization that dominated the Greek world between 1600 and 1200 B.C., a thousand years before Athens' Golden Age. The Mycenaeans were as distant and mysterious to the Golden Age Greeks as Plato and Socrates are to us today. Ancient Greek tourists visited the dramatic ruins of Mycenae and concluded that the Mycenaeans must have been the heroes who'd won the Trojan War, as related in Homer's epic poems, the *Iliad* and the *Odyssey*. They thought of the Mycenaeans as their ancestors, the first "Greeks."

Following the same ancient sandal-steps as the ancient Greeks, today's visitors continue to enjoy Mycenae's majestic set-

ting of mountains, valleys, and the distant sea. Exploring this still-impressive hilltop, you'll discover the famous Lion Gate, a fine little museum, an enormous domed burial chamber... and distant echoes of the Trojan War.

When it comes to unraveling the mystery of the Mycenaeans, modern historians—armed with only the slimmest written record—are still trying to sort out fact from legend. They don't know exactly who the Mycenaeans were, where they came from, or what happened to them. Here are the sketchy (and oft-disputed) details:

Around 1600 B.C., a Bronze Age civilization originating in Asia Minor developed an empire of autonomous city-states that covered the southern half of mainland Greece and a few islands. Their capital was the city of Mycenae, which also gave its name to the people and the era. From contact with the sophisticated Minoan people on the isle of Crete, the militaristic Mycenaeans borrowed elements of religion and the arts.

Sometime around the year 1200 B.C., the aggressive Mycenaeans likely launched an attack on Troy, a rich city on the northwest coast of Asia Minor (present-day Turkey). After a long siege, Troy fell, and the Mycenaeans became the undisputed rulers of the Aegean. Then, just as suddenly, the Mycenaeans mysteriously disappeared, and their empire crumbled. Whether the Mycenaeans fell victim to a sudden invasion by the Dorians (a Greek tribe), an attack of the mysterious tribes later dubbed the "Sea People," a drought, or internal rebellion—no one knows. Whatever the reason, by 1100 B.C., Mycenae was abandoned and burned, and Greece plunged into four centuries known as the Dark Ages.

Nearly three millennia later, in 1876, German archaeologist Heinrich Schliemann excavated this site and put it back on the archaeologists' (and tourists') map. Today a visit to Mycenae is a trip back into prehistory to see some of the oldest remains of a complex civilization in all of Europe—a thousand years older than Athens' Acropolis.

GETTING THERE

By Car: Mycenae is 18 miles north of Nafplio (follow signs to Athens, on the way to the major E-65 expressway). From the modern town of Mycenae/Μυκήνες (near the larger town of Fichti/Φιχτι), the ruins are about two miles north, dramatically perched atop a hill. If you're connecting Mycenae and Epidavros by car (allow 60 minutes), you can avoid driving all the way back into Nafplio by watching carefully for signs to either site, which direct you to a roundabout outside central Nafplio. At Mycenae, drivers can use the free parking lot near the entrance to the ruins and museum; if it's full, park along the road leading to the lot.

By Bus: Buses run from Nafplio directly to ancient Mycenae (Mon-Sat 2-3/day—likely at 10:00, 12:00, and 14:00; no buses on Sun; possibly fewer buses Oct-April, 45 minutes), but the timing for the return trip makes taking a bus a pain. You'll have either just 15 minutes to see the site (not enough) or 2.25 hours (a little too much for some people). For advice about connecting Mycenae and Epidavros in one bus-based day trip from Nafplio, see page 246. If you do take the bus, confirm that your bus goes to the archaeological site; other buses take you only as far as Fichti, two miles away (a €5 cab ride).

By Taxi: You can take a taxi to Mycenae from Nafplio (about €50-70 round-trip with time to sightsee). It's best to arrange your return in advance, but to arrange a return taxi from Mycenae on the spot, call mobile 694-643-1726.

ORIENTATION TO MYCENAE

Cost: €12 (€6 off-season) ticket includes archaeological site, museum, and Treasury of Atreus up the road.

Hours: Roughly May-Oct daily 8:00-20:00; closes an hour or two earlier in fall; Nov-April daily 8:00-15:00. As at other archaeological sites in Greece, Mycenae's hours can change without notice—ask your hotel or call the site to confirm before your visit; tel. 27510-76585 or 27520-27502, www.culture.gr.

Services: WCs are just above the museum, but none are on the actual site. A stand in the parking lot sells basic snacks.

Planning Your Time: As with most ancient sites with a museum, decide whether to see the museum first (to help reconstruct the ruins) or the site first (to get the lay of the land). To explore the cistern, bring a flashlight. To complement the information in this self-guided tour, read the chapter on Athens' National Archaeological Museum, where many Mycenaean artifacts are now displayed (see page 138).

Length of This Tour: Allow an hour for the site, a half-hour for the museum, and a half-hour for the Treasury of Atreus. Mycenae makes for a handy half-day side-trip from Nafplio. Drivers can combine it with the Theater of Epidavros for a full day of ancient site-hopping.

Pronunciation: Mycenae is pronounced my-SEE-nee by English-speakers; Greeks call the town Mykenes/Μυκήνες (mee-KEE-nehs), also spelled Mikenes. The ancient people are known as the Mycenaeans (my-seh-NEE-uhns).

Starring: The hilltop fortress at the center of the most ancient, powerful, and enigmatic of ancient Greek civilizations.

❷ SELF-GUIDED TOUR

The three main sightseeing areas at Mycenae are a few minutes' walk from one another. The **archaeological ruins** consist of the walled city of Mycenae atop the hill called the acropolis. Here you'll find the famous Lion Gate entrance, Grave Circle A (which yielded precious artifacts), and the ruins of the palace. Below the site is the **museum,** housing artifacts that were found here. Finally, as impressive as anything here is the **Treasury of Atreus**—a huge domed tomb located about 300 yards downhill from the main site (along the main road). A handful of other ruins and tombs are scattered around the area, but stick to these three to start your visit.

Note that some of the ruins (confusingly) have different names—for example, the Treasury of Atreus is also known as the Tomb of Agamemnon.

• *Buy your ticket for the archaeological site and enter, climbing the ramp up the acropolis.*

Archaeological Site

• *You'll enter the fortified complex through the...*

❶ Lion Gate and Wall

The grand Lion Gate (c. 1300 B.C.) guards the entrance to this fortress city on a hill. Above the doorway, two lionesses flank a column, symbolically protecting it the way the Mycenaean kings once protected the city. The lions' missing heads may have once turned outward, greeting visitors. The heads were made of stone or possibly of gold (anything made of a precious material like that would have been plundered long ago).

The lions form a triangle above the massive lintel (the crossbeam above the door). Mycenaean architects used the weak corbelled arch, less sturdy than the rounded Roman arch developed later. A simple horizontal stone spans the door, while heavy stones above it inch in to bridge the gap. The lintel is slightly arched to distribute the weight to the sides and add to its strength.

Apart from its rather fragile technology, Mycenaean architecture is really massive. The lintel weighs 18 tons—as much as a WWII B-17 bomber. The exterior walls that girdle the base of the hill (c. 1300 B.C.) were about 40 feet high, 20 feet thick, and 3,000 feet long. They were built with an estimated 14,000 boulders weighing 5 to 10 tons each. Marveling at the enormous scale, classical-era Greeks figured the legendary Perseus (who slew the Medusa) must have built the city with the help of the giant one-eyed Cyclopes, and dubbed the style "cyclopean." In reality, the Mycenaeans probably lifted these big stones into place the same way the Egyptians built the pyramids—by building ramps and rolling the stones up on logs drawn by oxen or horses.

Pass through the gate. Carved into the stone are **post-holes**

that held the wooden door. Just as you emerge, look left to see a square **niche** in the wall—this could have been a small shrine where statues of the gods who guarded the gates were displayed, or just a simple closet. Poke your head in to study the stonework.

• *Head up the ramp. About 30 yards ahead, you'll see (below and on the right) a circular wall that encloses rectangular graves. Walk a bit higher up the path and look down for the best view.*

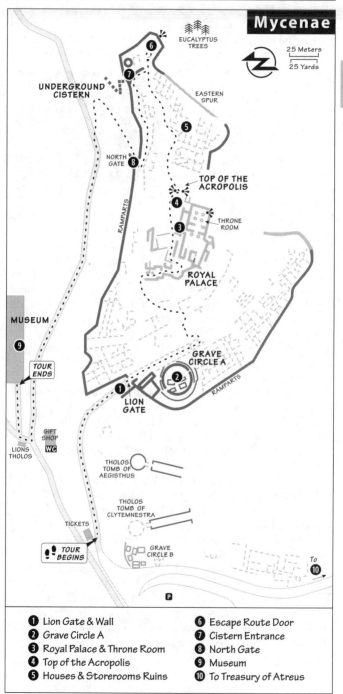

MYCENAE

Mycenae

EUCALYPTUS TREES

25 Meters
25 Yards

6

7

UNDERGROUND CISTERN

EASTERN SPUR

5

NORTH GATE 8

TOP OF THE ACROPOLIS

4

THRONE ROOM

3

RAMPARTS

ROYAL PALACE

MUSEUM

9

TOUR ENDS

GRAVE CIRCLE A

2

1

LION GATE

RAMPARTS

GIFT SHOP

WC

LIONS THOLOS

THOLOS TOMB OF AEGISTHUS

THOLOS TOMB OF CLYTEMNESTRA

TICKETS

TOUR BEGINS

GRAVE CIRCLE B

To 10

P

1 Lion Gate & Wall
2 Grave Circle A
3 Royal Palace & Throne Room
4 Top of the Acropolis
5 Houses & Storerooms Ruins
6 Escape Route Door
7 Cistern Entrance
8 North Gate
9 Museum
10 To Treasury of Atreus

❷ Grave Circle A (c. 1550 b.c.)

Judging from what was dug up in this round cluster of graves, Mycenaean royalty were buried here. The rectangular holes are called shaft graves, which were cut into the rock up to 20 feet deep. There are six such shaft graves here, each of which contained several bodies (19 total—9 women, 8 men, and 2 children). The bodies were found embalmed and lying on their backs along with their most precious belongings, with their heads facing east—toward

the rising sun—indicating a belief in an afterlife. Gravestones atop the graves (like the one displayed in the museum) were decorated with a spiral, possibly a symbol of continuous existence.

In 1876 these graves were unearthed by the famed German archaeologist Heinrich Schliemann. Schliemann had recently discovered the long-lost city of Troy, finally giving some historical credibility to Homer's tales. He next turned his attention to Mycenae, the legendary home of Agamemnon. In Grave Circle A, he found a treasure trove of gold swords, spears, engraved cups, and ritual objects buried with the dead—30 pounds in all, confirming Homer's description of Mycenae as a city "rich in gold."

The prize discovery was a gold mask showing the face of a bearded man. Masks like this were tied onto the faces of the deceased. This one was obviously for an important warrior chieftain. Schliemann was convinced the mask proved that Homer's tales of the Trojan War were true, and he dubbed it the "Mask of Agamemnon." This mask and other artifacts are now in the National Archaeological Museum in Athens.

Could it really be the Mask of Agamemnon? No. Not only is it unlikely that Agamemnon ever really existed, but the mask is from the 16th century b.c.—at least 300 years before the legendary king supposedly burned Troy.

The Mycenaeans practiced several different types of burial: interred in a pit (for the poorest), encased in a ceramic jar called a cist grave (for wealthier folks), laid in a shaft grave (for royalty), or placed in an elaborate domed chamber called a *tholos* (like the Treasury of Atreus, which we'll visit at the end of this tour).

• *Continue to climb up the paths, zigzagging past the ruins of former houses and shops, to the top of the acropolis. On the right, below you, are the rectangular foundations of the former...*

Mycenae and Troy: Fact or Fiction?

Several sites at Mycenae bear legendary names—"Agamemnon's Palace," the "Tomb of Clytemnestra," the

"Tomb of Agamemnon," and so on. Although these names are fanciful with no basis in fact, real-life Mycenae does sound eerily similar to the legends found in writings attributed to the poet Homer (c. 850 B.C.) and other ancient scribes.

The tales of the Trojan War are set during the time when the Mycenaeans dominated the Greek world and had the power to conquer Troy. They tell of the abduction of the beautiful Helen (who had "the face that launched a thousand ships") by Paris, a prince of Troy. Outraged at the loss of his bride, Menelaus, king of Sparta, convinced his brother Agamemnon, king of Mycenae, to lead the Greeks in an attack on Troy. But the winds were not favorable for launching the fleet. An oracle told Agamemnon that he had to sacrifice his daughter to get underway, so he lied to his wife, Clytemnestra, and ordered the priests to kill their daughter.

After the sacrifice, the Greek ships finally made it to Troy. When a long siege failed to defeat the Trojans, Odysseus suggested tricking the enemy by building a wooden idol (the famous "Trojan horse"), leaving it outside the city walls, and pretending to withdraw. The Trojans took the bait, brought the horse inside, and were met with an unpleasant surprise: The greatest warriors of Greece emerging from inside the horse to complete the conquest of Troy. The famous heroes of the Trojan War include Achilles and Ajax on the Greek side, and Paris' brother Hector—all of whom died by the war's end.

Homer's *Odyssey* tells of the homeward journey of Odysseus, who survived the war, only to wander for 10 years, thwarted by the god Poseidon, before finally reaching home. Agamemnon's fate is also told in the epic. After sacking Troy, Agamemnon returned to Mycenae with his Trojan concubine, where he was murdered by his wife (who was still brooding over her daughter's sacrifice and not very happy about the new competition). Not that Clytemnestra was a dutiful spouse—her new lover helped her murder Agamemnon and the concubine.

Metaphorically, Agamemnon's tragic story matches that of the historical Mycenaeans—no sooner had they returned home victorious from Troy than their own homes were destroyed. These legends of ancient Mycenae were passed down through oral tradition for centuries until, long after the fall of both Troy and Mycenae, they were preserved for posterity in Homer's *Iliad* and *Odyssey* as well as other ancient epics.

❸ Royal Palace and Throne Room (Megaron)

Kings ruled the Mycenaeans from this palace, which consisted of a line of several rectangular rooms (about all that remains today are the outlines of the rooms).

Imagine entering the palace and walking through a series of rooms. You'd start in an open-air courtyard—that's the biggest rectangle to the far right (west, toward the parking lot). Then you'd enter the palace itself, passing between two columns (see the remaining bases) onto a covered porch. Next, at the far end of the porch, was a small anteroom. Finally, you'd spill into the main hall—the throne room—at the east end. This great hall, or *megaron*, contains the outlines of a round hearth, which is where a fire burned. Here you could make burnt offerings to the gods. The four remaining bases around the hearth once held four inverted columns that supported the roof, which had a sunroof-type hole to let out the smoke. Against the wall to the right (the south wall) sat the king on his throne—the very center of power of the Mycenaean empire. The walls and floors were brightly painted with a pattern of linked spirals.

The same type of palace was found in every Mycenaean city, and later became the standard layout of the Greek temple—courtyard, colonnaded porch, small room *(pronaos)*, and main hall with its sacred *cella* area toward the back, where only the priest could go.
• *While we're on the top of the acropolis, check out the view and imagine the city/fortress at its peak.*

❹ Top of the Acropolis: Mycenae the Fortress-City

Mycenae was a combination citadel, palace, residence, and administrative capital of the extended empire of Mycenaean cities. But first and foremost, it was a for-tress, occupying a superb natu-ral defensive position guarding a major crossroads in Greece. The hill is flanked by steep ravines. To the south there are spacious views across the fertile plains of Argos to the Argolic Gulf, giv-ing the inhabitants ample time to prepare for any attack by sea. The cone-shaped hill in the dis-

tance ringed with walls near the top was the fortress of Argos. The port of Mycenae controlled trade on the road from Corinth to Naf-plio, and sea trade from Nafplio to points beyond.

In case of siege, Mycenae could rely on natural springs located on the mountainside to the east (away from the entrance—near the eucalyptus trees, a little above acropolis level, with a patch of exposed reddish hillside behind it). The water was channeled through clay pipes underground to a cistern dug inside the acropolis.

Though Mycenae was fundamentally a fortress, up to 60,000 people lived here.

• *Facing the distant bay, find the Acropolis of Argos in the distance, and imagine the torches and bronze plates once used to reflect and flash messages across long distances. Now, work your way eastward (farther away from the entrance, and a bit downhill), noticing natural defenses provided by cliffs on the right, before descending to the...*

Cistern and Other Sights at the East End

The ruins at this end were once mostly ❺ **houses and storerooms.** At the far eastern end, notice the doorway in the wall (now covered with a gate). This was ❻ an **escape route** out the back.

Find the gaping cave-like opening of the ❼ **cistern,** where 99 (slippery!) steps lead 50 feet down. Peering inside, you can see...

absolutely nothing, unless you've packed a flashlight. The cistern stored water from springs within the hillside, in case of siege or drought.

• *Head back toward the entrance—but bear to the right, following the north (outer) wall. Walk down the stairs and look for a gate on the right.*

This ❽ **North Gate,** smaller than the Lion Gate, has a similar rectangular crossbeam shape and heavy lintel. The wooden door is a reconstruction similar to the original, fit into the original holes cut in the lintel stone. Next to the North Gate is a niche in the wall (similar to the one at the Lion Gate) to display guardian gods.

• *From here you can explore your way along the ramparts back to the Lion Gate, or head directly to the museum. If you're ready to move on, exit through the North Gate, and bear left/downhill along the serpentine path to the museum, the modern building on the hillside below.*

❾ Museum

Whereas the ruins give a sense of the engineering sophistication of these people, the museum emphasizes their artistic, religious, literary, and cultural sides. You'll see various funeral objects from the graves, plus everyday objects that show influences from the Egyptian, Minoan, and Hittite cultures.

• *Follow the one-way, counterclockwise route through the collection, beginning in the...*

MYCENAE

Entrance Hall

The model of the Mycenae acropolis in the center of the room helps you visualize the city as it once was. Otherwise, the information posted here is pretty dull (on one side, a description of myths relating to this city; on the other, a dry history of the excavation).

• *From the entrance hall, move into the next room, on your right, where you'll find...*

Religious Symbols

This room shows off religious items found in temples. Snakes were believed to have sacred connections and were used for bridging the worlds of the living and the dead. The mysterious two-foot-tall figurines were likely used by priests in rituals to scare away evil. Pottery items found in homes were simply practical in an age without plastic storage. Notice the well-preserved elegant designs and colors that were baked into the clay.

• *Descend to the lower level to see...*

Funeral Objects

This room is filled with items found in tombs from about 1500 B.C. In the octagonal case, you'll see reproductions of the famous

Mask of Agamemnon and other golden items (such as crowns and medallions). These objects were discovered here in graves. (The originals are now in Athens' National Archaeological Museum.) On the wall behind the mask is a highly decorated funeral *stele* (gravestone) from Grave Circle B.

Diagrams below the artifacts show where each object on display was found in relation to the skeleton of the deceased. Back then, you *could* take it with you. Those with the means were sure to pack along jewelry, tools, kitchen utensils, even children's toys and sippy cups.

The miniature furniture was necessary for packing light. Tiny figurines may have represented the Goddess Earth. Notice the small baby coffin (a clay box with a lid, immediately left of the entry door).

• *As you continue into the next room, notice (on your left) a big clay urn used as a coffin for burial, with a band of spiral designs across the middle. Many funeral objects (such as this urn) were engraved with a spiral pattern—possibly a symbol of the never-ending path of life.*

Mycenaean Writing and Everyday Objects

In the case at the end of the room's partition are fragments of clay tablets inscribed in the Mycenaean written language known to scholars as Linear B. Each character represented a syllable. These fragments concern distinct subjects, including "Religion," "Lists of Names," "Products," inventories, and so on. Very few written documents survived from the Mycenaean era—no literature or history or stories—so we know very little of the Mycenaeans' inner thoughts.

On the other side of the partition, a glass case displays seal-stones, used to put a person's mark in wax or clay on a sealed document or box, to ensure it reached the intended recipient unopened. The Mycenaeans led an active trading life, and every businessman would have had one of these. The red one on top, in the center (#14), has the symbol from the Lion Gate on it.

To the left a large map shows the vast Mycenaean trading world. The Mycenaeans were seafarers, bringing back gold from Egypt, lapis lazuli from Afghanistan, amber from Scandinavia, ivory from Syria, jewelry from Spain, and more. Near the door, the display on "Women of the Mycenaean World" makes it clear they had plenty of toiletry and jewelry items: combs, tweezers, mirrors, beads, pendants, and so on.

• *Leaving the museum, take the ramp back up to the parking lot. (Just below the WC next to the museum, on your right, is the broken but interesting **Tholos Tomb of the Lions**.) At the parking lot, continue to the last area, one of the highlights of Mycenae: the tomb known as the **Treasury of Atreus**. It's located about 300 yards south of the ruins, along the road back toward the modern town of Mycenae. You can walk there in less than 10 minutes. Or, if you have a car, stop at the Treasury on your way out of the site—there's a small parking lot there. Show your entry ticket once more and follow the crowds gradually up-hill to get to the...*

MYCENAE

⓾ Treasury of Atreus (a.k.a. Tomb of Agamemnon, 13th century B.C.)

Mycenae's royalty were buried in massive beehive-shaped underground chambers called *tholoi*, which replaced shaft graves (like the ones at Grave Circle A) beginning in the 15th century B.C.

The entryway to this *tholos* itself is on a grand "cyclopean" scale—110 feet long and 20 feet wide. Imagine entering in a funeral procession carrying the body of the king. The walls rise at a diagonal up to the entrance, giving the illusion of swallowing you up as you enter.

The lintel over the doorway is mind-bogglingly big—26 feet across by 16 feet by 3 feet—and weighs 120 tons. (For comparison, the biggest stones of the Egyptian pyramids were 30 tons.) Notice before entering the hints of doorway hinges and ornamental pillars that once stood here.

Step inside and hear the 3,300-year-old echoes of this domed room. The round chamber is 47 feet in diameter and 42 feet tall, with an igloo-style dome made of 33 rings of corbelled (gradually projecting) stones, each weighing about 5 tons. The dome was decorated with bronze ornaments (you can see a few small nail holes where they were attached in the fifth row of stones up). The soot on the dome is from the campfires of fairly recent shepherds.

Kings were elaborately buried in the center of the room along with their swords, jewels, and personal possessions. There is also a side chamber (the door to the right) whose purpose can only be guessed at. After the funeral was over, the whole structure was covered with a mountain of dirt. But grave robbers got in anyway, and modern archaeologists have not found any bodies or treasures.

So why didn't the dome collapse? The weight of the dome is distributed by two triangular niches—one over the main lintel, and one over the side doorway. Notice how the main lintel has a crack in it. That crack is to the side of the doorway, right where the triangular niche spills all the weight of the dome onto it. Without this arch, the lintel would have cracked in the center and the dome would have collapsed. Look carefully at the smaller triangle above the smaller side-door arch to find its little crack (on the left). Again, without the arch, the weight over the door would have caused the lintel to break—and you wouldn't be standing here marveling at 3,300-year-old Mycenaean engineering.

• *Our tour's over. While only about 10 percent of the site has been excavated, I've Mycenae-n enough.*

OLYMPIA

ΑΡΧΑΊΑ ΟΛΥΜΠΊΑ / Αρχαία Ολυμπία

A visit to Olympia—most famous as the site of the original Olympic Games—offers one of your best opportunities for a hands-on experience with antiquity. Take your mark at the original starting line in the 2,500-year-old Olympic Stadium. Visit the Temple of Zeus, former site of a gigantic statue of Zeus that was one of the Seven Wonders of the Ancient World. Ponder the temple's once-majestic columns—toppled like towers of checkers by an earthquake—which are as evocative as anything from ancient times. Take a close look at the Archaeological Museum's gold-medal-quality statues and artifacts. And don't forget to step back and enjoy the setting itself. Despite the crowds that pour through here, Olympia remains a magical place, with ruins nestled among lush, shady groves of pine trees.

The modern-day town of Olympia (pop. 13,000) is far less inspiring—a concrete community custom-built to cater to the needs of the thousands of tourists who flock here year-round to visit the site. For convenience while sightseeing, you might want to spend one night in town; more time isn't necessary (though limited bus connections might require a two-night stay). While not romantic, Olympia is tidy, straightforward, functional, and pleasant enough.

Orientation to Olympia

The Sanctuary of Olympia sits in the fertile valley of the Alphios River in the western Peloponnese, 12 miles southeast of the regional capital of Pyrgos. The archaeological site curves along the southeastern edge of the tidy modern village of Archaia (Ancient) Olympia. The town's layout is basically a low-lying, easy-to-manage grid, five streets wide by eight streets long. The main road (called Praxitelous Kondyli) runs from Pyrgos in the north and leads right into a parking lot (and bus stop) at the south end of town. From here the museum and site are due east, over the Kladeos River.

Tourist Information: There's no TI, but your hotelier should be able to answer most questions. For current hours of the main sights, you can check local guide Niki Vlachou's **Olympia Travel Guide,** which contains updated information on sights—opening times, entry fees, discounts, etc.—and a detailed interactive map of the area (www.olympiatravelguide.com). She'll also answer questions from my readers free of charge (see her listing later, under "Helpful Hints").

ARRIVAL IN OLYMPIA

For driving directions into and out of Olympia, as well as options on reaching Olympia from the cruise-ship port of Katakolo, see "Olympia Connections," later.

By Bus: The bus drops you off just before the retail strip on the main street, a quick walk from the well-signed sights.

By Car: Parking is free and easy. It's fine to park on the streets in town. The best parking lots are near the Archaeological Museum, behind the main road next to the train station (see "Olympia Town" map). Avoid the bus lot near the Museum of the History of the Olympic Games in Antiquity, where you may get a ticket.

HELPFUL HINTS

Services: Olympia's main street has wide sidewalks, countless gift shops, and ample hotels, eateries, minimarkets, ATMs, and other tourist services.

Taxis: There's a taxi stand in town a block off the main street on the shady, angled side street called Georgiou Douma (tel. 26240-22555).

Local Guide: Consider hiring fantastic **Niki Vlachou** to show you around Olympia's ruins and museums (reasonable and negotiable rates, contact for exact price; also arranges transportation, wine tastings, olive press visits, cooking classes, and meals in local homes; mobile 697-242-6085, www.olympictours.gr, niki@olympictours.gr).

Don't count on finding a local guide to hire once you arrive—unlike many other popular ancient sites, the Sanctuary of Olympia is not surrounded by hopeful guides-for-hire.

Sights in Olympia

There are three parts to an Olympia visit: the Sanctuary of Olympia archaeological site, the Archaeological Museum, and the smaller Museum of the History of the Olympic Games in Antiquity (with the tiny adjacent Museum of the History of Excavations).

OLYMPIA

OLYMPIA

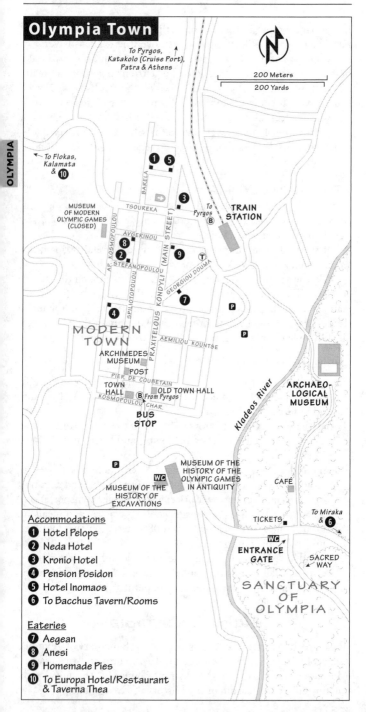

Olympia Town

To Pyrgos,
Katakolo (Cruise Port),
Patra & Athens

200 Meters
200 Yards

To Flokas,
Kalamata & ⑩

MUSEUM
OF MODERN
OLYMPIC GAMES
(CLOSED)

BARELA

TSOUREKA

AYGERINOU

AP. KOSMOPOULOU

SPILIOTOPOULOU

STEFANOPOULOU

KONDYLI (MAIN STREET)

PRAXITELOUS

GEORGIOU DOUMA

AEMILIOU KOUNTSE

① ⑤

③

To
Pyrgos
Ⓑ

TRAIN
STATION

⑧

②

⑨

Ⓣ

⑦

④

Ⓟ

Ⓟ

MODERN
TOWN

ARCHIMEDES
MUSEUM

POST

PIER DE COUBETAIN

TOWN
HALL

OLD TOWN HALL

KOSMOPOULOU

Ⓑ From Pyrgos

CHAR

BUS
STOP

Ⓟ

WC

MUSEUM OF THE
HISTORY OF
EXCAVATIONS

MUSEUM OF THE
HISTORY OF THE
OLYMPIC GAMES
IN ANTIQUITY

CAFÉ

Kladeos River

ARCHAEO-
LOGICAL
MUSEUM

TICKETS

To Miraka
& ⑥

WC

ENTRANCE
GATE

SACRED
WAY

SANCTUARY
OF
OLYMPIA

Accommodations
① Hotel Pelops
② Neda Hotel
③ Kronio Hotel
④ Pension Posidon
⑤ Hotel Inomaos
⑥ To Bacchus Tavern/Rooms

Eateries
⑦ Aegean
⑧ Anesi
⑨ Homemade Pies
⑩ To Europa Hotel/Restaurant
& Taverna Thea

▲▲▲THE SANCTUARY OF OLYMPIA AND ARCHAEOLOGICAL MUSEUM

Olympia was the mecca of ancient Greek religion—the location of its greatest sanctuary and one of its most important places of worship. In those times, people didn't live here: The sanctuary was set aside as a monastery and pilgrimage site; the nearest city was 30 miles away. Ancient Greeks came here only every four years, during the religious festival that featured the Olympic Games. The heart of the sanctuary was a sacred enclosure called the Altis—a walled-off, rectangular area that housed two big temples, multiple altars, and statues to the gods.

Whereas Delphi served as a pilgrimage destination mostly for groups of wealthy men on a particular mission, every four years Olympia drew 40,000 ordinary dudes (men only) for a Panhellenic party: the Olympic Games.

Cost: A €12 combo-ticket (€6 off-season) covers the archaeological site and all three museums (Archaeological Museum, Museum of the History of the Olympic Games in Antiquity, and Museum of the History of Excavations). Entry is free for ages 18 and under (be prepared to show ID).

Hours: Generally daily 8:00-20:00, Sept until 19:00, Oct until 18:00, Nov-March 8:30-15:00. Schedules vary by season and can change without warning, so confirm these times locally—either with your hotelier or at signs outside the sights.

Information: Tel. 26240-22742, www.culture.gr.

Getting There: If staying in Olympia, it's an easy five-minute **walk** from the town center to either the site or the Archaeological Museum. If arriving by **car,** park for free near the Archaeological Museum at one of two small lots at the east edge of town, south of the train station (see "Olympia Town" map, earlier; do not park near the site where the tour buses park, as you may get a ticket). To reach the museum and site from the parking lots, follow the path away from town, walking several hundred yards and crossing the Kladeos River. Up the stairs is the museum. For the site, take the path opposite the museum entry.

Planning Your Time: I recommend walking the archaeological site first, then touring the Archaeological Museum to reconstruct what you've seen. If you're passing the Archaeological Museum en route to the site anyway, buy your combo-ticket at the museum and stop in to see the site model in the entryway, which will spark your imagination as you stroll the site. Allow 1.5 hours for the site, and an hour for the Archaeological Museum.

Try to visit in the early morning or late afternoon (though the site can be very hot in the afternoon). These sights are most crowded between 10:00 and 13:00 (especially the Archaeological

OLYMPIA

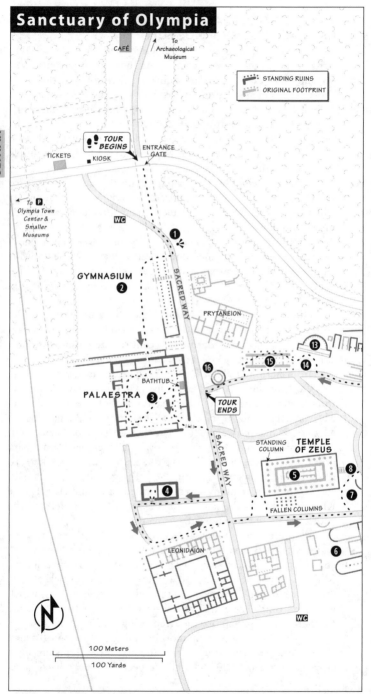

Sanctuary of Olympia

To Archaeological Museum

CAFÉ

STANDING RUINS
ORIGINAL FOOTPRINT

TICKETS
KIOSK

TOUR BEGINS

ENTRANCE GATE

To P, Olympia Town Center & Smaller Museums

WC

❶

GYMNASIUM ❷

SACRED WAY

PRYTANEION

❶❻

❶❸

❶❺ ❶❹

BATHTUB

PALAESTRA ❸

TOUR ENDS

STANDING COLUMN

TEMPLE OF ZEUS

❺ ❽

❼

FALLEN COLUMNS

SACRED WAY

❹

LEONIDAION

❻

WC

N

100 Meters

100 Yards

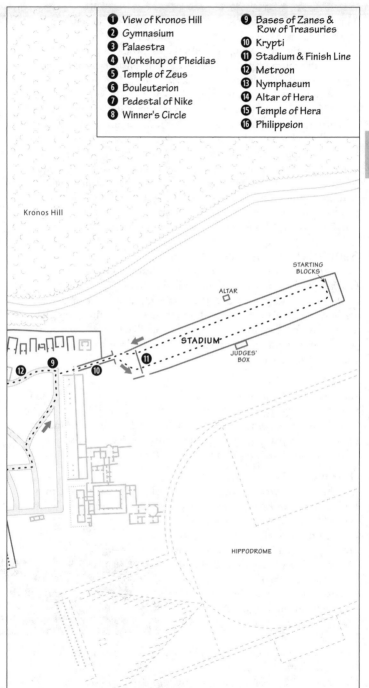

1. View of Kronos Hill
2. Gymnasium
3. Palaestra
4. Workshop of Pheidias
5. Temple of Zeus
6. Bouleuterion
7. Pedestal of Nike
8. Winner's Circle
9. Bases of Zanes & Row of Treasuries
10. Krypti
11. Stadium & Finish Line
12. Metroon
13. Nymphaeum
14. Altar of Hera
15. Temple of Hera
16. Philippeion

OLYMPIA

Kronos Hill

STARTING BLOCKS

ALTAR

STADIUM

JUDGES' BOX

HIPPODROME

Museum). Off-season, it's best to visit the site and museum in the morning, in case they close in the afternoon.

If coming into Olympia late in the day, you can use your combo-ticket to tour one place in the late afternoon and the other parts the next morning (one entry per place).

If you have all day for sightseeing, first hit the small Museum of the History of the Olympic Games in Antiquity, which provides background on the ancient games that'll help enliven your visit to the site (allow about a half-hour for this museum).

Services: There are WCs nearby (follow the signs). No food is allowed inside the site, though you can (and should) bring a water bottle. An open-air café is located between the site and the museum. The museum has a shop, WCs, and a café (outside, to the right as you face the entrance). The kiosk next to the ticket booth at the site sells guidebooks to the site and museum for €9.

Sanctuary of Olympia (The Site)

This center of ancient Greek religion dedicated to Zeus hosted the Olympic Games for more than a thousand years (c. 776 B.C.-A.D. 393). As you wander among these sporting arenas, temples, and statues, contemplate how the 100-meter dash was much more than a mere running race to the people of this civilization: It was a spiritual exercise that unified Greeks and expressed the most cherished values of Western civilization.

◐ Self-Guided Tour

Buy your tickets at the booth (stopping to use the WCs across the way if you need to), then head to the entrance gate. Inside, walk straight ahead (passing an orientation board) down into the ancient world of Olympia. This main path is called the Sacred Way.

• *Look to your left (through the trees) to catch glimpses of...*

❶ Kronos Hill

This hill was sacred to the ancient Greeks, who believed it to be the birthplace of Zeus—and the place where as a clever baby he escaped his father, Kronos, who'd tried
to eat him. Zeus later overthrew Kronos and went on to lead the pantheon of gods. (Other versions of the myth place this event on Mt. Olympus, in northern Greece, where the gods eventually made their home.) The hill was scorched by devastating wildfires in 2007—imagine how close the flames came to enveloping this ancient site. Locals replanted the hill, and it's once again green.

• *The Sacred Way leads down into a wide field scattered with ruins. To the left of the path was an enclosed area filled with various temples and altars; to the right were buildings for the athletes, who trained and lived in a complex of buildings similar to today's Olympic Village.*

Head to the right along the small path just before the two long rows of stubby columns. They mark the eastern edge of what was once the...

❷ Gymnasium

This was the largest building in the whole sanctuary, built in the

fourth century B.C. The truncated Doric columns once supported a covered arcade, one of four arcades that surrounded a big rectangular courtyard. Here athletes trained for events such as the sprint, discus throw, and javelin throw. The courtyard (about the size of six football fields, side-by-side along the Sacred Way) matched the length of the Olympic Stadium, so athletes could practice in a space similar to the one in which they would compete.

Because ancient Greeks believed that training the body was as important as training the mind, sports were a big part of every boy's education. Moreover, athletic training doubled as military training (a key element in citizenship)—so most towns had a gymnasium. The word "gymnasium" comes from the Greek *gymnos* ("naked"), which is how athletes trained and competed. Even today, the term "gymnasium" is used in many European countries (including Greece) to describe what Americans call high school.

Athletes arrived in a nearby town a month early for the Games, in order to practice and size up the competition. The Games were open to any freeborn Greek male (men and boys competed separately), but a good share of competitors were from aristocratic homes. Athletes trained hard. Beginning in childhood, they were given special diets and training regimens, often subsidized by their city. Many became professionals, touring the circuit of major festivals.

• *At the far end of the gymnasium ruins, stairs lead to a square space ringed by twin rows of taller, more intact columns. This is the...*

❸ Palaestra

Adjoining the gymnasium was this smaller but similar "wrestling school" (built around 300 B.C.). This square courtyard (216 feet on each side—about one acre), also surrounded by arcades, was used by athletes to train for smaller-scale events: wrestling, boxing, long jump (performed while carrying weights, to build strength), and

OLYMPIA

The Ancient Olympic Games

The Olympic Games were athletic contests held every four years as a way of honoring Zeus, the king of the gods. They were the culmination of a pilgrimage, as Greeks gathered to worship Zeus, the Games' patron.

The exact origins of the Games are lost in the mists of time, but they likely grew from a local religious festival first held at the Sanctuary of Olympia in about 1150 B.C. According to one legend, the festival was founded by Pelops, namesake of the Peloponnese; a rival legend credits Hercules. Sporting events became part of the festivities. A harmonious, healthy body was a "temple" that celebrated its creator by performing at its peak.

The first Olympic Games at which results were recorded are traditionally dated at 776 B.C. The Games grew rapidly,

attracting athletes from throughout the Greek world to compete in an ever-growing number of events (eventually taking up to five days in all). They reached their height of popularity around 400 B.C. Of the four major Greek games (including those at Delphi, Corinth, and Nemea), Olympia was the first, biggest, and most prestigious.

Besides honoring Zeus and providing entertainment, the Games served a political purpose: to develop a Panhellenic ("all-Greek") identity among scattered city-states and far-flung colonies. Every four years, wars between bickering Greeks were halted with a one-month "sacred truce" so that athletes and fans could travel safely to Olympia. Leading citizens from all corners would assemble here, including many second- and third-generation Greeks who'd grown up in colonies in Italy, France, or Africa. Olympia was geographically central, and for the length of the festivities, it was the symbolic heart of Greece.

This went on for 1,169 years, finally concluding in A.D. 393. Olympia today lives on in the spirit of the modern Olympic Games, revived in Athens in 1896. Every other year, athletes from around the world gather and compete in contests that challenge the human spirit and, it's hoped, foster a sense of common experience. Whether we're cheering on an American swimmer, a Chinese gymnast, or a Jamaican sprinter to go faster, longer, and better than any human has before, the Games bring the world together for a few weeks, much as they united the Greek world in this tranquil pine grove so many centuries ago.

pankration, a kind of ancient "ultimate fighting" with only two rules: no biting and no eye-gouging.

Picture athletes in the courtyard working out. They were always naked, except for a layer of olive oil and dust for a bit of protection against scrapes and the sun. Sometimes they exercised in time with a flute player to coordinate their movements and to keep up the pace. Trainers and spectators could watch from the shade of the colonnades. Notice that the columns are smooth (missing their fluting) on the lower part of the inside face. This way, when it rained, athletes could exercise under the arcade (or take a breather by leaning up against a column) without scraping themselves on the grooves.

In the area nearest the Sacred Way, notice the benches where athletes were taught and people gathered for conversation. You can still see the bathtubs that athletes used to wash off their oil-dust coating. (They also used a stick-like tool to scrape off the oily grime.)

Besides being training facilities, *palaestrae* (found in almost every city) were also a kind of health club where men gathered to chat.

• *Exit the* palaestra *on the left to continue down the Sacred Way, then take the next right. Climb the stairs at the far end, and peek into the ruined brick building that was once the...*

❹ Workshop of Pheidias

In this building, the great sculptor Pheidias (c. 490-430 B.C.) created the 40-foot statue of Zeus (c. 435 B.C.) that once stood in the

Temple of Zeus across the street (for details on how he constructed it, see the sidebar). The workshop was built with the same dimensions as the temple's *cella* (inner room) so that Pheidias could create the statue with the setting in mind. Pheidias arrived here having recently completed

his other masterpiece, the colossal *Athena Parthenos* for the Parthenon in Athens. According to ancient accounts, his colossal Zeus outdid even that great work.

How do we know this building was Pheidias' place? Because archaeologists found sculptors' tools and molds for pouring metals, as well as a cup with Pheidias' name on it (all now displayed in the museum). After the last ancient Games were held, this workshop was turned into a Christian church (fourth century A.D.—notice the semicircular part at the end facing east, which was added as an altar; see "Olympia's Legacy," later).

• *Head right out of the workshop, then loop back around to the left, past a large, open, rubble-strewn field (to the right) with dozens of thigh-high Ionic capitals. This was the site of the massive* **Leonidaion***, a luxury, four-star hotel—boasting 145 rooms, private baths, and a central pool— built in the fourth century B.C. to house dignitaries and famous athletes during the Games.*

Cross the Sacred Way, head up the ramp/stairs, then veer left toward Olympia's main sight: the ruins of the Temple of Zeus, marked by a single standing column.

❺ Temple of Zeus

The center of ancient Olympia—both physically and symbolically—was the massive temple dedicated to Zeus, king of the gods and patron of the Games. It was the first of the Golden Age temples, one of the biggest (not much smaller than the Parthenon), and is the purest example of the Doric style.

The temple was built in the fifth century B.C. (470-455 B.C.), stood for a thousand years, and then crumbled into the evocative pile of ruins we see today, still lying where they fell in the sixth century A.D.

Stand in front of the rubble field strewn with big gray blocks, two-ton column drums, and fallen 12-ton capitals. They're made

not of marble but of cheaper local limestone. Look closely and you can see the seashell fossils in this porous (and not terribly durable) sedimentary rock. Most of the temple was made of limestone, then covered with a marble-powder stucco to make it glisten as brightly

Statue of Zeus

Imagine yourself as a visitor to the Temple of Zeus in ancient times. You'd enter the temple from the east end (the end opposite the Sacred Way). Peering to the far side of the temple, you'd see the monumental statue of Zeus sitting 40 feet high on a golden throne. The statue gleamed gold and white, with colored highlights. In his right hand Zeus held a winged statue of Nike (goddess of victory), and in his left hand was a scepter topped with an eagle. Zeus completely filled the space. His head almost touched the ceiling (which was higher than the exterior columns), and his arms almost touched the sides, making the colossal statue appear even bigger. A cistern of olive oil on the temple floor reflected golden hues onto the statue.

Pheidias made the statue with a core of wood. He covered that with plates of ivory (soaked, carved, and worked into shape) to make Zeus' skin and 500 pounds of gold plates for the clothes and the throne. (Such statues, when decorated with gold and ivory—as many religious statues in ancient Greece were—are called "chryselephantine.") Pheidias' assistants painted the throne with scenes of the gods.

The statue was considered by ancient people as one of the Seven Wonders—a list of tourist musts that also included the Colossus of Rhodes and the pyramids of Egypt. We know the general outlines of the statue because it appeared on coins of the day.

We also know that the statue stood for 900 years, but no one knows what became of it. It may have been melted down by Christians or destroyed in the earthquakes that toppled the temple. Others think the pieces were carried off to Constantinople and accidentally burned in that city's catastrophic fire of A.D. 476.

as if it were made of pure marble. The pediments and some other decorations were made of expensive white marble from the isle of Paros.

An olive tree near the temple's southwest corner (to your left) marks the spot of the original tree (planted by Hercules, legends say) from which the winners' wreaths were made. Then as now, olives were vital to Greece, providing food, preservatives, fuel, perfumes...and lubrication for athletes.

You're standing near the back (west) end of the temple, near its most sacred part: The *cella*, where Pheidias' statue of Zeus stood. The interior of the temple is closed indefinitely; to get a good look you'll have to head back to the path that runs along what was once the south porch of the temple—the side facing away from Kronos Hill.

As you walk around the temple, try to reconstruct it in your mind. It was huge—about half an acre—and stood six stories tall. The lone standing column is actually a reconstruction (of original pieces, cleaned and restacked), but it gives you a sense of the scale: It's 34 feet tall, 7 feet thick, and weighs 9 tons. This was one of 34 massive Doric columns that surrounded the temple: 6 on each end and 13 along the sides (making this a typical peripteral/peristyle

temple, like Athens' Parthenon and Temple of Hephaistos in the Ancient Agora).

The columns originally supported a triangular pediment at each end (now in the Archaeological Museum), carved with scenes of the battle of the Lapiths and centaurs (west end) and Pelops and the chariot race (east end, which was the main entrance).

Along the south side of the temple, you'll see five huge fallen columns, with their drums lined up in a row like dominos. To the right of the path (across from the fallen columns) are the ruins of the ❻ **Bouleuterion,** the council chamber where, by stepping on castrated bulls' balls, athletes took an oath not to cheat. As this was a religious event, and because physical training was a part of moral education, the oaths and personal honor were held sacred.

Continue down the path to the front (east) end of the temple and duck off the path to the left to find the 29-foot-tall, white-marble, triangular ❼ **Pedestal of Nike.** It's missing its top, but it once held a famous statue (now in the museum) of the goddess Nike, the personification of victory.

She looked down upon the ❽ **Winner's Circle,** here at the main entrance to the temple, where Olympic victors were

announced and crowned. As thousands gathered in the courtyard below, priests called the name of the winner, who scaled the steps to the cheers of the crowd. The winner was crowned with a wreath of olive (not laurel) branches, awarded a statue in his honor—and nothing more. There were no awards for second and third place and no gold, silver, or bronze medals—those are inventions of the modern Olympics. However, winners were usually showered with gifts and perks from their proud hometowns: free food for life, tax exemptions, theater tickets, naming rights for gymnasiums, statues, pictures on ancient Wheaties boxes, and so on.

In the courtyard you can see pedestals that once held statues of winners, who were considered to be demigods. The inscriptions listed the winner's name, the date, the event won, his hometown, and the names of his proud parents.

The ruined building directly east of here was the Echo Hall, a long gallery where winners were also announced as if into a microphone—the sound echoed seven times. Just in front of the Echo Hall is a recently renovated marble column, which was built in 270 B.C. to honor Egyptian King Ptolemy II, the son of one of Alexander the Great's generals. After an eight-year restoration, the column now is at its original height, allowing visitors to better visualize the scale of Olympia's monuments.

• *With the main entrance of the Temple of Zeus at your back, walk out to the path, passing several of the inscribed pedestals. Turn left at the tree, then follow the right fork until you bump into the low wall at the base of Kronos Hill. The foot of that hill is lined with a row of pedestals, called the...*

❾ Bases of Zanes and Row of Treasuries

These 16 pedestals once held bronze statues of Zeus (plural "Zanes"). At the ancient Olympic Games, as at the modern ones, it was an honor just to compete, and there was no shame in not finishing first. Quitters and cheaters were another story. The Zeus statues that once lined this path were paid for with fines levied on cheaters, whose names and ill deeds were inscribed in the bases. As people entered the stadium (straight ahead), they'd spit on the names on the bases. Offenses ranged from doping (using forbidden herbs) or bribing opponents, to failing to train in advance of the

Games or quitting out of cowardice. Drinking animal blood—the Red Bull of the day—was forbidden. Official urine tasters tested for this ancient equivalent of steroids.

Just behind the statues (and a few feet higher in elevation) is a terrace that once held a row of treasuries. These small buildings housed expensive offerings to the gods. Many were sponsored by colonies as a way for Greeks living abroad to stay in touch with their cultural roots.

• *Turn right and pass under the arch of the...*

❿ Krypti

As you enter the stadium through this tunnel, imagine yourself as an athlete who has trained for years and traveled for days, carrying

the hopes of your hometown on your shoulders...and now finally about to compete. Built around 300 B.C., this tunnel once had a vaulted ceiling; along the walls are niches that functioned as equipment lockers. Just like today's NFL players, Olympia's athletes psyched themselves up for the big contest by shouting as they ran through this tunnel, then emerging into the stadium to the roar of the crowd.

• *On your mark, get set, go. Follow the Krypti as it leads into the...*

⓫ Stadium

Line up on that original marble-paved starting line from the ancient Olympic Games and imagine the scene. The place was filled

with 45,000 spectators—men, boys, and girls—who sat on the man-made banks on either side of the track. One lone adult woman was allowed in: a priestess of the goddess Demeter Chamyne, whose altar rose above the sea of testosterone from the north (left) bank (still visible today).

The stadium (built in the fifth century B.C.) held no seats except those for the judges, who sat in a special box (visible on the south bank, to your right). These Hellanodikai ("Judges of the Greeks") kept things on track. Elected from local noble families and carefully trained over 10 months for just a few days of Games, these referees were widely respected for their impartiality.

The stadium track is 192 meters (640 feet) from start to finish line. The Greek word *stadion* literally means a course that is 600 traditional Olympic feet long, supposedly first marked out by Hercules. The line at the near (west) end marked the finish, where all races ended. (Some started at this end as well, depending on how

many laps in the race, but most started at the far end.) The racers ran straight up and back on a clay surface, not around the track. There were 20 starting blocks (all still visible today), each with two grooves—one for each foot (athletes competed barefoot). Wooden starting gates (similar to those used in horse races today) made sure no one could jump the gun.

The first Games featured just one event, a sprint race over one length of the stadium, or one *stadion*. Imagine running this distance in 19.3 seconds, as Usain Bolt of Jamaica did at the 2012 Olympic Games. Over time, more events were added. There were races of two *stadia* (that is, up and back, like today's 400-meter event), 24 *stadia* (similar to today's 5K race), and a race in which athletes competed in full armor, including shields.

At the height of the Games (c. 400 B.C.), there were 13 events held over five days (most here in the stadium). Besides footraces, you'd see events such as the discus, javelin, boxing, wrestling, long jump, *pankration* (a wrestling/boxing/martial arts mix), and the pentathlon. (The decathlon is a modern invention.) During the 2004 Games in Athens, the shot-put competition was held in this stadium. South of the stadium was the hippodrome, or horse-racing track, where riding and chariot races took place.

Compare this stadium and the events held here with the gladiatorial contests in ancient Rome several centuries later: In the far more massive Colosseum, the sensationalistic events weren't about honor, athletic glory, or shared humanity, but a bloody fight to the death, staged to remind the citizens of the power of the state. Good thing it's the Greek games we now emulate.

• *Backtrack through the tunnel and continue straight past the pedestals for the Zeus statues. You'll bump into some rectangular foundations, the ruins of the...*

⓰ Metroon and the Altar of Zeus

The Metroon (mid-fourth century B.C.) was a temple dedicated to the mother of the gods, Rhea (also known as Cybele). The site also honored the mother-goddess of the earth, worshipped as "Gaia."

Somewhere near here once stood the Altar of Zeus, though no one knows exactly where—nothing remains today. At this altar the ancient Olympians slaughtered and burned animals in sacrifice to Zeus on a daily basis. For special festivals, they'd sacrifice 100 cattle (a "hecatomb"), cook them on the altar, throw offerings into the flames, and feast on the flesh, leaving a pile of ashes 25 feet high.

In the middle of the wide path, under an olive tree, is a **sunken apse,** only recently excavated. It's actually the foundation of a 3,000-year-old house—i.e., more than 1,000 years older than the ancient ruins we've seen elsewhere—more evidence that this site was important long before the Olympic Games and the Golden Age of ancient Greece.

• *To the right are the ruins of a semicircular structure built into the hillside, the...*

⓭ Nymphaeum

This was once a spectacular curved fountain, lined with two tiers of statues of emperors, some of which are now in the Archaeologi-

cal Museum. The fountain provided an oasis in the heat and also functioned as an aqueduct, channeling water throughout the sanctuary. It was built toward the end of the sanctuary's life (around A.D. 150) by the wealthy Roman Herodes Atticus (who also financed construction of the famous theater at the base of the Acropolis in Athens—the Odeon of Herodes Atticus).

When the Romans conquered Greece, in the second century B.C., they became fans of Greek culture, including the Olympics. The Romans repaired neglected buildings and built new structures, such as this one. But they also changed (some say perverted) the nature of the Games, transforming them from a Greek religious ritual to a secular Roman spectacle. Rome opened up the Games to any citizen of the Empire, broadening their appeal at the cost of their Greekness.

Rome's notorious Emperor Nero—a big fan of the Olympics—attended the Games in the mid–first century A.D. He built a villa nearby, started music contests associated with the Games, and entered the competition as a charioteer. But when he fell off his chariot, Nero ordered the race stopped and proclaimed himself the winner.

• *Directly in front of the Nymphaeum are the rectangular foundations of what was once the...*

⑭ Altar of Hera

These humble foundations provide a bridge across millennia, linking the original Olympics to today's modern Games. Since 1936, this is where athletes have lit the ceremonial Olympic torch (for both the summer and winter Games). A few months before the modern Games begin, local women dress up in priestess garb and solemnly proceed here from the Temple of Hera. A curved, cauldron-shaped mirror is used to focus the rays of the sun, igniting a flame. The women then carry the flame into the stadium, where runners light a torch and begin the long relay to the next city to host the Games—a distance of more than 9,000 miles to Pyeongchang, South Korea, where the 2018 Winter Games were held, and 6,000 miles to Tokyo, site of the 2020 Summer Games.

• *Fifteen yards farther along are the four standing Doric columns that mark the well-preserved...*

⑮ Temple of Hera

First built in 650 B.C., this is the oldest structure on the site and one of Greece's first monumental temples. The temple originally honored both Hera and her husband Zeus, before the Temple of Zeus was built.

The temple was long but not tall, giving it an intimate feel. Its length-to-width ratio (and number of columns: 6 on the short sides, 16 on the long ones) is 3:8, which was considered particularly harmonious and aesthetically pleasing, as well as astronomically significant (the ancients synchronized the lunar and solar calendars by making the year three months longer every eight years).

The temple was originally made of wood. Over time, the wooden columns were replaced with stone columns, resulting in a virtual catalog of the various periods of the Doric style. The columns are made from the same shell-bearing limestone as most of the site's buildings, also originally covered in marble stucco.

Inside, a large statue of Hera once sat on a throne with Zeus standing beside her. Hera's priestesses wove a new dress for the statue every four years. The temple also housed a famous statue of Hermes and was topped with the Disk of the Sun (both are now in the museum).

Though women did not compete in the Olympics, girls and maidens competed in the Heraean Games, dedicated to Hera. The Heraean Games were also held here every four years, though not in the same years as the Olympics. They were open only to unmarried virgins—no married women allowed. Wearing dresses that left one shoulder and breast exposed, the girls raced on foot (running five-sixths of a *stadion*, or 160 meters/525 feet). Like the men, the winners received olive wreaths and fame, as well as a painted portrait displayed on a column of the Temple of Hera.

• *Walking out the back of Hera's temple, you'll reach our last stop: a round temple with three reconstructed Ionic columns. This was the...*

⓰ Philippeion

The construction of the Philippeion marked a new era in Greece: the Hellenistic era. (Compare these gracefully slender Ionic columns to the earlier, stouter Doric columns of the Temple of Hera—in the centuries between when they were built, Greek ideals of proportion had shifted away from sturdiness and strength to a preference for elegant beauty.)

Philip of Macedon built this monument to mark his triumph over the Greeks. The Macedonians spoke Greek and had many similar customs, but they were a kingdom (not a democracy), and the Greeks viewed them as foreigners. Philip conquered Greece around 340 B.C., thus uniting the country—by force—while bringing its Classical Age to an end.

The temple—the first major building visitors saw upon entering the sacred site—originally had 18 Ionic columns of limestone and marble stucco (though today it appears dark, as the gleaming stucco is long gone). Inside stood statues of Philip and his family, including his son, the man who would bring Greece to its next phase of glory: Alexander the Great.

Just north of the Philippeion, bordering the Sacred Way and difficult to make out, are the scant remains of the Prytaneion, the building that once housed the eternal Olympic flame.

Olympia's Legacy

After the Classical Age, the Games continued, but not in their original form. First came Alexander and a new era of more secular values. Next came the Romans, who preserved the Games but also commercialized them and opened them up to non-Greeks. The Games went from being a somber celebration of Hellenic culture to being a bombastic spectacle. The lofty ideals for which the games were once known had evaporated—along with their prestige. As Rome/Greece's infrastructure decayed, so did the Games. A series of third-century earthquakes and the turmoil of the Herulian invasion (in A.D. 267) kept the crowds away. As Greece became Christian, the pagan sanctuary became politically incorrect.

The last ancient Games (the 293rd) were held in A.D. 393. A year later, they were abolished by the ultra-Christian emperor Theodosius I as part of a general purge of pagan festivals. The final blow was delivered in 426, when Theodosius II ordered the temples set ablaze. The remaining buildings were adopted by a small early Christian community, who turned Pheidias' workshop into their church. They were forced to abandon the area after it was hit by a combination of earthquakes (in 522 and 551) and catastrophic floods and mudslides. Over the centuries, two rivers proceeded to bury the area under 25 feet of silt, thus preserving the remaining buildings until archaeologists started excavations in 1875. They finally finished digging everything out in 1972.

• *The Archaeological Museum is 200 yards to the north and well-signed.*

Archaeological Museum

Many of Olympia's greatest works of art and artifacts have been removed from the site and are now displayed, and well-described in English, in this compact and manageable museum.

➲ Self-Guided Tour: This tour takes you past the highlights, but there's much more to see if you have time. As you enter, ask for the free pamphlet that includes a map of the museum (and the site).

• *In the entrance lobby, to the right of the ticket desk, is a...*

❶ Model of the Site, Reconstructed: Looking at Olympia as it appeared in its Golden Age glory, you can see some of the artifacts that once decorated the site (and which now fill this museum). On the Temple of Zeus, notice the pediments, topped with statues and tripods. Southeast of the temple is the Pedestal of Nike, supporting the statue of Nike. Find Pheidias' workshop and the Temple of Hera, topped with the Disk of the Sun. We'll see all of these items on this tour.

• *Continue straight ahead into the main hall. On the right wall are...*

❷ Statues from the West Pediment of the Temple of Zeus: These statues fit snugly into the 85-foot-long pediment that stood over the back side of the temple (facing the Sacred Way). Study the scene depicting the battle of the Lapiths and centaurs: The centaurs have crashed a human wedding party in order to carry off the women. See one dramatic scene of a woman and her horse-

Olympia Archaeological Museum

OLYMPIA

MAIN
HALL

BULL

ENTRANCE

CAFE, SHOP
& WC

① Site Model
② Temple of Zeus:
   West Pediment
③ Temple of Zeus:
   East Pediment
④ Nike of Paeonius
⑤ Helmet of Miltiades
⑥ Workshop of Pheidias
⑦ Hermes of Praxiteles
⑧ Nymphaeum Statues
⑨ Zeus & Ganymede
⑩ Disk of the Sun
⑪ Griffins
⑫ Tripods

man abductor just left of center. The Lapith men fight back. In the center, a 10-foot-tall Apollo stands calmly looking on. Fresh from their victory in the Persian Wars, the Greeks were particularly fond of any symbol of their struggle against "barbarians."

The statues from the West Pediment are gorgeous examples of the height of Golden Age sculpture: Notice the harmony of the poses and how they capture motion at the perfect moment without seeming melodramatic. The bodies, clearly visible under clothing, convey all the action, while the faces (in the statues that still have them) are stoic.

• *On the opposite side of the hall are...*

   ❸ **Statues from the East Pediment of the Temple of Zeus:** Olympic victors stood beneath this pediment—the temple's main entrance—as they received their olive wreaths. The statues

tell the story of King Pelops, the legendary founder of the Games. A 10-foot-tall Zeus in the center is flanked by two competing chariot teams. Pelops (at Zeus' left hand, with the fragmented legs) prepares to race King Oenomaus (at Zeus' right) for the hand of the king's daughter Hippodamia (standing beside Pelops). The king, aware of a prophecy predicting that he would be murdered by his son-in-law, killed 13 previous suitors after defeating them in chariot races. But Pelops wins this race by sabotaging the king's wheels (that may be what the crouching figure is up to behind the king's chariot), causing the king to be dragged to his death by his horses (just like that chariot race in *Ben-Hur*). Pelops becomes king and goes on to unify the Peloponnesian people with a festival: the Olympic Games.

As some of the first sculpture of the Golden Age (made after the Persian invasion of 480 B.C.), these figures show the realism and relaxed poses of the new age (note that they're missing those telltale Archaic-era smiles). But they are still done in the Severe style—the sculptural counterpart to stoic Doric architecture—with impassive faces and understated emotion, quite different from the exuberant West Pediment, made years later. Still, notice how refined the technique is—the horses, for example, effectively convey depth and movement. But seen from the side, it's striking how flat the sculpture really is.

• *Continue straight ahead, where you'll see a statue rising and floating on her pedestal. She's the...*

❹ **Nike of Paeonius:** This statue of Victory (c. 421 B.C.) once stood atop the triangular Pedestal of Nike next to the Temple of Zeus. Victory holds her billowing robe in her outstretched left hand and a palm leaf in her right as she floats down from Mt. Olympus to proclaim the triumph of the Messenians (the Greek-speaking people from southwest Peloponnese) over Sparta.

The statue, made of flawless pure-white marble from the island of Paros, is the work of the Greek sculptor Paeonius. It was damaged in the earthquakes of A.D. 522 and 551, and today, Nike's wings are completely missing. But they once stretched behind and above her, making the statue 10 feet tall. (She's about seven feet today.) With its triangular base, the whole monument to Victory would have been an imposing 36 feet tall, rising above the courtyard where Olympic winners were crowned.

• *In the glass case to the right as you face Nike are two bronze helmets. The green battered one (#2) is the...*

❺ **Bronze Helmet of Miltiades:** In September of 490 B.C., a huge force of invading Persians faced off against the outnumbered

Greeks on the flat plain of Marathon, north of Athens. Although most of the Athenian generals wanted to wait for reinforcements, Miltiades convinced them to attack. The Greeks sprinted across the plain, into the very heart of the Persians—a bold move that surprised and routed the enemy. According to legend, the good news was carried to Athens by a runner. He raced 26 miles from Marathon to Athens, announced "Hurray, we won!"...and dropped dead on the spot.

The legend inspired the 26-mile race called the marathon— but the marathon was not an Olympic event in ancient times. It was a creation for the first modern Games, revived in Athens in A.D. 1896.

• *Pass the helmet and walk into the room with the Zeus statue painting.*

❻ **Workshop of Pheidias Room:** The poster shows Pheidias' great statue of Zeus, and a model reconstructs the workshop where he created it. In the display case directly to the left as you enter, find exhibit #10, the clay cup of Pheidias. The inscription on the bottom (hence the mirror) reads, "I belong to Pheidias." The adjacent case holds clay molds that were likely used for making the folds of Zeus' robe. The case in the opposite corner contains lead and bronze tools used by ancient sculptors to make the statues we've seen all day.

• *The room hiding behind the Zeus poster contains...*

❼ **Hermes of Praxiteles:** This seven-foot-tall statue (340-330 B.C.), discovered in the Temple of Hera, is possibly a rare original by the great sculptor Praxiteles. Though little is known of this fourth-century sculptor, Praxiteles was recognized in his day as the master of realistic anatomy and the first to sculpt nude women. If this statue looks familiar, that's because his works influenced generations of Greek and Roman sculptors, who made countless copies.

Hermes leans against a tree trunk, relaxed. He carries a baby—the recently orphaned Dionysus—who reaches for a (missing) object that Hermes is distracting him with. Experts guess the child was probably groping for a bunch of grapes, which would have hinted at Dionysus' future role as the debauched god of wine and hedonism.

Circle the statue counterclockwise and watch Hermes' face take on the many shades of thoughtfulness. From the front he appears serene. From the right (toward the baby), he seems sad. But from the left (toward his outstretched arm), there's the hint of a smile. (And, from the back, nice cheeks!)

The statue has some of Praxiteles' textbook features. The body has the distinctive S-curve of Classical sculpture (head tilted one way, torso the other, legs another). Hermes rests his arm on the tree stump, over which his robe is draped. And the figure is interesting from all angles, not just the front. The famous Praxiteles could make hard, white, translucent marble appear as supple, sensual, and sexual as human flesh.

• *Back in the Pheidias room, detour left to see more statues, from the Roman Nymphaeum fountain. (If you're in a rush, skip this section and head for the Disk of the Sun.)*

❽ **Nymphaeum Statues:** The grand semicircular fountain near the Temple of Hera had two tiers of statues, including Roman

emperors and the family of the statue's benefactor, Herodes Atticus. Here you can see some of the surviving statues, as well as a bull (in the center of the room) that stood in the middle of the fountain. The bull's inscriptions explain the fountain's origins. Compared to the energetic statues we just saw from the west pediment of the Temple of Zeus, these stately statues are static and lackluster.

The next (smaller) room holds more Roman-era statues, from the Metroon and the Temple of Hera.

• *Return to the Workshop of Pheidias Room, then backtrack past the helmets and Nike to find the glass case with the smaller-than-life-size...*

OLYMPIA

❾ Statue of Zeus Carrying Off Ganymede: See Zeus' sly look as he carries off the beautiful Trojan boy Ganymede to be his cup-bearer and lover. The terra-cotta statue was likely the central roof decoration (called an *akroterion*—see the nearby diagram) atop one of the treasury houses.

• *Continue into the long hall with the large, decorated terra-cotta pediments, reminding us that these temples were brightly painted, not the plain-white marble we imagine them today.*

❿ Disk of the Sun: This terra-cotta disk—seven-and-a-half feet across and once painted in bright colors—was the *akroterion*

that perched atop the peak of the roof of the Temple of Hera. It stood as a sun- or star-like icon meant to ward off bad juju and symbolize Hera's shining glory.

• *Along the left wall is an assortment of cool-looking...*

⓫ Griffins: Because Greeks considered the lion the king of the beasts, and the eagle the top bird, the half-lion-half-eagle griffin was a popular symbol of power for the ancient Greeks, even if no such animal actually existed.

• *The rest of this long room contains several...*

⓬ Tripods: These cauldrons-with-legs were used as gifts to the gods and to victorious athletes. For religious rituals, tripods were used to pour liquid libations, to hold sacred objects, or to burn incense or sacrificial offerings. As ceremonial gifts to the gods, tripods were placed atop and around temples. And as gifts to athletes, they were a source of valuable bronze (which could easily be melted down into some other form), making for a nice "cash" prize.

OTHER OLYMPIA MUSEUMS

While the core of Olympia's collection is displayed at the newer, more modern museum described earlier, two related museums (one tiny and skippable, the other a bit bigger and more worthwhile) are perched on a low hill above the southern parking lot housed in what used to be Olympia's original archaeological museum and the town's first hotel for antiquity-loving tourists.

In Olympia town, the Archimedes Museum will appeal to engineering nuts. You may also see signs pointing to the Museum of the Modern Olympic Games, housed in a low building in the middle of town, but it's currently closed (supposedly for a badly needed renovation), and locals don't expect it to open anytime soon.

▲▲Museum of the History of the Olympic Games in Antiquity

Most people are familiar with the modern-day Olympics, but the games played by those early Olympians were a very different operation. The collection offers
a handy "Ancient Olympics 101" lesson that helps bring the events to life and nicely complements the other attractions in Olympia. If you can spare the 30-45 minutes it takes to see this museum, stop by here first to get your imag-

ination in gear before seeing the ancient site.

Just inside the entrance are models of the site from four different eras. The rooms around the perimeter of the building tell the story of the original Games—you'll see the awards and honors for the victors, and, in the corner, a beautiful mosaic floor (c. A.D. 200) depicting some of the events. The main central hall focuses on the athletic events themselves, displaying ancient discuses, javelin heads, halters (weights used in the long jump), and large shields that were carried by fully armor-clad runners in some particularly exhausting footraces.

Cost and Hours: Covered by €12 combo-ticket; Mon 10:00-17:00, Tue-Sun 8:00-15:00 (closed Sat-Sun off-season); WCs outside building behind excavations museum.

Museum of the History of Excavations

This one-room exhibit, in the small building near the Museum of the History of the Olympic Games in Antiquity, explains the various waves of excavations that have taken place since the site of Olympia was identified in the mid-18th century. While early investigations were done by archaeologists from France (in the 1820s) and Germany (in the 1870s), most of the site was systematically uncovered to the point you see today by Germans between 1936 and 1966. (When Berlin hosted the 1936 Olympics, Germany took a special interest in the history of the original Games.) You'll see old maps, photos, and archaeologists' tools.

Cost and Hours: Covered by €12 combo-ticket, same hours as museum above.

Archimedes Museum

Located on the main drag in Olympia, this museum shows off replicas of ancient Greek technologies, such as the Archimedes screw, the crane used to build the Parthenon, the Antikythera mechanism (ancient computer thought to have been used in astronomy), and the pantograph (the original photocopier). The models (and museum) were created by Konstantinos Kotsanas, who studied mechanical engineering at a university in Patra.

Cost and Hours: Free, donations accepted, daily 10:00-20:00, off-season until 15:00.

OLYMPIA

Sleeping in Olympia

Olympia's impressive archaeological site and museum—and the town's inconvenient location far from other attractions—make spending the night here almost obligatory. Fortunately, there are enough good options to make it worthwhile, including one real gem (Hotel Pelops). If you have a car, consider sleeping above Olympia in the more charming village of Miraka.

IN OLYMPIA

For locations, see the "Olympia Town" map, earlier.

$$ Hotel Pelops is Olympia's top option, with 18 comfortable rooms—try this place first. Run by the warm, welcoming Spiliopoulos clan—father Theodoros, Aussie mom Susanna, and children Alkis, Kris, and Sally—the hotel oozes hospitality. They're generous with travel advice and include free tea and coffee in each room. On the wall of the breakfast room, look for the four Olympic torches that family members have carried in the official relay: Tokyo 1964, Mexico City 1968, Athens 2004, and Rio 2016 (elevator, cooking classes extra—arrange well in advance, Varela 2, tel. 26240-22543, www.hotelpelops.gr, hotelpelops@gmail.com).

$$ Neda Hotel has 44 in-need-of-modernization rooms. But there are two reasons to consider staying here: It's the only place in town with a swimming pool (decent size, surrounded by chaises, café tables, and a small bar), and its top-floor dining room, where the buffet breakfast is served, has outdoor seating and lovely views of Olympia (elevator, Karamanli 1, tel. 26240-22563, www.hotelneda.gr, info@hotelneda.gr, Tyligadas family).

$ Kronio Hotel, run by friendly Panagiotis Asteris, rents 23 straightforward rooms along the main street; all but one have balconies and bathtubs (elevator, Tsoureka 1, tel. 26240-22188, www.hotelkronio.gr, hotelkronio@hotmail.com).

$ Pension Posidon is a good budget option, with 10 simple but clean rooms in a homey, flower-bedecked house just two blocks above the main street (most rooms have balconies, breakfast extra, rooftop patio, Stefanopoulou 9, tel. 26240-22567, mobile 697-321-6726, www.pensionposidon.gr, info@pensionposidon.gr, Liagouras family).

$ Hotel Inomaos has 25 basic crank-'em-out rooms on the main street, each with a no-nonsense balcony (family rooms, elevator, tel. 26240-22056, hotelinomaos@hotmail.com).

NEAR OLYMPIA, IN MIRAKA

The village of Miraka, which sits on a hill above Olympia, is the site of the ancient settlement of Pissa (Archea Pissa/Αρχαια Πισα). Today it offers an authentic-feeling Old-World village experience and a scenic perch with fine views over the fire-charred (but gradually reviving) olive groves in the valley below.

$$ Bacchus Tavern (also a recommended restaurant) rents 11 modern, comfortable rooms in a traditional village a 10-minute drive above Olympia. This is a luxurious-feeling retreat from the drabness of modern Olympia (family rooms, apartment, inviting terrace and swimming pool, tel. 26240-22298, mobile 693-714-4800, www.bacchustavern.gr, bacchuspension@gmail.com, Kostas and Achilleas).

Getting There: It's about a 10-minute drive from Olympia's town center: Take the main road out of town toward Pyrgos, then turn right toward Tripoli and twist uphill on the new, modern highway. After the fourth tunnel, exit to the left and curve around to reach Miraka. Bacchus Tavern is on the right as you enter town (look for the parking lot).

Eating in Olympia

Because its restaurants cater to one-nighters, Olympia has no interest in creating return visitors—making its cuisine scene uniformly dismal in the middle of town. For something more special, it's worth the drive (or taxi ride) to one of the more interesting places in the hills above town. See the "Olympia Town" map, earlier, for locations.

IN THE TOWN CENTER

The shady, angled side-street called Georgiou Douma is lined with touristy places serving mediocre food; but if you're attracted to the area's convenient location and leafy scene, try **$$$ Aegean** (Αιγαίο), right off the main street, where the meals are cooked by the owner (good salads, tasty vegetarian options, open daily for lunch and dinner, closed Nov-March, tel. 26240-22540).

$$ Anesi, located just outside the tourist zone, has zero atmosphere but is the local favorite for grilled meat (open daily for lunch and dinner, closed Nov-Dec, one block off main street at corner of Avgerinou and Spiliopoulou, tel. 26240-22644).

$ Fresh Cheese Pies: Takis opens at 7:00 and closes when he runs out of his freshly baked pies, made with handmade dough and various fillings (along the main street, look for the sign that says *Homemade*).

IN THE HILLS ABOVE OLYMPIA

The town's best dining experiences are up in the hills above town, where locals head to enjoy the food and views. The two places to the west are a five-minute ride out of town—you could walk to either of these with enough time (20-30 minutes each way), but I'd drive or spring for a taxi. Bacchus, to the east, is far beyond walking distance.

West of Town

$$$ Europa Hotel's elegant garden restaurant, on the hills overlooking Olympia, is a 20-minute uphill hike or a 5-minute drive/taxi ride (it's well-signed; from middle of town, follow the small road behind Hotel Hercules). Chef Alki practices his art on fresh products from the hotel's farm. His "farm dish" consists of layers of Talagani cheese and roasted vegetables—a refreshing break from traditional Greek salad; the grilled meats and fish are savory and satisfying. Drink in the magnificent terrace dotted with olive trees, rose bushes, and grapevine arbors—in the fall, Alki will cut off clumps of grapes and bring them to your table for dessert (open daily for dinner starting at 19:00, 1 Drouva street, tel. 26240-22650).

$$ Taverna Thea (ΘEA), a few more minutes farther into the hills, is a homier (and cheaper) alternative to dining at the Europa Hotel. Greek Andreas and Swedish Erika proudly serve a standard menu plus some regional specialties to happy locals, who usually gather in the garden terrace after dark, and in-the-know tourists who enjoy the balcony views earlier in the evening (fresh fish specialties, open daily for dinner starting at 18:00, tel. 26240-23264). From the middle of town, follow signs to Europa Hotel (listed above); near the top of the hill, take the fork to the right, following *Krestena, Floka,* and/or *theatre/*ΘEATPO signs, then stay on the same road as it crests the hill, while looking for the *TABEPNA* sign on the left, across the street from the taverna itself.

East of Town

$$$ Bacchus Tavern, with a striking setting and pleasant decor that mingles new and old, is the best eatery in the area. The Zapantis family is proud of their traditional, homemade Greek cuisine with creative flair. Olympians favor their lamb baked in oregano and olive oil. Ask owner Kostas how he used water from the swimming pool to save his tavern from the 2007 wildfires (affordable fixed-price meals, good vegetarian options, daily 12:00-24:00, Fri-Sun only in Jan-Feb, tel. 26240-22298). For driving directions, see the Bacchus Tavern hotel listing, earlier.

Olympia Connections

BY BUS

For all connections, you'll transfer first in **Pyrgos** to the west (about hourly Mon-Fri, 7/day Sat-Sun, last bus leaves Olympia at 22:15, 35 minutes).

From Pyrgos you can connect to **Athens** (8/day, 4.5 hours), **Patra** (8/day, 2 hours, some onward connections to **Delphi**), **Kalamata** (2/day, 2.5 hours, onward connections to **Kardamyli, Sparta,** and **Monemvasia**), and **Tripoli** (3/day, 3 hours, some onward connections to **Nafplio**). For the Pyrgos bus station, call 26210-20600. For schedules, see the KTEL website for this region (www.ktelileias.gr).

BY CRUISE SHIP

Cruise ships stop at the village of Katakolo (kah-TAH-koh-loh), about 18 miles west of Olympia. Along the waterfront is a pedestrian promenade with several restaurants. This is a good place to try seafood and kill time before reboarding your ship.

Getting to Olympia from Katakolo

By Train: Trains run from Katakolo to Olympia, but not always on a predictable schedule. Generally one train leaves Katakolo in the early morning (before 9:00), and one train returns from Olympia in the late morning (before noon), but more trains may be added if several large ships are in town. Since there's no reliable way to look up an updated schedule, it's best to go straight from your ship to the train station to ask. The station is about a 10-minute walk from the port parking lot: Head down Katakolo's tacky tourist street a few blocks until you reach the park. The train platform and ticket booth are to the right. The train ride takes about 50 minutes, followed by an additional 10-minute walk from the Olympia train station to the site (€10 round-trip, buy tickets at booth—not on train, double-check return times, tel. 26210-22525, www.trainose.gr/en/tourism-culture).

By Big Bus: For the same price you can also take a big bus from one of several agencies on the main street (€10 round-trip; ask how much time you'll have in Olympia—most offer between 1.5 and 3 hours, you'll want at least 2). These places understand how much you don't want to miss your boat—and all but guarantee you won't. But note that you may have to wait up to 30 minutes in Katakolo until they collect enough passengers to make the trip worthwhile. If there's a train leaving soon after you dock, I'd take that instead.

By Tour: Olympic Traveller offers various packages combining round-trip transport to Olympia with a two-hour guided tour of the site and museum, likely with recommended local guide Niki Vlachou (€48-69/person, groups never larger than 25, mobile 697-320-1213, www.olympictraveller.com, info@olympictraveller.com). For €25 you can skip the guided tour in Olympia, but enjoy a narrated ride, quick pick-up times (they won't dally at the port waiting for the bus to fill up), and guaranteed on-time return to your cruise ship.

By Taxi: Taxis descend upon the dock, hoping to pick up passengers; the round-trip fare for a one-hour visit to Olympia runs €80, while a two-hour visit costs €100 (talk to a few drivers to find a good match). For the best prices and service, book in advance. Consider Takis Tsaparas (mobile 694-543-4913, www.taxikatakolon.gr).

By Rental Car: Avoid the sleazy rental agency on the main street as you leave the dock. Try Avis, just uphill from the main street, marked with a big red sign (€45/day plus gas for smallest manual-transmission car with air-con, best to book ahead in July-Aug, tel. 26210-42200, mobile 694-700-2290, www.katakolo-rentacar.com, helpful Kostas). The route is an easy 30-minute drive that bypasses any towns; ask the rental agent for directions.

Wine Tasting and a Beach: If you don't want to visit Olympia, one option is to ride the hop-on, hop-off tourist train, which stops at Mercouri winery and at rocky Agioas Andreas Beach, where you'll find a few restaurant/beach bars. Catch it in Katakolo, in the square next to the church at the end of the promenade (€6, every 30 minutes, last train one hour before cruise ships leave, Katakolo Train Tours, mobile 694-777-8842).

ROUTE TIPS FOR DRIVERS

Olympia is situated in the hilly interior of the Peloponnese, connected to the outside world by one main highway, called E-55. You can take this west to **Pyrgos** (30 minutes), where E-55 forks: Take it north to **Patra** (2 hours from Olympia) and **Delphi** (4 hours from Olympia—see Delphi's "Route Tips for Drivers" on page 369); or south to **Kalamata** (2.5 hours from Olympia) and on to **Kardamyli** (3.5 hours from Olympia). Or, from Olympia, you can take E-55 east on its twisty route to **Tripoli** (2.5 hours), then get on the major E-65/A-7 expressway to zip to **Nafplio** (3.5 hours from Olympia) or **Athens** (4.5 hours from Olympia).

Near Olympia: Patra

The big port city of Patra (Πάτρα, sometimes spelled "Patras" in English, pop. 170,000) is many visitors' first taste of Greece, as it's the hub for boats arriving from Italy (and from the Ionian Islands, such as Corfu). While it's not a place to linger, Patra has rejuvenated its main thoroughfare to become a fairly enjoyable place to kill a little time waiting for your boat or bus.

Patra sprawls along its harborfront, which is traced by the busy road called Othonos Amalias. Patra's transit points line up along here (from north to south, as you'll reach them with the sea on your right): the North Port Terminal for some local ferries, a ragtag main bus station, the low-profile train station, and the South Port Terminal where ferries from Italy dock.

Visiting Patra: Patra has several enjoyable pedestrian zones that bustle with a lively, engaging chaos you'll find only in a Mediterranean port town. Stretching west from the bus station, the pedestrianized Riga Fereou (two blocks inland from Othonos Amalias) is where locals spend their time eating, drinking coffee, and shopping. Riga Fereou intersects with another pedestrian zone, called Agiou Nikolaou. Both streets are lined with al fresco cafés, restaurants, and shops—and are fine places to feel the pulse of urban Greece.

Patra has several worthwhile sights. The **archaeological museum,** housed in a modern building on the north side of town, displays artifacts from the city and surrounding area, and focuses on themes of private life, public life, and cemeteries (about 1.5 miles from city center—best to take a taxi or drive, tel. 26136-16100). The town **castle,** built by the Emperor Justinian in the sixth century, is reachable from a staircase at the top of Agiou Nikolaou (tel. 26106-23390). Near the castle, the impressively restored **ancient** *odeon* (theater) dates from Roman times (tel. 26102-20829). And along the waterfront, south of the main transit zone, the vast **Church of Agios Andreas** is the city's *mitropolis* (like a cathedral). See www.patrasinfo.com for more information on these sights and the town itself.

Sleeping in Patra: If you're stuck here overnight, these options are handy to the boats, buses, and trains: **$$ Olympic Star** (luxurious touches, four blocks up from the port and just below the old town and castle, Agiou Nikolaou 46, tel. 26106-22939, www.olympicstar.gr) or **$$ Hotel Acropole** (business-class rooms across from train station, Agiou Andreou 32, tel. 26102-79809, www.acropole.gr).

Patra Connections: You can sail by **boat** from Patra to several towns in Italy, including Bari, Ancona, Brindisi, and Venice;

OLYMPIA

many boats stop at the Greek island of Corfu en route (check Superfast Ferries—www.superfast.com, Grimaldi Lines—www.grimaldi-lines.com, Minoan Lines—www.minoan.gr, and ANEK Lines—www.anek.gr). **Buses** connect Patra directly to Athens and Pyrgos (with onward connections to Olympia); see www.patrasinfo.com for more information.

OLYMPIA

KARDAMYLI & THE MANI PENINSULA

ΚΑΡΔΑΜΎΛΗ / Καρδαμύλη •
ΜΆΝΗ / Μάνη

The Mani Peninsula is the southernmost tip of mainland Greece (and of the entire European continent, east of Spain)—and it really does feel like the end of the road. Sealed off from the rest of Greece by a thick ring of mountains, the peninsula has seen its population ebb and flow throughout history with tides of refugees fleeing whatever crises were gripping the rest of Greece. The only part of Greece that never completely fell to the Ottoman invaders, the Mani became the cradle of the 1821 revolution that finally brought independence to the Greeks.

In the Mani, travelers discover a timeless region of rustic villages and untrampled beaches. A day's drive around this desolate, rural peninsula offers dramatic mountain scenery and bloody history all tied up in a hardscrabble and evocative package—making hedonism on the Mani coast feel all the more hedonistic. At the end of the day, you can retire to charming Kardamyli.

PLANNING YOUR TIME

Two nights and a full day is a minimum for this area. To really be on vacation, add more nights. Sleep in Kardamyli. With one day, first take my self-guided walk of Kardamyli to get your bearings, then head up to Old Kardamyli. In the afternoon, go for a hike or hit the beach. With a second day and a car, drive the Mani Peninsula. Those with three days here can do the driving tour at a more leisurely pace, saving the Pyrgos Dirou Caves and the detour to Kastania for a separate side-trip from Kardamyli (or as a detour en route to or from Monemvasia).

Instead of returning to Kardamyli, you can head from the Mani loop directly to Monemvasia.

Kardamyli

The village of Kardamyli (kar-dah-MEE-lee) is the gateway to the Mani Peninsula and its best home base. It's an atypical resort that delicately mixes chic hotels and conscientious travelers with real-world Greece. Relax and tune in to the pace of country life. On Kardamyli's humble but fascinating main drag, locals-only mom-and-pop shops mingle with trendy tourist stalls.

Little Kardamyli is one of the oldest city names in Greek history. In the *Iliad*, Homer described "well-peopled" Kardamyli as one of seven cities presented to the Greek hero Achilles to persuade him to return to the siege of Troy. Achilles' son Pyrrhus sailed to Kardamyli, then walked to Sparta to claim the hand of Ermioni. And the legendary Gemini twins—Castor and Pollux—are said to be buried here.

Kardamyli is wedged between the sparkling pebble beaches of the Messenian Gulf and towering Mount Profitas Ilias (7,895

feet)—the Peloponnese's highest peak, which is snowcapped from November to early May. Between the sea and the distant mountain-top, dramatic hills and cliffs are topped with scenic villages, churches, and ruined towers. As throughout the rest of the Mani, in the sixth century A.D. Kardamyli's residents fled from pirates into these hills—returning to sea level only in the 18th century, after the construction of Old Kardamyli's defensive tower house made it safe.

Visitors can enjoy hiking into the hills, learning about the region's rough-and-tumble history at Old Kardamyli, swimming at the town's Ritsa Beach, and driving deeper into the Mani Peninsula, but the real charm of Kardamyli is its low-key ambience—the place works like a stun gun on your momentum. I could stay here for days, just eating well and hanging out. It's the kind of place where travelers plan their day around the sunset.

Orientation to Kardamyli

Tiny Kardamyli—with just 230 year-round residents—swells with far more visitors in the summer months. The town is compact, gathered around a convenient central spine (the main road running south from Kalamata). Kardamyli is small enough to feel like a cozy village, but big enough to serve the needs of its many visitors—with small grocery stores, ATMs, a post office, and more.

Tourist Information: Because Kardamyli has no TI, hoteliers pick up the slack, sometimes offering free hiking maps and usually eager to direct visitors to the best restaurants and activities. The helpful official town website has lots of good information, including accommodations (www.kardamili-greece.com, run by energetic Luna).

Arrival in Kardamyli: For specifics on driving into town, see "Route Tips for Drivers," later.

Local Guide: Elias Polimeneas is a soulful native who proudly introduces visitors to his town and region. If you'd like to explore Kardamyli with a Kardamylian, or see the Mani Peninsula, Elias is your man (reasonable and negotiable rates, tel. 27210-73453, antoniasapartments@yahoo.gr).

Kardamyli Walk

You could walk from one end of Kardamyli to the other in 10 minutes, but you'd miss the point. Slow down, and keep an eye out for intriguing pockets of traditional Greek village culture. This leisurely self-guided stroll lasts about an hour.

• Start at the beginning of town, by the...

Village Church

The modern Church of St. Mary, with its thriving congregation, is the heart of this town. Notice the loudspeakers outside, which allow overflow crowds to take part in the service on very important days, such as Easter. Kardamyli takes its Easter celebration very seriously: On Good Friday, a processional passes through the town and the priest blesses each house. At midnight on Holy Saturday, everyone turns off  their lights and comes to this main square. The priest emerges from the church with a candle, passing its flame through the candle-

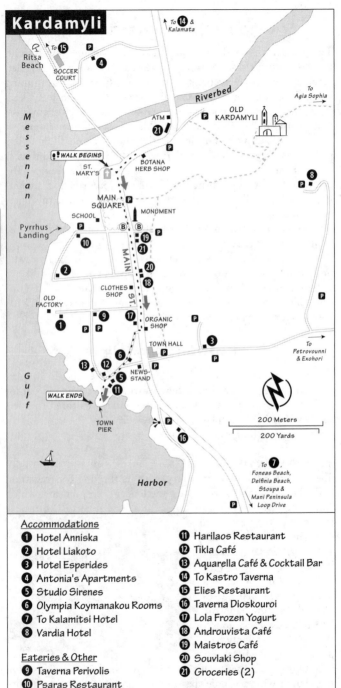

Kardamyli

Ritsa Beach

SOCCER COURT

Messenian

Riverbed

OLD KARDAMYLI

To Agia Sophia

ATM

WALK BEGINS

ST. MARY'S

BOTANA HERB SHOP

MAIN SQUARE

MONUMENT

SCHOOL

Pyrrhus Landing

CLOTHES SHOP

OLD FACTORY

ORGANIC SHOP

TOWN HALL

Gulf

NEWS-STAND

WALK ENDS

TOWN PIER

Harbor

To Kalamata

To Petrovounni & Exohori

200 Meters

200 Yards

To Foneas Beach, Delfinia Beach, Stoupa & Mani Peninsula Loop Drive

KARDAMYLI & MANI PENINSULA

Accommodations

1. Hotel Anniska
2. Hotel Liakoto
3. Hotel Esperides
4. Antonia's Apartments
5. Studio Sirenes
6. Olympia Koymanakou Rooms
7. To Kalamitsi Hotel
8. Vardia Hotel

Eateries & Other

9. Taverna Perivolis
10. Psaras Restaurant
11. Harilaos Restaurant
12. Tikla Café
13. Aquarella Café & Cocktail Bar
14. To Kastro Taverna
15. Elies Restaurant
16. Taverna Dioskouroi
17. Lola Frozen Yogurt
18. Androuvista Café
19. Maistros Café
20. Souvlaki Shop
21. Groceries (2)

carrying crowd, who then take the light home with them...gradually illuminating the entire town. And then the fireworks begin.

Before we head into the middle of town, walk a few yards up the main street, away from the church and the main square, and look for a worn wooden fence on the right (before the two grocery stores). Behind the fence is the **Botana Herb Shop,** a celebration of what grows in the hills above Kardamyli. Welcoming owner Yiannis Dimitreas, a walking encyclopedia on local foraging, offers free tastes of his organic produce—marinated olives, fresh olive oil, and local honey—and also sells homemade herbal teas, soaps, and skin creams (generally open daily).

• *Extending toward town from the church is the leafy...*

Main Square

Most of the year, this spot is a popular playground for Kardamylian kids, who play under the eucalyptus trees (on the site of the ancient gymnasium). But on New Year's Day, a local club fills the square with truckloads of snow from the mountains, turning it into a playground for giddy grown-ups as well.

Walk to the end of the square. In the little park is the town water spigot and an oddball collection of **monuments.** Find the busts of two almost comically medal-laden generals who fought in the Greek Revolution and Macedonian Wars. The modern sculpture between them, called *Unity,* evokes the many fortified towers that dot the Mani Peninsula. Despite the vendettas that frequently cropped up among the peninsula's inhabitants, today Maniots generally feel united with one another.

Across the street, on the pedestal, is a **monument to the heroes** who have fought for Greek unity and independence since antiquity. Next to the palm branch is the Greek motto "Freedom or Death." While two wars are highlighted in the wreath below (the 1821 Greek War of Independence, and the 1912-1913 First Balkan War), the monument is a reminder that the ideals behind those conflicts date back to the ancients.

The cobbled path just behind this monument takes hikers (in about 10 minutes) to the restored ruins and museum of **Old Kardamyli** (described later, under "Sights in Kardamyli").

Back across the street at the end of the square, look down to the **waterfront.** The primary school (with a small playground) sits just behind the square. The school has a disproportionate number of Albanian kids, because as a couple of generations of young people moved to Athens in search of work, Albanian workers migrated here to do stone work and other manual labor jobs. And most recently, Greeks who are struggling economically are unable to afford a family.

Now look in the opposite direction, up at the **hillsides.** From here you can see two of the most popular nearby hiking destinations: On the left is the little hilltop church of Agia Sophia, and to the right is the village of Petrovouni. An enjoyable three-hour loop covers both of these sights (described later, under "Hiking").

• *Across from the end of the park begins the commercial zone of...*

Kardamyli's Main Street

The next few blocks reveal a fascinating blend of traditional Greek village lifestyles side-by-side with a pleasantly low-key tourism. In

most Greek towns with such a fine seaside setting, the beaches are lined with concrete high-rise hotels, and the main streets are a cavalcade of tacky T-shirt shops. But the people of Kardamyli are determined to keep their town real—a hard-fought local law prohibits new construction over a certain height limit (ruling out big resorts), and the town has made long-term sustainability a priority over short-term profit. (It also helps that the beach has pebbles instead of sand, which keeps away the party crowds.) Its residents have created a smart little self-sustaining circle: The town keeps its soul even as it profits from visitors...allowing it to attract the caliber of travelers who appreciate Kardamyli for what it is.

Take a walk down the main street for examples of both faces of Kardamyli. Notice that with the exception of the empty red eyesore a half-block down—which only locals seem to notice (and won't reveal to visitors even when you ask nicely)—all of the buildings are traditionally built, using stone from this area. Even newer buildings (such as the café right at the start of the street) match the old style. As you stroll you'll see:

Maistros Café (on the left, with breakfast and backgammon): This is Kardamyli's closest thing to a place where the "old boys" hang out.

The **pharmacy** (left, after the handy little supermarket): Pop inside to see how tastefully it's been renovated.

Psaltiras Wine and Olive Oil Shop (left): Nicos Psaltiras speaks English and loves to share his quality local products.

2407 Kardamili Mountain Shop (left): Named for the height in meters of the tallest mountain in the Peloponnese, this is the go-to place for outdoor equipment, bike rentals, and advice on walks and treks. See www.2407m.com for their weekly schedule of excursions and tours.

Souvlaki Shop (left): Here you'll find local-style "fast food" dished up by shepherds serving their own freshly butchered meat.

Androuvista Café (left): This delightful little café bakes its much-loved walnut cake daily.

Blauel Olive Shop (right): This shop is a pioneer in organic olive oil production. Katerina loves offering tasty samples.

The **butcher** (left): Peek inside to see a classic butcher block and a row of hooks with tools and smocks. Local shepherds produce lots of goats.

Lola Frozen Yogurt (right): Try this fun stop for homemade ice cream, tempting cakes, and a peaceful courtyard out back.

Mountain Herbs Shop (left): Pop in for homegrown goodies—and possibly some samples of olive oils and honeys.

Finish your Main Street stroll with the **bank** (with ATM) and **real estate office** (one of two in town for visitors smitten with the desire to have a vacation home here). Farther down are the **City Hall, hardware store** (supplying out-of-towners working on their fixer-upper retirement/vacation properties), and an old-school **newsstand.**

• *Turn right (toward the water) at the Piraeus Bank to find yourself among...*

Kardamyli's Back Streets

As you step off the main drag, notice how civilization seems to melt away as back streets quickly turn into cobbles, then gravel, then red dirt.

Continuing down the road past small shops to the sea, you'll see some signs advertising **rooms** (ΔΩΜΑΤΙΑ, *dhomatia*) for visitors—a great value for cheap sleeps. If you look like you need a roof over your head tonight, someone might offer you a room as you pass.

• *Continue down to the water, walk out on to the concrete pier, and look around at...*

Kardamyli's Waterfront

Until a few generations ago, no roads connected Kardamyli to the rest of civilization. This pier was the main way into and out of the area, providing a link to the big city of Kalamata and bustling with trade and passengers. The old smokestack (behind your right shoulder as you face the water) marks the site of a once-thriving olive-oil factory. The oil was shipped from this pier. (The factory has been deserted since the 1950s, and much of the original equipment is rusty but intact. There's talk of turning it into a museum.)

Between the 1950s and the 1970s, the ever-improving network of roads made this port obsolete. Today only one professional fisherman works out of Kardamyli. He brings his catch right here to the pier to sell to locals, tourists, and restaurateurs. To the left, a set of concrete steps leads around a watery curve to a rocky alcove where there may be a handful of swimmers. The small harbor across the bay has only a few boats. Even without its traditional industries, Kardamyli still thrives, and most of its traditional lifestyles remain intact...thanks in part to respectful visitors like you.

Above the harbor the Mirginos Tower completes the ring of fortifications that starts at the other end of town at Old Kardamyli. The little island offshore (Miropi) holds the barely visible ruins of an old church.

• *Our walk is finished—time to take a deep breath of sea air, relax, and soak in the slow pace of Kardamyli life. There are a couple of relaxing bars with fine sea views within a few steps.*

Sights in Kardamyli

Old Kardamyli

The fortified compound of Old Kardamyli perches just above today's modern town. On the ancient Mani Peninsula, "old" is relative—this settlement, marked by a fortified tower, was established by the first families (who were forced into the hills in the Middle Ages by pirates) to return to flat ground at the end
of the 17th century. After sitting in ruins for centuries, the complex

has recently been partially restored and converted into a little museum about the Mani Peninsula and its traditional architecture. It's worth the 10-minute hike through an olive grove to poke around the fortified cluster and visit the museum.

The trail to Old Kardamyli begins just behind the monument to the heroes along the main street. From here it's an up-and-down 10-minute walk—just follow the cobbled path, lined with lampposts, which leads through an up-close slice of traditional village life and an olive grove. As you approach the site, behind the ruined building on the right (under a eucalyptus tree near the final lamppost) is an old cistern once used to draw and carry water back home. Curl around the right side of Old Kardamyli to hike up into the

complex. Standing inside the fortified complex, imagine the stark reality of life within these walls, where a church, olive press, iron smith, garden, and cistern were the necessities for the frightened community to survive.

Passing through the archway, on the right you'll see the **Church of St. Spyridon** (circa 1750). Though it's not open to visitors, the exterior is interesting for its bell tower and its (typical-in-Greece) use of fragments of older buildings in its construction (such as the 3,500-year-old Mycenaean-age sill, wall chunks plundered by the Venetians, and Byzantine marble frames that surround the door and windows). Over the window and door, notice the crowned double-headed eagle, a symbol of the Byzantine Empire and the Orthodox Christian Church.

Now head toward the tower complex itself. The **Mourtzinos Tower** was built by the powerful Troupakis family at the beginning of the 18th century. It's named after the leader of the Troupakis clan, who was known for his scowling face *(mourtzinos)*, during the War of Independence.

Attached to the tower, the former **Troupakis residence** now houses a multilevel museum (€2, Tue-Sun 8:30-17:00, later in summer, closed Mon and Dec-March). Poke into all the little doors to see exhibits about the Maniots' terraces, cisterns, beekeeping, agricultural production, salt pans, and quarries. On the top floor you can learn about the different subregions of the Mani.

The cute little blue-and-white church just uphill from the complex, **Agia Sophia,** marks the beginning of a cobbled path that leads up, up, up to the distant church on the hilltop (also called Agia Sophia). High above on the bluff was the site of the acropolis of Homeric-era Kardamyli (from 1250 B.C.). You can do the whole strenuous loop up to the church, then walk around to the adjacent village of Petrovouni (see "Hiking," later). Or, for just a taste, hike about five minutes up the cobbled trail to find two graves burrowed into a rock (on the right, behind the green gate). These are supposedly the **graves of Castor and Pollux,** the "Gemini twins" of mythology. These brothers of Helen of Troy had different fathers. When Castor died, Pollux—who was immortal because he was fathered by Zeus—asked his dad to bond the brothers together in immortality. Zeus agreed and turned them into the Gemini constellation. These brothers, so famous for their affection for each other, remain in close proximity even in death: Notice the connecting passage at the back of the graves.

Beaches

Many visitors come to Kardamyli to enjoy the beach. Most simply head for nearby **Ritsa Beach,** a pleasant pebbly stretch that begins just beyond the village church. You can swim anywhere along its length, but most beach bums prefer the far end, where the water gets deeper quicker (no showers).

Ritsa Beach is bookended by twin restaurants with outdoor seating. Recommended **Elies,** at the far end, is everyone's favorite (see "Eating in Kardamyli," later).

If you have a car and want to get out of town, you could day-trip to two more good sand/fine gravel beaches that lie to the south, near the hamlet of Neo Proastio on the way to Stoupa: **Foneas Beach** (a cove flanked by picturesque big rocks) and **Delfinia Beach.** The resort town of **Stoupa** also has some good sandy beaches and a promenade perfect for strolling.

As elsewhere in Greece, water shoes are recommended to avoid stepping on spiny sea urchins. Locals claim that the water's warm enough for swimming year-round, except in March, when it's chilled by snowmelt runoff from the mountains.

Hiking

Hiking vies with beach fun as Kardamyli's biggest attraction. Especially in spring and fall, visitors head away from the sea to explore the network of color-
coded trails that scramble
up the surrounding hills.
Many of these follow the
ancient *kalderimi* (cobbled
paths) that until fairly recently were the only way of
traveling between villages.
Ask your hotel for a map
that explains the routes
and codes; for serious hikes, buy a more detailed hiking map. As
the hikes tend to be strenuous—uphill and over uneven terrain—
wear good shoes and bring along water and snacks (some walks do
pass through villages where you can buy food and drinks).

The most popular destinations sit on the hillsides just behind
Kardamyli: the hilltop church of **Agia Sophia** and the village of
Petrovouni. You can hike to either one or (with more time and
stamina) do a loop trip that includes both. Consider this plan: Start
by visiting Old Kardamyli, then continue past the smaller blue-
and-white Agia Sophia church and the ancient graves of Castor
and Pollux (described earlier) to the higher church of Agia Sophia.
Then, if your energy holds, follow the path around to Petrovouni,
from which you can head back down into Kardamyli. The paths are
very steep (there's about a 650-foot elevation gain from Kardamyli
to Petrovouni), and the round-trip takes about 1.5 hours at a good
pace with few breaks (follow the yellow-and-black trail markings).
Other trips lead farther into the hills, to the remote village of **Exohori.** To avoid brutal heat in the summer, time your hike to finish
by 10:00.

Sleeping in Kardamyli

Most of Kardamyli's accommodations cater to British, European,
and Australian tourists who stay for a week or more. Rather than
traditional hotels, you'll find mostly "apartments" with kitchenettes, along with simpler and cheaper rooms *(dhomatia)*. While
some places do offer breakfast, most charge extra, assuming that
you'll make your own in your kitchenette or get a pastry and a coffee at a bakery or café. If you want breakfast, be sure to tell your
host the day before (they'll likely buy fresh bread for you in the
morning).

IN THE TOWN

$$$ Hotel Anniska and **Hotel Liakoto** ("Sunny Place") rent nicely appointed, resort-feeling apartments with kitchenettes. The Anniska has 22 apartments that share an inviting lounge and a delightful seaview terrace (breakfast extra, free Wi-Fi in reception area, tel. 27210-73601). The Liakoto's 25 apartments cluster around a swimming-pool courtyard oasis, all with sea views that turn golden at sunset (breakfast extra, tel. 27210-73600). Both hotels are run by friendly British-Australian-Greek couple Ilia and Gerry (www.anniska-liakoto.com, anniska@otenet.gr).

$$ Hotel Esperides has 19 rooms and apartments with kitchenettes, all surrounding a pleasant garden veranda just a few steps up from the main road. You'll enjoy a friendly welcome and lots of travel advice (breakfast extra, closed Nov-March, arrange arrival time in advance because reception isn't open 24 hours, tel. 27210-73173, www.hotelesperides.gr, info@hotelesperides.gr).

$$ Antonia's Apartments sit among the olive trees, just up from Ritsa Beach and a short walk from the town center (turn right after the first beach restaurant). Its two newer apartments in the tower house are stylishly furnished with thoughtful touches that put them several notches above the norm. The two older units, while more old-fashioned, are a bit bigger, with two separate bedrooms. All four apartments have seaview verandas (lending library, tel. 27210-73453, antoniasapartments@yahoo.gr, lovingly tended by recommended local guide Elias).

$$ Studio Sirenes has four well-priced rooms over a busy restaurant. The rooms are simple, but all have kitchenettes and balconies overlooking Kardamyli's little harbor (good windows block out most of the dining noise, mobile 698-034-2020, www.lessireneskardamili.com, e.sirenes@gmail.com).

$ *Dhomatia:* You'll see signs advertising rooms (ΔΩΜΑΤΙΑ) all over town. Though air-conditioning is a safe bet, rooms are generally quite simple, with kitchenettes but no breakfast. English can be limited, credit cards aren't accepted, and value can vary. If you're in a pinch, check out a few, pick the best, and don't be afraid to haggle. Try warm and welcoming **Olympia Koymanakou,** who rents five rooms on the cobbled lane just up the road from the harbor and speaks just enough English (shared kitchen, Paraleia street, tel. 27210-73623, mobile 693-479-2259).

JUST OUTSIDE KARDAMYLI

These enjoyable retreats sit a bit farther from Kardamyli's main street. While walkable, they're more enjoyable if you have a car (especially the Kalamitsi).

$$$ Kalamitsi Hotel is a charming enclave hovering above its own bay, beach, and olive grove a two-minute drive down the road from Kardamyli (toward Areopoli, just around a big curve in the road). In addition to 17 rooms in the main building, it has 15 bungalows that bunny-hop across its plateau (suites, breakfast extra, dinner available, tel. 27210-73131, www.kalamitsi-hotel.gr, info@kalamitsi-hotel.gr).

$$ Vardia Hotel is a stony retreat huddled on a hilltop just above town. All of its 18 studios and apartments have balconies overlooking town and the sea beyond, and a steep, stony path leads from the hotel's grand-view veranda directly to Old Kardamyli (breakfast extra, tel. 27210-73777, mobile 694-611-9741, www.vardia-hotel.gr, info@vardia-hotel.gr).

Eating in Kardamyli

Kardamyli prides itself on pleasing a huge group of return visitors, who come here on holiday year after year. Consequently, quality is high and value is good. When you ask locals where to dine, they shrug and say, "Anywhere is good"...and you sense it's not just empty town pride talking. As you dine, notice the dignified European visitors conversing quietly around you...and try to imitate them.

IN TOWN

$$ Taverna Perivolis, run by Peter and his Greek-Australian family, lacks a view but offers good value in a garden setting. Their list of daily specials often includes *pastitsio* (Greek lasagna) and freshly grilled meat (daily 19:00-24:00 except likely closed Mon off-season, tel. 27210-73713). It's near the water, across the street from the deserted factory.

$$ Psaras Restaurant overlooks Pyrrhus landing, an appropriate location given the fish-forward menu. Rustic wood tables under a covered patio and the sound of lapping waves make this a great spot for a memorable meal (daily 11:00-22:00, tel. 27210-73365).

ON THE WATER, WITH SEA VIEWS

These three places are side-by-side overlooking the harbor and designed for enjoying sea views. All have fine interiors if the weather is disagreeable. The first is a serious restaurant, while the next two are bars that serve food.

$$$ Harilaos Restaurant seems to be open when others are not. It's bright and elegant, boasts fine views over the harbor, and serves fresh fish and classic Greek dishes (tel. 27210-73373).

$$ Tikla Café, with a stylish covered terrace and a stony-mod interior, offers a short menu of updated Greek cuisine (American breakfast, free Wi-Fi, long hours daily but may close 14:00-18:00 at slow times, tel. 27210-73223). It's also a fine café/bar for just hanging out with good coffee, cocktails, and music until noon.

$$ Aquarella Café and Cocktail Bar is youthful and hip, taking full advantage of its romantic seaside setting with sofas under trees and backgammon boards. Relax with drinks and snacks—there are even cigars on the menu. They also serve breakfast (open daily until late, tel. 27210-75010).

JUST OUTSIDE KARDAMYLI

$$ Kastro Taverna is a gourmet's delight and a splurge for your taste buds (but no pricier than most other restaurants in town). Sitting amid an olive grove just outside town toward Kalamata, it's a 15-minute walk or quick drive from the town center. The trek is worth it—the chef uses local products for his daily specials, including meat and produce from his farm in the hills above town. A highlight is the *keftedes* (meatballs) in a savory tomato sauce, but it's hard to go wrong with anything on the menu. Choose between the cozy fireplace interior and the broad veranda with distant sea views (daily starting at 19:00, possibly closed in winter, tel. 27210-73951).

$$ Elies (Ελιές), with what most locals consider the best lunch around, is a 15-minute walk up from the town center, on Ritsa Beach. Relax with beachgoers at pastel tables in the shade of olive trees, and enjoy their excellent Greek cuisine. They serve simple, traditional Greek dishes for lunch from April through October and offer a fancier dinner menu from mid-June through mid-September (daily, tel. 27210-73140). Kids enjoy their playground.

$$ Taverna Dioskouroi sits in a lovely setting on the headland overlooking Kardamyli's adorable little harbor, on the southern end of the village (daily specials, long hours daily, on the right 200 yards south of the village, tel. 27210-73236).

OTHER OPTIONS

Breakfast: If you're not eating breakfast at your hotel consider these options. Bohemian-chic **Aquarella** and smarter **Tikla** are side-by-side (listed above). Several places mentioned on my self-guided walk offer breakfast fare: **Lola Frozen Yogurt** (dainty setting, garden tables out back) has light bites and good coffee, **$$ Androuvista Café** serves walnut cake, a beloved local specialty, and **$$ Maistros Café,** on the main square, is an old-school cafeteria with local clientele and full array of breakfast options. Or consider a neighboring place with tables on the square.

$$ Cafés: Kardamyli enjoys a wide range of delightful cafés with traditional/chic decor and basic food; several line the main drag. Most of these have indoor and outdoor seating and serve drinks as well as light food, including breakfast.

Picnics: There are two grocery stores at the entrance to town, and one on the main street just past the square (all open long hours daily). For a fast bite, the **souvlaki shop** on the main street is good (described earlier, on my self-guided walk).

Kardamyli Connections

Kardamyli's biggest disadvantage is its tricky-to-reach position on the far-flung Mani Peninsula. The nearest major city (with good bus connections to the rest of Greece) is Kalamata, about 24 twisty miles to the north. Kardamyli is connected to **Kalamata** by bus (3/day Mon-Fri—first bus around 7:30, last at around 20:30; 2/day Sat-Sun, 1 hour; in Kardamyli, catch bus at main square). For Kalamata bus information, call 27210-22851. KTEL, the national bus system, has a minimal website (www.ktelbus.com).

You can also get to Kalamata by taxi for around €55—a handy option for catching early buses out of Kalamata off-season, when buses from Kardamyli to Kalamata might not run early enough. Ask your hotelier for help booking a taxi.

ROUTE TIPS FOR DRIVERS

The Mani Peninsula's mountains make driving slow going, but if you don't mind spending a few euros on tolls, A-7 allows you to bypass the town of Kalamata, shaving 30 minutes off your travel time. Cheapskates driving through Kalamata should follow signs reading *Port, Seafront,* or *Areopoli.* Once past the port, keep driving in the same direction, with the water on your right. The road to Kardamyli is badly signed—you might see directions in Greek for Καρδαμύλη (Kardamyli) or Μάνη (Mani)—but as long as you keep the water on your right, you'll end up on the highway.

Either way, heading south from Kalamata, you'll twist over a suddenly remote-feeling terrain of dramatic mountains and emerge overlooking a grand bay with views over Kardamyli.

After going through Kardamyli, the road continues south, passing near—or directly through—a string of scenic villages before climbing back up over mountains and around a dramatic bay to the regional capital of Areopoli.

From Areopoli you can head east to Gythio and then on to Monemvasia (about 2 hours total), or head south for a loop of the Mani on lesser roads (described next).

The Mani Peninsula

The Mani Peninsula is where the rustic charm of Greece is most apparent. For many travelers, this peninsula is the rural slice of Greek coast-and-mountains that they came to this country to see.

The region's dramatic history has left behind a landscape that's at once eerily stark and remarkably scenic. While mountains edged with abandoned terraces hint that farming was once more extensive, olives have been the only Mani export for the last two centuries. Empty, ghostly hill towns cling barnacle-like onto distant ridges, still fortified against centuries-old threats. Cisterns that once caught rainwater to sustain hardy communities are now mucky green puddles that would turn a goat's stomach. The farther south you go, the bleaker conditions become. And yet many Mani towns feature sumptuous old fresco-slathered churches...pockets of brightness that survive in this otherwise parched land.

This region is difficult to fully experience without a car. To really delve into this rustic corner of Greece, follow this loop drive from Kardamyli.

PLANNING YOUR DRIVE

To hit all the places described here in one day, you'll need to get an early start and not linger too long in any one place. It takes about eight hours to drive the entire loop, pausing just long enough to stretch your legs and snap a few photos at each sight.

If you prefer a later start or a more relaxed day, you could skip Kastania or the cape (saving you about an hour each). The major towns worth stopping at are Agios Nikolaos, Areopoli, and Gerolimenas. Also worthwhile are the Pyrgos Dirou Caves, which you can visit at the beginning or end of the drive, as you'll pass by them on your return to Kardamyli (but bear in mind what time they close).

Along the way, you'll experience stunning coastal vistas equal to California's Big Sur or the French Riviera. But keep a firm grip on the wheel—the route is a string of hairpin curves, missing guardrails, and blind corners in ancient stone villages. Allow time to pull over frequently for photos and to soak it all in.

Sightseeing Tip: The light inside old churches can be very dim—if you have a flashlight, bring it along to illuminate the frescoes.

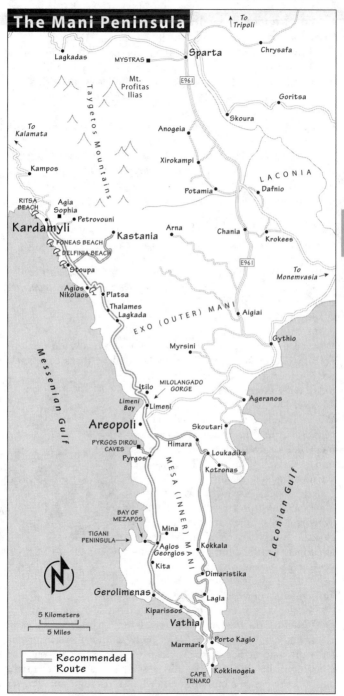

The Mani Peninsula

To Tripoli

To Kalamata

To Monemvasia

Lagkadas
MYSTRAS
Sparta
Chrysafa

Mt. Profitas Ilias

E961

Goritsa

Skoura

Anogeia

Xirokampi

Kampos

Potamia

LACONIA

Dafnio

RITSA BEACH
Agia Sophia
Petrovouni
Kardamyli
FONEAS BEACH
DELFINIA BEACH
Kastania
Arna
Chania
Krokees

Taygetos Mountains

Stoupa

Agios Nikolaos
Platsa
Thalames
Lagkada

EXO (OUTER) MANI

E961

Aigiai

Myrsini

Gythio

Itilo
MILOLANGADO GORGE

Limeni Bay
Limeni

Messenian Gulf

Ageranos

Areopoli

Skoutari

PYRGOS DIROU CAVES
Himara
Loukadika

Pyrgos

Kotronas

MESA (INNER) MANI

Laconian Gulf

BAY OF MEZAPOS

Mina

TIGANI PENINSULA
Agios Georgios
Kokkala

Kita

Dimaristika

Gerolimenas

Lagia

Kiparissos

Vathia

5 Kilometers
5 Miles

Porto Kagio

Marmari

Kokkinogeia

CAPE TENARO

Recommended Route

MANI PENINSULA DRIVING TOUR
From Kardamyli to Kastania

Head south from Kardamyli on the main road. After a few miles you'll pass the attractive little resort town of **Stoupa.** While Kardamyli turns its back to the sea, Stoupa embraces it—with a fine sandy beach arcing right through its center. (Stoupa also works as a separate jaunt from Kardamyli.)

• *Just after Stoupa is the turnoff for our first stop, Kastania (Καστανεα). Note that Kastania is a time-consuming detour from the main road (allow 90 minutes for the round-trip, including 30 minutes to walk around). If short on time, you might want to skip it for now and consider making it a separate side-trip from Kardamyli or a detour en route to Monemvasia.*

If you are going to Kastania, look for the turnoff from the main road. It may not be well-signed: Keep an eye out for a small brown sign pointing toward the road up through the olive orchard, on the left, opposite the prominent rocky hill (it's just before a tiny church on your right). Follow any signs to Neochori, which is en route to Kastania. Leaving the main road, head uphill, passing through two other villages along the way. Keep going, following the well-traveled blacktop.

Kastania

Wedged in a gorge, the village of Kastania offers you a rare opportunity to explore a traditional Mani village that's completely off the tourist track. It may feel sleepy today, but Kastania was once a local powerhouse. During the 19th-century Greek War of Independence, it boasted no fewer than 400 "guns" (as Maniots called their menfolk), gathered under a warlord whose imposing family tower still stands over the town square. The town also had many churches, some of which still feature remarkably well-preserved old frescoes. (Unfortunately, the churches are often closed. If you come across one that doesn't look open, try the door. If it's locked and you see people nearby, ask if they know how to get inside—sometimes there's a key hidden somewhere close by.)

Kastania is nestled in a strategically hidden location: You don't even see the town until you're right on top of it. As you enter the town, you'll pass the first of many Byzantine churches on the left—this one dedicated to St. John (Ag. Ioannis). Beyond the church, just before the traffic mirror and big blue sign, turn right and squeeze past the buildings into what seems to be an alley. It's actually the link to the main square, which is watched over by the Church of the Assumption and the town's tower house (built by the local Dourakis clan and now mostly ruined, but may be renovated to become one of seven planned Mani museum towers). Park your car wherever you can near the square, and poke into one of the very traditional cafés for a coffee. The one at the top of the square is a real time warp, where old-timers gather around simple tables, smoking and chatting.

Consider hiking uphill from the square to take in the back streets and some deep breaths of mountain air. Along a rustic

lane near the old cistern at the upper end of town is the **Church of St. Peter** (Ag. Petros), which dates from around 1200 and is the oldest of the town's Byzantine churches. It appears to be cobbled together using bits and pieces of antiquity. If it's open, go inside—it's richly adorned with frescoes that have told Bible stories

to this community since the 14th century. While the lighting may be jerry-rigged and a destructive mold has hastened the aging of its precious art, the spiritual wonder of the place remains intact. The olive-oil lamp burns 24 hours a day, tended by a caretaker family. Even if the church is closed, stop to enjoy the views over town from this perch.

• *Back in your car, backtrack to the main road and turn left (south). Continue driving...*

From Stoupa to Areopoli

As you drive you may notice rooftop **solar panels** attached to cylindrical tanks—an efficient way to heat water in this sunny climate. All along the route, set on roadside pedestals, are those little **miniature churches** you've seen throughout Greece. Most of these are "votive churches," erected as a thank-you gesture to God by someone who was spared in an accident. Little churches with a photograph of a person, however, are memorials to someone killed in an accident.

Heading south, you'll pass another fine beach town, **Agios Nikolaos** (St. Nicholas). About a kilometer (half-mile) off the road, this is a little fishing port with wild rocks, a tiny bell tower, a scrawny lighthouse, a tough fleet of little fishing boats, inviting stay-a-while cafés, and harborfront restaurants selling fresh fish to

History of the Mani Peninsula

The Mani feels as wild as its history. The region was supposedly first developed around 200 B.C. by breakaway Spartans (from the famously warlike city to the north). Spartan stubbornness persisted in the Mani character for centuries—and made Maniots slow to adopt Christianity. In the 10th century, St. Nikon finally converted the Maniots, and a flurry of Byzantine church-building followed.

Most coastal Mani towns (including Kardamyli) were slowly deserted in the Middle Ages as marauding pirate ships forced people to flee into the hills. There they hid out in villages tucked in the folds of the mountains, far from the coast. (Later, in the 18th century, the construction of protective tower houses allowed Maniots to tentatively begin to return to their coastal settlements.)

Fertile land here was at an absolute premium and hotly contested. In the 17th and 18th centuries, this hostile corner of Greece was known to travelers as the "land of evil counsel" *(Kalavoulia)* because of its reputation for robbery and piracy—a more reliable way to survive than trying to eke out an honest living by farming. Maniots banded together in clans, whose leaders built the characteristic tower settlements *(kapitanias)* that are a feature of the region. Each *kapitania* controlled its own little city-statelet of land. Some larger towns were occupied by several rival *kapitanias*. Honor was prized even more than arable land, and each clan leader had a chip on his shoulder the size of a big slab of feta cheese. Vendettas and violent bickering between clans—about control of territory or sometimes simply respect—became epidemic. If Greece had

stray travelers. The waterfront eatery **Vesuvius** has a ladder down to the sea from its terrace, so you can combine swimming, basking, and eating.

After Agios Nikolaos the road begins to curve up the mountain, passing through **Platsa** (with the interesting church of St. John/Ag. Ioannis). If the church is open, poke inside to see the ceiling fresco with Jesus surrounded by zodiac symbols—a reminder of the way early Christians incorporated pre-Christian mythology. Higher up, the village of **Thalames**—its square shaded by a giant plane tree—is known for its olive-oil production (several shops on the square sell it). Then, in **Lagkada,** watch (on the left) for the rea Tombstone and an OK Corral, this is where they'd be.

When they weren't fighting each other, the Maniots banded together to fight off foreign invaders. Locals brag that the feisty Mani—still clinging to the stubborn militarism of the ancient Spartans—remained the only corner of Greece not fully under the thumb of the Ottoman Turks. During nearly four centuries of Turkish rule, the sultan struck a compromise to appoint more or less Ottoman-friendly Maniots as regional governors. After a failed Greek uprising against the Turks in the late 18th century, Greeks from all over the country flooded into the Mani to escape harsh Ottoman reprisals. As the population boomed, competition for the sparse natural resources grew even fiercer.

Perhaps not surprisingly, the hot tempers of the Maniots made the peninsula the crucible for Greek independence. On March 17, 1821, Maniot Petros Mavromichalis, the Ottoman-appointed governor *(bey),* led a spirited rebellion against his Turkish superiors. Mavromichalis succeeded in taking Kalamata six days later, and the War of Independence was underway. What began in the remote hills of the Mani quickly engulfed the rest of Greece, and by 1829 the Ottomans were history and Greece was free.

Looking around today at the barren landscape of the Mani Peninsula, which now barely supports 5,000 people, it's hard to believe that 200 years ago it sustained a population of almost 60,000. Over time that number was depleted by blood feuds, which raged into the early 20th century. The end of Ottoman rule in the early 19th century and the devastating Greek Civil War of the mid-20th century sparked population shifts out of the region, as Maniots sought easier lifestyles elsewhere in Greece, or set out for the promise of faraway lands, primarily America, the UK, and Australia. But these days, as the Mani emerges as a prime tourist destination, many Maniot emigrants are returning home—bringing back with them an array of accents from around the world.

markably well-preserved Byzantine Church of the Metamorphosis, lavishly decorated with terra-cotta designs.

As you ascend ever higher, notice how the landscape fades from green to brown. From here on out, the Mani becomes characteristically arid. You'll also begin to see **terraces** etched into the mountainsides, a reminder of how hard Maniots had to work to earn a living from this inhospitable land. They'd scrape together whatever arable soil they could into these little patches to grow olive trees and wheat. Some of the larger stone walls surrounding the terraces demarcate property boundaries.

Soon you cross the "state line" that separates the Exo (Outer)

Mani from the Mesa (Inner) Mani—its southern tip and most striking area.

As you reach the lip of the dramatic Milolangado Gorge, the town of **Itilo** (EE-tee-loh) comes into view. Like Kardamyli, this

town was mentioned in Homer's *Iliad*. The fortifications on the southern side of the gorge belong to Kelefa Castle, built by the Ottomans in 1670 in a short-lived attempt to control the rebellious Maniots. Enjoy the views before heading down to Limeni Bay, where you'll pass the settlements of Neo ("New") Itilo and **Limeni** (birthplace of the war hero Petros Mavromichalis, whom we'll meet shortly). Fish lovers detour into Limeni for lunch at Takis Taverna, overlooking the harbor, while adventure seekers enjoy hiking the 3.5 miles up from the bayside road into the gorge itself.

• *Continuing up the other side of the gorge, and then cresting the top, you'll shortly arrive in...*

Areopoli

Areopoli (ah-reh-OH-poh-lee)—named after Ares, the ancient god of war—is the de facto capital of the Inner Mani. Less charming but more lived-in than other Mani towns, Areopoli is the region's commercial center.

As you arrive from Itilo, turn right at the stop sign, veer left following the sign to *Dirou Caves,* then turn right just past the su-

permarket and stone wall into a modern main square, **Plateia Athanaton** (where you should be able to find a place to park). Dominating the square is a statue of Petros Mavromichalis (1765-1848). This local-boy-done-good was selected to rule the region by the Ottoman overlords, who assumed they could corrupt him with money and power. But they underestimated his strong sense of Mani honor. On March 17, 1821, Mavromichalis gathered a ragtag Maniot army here in Areopoli and marched north to Kalamata, launching the War of Independence. Mavromichalis looks every inch a warrior, clutching a mighty curved sword, with a pistol tucked into his waistband.

The square hosts a lively market on Saturday mornings. At

other times, everything else of interest is to be found about 500 yards west of here, around the old main square, **Plateia 17 Martiou.** If Mavromichalis jumped off his pedestal, marched toward the candy-colored cafés, and headed left, he'd reach the old center of town in five minutes: a stony fortified village settlement circling a stone church. This is the spot where Petros mustered his men for the march to Kalamata, a moment commemorated by a plaque on the northern wall. The square is dominated by the 18th-century Church of Taxiarhes ("Archangels"), sporting an impressive four-story bell tower. The carvings above the main door (around the left side) show the archangels Gabriel and Michael, flanked by the saints Georgios and Dimitrios on horseback. Under the bell tower is a private war museum of rough artillery. Just behind the church (ΑΡΤΟΠΟΙΕΙΟ sign, near the well), find the rustic bakery run by Milia, who makes bread and savory pies in a wood-fired oven. For an edible souvenir, survey the bags of cookies on the rack by the door.

With your back to the war museum's doorway, take the path straight in front of you, skirting around the ruins of the war tower

of Petros Mavromichalis. Follow this alley as it winds its way next to a church. At the end of the alley, jog left, then right. On this second alley are the Church of St. John and the Pikoulakis Tower—home to the two-room **Mani Museum of Religion,** which documents the long history of Christianity on the peninsula (closed Mon).

• *Your next stop is the Pyrgos Dirou Caves, about six miles south of Areopoli. (If you're skipping the caves, or saving them for the end of your drive, follow signs toward* Kotronas/ Κότρωνας *just south of Areopoli—take the left turn at the fork—and pick up this tour at "Eastern Mani," later.)*

Continuing south of Areopoli, follow the well-marked signs for Diros Caves; *the turnoff is marked with a blue sign in the center of town. If you go past Pyrgos and reach the turnoff sign for* Γκλεζι, *you've gone too far—backtrack into Pyrgos. The cave entry is along a small bay, reached by a steep road that twists down to the water.*

▲Pyrgos Dirou Caves
(a.k.a. Diros Caves and Vlychada Cave)

These remarkable cave formations—discovered by locals in the 1870s and opened to the public in 1963—rank among Europe's best. The formations range from stout stalactites and stalagmites to delicate hair-like structures—many of them surprisingly colorful, thanks to reddish iron deposits.

Cost and Hours: €13; daily 9:00-17:00, Oct-April 8:30-15:30; tel. 27330-52222. Because this is a very popular attraction, you might be in for a wait during busy summer months (lines are worst from noon to 14:00 and any time in August). Figure about an hour total to tour the caves (not counting wait time).

Visiting the Caves: Buy your ticket at the gate, then walk five minutes down to the cave entrance to wait for your appointed entry time (if the gate's open, you can also drive right down to the cave entrance after getting your ticket). The temperature in the caves is usually between 60 and 65 degrees Fahrenheit—you may want a sweater. (Be sure to pick up the English brochure, which says about as much as your Greek guide.)

After you've boarded a little boat, your guide poles you along underground canals, softly calling out (usually in Greek only) the creative names for each of the spectacular formations: "Hercules' columns," "palm forest," "golden rain," "crystal lily," and so on. Stalactites drip down directly overhead, and damp cave walls, beautifully lit, are inches away—you'll need to duck or bend from time to time as the boat glides through some of the narrower passageways. In some places the water beneath you is 100 feet deep...you're actually floating near the ceiling of a vast, flooded cavern. (Life preservers are provided.) Pinch yourself: This isn't a movie or a Disney ride, but the real deal. After your three-quarter-mile boat trip, you return to dry land and walk another quarter-mile for up-close views of more limestone formations.

Museum: If you have more time and interest after your cave visit, consider touring the little museum on the hillside between the entrance and ticket office. It shows off human bones and Neolithic artifacts found in similar caves in this area (€2, Tue-Sun 8:30-15:00, closed Mon, well-described in English).

Eastern Mani

To experience the Mani's most rugged and remote-feeling area,

cross over the spine of the peninsula to the eastern coast. The few tourists you encounter melt away the farther south you drive, until it's just you, sheer limestone cliffs, fortified ghost towns, olive trees, and tumbling surf. Here the terrain seems even more desolate than what you've seen so far.

As you explore the countryside you'll notice huge building projects, hotel developments springing up like mushrooms—including the luxury Tzokeika Traditional Settlement just north of Platsa at the beginning of this drive—and decadent private mansions. (Athenian big shots like to have a Mani escape.) The impressive stonework is generally done by Albanian workers. Mixed in are tiny 13th-century Byzantine churches clinging to the stark land like barnacles and lots of mobile "honey farms." Bee farmers chase the sage and thyme, setting up their hives where the pollen is best. The honey of the Mani is the most expensive and prized in Greece. With so much to see, you'll need to drive carefully. You don't want to become just another of the many roadside shrines.

After taking the right turn for **Kotronas/Κότρωνας** just south of Areopoli, head overland through stark scenery. Cresting the hills at **Himara/Χιμαρα,** you'll begin to glimpse the Mani's east coast. At **Loukadika/Λουκαδικα,** bear right (south) along the main road toward **Kokkala/Κοκκαλα,** and you'll soon find yourself traversing the top of a cliff above some of the best scenery on the Mani. Heading south you'll see more and more fortified towers climbing up the rocky hillsides. Imagine that each of these towers represents the many ruthless vendettas that were fought here.

Approaching **Dimaristika/Διμαριστικα,** notice the three tower settlements that dot the hill at three different levels. It's easy to imagine why the Ottomans never took this land—the villages could see them coming by ship from miles away and bombard them with cannonballs. And if the Ottomans managed to make landfall, they'd have to climb up, up, up to overtake the forts. It just wasn't worth the trouble.

The village of **Lagia/Λαγια** was supposedly the site of the last Mani vendetta, a scuffle in the 1930s. The town seems almost abandoned today, but most of these houses are owned by Maniots who now live in Athens and come back for the holidays. On the square (along the main road through town) is a monument honoring Panagiotis Vlahakos, a villager who died in a 1996 conflict over a small Aegean island (called Imia in Greek, or Kardak in Turkish) claimed by both Greece and Turkey. The Ottomans left

KARDAMYLI & MANI PENINSULA

this country close to two centuries ago, but Greek-Turkish relations are still raw.

• *Leaving Lagia, continue straight ahead. After about five minutes, you'll reach a fork. If you're ready to head back around to the western Mani coast, take the right turn (direction: Lagia—and skip down to the "Vathia" section of this tour). But to reach the most distant corner of mainland Greece, Cape Tenaro, bear left toward the long list of Greek names (including Kokkinogeia/Κοκκινόγεια). Switchback your way tightly down toward the sea, always following signs for* Kokkinogeia/ Κοκκινόγεια; *if highway signs are missing, look for smaller hiking-route signs that mark the* Tenaro Archaeological Site *(not* Porto Kagio*). After cresting the small isthmus over to the west side of the cape, with both bays in front of you, you'll come to a completely unmarked fork just after a stone shed; bear right, then take a sharp left. You'll shortly pass near Marmari/Μαρμαρι (but not through it; it'll be below and to the right as you follow hikers' signs to take an uphill left fork). Then keep following signs to* Tenaro/Ταίναρο *and* Sanctuary and Death Oracle, *staying left. You'll come to the literal end of the road.*

Imagine the work it takes to eke out a subsistence living in this god-forsaken corner of Greece, and spending your days digging up stones to build the fortified tower houses you see capping the hills.

Cape Tenaro (a.k.a. Cape Matapan): Greece's "Land's End"

Drive out to the tip of the rocky promontory known as the "Sanctuary of the Dead." As the farthest point of the known world, this was where the ancient Greeks believed that the souls of the deceased came to enter the underworld. An underwater cave here was thought to belong to Hades, god of the underworld. It was also the site of a temple and oracle devoted to Poseidon, the god of the sea (marked today by a ruined Christian church).

Visitors can still explore the scant unexcavated ruins of an ancient town that was called Tenaron (mentioned in the *Iliad*). An inviting restaurant also offers travelers a good opportunity for a break.

Just below the parking lot are the ruins of an early Christian church, likely constructed using giant blocks scavenged from the temple upon which it sits. To visit the poorly marked ruins of Tenaron, walk down from the parking lot toward the water, then bear right around the far side of the bay. You'll soon be able to pick out the footprints of ancient Greek and Roman structures. Hiding behind one of these low walls, about a five-minute walk around the tiny bay, is a surprisingly intact floor mosaic from a Roman villa, just sitting out in the open. If you've got time to kill and are up for a longer hike, trudge another 30 minutes out to a lighthouse at the end of the world. A busy shipping channel lies just offshore; you can count the vessels

heading east to Athens or to ports to the west.

• *Retrace your tracks back to civilization. Reaching the first fork (unmarked, with the stone shed), turn left and head up the west coast of the Mani (toward Vathia/Βαθειά—not the direction you came down from). Soon you'll be treated to views of the classic Mani ghost town. The pullout on the left, 100 yards before the town, offers the best view. Then continue and park near the double phone booth. From there you can walk into the stony village. Circle it clockwise (a former donkey mill is inside the first house on the left). Consider how a settlement like this with no roads and only footpaths can't survive in the modern age.*

Vathia

The most dramatic of all the Mani tower villages, Vathia is Vendetta-ville—it seems everyone here barricaded themselves in forts.

The more towers a town had, the more dangerous it was—and it's hard to imagine cramming more towers into a single town than they did in Vathia. Built on a rocky spur and once famed for its olive oil, Vathia was an extreme example of what can happen when neighbors don't get along. The 80-some houses were split north/south into two rival camps, which existed in a state of near-permanent hostility. Now Vathia is mostly uninhabited. Once-intimidating towers are now haunting ruins, held together with boards and steel cables.

• *Driving north, you'll pass through the larger town of Kiparissos—originally Kenipolis ("New City"), which was settled by those who left ancient Tenaron—then turn off (signs in Greek only) to reach the town center and port of...*

Gerolimenas

Gerolimenas (yeh-roh-LEE-meh-nahs, roughly "sacred port"),

nestled at the back of a deep sheltered bay, is a cute fishing town kept alive by tourism. The waterfront is lined with cafés and restaurants, and the water is good for a swim—making it an all-around enjoyable place to take a break and watch the surf.

• *Continue back out to the main road and turn left, toward* **Kita.** *This town was the setting for the Mani's final major feud in 1870, which raged for weeks until the Greek army arrived, artillery in tow, to enforce a truce.*

For one last little detour, hang a left turn at the village of Agios Georgios (toward Μέζαπος/*Mezapo/Beach*), *and go a bit more than a mile down to the...*

Bay of Mezapos

At the cove at Mezapos (MEH-zah-pohs), carved out of lime-stone by the surf, boats bob picturesquely in the protective harbor, watched over by an extremely sleepy hamlet. Mezapos was once a notorious haven for pirates. It's easy to see why, if you look across the bay to see the long, naturally fortified peninsula aptly named Tigani ("frying pan"). This was once thought to be the site of the Frankish castle of Maina (roughly, "clenched fist"), which some believe to be the namesake of the Mani.

• *Continuing north you'll first pass the village of Pyrgos—with the turn-off for the caves—then arrive back at Areopoli. From here retrace your route around Itilo Bay back to Kardamyli; or, if you're continuing on-ward, head east just beyond Areopoli to reach Monemvasia.*

MONEMVASIA

MONEMBASIA / Μονεμβασία

Monemvasia (moh-nehm-vah-SEE-ah), a gigantic rock that juts improbably up from the blue-green deep just a few hundred yards offshore, is a time-warp to the medieval Peloponnese. Its little Lower Town hamlet hides on the seaward side of the giant rock, tethered to the mainland only by a skinny spit of land. This remarkably romantic walled town—with the remains of an even bigger Upper Town scattered along the peak high above—is a stony museum of Byzantine, Ottoman, and Venetian history dating back to the 13th century. Summiting Monemvasia is a key experience on any Peloponnesian visit.

Monemvasia means "single entry"—and the only way to get here is to cross the narrow causeway. At the mainland end of the causeway is the nondescript town of Gefyra (YEH-fee-rah), a smattering of hotels, restaurants, shops, and other modern amenities that offer a handy 21st-century base and springboard for exploring the Rock.

Heading to or from Monemvasia, consider a stop at Mystras, near Sparta. Although the town of Sparta has little of touristic interest, the site of Mystras has well-preserved Byzantine churches (dating from the 13th to 14th century) that evoke the grandeur of the Byzantine Empire before it fizzled.

PLANNING YOUR TIME

It takes only a couple hours to see Monemvasia—a stroll through the Lower Town, a hike to the Upper Town, and you've done it all. Though doable as a day trip from Kardamyli or Nafplio (2.5-3 hours by car each way), I don't recommend it. Spending the night in Monemvasia (or mainland Gefyra) allows you to linger on the floodlit cobbles and makes the long trip down here more worthwhile.

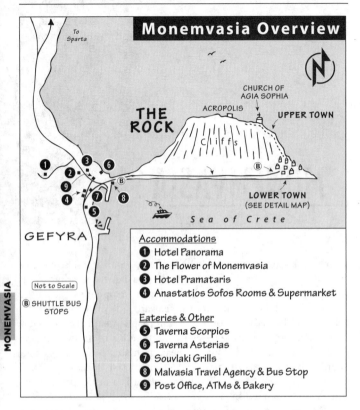

Monemvasia Overview

To Sparta

CHURCH OF
AGIA SOPHIA

ACROPOLIS

THE ROCK

UPPER TOWN

Cliffs

LOWER TOWN
(SEE DETAIL MAP)

Sea of Crete

GEFYRA

Not to Scale

Ⓑ SHUTTLE BUS
STOPS

Accommodations
❶ Hotel Panorama
❷ The Flower of Monemvasia
❸ Hotel Pramataris
❹ Anastatios Sofos Rooms & Supermarket

Eateries & Other
❺ Taverna Scorpios
❻ Taverna Asterias
❼ Souvlaki Grills
❽ Malvasia Travel Agency & Bus Stop
❾ Post Office, ATMs & Bakery

MONEMVASIA

Orientation to Monemvasia

Monemvasia is moored to the mainland at the village of Gefyra, where most of its services are located. The road into Gefyra from Sparta becomes the main street, where you'll find—clustered where the road bends left toward the Rock—the post office, a few ATMs, and an excellent bakery (with a supermarket just up the street). The Malvasia Travel Agency sells bus and shuttle tickets and serves as the town's bus stop (located at the start of the causeway across from the shuttle bus stop).

After passing through Gefyra, the main road leads to the causeway across to the Rock (Vraxos). The hamlet of Monemvasia itself, which locals call To Kastro ("The Castle"), is out of sight around behind the Rock. To Kastro is divided into the Lower Town (with shops, hotels, and restaurants) and the ruins of the Upper Town high above. Only a dozen or so people actually live in Monemvasia, and it's fair to say every business there caters to tourists.

ARRIVAL IN MONEMVASIA

A road runs around the base of the Rock from the causeway to Monemvasia's Lower Town. To get from Gefyra on the mainland to the Lower Town, you have three options: walk (across the causeway, then around the Rock, about 20 minutes); drive (go all the way to the castle gate and then circle back to grab the closest roadside parking spot); or take a shuttle bus (see next).

HELPFUL HINTS

Gefyra-Monemvasia Shuttle Bus: Use this handy service to avoid the long, hot, and boring walk between Gefyra and old Monemvasia (2/hour, leaves Gefyra on the half hour 8:00-24:00—until 14:00 off-season—and departs the castle a few minutes later, €1.10 each way, buy tickets at **Malvasia Travel Agency** mentioned earlier or pay driver directly if office is closed; bus is signed *Kastro*, which means "castle").

Name Variation: In English the town's name can also be spelled Monemvassia, Monembasia, or Monembacia. During the Venetian period it was called Malvasia.

Addresses: Locals don't bother with street numbers, or even names—both Monemvasia and Gefyra are small enough that everyone knows where everything is. If you can't find something, just ask around. On the Rock, businesses are only allowed on the main drag.

Don't Needlessly Fry: If climbing to the top of the Rock in the summer, go early or late, as it can be brutally hot at midday. Wear good shoes and bring sun protection (there's very little shade up there) and carry water (there are no shops up top, but you can buy water at gift shops along the Lower Town's main drag).

Monemvasia Walk

There are only two things to see in Monemvasia: the walled Lower Town and the castle ruins of the Upper Town high above (free and open 24 hours daily). This self-guided walk covers both.

Lower Town

Begin outside the 17th-century **main gate,** designed by the Ottomans who were occupying the town at the time (and who knew a thing or two about designing—and breach-

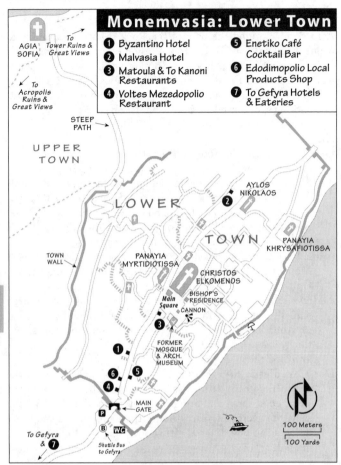

Monemvasia: Lower Town

1 Byzantino Hotel
2 Malvasia Hotel
3 Matoula & To Kanoni Restaurants
4 Voltes Mezedopolio Restaurant
5 Enetiko Café Cocktail Bar
6 Edodimopolio Local Products Shop
7 To Gefyra Hotels & Eateries

AGIA SOFIA

To Tower Ruins & Great Views

To Acropolis Ruins & Great Views

STEEP PATH

UPPER TOWN

LOWER

TOWN

AYLOS NIKOLAOS

PANAYIA KHRYSAFIOTISSA

TOWN WALL

PANAYIA MYRTIDIOTISSA

CHRISTOS ELKOMENOS

Main Square

BISHOP'S RESIDENCE

CANNON

FORMER MOSQUE & ARCH. MUSEUM

MAIN GATE

P

B

WC

To Gefyra & 7

Shuttle Bus to Gefyra

100 Meters

100 Yards

MONEMVASIA

ing—gates like this one). The only public WCs are to the right, in front of the gate.

Look up to the cliff and down to the sea, appreciating how successfully the crenellated wall protected this mighty little nugget of Byzantine power. There are only four entrances: two on this side, one on the opposite side, and one from the sea. Combine that with the ridiculously easy-to-defend little causeway (once equipped with a drawbridge) and the perfect bird's-eye view from the top of the Rock (ideal for spotting would-be invaders from miles and miles away), and Monemvasia was a tough nut to crack.

Enter the gate. (The stairway inside leads left up to a terrace with a monument noting the fact that the 20th-century poet Yiannis Ritsos—beloved by Greeks but unknown abroad—spent much of his life here.) Inside the gate, notice that the road jogs, prevent-

Monemvasia's History

Mighty Monemvasia, a Gibraltar-like rock with a Crusader-style stone town at its base, has ruins scattered all across its Masada-like plateau summit.

Monemvasia's Upper Town may have been founded in the sixth century A.D. by refugees fleeing Slavic raids into the Peloponnese. Gradually the settlement spread down the hill and, thanks to its uniquely well-defended position, became a powerful town. It was a center of both trade and military importance, with merchants living below and the nobility living above. In the declining days of the Byzantine Empire (1262-1460), when nearby Mystras was its ecclesiastical base, Monemvasia was its main city and one of the great commercial centers of the Byzantine world, with a thriving population in the tens of thousands. It was known for its Malvasia wine, a lightly fortified red that was prized at the royal courts of Europe. Over the next several centuries, highly strategic Monemvasia changed hands again and again—mostly back and forth between the Venetians and the Ottomans. While most of the buildings that survive today date from the second period of Venetian rule (1690-1715), foundations and architectural elements from each chapter survive.

By the 18th century, Monemvasia slipped into decline... until it was rediscovered by tourists in the 1970s. Today Monemvasia is a leading destination both for international visitors and for wealthy Athenians, who are converting its old houses into weekend retreats.

MONEMVASIA

ing you from even getting a peek at the town until you emerge on the other side—another defensive measure. And then...

You're at the start of Monemvasia's narrow, cobbled **main street.** Bear uphill (left) at the fork, through a gauntlet of tourist shops, hotel offices (renting rooms in buildings scattered all over town), and cafés with inviting terraces stretching toward the sea. Elsewhere in town, doors and windows are small, but here—on what's always been the main commercial drag—the wide, arched windows come with big built-in counters for displaying wares. Enjoy this atmospheric lane, scouting cafés and restaurants for later (see "Eating in Monemvasia").

At the **Edodimopolio local products shop** (on the left, near the entry gate), energetic Fotini stocks all sorts of gifty edibles and is happy to offer samples of her honey-wine and olive oil.

The lane leads to the town's **main square,** Plateia Dsami—literally "Mosque Square," a very rare-in-Greece tip of the hat to Ottoman rule. The namesake mosque still stands (the blocky building with the small red dome, on the right). In the middle of the square, notice two symbols of the town: a cannon (Monemvasia was nothing if not well-defended) and a well. Monemvasia is honeycombed with cisterns for catching rainwater...the one thing that a city clinging to a rock floating in the sea needs to survive. Virtually every house—in both the Upper and Lower Towns—had a roof designed to catch water, with pipes plumbed into its walls and its own cellar cistern.

Walk to the edge of this square and survey the rooftops of the **Lower Town.** Notice a unique feature of Monemvasia houses:

sharply angled rooflines, which allowed built-in tile gutters to carefully channel water into those cellar cisterns. Houses are built of stone quarried from right here on the Rock—a very efficient way to get building materials. Whereas the stone walls of many houses are exposed today, historically most houses were covered with plaster (some

still are), which once gave the skyline Santorini-like soft edges.

Now turn around and face the Rock and the **Upper Town.** Notice the stoutly walled, zigzagging path that climbs the cliff face. Halfway up and a little to the right, notice the small cave (with the white entrance) burrowed into the cliff—a humble chapel reached by a precarious footpath. You can see from here that most of the Upper Town is in ruins...but it is fun to explore (described later).

Before leaving the square, do a little sightseeing. The old mosque—which has also served as a church, prison, and coffee shop—today hosts a modest **archaeological museum** (€2, Tue-Sun 8:00-15:00, closed Mon, tel. 27320-61403). The one-room display, though sparse, is well-presented and well-described in English: pottery fragments, the stone chancel screen (iconostasis) from a long-gone Byzantine church, and an explanation of how many ancient architectural elements were scavenged to build early Christian churches.

Across from the mosque/museum is the whitewashed, 11th-century **Church of Christos Elkomenos** ("Christ in Pain"). In its

day, this was a very important Byzantine church. (The twin platforms in the rear are said to be for the thrones used when the emperor and empress visited from Constantinople.) While this was originally a Byzantine church, the Venetians substantially expanded it: Notice the elaborately carved lintel above the entrance, a sure sign of Venetian influence. The peacock relief above the lintel was added after independence (1820s), as was the bell tower. If open (generally daily 9:00-14:00 & 16:00-20:00), step into the tidy white interior for a serene visit to an Orthodox church. If you're so moved, drop a coin in the box, light a candle, and say a prayer. Hiding behind the marble iconostasis (peek behind the curtain) is a small reminder of the church's humble Byzantine origins: old amphitheater-like stone risers where bishops once stood.

The artistic highlight of the entire region is in a small chapel to the right: a precious icon of the Crucifixion dating from around 1300, the peak of the Byzantine Renaissance. As this is the world in which El Greco trained, you could consider it "proto-El Greco." The emotions portrayed were groundbreaking for the age (English description outside the door). This icon was stolen in the 1970s,

making headlines across the country, and is displayed now only with high security.

Although it's a little town today, Monemvasia was once important enough to be a bishopric. Back outside, to the right as you face the church, notice the entrance to the bishop's former residence—with the Venetian coat of arms (the winged lion of St. Mark) above the door. You'll also see that the church is attached by an archway to a small chapel.

Before huffing up to the Upper Town, poke around the Lower Town's twisty lanes. Descend through the archway to the right of the church. The steps lead down through a maze of steeply cobbled streets to the seawall. A gate (tiny and therefore easy to defend) at the center of the wall leads out to a rocky platform with ladders into the sea for swimmers (there's a handy shower here).

As you explore, keep in mind that the streets of Monemvasia contain a variety of architectural influences: Byzantine, Venetian, and Ottoman. Wandering the streets of the Lower Town, you might notice pointed archways or large lintels (stones over windows), which are distinctively Venetian; or occasional tulip-shaped windows (curling on top with a little peak in the middle), which are unmistakably Turkish. Notice the many arched passageways spanning narrow lanes—the only way a crowded, walled town could grow. Quite a few houses are still in ruins, but with Monemvasia's tourism on the rise, many of these are now being excavated and rebuilt. Because the town is protected, restoration requires navigating a lot of red tape and giving painstaking attention to historical accuracy.

You'll notice lots of little churches. In Byzantine times, ecclesiastical and political power overlapped, and building a church gave a wealthy family more prestige and power. Also, a trading town like this would have been home to communities from different lands—each with its own style of worship and particular church.

Each significant site around town is numbered and explained by posted information...but there's no need to get bogged down by those details. Just have fun with the perfect medieval streetscapes awaiting discovery around each turn.

When you're ready to climb the Rock, make your way to the top of town and huff up the steep path to the...

Upper Town

The ruins of the Upper Town are spread across a broad, rolling plateau at the summit of the Rock. Unlike the well-preserved Lower Town, very little of the Upper Town has survived intact. The last weary resident left the plateau nearly a century ago, and it is now a wasteland of ruined old buildings, engulfed by a sea

of shrubs and wildflowers that seem to sprout from the rocks. As you explore up here, watch your step—sudden cliffs, slippery rocks (especially treacherous when wet), and open cisterns are genuine hazards.

Nearing the top of the trail, curl through yet another defensive gateway. The door here, with its metal casing, is likely 18th-century Ottoman—and is probably the best artifact surviving in the Upper Town. As you emerge onto the top, observe the collection of buildings to your right at the gate (with fine views onto the Lower Town from the tiny square) and the Church of Agia Sophia above you to the left. The best way to enjoy the top of the Rock is to let your inner child take over for a king- or queen-of-the-castle scramble across the ramparts and ruins.

Follow the trail up to the 12th-century Byzantine **Church of Agia Sophia.** Thanks to recent erosion, the church hangs precari-

ously (and scenically) close to the edge of a sheer cliff. Like so many buildings here, the church has elements from various eras of history: a Byzantine core (it retains its original octagonal design), with Ottoman elements (most now gone, but you can still see the prayer niche, or mihrab), and a triple-arched loggia graft- ed onto the front in the 16th century by the Venetians. The interior was whitewashed when it was converted into a mosque under Turkish rule, but fragments of original frescoes survive.

MONEMVASIA

From here you can climb high- er up the hill for good **views** back down onto the church. If you want to lengthen your hike, you can climb all the way to the **acropolis,** the for- tification near the peak of the Rock (visible from here). Or, for an easier walk, head downhill to the crenel- lated watchtower area out toward the sea; this **promontory** has the best views back up to the church.

As you explore the site, re- member that this was regarded as the mightiest fortress in Byzantine

Greece. Not surprisingly, it was never captured in battle—only by a protracted starve-'em-out siege. Monemvasia's Achilles' heel was its dependence on the mainland for food. And though some basic

supplies were cultivated atop the Rock, it wasn't enough to sustain the entire town for very long.

Back near the entrance gateway, consider heading right along the wall (as you face the Lower Town and water) for good views back down onto the Lower Town. If you continue farther along this path, you'll reach an old Turkish house, and then the granddaddy of all the town's cisterns: a **cavernous vaulted hall.**

Our tour of the Rock is finished. When you're done enjoying the views and the evocative ruins, head back down the way you came up.

Evenings in Monemvasia

Monemvasia is touristy yet peaceful and romantic after dark, with several bars and cafés open late, and plenty of rooftop seating. Everything of interest is along the one business street or on the town square. My choice for a drink is the **Enetiko Café Cocktail Bar** (about 100 yards in from the gate, with great cocktails, a chill vibe, and a view terrace).

The long walk between the mainland and the old town can be nerve-wracking at night with little light and cars dodging pedestrians. I'd take advantage of the shuttle bus that goes on the half-hour until midnight in high season (see "Helpful Hints," earlier). Evenings along the harborfront in **Gefyra** can be delightful, too, with plenty of places for a drink or meal.

Sleeping in Monemvasia

Peak-season demand drives prices up in July and August—especially on weekends, when this is a popular retreat for Athenians. Off-season, you can usually get a deal.

ON THE ROCK

Sleeping in Monemvasia's old Lower Town, romantic and appealing to many, is a lot of work because you can't park nearby. Various hotels rent rooms scattered through old buildings. All of them have decor that mixes new and old, with old-fashioned Monemvasia flourishes (such as low platform beds, tight bathrooms, head-banging archways, and stone shower enclosures without curtains). Keep in mind that Monemvasia is a honeycomb of cobblestone alleys and stairs. Luggage with wheels won't work here. If you stay on the Rock, be prepared to carry your luggage to your hotel (drivers might want to cram essentials into a daypack).

I've listed two "hotels" that are actually a reception desk near the entry gate managing mostly elegantly remodeled rooms scattered throughout the Lower Town. Review their websites and compare what they offer.

$$ Byzantino Hotel rents 25 tastefully old-fashioned rooms in the Lower Town, some with sea views and balconies (breakfast extra at their café, tel. 27320-61351, www.hotelbyzantino.com, info@hotelbyzantino.com). Avoid the pricey rooms in their Lazareto Hotel, outside the Lower Town, just across the causeway from the mainland.

$$ Malvasia Hotel is a collection of 25 rustic but atmospheric rooms around town in three different buildings (tel. 27320-61160, www.malvasiahotel-traditional.gr, malvasia@otenet.gr).

IN GEFYRA

Sleeping in the mainland town of Gefyra lacks the romance of spending the night in old Monemvasia, but it's less expensive and easier. The following listings are each a solid value if rooms in Monemvasia are booked up, or for those who'd rather trade atmosphere for the convenience of parking a few steps from their room.

$$ Hotel Panorama is well-run by friendly Angelos and Rena Panos. At the top of Gefyra, a 10-minute hike up from the main street, it's quiet and comes with great views. Its 27 comfy rooms all have balconies; some have sea views (family rooms, no elevator, tel. 27320-61198, www.panoramahotel-monemvasia.gr, info@panoramahotel-monemvasia.gr).

$$ The Flower of Monemvasia is a pleasant family-run hotel along the main road near the causeway with 20 rooms, most with a balcony (breakfast extra, no elevator, tel. 27320-61395, www.flower-hotel.gr, info@flower-hotel.gr).

$$ Hotel Pramataris offers 22 good-value rooms across the street from The Flower of Monemvasia. All rooms have balconies; most have views of the Rock (no elevator, tel. 27320-61833, www.pramatarishotel.gr, hotelpr@hol.gr).

$$ Anastatios Sofos is the cheaper option, with eight bare-bones rooms along the main road (no breakfast, tel. 27320-61202, speaks just enough English).

Eating in Monemvasia

ON THE ROCK

The first two eateries are along the main pedestrian artery of Monemvasia's Lower Town, just before the main square.

$$$ Matoula (Ματούλα), with its delightful vine-shaded

terrace looking out to sea, is the most appealing of the restaurants on the Rock. Amid all the pretense of this town, it serves good traditional Greek dishes at fine prices. Consider the daily specials and *barbounia* (red mullet), or ask owner Venetia about the daily specials (seafood splurges, daily 12:00-late, tel. 27320-61660).

$$$ To Kanoni ("The Cannon"), next door to Matoula, is another good choice, with a cozy interior and a scenic upper veranda (pricier seafood dishes, daily 10:00-late, tel. 27320-61387, say hi to Petros). I like the tables on the cool rooftop terrace with a view down on the old square.

$$ Voltes Mezedopolio, a cozy little place just inside the gate, is run by two hardworking brothers and makes a good stop for *mezes* to enjoy family-style. The restaurant has no view, but the atmosphere is friendly and the prices are very good.

IN GEFYRA

A collection of interchangeable eateries cluster like barnacles at the Gefyra end of the causeway. In good weather, it's pointless to eat anywhere here without a view of

the Rock. I like to walk along the water (on either side of the causeway) and survey the options.

At **$$ Taverna Scorpios,** Vasillis and Julie share duties cooking and taking good care of diners at rustic white tables under a blue canopy. It has a castaway ambience and my favorite views of the Rock (daily 12:00-24:00, tel. 27320-62090).

$$ Taverna Asterias is a place where your chair can settle into the pebbles of the beach while friendly Spiro cooks fresh fish daily for lunch and dinner. When it's cold, dine indoors by the cozy open fireplace (to the left of the causeway as you face the Rock, tel. 27320-61633).

Fast Food and Picnics: For a quick snack, two side-by-side **$ souvlaki grills** are equally good for souvlaki and gyros (eat-in with the locals or takeaway; located in the center a block from the causeway). The bakery on Gefyra's main street (near the post office) is wonderful, and the supermarket just up the side street from there will help you round out your moveable feast for the top of the Rock. While you can buy basic drinks and snacks in Monemvasia's Lower Town, there's no grocery store there—do your shopping in Gefyra.

Monemvasia Connections

By Bus: Monemvasia is not well connected by bus and has no bus station. Buses stop across the street from the Malvasia Travel Agency, just before the causeway; you can buy tickets on the bus or at the travel agency (recommended a day in advance in busy times, tel. 27320-61752).

Four to five buses leave for **Sparta** each day (likely at 4:45, 7:15, 14:15, and 17:30; Mon and Fri also at 8:30; 2 hours); these continue on to **Tripoli** (4 hours total) and then **Athens** (6 hours total). You'll need to change in Sparta to reach just about anywhere else, such as **Areopoli** on the Mani Peninsula (3 hours from Sparta). Change in Tripoli for **Nafplio** (1.5 hours from Tripoli).

By Shared Taxi: Hotels can arrange a shared taxi to **Athens** (€40/person, 4 hours, departs early each morning).

ROUTE TIPS FOR DRIVERS

Monemvasia's a bit out of the way, but the trek is worth it. Allow 2.5 hours from **Kardamyli** (consider a pit stop in Gythio, a workaday port town with fine harborfront restaurants, about 1.5 hours from Monemvasia) or roughly 3 hours from **Nafplio** (on the fast road via Sparta and Tripoli). If you pass through Sparta en route, you can easily fit in a visit to the nearby Byzantine city and churches of Mystras (see next section).

You can speed on the highway for most of the route between Nafplio and Monemvasia, but you'd be missing one of the most stunning scenic drives in Greece: The coastal road between Nafplio and cute little Leonidio is very pretty, and the twisty cliffside uphill from (or downhill to) Leonidio is jaw-dropping. The mountain town of Kosmas is good for a quick break. Between Monemvasia and Kosmas, look for signs to Skala and Vrontamas. The route requires a little planning (as roads aren't well marked) and isn't for the squeamish. Even with a GPS on board, it's a good idea to ask your hotelier for route tips.

Sparta and Mystras

Located roughly between Kardamyli, Monemvasia, and Nafplio, the town of Sparta (which is nothing much) is near the site of Mystras, which is worth a stop. Its impressive Byzantine churches are fine examples of the empire's last Golden Age.

SPARTA

Sparta (Σπάρτη)—where mothers famously told their sons to "come home with your shield...or on it"—is a classic (and, I hope, thought-provoking) example of how little a militaristic society leaves as a legacy for the future.

The ancient Sparta that dominated Greek affairs in the sixth and fifth centuries B.C. isn't one visitors can experience: The various excavation sites around town go down no farther than the level of Roman Sparta, which was built on the foundations of the classical city from the first century B.C.

One reason why so little remains is that the town was abandoned in the 13th century, and its buildings were dismantled for reuse in the construction of nearby Mystras. Sparta was reestablished in 1834 on the initiative of King Otto and his Bavarian court, whose classical education had given them a strong appreciation of Sparta's place in history. Otto ordered his planners to create a city of wide boulevards and parks; today Sparta looks more like 19th-century Bavaria than the home of Spartan hero King Leonidas.

Sparta, built on a grid system, is easier to navigate than many Greek cities. Coming from Monemvasia or Gythio, you'll enter on Palaeologou and head through town, past the main square, until the main drag reaches a statue of King Leonidas. (Below the statue is written his famous taunt before the Persians slaughtered him and his last 300 troops in 380 B.C.: "Come and get it.") A block before the statue, in the median, a monument honors 27 centuries of hometown athletes—medalists in Olympic Games from 720 B.C. to A.D. 1996 (mostly for running and wrestling).

The acropolis of ancient Sparta is signposted from the statue of Leonidas. It's a pleasant 10-minute walk, but the ruins that lie scattered among the olive trees are Roman-era or later. The main feature of the excavations is an impressive Roman theater; however, much of its stone seating was removed and used in the defensive wall built around the city's acropolis in the fourth century A.D.

MYSTRAS

Mystras (Μυστράς), four miles west of Sparta, is the most important Byzantine site in Greece. It was here, in the foothills of the Taygetos Mountains, that the Byzantine Empire enjoyed a final dazzling period of creative energy (1262-1460) before it was swallowed up by the Ottomans.

The main attractions in Mystras are its churches—regarded as some of the finest surviving examples of late Byzantine architecture in Greece. The extravagantly decorated frescoes were painted by the empire's greatest artists (although their names sadly went unrecorded). Because of ongoing restoration work, some of the churches may be closed when you visit.

Cost and Hours: €12, €6 off-season, Mon-Sat 8:00-20:00, Sept until 13:30, Oct until 17:30, Nov-March until 15:00; Sun

8:00-15:00 year-round (ticket valid for same-day reentry); tel. 27310-83377.

Services: There's a good restaurant a block below the entrance. If you have a car, consider driving to the next village, Pikoulian-ika, which has a handful of rustic tavernas, including Restaurant Chromata (open for dinner), offering good views over Mystras and Sparta (5 minutes from the Upper Gate—follow signs). The only WC in the site is before entering.

Background

The last rulers of the Byzantine Empire were the Palaiologos "des-pots"—but they were not tyrants; the name comes from a subdi-vision of the Byzantine church called a "despotate." Under the Palaiologos family, Mystras became the Byzantine Empire's cul-tural and intellectual capital. It was home to many great artists and to the philosopher Plethon, who was responsible for the revival of Plato's teachings. Plethon and other scholars based here had a major impact on the Italian Renaissance, especially after he visited Florence in 1438.

After the fall of Constantinople to the Ottomans in 1453, the Byzantine emperors retreated here, and Mystras became the last outpost of their empire. But Mystras' Golden Age came to an end when the city surrendered to the Turks a few years later in 1460.

While Mystras is many centuries old, it was a thriving center until more modern times: Mystras had about 15,000 people living within its walls even during Muslim Ottoman rule (1460-1828). During that period, the sultan appointed the Orthodox patriarch, who was allowed to carry on if he didn't cause trouble. You'll see only one mosque in the entire site (built for the sultan's bureau-cracy).

Then, with Greek independence in the early 1800s, the Ot-tomans were expelled. King Otto consolidated power in part by dissolving the Orthodox monasteries and nationalizing the Greek Orthodox Church. He shut down Mystras and turned the great city into a quarry, providing stone for the building of modern Spar-ta. (He dreamed of making Sparta and Athens twin cities for his new Greece.) It's interesting to note that ancient Sparta served as a quarry for the building of Mystras, and then Mystras served as a quarry for the rebuilding of 19th-century Sparta.

Visiting the Site

The gangly site stretches halfway up the mountain. Tour groups start at the top Upper Gate entrance (about a mile up the road) and see Mystras as a long downhill walk—convenient if you can find a ride to the top entrance. Drivers can strategically divide the visit in two segments—park and start at the lower Main Gate entrance, then drive to the top for the rest of the site (showing your ticket to reenter). I'll assume you'll park at the Main Gate and see the site by zigzagging uphill and then retracing your steps back down to leave. Here are the main stops from the bottom to the top.

Metropolis (St. Demetrius Cathedral): The cathedral was built in 1270 and dedicated to St. Demetrius. Stepping into the courtyard, you see columns recycled from ancient Sparta, the bishop's residence, and a fountain built with a mishmash of ancient plunder. Inside the cathedral are more ancient columns. The double-headed eagle relief set into the floor in the center commemorates the coronation of the last Byzantine emperor, which took place here in 1449. (Since ancient times, the double-headed eagle has been the symbol of anyone considering himself the successor of the Roman emperor—like Byzantine emperors, Habsburg rulers, and Holy Roman Emperors.)

Museum: From the courtyard, steps lead to a small museum (featuring old holy books, marbles, artifacts from local graves). Before leaving the courtyard enjoy the uphill view of the rest of Mystras. The lower zone was for the common people and merchants (and this cathedral). The upper zone was for the nobility and ruling elite. The intact building directly above is the Palace of the Despots (described later). Imagine the despot surveying his realm from that perch.

Churches of Theodoros and Aphentiko: Beyond the Metropolis, a path slopes gently uphill to the right. This takes you to the churches of Agios Theodoros and Aphentiko, nestled below a grove of tall cypress trees. It's worth the detour just to admire the frescoes and the magnificent, multiple red-tiled domes of the Aphentiko.

Convent and Church of Pantanassa: Opposite the Metropolis, a steep path leads up toward the imposing Church of Pantanassa. The only living part of Mystras, it's home to six sweet, elderly, black-veiled nuns who live in a row of small rooms (on the left as you enter the church's walled compound). They tend the flower gardens and produce linen embroidered with Byzantine motifs, sold in the small shop at the end of the row. (A sister told me they actually have my guides and me on their prayer list in thanks for the thoughtful visitors who come here with this book and on our tours and buy their handmade embroidery work. Please, buy their delightful little souvenirs...I can use the prayers.) The church here is home to Mystras' best collection of frescoes and more columns and capitals plundered from ancient Sparta.

Monemvasia Gate: From the convent, retrace your steps to the path where you arrived below and continue uphill, following signs to the palace through the well-fortified gate (the name means "only one entrance"). The gate provided the only access between the lower town and the upper town, where the noble and powerful lived.

Palace of the Despots: The original palace is the closest wing of the building on the right, which was built by the Crusaders. Although the palace has been closed to the public for many years, you can check out the pointed Gothic arches of the top-floor windows—a favorite motif found at other Crusader castles around the Peloponnese. In the final decades of their rule, the Palaiologos despots built the second wing. Its massive central hall, which covers the entire second floor, served as their throne room. From here, drivers can choose to retrace their steps back to the exit and drive to the Upper Gate—saving more energy than time—or continue on foot.

St. Nicholas Church, Church of St. Sofia, Top Entry, and Crusader Castle: The top part of the site is a long climb (not worth the sweat for many if it's hot). The St. Nicholas Church (which comes first) is most interesting and worth hiking up to see. It was built in the early 1600s, during Ottoman rule. Near the top entry is the Church of St. Sofia. High above, capping the mountain, stands the Crusader Castle, built in 1249 and offering a commanding view into a 400-yard-deep gorge and out across the Peloponnese.

MONEMVASIA

BEYOND
ATHENS

DELPHI
ΔΕΛΦΟΊ / Δελφοί

Perched high on the southern slopes of Mt. Parnassos, and over-looking the gleaming waters of the Gulf of Corinth, Delphi (Greeks pronounce it "thell-FEE" or "dell-FEE," not "DELL-fye") is without doubt the most spectacular of Greece's ancient sites.

Back then, Delphi was famous throughout the world as the home of a prophetess known as the oracle (a.k.a. the Pythia). As the mouthpiece of Apollo on earth, she told fortunes for pilgrims who came from far and wide seeking her advice on everything from affairs of state to wars to matrimonial problems. Delphi's fame grew, and its religious festivals blossomed into the Pythian Games, an athletic contest that was second only to the Olympics.

Today Delphi offers visitors several worthwhile sights. The archaeological site contains the ruins of the Sanctuary of Apollo. Next door is the great Archaeological Museum, where statues and treasures found on the site help bring the ruins to life. And a short walk from the site are still more ruins—including the Kastalian Spring and the photogenic Sanctuary of Athena, taking you back to Delphi's prehistoric origins.

It's possible to visit Delphi as a day trip from Athens, but it's more relaxed as an overnight stop, allowing you to enjoy the pleasant modern town and craggy mountainside setting (suitably awesome for the mysterious oracle). Though the town is crammed with tourists, it still feels laid-back, offering sweeping vistas of the valley below and the Gulf of Corinth in the distance. (It's hard to find a hotel or restaurant that doesn't boast grand views.)

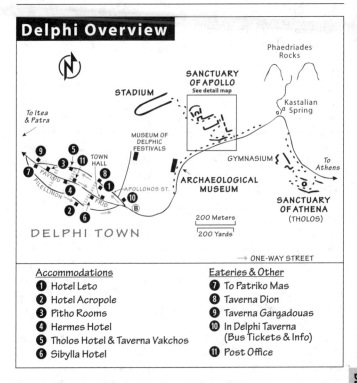

Delphi Overview

Phaedriades Rocks

SANCTUARY OF APOLLO
See detail map

STADIUM

Kastalian Spring

To Itea & Patra

MUSEUM OF DELPHIC FESTIVALS

GYMNASIUM

To Athens

TOWN HALL

ARCHAEOLOGICAL MUSEUM

PAVLOU

FILELLINON

APOLLONOS ST.

FRID

SANCTUARY OF ATHENA (THOLOS)

DELPHI TOWN

200 Meters
200 Yards

→ ONE-WAY STREET

Accommodations	Eateries & Other
❶ Hotel Leto	❼ To Patriko Mas
❷ Hotel Acropole	❽ Taverna Dion
❸ Pitho Rooms	❾ Taverna Gargadouas
❹ Hermes Hotel	❿ In Delphi Taverna
❺ Tholos Hotel & Taverna Vakchos	(Bus Tickets & Info)
❻ Sibylla Hotel	⓫ Post Office

DELPHI

Especially after a stay in bustling Athens, Delphi is an appealing place to let your pulse slow.

Orientation to Delphi

Visitors flock from all over Greece to walk the Sacred Way at Delphi. Many don't bother to spend the night. But the town, a half-mile west of the archaeological site and museum, is a charming place in its own right. Delphi, sometimes spelled Delfi or Delfoi in English (pop. 2,300), was custom-built to accommodate the hordes of tourists. The main street, Vasileos Pavlou-Friderikis, is a

tight string of hotels, cafés, restaurants, and souvenir shops. Two other streets run roughly parallel to this main drag (Apollonos is one block uphill/north, and Filellinon is one block downhill/

south), connected periodically by steep stairways. The three streets converge at the eastern end of town.

TOURIST INFORMATION

Delphi has no TI. The Town Hall office on the main drag posts current hours for the museum and archaeological site (at Pavlou-Friderikis 12, on the sanctuary end of town). Its entryway has a model of the Sanctuary of Apollo in ancient times—before you head out to the sanctuary, stop here to give it a good look; compare it to the map later in this chapter to locate what you'll see at the site.

ARRIVAL IN DELPHI

Delphi is three hours north of Athens, and is reachable by bus or by car.

By Bus: Buses to Delphi depart Athens 4-5 times a day from Terminal B (check local schedules—you can get one at the Athens TI or go to www.ktel-fokidas.gr; online tickets available). Most buses have air-conditioning but no WC and make a café rest stop en route. The drive takes you past Thiva (ancient Thebes) and has nice views of Mt. Parnassos as you approach.

Buses drop you off at the sanctuary (east) end of town. It's smart to buy your return ticket as soon as you arrive, because buses can fill up. Buy tickets from the In Delphi taverna (signed ἐN ΔΕΛΦΟἰζ): From the stop, walk toward town past a storefront or two, staying on the right (uphill) side of the road. The restaurant doubles as the town's ersatz bus station; waiters sell bus tickets and can tell you today's schedule. For more on buses back to Athens, see "Delphi Connections," later.

Many Athens-based companies offer convenient one-day **package tours** to Delphi, which include transportation, a guided tour, and lunch. Ask at your Athens hotel for details.

By Car: For tips on getting to Delphi by car, see "Route Tips for Drivers" at the end of this chapter. Note that Delphi's town streets are one-way. When arriving from the east, you'll go right at the fork onto the uppermost of three streets, Apollonos. While it's possible to park at the site/museum, space is limited: Leave your car in town and walk (10 minutes). Park anywhere where the street doesn't have a double-yellow line.

HELPFUL HINTS

Unpredictable Hours: Don't count on the opening hours given here: They're likely to fluctuate. Check locally before planning your day.

Services: The main drag, Pavlou-Friderikis, has just about everything you might need, including a post office (at the east end), ATMs, and several cafés and shops.

Delphi: From Legend to History

Delphi's origins are lost in the mists of time and obscured by many different, sometimes conflicting, legends.

The ancients believed that Delphi was the center of the world. Its position was determined by Zeus himself, who released two eagles from the opposite ends of the world and noted where they met.

It was here that a prophetess (the sibyl) worshipped Gaia, the mother of the gods. A serpent (python) guarded the ravine of the Kastalian Spring. Apollo, the god of the sun and music, arrived in the guise of a dolphin (*delfini*, hence Delphi) and killed the snake. The sibyl's role was later taken on by an oracle priestess, the Pythia, and she and the place now served Apollo.

Historically speaking, the site was probably the home of a prophetess as early as Mycenaean times (1400 B.C.). The worship of Apollo grew, and the place gained fame for the oracle and for its religious festivals. Every four years, athletes and spectators gathered here to worship Apollo with music and athletic competitions: the Pythian Games, which soon rivaled the Olympics. The Sanctuary of Apollo reached the height of its prestige between the sixth and fourth centuries B.C., by which time Delphi so dominated Greek life that no leader would make a major decision without first sending emissaries here to consult the oracle. The sanctuary was deemed too important to be under the control of any one city-state, so its autonomy was guaranteed by a federation of Greek cities.

Even when Greece was conquered by the Macedonians (Alexander the Great) and Romans, the sanctuary was preserved and the conquerors continued to consult the oracle. For a thousand years, Apollo spoke to mortals through his prophetess, until A.D. 394, when Christians shut down the pagan site.

Local Guide: Penny Kolomvotsou is a great guide who can resurrect the ruins at Delphi and tailor a tour to your particular interests (reasonable prices, great with families, mobile 694-464-4427, kpagona@hotmail.com). Penny can also arrange activities in Delphi such as hiking and pottery classes.

Weather: Delphi is in the mountains and can be considerably cooler and rainier than Athens. Check the forecast (ask at your hotel) and dress accordingly, especially off-season.

Sights in Delphi

Delphi's most important sights are its archaeological site (with the Sanctuary of Apollo) and the adjacent Archaeological Museum. Nearby are other Sanctuary of Apollo sites (Kastalian Spring, the gymnasium, and the Sanctuary of Athena). The skippable Museum of Delphic Festivals is in Delphi town.

▲▲▲THE SANCTUARY OF APOLLO AND ARCHAEOLOGICAL MUSEUM

Ancient Delphi was not a city, but a sanctuary—a place of worship centered on the Temple of Apollo, where the oracle prophesied.

Surrounding the temple is what remains of grand monuments built by grateful pilgrims. And the Pythian Games produced what are perhaps the best-preserved theater and stadium in Greece.

Planning Your Time: Allow 1.5-2 hours for the archaeological site (hiking to the stadium alone is nearly a half-hour round-trip) and another 45-60 minutes for the museum. You can do the archaeological site and the museum in either order. Crowds and weather might help you decide. If it's hot or raining, do the museum first to hedge your bets for better conditions for the site. With all things being equal, I recommend doing the site first: You'll have more energy for the climb (there's a 700-foot elevation gain from the entrance to the stadium), and later, when you tour the museum, you can more easily imagine the original context of the items on display.

On your way to the site, stop at the museum to check the day's opening hours, posted on the wall just up the steps (before the ramp). If arriving later in the day, consider visiting one sight when you arrive and the other the next morning: Your combo-ticket is good over two days (but only one visit per sight).

To visit the other sights to the east of the Sanctuary of Apollo, allow another 30-45 minutes by foot (though you can view two of them, distantly, from in front of the site).

Cost: It's €12 to enter both the site and museum (€6 off-season, 18 and under free—be prepared to show ID).

Hours: Both the site and museum are open daily 8:00-20:00 in summer (generally April-Oct). In winter, both are open daily at least 9:00-15:00 (generally Nov-March). Upon arrival in Delphi, confirm opening times either with your hotel or by stopping by the museum.

Information: Tel. 22650-82312, www.culture.gr.

Closures: Parts of the site—especially the path to the stadium, above the theater—can be closed after heavy rains (to keep visitors safe from possible rock slides).

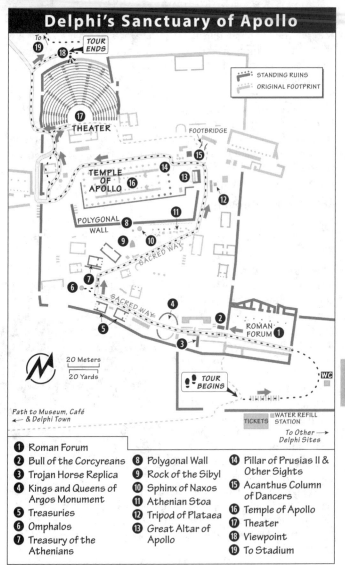

Delphi's Sanctuary of Apollo

- To 19
- TOUR ENDS
- 18

STANDING RUINS
ORIGINAL FOOTPRINT

- 17 THEATER
- FOOTBRIDGE
- 15
- TEMPLE OF APOLLO 16
- 14
- 13
- 12
- 11
- POLYGONAL WALL 8
- 9
- 10
- (SACRED WAY)
- 7
- SACRED WAY
- 6
- 4
- 2
- ROMAN FORUM 1
- 5
- 3

20 Meters
20 Yards

TOUR BEGINS

Path to Museum, Café
& Delphi Town

WC

TICKETS WATER REFILL STATION

To Other
Delphi Sites

DELPHI

- 1 Roman Forum
- 2 Bull of the Corcyreans
- 3 Trojan Horse Replica
- 4 Kings and Queens of Argos Monument
- 5 Treasuries
- 6 Omphalos
- 7 Treasury of the Athenians
- 8 Polygonal Wall
- 9 Rock of the Sibyl
- 10 Sphinx of Naxos
- 11 Athenian Stoa
- 12 Tripod of Plataea
- 13 Great Altar of Apollo
- 14 Pillar of Prusias II & Other Sights
- 15 Acanthus Column of Dancers
- 16 Temple of Apollo
- 17 Theater
- 18 Viewpoint
- 19 To Stadium

Getting There: The archaeological site and museum are about a half-mile east of the modern town of Delphi. Parking is limited, so it's best to leave your car in town and walk (10 minutes). You'll reach the museum first; to reach the site, continue along the path past the museum.

Services: A WC and a café (with slushie-style drinks and little else) are outside the museum. At the site itself, you'll find only a water refill station to the right of the ticket booth (you can bring a water bottle but no food inside the site). The sanctuary's WC is just above the entrance, up the first set of stairs, after you've scanned your ticket (inhaling the fumes there is not guaranteed to give you any prophetic visions).

The Sanctuary of Apollo

Looking up at the sheer rock face, you see the ruins clinging to a steep slope. From here you ascend a switchback trail that winds up, up, up: through the ruins to the Temple of Apollo, the theater, and the stadium, 700 feet up from the road. Every pilgrim who visited the oracle had to make this same steep climb.

◑ Self-Guided Tour

• *Start up the path, going to the right up a set of stairs (WCs at the top). After you double back on the switchback path, you enter a rectangular area with 10 gray columns, marking the…*

❶ Roman Forum

This small public space stood outside the sanctuary's main gate. The columns supported an arcade of shops (check out the illustration on the information plaque). Here pilgrims could pick up handy last-minute offerings—small statues of Apollo were popular—before proceeding to their date with the oracle. At festival times, crowds of pilgrims (all of them men) gathered here for parades up to the temple, theater, and stadium.

Gaze up at the hillside and picture the ruins as they were 2,000 years ago: gleaming white buildings with red roofs, golden statues atop columns, and the natural backdrop of these sheer gray-red rocks towering up 750 feet. It must have been an awe-inspiring sight for humble pilgrims, who'd traveled here to discover what fate the fickle gods had in store for them.

The men began their ascent to the oracle by walking through the original entrance gate, between 10-foot walls, entering the sanctuary on the street known as the Sacred Way.

• *A huge wall once enclosed the whole sanctuary, forming a rough rectangle, with the Temple of Apollo in the center. As you climb the five steps out of the forum, you're passing through a gate in the walls and beginning your walk along the…*

Sacred Way

The road is lined with ruins of once-glorious statues and monuments financed by satisfied pilgrims grateful for the oracle's advice. Immediately to the right is a pedestal of red-gray blocks, 17 feet long. This once held a huge bronze statue, the ❷ **Bull of the Corcyreans** (c. 580 B.C.), a gift from the inhabitants of Corfu to thank the oracle for directing them to a great catch of tuna fish.

A dozen or so steps farther along (left side) was an even bigger statue, a colossal bronze replica of the ❸ **Trojan Horse.**

Just beyond that (right side) is a semicircle 40 feet across, which was once lined with 10 statues of the legendary ❹ **Kings**

and Queens of Argos, including Perseus, Danae, and Hercules.

Next comes a row of so-called ❺ **Treasuries** (left side), small buildings that housed precious gifts to the gods. These buildings and their contents were paid for by city-states and kings to thank the oracle and the gods for giving them success (especially in war). From the outside they looked like mini temples, with columns, pediments, statues, and friezes. Inside they held gold, jewels, bronze dinnerware, ivory statues, necklaces, and so on. The friezes and relief sculptures that once adorned the Sikyonian and Siphnian Treasuries are now in the museum.

• *At the corner where the path turns to go uphill is a cone-shaped stone called an...*

DELPHI

❻ **Omphalos**

The ancients believed that Delphi was the center of the world and marked that spot with a strange cone-shaped monument called an

omphalos (navel). The omphalos was also a symbolic tombstone for the python that Apollo slew.

Several omphalos stones were erected at different places around the sanctuary. The original was kept inside the Temple of Apollo. A copy graced the temple's entrance (it's now in the museum). Another copy stood here along the Sacred Way, where this modern replica is today.

As the center of the world, Delphi was also the starting point for history. From here the oracle could predict the course of human destiny.

• *Rounding the bend up the stairs, on the left you'll face the...*

❼ Treasury of the Athenians

The Athenians built this temple to commemorate their victory over the Persians (ancient Iranians) at the Battle of Marathon in

490 B.C. The tiny inscriptions on the blocks honor Athenian citizens with praise and laurel-leaf wreaths, the symbol of victory at Delphi's Pythian Games. When the ruins were rebuilt (1904-1906), the restorers determined which block went where by matching up pieces of the inscriptions.

The structure's ceremonial entrance (east end) has two Doric columns of expensive marble from Paros. They support six metopes (reconstructed; the originals are in the museum) that feature the Greeks battling the legendary Amazon women—symbolizing the Greek victory over the barbaric Persians at Marathon.

• *Follow the path as it continues uphill. By now you have a great view to the left of the...*

❽ Polygonal Wall and Other Ancient Features

The retaining wall (sixth century B.C.) supports the terrace with the Temple of Apollo. It runs across the hillside for some 250 feet at heights of up to 12 feet. It has survived in almost perfect condition because of the way that the stones were fitted together (without mortar). This created a "living" wall, able to absorb the many

earthquakes for which the region is renowned (earthquakes caused the other buildings here to crumble).

Near the wall, just above the Treasury of the Athenians, the 10-foot ❾ **Rock of the Sibyl** hearkens back to the murky prehistoric origins of this place as a sacred site. According to legend, the oracle's predecessor—called the sibyl—sat atop this rock to deliver her prophecies, back when the area was sacred to Gaia, the mother of the gods.

Just behind that rock, near the stubby white column (walk up the path to get a better view), is a pile of rocks with a black slab pedestal. This was once a 35-foot-tall pillar holding the statue of the ❿ **Sphinx of Naxos** (c. 570-560 B.C., now in the museum). Inhabitants of the isle of Naxos used their best marble for this gift to the oracle, guaranteeing them access to her advice even during busy times.

A few more steps up, the three white fluted Ionic columns along the wall belonged to the ⓫ **Athenian Stoa,** a 100-foot-long

open-air porch. Here the Athenians displayed captured shields, ships' prows, and booty from their naval victory over Persia at the decisive Battle of Salamis (480 B.C.). It was the oracle of Delphi who gave Athens the key to victory. As the Persian army swarmed over Greece, the oracle prophesied that the city of Athens would be saved by a "wooden wall." The puzzled Athenians eventually interpreted the oracle's riddle as meaning not a city wall, but a fleet of wooden ships. They abandoned Athens to the Persian invaders, then routed them at sea. Once the enemy was driven out, Greece's cities ceremonially relit their sacred flames from the hearth of Delphi's temple.

• *Continue up the Sacred Way and follow it as it turns left, up the hill. As you ascend, along the right-hand side you'll pass a square gray-block pedestal that once supported a big column. This monument, the ⓬ Tripod of Plataea, was built to thank the oracle for victory in the Battle of Plataea (479 B.C., fought near Thebes), which finally drove the Persians out of Greece. The monument's 26-foot bronze column of three intertwined snakes was carried off by the Romans to their chariot-racing track in Constantinople (now Istanbul), where tourists snap photos of what's left of it.*

At the top of the path, turn left and face the six Doric columns and ramp that mark the entrance to the Temple of Apollo. In the courtyard in front of the temple are several noteworthy ruins.

The Temple Courtyard

Take in the temple and imagine the scene 2,000 years ago as pilgrims gathered here at the culmination of their long journey. They'd come seeking guidance from the gods at a crucial juncture in their lives. Here in the courtyard they prepared themselves before entering the temple to face the awe-inspiring oracle.

Opposite the temple entrance, pilgrims and temple priests offered sacrifices at the (partially restored) gray stone ⓭ **Great Altar of Apollo.** Worshippers would enter the rectangular enclosure, originally made of black marble with white trim. Inside they'd

DELPHI

sacrifice an animal to Apollo—goats were especially popular. One hundred bulls (a hecatomb) were sacrificed to open every Pythian Games.

To the right of the temple (as you face it) once stood several monuments that dazzled visitors. Imagine a 50-foot **Statue of Apollo Sitalkas** towering over the courtyard, where only a humble rectangular base remains today. Next to it (on the left) is the still-impressive 20-foot-tall rectangular ❶ **Pillar of Prusias II.** Atop this was a statue of a second-century king on horseback who traveled here from Turkey to consult the oracle. To the right of the pillar are **three round column stubs** that once held ceremonial tripods. Behind them rose the tall ❶ **Acanthus Column of Dancers,** three young women supporting a tripod (now in the museum).

• *But these sights paled in comparison to the...*

❶ Temple of Apollo

This structure—which in its day must have towered over the rest of the site—was the centerpiece of the whole sanctuary. It was dedicated to the god who ruled the hillside, and it housed the oracle who spoke in his name. This was the third and largest temple built on this site (completed 330 B.C.), replacing earlier versions destroyed by earthquake and fire. It was largely funded by Philip of Macedon and dedicated in the time of Alexander the Great.

The temple was gleaming white, ringed with columns, with a triangular pediment over the entrance and a roof studded with statues. Above the entrance, the pediment statues showed Apollo arriving in Delphi in a four-horse chariot (now in the museum). The six huge Doric columns that stand near the entrance today (reassembled in 1904) were complemented by 15 columns along each side. (Sections from a toppled column lie on the hillside below the temple's left side, near the Polygonal Wall, giving an idea of the temple's scale; to see this, backtrack down the hill.) Though the temple appeared all white, it was actually constructed with a darker local limestone. The columns were coated with a stucco of powdered marble to achieve the

The Oracle

The oracle was a priestess of Apollo who acted as a seer by "channeling" the god's spirit. Always female, she was usually an older empty-nester with a good reputation, but we don't know any of Delphi's oracles by name. These women were not the focus—rather, they were vessels for the words of Apollo as interpreted by priests.

Early on, there was one oracle, who prophesied only on auspicious days. At Delphi's peak, two or three oracles worked shifts every day. The oracle purified herself in the Kastalian Spring, dressed in white, and carried a laurel branch—a symbol of Apollo. Why the oracle sat on a tripod—a ritual cauldron on three legs—no one knows for sure.

The oracle presumably prophesied in a kind of trance, letting the spirit of Apollo possess her body and speaking as if she were the god himself. Many think she was high on vapors that rose from the natural chasm in the inner sanctum floor. Science has found no evidence of the supposed chasm, though ravines and springs nearby do emit psychotropic gases. The trance might also have been caused by the oracle eating or inhaling burned laurel leaves. Regardless of the source, the oracle's ultimate message was tightly controlled by the priests.

The oracle addressed all kinds of questions. Travelers came to Delphi before journeys. Rulers came to plan wars. Explorers wanted advice for getting newfound colonies off to a good start. Philosophers asked the oracle to weigh in on ethical dilemmas. Priests sought approval of new rituals and cults. Ordinary people came because their marriages were rocky or simply to have their fortunes told.

Apollo was considered a god of peace, order, and personal virtue. As the priestess of Apollo, the oracle could address moral questions and religious affairs. And because Delphi was considered the center of the world, the words of the oracle were the source of fate and the fortunes of men.

Many famous people made the pilgrimage. A young Socrates was so inspired by the phrase "Know Thyself" (inscribed on the Temple of Apollo) that he pursued the path of self-knowledge. The oracle was visited by foreign kings such as Midas (of the golden touch) and the ancient billionaire Croesus (of "rich-as" fame). The historian Plutarch served here as a priest, interpreting the oracle's utterances. Roman Emperor Nero visited, participated in the Pythian Games, and was warned about his impending assassination. Alexander the Great asked the oracle whether he'd be successful in conquering the world. When the oracle hesitated, Alexander grabbed her by the hair and wouldn't let go. The helpless oracle cried, "You're unstoppable." Alexander said, "I have my answer."

white color. Only the pediments and other decorations were made from costly white marble shipped in from the isle of Paros.

Imagine yourself an ancient pilgrim finally preparing to meet the oracle after the long trek to the center of the world. You've just bathed with the priests at the Kastalian Spring in the ravine east of the sanctuary. You've paraded ceremonially to the temple, up the same Sacred Way tourists walk today. At the Great Altar, you just offered a sacrifice, likely of goat (a loaf of bread was the minimum cover charge). At last, you're about to enter the temple with the priests, climbing the ramp and passing through the columns to learn your fate. Inscribed at the entrance are popular proverbs, including "Know Thyself," "Nothing in Excess," and "Stuff Happens."

Inside, the temple is cloudy with the incense of burning laurel leaves. You see the large golden statue of Apollo and the original omphalos stone, a reminder that you've arrived at the center of the world. After offering a second sacrifice on the hearth of the eternal flame, it's time to meet the oracle.

The priests lead you into the *adyton*—the farthest back, holiest chamber of the *cella*. There, amid the incense, is the oracle—an older woman, dressed in white, seated in the bowl of a tripod, perhaps with an unsettling gleam in her eye. The tripod may be balanced over a hole in the floor of the temple, exposing a natural ravine where a spring bubbles up. While you wait, the priests present your question to the oracle. She answers—perhaps crying out, perhaps muttering gibberish and foaming at the mouth. The priests step in to interpret the oracle's meaning, rendering it in a vague, haiku-like poem.

Then you're ushered out of the temple, either enlightened or confused by the riddle. For many pilgrims—like Socrates, who spent much of his life pondering the oracle's words—a visit to Delphi was only the beginning of their life's journey.

• *Uphill, to the right of the Temple of Apollo, stands Delphi's stone theater. Climb up—I'll meet you there.*

⓱ Theater

One of Greece's best-preserved theaters (fourth century B.C.) was built to host song contests honoring Apollo, the god of music. With 35 rows of white stone quarried from Mt. Parnassos, it could seat 5,000. The action took place on the semicircular area (60 feet across, surrounded by a drainage ditch)

known as the orchestra. As at most ancient theaters, it would have been closed off along the street by a large structure that created a backdrop for the stage and served as the theater's grand entryway. The famous *Bronze Charioteer* statue (now in the museum) likely stood outside the theater's entrance, in the middle of the road, greeting playgoers. The theater was designed so that most spectators could look over the backdrop, taking in stunning views of the valley below even as they watched the onstage action.

The theater's original and main purpose was to host not plays, but song contests—a kind of "Panhellenic Idol" competition that was part of the Pythian Games. Every four years, singer-songwriters from all over the Greek-speaking world gathered here to perform hymns in honor of Apollo, the god of music. They sang accompanied by flute or by lyre—a strummed autoharp, which was Apollo's chosen instrument.

Over time, the song competition expanded into athletic contests (held at the stadium), as well as other events in dance and drama. The opening and closing ceremonies of the Pythian Games were held here. One of the games' central features was a play that re-enacted the dramatic moment when Apollo slew the python and founded Delphi...not unlike the bombastic pageantry that opens and closes today's Olympic Games.

• *A steep path continues uphill to a stunning...*

⑱ View from Above the Theater

With craggy cliffs at your back, the sanctuary beneath you, and a panoramic view of the valley in the distance, it's easy to see why the ancients found this place sacred.

We're 1,800 feet above sea level on the slopes of Mt. Parnassos (8,062 feet). The area's jagged rocks and sheer cliffs are made of gray limestone, laced with red-orange bauxite, which is mined nearby. The cliffs have striations of sedimentary rocks that have been folded upward at all angles by seismic activity. The region is crisscrossed with faults (one runs right under the temple), pocked with sinkholes, and carved with ravines.

Two large sections of rock that jut out from the cliff (to the left) are known as the Phaedriades Rocks, or "Shining Ones," because of how they reflect sunlight. At the foot of one of the rocks lies the sanctuary. Between the two rocks (east of the sanctuary) is the gaping ravine of the Kastalian Spring.

Looking down on the entire sanctuary, you can make out its

> ## Delphi's Decline and Rediscovery
>
> After reaching a peak during the Classical Age, the oracle's importance slowly declined. In Hellenistic times, traditional religions like Apollo-worship were eclipsed by secular philosophy and foreign gods. By the third century B.C., the oracle was handling more lonely-hearts advice than affairs of state. The Romans alternated between preserving Delphi (as Hadrian did) and looting its treasuries and statues. Nero famously stole 500 statues for his home in Rome (A.D. 66), and Constantine used Delphi's monument to decorate his new capital. As Rome crumbled, barbarians did their damage. Finally, in A.D. 394, the Christian Emperor Theodosius I closed down the sanctuary, together with all the other great pagan worship centers.
>
> The site was covered by landslides and by the village of Kastri until 1892, when the villagers were relocated to the modern village of Delphi, about a half-mile to the west. Excavation began, the site was opened to tourists, and its remaining treasures were eventually put on display in the museum.

shape—a rough rectangle (640 feet by 442 feet—about twice as big as a football field) enclosed by a wall, stretching from the top of the theater down to the Roman Forum. Trace the temple's floor plan: You'd enter where the columns are, pass through the lobby *(pronaos)*, into the main hall *(cella)*, and continue into the back portion *(adyton)*, where the oracle sat (they say) above a natural chasm.

In the distance, looking south, is the valley of the Pleistos River, green with olive trees. Beyond that (though not visible from this spot) are the turquoise waters of the Gulf of Corinth.

• *If you're winded, you can make your way back down now. But you've come so far already—why not keep going? Hike another 10 minutes up the steep, winding path to the...*

⓳ Stadium

Every four years, athletes and spectators from across Greece gathered here to watch the same kinds of sports as at the ancient Olympics. The Pythian Games (founded at least by 582 B.C.) were second only to the (older, bigger) Olympic Games in prestige. They were one of four Panhellenic Games on the athletics calendar (Olympia, Corinth, Nemea, and Delphi).

The exceptionally well-preserved stadium was built in the fifth century B.C. (Though you aren't allowed to walk through its cen-

ter, you can still get a good look down into it from the far end.) It was remodeled in the second century A.D. by the wealthy Herodes Atticus, who also built a theater in Athens and a fountain in Olympia (the Nymphaeum). There was stone seating for nearly 7,000, which was cushier than Olympia's grassy-bank stadium. Among the seats on the north side, you can still make out the midfield row of judges' seats. The track—580 feet long by 84 feet wide—is slightly shorter than the one at Olympia. The main entrance was at the east end; the thick pillars once supported a three-arched entry. The starting lines (one at either end, depending on the length of the race) are still here, and you might be able to make out the postholes for the wooden starting blocks.

The Pythian Games lasted about a week and were held in the middle of a three-month truce among warring Greeks that allowed people to train and travel safely. Winners were awarded a wreath of laurel leaves (as opposed to the olive leaves at the Olympic Games) because Apollo always wore a laurel-leaf wreath. For more on the types of events held here during the games, see the Olympia chapter.

• *Wind your way back down to the exit. The museum is located 200 yards west of the Sanctuary of Apollo. Before heading in that direction, you might consider venturing a little farther out of town to reach the Kastalian Spring, gymnasium, and/or Sanctuary of Athena (all described later, under "Other Delphi Sights").*

DELPHI

Archaeological Museum

Delphi's compact-but-impressive museum houses a collection of ancient sculpture matched only by the National Archaeological and Acropolis museums in Athens.

❂ Self-Guided Tour

Follow the one-way route, looking for the following highlights. Everything is well described in English.

• *Scan your ticket and head right into the...*

❶ First Room: This room holds the earliest traces of civilization at Delphi. Near the entry, find the picture depicting French architect Albert Tournaire's romantic rendering of how the Sanctuary of Apollo would have looked at its ancient peak. Also in this room is a giant

bronze cauldron, which was once adorned with grotesque griffin heads.

• *Proceed into the next room, then turn right to find the...*

❷ **Sphinx of Naxos** (c. 570-560 B.C.): This marble beast—a winged lion with a female face and an Archaic smile—was once brightly painted, standing atop a 40-foot Ionic column in the sanctuary. The myth of the sphinx is Egyptian in origin, but she made a splash in Greek lore when she posed a famous riddle to Oedipus at the gates of Thebes: "What walks on four legs in the morning, two at noon, and three at night?" Oedipus solved it: It's a man—who crawls in infancy, walks in adulthood, and uses a cane in old age.

• *Across the room, find the...*

❸ **Frieze from the Siphnian Treasury:** This shows how elaborate the now-ruined treasuries in the sanctuary must have been. The east frieze (left wall) shows Greeks and Trojans duking it out. The gods to the left of the battle are rooting for the Trojans, with the Greek gods to the right. The north frieze (back wall) features scenes from the epic battle between the Greek gods and older race of giants.

• *Backtrack into the previous room, then turn right. You're face-to-face with...*

❹ **Twin Kouros Statues** (c. 600-580 B.C.): These statues have the typical features of the Archaic period: placid smiles, stable

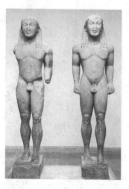

poses facing the front, braided dreadlocks, and geometrical anatomy. These sturdy seven-foot-tall athletes are the legendary twins of Argos, who yoked themselves to their mother's chariot and pulled her five miles so she wouldn't be late for the female Games (the Heraia). Upon arrival, the exhausted twins fell into a sleep so deep they never woke up.

• *In the small room behind the twins (to the right) is what's left of a...*

❺ **Silver Bull:** These silver-and-gold plates are the surviving fragments that once covered a life-size bull statue from the sixth century B.C. This bull and the other objects in the room were buried in ancient times (perhaps for safekeeping) and were discovered in the 20th

Delphi's Archaeological Museum

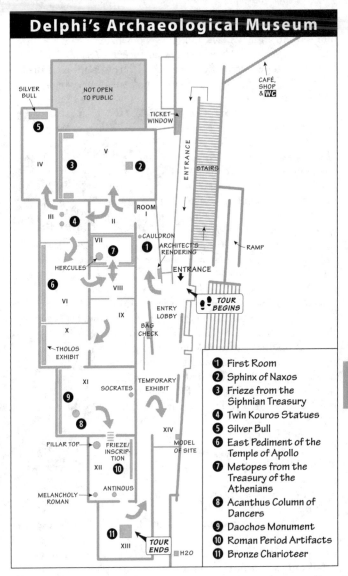

SILVER
BULL

NOT OPEN
TO PUBLIC

CAFÉ,
SHOP
& WC

TICKET
WINDOW

5

ENTRANCE

STAIRS

V

IV **3** **2**

ROOM
I

III
4 II

CAULDRON

1 ARCHITECT'S
RENDERING

RAMP

VII
7

HERCULES

6 VIII

VI

IX

ENTRY
LOBBY

BAG
CHECK

X

TOUR
BEGINS

ENTRANCE

THOLOS
EXHIBIT

XI

SOCRATES

TEMPORARY
EXHIBIT

9

8

PILLAR TOP

FRIEZE/
INSCRIP-
TION

XIV

MODEL
OF SITE

XII **10**

ANTINOUS

MELANCHOLY
ROMAN

11

XIII

TOUR
ENDS

H2O

DELPHI

1 First Room
2 Sphinx of Naxos
3 Frieze from the
Siphnian Treasury
4 Twin Kouros Statues
5 Silver Bull
6 East Pediment of the
Temple of Apollo
7 Metopes from the
Treasury of the
Athenians
8 Acanthus Column of
Dancers
9 Daochos Monument
10 Roman Period Artifacts
11 Bronze Charioteer

century in a pit along the Sacred Way, near the Treasury of the Athenians.

• *In the room after the twins, find the...*

6 **East Pediment of the Temple of Apollo:** This is what greeted visitors as they stood before the temple entrance. Though it's mostly fragments today, in the center you can make out some of the four horses that pulled Apollo in his chariot. To the right, a lion jumps on an animal's back and takes it down.

• *Continue left into the next room, then turn left to find the...*

❼ **Metopes from the Treasury of the Athenians (510-480 B.C.):** These carvings from the sanctuary's small surviving treasury include (among other themes)

six of the Twelve Labors of Hercules. In the most intact carving (directly to the left as you enter), **Hercules** is the one with curly hair and beard, inscrutable Archaic smile, and lion skin tied preppy-style around his neck.

• *Proceed through the next three rooms (the third of which has an exhibit with some pieces from the round* tholos *monument, at the Sanctuary of Athena). You'll wind up in a room with two monuments from the era of Alexander the Great, which once stood side by side in the sanctuary.*

❽ **Acanthus Column of Dancers:** This giant leafy sculpture sat atop a 40-foot column to the right of the Temple of Apollo (on

the same level as the theater). The three dancing girls originally carried a bronze tripod on their shoulders. Scholars now believe that this tripod supported the **omphalos**—the gigantic pinecone-shaped stone, which represented the "navel" of the world. The omphalos, now resting next to the column, is not the original stone marking the center of the earth, but a Roman-era copy. Nearby is the bottom of the column, which appears to be sprouting out of the ground.

• *Then, as now, next to the column stand statues from the...*

❾ **Daochos Monument** (c. 336-332 B.C.): Out of the nine original statues (count the footprints), today seven survive (OK, six—one is just a sandal). They have the relaxed poses and realistic detail of Hellenism. Daochos (center, wearing a heavy cloak) was a high-ranking army commander under Alexander the Great. His family flanks him, including two of the three sons who were famous athletes, all of whom won laurel crowns at the same Pythian Games. Nude Agelaos (also in the center, armless, with sinuous *contrapposto*) won running contests in Delphi. Aghias (to the right, with two partial arms and genitals) swept all four Panhellenic Games in *pankration*, a brutal sport that combined wrestling and boxing with few holds barred.

• *Across the room and facing these gents, notice the sculpture of bearded, balding Socrates, who was inspired by the mystery of this place. Up the stairs, the next room features artifacts from the...*

❿ Roman Period (191 B.C.-A.D. 394): The Romans made Delphi their own in 191 B.C. and left their mark. On the left you'll see the **frieze** that decorated the proscenium of the theater and (high on the wall) an inscription from the proud Emperor Domitian, crowing that he had repaired the Temple of Apollo.

Across the room is the rectangular **top of a pillar,** erected by the arrogant King Perseus in anticipation of a military victory. Instead, the king was soundly defeated by Aemilius Paulus, who topped the pedestal with his own equestrian victory statue (pictured nearby) and adorned it with this frieze of scenes depicting Perseus' defeat. This sculpture is particularly exciting for historians, as it's the oldest relief work (in Western history, at least) narrating an actual event. For centuries after this, battles would be recounted in similar 3-D carvings (think of Trajan's Column in Rome or Nelson's Column in London).

Also worth noting here is the **circular altar** decorated with a graceful relief sculpture showing young women gussying up the sanctuary for a festival performance.

At the end of the room are two noteworthy sculptures. The small, lightly bearded head dubbed the **"Melancholy Roman"** (likely Titus Quinctius Flamininus, who proclaimed autonomy for the Greek state in 197 B.C.) demonstrates a masterful sense of emotion. Standing next to him is a full-size nude statue (minus its forearms) of Emperor Hadrian's young lover, **Antinous.** The handsome curly-haired youth from Asia Minor

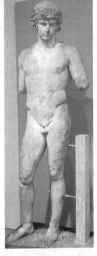

(today's Turkey) drowned in the Nile in 130 B.C. A heartbroken Hadrian declared Antinous a god and erected statues of him everywhere, making him one of the most recognizable people from the ancient world. Notice the small holes around his head, which were used to affix a bronze laurel wreath. Next to the sculpture, find the photo of excited archaeologists unearthing this strikingly intact specimen.

• *The grand finale is the museum's star exhibit, the...*

DELPHI

❶ **Bronze Charioteer:** This young charioteer has just finished his victory lap, having won the Pythian Games of 474 B.C. Standing ramrod straight, he holds the reins lightly in his right hand, while his (missing) left hand was raised, modestly acknowledging the crowd.

This surviving statue was part of an original 3-D ensemble that greeted playgoers at the entrance to the theater. His (missing) chariot was (probably) pulled by four (mostly missing) horses, tended by a (missing) stable boy. Nearby, a case displays scant surviving chunks of the cart, the horse, and the stable boy's arm.

The statue is life-size (5'11") and lifelike. His fluted robe has straps around the waist and shoulders to keep it from ballooning out in the wind. He has a round-

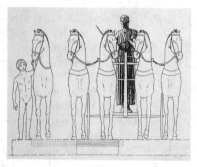

ed face, full lips, awestruck eyes (of inset stones and enamel), and curly hair tied with the victor's headband.

The most striking thing is that—having just won an intense and dangerous contest—his face and attitude are calm and humble. The statue was cast when Greece was emerging from the horrors of the Persian invasion.

The victorious charioteer expresses the sense of wonderment felt as Greece finally left the battle behind, gazed into the future, and rode triumphantly into the Golden Age.

As you exit the museum, examine the small model (in the lobby) of the sanctuary as it appeared in ancient times.

OTHER DELPHI SIGHTS

The related Sanctuary sites, especially the Temple of Athena Pronea, are worth a visit. There are also a number of hikes from Delphi—ask your hotelier for ideas.

Sanctuary of Apollo Sites

These three sites, located along the main road beyond (to the east of) the site, are associated with the Sanctuary of Apollo and free to view. I've listed them in order, from nearest to farthest (you can walk to any of them, or you can simply view the gymnasium and the Sanctuary of Athena from the road in front of the site and museum).

Kastalian Spring: On the left side of the road, 800 yards past the archaeological site (around the jutting cliff), a spring bubbles forth from the ravine between the two Phaedriades Rocks. It was here that Apollo slew the python, taking over the area from the mother of the gods. Pilgrims washed here before consulting the oracle, and the water was used to ritually purify the oracle, the priests, and the Temple of Apollo. Inside are two ruined fountains (made of stone, with courtyards and benches to accommodate pilgrims) that tapped the ancient sacred spring, but because of rock slides, the ravine is closed to visitors (you can still see and hear the gurgling spring water).

Gymnasium: On the right side of the road, look for running tracks and a circular pool, where athletes trained for the Pythian Games.

Sanctuary of Athena Pronea: Farther along (also on the right side of the road) is a cluster of ruined temples. Because of the ar-

ea's long association with Gaia, Athena was worshipped at Delphi along with Apollo. The star attraction is the *tholos* (c. 380 B.C.), a round structure whose exact purpose is unknown. Although presumably less important than the Sanctuary of Apollo, its three reconstructed columns (of 20 Doric originals that once held up a conical roof) have become the most-photographed spot in all of Delphi.

Museum of Delphic Festivals
Perched high on the hill above town, this old mansion explains the quest of beloved poet and resident Angelos Sikelianos to create a new "Delphic Festivals" tradition in the 1920s. There's not much to see, aside from photos, costumes, and props of the event—which was held twice (in 1927 and 1930)—and some artifacts from Sikelianos' life. It's only worthwhile as an excuse for a strenuous hike (or quick drive) above town to grand vistas.

Cost and Hours: €1, open hours vary—ask your hotelier to call ahead, tel. 22650-82175.

Sleeping in Delphi

Spending the night in Delphi is a pleasant (and much cheaper) alternative to busy Athens. The town is squeezed full of hotels, which makes competition fierce and rates very soft—hoteliers don't need much of an excuse to offer a discount in slow times.

$$ Hotel Leto is a class act, with 22 smartly renovated rooms right in the heart of town (RS%, elevator, Apollonos 15, tel. 22650-82302, www.leto-delphi.gr, info@leto-delphi.gr, Petros.

$$ Hotel Acropole is a big but welcoming group-oriented

DELPHI

hotel along the lower road. It's quieter and has better vistas than my other listings. Most of the 42 rooms feature view terraces for no extra charge; try to request one when you reserve (RS%, family suite with fireplace, elevator, 13 Filellinon, tel. 22650-82675, www.delphi.com.gr, delphi@delphi.com.gr, say hi to Effie).

$$ Pitho Rooms has eight good rooms above a gift shop on the main street. Your conscientious hosts, George and Vicky, pride themselves on offering a good value; they'll make you feel like part of the family (RS%, no elevator, Pavlou-Friderikis 40A, tel. 22650-82850, www.pithohotel.gr, pitho_rooms@yahoo.gr).

$ Hermes Hotel explodes with polished wood, cut glass, artwork, and sculptures in its public areas. Upstairs, its 36 rooms have spare but stately furniture; nearly all face the valley and have balconies (elevator, Pavlou-Friderikis 37, tel. 22650-82318, www. hermeshotel.com.gr, info@hermeshotel.com.gr).

$ Tholos Hotel has 19 quasi-Scandinavian rooms on the upper street, some with view balconies (breakfast extra, no elevator, Apollonos 31, tel. 22650-82268, www.tholoshotel.com, hotel_tholos@yahoo.gr).

$ Sibylla Hotel rents eight simple rooms at youth-hostel prices without a hint of youth-hostel grunge. No elevator, no air-conditioning...just good value. All have balconies: four with valley views, four over the street (no breakfast, ceiling fans, Pavlou-Friderikis 9, tel. 22650-82335, www.sibylla-hotel.gr, info@sibylla-hotel.gr, Christopoulos family).

Eating in Delphi

Delphi's eateries tend to cater to tour groups, with vast dining rooms and long tables stretching to distant valley-and-gulf views. The following restaurants distinguish themselves by offering high quality and good value. Look for the regional specialty, fried *formaela* cheese (spritz it with fresh lemon juice, then dig in). All of my listings are open daily for both lunch and dinner (around 12:00 until 22:30 or 23:00). Some places close for a midafternoon siesta (roughly 16:00-18:30).

$$$ Taverna Vakchos is homey and woody, with down-home, family-run charm. The focus is on tasty traditional dishes, such as *kokoras kokkinisto* (rooster cooked in red wine) and baked lamb with lemon sauce. For dessert, try the locally produced farm-fresh yogurt with honey or ask what topping is in season (Apollonos 31, tel. 22650-83186).

$$$$ To Patriko Mas ("Our Family's Home") is more upscale, with a classy stone-and-wood interior and a striking outdoor terrace clinging to the cliff face (reservations suggested for view table, Pavlou-Friderikis 69, tel. 22650-82150, Konsta family).

$$ **Taverna Dion** serves standard Greek fare at reasonable prices and specializes in grilled meats. Their good-value fixed-price meals include three plates plus dessert (Apollonos 30, tel. 22650-82790).

$$ **Taverna Gargadouas** is proud *not* to cater to tour groups (it's too small). This simple taverna has a blaring TV in the corner and locals mixed in with the tourists, all here for affordable, unpretentious, traditional cuisine (on main drag at end of town farthest from sanctuary, tel. 22650-82488).

Picnics: Grocery stores and bakeries are well-marked along the main street. And though picnics are not allowed inside the archaeological site, you could choose a perch along the road overlooking the vast valley.

Delphi Connections

BY BUS

Delphi's one disadvantage, from a traveler's perspective, is its distance from the other attractions described in this book. Delphi is well-connected by bus to **Athens** (4-5/day—check times locally, 3-hour trip, €17 one-way). Connecting to the **Peloponnese** is long and complicated. For the eastern Peloponnese (such as **Nafplio**), it's best to go via Athens (see the Athens Connections chapter). To the western Peloponnese, you'll connect through **Patra** (one bus per day from Delphi, departs around 13:10; a second bus may leave Sun evening around 17:00; 3 hours, €15 one-way). From Patra you can continue on to **Olympia** (via Pyrgos) or **Kardamyli** (via Kalamata). Either is a very long trip, and the Delphi-Kardamyli trip can't be done in one day.

For bus information, go to www.ktel-fokidas.gr (online tickets available).

ROUTE TIPS FOR DRIVERS

From Athens to Delphi: Head north (toward *Lamia/Λαμία*) on national road 1/expressway E-75 (one toll booth). Take the second exit for ΘΕΒΑ/*Theba/Thiva*, which is also marked for *Livadia/Λιβαδειά* (another tollbooth). From the turnoff, signs lead you (on road 3, then road 48) all the way to *Delphi/Δελφοί*. As you get farther up into the mountains, keep an eye out for ski resorts—Athenians come here to ski from December to March.

From Delphi to the Peloponnese: As with the bus, for sights in the eastern Peloponnese (such as **Nafplio** or **Monemvasia**), it's faster to backtrack through Athens. (See the Athens Connections chapter for more driving tips.)

To reach the western Peloponnese (such as **Olympia** or **Kardamyli/Mani Peninsula**), first follow the twisting road from

Delphi down toward Itea (Ιτέα) on the Gulf of Corinth, then follow signs toward *Galaxidi/Γαλαξίδι* (a charming port city worth a quick stop). Trace the gulf on a magnificently scenic, two-hour westward drive along road E-65 (toward *Nafpaktos/Ναύπακτος*). Take your time and use the pullouts to enjoy the views. In Antirrio, follow signs for *Patra/Πάτρα* across the Rio-Antirrio suspension bridge (toll) to the town of Rio. You'll enter the Peloponnese just north of the big port city of Patra (Πάτρα, described at the end of the Olympia chapter); skirt this city and head south another 1.5 hours along road E-55 toward *Pyrgos/Πύργος*—be sure to get on the faster highway, with a green sign, instead of the slower regional road. (Note that attempting to "shortcut" through the middle of the Peloponnese takes you on some very twisty, slow, and poorly signed mountain roads—avoid them unless you value scenery more than time.)

Once at Pyrgos, you can head east/inland to Ancient Olympia (Αρχαία Ολυμπία, well-marked with brown signs); or continue south to Kyparissia and Pylos, then eastward to Kalamata/ Καλαμάτα (about two hours beyond Pyrgos; note that the Kalamata turnoff, just before Kyparissia, is not well-marked). From Kalamata, continue south another hour to Kardamyli.

GREEK ISLANDS

For many people, Greece is synonymous with islands. If you need a vacation from your busy mainland Greek vacation, the islands exert an irresistible pull.

Explore a tight, twisty maze of whitewashed cubic houses with vibrant trim. Dig your toes into the hot sand while basking

under a beach umbrella. Go for a dip in the crystal-clear, bath-water-warm Aegean. Sip an iced coffee along a bustling harbor-front, watching fishermen clean their catch while cuddly kittens greedily beg below. Indulge in fresh seafood at a rustic seaside taverna, and chat with the big personality whose family has owned the place for generations, all while watching the sun gradually descend into the sea. The Greek islands really do live up to their worldwide acclaim.

While I appreciate a healthy dose of restorative island time, I prefer to spend the bulk of my Greek vacation visiting the country's amazing wealth of ancient sites. That's why I've focused this book on the bustling capital of Athens and Greece's "heartland," the Peloponnese, where—compared to the islands—prices are much lower, tourism is less suffocating, and travelers have more exciting opportunities to peel back layers of history. Still, a visit to Greece isn't complete without at least one island stay. This book covers three island destinations: Hydra, Mykonos, and Santorini.

GREECE'S ISLAND GROUPS

Greece's roughly 3,000 islands and islets (227 of which are inhabited) are scattered far and wide across the eastern Mediterranean. Most are in the Aegean Sea (south and east of mainland Greece), while a few are in the Ionian Sea (west of the mainland). The islands are divided into clusters:

The **Ionian Islands,** closer to Albania and Italy than to Athens, are Greece's northwest gateway to the Adriatic and the rest of Europe—they've had more foreign invaders and rulers (from Venice, France, Britain, Russia, Austria, and so on) than  anywhere else in the country. The main island is Corfu (Kerkyra in Greek), with a bustling, architecturally eclectic main town and a lush, green islandscape dotted with attractions and beaches.

The **Saronic Gulf Islands** (Argosaronikos), conveniently wedged between the Peloponnese and Athens, ooze lots of island charm and give you a chance to get away from it all without actually going very far. **Hydra,** my favorite, is in this group.

The **Sporades Islands,** due east of Athens, are dominated

by the giant Evia island, which is attached to the mainland by a bridge. Thickly forested and less touristed by international visitors, the Sporades are a popular and handy weekend getaway for Athenians.

The **Cycladic Islands** (or simply Cyclades)—a bit farther south, between Athens and Crete—are the prototypical "Greek islands," boasting chalk-white houses with colorful windowsills and doorways; rocky, sun-parched landscapes; delightful beaches; old-fashioned white windmills topped with tufts of grass like unkempt hair; and an almost overwhelming crush of international visitors. **Mykonos** and **Santorini** are the two best and most famous of the

Cyclades. Near Mykonos is the archaeological site of **Delos** (one of the most important locales of the ancient world).

The **Dodecanese Islands,** at the sunny, southeastern end of the Greek lands, are more rustic and less developed than the Cyclades. Their proximity to Turkey and historic ties to Venice give them a hybrid Turkish-Venetian flavor (though the population is mostly ethnic Greek, these islands merged with Greece only after World War II). Rhodes, with an appealing and very real-feeling old town, is the biggest of these islands.

The **North Aegean Islands,** relatively untrampled and remote-feeling, lie roughly between Turkey and Thessaloniki (at the northern end of mainland Greece). The southernmost of these, Samos, is a particularly handy springboard for Turkey, as it's very close to the Turkish port city of Kuşadası (near the remarkable ancient site of Ephesus).

Crete is Greece's biggest island and practically a ministate of its own (in fact, from 1897 to 1913 it was an autonomous state within the Ottoman Empire). While many of Greece's smaller is-

lands merit a day or two of fun in the sun, Crete could occupy even a busy traveler for a week or more. Historically, Crete was home to the Minoans—the earliest advanced European civilization, peaking around 1950 B.C., centuries before "the ancient Greeks" of Athens. While Crete's modern main city, Iraklio, is drab and uninviting, the rest of the island offers an engaging diversity of attractions: Minoan ruins, scenic mountains, enticing beaches, characteristic rustic villages, and dramatic caves and gorges (including the famous Samaria Gorge).

CHOOSING AN ISLAND

For this book I've chosen to cover three of the most popular escapes. **Hydra** is my favorite, thanks to its speedy connections to Athens and the Peloponnese, relaxing car-free ambience, easily reached beaches, and charming harbor that invites you to linger. Two of the most popular Greek islands are Mykonos and Santorini; both are relatively well connected to Athens. **Mykonos** is an adorable, windmill-topped fishing village slathered in white and thronged by a hard-partying international crowd, enjoying its many beaches and side-tripping to the ruins on nearby Delos. **Santorini** is the most geologically interesting of all the Greek islands, and arguably the most picturesque, with idyllic villages perched on the rim of a collapsed and flooded volcano crater.

If you're choosing just one island, I'd go with Hydra. Farther-flung Mykonos and Santorini can easily be connected in a loop—

they are linked to Athens' port (Piraeus), and to each other, by boat and plane. If your travels take you to islands beyond these three, pick up another guidebook to supplement the information here.

While each Greek island has its own personality and claims to fame, most offer the same basic ingredients: a charming fishing village, once humble and poor, now a finely tuned machine for catering to (and collecting money from) a steady stream of tourists; a rugged interior and rough roads connecting coastal coves; appealing beaches with rentable umbrellas and lounge chairs, presided over by tavernas and hotels; maybe a few dusty museums collecting ancient artifacts or bits and pieces of local folklore; and occasionally a good or even great ancient site to tour.

Many islands have a main town, which is sometimes named for the island itself, or might be called Chora or Hora (Χώρα), which literally means "village." This is generally the hub for transportation, both to other islands (port for passenger ferries and cruise ships) and within the island (bus station and taxi stand). Some islands—such as Rhodes, Corfu, and Crete—have sizeable cities as their capitals.

GETTING AROUND THE GREEK ISLANDS

Many passenger boats crisscross the Aegean Sea, making it quick and fairly easy to reach your island getaway. Be warned, however, that gathering ferry infor-

mation takes some work, as routes can be covered by multiple companies and schedules can change. Prior to your trip, look up schedules online, then confirm the details on arrival in Greece at any travel agency (or two or three, as you may get slightly different information from different agencies). For more tips on schedules and tickets, see the Practicalities chapter; for connections from Piraeus (Athens' port), see the Athens Connections chapter. Note that boats can be cancelled due to bad weather (more likely off-season).

To save time, consider flying between Athens and Mykonos or Santorini. Compared with boats, flights are less likely to get delayed or cancelled, tend to offer more frequent connections, and are much faster—but often more expensive. Two major Greek carriers that offer daily flights from Athens to many Greek islands are **Olympic Airlines** (www.olympicair.com) and **Aegean Airlines** (www.aegeanair.com). Also consider **Astra Airlines** (www.astra-airlines.gr) and **Sky Express** (www.skyexpress.gr).

The Greek islands are made-to-order for cruising and a major destination for cruise ships. If you're coming on a cruise, your challenge is to beat the hordes: You'll arrive in town at precisely the same time as 2,000 other visitors, all hoping to fit the maximum amount of sightseeing, shopping, or beach time in a single day. Get as early a start as possible, and explore the back lanes and beaches when the main drag gets too congested.

If you're not cruising, it's smart to be aware of when ships are scheduled to show up. If you're planning to visit outlying sights or beaches, do it when the ships are in port—by the time you return to town in the afternoon, the cruise-ship passengers will be loading up to leave again.

ISLAND ACCOMMODATIONS

Greek-island accommodations range from rustic *dhomatia* to designer hotels with spectacular views. Even out-of-the-way islands get heavy tourist traffic in the summer, so options abound.

At the busiest times (July-Sept, peaking in Aug), visitors can outnumber beds; to get your choice of accommodations, book far ahead. Expect to pay (sometimes wildly) inflated prices in high season—in the most popular destinations, such as Mykonos and Santorini, prices for even budget hotels can more than double. Prices for other services—such as car rentals and restaurant meals—also increase when demand is high. For the best combination of still-good weather, fewer crowds, and more reasonable prices, visit just before or after these busy times.

Whenever you visit, enjoy your time here and simply give yourself over to the Greek islands. With a few exceptions, the "sights" (museums and ruins) are not worth going out of your way for—you're here to relax on the beach and explore the charming towns. Make the most of it.

HYDRA

ΎΔΡΑ / Ύδρα

Hydra (pronounced EE-drah, not HIGH-drah)—less than a two-hour boat ride from Athens' port, Piraeus—is a glamorous getaway that combines practical convenience with idyllic Greek island ambience. After the noise of Athens, Hydra's traffic-free tranquility is a delight. Donkeys rather than cars, the shady awnings of well-worn cafés, and memorable seaside views all combine to make it clear...you've found your Greek isle.

The island's main town, also called Hydra, is one of Greece's prettiest. Its busy but quaint harbor—bobbing with rustic fishing boats and luxury yachts—is surrounded by a ring of rocky hills and blanketed with whitewashed homes. From the harbor, a fleet of zippy water taxis whisks you to isolated beaches and tavernas. Hydra is an easy blend of stray cats, hardworking donkeys, welcoming Hydriots (as locals are called), and lazy tourists on "island time."

One of the island's greatest attractions is its total absence of cars and motorbikes. Sure-footed beasts of burden—laden with

everything from sandbags and bathtubs to bottled water—climb stepped lanes. While Hydra is generally quiet, dawn teaches visitors the exact meaning of "cockcrow." The end of night is marked with much more than a distant cock-a-doodle-doo; it's a dissonant chorus of catfights, burro honks, and what sounds like roll call at an asylum for crazed roosters. After the animal population gets all that out of its system, the island slumbers a little longer.

Hydra's Hystory

Though it may seem tiny and low-key, overachieving Hydra holds a privileged place in Greek history. The fate of Hydriots has always been tied to the sea, which locals have harnessed to their advantage time after time.

Many Hydriot merchants became wealthy running the British blockade of French ports during the Napoleonic Wars. Hydra enjoyed its glory days in the late 18th and early 19th centuries, when the island was famous for its shipbuilders. Hydra's prosperity earned it the nickname "Little England." As rebellion swept Greece, the island flourished as a safe haven for those fleeing Ottoman oppression.

When the Greeks launched their War of Independence in 1821, Hydra emerged as a leading naval power. The harbor, with its twin forts and abundance of cannons, housed and protected the fleet of 130 ships. Hydriots of note from this period include the naval officer Andreas Miaoulis, who led the "firebrands" and their deadly "fireships," which succeeded in decimating the Ottoman navy, and Lazaros Kountouriotis, a wealthy shipping magnate who donated his fleet to the cause (more on both of these figures later in this chapter).

Greece won its independence, but at a great cost to Hydra, which lost many of its merchant-turned-military ships to the fighting...sending the is-land into a deep economic funk. During those lean post-war years, Hydriots again found salvation in the sea, farming the sponges that lived below the surface (sponge divers here pioneered the use of diving suits). Gathering sponges kick-started the local economy and kept Hydra afloat.

In 1956 Sophia Loren came here to play an Hydriot sponge diver in the film *Boy on a Dolphin,* propelling the little island onto the international stage. And the movie's plot—in which a precious ancient sculpture is at risk of falling into the hands of a greedy art collector instead of being returned to the Greek government—still resonates with today's Greeks, who want to reclaim their heritage for the Acropolis Museum.

Thanks largely to the film, by the 1960s Hydra had become a favorite retreat for celebrities, well-heeled tourists, and artists and writers, who still draw inspiration from the idyllic surroundings. Canadian songwriter Leonard Cohen lived here for a time—and was inspired to compose his beloved song "Bird on the Wire" after observing just that here on Hydra. Today visitors only have to count the yachts to figure out that Hydra's economy is still based on the sea.

HYDRA

Little Hydra—which has produced more than its share of military heroes, influential aristocrats, and political leaders—is packed with history. Rusted old cannons are scattered about town; black, pitted anchors decorate squares; and small museums hold engaging artifacts. But most visitors enjoy simply being on vacation here. Loiter around the harbor. Go on a photo safari for donkeys and kittens. Take a walk along the coast or up into the hills. Head for an inviting beach, near or far, to sunbathe and swim. Hang out past your bedtime in a cocktail bar. Hydra's the kind of place that makes you want to buy a bottle of ouzo and toss your itinerary into the sea.

PLANNING YOUR TIME

While Hydra can be done as a long day trip from Athens, it's better to spend at least two nights to take full advantage of the island's many dining options, and to give yourself a whole day to relax. Even if you're visiting Mykonos, Santorini, or other Greek islands, Hydra has a totally different vibe and is still the best place I know of to take a vacation from your Greek vacation.

To get your bearings, take my brief self-guided walk as soon as you arrive. While the walk gives you the historic context of the town, it also points out practical stops that will make your stay more efficient and enjoyable (and finishes at a wonderful little bakery). You'll still have ample time for your choice of activities: Dip into a museum that tickles your curiosity, enjoy a drink at a café, go for a hike into the hills, walk along the water to nearby villages and beaches, or catch a shuttle boat or water taxi for a spin around the island.

Orientation to Hydra

Remember, Hydra is the name of both the island and its main town (home to about 90 percent of the island's 2,000 residents). Hydra

town climbs up the hill in every direction from the port.

Branching off from the broad café-lined walkway at the bottom of the harbor are four major streets. In order from the boat dock, these are called Tompazi, Oikonomou, Miaouli, and Lignou. Not that street names mean much in this town—locals ignore addresses, and few lanes are labeled. Though the island is small, Hydra's streets twist defiantly to and fro. If seeking a specific location, use the map in this chapter or ask a local (note that most maps of Hydra, including mine, show

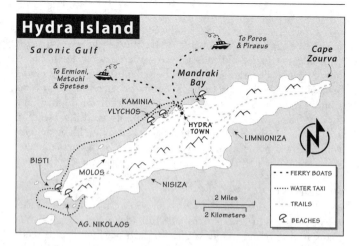

Hydra Island

the harbor—which is actually to the north—at the bottom). Expect to get lost in Hydra...and enjoy it when you do.

Consider venturing beyond Hydra town to settlements and beaches elsewhere on the island. The most accessible is the tiny seaside hamlet of Kaminia, which lies just over the headland west of the harbor (with a good recommended restaurant).

Tourist Information: Hydra has no TI, but most of the hoteliers I've listed here are happy and willing to help. You can also check www.hydra.gr and the more basic www.hydra.com.gr.

ARRIVAL ON HYDRA

All ferry boats dock in the heart of Hydra town's harbor, along its eastern edge (for details on how to get to Hydra, see "Hydra Connec-

tions" at the end of this chapter). Nearly all of my recommended accommodations are within a 10-minute walk of the harbor. At the port you can hire a donkey to carry your bags (€10-15, establish the price up front). If you ask, better hotels will often meet you at the boat and help with your bags.

GETTING AROUND HYDRA

As there are no cars, your options are foot, donkey, or boat. You'll walk everywhere in town. You can hike to neighboring beaches, but it's fun to hop a **shuttle boat** (about €3 to Vlychos—due to Greek laws you may have to pay for a round-trip ticket even if you only use it one-way; departures about every 30 minutes in high season from in front of Hotel Sophia) or take a **water taxi** (much more expensive unless you're a small group—same rate for one person or eight). You'll see the red taxi boats stacked and waiting near the donkeys on the harborfront. Sample taxi fares: €12 to Kaminia, €17 to Vlychos (there's a fare board lashed to the pole by the taxi dock, with the English translation hiding on the back side). To get back to town by water taxi, call 22980-53690.

HELPFUL HINTS

Summer Weather: Hydra can get extremely hot, especially in July and August when temperatures can reach near scorching. While other islands receive bursts of breezy north winds granting temporary reprieve, the entire island of Hydra is cut off from nature's air-conditioning by the Attica peninsula. Before you head out for the day, make sure you're prepared with sunscreen and plenty of water.

Drinking Water: The island's name means "water" in ancient Greek, but it was named a long, long time ago: Today there's no natural water source on Hydra (other than private cisterns). Until recently, water was barged in daily. But with EU help, Hydra now has a seawater desalination plant, giving the island a reliable water supply and drinkable tap water.

Hydra Harbor Walk

Hydra clusters around its wide harbor, squeezed full of fishing boats, pleasure craft, luxury yachts, and the occasional Athens-bound ferry. Get the lay of the land with this lazy 30-minute self-guided stroll.

• *Begin at the tip of the port (to the right, as you face the sea). Climb the stairs (by the wall of cactus) to the cannon-studded turret. From here you have a fine...*

View of the Harbor

The harbor is the heart and soul of Hydra. Imagine it as an ancient theater: The houses are the audience, the port is the stage, the boats are the actors...and the Saronic Gulf is the scenic backdrop.

This little town has a history rich with military might, political power, and artistic sophistication. Looking at the arid, barren mountains rising up along the spine of the island, it's clear that not much grows here—so Hydriots have always turned to

HYDRA

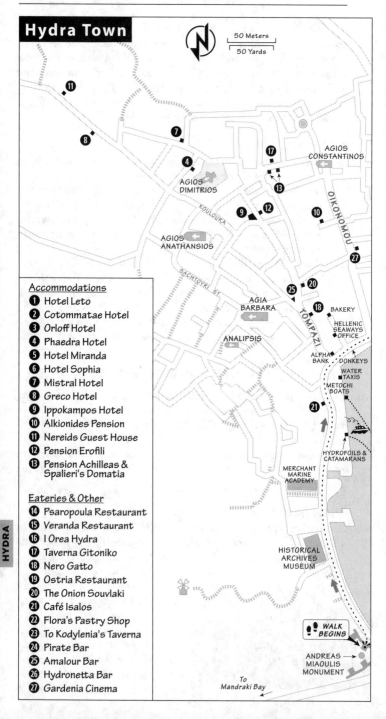

Hydra Town

50 Meters
50 Yards

AGIOS CONSTANTINOS

AGIOS DIMITRIOS

KOULOURA

AGIOS ANATHANSIOS

SACHTOYRI ST.

OIKONOMOU

AGIA BARBARA

ANALIPSIS

TOMPAZI

BAKERY

HELLENIC SEAWAYS OFFICE

ALPHA BANK

DONKEYS

WATER TAXIS

METOCHI BOATS

HYDROFOILS & CATAMARANS

MERCHANT MARINE ACADEMY

HISTORICAL ARCHIVES MUSEUM

WALK BEGINS

ANDREAS MIAOULIS MONUMENT

To Mandraki Bay

Accommodations
1. Hotel Leto
2. Cotommatae Hotel
3. Orloff Hotel
4. Phaedra Hotel
5. Hotel Miranda
6. Hotel Sophia
7. Mistral Hotel
8. Greco Hotel
9. Ippokampos Hotel
10. Alkionides Pension
11. Nereids Guest House
12. Pension Erofili
13. Pension Achilleas & Spalieri's Domatia

Eateries & Other
14. Psaropoula Restaurant
15. Veranda Restaurant
16. I Orea Hydra
17. Taverna Gitoniko
18. Nero Gatto
19. Ostria Restaurant
20. The Onion Souvlaki
21. Café Isalos
22. Flora's Pastry Shop
23. To Kodylenia's Taverna
24. Pirate Bar
25. Amalour Bar
26. Hydronetta Bar
27. Gardenia Cinema

HYDRA

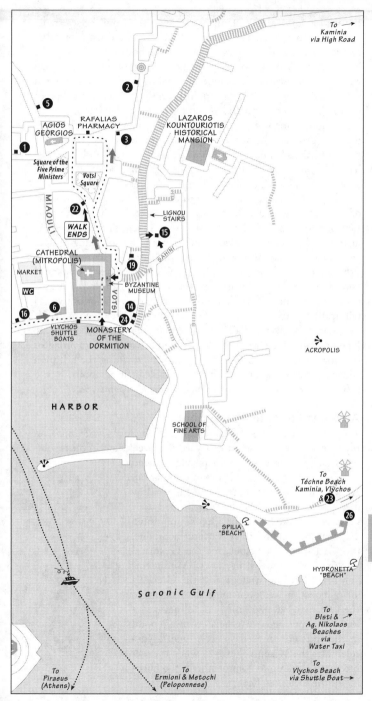

To →
Kaminia
via High Road

❺ AGIOS GEORGIOS

❷

RAFALIAS PHARMACY

❸

LAZAROS KOUNTOURIOTIS HISTORICAL MANSION

❶

Square of the Five Prime Ministers

Votsi Square

MIAOULI

㉒ WALK ENDS

LIGNOU STAIRS

CATHEDRAL (MITROPOLIS)

⑮

SAHINI

MARKET

WC

⑲

VOTSI

BYZANTINE MUSEUM

⑯ ❻

⑭

VLYCHOS SHUTTLE BOATS

㉔

MONASTERY OF THE DORMITION

ACROPOLIS

HARBOR

SCHOOL OF FINE ARTS

To
Téchne Beach
Kaminia, Vlychos
& ㉓

㉖

SPILIA "BEACH"

HYDRONETTA "BEACH"

Saronic Gulf

To
Bísti &
Ag. Nikolaos
Beaches
via
Water Taxi

To
Piraeus
(Athens)

To
Ermioni & Metochi
(Peloponnese)

To
Vlychos Beach
via Shuttle Boat →

HYDRA

the sea for survival. As islanders grew wealthy from the sea trade, prominent local merchant families built the grand mansions that rise up between the modest whitewashed houses blanketing the hillsides. One of these—the Lazaros Kountouriotis Historical Mansion—is open to the public (the yellow mansion with the red roof and open terrace facing you, high on the hill across the harbor to the right, near the small red bell tower; described later).

Another mansion, the rough-stone four-story building directly across from the port (behind the imposing zigzag wall), now houses Hydra's School of Fine Arts. Artists—Greek and foreign—have long swooned over the gorgeous light that saturates Hydra's white homes, brown cliffs, and turquoise waters.

Look directly across the mouth of the harbor. Along the base of the walkway, under the seafront café tables, is the town's closest "beach," called Spilia ("Cave")—a concrete pad with ladders luring swimmers into the cool blue. For a more appealing option, you can follow the paved, mostly level path around this point to the fishing hamlet of Kaminia (with a scenic recommended restaurant) and, beyond that, to Vlychos (for the best beach around). Visually trace the ridgeline above that trail, noticing the remains of two old windmills—a fixture on many Greek islands, once used for grinding grain and raw materials for gunpowder. The windmills' sails are long gone, but the lower one was restored for use as a film prop (for the Sophia Loren film *Boy on a Dolphin*). Crowning the hill high above are the scant ruins of Hydra's humble little acropolis.

• *Turn your attention to the centerpiece of this viewpoint, the...*

Andreas Miaoulis Monument

The guy at the helm is Admiral Andreas Miaoulis (1768-1835), an Hydriot sea captain who valiantly led the Greek navy in the revolution that began in 1821. This war sought to end nearly four centuries of Ottoman occupation. As war preparations ramped up, the wealthy merchant marines of Hydra transformed their vessels into warships. The Greeks innovated a clever and deadly naval warfare technique: the "fireship." (For details, see the Historical Archives Museum listing, later.) While this kamikaze-burning strategy cost the Greeks a lot of boats, it was even more devastating to the Ottoman navy—and Miaoulis' naval victory was considered a crucial turning point in the war. For three days each June, Hydra celebrates the Miaoulia Festival, when they set fire to an old ship to commemorate the burning of the Ottoman fleet.

On the monument, the cross that hangs from the steering column represents the eventual triumph of the Christian Greeks over the Muslim Ottomans. Miaoulis' bones are actually inside the stone pedestal under the statue.

• *Head back down the stairs and begin walking along the harborfront.*

Along the Harbor

About 50 yards down is the stout stone mansion that houses the **Historical Archives Museum.** This small but good collection (described later, under "Sights and Activities in Hydra") does its best to get visitors excited about Hydra's history. The gap after the museum is filled with monuments honoring Hydriot heroes. The green plaque in the pillar is a gift from Argentina to honor an Hydriot aristocrat who fought in the Argentinean war for independence. The next building is the Merchant Marine Academy, where Hydra continues to churn out sailors—many of whom often hang around out front. (During the WWII occupation of Greece, this building was used as a Nazi base.) Next, the row of covered benches along the water marks the embarkation point for the ferries ("Flying Dolphin" hydrofoils and "Flying Cat" catamarans) that connect Hydra to Athens and other Greek islands for those of us who lack yachts of our own.

Notice the three flags to the right—specifically, the **flag of Hydra.** Dating from the uprising against the Ottomans, it's loaded with symbolism: the outline of the island of Hydra topped with a flag with a warrior's helmet, a cross, and an anchor—all watched over by the protective eye of God. The inscription, Η ΤΑΝ Η ΕΠΙ ΤΑΣ, means "with it or on it," and evokes the admonition of the warlike Spartans when sending their sons into battle with their huge shields: Come back "with it," victorious and carrying your shield; or "on it," dead, with your shield serving as a stretcher to carry your body home.

When you reach the corner of the harbor, you'll likely see **donkeys and mules** shooing flies as they wait to plod into town

with visitors' luggage lashed to their backs. The donkeys are not just a touristy gimmick, but also a lifestyle choice: Hydriots have decided not to allow any private motorized vehicles on their island, keeping this place quiet and tranquil, and reducing pollution (now just donkey poop). This means that, aside from a few garbage trucks or emergency vehicles, these beasts of burden are the only way to get around. It's not unusual to see one with a major appliance strapped to its back, as it gingerly navigates the steps up to the top of town. Locals dress their burros up with rugs, beads, and charms. Behind each mule-train toils a human pooper-scooper. On Hydra a traffic jam looks like a farm show. And instead of the testosterone-fueled revving of moped engines, Hydra's soundtrack features the occasional distant whinnying of a donkey echoing over the rooftops.

In the same corner as the donkeys is the dock for the feisty fleet of red **water taxis.** These zip constantly from here to remote points around the island. Meanwhile, simple fishing boats squeeze between the luxury yachts to put in and unload their catch...eyed hungrily by scrawny cats.

Hang a right and continue along the bottom of the harbor. At this corner (next to the Alpha Bank) is Sahtouri street, which soon becomes Tompazi, and quickly devolves into a twisty warren of lanes with many hotels. Continue along the harbor, past a tiny dead-end lane leading to a good bakery. As you stroll, window-shop the **cafés** and choose one to return to later. Overhead, notice the ingenious rope system the seafaring Hydriots have rigged so that they can quickly draw a canopy over the seating area—like unfurling the sails on a ship—in the event of rain...or, more commonly here, overpowering sunshine. Next, skinny Oikonomou street leads to shops and the open-air Gardenia Cinema. A few steps farther, another narrow lane leads to the post office, public WC, and Hydra's ramshackle little market hall.

Hydra is known for its **jewelry.** A few shops right here on the harbor, such as Zoe's and Elena Votsi, sell the handiwork of Hydriot designers and artists (Votsi is locally famous as the designer of the 2004 Olympic medals). Many Hydra hoteliers supplement their income by running jewelry and souvenir shops, often with the same name as their hotels (good to know if you need to find your hotelier at midday). The next street, Navarhou Miaouli, bustles with appealing **tavernas.**

Shuttle boats line up along the next stretch of the quay. They offer cheap rides to points around the island—a service much appreciated by the owners of Hydra's many remote cafés and tavernas (but which annoys the water-taxi drivers).

• Near the far corner of the harbor stands a symbol of Hydra, the clock tower of the...

Monastery of the Dormition

Hydra's ecclesiastical center is dedicated to the Dormition of the Virgin. "Dormition"—as in "sleep"—is a Greek euphemism for death. Orthodox Christians believe Mary died a human death, then (like her son) was resurrected three days later, before being assumed into heaven.

Go through the archway under the tower, and you'll emerge into what was, until 1832, an active monastery. The double-decker

arcade of cells circling the courtyard was once the monks' living quarters; it now houses the offices of the city government and mayor.

The monastery's church, which doubles as Hydra's *mitropolis* (cathedral), is free to enter. Stepping inside, it's clear that this was a wealthy community—compare the marble iconostasis, silver chandelier, gorgeous *Pantocrator* dome decoration, rich icons, and frescoes with the humbler decor you'll see at small-town churches elsewhere in Greece. Just inside the door (to the left), the icon of the Virgin and Child is believed to work miracles. Notice the many votive rings and necklaces draping it as a thank-you for prayers answered.

Back in the courtyard, you'll see war memorials and monuments to beloved Hydriots. The humble Byzantine Museum (also called the "Ecclesiastical Museum"—up the stairs across the courtyard) has a few rooms of glittering icons, vestments, and other paraphernalia from this monastery and church (€4, €2 off-season, some English labels, Tue-Sun 10:00-14:30, closed Mon).

• *If the doorway's open under the museum, exit here onto Votsi street (otherwise, return to the harborfront, then hang a left up the next street). From this spot (either straight ahead or around the right side of the yellow butcher's shop) stairs head to the upper reaches of town, and eventually lead over the headland and down to the village and little harbor of Kaminia. For now though, keep to the left, walking toward the orange-tree-filled square.*

Upper Town Squares

Tidy **Votsi Square** has lots of cats. Hydriots love their cats, perhaps because they share a similar temperament: tender, relaxed, but secretly vigilant and fiercely independent. At the bottom of the square (on the left) is Flora's Pastry Shop, where we'll finish our stroll.

For now, keep walking about 100 feet above the square until the lane hits the old-time **Rafalias Pharmacy.** The pharmacy is an institution in town, and Vangelis Rafalias has kept it just as his grandfather did. He welcomes the browsing public, so take a look. Just inside the window, on the far right wall, is a photo of Jackie Onassis visiting Hydra.

With your back to the pharmacy, one lane leads to the left,

HYDRA

heading uphill to the site of the original town, which was positioned inland to be safely away from marauding pirates. We'll head
in the other direction, right, and slightly downhill, rounding the
building on the left to the little **Square of the Five Prime Ministers.** The monument, with five medallions flanked by cannons,
celebrates the five Hydriots who were chosen for Greece's highest
office in the nearly two centuries since independence. It's an impressive civic contribution from a little island town, perhaps due
to Hydra's seafaring wealth and its proximity to the Greek capitals
(Nafplio, then Athens). From here, narrow, stepped, cobblestone
lanes invite exploration of Hydra's quiet side.

But for now, continue left and downhill, back to Votsi
Square. The recommended **Flora's Pastry Shop** (signed
ZAXAPOΠΛΑΣΤΕΙΟ) is at the bottom of the square, on the right
(see "Eating in Hydra," later). Treat yourself to a homemade ice
cream or baklava. Or, for something more traditional, try the local
favorite—*galaktoboureko* (gha-lahk-toh-boo-re-KOH), which is
cinnamon-sprinkled egg custard baked between layers of phyllo.

Sights and Activities in Hydra

MUSEUMS
▲Historical Archives Museum
This fine little museum, in an old mansion right along the port,
shows off a small, strangely fascinating collection of Hydra's history and has good English descriptions throughout.

Cost and Hours: €5, includes temporary art exhibits; daily
9:00-16:00, also 19:30-21:30 in June-Sept; along the eastern side
of the harbor near the ferry dock, tel. 22980-52355, www.iamy.gr.

Visiting the Museum: The core of the exhibit is upstairs. At
the top of the stairs, look straight ahead for a tattered, yellowed **old
map** by Rigas Feraios from 1797.
Depicting a hypothetical and
generously defined "Hellenic
Republic," it claims virtually the
entire Balkan Peninsula (from
the Aegean to the Danube) for
Greece. The map features historical and cultural tidbits of the
time (such as drawings of coins
from various eras), making it a
treasure trove for historians. Drawn at a time when the Greeks
had been oppressed by the Ottomans for centuries, the map—with
1,200 copies printed and distributed—helped to rally support for
what would become a successful revolution starting in 1821.

The stairwell is lined with portraits of **"firebrands"**—sailors (many of them Hydriots) who burned the Ottoman fleet during the war. They were considered the "body and soul" of the Greek navy in 1821. To learn more about their techniques, head behind the map and into the room on the left; in its center, find the **model of a "fireship"** used for these attacks. These vessels were loaded with barrels of gunpowder, with large ventilation passages cut into the deck and hull. Suspended from the masts were giant, barbed, fishing-lure-like hooks. (Two actual hooks flank the model.) After ramming an enemy ship and dropping the hooks into its deck to attach the two vessels, the Greek crew would light the fuse and escape in a little dinghy...leaving their ship behind to become a giant firetrap, engulfing the Ottoman vessel in flames. Also in this room are nautical maps and models and paintings of other Hydriot vessels.

In the biggest room (immediately behind the old map), you'll see a Greek urn in the center containing the actual, embalmed **heart** of local hero Andreas Miaoulis. On the walls are portraits of V.I.H.s (very important Hydriots). Rounding out the collection on this floor is a room filled with **weapons** and 18th- and 19th-century **Hydriot attire.**

Lazaros Kountouriotis Historical Mansion

Because of Hydra's merchant-marine prosperity, the town has many fine aristocratic mansions...but only this one is open to the public.

Lazaros Kountouriotis (koon-doo-ree-OH-tees, 1769-1852) was a wealthy Hydriot shipping magnate who helped fund the Greek War of Independence. He donated 120 of his commercial ships to be turned into warships, representing three-quarters of the Greek navy. Today Kountouriotis is revered as a local and national hero, and his mansion offers visitors a glimpse into the lifestyles of the 18th-century Greek rich and famous.

Cost and Hours: €4; daily 10:00-16:00, off-season until 14:00, Nov-March by appointment only; on the hillside above town, signposted off the stepped Lignou street—turn right after Veranda Restaurant, tel. 22980-52421, www.nhmuseum.gr/en/exhibitions/ydra.

Visiting the Mansion: The main building of Kountouriotis' former estate is a fine example of aristocratic Hydriot architecture of the late 18th century, combining elements of Northern

HYDRA

Greek, Saronic Gulf Island, and Italian architecture. The house has changed little since its heyday.

You'll enter on the second floor, with several period-decorated rooms. These reception rooms have beautiful wood-paneled ceilings, and are furnished with all the finery of the period. Included is the statesman's favorite armchair, where you can imagine him spending many hours pondering the shape of the emerging Greek nation. Then you'll head outside and upstairs to see a collection of traditional costumes and jewelry from throughout Greece, labeled in English. The lower floor displays the art of the local Byzantinos family: father Pericles (hazy Post-Impressionistic landscapes and portraits) and son Constantinos (dark sketches and boldly colorful modern paintings).

BEACHES

Although Hydra's beaches are nothing to get excited about, there's no shortage of places to swim. There are a few basic swimming spots in Hydra town—the rest are reachable by foot, shuttle boat, or water taxi. Three decent beaches within a pleasant, easy walk of Hydra are Mandraki Bay, Kaminia Castello, and Vlychos. Distant beaches on the southwestern tip of the island (Bisti and Ag. Nikolaos) really get you away from it all, but are best reached by boat.

Spilia

The main spot to swim in town is Spilia ("Cave"), at the western entrance to Hydra harbor. There you'll find steps that lead down to a series of small concrete platforms with ladders into the sea—but no showers or changing rooms. (Spilia appears to belong to the adjacent café, but anyone is welcome to swim here.)

Hydronetta and Téchne

You'll find two more rocky, cement "beaches" just outside the town center, on the way to Kaminia. Both are associated with namesake restaurants, and neither has showers or changing rooms. The first, Hydronetta, sits just below the cannons along the ramparts (no shoreline, just a small diving terrace and ladder into the water). The bar's umbrella-shaded tables are good for between-dip refreshments. Téchne, two minutes down the same path, is the largest swim spot in Hydra town. A zigzagging staircase leads down to a rocky outcrop with two rock platforms, a small pebble cove, and an upmarket **$$$$ restaurant** featuring neo-Greek fare.

Mandraki Bay

This pebble beach is to the east of Hydra, near the main coastal path (30-minute walk from the eastern end of the harbor, €6 round-trip shuttle boat from Hydra). If it's sun you're after, Mandraki is best earlier in the day, as the hills around it bring shade in the late afternoon. The private beach is well maintained, with tidy rows of lounge chairs and umbrellas (€12 for two chairs with an umbrella).

Kaminia Castello Beach

To the west of town is the delightful little harbor of Kaminia and the recommended Kodylenia's Taverna (15-minute walk). Just beyond that you'll find another restaurant and bar called Castello above the small Kaminia Castello Beach. While handy, the beach can be overwhelmed by the musical taste of the kids who run the bar, and is often crowded with lots of families. For walking directions, see "Walks," below.

Vlychos Beach

Located past Kaminia, Vlychos is my favorite. Like a little tropical colony, 20 thatched umbrellas mark a quiet stretch of pebbly beach (€8 for two lounge chairs and an umbrella). You'll find other amenities, including the **$$ Marina Taverna,** a pleasant place for a meal (open daily for lunch and dinner, tel. 22980-52496), and showers at the beach of the nearby hotel. In peak tourist season, a shuttle boat  zips from Hydra to Vlychos twice an hour until sunset (confirm last boat time, €6 round-trip). The 40-minute walk from Hydra to Vlychos is great (described next).

WALKS

Hydra to Kaminia and Vlychos

The walk from Hydra town to the cute cove of Kaminia and the excellent beach at Vlychos (both described above) is one of my favorites. While the walk leads to two beaches, it's perfectly pleasant whether or not you take a dip.

For the easy approach, simply follow the mostly level coastal path that runs west from Hydra town to the villages of Kaminia and Vlychos. As you curve out of Hydra, you'll pass the town's best-preserved windmill, which was reconstructed for the 1957 Sophia Loren film *Boy on a Dolphin*. Up the steps to the windmill is a statue honoring the film that attracted many celebrities to Hydra.

Continuing along the path, you'll find yourself at the delightful harbor in **Kaminia** after about 15 minutes, where two dozen tough little fishing boats jostle within a breakwater. With cafés, a tiny beach, and a good taverna (see "Eating in Hydra," later), this is a wonderful place to watch island life go by.

Follow the water past the harbor where the stone path hugs a hillside, passing above Kaminia Castello Beach. Soon you're all alone with great sea views. Ten minutes or so later, you round a bluff, descend across an Ottoman-style single-arched bridge, and drop into **Vlychos,** with its welcoming little beach.

From Vlychos, an inland trail leads back to upper Hydra, passing donkey-strewn terraced pastures and a small cemetery. Leaving Vlychos, go under the Ottoman Bridge, across the footbridge, and straight onto the path (30 minutes to reach the top of Lignou stairs, lit at night).

The Hydra-Kaminia High Road: On this alternate inland route, you'll feel your way up and over the headland, then descend into Kaminia. Here shabby homes enjoy grand views, tethering off-duty burros seems unnecessary, and island life trudges on, oblivious to tourism. Along the way, look for dry, paved riverbeds, primed for the flash floods that fill village cisterns each winter. (You can also climb all the way up to the remains of Hydra's humble acropolis, topping the hill due west of the harbor.) From Hydra, start by climbing the Lignou staircase. Near the top, take the turnoff on your right (look for two large telephone poles and signs pointing to Hotel Oceano). About 200 yards ahead you'll see an orange grocery store on the left, Hotel Oceano on the right, and the acropolis straight ahead and above. Follow the road downhill, then down the staircase, staying to the left. After five minutes you'll see a large community cistern and dry riverbed that leads down to Kaminia's harbor.

More Walks and Hikes

Beyond walking to a nearby beach, Hydra is popular for its network of ancient paths that link the island's outlying settlements, churches, and monasteries. Most of the paths are well maintained and clearly marked. Review the handy signpost map of the island at the harbor (opposite the monastery) for an overview and ask your hotel for a trail map. Serious hikers should buy a detailed hiking map (sold locally). If you do venture into the hills, wear sturdy shoes, sunscreen, and a hat, and take your own water and picnic supplies.

Nightlife in Hydra

Locals, proud of the extravagant yachts that flock to the island, like to tell of movie stars who make regular visits. But the island is so quiet that by midnight, all the high-rollers seem to be back onboard watching movies.

And yet there are plenty of options to keep visitors busy. People enjoy watching a film at the town's outdoor cinema or nursing a drink along the harborfront—there are plenty of mellow cocktail bars proudly serving "Paradise in a Glass" for €8.

Pirate Bar is run by a hardworking family serving homemade breakfast and lunch until 17:00 and fine drinks until late. It sits on a prime spot on the water, at the little lane just past Lignou. The son, Zeus, runs the night shift and is famous for his inven-

tive cocktails—try his Greektini, made with mastic. This is a mellow, trendy spot to be late at night (tel. 22980-52711).

Amalour Bar, run by Vasilis, is "the place to fall in love" (or just enjoy wonderful music and good drinks). There's no sea view here—just cool music played at the right volume inside, and tables outside tumbling down a cobbled lane. It's mellow tunes until midnight, and then harder music (just up Tompazi street from the harbor, mobile 697-746-1357).

Hydronetta Bar, catering to a younger crowd with younger music, offers great sea views from under the "Sofia Loren wind-

mill," with a bunch of romantic tables nestled within the ramparts and cannons plus a small swimming hole described earlier (tel. 22980-54160). Reach it by walking along the coastline past Spilia Beach and through the Sunset Restaurant. This and the neighboring Spilia

cocktail bar are the most touristy of Hydra's nightlife choices.

Gardenia Cinema is part of a great Greek summer tradition:

watching movies in the open air. Hydra's delightful outdoor theater, lovingly run by the local cinema club, is right in the center of town on Oikonomou street; it shows movies in the original language on summer weekends (runs for 40 nights in the height of summer, nightly at 21:00 and 23:00, tel. 22980-53105).

Sleeping in Hydra

Hydra has ample high-quality accommodations. But the prices are also high—more expensive than anywhere on the Peloponnese, and rivaling those in Athens. Prices max out in the summer (June-mid-Sept). Outside of these times, most accommodations offer discounts—always ask. Longer stays might also garner you a deal. Some cheaper hotels don't provide breakfast, in which case you can eat for about €7 at various cafés around town. Communication can be challenging at a few of the cheaper places (as noted). The only hotel with an elevator is the Leto (though no hotel has more than three stories). Because Hydra has a labyrinthine street plan and most people ignore street names, I list no addresses. To find your way, use my "Hydra Town" map (earlier), and follow signs posted around town. Most accommodations in Hydra close for the winter (typically Nov-Feb, sometimes longer).

$$$$ Hotel Leto is the island's closest thing to a business-class hotel, offering executive service and a professional vibe, 22 well-appointed rooms, and inviting public spaces (small elevator, spa treatments, tel. 22980-53385, www.letohydra.gr, info@letohydra.gr).

$$$$ Cotommatae Hotel lives up to its grand pedigree as a former mansion with elegant public areas, a restful garden, and seven carefully styled, palatial rooms. Of all the restored houses in Hydra, this one feels the most luxurious (suites available, closed Dec-mid-Feb, tel. 29980-53873, www.cotommatae.gr, info@cotommatae.gr).

$$$$ Orloff Hotel is a lovingly maintained historic Hydriot house decorated in the traditional style. All eight rooms in this former Russian count's home have an Old-World-meets-21st-century charm (closed Nov-March, tel. 22980-52564, www.orloff.gr, hotel@orloff.gr).

$$$ Phaedra Hotel rents seven spacious and tasteful rooms in what was once a carpet factory. Helpful owner Hilda takes pride in her hotel, and it shows (family studio, 2-bed 2-bath suite with private veranda, great breakfast, open year-round, tel. 22980-53330, mobile 697-221-3111, www.phaedrahotel.com, info@phaedrahotel.com).

$$$ Hotel Miranda, in a sea captain's house from the early 19th century, is filled with an elegant nautical charm that feels almost New England-y—it's the most atmospheric of my listings. Its 10 stylish rooms are bright with whitewashed stone, and surround a classy terrace (tel. 22980-52230, www.mirandahotel.gr, mirandahydra@hol.gr).

$$$ Hotel Sophia is a plush little boutique hotel right above the harbor restaurant strip. It's been family-run since 1934; today English-speaking sisters Angelika and Vasiliki are at the helm. The six thoughtfully appointed rooms, while a little tight, are stony-chic, with high ceilings, heavy exposed beams, tiny-but-posh bathrooms, and good windows that manage to block out most of the harbor noise. Three rooms come with private balconies while the others have access to a shared veranda, giving you a royal box seat overlooking all the harbor action (RS%, closed Nov-March, tel. 22980-52313, www.hotelsophia.gr, hydra@hotelsophia.gr). Ask to see the family museum filled with items from the original hotel.

$$$ Mistral Hotel is a well-run place offering 17 rooms in a comfortable, modern-equipped, ivy-covered stone building with a central lounge and a breezy courtyard. It's a fine value at the very quiet top part of town (Wi-Fi in lobby and courtyard, tel. 22980-52509, www.hotelmistral.gr, info@hotelmistral.gr, Theo and Jenny serve a particularly good breakfast).

$$ Greco Hotel rents 16 rooms set above one of the shadiest, lushest gardens in town. It's where lovely owner Maria Keramidas serves a homemade buffet breakfast...and where you'll be tempted to just relax and do nothing all afternoon (closed Nov-March, tel. 22980-53200, www.grecohotel.gr, grecohotelhydra@gmail.com; Maria speaks little English, but son Alkis is around to help).

$$ Ippokampos Hotel has 16 pleasant rooms around a cocktail-bar courtyard. The four top-floor rooms open right onto a seaview patio. The suite is a few notches up in quality and amenities, with its own private veranda (bar closes at 23:00, closed Nov-March, tel. 22980-53453, www.ippokampos.com, ippo@ippokampos.com, Sotiris and Voula).

$$ Alkionides Pension offers 10 smartly renovated rooms around a beautiful and relaxing courtyard, and is buried in Hydra's back lanes (apartment, breakfast extra, tel. 22980-54055, mobile 697-741-0460, www.alkionidespension.com, info@alkionidespension.com, Kofitsas family).

$$ Nereids Guest House is a bit farther from the harbor than my other listings, but the nine stony rooms offer good atmosphere and space for the price (no breakfast, two minutes past Greco Hotel, tel. 22980-52875, www.nereids-hydra.com, nereids@otenet.gr).

$$ Pension Erofili is a reliable budget standby in the heart of town, renting 12 basic but tasteful rooms just off (or over) a relaxing little courtyard (RS%, apartment, homemade breakfast extra, tel.

22980-54049, mobile 697-768-8487, www.pensionerofili.gr, info@
pensionerofili.gr, George and Irene).

$$ Pension Achilleas rents 13 decent rooms in an old mansion with a relaxing courtyard terrace and a gorgeous seaview roof patio. Request one of the upstairs rooms (they're brighter), and try to land one with a balcony (apartment, cash only, breakfast extra, tel. 22980-52050, www.achilleaspension.gr, kofitsas@otenet.gr, Dina or Demitris speak only a little English).

$$ Spalieri's Dhomatia has five rooms in a cheery home with a welcoming garden courtyard. The units, though simple, are spacious. Staying with the Spalieri family provides a homier experience than at most other places in town (breakfast extra, on the corner next to Pension Achilleas, tel. 22980-52894, mobile 694-414-1977, spalsteff@ath.forthnet.gr, minimal English).

Eating in Hydra

There are dozens of places to eat, offering everything from humble gyros to slick modern-Mediterranean cuisine. Harbor views come with higher prices; places farther inland typically offer better value.

IN HYDRA TOWN

$$$$ Psaropoula Restaurant, at the southwest corner of the harbor, fills a top-floor terrace in a prime spot overlooking all of the action. They specialize in seafood but also have pasta and meat dishes. Ask to see what's cooking in the kitchen, or peek inside their drawers full of fresh fish to see what looks good for dinner (daily 12:00-23:00, reservations smart in summer—especially for view tables, tel. 22980-52573, www.psaropoula.org).

$$$ Veranda Restaurant, perched on a terrace with fine views over the town and harbor, wins the best ambience award. It's great on a summer evening; enjoy a cold drink before selecting from a menu that offers pasta served a dozen different ways and a creative assortment of salads (better-than-average wine list, daily 18:00-late, halfway up the steep steps on Sahini lane or along the Lignou steps, reservations smart in summer, tel. 22980-52259, Andreas).

$$$ I Orea Hydra (Η Ωραία Ύδρα) is a serious seafood restaurant highly regarded by locals for their modern approach to Greek cuisine (daily 11:30-16:00 & 18:00-23:00, closed Nov-March, try to reserve one of the balcony tables for an even more romantic experience, tel. 22980-52556).

$$ Taverna Gitoniko is a tricky-to-find taverna with a delightful rooftop garden, but it's worth seeking out for a memorable meal. The kitchen works magic with the produce they snap up fresh from the market. Order a selection of creative first courses and check their daily specials (daily for lunch and dinner, closed Nov-Feb, on Spilios Haramis street, tel. 22980-53615).

$$$ Nero Gatto is a modern Italian eatery, with tables inside or out on lively Tompazi street. Here you'll find good food, a friendly owner, and just the right mix of trendy and casual (open daily 14:00-late, closed mid-Oct-mid-April, a minute up from the harbor on Tompazi, tel. 22980-54030).

$$$ At **Ostria Restaurant,** handwritten menus in spiral-bound notebooks look more like grocery lists than dinner options, making it feel as though you're eating in a local's dining room. In this family-run taverna known for authentic food at reasonable prices, no-nonsense Tassoula runs the show while laid-back Stathis does the cooking—if you're lucky he'll be preparing freshly caught calamari, his specialty (daily 11:00-15:00 & 19:00-23:00, tel. 22980-54077).

$$-$$$ Tavernas on Miaouli Street: This street leading up from the port (to the left of the monastery bell tower) is crammed with appealing little tavernas that jostle for your attention with outdoor seating and good food.

$ Souvlaki: For a quick, cheap meal, souvlaki is your best bet. For a civilized, sit-down souvlaki experience, drop by **The Onion Souvlaki** (Και Κρεμμύδι), a cute eatery filling a charming corner up Tompazi street, across from the Amalour Bar.

Cafés on the Harbor: Enjoy the scene as you nurse a drink here—drivers rolling their pushcarts, donkeys sneezing, taxi-boat drivers haggling, big boats coming and going. For a meal, try **$$$ Café Isalos** ("Waterline"), with a fun menu of light bites, including salads, sandwiches, pastas, and pizzas. In the early evening, watch for yachts trying to dock; some are driven by pros and others aren't, providing a comedic scene of naval inexperience.

Dessert: Flora's Pastry Shop is a hardworking little bakery cranking out the best pastries and homemade ice cream on the island. Flora has delightful tables that overlook Votsi Square, just behind the monastery. She sells all the traditional local sweets, including honey treats such as baklava. Many of her ingredients come from her farm on the nearby island of Dokos (daily 7:00-24:00).

EATING NEAR HYDRA, IN KAMINIA

A great way to cap your Hydra day is to follow the coastal path to the rustic and picturesque village of Kaminia, which hides behind the headland from Hydra. Kaminia's pocket-sized harbor shelters the community's fishing boats. Here, with a glass of ouzo and some munchies, as the sun slowly sinks into the sea and boats become silhouettes, you can drink to the beauties of a Greek isle escape. Consider combining dinner with a late-afternoon stroll along the seafront (see "Walks—Hydra to Kaminia and Vlychos," earlier).

$$$ Kodylenia's Taverna is perched on a bluff just over the Kaminia harbor. With my favorite irresistible dinner views on Hydra, this scenic spot lets you watch the sun dip gently into the Saronic Gulf, with Kaminia's adorable port in the foreground. Owner Dimitris takes his own boat out early in the morning to buy the day's best catch directly from the fishermen. For meals, you can sit out on the shady

covered side terrace above the harbor—check the chalkboard to see what's freshest today. For drinks, sit out front on the porch. Relax and take in a sea busy with water taxis, ferries that connect this oasis with Athens, old freighters—like castles of rust—lumbering slowly along the horizon, and cruise ships anchored as if they haven't moved in weeks (visit their display case and see what's cooking, daily 12:00-23:30, may close earlier off-season, closed mid-Nov-Feb, tel. 22980-53520).

Hydra Connections

Note that there are no direct ferry routes between Hydra and Mykonos or Santorini—to reach either from Hydra you'll first have to backtrack to Piraeus before continuing to your final destination.

GETTING BETWEEN ATHENS AND HYDRA

Hydra is easily reached from Athens's port at Piraeus via the Hellenic Seaways ferry, either the "Flying Dolphin" hydrofoil or the slightly larger "Flying Cat" catamaran (6-8/day June-Sept, 4/day Oct-May, 1.5-2 hours). If traveling to Hydra from Athens, then on to the Peloponnese, note that it's not necessary to return to Athens to pick up a car. You can go by ferry from Athens to Hydra, then continue by ferry from Hydra to Ermioni on the coast of the Peloponnese, where you can pick up a rental car (described later).

When to Buy Tickets: Because these boats are virtually the only game in town, it's wise to book in advance (at least a week ahead in summer). They can sell out during summer weekends, when boats are packed with Athenians headed to or from their Hydra getaway. Outside of summer, tickets should be available up to a day or two in advance.

Where to Buy Tickets: If you book ahead on the **Hellenic Seaways website** (www.hellenicseaways.gr), there are a few ways to get your actual ticket. You can either check in online (anytime between 30 minutes and 48 hours before departure) and have an eticket sent to you. Or you can pick up a paper ticket at a travel

agency, a Hellenic Sea-
ways ticket office, or at
a self-service machine at
Piraeus.

It's also possible to
buy a ticket in person soon
after you arrive in Greece
(tickets sold for the same
price at any **travel agency**).
Check the cancellation policy before buying your ticket.

In Hydra you can buy tickets at the **Hellenic Seaways office,**
just down an alley near the Alpha Bank (open long hours daily in
summer, tel. 22980-54007 or 22980-53812).

Boat Cancellations: Be aware that boats can be delayed, or
even cancelled, if the weather's bad enough (mostly a concern in
off-season). For more advice on navigating the Greek ferry system,
see page 532 of the Practicalities chapter.

GETTING BETWEEN HYDRA
AND THE PELOPONNESE

You have several options for connecting Hydra and the Peloponnese via several spots on the coast of the peninsula: Metochi,
Ermioni, or Tolo. Drivers can leave their cars in long-term parking
at either Metochi (frequent crossings to Hydra on small passenger
boats, just show up) or Ermioni (larger, less-frequent ferries, can be
booked in advance). You can also connect Nafplio and Ermioni by
public transportation (with some effort) or pick up a rental car in
Ermioni to begin a tour of the Peloponnese. Another option is to
day-trip from Tolo (near Nafplio) to Hydra.

Metochi (drivers only): Metochi is the spot on the mainland
closest to Hydra (under 2 hours from Nafplio, 3 hours from Athens). It's at the end of a dirt road with nothing there except a couple
of ticket stands and a small boat pier. You can park on the road
or in the small dirt lot for free, or use the pay lot (€5/day). Both
the **Freedom Boat** (mobile 694-424-2141, www.hydralines.gr) and
Metoxi Express (tel. 22980-53000, www.hydracelebrity.gr) sail to
Hydra quickly and frequently (€5-6.50, hop on the one that's leaving next, about hourly in summer, less frequent in spring and fall,
20-30 minutes, no boats Jan-March). Another option is a **water
taxi** (these may be waiting in Metochi, otherwise call Hydra's sea
taxi service at tel. 22980-53690, about €45 but confirm upfront).

Ermioni (drivers and those without cars): Ermioni (a.k.a.
Hermioni) is an actual town with some amenities, and a little
closer to Nafplio (1.5 hours). It's a 25-minute boat ride between
Ermioni and Hydra on a **Hellenic Seaways** ferry (€8, 3-4/day in
summer, fewer off-season, www.hellenicseaways.gr).

HYDRA

If you're visiting Hydra early in your trip and then continuing to the Peloponnese, a good plan is to ride the ferry from Athens to Hydra, then take the ferry from Hydra to Ermioni, where you can rent a car (try Pop's Car, www.popscar.gr, a five-minute walk from the ferry dock, ask about fee for dropping the car in Athens or at the airport; you can also ask your Hydra hotelier to help with car rental).

Without a car, you can connect Ermioni and Nafplio by taxi and bus, though this is more complicated than it should be (see "Nafplio Connections" on page 243).

Tolo, near Nafplio (day trippers only): **Pegasus Tours** operates an excursion boat from the port at Tolo, near Nafplio, but it runs only a few times a week, can be cancelled on short notice (if not enough passengers—mainly off-season), and requires an early-morning (though short) bus ride. Stopping in both Spetses and Hydra, it's a good option only for travelers without a car who can't devote an overnight to Hydra (3 boats/week July-mid-Sept, 2/week May-June and mid-Sept-Oct, some sailings March-April, €34, tel. 27520-59430, www.pegasus-cruises.gr, easiest to book through Stavropoulos Tours in central Nafplio—see page 221).

HYDRA

MYKONOS

MYKONOΣ / Μυκονοσ

At its heart, Mykonos (MEE-koh-nohs) is the very picture of the perfect Greek island town: a seafront village crouched behind a sandy harbor, thickly layered with blinding white stucco, bright blue trim, and purple bougainvillea. (Thank goodness for all that color; otherwise, this island—one of Greece's driest—would be various shades of dull brown.) On a ridge over town stretches a trademark row of five windmills, overlooking a tidy embankment so pretty they call it "Little Venice."

Mykonos' Old Town seems made for exploring. Each picture-perfect lane is slathered with a thick layer of stucco, giving the place

a marshmallow-village vibe. All that white is the perfect contrast to the bright blue sky and the vivid trim. Sometimes described as "cubist" for its irregular jostle of angular rooflines, Mykonos' townscape is a photographer's delight. Enjoy getting lost, then found again.

While Mykonos was once a sleepy, backwater fishing village, those days are a faint memory. Today's Mykonos is easily one of the most expensive, most exclusive places in Greece. Prices are stunningly high here, and the island is crammed through the summer season (especially in August).

As one of the Mediterranean's premier party destinations, the entire Old Town throbs with a cacophony of nightclub beats well into the wee hours. This is fun if you're seeking late-night activity...but otherwise, it can be miserable. If you're seeking a peaceful getaway, time your visit for shoulder season—May or late September/early October—when suitable beach weather is still likely, but the town is less crowded, less noisy (except on weekends), and less expensive. On October 1, hotels drop their prices in half. And in winter (around Nov-March), the island essentially shuts down, as many restaurants and hotels close for the season.

Whenever you visit, find ways to enjoy the traditional soul of Mykonos. If you grow tired of the fashionista tourists and the high-end boutiques, climb just a block or two in either direction from the core of town, and you'll enter truly local neighborhoods relatively untrampled by tourism. Fishermen still hang out on the benches by the harbor, wearing their traditional caps (Mykonian men are famous among Greeks for their baldness).

The island's arid but idyllic terrain, with lots of hidden coves, is a favorite backdrop for filmmakers (*Shirley Valentine, Mamma Mia!, The Bourne Identity, Before Midnight*). A string of inviting beaches lines up on the sandy, pebbly coves along the jagged south coast—each with a personality of its own, and all reachable by a cheap and easy bus ride from town.

For armchair historians, the highlight here is a 30-minute boat trip to the island of Delos—one of the Greek islands' top sites, with the remains of important ancient temples honoring the birthplace of the twin gods Apollo and Artemis. Delos was a pilgrimage site for believers who came from all over to worship this "birthplace of light." Judging by the present-day sun worshippers who scramble for the best patch of sand on Mykonos each summer, things haven't changed much.

PLANNING YOUR TIME

Mykonos, a delightful place to be on vacation, merits at least a full day and two overnights; more time lets you squeeze in more beaches.

On a short visit, begin with my self-guided Mykonos Walk to get your bearings to the town, dip into any museums that interest you, and grab an early lunch. In the afternoon, historians can side-trip to Delos (easy 30-minute boat trip each way, figure 3-4 hours round-trip), while vacationers can head to a beach. (As Mykonos's beaches are good-quality and easy to reach by bus, it's the perfect place to squeeze in some quality beach time.) Enjoy the sunset from a beach or while nursing a cocktail near the "Little Venice" zone, then have a late dinner.

Orientation to Mykonos

Mykonos' main town is called Chora (or Hora, Χώρα; roughly "village") but it's often referred to as "Mykonos town."

Mykonos town is the main point of entry for the island. The Old Town clusters around the south end of the Old Port—the har-

Mykonos Island

To Piraeus

Aegean Sea

N

MERCHIAS

AGIOS STEFANOS

NEW PORT

OLD PORT

TOURLOS

FTELIA

ANO MERA

MYKONOS TOWN

AIRPORT

KALAFATI

KAPARI

ORNOS

PLATIS GIALOS

AGRARIA

ELIA

AGIOS IOANNIS

PSAROU

SUPER PARADISE

PARAGA

PARADISE

2 Kilometers

2 Miles

To Delos

To Paros, Santorini & Crete

······ Shuttle Boat
—— Roads
R Beaches

bor area bookended by two piers. To the north is the Old Port pier and bus stop, and to the southwest is the pier for boats to Delos and the Sea Bus to the New Port, where most ferries and cruise ships arrive. Squeezed between the harbor and the main road (passing above town on the gentle hill) is the Old Town's tight maze of whitewashed lanes.

To get your bearings, look at a map and notice that three "main" roads (barely wide enough for a moped) form a U-shaped circuit facing the harbor: Kouzi Georgouli, Enoplon Dinameon, and Matogianni. While some streets have names, others don't, and in any case, locals never use them—they just know where things are. If you can't find something, ask.

You'll find travel agencies, ATMs, launderettes with drop-off service, minimarkets, pharmacies, and other helpful services scattered around the Old Town. For the highest concentration of services (and tattoo parlors), head for the area around the Fabrika bus station.

Tourist Information: Mykonos doesn't have a TI. Hoteliers, travel agents, and other friendly locals can answer basic questions. Look for town maps, or consult www.mykonos.gr, the island's official website.

Private Guide: Antonis Pothitos is an excellent local guide who enjoys introducing visitors to the hidden nooks and crannies of Mykonos. In addition to town walks and tours of the Delos archaeological site, he enjoys leading a 2.5-hour "Food on Foot" town walk, with tasting stops, and an all-day "Ambrosial Mykonos" experience, including a town walk and a drive around the island to an artisanal creamery, brewery, and vineyard, plus a beach break (4-person minimum, contact Antonis for prices, mobile 693-660-6640, www.delosguide.com, antonis@delosguide.com).

ARRIVAL IN MYKONOS

At the port and airport, hotel representatives toting signs wait to transfer guests into town. To make it easy, ask your hotel in advance about this option.

By Boat: Most travelers coming by boat arrive at the **New Port,** a mile north of the Old Town, at the far end of the bay. (This serves most ships from Piraeus and Santorini, as well as many cruise ships.) You have several options for getting to the Old Town: Easy and pleasant, the Sea Bus water taxi runs between the New Port and Mykonos town (may stop at the Old Port pier en route; €2, 1-2/hour, runs 7:00-23:00, mobile 697-883-0355). By land, you can take a taxi (€15-20 one-way), ride a public bus to the Old Port bus stop (2/hour, €1.80), or, if arriving on a cruise, pay for the cruise line's shuttle bus. In a pinch, you could do the dreary 25-minute walk along the coast into town (turn right, follow the water, and just keep going—you can see the gaggle of white houses across the bay).

A few smaller, passenger-only ferries from other islands dock at the **Old Port Pier**—just a five-minute walk from the Old Town harborfront. And if your cruise ship is tendered, you'll disembark at the pier at the opposite end of the harbor (where boats to Delos come and go). Just walk down the pier and you're at the harbor (there's a public WC on the right, along the water).

By Plane: Mykonos is well connected by air to Athens, as well as to many other European cities (code: JMK, tel. 22890-22327). The small airport sits just two miles outside town, easily connected by a short but pricey taxi ride (€15-20). There are also infrequent public buses—worthwhile only if a bus happens to be there when you arrive (see www.mykonosbus.com). If flying out from the airport, note that there are separate check-in terminals for international departures (on the right) and domestic flights (on the left); both use the same arrivals area.

GETTING AROUND MYKONOS

Mykonos is a fun and easy island to explore. For bus station/stops and taxi stand locations, see the Mykonos Town map.

By Bus: Mykonos' bus network easily connects travelers to the island's many fine beaches (and it's much cheaper than going by taxi). And because this is a party island, buses run late into the night in peak season. Schedules are posted on chalkboards at stops and in most hotel reception areas; tickets cost around €2—buy from the driver, or (in Mykonos town) at the ticket kiosk at the Fabrika bus station.

In town, the **Fabrika bus station** (serving beaches on the south side of the island) is a 10-minute walk up from the harbor, just under the main ring road. The **Old Port stop** (serving the eastern half of the island) is at the northeast edge of the Old Town, along the pier below the Archaeological Museum (look for the clearly marked ramp along the beach near the old harbor).

By Taxi: Taxis are extremely expensive (with fixed rather than metered prices), and there are generally not enough to accommodate demand. There are no cars allowed in Mykonos town, so you'll wait for a taxi at one of two places: the stand behind the large building labeled *Remezzo* (behind the Archaeological Museum at the north end of town); or at the Fabrika bus stop (see above).

By Motorized Scooter or All-Terrain Vehicle (ATV): On Greek islands, tourists are notorious for renting a scooter or an ATV, overestimating their abilities to control a machine they've never driven before, and denting someone's fender or leaving a strip of knee or elbow skin on the pavement...or worse. That said, and keeping in mind the risks inherent in renting wheels here, it can be an affordable, efficient, and memorably fun way to connect distant beaches. If I were renting a scooter or an ATV on a Greek isle, I'd do it on Mykonos—where the roads are not too heavily trafficked (you'll pass more fellow scooters and ATVs than cars), and an appealing variety of idyllic beaches are a short ride away. Travel agencies all over town rent both types of wheels for reasonable all-day rates (€10-25/day for a scooter or an ATV, some places may charge €7-10/day extra for insurance, rates depend on time of year). Two people can ride one machine, and both should ask for helmets.

Once on the road, be especially careful on turns, where steering becomes more difficult. On a slow-moving ATV, figure 15-20 minutes from Mykonos town to most of the beaches I list (Super Paradise is the farthest). Find rental details under "Getting to the Beaches," later.

By Car: You can rent a car for as little as €35 per day; look for car-rental signs at several agencies around town—especially near the Fabrika bus station—and negotiate a good bargain if you're here outside peak season. The island is less satisfying to explore by car than Santorini—it's basically similar beaches and remote villages.

MYKONOS

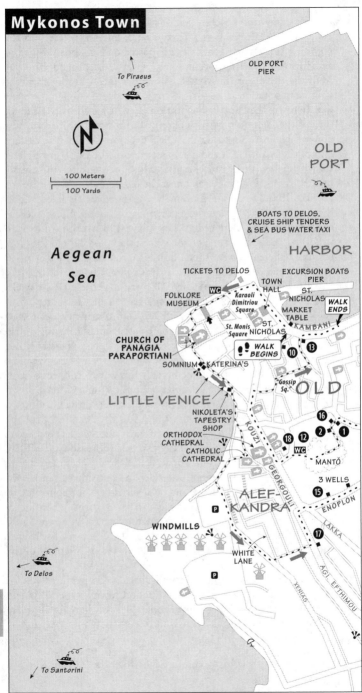

Mykonos Town

To Piraeus

OLD PORT PIER

OLD PORT

100 Meters
100 Yards

Aegean
Sea

BOATS TO DELOS,
CRUISE SHIP TENDERS
& SEA BUS WATER TAXI

HARBOR

TICKETS TO DELOS

EXCURSION BOATS
PIER

TOWN
HALL

ST.
NICHOLAS

WALK
ENDS

FOLKLORE
MUSEUM

WC

Karaoli
Dimitriou
Square

MARKET
TABLE

St. Monis
Square

ST.
NICHOLAS

KAMBANI

CHURCH OF
PANAGIA
PARAPORTIANI

WALK
BEGINS

10

13

SOMNIUM   KATERINA'S

Gossip
Sq.

OLD

LITTLE VENICE

NIKOLETA'S
TAPESTRY
SHOP

16

ORTHODOX
CATHEDRAL

18

12

2

1

CATHOLIC
CATHEDRAL

WC

MANTO

3 WELLS

ALEF-
KANDRA

15

ENOPLON

LAKKA

P

WINDMILLS

17

WHITE LANE

P

To Delos

XENIAS

AGI. EFTHIMOU

To Santorini

MYKONOS

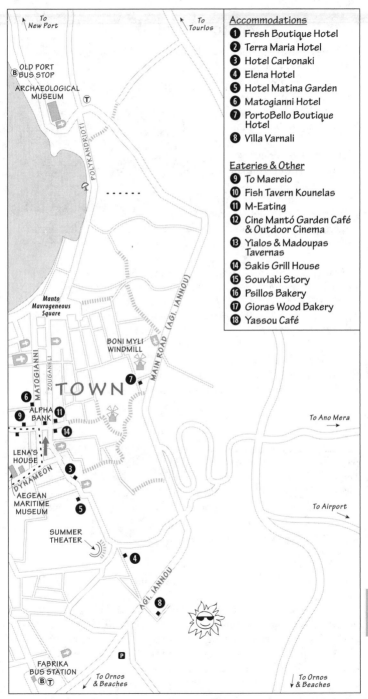

Accommodations

1 Fresh Boutique Hotel
2 Terra Maria Hotel
3 Hotel Carbonaki
4 Elena Hotel
5 Hotel Matina Garden
6 Matogianni Hotel
7 PortoBello Boutique Hotel
8 Villa Varnali

Eateries & Other

9 To Maereio
10 Fish Tavern Kounelas
11 M-Eating
12 Cine Mantó Garden Café & Outdoor Cinema
13 Yialos & Madoupas Tavernas
14 Sakis Grill House
15 Souvlaki Story
16 Psillos Bakery
17 Gioras Wood Bakery
18 Yassou Café

To New Port
To Tourlos
OLD PORT BUS STOP
ARCHAEOLOGICAL MUSEUM
POLYKANDRIOTI
Manto Mavrogeneous Square
BONI MYLI WINDMILL
MAIN ROAD (AGI. IANNOU)
TOWN
MATOGIANNI
ZOUGANELI
ALPHA BANK
LENA'S HOUSE
DYNAMEON
AEGEAN MARITIME MUSEUM
SUMMER THEATER
AGI. IANNOU
To Ano Mera
To Airport
FABRIKA BUS STATION
To Ornos & Beaches
To Ornos & Beaches

MYKONOS

Mykonos Walk

The core of town is literally a maze, designed by Mykonians centuries ago to discourage would-be invaders from finding their way.

That tactic also works on today's tourists. But I can think of few places where getting lost is so enjoyable.

This self-guided walk is designed to orient you to Mykonos' main landmarks in about 1.5 hours. This town is notoriously difficult to navigate: Even if you follow my directions to a T and use my map, be prepared to get lost from time to time. But with this walk under your belt, the town becomes more manageable.

• *The walk begins at the harbor, in the heart of Mykonos. If you're arriving on a cruise ship tender, you'll land right here; if you're coming from elsewhere on the island, you can't miss this sandy centerpiece of town. Position yourself near the marble fish-washing table/market stalls, right along the harbor, near the blue-domed church at the pier.*

Old Town Harbor

Mykonians describe this delightful swath of land as their "downtown." Unlike many other Greek island towns—which have built

up bulky concrete embankments—Mykonos has kept its traditional waterfront, where the cobbles taper into a sandy beach, preserving the Mykonians' connection to the Aegean. Glancing offshore, you'll see humble fishing boats bobbing in the foreground, with 2,000-passenger cruise ships looming in the distance.

A row of cafés and restaurants lines the harborfront, including some near you: Madoupas, near the red-domed church, and Yialos (Γυαλός). Mykonians appreciate cafés like these that stay open through the winter to cater to natives (since most businesses close up shop after cruise season ends). You're most likely to catch a few Mykonians (or in-the-know expats) hanging out here in the morning. Pull up a rustic table, nurse an iced coffee, and watch the tide of tourists wash over village life. At the marble table by the beach, fisherfolk sort and clean their catch each morning (while stray cats gather below). Nearby, old-timers and kids alike toss fishing lines into the water.

You may even see one of the resident **pelicans**—Petros, Nikolas, or Irini. Ever since a local fisherman found an ailing pelican and nursed it back to health half a century ago, these odd birds have been the town's mascots. They hang out at the harbor, or you may see them elsewhere in town, as well—always surrounded by an entourage of paparazzi tourists.

At the far end of this sandy harbor (we'll go there later) is the piazza known as **Manto Square**. This is marked by a bust of Manto Mavrogenous (1796-1848), a heroine of the Greek War of Independence. A wealthy aristocrat of Mykonian heritage, she spent her fortune supplying Greek forces in a battle against their Ottoman rulers. Mavrogenous—who, despite her contributions, was denied a Greek pension—ended her life destitute on the island of Paros, never regretting the sacrifices she made for Greece's freedom. Today locals still celebrate her brave spirit.

• *Turn with the water on your right, and walk about 50 yards to the little, blue-domed...*

Church of St. Nicholas (Agios Nikolakis)

This is one of an estimated 90 small churches that dot the Old Town of Mykonos (with hundreds more scattered all over the island).

Why so many? First, while these belong to the Greek Orthodox Church, each one was built by, and is still maintained by, a private local family—usually to honor a namesake saint. Having a chapel is a matter of familial pride. On that saint's feast day, the family invites a priest to preside over a service here, followed by a big party to which the entire community is invited. (On the day of a popular saint, many families host dueling parties.) Chapels were often built to give thanks for the safe return of a relative—and in this seafaring town, this was often necessary.

This harborfront location—which was originally on its own little island, connected by a bridge—makes sense for St. Nicholas, the patron saint of sailors and fishermen. In fact, St. Nicholas is so important that there are two churches dedicated to him in this same area: This one is officially "St. Nicholas of the Chain"—named for the chain that was once pulled across the mouth of the harbor from here in times of enemy threat. And the red-domed church just around the harbor is "St. Nicholas of the Wind," since it faces into the prevailing northerly winds.

Step inside this votive chapel to see a container of lit candles. Many local fishermen still light a candle here each morning before heading out to sea. Originally, each chapel also served as a family mausoleum, where departed relatives were interred. This unhygienic practice ended in the 18th century, when Mykonos established a cemetery just outside town. But a loophole allows locals to dig up a loved ones' remains five years after burial, and reinter them in the family chapel. Notice the plaques on the walls and floor marking the final resting places of several Mykonians. The one on the left wall just inside the door is significant: It marks the remains of Captain Petros I. Drakopolos, who—the plaque explains—was executed by Germans during the Nazi occupation in September 1944. (This local hero is the namesake of the first pelican mascot of Mykonos.)

• *Head back outside.*

Town Hall and Delos Pier

The big, boxy building facing St. Nicholas is the **Town Hall** (labeled in Greek and English), with the only red terra-cotta roof on the island. This was built in 1780, during a brief period of Russian occupation, when Czarina Catherine the Great sent a governor to rule over the island. (St. Nicholas was built at the same time.) The building's few marble pillars are most likely scavenged from the ancient ruins on the nearby  isle of Delos, as is the well-worn marble bench under its porch. In general, anytime you see irregular bits and pieces of marble incorporated into Mykonos buildings (thresholds, window sills, and so on)—they probably came from Delos.

Now walk with the harbor on your right. Soon you'll spot the ticket kiosk for boat trips to the ancient site at Delos (more on that in a moment). Just behind that is the town dumpster and trash compactor—convenient for shipping garbage to the mainland. And just after that you'll see some handy pay WCs.

Continue along the deserted-feeling embankment. Straight ahead, on the horizon, is the isle of **Delos**—said to be the birthplace of the god Apollo and home of one of the ancient world's most important sites. In antiquity, this was a busy commercial port and financial center, and today it contains some fascinating ruins. Nearby, you will likely also see a cruise ship, which is fitting. In the early days of cruising—the 1920s—ships came to this area for the ruins at uninhabited Delos, and then made a pit stop on Mykonos—which slowly became a tourist destination in its own right. The town's popularity boomed in the 1950s, when celebrities discovered its allure; and again in the 1980s, when it became a mecca for gay tourists; and again in the early 2000s, with the most recent cruise-ship surge. Today Mykonos is arguably Greece's most popular island.

• *Reaching the end of the embankment, hook left and walk uphill to the top of the little bluff. You are in the heart of the...*

Old Venetian Quarter

This strategic spit of land—with visibility over the water in three directions—has always been an important point in Mykonos (the site of its acropolis in ancient times). Like many other Greek islands, Mykonos fell under Venetian rule after the Fourth Crusade (early 13th century). The Venetians fortified this point, enclosing the entire peninsula with a stout fortress that contained some 4,000 people. While that fortress is long gone, soon we'll walk through tight lanes that make it easy to imagine those crowded conditions.

But first, turn your attention to the giant melting-marshmallow building on your right—the Church of Panagia Paraportiani.

This striking architectural oddity is actually a hodgepodge of five small chapels draped together in a thick layer of whitewashed stucco. The four chapels at the base are interconnected; the chapel on top is separate and gives its name to the entire complex: "Panagia" refers to St. Mary—who, according to Byzantine tradition, was often the guardian at the entrance to a town—and "Paraportiani" marks the secondary *(para)* gate *(port)* in the Venetian fortress complex. While the interior is usually closed, you may occasionally find one of the chapels open, the small space filled with the rich aroma of incense.

Now head down the tight lane just behind the church, marked with the sign for *Kastro's Bar-Restaurant*. The houses on the right side of this street belonged to local sea captains. Here in the fickle Aegean, seafarers might be part-time merchants and traders, and part-time pirates, depending on the tenor of the times. These houses were actually the fortified outer seawall of the Venetian fortress.

A few doors down on the right, peek into the **Somnium shop,** which sells upscale medieval kitsch and offers a peek at an authentic old house interior. Notice the walls are made of heavy local granite and mica stone, with wooden beams mixed in. This wood—imported from the mainland to this nearly treeless island—gave some flex to buildings, and therefore made them earthquake-resistant. The window at the far (seaward) end was added later; originally this was a solid chunk of the city wall, and the only opening was a small passage at the base that allowed the captain to come and go more easily.

The house next to Somnium, **Katerina's,** is named for the first female sea captain from Mykonos, Katerinas Xidaki (you can see old photos of her just inside the door...and may see her in the flesh hanging out inside).

Continue downhill on this narrow lane, keeping right at the fork. You'll pass a row of shops, bars, and restaurants. Peek through the ones on the right to see the windows overlooking the water.

When you reach the busy little intersection, turn right toward the water. A few steps down this lane, on the right, drop into **Nikoleta's weaving shop.** You'll likely be greeted by Nikoleta herself, and there in the back of her shop is her *very* old-fashioned loom—similar to one described by Homer—which she still uses to create handwoven knitwear. Nikoleta enjoys showing off tattered old clippings about her work, but she laments that her competitors selling made-in-China wares just up the street can easily undersell her to tourists. She can no longer buy actual Greek wool (the last textile mills have closed), so she uses imported yarn instead. But she has trained her daughter to carry on the family tradition and continues to create beautifully crafted one-of-a-kind hats, blankets, and scarves. Nikoleta finds she spends most of her time posing for photographs, and is understandably cranky when this distracts her from her work (at which point she flashes a *1 photo = 1€* sign).

Continue past Nikoleta's shop, turn left, and walk along the bar tables that perch just above the seawall. At the end of this row, look back along the waterline for a wonderful view of the area called Little Venice (Mikri Venetia). You'll see how the formerly fortified seawall has opened up with windows and brightly painted wooden balconies. The name is inspired both by the builders of that original wall, and to conjure compari-

sons with the many fine palazzos that rise up from Venice's Grand Canal. Looking the other way, you'll enjoy fine views of the town's trademark windmills (we're heading up there soon). This scenic spot is a favorite vantage for enjoying the sunset over a pricey cocktail; pick a spot to reserve for tonight.

• *Turn with your back to the water and walk up past the remaining few café tables, then turn right down the little lane. Follow this until you pop out at a tiny square with a big bell tower.*

Alefkandra Neighborhood

The church on your left, with the square bell tower, is Mykonos' **Greek Orthodox cathedral** (or "metropolitan" church). And

straight ahead of you is the side of the local **Catholic cathedral.** Jog to the right, around to the front door of the Catholic church (facing the water). While the Venetians left their mark with their fortress, their cultural legacy is minimal. This small chapel was built by the only Catholic family on Myko-

nos—and so, as the only Catholic church, it's the default cathedral. Services are posted to the right of the door; a priest who serves the surrounding islands (especially Tinos, with a much larger Catholic population) comes here periodically to worship. Step inside to see the architectural mix of Catholic (with depictions of the Virgin Mary) and Orthodox (the candle reservoir).

Continue past the Catholic church, and look for the little dry channel leading to the sea. Once a gushing stream, this gave the Alefkandra neighborhood its name: *lefkos* means "whiten," and this stream was where locals would launder—or whiten—their textiles. Follow this channel to the waterfront, where again you enjoy views to Little Venice (right) and the windmills (left).

• *Now turn left and climb up to those windmills. You can either use the ramp (step over the parking barrier) or the grand, white staircase— where celebrities of the 1950s and 1960s famously posed, with the iconic windmills in the background, helping to put Mykonos on the map.*

Windmills

Mykonos is infamously windy, and Mykonians have special names for the different winds that blow through: "the bell ringer," "the chair thrower," and "the unseater of horsemen." Today, locals are

most concerned when the wind is bad enough to prevent cruise ships from docking or the Delos excursion boats from running.

This ridge—called **Kato Myloi**—is perfectly positioned to catch both northerly and southerly winds—which, combined, blow nine days out of ten. You'll see five intact windmills, plus the bases of two others. As in many Greek island towns, Mykonos' old-fashioned windmills harnessed this natural power in order to grind grain to supply its ships. Notice how the windmills are strategically located over the water, making it easy to load up ships. Traditionally, the windmills were owned not by individuals, but by little committees made up of five different factions: priests, merchants, millers, bankers, and carpenters. While there's nothing to see inside these buildings, they make for a fine photo op and offer great views over town. If you'd like to enter a windmill, you'll need to head to the opposite (east) end of the Old Town, where the Boni Myli windmill is open to visitors each evening (free but donations appreciated, June-Sept Mon-Sat 17:30-20:30, closed Sun and Oct-May, tel. 22890-22591).

• *When you're done exploring the windmills, continue up the path through the middle of the adjacent parking lot (with the mills on your right). After the base of the final windmill—now an Airbnb rental—turn left down the narrow, unmarked street. Let's explore...*

Backstreets Below the Windmills

Walk downhill on this sleepy lane, through a rare corner of Mykonos that's still predominantly residential—locals really live here (as you can tell from the laundry drying). The first side street on the left is particularly evocative, offering a rare glimpse of Mykonos before it was glitzy.

The maze of meandering, skinny lanes helped buffer the howling winds...and discouraged pirates and invaders. As you explore here, tune into the details of Mykonos' unique architecture: Houses and public space (sidewalks and curbs) all blend together, with little concern about who owns what. Everything is painted a blinding white, including the seams between the paving stones. Today this is decorative, but originally it was practical: By painting the lanes with lime, a natural disinfectant, locals offset the unhygienic living conditions (people living on top of each other, and emptying their chamber pots in the streets). And the rooftops were painted with lime, too—they collected precious rainwater, which was carried

through a network of gutters to cisterns down below. (Fresh water is hard to come by on an arid island.) Houses generally had the kitchen and living room on the main floor, a couple of bedrooms upstairs, and a tiny toilet under the stairs (exploring town, look for a few surviving under-the-stairs doors today—now mostly used for storage). Today those staircases and trim are painted bright, cheery colors, giving Mykonos its distinctive look.

Continue down the lane until you reach a T-intersection. Across the street and a bit to the right is **Gioras Wood Bakery,** an old-fashioned cellar bakery selling sweet and savory pastries. Until recently, they really did use a wood oven and mainly baked breads for locals, as it's been done for some 500 years; today they focus on tourist-friendly pastries, but maintain their charming and historic interior.

• *From the bakery, head downhill on the lane, past several shops. At the intersection, head right along one of the town's most bustling streets, Enoplon Dinameon.*

Enoplon Dinameon and Matogianni Streets

Strolling the lane called Enoplon Dinameon, you'll pass a school on the right. Then (just after Louis Vuitton on the left) look for

three old wells. These were the town's main source of drinking water until the arrival of modern plumbing in the 1950s—and, as such, this was the place to see and be seen, to gossip, and to court. It was said that if a visitor was offered water from the three wells, they were really respected by a Mykonian.

Continue past the wells, between two churches. On the left you'll see the **Maritime Museum,** with a well-presented exhibit about Mykonos' seafaring history, and **Lena's House,** an open-only-in-the-evening glimpse into a traditional old home (both described under "Sights in Mykonos").

Keep going on Enoplon Dinameon as the colors—and crowds—crescendo, and you pass under a brilliant purple bougainvillea. (Good luck dodging all the impromptu photo shoots.) After dark, the clientele from the bars and cafés in this area all merge into one big, open-air cocktail party under purple petals.

Soon you'll come to the wide cross street called

Matogianni, nicknamed the "Catwalk of Mykonos" for its lineup of top-end boutiques. Turn left here and appreciate the traditional architecture-meets-modern couture vibe.

After just one block, you'll run into **Alpha Bank;** from here, the streets on either side of the bank lead you straight down to the harbor.

• *But if you're up for more exploring, stay with me a few more minutes for a look at some back lanes that many visitors miss.*

Backstreets to the Harbor

Stick with me, now: At Alpha Bank, turn left, passing the recommended To Maereio restaurant (on your right). The street curves a bit; then, turn left immediately past Fresh Boutique Hotel. On this little lane, the red-doored house on the right is the recommended Psillos bakery, where locals buy sweet and savory pies. Continuing past the bakery, bear left with the street at Terra Maria Hotel, and watch on your right for the low-profile door to **Mantó Garden Café/Cine Mantó.** Step inside to a peaceful, verdant world unto itself—called the "public garden"—sheltered from the wind, filled with giant cactus and pomegranate trees, and cooled by a goldfish pond. Locals appreciate its calm, natural atmosphere, public WCs, and free Wi-Fi. Consider a drink or light meal at the café, then walk to the far end of the garden, where you'll find the screen and chairs for the delightful open-air movie theater. Exit the far end of the complex, near the theater. (If this part is closed for some reason, backtrack past the bakery, then make four successive lefts. I'll meet you there.)

Outside the garden gate, enjoy the little square with the big tree; the nearby **Yassou café** is a good spot to try piping-hot, fresh *loukoumades* (Greek doughnut holes—choose cinnamon and honey or Nutella).

Facing Yassou café, turn left, then head right on the busy lane just past the outdoor tables for Kostas. You'll pass the back end of the Greek Orthodox cathedral we saw earlier. Continue straight through this mazelike area, bearing right where the street widens. Head a couple of short blocks down this shop-lined lane. At the Happiness shop, bear right at the fork, then take the next right, up the narrow alley. Suddenly  you find yourself alone with Mykonos, at a little square with five churches and three trees. Known locally as **"Gossip Square"** (for the way the churches seem to be gathering to swap local news), this forgotten slice of old Mykonos is entirely surrounded by today's trendy bustle.

Exit this square to the left of the three red-doored churches. From here, I'll let you find your own way down to the harbor—because you couldn't possibly follow my directions anyway. The general idea is to bear right, then listen for the surf, for the horns of the ships, or for the howl of the northerly wind. (*KOUNELAS* signs, to the recommended fish tavern just off the harbor, are helpful.) Enjoy getting lost in the maze, likely having some lanes to yourself.

• *You'll wind up more or less where we started, at the harbor. Your walk is finished, and you've seen a good slice of Mykonos. Circle back to any museums you'd like to see, or consider heading around the right side of the harbor for a look at the Archaeological Museum. Or, if you have time and the seas are calm, take a boat out to Delos (see later in this chapter for details).*

Sights in Mykonos

MUSEUMS
Mykonos Archaeological Museum

This small museum, just uphill from the Old Port, displays artifacts found on the nearby island of Rheneia, which the Athenians re-

served as a burial isle for Delos in order to keep the sacred isle pure (see sidebar on page 426). With limited English labels and almost no descriptions, most of what's here—vases, jewelry, and statue fragments—is pretty dull. One item, however, makes a visit worth considering: a large vase (in room just beyond entry, dead center along the back wall) clearly showing the Trojan Horse filled with Greek soldiers sporting gleeful archaic smiles, and cartoon-like panels telling the story of the massacre that followed when they jumped out. Dating from roughly 670 B.C., it's the oldest depiction of the Trojan Horse ever found. Unlike the museum's other pieces, it wasn't excavated from the Rheneia graves, but found right here on Mykonos, discovered in 1961 by a (surely very surprised) farmer who'd set out to dig a well. Out back you'll find a courtyard ringed with intricately carved stone grave markers.

Cost and Hours: €4; April-Oct Mon 15:00-22:00, Tue and Thu-Sun 9:00-22:00, Wed until 16:00; Nov-March shorter hours and closed Mon; tel. 22890-22325.

Aegean Maritime Museum

This tight but endearing collection traces the story of the local mercantile shipping industry. A desert isle of history in a sea of wealthy tourism, this little place takes its subject very seriously. In its three rooms you'll find amphora jugs, model ships, portraits of great sailors, and more. The tranquil garden in back displays the actual, original lighthouse from the island's Cape Armenistis, as well as replicas of ancient sailors' gravestones. The good English descriptions offer a fine history lesson for those willing to read them.

Cost and Hours: €4, April-Oct daily 10:30-13:00 & 18:30-21:00, closed Nov-March, Enoplon Dinameon 10, tel. 22890-22700.

Lena's House

This little museum (affiliated with the Mykonos Folklore Museum) shows part of a typical middle-class Mykonian house dating from the late 19th century, complete with original furnishings and artwork.

Cost and Hours: Free, donations appreciated; April-Sept Mon-Sat 18:30-21:30, Sun 19:00-21:00; closed Oct-March; Enoplon Dinameon, tel. 22890-22390.

Mykonos Folklore Museum

Housed in a typically Cycladic former sea captain's residence just up the bluff from the harbor, this museum is deceptively sprawling. Exploring its interior, you'll peruse a random mix of traditional folk items from around the island, as well as a typical kitchen and bedroom. In the basement are fragments of the Venetian castle that one stood here, discovered only in the 1970s.

Cost and Hours: Free but donations appreciated, April-Sept daily 10:30-14:00 & 17:30-20:30, closed Oct-March, tel. 22890-22591.

BEACHES

Mykonos' beaches rival those of any Greek island. Each beach seems to specialize in a different niche: family-friendly or party; straight, gay, or mixed; nude or clothed; and so on. (Remember, even "family-friendly" beaches can have topless sunbathers.) Get local advice to find the one that suits your beach-bum preferences, or choose from the options below.

All of these beaches have beach bars or restaurants that rent comfortable lounge chairs with umbrellas out on the sand (around €15-30 for two chairs that share an umbrella; can be much more at exclusive beaches). Just take a seat—someone will come by to collect money. The bars usually sell cocktails and typical Greek-island meals. You can often order from your beach chair, but heading inside can be a welcome escape from the sun. Be warned that in peak season (July and especially Aug), all beaches are very crowded, and it can be difficult to find an available seat.

Getting to the Beaches: The beaches I've recommended are all on the south coast of the island, and listed here roughly in order, from west to east, as you would approach them from Mykonos town. All are within a 10- to 20-minute drive, ATV/scooter outing, or bus ride from town.

Throughout the season, **buses** run to major beaches twice hourly during the day, usually leaving from the Fabrika stop in town at :00 and :30 past each hour; most rides cost around €2. Confirm the schedule at the little ticket kiosk, then find the bus marked with your destination and hop on. As buses can be crowded at prime times, it can be smart to line up early to ensure getting a seat.

A **taxi** to the beach from town will run €15-20; some of the farther beaches can go up to €25. There are rarely taxis standing by at beaches; when you're ready to leave, call for one (tel. 22890-22400) or ask a taverna to call for you (if you've paid for chair rental or drinks, they're generally happy to do this). You may be charged a few extra euros for calling rather than hailing a taxi.

To explore a variety of beaches in one day, you can also connect some of the major beaches—Platis Gialos, Paraga, Paradise, Super Paradise, Agrari, and Elia—by regular **shuttle boat** (€10 round-trip for one hop, or €20 for an all-day hop-on, hop-off ticket). Note that these run between the beaches, but not from Mykonos town.

▲Agios Ioannis

Pronounced AH-yohs yoh-AH-nees, this appealingly remote patch of pebbly sand, tucked behind a mountain ridge, has the feeling of being on a castaway isle. You'll enjoy views across to the important isle of Delos. From Mykonos town, go to Ornos, then head toward Kapari; on your way down the hill, turn off on the left at the low-profile beach signs (one directs you to ΠΥΛΗ, one of the

restaurants on the beach); this is also where buses stop, a short but steep hike above the beach. You'll drop down this road to an idyllic Robinson Crusoe spot. The two main restaurants here are the trendy, pretentious Hippy Fish (where the film *Shirley Valentine* was filmed), and the nice but more accessible Pili (ΠΥΛΗ); both rent chairs and have full food and drink menus.

For the even more secluded **Kapari** beach, continue down the road past the Agios Ioannis turnoff, then swing right at the white church.

Ornos

This easy-to-get-to, family-friendly beach is right in the middle of the sizeable town of Ornos. It's one of the more functional beaches of those I list (and has better lounge-chair values). Even though it's in a built-up area, the whole place has an unpretentious charm.

Psarou and Platis Gialos

These two beaches are along the next cove east of Ornos. The main landmark here is **Platis Gialos,** a crowded, densely developed

stretch of beach just below the main bus stop. You'll find a row of beach hotels, plenty of beach-chair rentals, and an array of other water activities—but it can feel a little claustrophobic (the far end from the bus stop/parking is less jammed).

I prefer to walk 10 minutes to the less developed **Psarou** (psah-ROO)—head back up the way the bus came, and watch on your left (through a little parking lot) for a fine trail that leads above the waterline down to an idyllic cove. (You can also get off the bus a stop early, but from there it's a steep hike down—along rocky, uneven steps—to the beach.) Psarou, one of the most sheltered beaches on the island, is a broad, sandy stretch with luxury yachts moored just offshore. It has an exclusive reputation, thanks to the big, fancy Mykonos Blu beach hotel and the top-end Nammos restaurant (which charges an exorbitant fee for its chair rentals). But right in the middle is the more affordable Cavo Psarou, a humbler beach bar with chair rentals priced within reach of mere mortals. This beach is relatively uncrowded, and the sand is fine—making it my favorite place for a day at the beach.

Paradise and Super Paradise

Mykonos' famous "meat-market" party beaches are a magnet for young people in the Aegean, and more of a destination than the other beaches listed here. While a bit too lively for my typical reader, they're a little calmer in the shoulder season.

Located at the southern tip of the island, **Paradise** (a.k.a. Kalamopodi) is presided over by hotels that run party-oriented bars for young beachgoers—perfect if you want to dance in the sand all night with like-minded backpackers from around the world. By day, it's less crowded and more accessible, but still comes with thumping music. As you approach, the last stretch is through thick, high grasses, giving the place an air of secrecy; then you'll pass long rows of lockers before popping out at the party.

The next cove over hosts **Super Paradise** (Plintri) beach, which has eclipsed the original as the premier party beach on the island. Super Paradise tries to be a bit more elegant than plain old Paradise—rather than grungy backpackers, it skews slightly older, with posh thirtysomethings.

Nightlife in Mykonos

Covering the fast-changing lineup of trendy clubs is beyond the scope of this book. But here is a pair of enjoyable evening activities.

Cocktails at Sunset: The Little Venice embankment is lined with cocktail bars and cafés, crowded every night with throngs of visitors enjoying the island's best spot to watch the sunset—one of the highlights of visiting Mykonos. Plan on cocktails in the €15-20 range, with wine or beer around €10. While it's fun to window-shop your options here before settling in at your pick, reputable choices include **Scarpa, Galleraki,** and **Caprice.**

Open-Air Cinema: In summer, locals and vacationers sit back and enjoy the movies under the palm trees at **Cine Mantó,** in a lovely public garden smack in the middle of town (films shown in original language—usually English, June-Sept only, usually two showings a night—check signs around town for times, tel. 22890-26165, www.cinemanto.gr). You can combine this with a dinner from the adjoining café/grill for an affordable-for-Mykonos €16 (café open all day long; see under "Eating in Mykonos").

Sleeping in Mykonos

Mykonos is an extremely expensive place to overnight—especially from mid-June to mid-September, and peaking in mid-July through August. During these premium times, even "budget" hotels dramatically increase their rates...which means you should lower your value-for-money expectations. If you can come outside this busy period, you can save more than half; it's worth comparison-shopping in shoulder season to find the best deal. If you do come in peak season, book as far ahead as possible—most of the smaller hotels get filled up with repeat customers.

In this party town, nighttime noise—dance clubs, people ca-

MYKONOS

rousing in the streets, and so on—is epidemic; plan to wear earplugs, and if you're a light sleeper, try requesting a hotel's quietest room. I've tried to recommend places on streets that are less raucous than the norm, but they're also very central, so no promises.

IN THE OLD TOWN

$$$$ Fresh Boutique Hotel is buried deep in the heart of Mykonos. Its 10 rooms, some with balconies, are thoroughly modern. While it has hardly any public spaces, its sleek garden restaurant (which can be noisy) serves as an ersatz lounge. With dramatic price drops outside peak season, this can be a particularly good value in slow times (breakfast extra, closed Dec-Feb, N. Kalogera 31, tel. 22890-24670, www.hotelfreshmykonos.com, info@hotelfreshmykonos.com).

$$$$ Terra Maria, just around the corner from Fresh, feels even more upscale, with 18 rooms and a rare elevator. It's next to the appealing Mantó café and outdoor cinema (breakfast extra, N. Kalogera 18, tel. 22890-24212, www.terramariahotel.com, mykonos@terramariahotel.com).

$$$$ Hotel Carbonaki, loosely run by the welcoming Rousounelos family, rents 21 fine but faded rooms around an oasis courtyard with a Jacuzzi. It's conveniently located a few steps above the busiest downtown streets (breakfast extra, closed Nov-Feb, Panachrantou 23, tel. 22890-24124, www.carbonaki.gr, info@carbonaki.gr, Theodore).

$$$$ Elena Hotel, even higher up than Carbonaki (and therefore a bit more peaceful), has 30 modern rooms, helpful staff, and a pleasant veranda lounge/breakfast area with a bit of a sea view (Rochari street, tel. 22890-23457, www.elenamykonos.gr, info@elenamykonos.gr).

$$$$ Hotel Matina Garden is charming. Humble but nicely maintained, it's been family-run since 1958 (Julia is the third generation), with rooms surrounding a tranquil garden near the top end of town. Their 12 "hotel" rooms are priced similarly to other midrange hotels in town, but they also have seven cheaper "pension" rooms with shared bathrooms (Fournakia 3, tel. 22890-22387, www.hotelmatina-mykonos.com, hotelmatina@marinet.gr).

$$$ Matogianni Hotel, with 25 rooms facing a garden in the heart of town, keeps its prices reasonable while offering a sense of contemporary style unusual for this price range. It has an on-site café and a long, pleasant front porch filled with wicker chairs (breakfast extra, closed Dec-Feb, Matogianni street, tel. 22890-22217, www.matogianni.gr, info@matogianni.gr, helpful Nancy).

HIGHER UP

These places get you up above the rooftops of Mykonos. This helps cut down on party noise—but, as they're closer to the main road around town, can come with some traffic noise.

$$$$ PortoBello Boutique Hotel is the place for well-heeled mountain goats. Perched high above town near the windmill museum (a steep 5-minute walk down, or 10-minute walk up), it has 17 rooms—some with spectacular views for higher rates—plus a swimming pool and a popular sunset-view bar. It feels modern, fresh, and tidy (tel. 22890-23240, www.portobello-hotel.gr, info@portobello-hotel.gr).

$$$$ Villa Varnali has seven small but modern rooms and a pool with a view just above the main road at the top of town—a few steps above some of my other recommendations (mobile 694-486-8172, villavarnali@gmail.com, Andreas).

Eating in Mykonos

The twisting streets of the Old Town are lined with tourist-oriented restaurants. Don't look for good value here—Mykonos is ex-

pensive. Simply choose the spot with the menu and ambience that appeal to you: The harborfront has the workaday action, while the places in Little Venice are more romantic—especially at sunset. A few steps inland, tucked in the town's winding back lanes, are countless charming restaurants filling hidden gardens under trellises of bougainvillea, some with tables out on a busy pedestrian lane. Take mental notes as you explore by day, then come back to the place that most appeals.

PRICEY DINNER RESTAURANTS

These places are open only for dinner.

$$$$ At **To Maereio** (Τό Μαερειό), in-the-know diners choose from a small but reasonably priced, inventive menu that includes some Mykonian specialties and plenty of meat options. The seating is almost entirely indoors. Out front you'll often see a long line of hopeful diners—arrive early, or be prepared to wait (daily from 19:00, Kalogera 16, tel. 22890-28825).

$$$$ Fish Tavern Kounelas, buried a few winding streets off the harbor, feels friendly and unpretentious. They offer a warm welcome, tight and atmospheric outdoor seating, a nondescript interior, and a typical taverna menu focusing on fish and seafood. Notice the little grill right out on the tiny alley where they prepare your fish (daily from 18:30, near St. Monis Square—look for blue-and-white *KOUNELAS* signs, tel. 22890-28220).

$$$$ M-Eating serves up high-end, creatively presented, modern Mediterranean cuisine with a homegrown influence. Most diners vie for their outdoor covered terrace seating; you might have better luck snagging one of the few small tables inside. Among Mykonos' posh eateries, this one distinguishes itself by delivering quality food and polished service. As it's popular, book ahead (daily from 19:00, 10 Kalogera, tel. 22890-78550, www.m-eating.gr).

MIDRANGE LOCAL OPTIONS

While these centrally located places are welcoming to tourists, they're popular with value-seeking locals and expats, too.

$$$ Cine Mantó Garden Café, filling a beautiful oasis-garden in the heart of Mykonos, is best known as an outdoor movie venue (see "Nightlife in Mykonos," earlier). But the café here—with outdoor tables under palm trees—is open all day long, and it's an ideal respite from the busy town for a drink or light meal (daily 9:00-24:00, tel. 22890-26165, www.cinemanto.gr).

Lowbrow Tavernas on the Harbor: Mykonos' harborfront has a cluster of simple tavernas that draw locals with relatively good prices and enjoyable water views (provided the wind doesn't blast you away). **$$$ Yialos** (Γυαλός) and **$$$ Madoupas,** near each other and the red-domed church, are decent places for a straightforward meal (both open long hours daily). Even if you're not up for a full meal, consider enjoying a *freddo cappuccino* or *frappé* from this comfortable perch, which offers some of Mykonos' best people-watching (and, sometimes, cat- and pelican-watching).

CHEAP EATS AND EASY LUNCHES

It's difficult to have a sit-down meal in Mykonos without dropping at least €20 per person. Here are some less expensive alternatives.

Souvlaki: A variety of souvlaki stands are scattered around town (for more on this classic Greek street food, see page 186). Most cater to tourists, and Mykonos lacks a stellar souvlaki joint. But relatively reliable choices include the classic **$$ Sakis Grill House** (Kalogera 7) and the upscale **$$ Souvlaki Story** (Enoplon Dinameon 37), both right in the heart of the Old Town.

Bakeries: Locals still shop at **Psillos,** a family-run, unsigned hole-in-the-wall where they bake everything on site. Grab something from the bins of breads, cookies, and other items lining the wall, or try a cheap meat or cheese pie. It offers a bit of affordability and local flavor in the center of this pricey, touristy town (daily until 15:30, find it between Fresh and Terra Maria hotels on Klaous street). **Gioras Wood Bakery,** filling a traditional cellar on a quiet street below the windmills, also has savory and sweet pastries, and atmospheric indoor seating (daily 9:00-late, Efthiniou street, tel. 22890-27784).

Mykonos Connections

BY BOAT

All bigger boats and car ferries leave from the New Port, about a mile north of town (see page 404 for information on getting there from Mykonos town). That includes most boats to Piraeus and Santorini. The rest of the boats leave from the Old Port. Be sure to check locally to confirm which port your ferry is departing from. For ferry tips, see page 532.

To Piraeus: Generally 3/day in high season (1 fast boat, 3 hours, www.seajets.gr; 2 slow boats, 5.5 hours, www.hellenicseaways.gr or www.bluestarferries.com). Off-season (Nov-mid-March) there is likely one slow boat daily (confirm, especially Jan-March).

To Santorini: Generally 2-4/day April-mid-Oct, none in winter, 3 hours, 1-2 stops en route, www.hellenicseaways.com or www.seajets.gr.

Delos

As popular as Mykonos is today, it was just another island centuries ago. The main attraction was the island next door, Delos, worth ▲. In antiquity, Delos lived several lives: as one of the Mediterranean's most important religious sites, as the "Fort Knox" of Greek city-states, and as a busy commercial port for the ancient world. Its importance ranked right up there with  Athens, Delphi, or Olympia. Today the island is a ghost town—but because no modern buildings were ever erected here, these ruins are nearly undisturbed. Highlights of your visit include some much-photographed lion statues (the Lion Terrace), some nice floor mosaics, the view from Mount Kynthos, and a windswept setting pockmarked with foundations that hint at Delos' rich history.

MYKONOS

The Rise and Fall of Delos

Delos entered history 3,000 years ago as a sacred cult center, where gods were worshipped. Blessed with a prime location in the center of the Greek islands but cursed with no natural resources, the barren island survived as a religious destination for pilgrims.

According to myth, the philandering Zeus impregnated the mortal Leto. Zeus' furious wife, Hera, banished Leto from the earth, but Zeus implored his brother Poseidon to create a refuge for her by raising up the underwater world of "Invisible" (*Adelos*) to create an island that was "Visible" (*Delos*). Here Leto gave birth to twins—Apollo (god of the sun) and Artemis (goddess of the moon). Their human followers built temples in their honor (ninth century B.C.), and pilgrims flocked here with offerings.

As Athens began to assert control over the Aegean (sixth century B.C.), it made sure that spiritually influential Delos stayed politically neutral. The Athenians ordered a purification of the island, removing dead bodies from the cemeteries. Later, they also decreed that no one could be born or die there—there were to be no permanent residents. The Delians were relocated to an adjacent larger island called Rheneia. Ostensibly, this was to keep Delos pure for the gods, but in reality it removed any danger of rivals influencing the island's native population.

Because of its neutral status and central location, Delos was chosen in 478 B.C. as the natural meeting place for the powerful Delian League—an alliance of Greek city-states formed to battle the Persians and to promote trade. The combined wealth of the league was stored here in the fabulously rich bank of Delos. But all that changed in 454 B.C., when Pericles moved the treasury to Athens, and Delos reverted to being a pilgrimage site.

Centuries later, under the Romans, Delos' course changed dramatically once more. Thanks to its strategic location, the island was granted the right to operate as a free port (167 B.C.). Almost overnight, it became one of the biggest shipping centers in the known world, complete with a town of 30,000 inhabitants.

Then, in 88 B.C., soldiers from the Kingdom of Pontus, an enemy of Rome, attacked and looted the town, slaughtering 20,000 of its citizens. Delos never really recovered. Plagued by pirate attacks and shifting trade routes, Delos faded into history. Its once-great buildings were left to decay and waste away. In 1872, French archaeologists arrived (so far, scientists have excavated about one-fifth of the site), and Delos' cultural treasures were revealed to the modern world.

GETTING THERE

Delos is a 30-minute boat ride from Mykonos. Boats depart from the pier extending straight out from the Old Town; buy the €20 round-trip ticket at the kiosk at the base of the pier (generally departing Mykonos at 9:00, 10:00, and 11:30; returning from Delos at 12:00, 13:30, and 15:00). You can take any boat back. There may also be a late-afternoon boat from Mykonos (around 17:00) that returns in the early evening (around 19:30; times differ outside peak season). Times can change depending on weather, cruise-ship arrivals and departures, and other factors, so check locally.

ORIENTATION TO DELOS

Cost and Hours: €12 admission includes the site and museum, open daily from the arrival of the first boat to the departure of the last one; tel. 22890-23413.

Planning Your Time: Most visitors find that two hours on the island is plenty to wander the site and see the museum; add more time if you want to climb Mount Kynthos.

Tours: Local guides meet arriving boats (€10 for a 1-1.5 hour tour—you'll need more time to actually hike around the site and see the museum). Travel agencies in Mykonos town sell package excursions to Delos that include the boat, museum entry, and a guided tour (overpriced at roughly €40, though these tours last longer than those offered by on-site guides).

Services: A café next to the museum sells coffee, juice, and basic snacks; behind the café are WCs.

Be Prepared: Delos has virtually no shade and minimal services. Wear good shoes, and bring sun protection and plenty of water.

⊙ SELF-GUIDED TOUR

• *From the boat dock, walk to the entrance, buy your ticket, pick up the helpful included map, and enter the gate.*

Pause and survey the site. The commercial harbor was to your right, and the sacred harbor to your left. Ahead and to the right are the foundations of shops and homes that constituted one of the Aegean's finest cities in Hellenistic times. Standing above those ruins is Mount Kynthos, its hillsides littered with temple remains. The Agora of the Competaliasts—one of the main squares in town—is straight ahead (with the museum building poking up behind). The religious area (with the temples

MYKONOS

of Apollo) is ahead and to the left, at the end of the Sacred Way. And far to the left was the Sacred Lake (now a patch of trees), overlooked by the famous Terrace of the Lions.

• *Start by wandering through the long rows of foundations on your right. You can circle back to these at the end, or poke around now.*

❶ Residential and Commercial District

Most of the remains here were either homes or shops. In the second century B.C. (when Delos was a bustling commercial port),

you could buy just about anything from one of the many shops, and the elaborate homes of wealthy merchants and shippers covered the hillsides above. Delos was considered the most important commercial center in the known world. (One of its primary commodities was human beings—it was a major center in the ancient

slave trade.) The city was cosmopolitan, with 30,000 residents and distinct ethnic groups, each with its own linguistic and cultural neighborhood (Greeks, Syrians, Beirutis, Italians, and so on). Remains of these same neighborhoods can still be seen today.

Poke into some of the **house foundations.** Homes were generally organized around a central courtyard above a giant cistern. Look for fragments of elaborate mosaic floors (intact portions are on display inside the museum), as well as marble structures that once decorated the place. The city even had a surprisingly advanced sewer system. Because wood was rare on the arid Cycladic Islands, most buildings were constructed from dry-stone walls; wood was a status symbol, used only by the wealthiest to show off. Delos had some of the biggest homes of ancient Greece in part because residents could build big here without fear of the devastating earthquakes that plagued other locations in the islands. The Greeks attributed this to divine intervention, while modern seismologists have found that Delos sits away from major fault lines.

• *Now head toward the agora that's near the ticket building.*

❷ Agora of the Competaliasts

This was the main market square of the Roman merchants who worshipped the deities called *lares compitales,* who kept watch over the crossroads. This is not *the* agora, but one of many agoras (marketplaces) on Delos—a reminder that several different communities coexisted in this cosmopolitan trading city.

• *Just above the upper-left corner of this agora, the Sacred Way leads off to the left. Follow the same path ancient pilgrims walked as they approached the Sanctuary of Apollo (look for the blue arrows to guide you).*

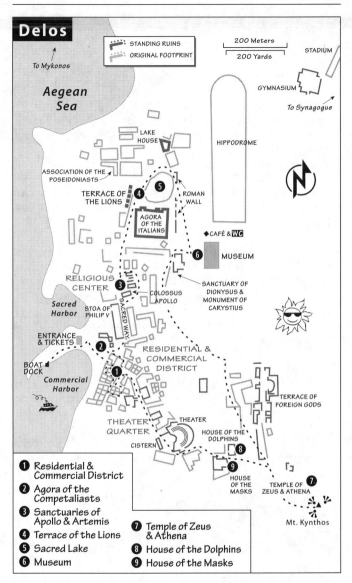

Delos

STANDING RUINS
ORIGINAL FOOTPRINT

200 Meters
200 Yards

To Mykonos

Aegean Sea

STADIUM

GYMNASIUM

To Synagogue

LAKE HOUSE

HIPPODROME

ASSOCIATION OF THE POSEIDONIASTS

TERRACE OF THE LIONS **4** **5** ROMAN WALL

AGORA OF THE ITALIANS

◆CAFÉ & WC

6 MUSEUM

RELIGIOUS CENTER **3**

COLOSSUS APOLLO

SANCTUARY OF DIONYSUS & MONUMENT OF CARYSTIUS

Sacred Harbor

STOA OF PHILIP V

SACRED WAY

ENTRANCE & TICKETS

2

BOAT DOCK

Commercial Harbor

1

RESIDENTIAL & COMMERCIAL DISTRICT

TERRACE OF FOREIGN GODS

THEATER QUARTER

THEATER

CISTERN

HOUSE OF THE DOLPHINS

8

HOUSE OF THE MASKS

9

HOUSE OF THE MASKS

TEMPLE OF ZEUS & ATHENA **7**

Mt. Kynthos

1 Residential & Commercial District
2 Agora of the Competaliasts
3 Sanctuaries of Apollo & Artemis
4 Terrace of the Lions
5 Sacred Lake
6 Museum
7 Temple of Zeus & Athena
8 House of the Dolphins
9 House of the Masks

*Along the left side of the road runs the long ledge of the pediment (with recognizable triglyphs) from the **Stoa of Philip V** (what we see here as the "bottom" actually ran along the top of the building). At the end of the Sacred Way is the...*

Religious Center

Both the **3 Sanctuary of Apollo** and, beyond that, the **Sanctuary**

of Artemis consisted of several temples and other ceremonial buildings. In its day, Apollo's sanctuary had three large, stern Doric temples lined with columns. The biggest temple was nearly 100 feet long. The nearby Porinos Naos served as the treasury of the Delian League.

Other treasuries once held untold riches—offerings to the gods brought by devout pilgrims.

• *Follow the route to the right, then left, then left again around the Sanctuary of Apollo. Before heading off to the right down the main path, pause at the giant marble pedestal that once held the...*

Colossus Apollo Statue

The 35-foot statue (seventh century B.C.) was a gift from the Naxians and was carved from a single block of marble. It's long gone now, but a few bits of its fingers are on display in the museum.

• *Continue down the path, beyond the Sanctuary. You'll pass the foundations that surround the spacious **Agora of the Italians** (on the right) on the way to the...*

❹ Terrace of the Lions

This row of five lion statues is the main, iconic image of this site. These are replicas, but five of the original marble statues (seventh

century B.C.) are in the museum. One of the originals was stolen by the Venetians, "repaired" with an awkwardly too-big head, and still stands in front of Venice's Arsenal building.

• *Northwest of the lions, up a small hill, are four columns marking the **Association of the Poseidoniasts,** the religious and commercial center for a guild of ship owners and merchants from Berytus (modern Beirut), in ancient Syria. Below the columns is the...*

❺ Sacred Lake

This was supposedly the source of Zeus' seed. When Leto was about to give birth to Zeus' children (according to the Homeric *Hymn to Apollo*), she cried out: "Delos, if you would be willing to be the abode of my son Apollo and make him a rich temple, your people will be well-fed by strangers bringing offerings. For truly your own soil is not rich." (French archaeologists drained the lake to prevent the spread of bacterial disease.)

• *Walk around the Sacred Lake. At the top, stop by the **Lake House**, providing a glimpse of a second-century B.C. Delian home. Now hike up toward the museum. Just before the museum, a path detours to the left far into the distance. You can follow it to find the remains of a gymnasium, a stadium, and a Jewish synagogue.*

Olympics-style games were held at Delos' **stadium** *every five years. Like the more famous games at Olympia and Delphi, these were essentially religious festivals to the gods, particularly Dionysus. Pilgrims from across the Greek world gathered to celebrate with sports, song contests, theatrical performances, and general merrymaking.*

Make your way to the...

❻ Museum

This scantily described collection includes statuary, vases, and other items. Inside the door is a model of the site in its heyday. Most of

the site's best pieces are in the National Archaeological Museum in Athens, but a few highlights remain, including a beautifully carved stone table, five of the original marble lions (in a room of their own), the fingers of Colossus Apollo (in the central hall, near the front door), and—perhaps the best part—several bits of striking floor mosaics.

For more body parts of other gods, exit the museum straight out, then go slightly left to stand in front of the **Monument of Carystius** (once part of the Sanctuary of Dionysus), with its large (broken-off) penis-on-a-pillar statues.

• *Past the museum, the path splits. If you stay right you'll wind back to the start. Or you can go left, which starts a hike up the hill toward more remains of houses and temples all the way up to Mount Kynthos (allow about 45 minutes).*

Mount Kynthos

At 370 feet, the island's highest point feels even taller on a hot day. To ancient Greeks, this conical peak looked like the spot from which Poseidon had pulled this mysterious isle up from the deep. Up here are the remains of the ❼ **Temple of Zeus and Athena.** As you observe the chain of islands dramatically swirling around Delos, you can understand why most experts believe that the

Cycladic Islands got their name from the way they circle (or cycle around) this oh-so-important islet.

• *Head back downhill, toward the theater and harbor. On your way down you'll pass the* ❽ *House of the Dolphins, with mosaics of cupids riding dolphins, and the* ❾ *House of the Masks, with a beautiful mosaic of a tambourine-playing Dionysus riding a leopard. As you return to the boat, you'll see the remains of a giant cistern and the 5,500-seat theater...starring a 360-degree view of the Cycladic Islands.*

SANTORINI

ΣΑΝΤΟΡΙΝΗ / Σαντορίνη;
a.k.a. Thira (ΘΗΡΑ / Θηρα)

Scenic, seismic Santorini is one of the world's most dramatic islands: a flooded caldera (a collapsed volcanic crater) with a long, steep, colorfully striped arc of cliffs, thrusting up a thousand feet above sea level. Sometimes called "The Devil's Isle," this unique place has captured visitors' imaginations for millennia and might have partly inspired tales of Atlantis. But the otherworldly appeal of Santorini (sahn-toh-REE-nee) doesn't end with its setting. Perched along the ridgeline is a gaggle of perfectly placed whitewashed villages punctuated with azure domes that make this, undeniably, one of Greece's most scenic spots. If this place didn't exist, some fantasy painter would have to conjure it up.

The main town, Fira (Φηρα, FEE-rah)—with Santorini's handiest services and best museum—is equal parts functional and scenic. But the village of Oia (Οια, EE-ah), on the northern tip of the island—with its chalk-white houses and vivid domes—is even more dramatic. Oia is the place you imagine first when you think "Santorini." Strolling through Oia is like spinning a postcard rack—it's tempting to see the town entirely through your camera's viewfinder. A complete visit to the island involves spending time in both towns (though Fira is, for a number of reasons, the more practical home base).

Santorini deserves more time than one-town islands Mykonos and Hydra. Besides the towns Fira and Oia, the rest of the island is also entertaining and fascinating—with charming villages, countryside wineries, ancient sites, unusual beaches, and a never-ending supply of

Santorini Island

Legend:
- ······ Excursion/Shuttle Boat
- —— Roads
- - - - Trail
- ♀ Beaches

To Mykonos & Piraeus

Oia
Riva
SIGALES WINERY
Finikia
THIRASSIA
Aegean Sea
Imerovigli
Firostefani
AGIOS THEODORI CHURCH
Manalos
CABLE CAR
NEA KAMENI
Fira
Old Port
Monolithos
Hot Springs
SEA DIAMOND SHIPWRECK WINES
SANTO WINES
EXO GONIA VILLAGE & METAXI MAS REST.
AIRPORT
KOUTSOYANNOPOULOS WINE MUSEUM
PALEA KAMENI
Athinios (New Port)
ARGYROS WINERY & SANTORINI BREWING CO.
Pirgos
Kamari
Akrotiri Town
VENETSANOS WINERY
LIGHTHOUSE (FAROS)
Emporio
ANCIENT THIRA
White Beach
Red Beach
Akrotiri Beach
AKROTIRI RUINS
Vlychada Port
Perissa
To Crete

2 Kilometers
2 Miles

stunning viewpoints (a boat trip in the caldera is a fun way to savor the area). In general, Santorini invites explorers to linger; even with several days, you won't run out of ways to enjoy yourself.

Santorini is hugely popular and can be very crowded in high season (roughly July-Sept, peaking mid-July-Aug). And it's expensive. I've done my best to find good-value accommodations and restaurants, but on a Greece-wide scale, they're still budget-busters. People coming to Santorini on a tight budget may find themselves eating lots of picnics and takeout souvlaki, and seeking accommodations with no views on the Airbnb market. Arriving via cruise ship helps control costs, even if it provides only a fleeting glimpse—but locals grumble that discount cruise lines and Airbnb are attracting a less wealthy clientele, who contribute less to the local economy.

They have reason to be concerned—tourism has helped make Santorini relatively wealthy. It's one of the few places in Greece where young people don't have to move away to find satisfying work. Fortunately, it's not difficult to break away from the main tourist rut and discover some scenic lanes of your own. In both Fira and Oia, the cliffside streets are strewn with countless cafés, all of them touting "sunset views"...the end of the day is a main attraction here.

SANTORINI OVERVIEW

The five islands that make up the Santorini archipelago are known to Greeks as Thira (Θηρα, THEE-rah). Most of the settlement is on the 15-mile-long main island, also called Thira. But most travelers call it Santorini (from the Venetian "Santa Irini," after an early Christian cathedral here)—and I do, too. The west side of Santorini is a sheer drop-off—the caldera (the crater of the former volcano), while the east side tapers more gradually to the water (the former volcano's base).

This archipelago's permanent population is officially around 15,000, but it nearly doubles with seasonal workers in the summer; Santorini gets around 80,000 visitors annually.

The primary tourist towns perch atop cliffs on the steep western side of Santorini: **Fira** is the island's capital and transportation hub, but the main attraction is **Oia,** a village six miles to the northwest. Sprawling north from Fira, along the road toward Oia, are the even higher, hill-capping villages of **Imerovigli** and **Firostefani.** The relatively level east and south areas have the ancient sites, most of the wineries, and the best beaches.

PLANNING YOUR TIME

For a speedy visit, Santorini deserves at least two nights and a full day divided between Oia and Fira. But if you have another day or two (or longer) to spare, Santorini has plenty more to offer. Three or four nights is ideal.

If your time on Santorini is short, make a beeline (by bus or taxi) to Oia to get your fill of classic Santorini views. Then, as the midday Oia cruise crowds begin to peak, return to Fira for a little sightseeing—follow my self-guided Fira Walk, then tour the Museum of Prehistoric Thira. Be sure to catch the sunset from somewhere along the caldera ridge (see sidebar later).

On a longer visit, rent a car or ride a bus or taxi to other points on the island, or take a boat trip in the caldera.

Don't rely on the opening hours for museums and archaeological sites given in this book; they can change at the whims of the government and the Greek economy. Check locally before planning your day.

Choosing a Home Base: Most travelers find Fira to be the handiest home base. It's plenty scenic, and has the best variety of accommodations, restaurants, and services. It's centrally located for exploring the island and has the best transportation connections. Wealthy romantics hang their hat in Oia—but it has some drawbacks. Oia feels remote (to get just about anywhere on the island, you first have to drive, taxi, or bus 25 minutes to Fira), extraordinarily expensive (even by Santorini standards), and is unbearably crowded around sunset...when your "private" terrace could suddenly be just steps below packs of shutterbugs.

You could also look for accommodations in the smaller villages of Firostefani or Imerovigli, which adjoin Fira to the north and also have fantastic views. If you'll have a car and want to settle into island life away from the crowds, it can be somewhat cheaper to find a countryside villa on the quieter eastern side of the island.

ARRIVAL IN SANTORINI
By Boat

Boats arrive in one of two places on Santorini: Ferries from Athens and the other islands arrive at the New Port at Athinios, about five miles south of Fira; cruise ships usually tender passengers to the Old Port, directly below Fira.

By Ferry at the New Port (Athinios): The Athinios port is a hive of activity, with ferries and cruise-ship tenders coming and going, and a row of cafés and car-rental offices facing the busy embankment. From here, a serpentine road twists up the hill. A taxi into Fira runs about €25 (more to Oia or other towns). Buses are much cheaper and meet arriving boats to bring passengers into Fira, where you can connect to other points on the island (there are many buses in this chaotic area—look for one marked *Local Bus*). As these buses can be very crowded in peak season, don't dawdle. You may also be accosted by transfer companies offering shared shuttle-bus rides into town (€20/2 people).

Visible from the road above Athinios, the ringed-off area in the bay just below the switchbacks is the site of the *Sea Diamond* shipwreck—a cruise ship that sank here in 2007; all but two of the 1,195 passengers were rescued. The ship rests in 450 feet of water. Concerned that it might slip deeper and that it's polluting the bay, islanders are hoping to pull it up.

For boat connections from Athinios, see "Santorini Connections" at the end of this chapter.

By Cruise Ship: Cruise ships anchor in the caldera below Fira. Passengers taking excursions get the first tenders, which go to the New Port at Athinios (described earlier) and are met by tour buses; after your excursion, the bus will likely drop you off in Fira (for info on returning to your ship, see later). Independent day-trippers are tendered to the Old Port directly below Fira.

From Fira's **Old Port,** there are three ways to reach the town center on the cliff above: Take a cable car, hike up, or ride a donkey. The **cable car** is the easiest option (€6 each way, more for luggage, daily 7:00-21:00, every 20 minutes, more frequent with demand, 3-minute ride to the top). However, the cable car is small

Santorini Sunsets

Watching the sunset from the caldera ridge is a ▲▲▲ experience that's worth planning ahead for. Find out what time the sun sets, and where (it gradually moves from north to south over the course of the summer).

Oia is the most famous place to enjoy the Santorini sunset. During July and August it provides unobstructed views, and all that whitewash beautifully captures the swirling colors of the sky. Be warned that sunset-watching in Oia is hardly a unique brainstorm—and as the shadows get long, the town's narrow streets become a tedious human traffic jam. Seriously—just before sunset, you can barely walk anywhere in the old center. If you are determined to ex-

perience an Oia sunset, arrive very early—and hour or more in peak season—and immediately stake out a spot at the prime vantage point: at or near the ruined fortress at the tip of town. But, to be honest, many travelers find it simply not worth the headaches involved.

Fira is arguably just as good for enjoying the sunset, and the crowds are less concentrated. Unlike Oia, Fira affords a view over the entire caldera rather than looking out to sea (so the sun sets over land, not just water). If your hotel doesn't offer a caldera-view perch, scout a bar or restaurant during the day, and reserve a table for sunset time. If you're improvising, simply belly up to the whitewashed wall (along with every other tourist in town) along the terrace in front of the Orthodox Cathedral.

And don't forget the many **other places on the island** for sunset-viewing—basically anywhere facing the caldera will work. Ask locals for tips. The villages of Firostefani and Imerovigli, just above Fira, are smaller (less crowded) and even higher up. Some of my recommended wineries on the southern part of the island (especially Venetsanos and Santo) boast spectacular sunset views. And if you're taking a cruise in the caldera, choosing one timed to coincide with sunset kills two sightseeing birds with one stone.

Remember: If you hope to watch the sunset from a particular café or winery, be sure to specifically reserve a sunset-view table well in advance.

When Santorini Blew Its Top

Situated on an edgy stack of tectonic plates, Santorini was created by volcanic activity that lasted more than two million years. The island was once a neatly circular "shield volcano," with a gentle slope that was built up gradually, over a series of volcanic eruptions.

The first major eruption of Santorini took place around 21,000 years ago. The middle of the volcano collapsed and filled with about a hundred feet of water—creating the caldera we see today. For millennia, it was a mostly intact, ring-shaped island—with just a small opening at one end, and a small island in the middle...a perfect natural harbor. The island prospered as a trade port. Experts believe that the island in the middle of the ring may have been the site of a thriving city (the one that, later, may have partly inspired tales of Atlantis). It went by two names: Strongili, meaning "Circular"; and Kalliste, meaning "Beautiful."

But then came the famous "Minoan Eruption" around 1630 B.C.—one of the largest in human history. It blew out 24 cubic

miles of volcanic material, at least four times the amount ejected by the 1883 explosion of Krakatoa in today's Indonesia. The volcano likely warned Santorini's inhabitants with a major earthquake and an initial small eruption before the full-scale eruption. No human skeletons and few valuable items from that time have been found here, suggesting that islanders were able to pack up and evacuate. Good thing. Soon afterward, large amounts of ash and pumice blasted out of the crater, and superheated pyroclastic flows swept down the is-

(maximum 36 people/trip)—so you might be in for a long wait if you arrive on a big ship. **Hiking** up the 588 steep steps is demanding, and you'll share them with fragrant, messy donkeys. You can pay €6 to ride partway up on a **donkey,** but the stench and the bumpy ride make this far less romantic than it sounds. And the donkeys don't take you all the way up, leaving you a steep uphill hike of around 100 steps at the end. The cable car and donkey trail converge at the same point up top, which is also the start of my self-guided Fira Walk.

land's slopes. Several walls of the ring collapsed; the island in the middle disappeared; and the caldera became much deeper—filled with more than a thousand feet of water. That's when the island took on the shape that visitors see today.

This eruption displaced enough seawater to send a tsunami screaming south toward Crete, less than 70 miles away. Archaeologists think that the tsunami (and perhaps earthquakes near the same time) caused severe hardship, eventually leading to the downfall of the Minoan civilization.

The volcano isn't done. Two little islets emerged from the bay quite recently, by geological standards. Palea Kameni ("Old Burnt Island") rose from the deep in 197 B.C., leaving islanders awestruck. They credited the sea god Poseidon and built a temple here, which was later destroyed in further eruptions. Then, in A.D. 1707, Nea Kameni ("New Burnt Island") appeared beside its older brother. Both Kameni islets grew even more in the 1860s. To this day, these islets sometimes sputter and steam, and earthquakes still wrack the entire archipelago (including a devastating one in 1956). The last small eruption (on Nea Kameni) was in 1950. Today, the "hot" springs on Palea Kameni are a popular tourist attraction.

Although the Minoan Eruption devastated the island, it also left behind a unique ecosystem and agricultural tradition (see sidebar on page 456). And, starting in the 19th century and ramping up in the early 20th century, the volcanic soil was also the basis for a local industry: The upper layer of pumice and volcanic ash was quarried, pulverized, and mixed with lime to create a very strong concrete (produced until recently in the blocky, abandoned building on the cliff at the southern edge of Fira). Santorini is the country's sole source of this material. But with the rise of tourism in the 1970s and 1980s, civic leaders realized that Santorini's pristine nature would be better in the long run than gaping quarries, most of which have halted production.

To **return to the Old Port,** you can take the cable car, ride a donkey, or walk down. Note that the line for the cable car can get comically long, snaking through town, as the ship's departure nears.

If, on arrival, you want to head from Fira's Old Port directly to **Oia,** shop around once on shore for local transport. A typical package, costing around €25, includes a fast boat from the Old Port to Ammoudi (Oia's port), a bus ride up the hill to Oia, several hours to explore Oia and have lunch, then a 30-minute bus ride back to Fira Town.

By Plane

Santorini's little, rustic airport sits along the flat area on the east (back) side of the island, about four miles from Fira (airport code: JTR, tel. 22860-28400; www.santorini-airport.com). It's about a 15-minute ride into Fira, either by taxi (around €20) or bus (around €2, roughly hourly—coordinated to meet some but not all flights).

GETTING AROUND SANTORINI

By Bus: Fira is the bus hub for the island. The bus station—a big parking lot with a little information kiosk—is a block below the main street, near the south end of town (just downhill from the Orthodox cathedral and Museum of Prehistoric Thira). Schedules are posted at the kiosk at the bottom end of the lot; buy tickets from the driver (cash only). Buses are a much cheaper alternative to taxis, but can be extremely crowded, especially in peak season—get there early to reduce the odds of having to stand on board. For bus connections, see "Fira Connections" later.

By Taxi: The main taxi stand is just uphill and around the corner from Fira's bus station, along the main street. There's often a line of people waiting for taxis, particularly when cruise ships have just arrived. If you need to head to the port or airport in the morning, book a taxi the night before through your hotel. You can also try calling for a taxi (tel. 22860-22555 or 22860-23951). Distances on the island are short, but prices are high (and can be slippery): Figure €25 to Oia, Athinios port, or Perissa; €20 to Kamari's beaches or the airport; and €30 to Akrotiri. Given these prices, it's tempting for those exploring the island to simply rent their own car (typically cheaper than two or three taxi rides)—see next.

By Car: If ever there's a Greek island where it's nice to have a car, Santorini's the one. Taxis are expensive, buses are crowded, and many outlying sights and viewpoints are well worth the trip. Driving around Santorini is reasonably straightforward. Roads are windy but wide (enough), drivers are aggressive but not reckless (drive defensively), towns are well signposted, and parking is usually free and easy. Traffic, however, can be a big problem at certain times of day and in peak season.

Offices renting cars, scooters, and ATVs abound in Fira (clustering at the northern end of town, along the main street), in Oia (at the entrance to town), and at the New Port and airport. Or ask your hotel—they likely have a partnership with a company that can make things easy. A small manual-transmission car with basic insurance runs around €45-60 for 24 hours; you'll pay more for an automatic, better insurance, and during the July and August high season. You can usually rent a car on the spot, but it's smart to prebook in July and August.

Renting an **ATV** is popular on Santorini...but I wouldn't. This island is hillier and more congested than most. Before renting one, let this sink in: Local hospitals report that, on a busy day in the summer, they treat as many as 25 injuries from ATV-related accidents. No matter how defensively you drive, you're sharing the roads with dangerous ATV novices. I'd spring a few more euros for the relative safety of a car.

By Guided Tour: Santorini Private Tours, run by Kostas and his select team of guides, does an excellent job of giving meaning to your Santorini visit. It offers a variety of excursions, including "highlights" tours around the island (€300/4.5 hours, €380/6 hours including Akrotiri, prices for up to 4 people), food and wine tours, and cooking classes. The guides work with both cruise passengers and independent travelers. Review the options and contact them through their website (www.santorini-private-guide.com).

Fira

The island's main town, Fira, is a practical hub with an extraordinary setting. Sit at a cliff-clinging café terrace, sip an iced coffee, and watch thousands of cruise-ship passengers flood into town each morning (on the cable car and donkey trail), then recede in the afternoon. All this built-in business has made Fira a bit greedy; its main streets (including

the aptly named "Gold Street") are lined with aggressive jewelry salespeople and restaurants with great views, high prices, and low quality.

But if you can ignore the tackiness in this part of town, you'll discover that Fira has a charm of its own—particularly in the cozy labyrinth of streets that burrow between its main traffic street and the cliff edge, and on the steeply switchbacked lanes that zigzag down the side of the cliff toward the caldera. Fira is also home to a pair of cathedrals (Orthodox and Catholic) and the island's top museum (the excellent Museum of Prehistoric Thira).

Remember that Fira is not the setting of all those famous Santorini photos—those are taken in Oia.

Orientation to Fira

The core of Fira is squeezed between the cliff and the busy, not particularly charming main road through town, called 25 Martou. Most places of interest to visitors are in the cluster of narrow streets

SANTORINI

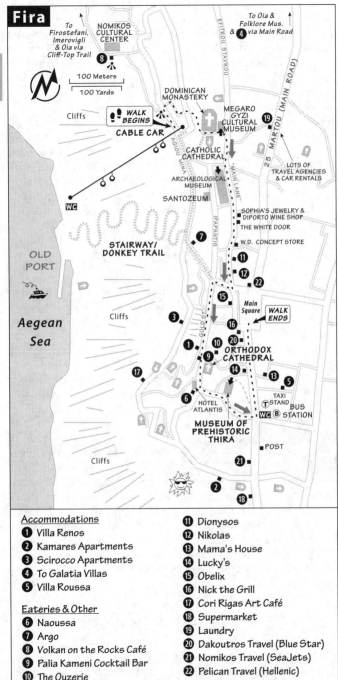

Fira

To Firostefani, Imerovigli & Oia via Cliff-Top Trail

NOMIKOS CULTURAL CENTER

To Oia & Folklore Mus. & ④ via Main Road

100 Meters
100 Yards

DOMINICAN MONASTERY

Cliffs

WALK BEGINS
CABLE CAR

CATHOLIC CATHEDRAL

MEGARO GYZI CULTURAL MUSEUM

⑲

25 MARTIOU (MAIN ROAD)

EFTIROU STAVROU

LOTS OF TRAVEL AGENCIES & CAR RENTALS

ARCHAEOLOGICAL MUSEUM

SANTOZEUM

WC

SOPHIA'S JEWELRY & DIPORTO WINE SHOP
THE WHITE DOOR
W.D. CONCEPT STORE

⑪
⑫
㉒

OLD PORT

STAIRWAY/ DONKEY TRAIL

MAIN LANE

IPAPANTIS

⑦

Aegean Sea

Cliffs

③

⑮

⑯

Main Square

WALK ENDS

GOLD ST.

①

⑩
⑨

⑳

ORTHODOX CATHEDRAL

⑰

⑭

⑬ ⑤

⑥

HOTEL ATLANTIS

TAXI STAND
WC Ⓑ BUS STATION

MUSEUM OF PREHISTORIC THIRA

POST

Cliffs

㉑

②

⑱

Accommodations
1. Villa Renos
2. Kamares Apartments
3. Scirocco Apartments
4. To Galatia Villas
5. Villa Roussa

Eateries & Other
6. Naoussa
7. Argo
8. Volkan on the Rocks Café
9. Palia Kameni Cocktail Bar
10. The Ouzerie

11. Dionysos
12. Nikolas
13. Mama's House
14. Lucky's
15. Obelix
16. Nick the Grill
17. Cori Rigas Art Café
18. Supermarket
19. Laundry
20. Dakoutros Travel (Blue Star)
21. Nomikos Travel (SeaJets)
22. Pelican Travel (Hellenic)

between here and the caldera. Even where street names exist, locals ignore them. Making navigation even more confusing, it's a very vertical town—especially along the cliff. Use a map, and don't be afraid to ask for directions.

Fira—and the island—has no real TI (there is a tiny kiosk between the bus station and the main square that dispenses brochures, but it's usually closed). For help, ask at your hotel, local travel agencies, or other businesses.

HELPFUL HINTS

Combo-Ticket: A €14 combo-ticket covers the ancient sites of Akrotiri (€12) and Ancient Thira (€4) outside of Fira, as well as the recommended Museum of Prehistoric Thira in Fira (€6)—a good value if you see all three. (Both Akrotiri and Ancient Thira have a history of unexpected closures, so carefully confirm in town that they're open before purchase.)

Laundry: Most launderettes in town offer drop-off service for €10-15 (generally closed Sun; ask at your hotel for the nearest location). **Penguin** has both self-service and full-service in about three hours, for the same price (Mon-Sat 8:30-21:00, Sun 9:00-17:00, on 25 Martou toward Oia side, tel. 22860-22168).

Grocery Store: Sklavenitis (ΣΚΛΑΒΕΝΙΤΗΣ), at the south end of town on the main road, is sizable (Mon-Sat 8:00-21:00, Sun 9:30-14:30); it shares a parking lot with a much smaller organic grocery store.

Ferry Tickets: Dakoutros Travel sells tickets for the slow Blue Star ferry to Mykonos and Athens; **Nomikos Travel** sells tickets for SeaJets; and **Pelican Travel** sells tickets for Hellenic Seaways. All of these are along Fira's main road.

Travel Blog: For informative, enjoyably lowbrow local travel information, see www.santorinidave.com.

Fira Walk

This self-guided orientation walk introduces you to Santorini and its main town. It can be done in about an hour; allow more time for sightseeing, photo stops, and hiking to better views. Be warned that this walk traverses the main streets, which can be jammed with tourists; it can be much more relaxing in late afternoon, or even after dark. Begin where most cruise passengers do: at the cable car station near the top of town. (The cable car is easy to find from anywhere in Fira—just look for the blue signs.)

• *With the cable-car station at your back, turn right—yes, away from town—and follow the cobbled path as it curves up and to the right, toward the cliff, between scenic restaurants. Pause along the wall in front of Zafora Restaurant for a...*

Big Orientation View of Santorini

You're looking at the glorious cliff-draping town of Fira—the capital of the archipelago known internationally as Santorini, and locally as Thira. This town is improbably perched along the lip of a flooded volcanic caldera—Spanish for "cauldron." And, like a cauldron indeed, Santorini bubbled over and blew its top about 3,600 years ago, obliterating what had been a tidy, ring-shaped archipelago with a busy island town in the middle (see the "When Santorini Blew Its Top" sidebar, earlier).

The crescent-shaped island you're on is called **Thira**. The next-biggest island—the smaller crescent facing Thira across the caldera—is called **Thirasia**. Its little port town, Manolas, is connected to the spine of the island by a rugged donkey path. The two chunky islands in the middle of the caldera are called **Nea ("New") Kameni** and **Palea ("Old") Kameni**—both of which remain volcanically active. Historically, Santorini has experienced volcanic activity about every 75 years, most recently in the mid-1950s. Do the math...and keep your eyes peeled for steam venting.

Scanning the cliffs, notice the **horizontal stripes** of black, gray, and red—indicating where the original volcanic island was

formed by a series of eruptions, each one building on the previous one, like the rings of a tree. The edge of the caldera was sheared off cleanly by an eruption 21,000 years ago, creating this cross-section of the striations—a unique opportunity to see eons of geology in one glance.

Now look down below, where a stepped **donkey** path twists all the way to the Old Port of Fira. You can pay €6 for the ride up or down. While this seems like a tourist gimmick, beasts of burden have been hauling cargo from the port up to the cliff-capping towns for centuries. In recent years, more progressive islanders have formed the Santorini Animal Welfare Association (SAWA) to educate the traditional donkey wranglers to treat their animals more humanely. If the cable car is totally jammed—and it usually is—you can hike down this path...but step carefully to avoid the donkey droppings.

Continue uphill past the restaurant, hiking up to better and better views. Go at least as far as the Da Costa restaurant (a 5-minute climb) and pause there. But if you have energy and want to (somewhat) escape even more crowds, you can hike all the way up to the boxy, orange Nomikos Cultural Center, which caps the trail's summit. You could continue another 10 minutes past that to the village of Firostefani with its classic blue-domed Agios Theodori Church (or even carry on two hours farther for the rugged, unforgettably scenic—and unforgettably strenuous—hike all the way to Oia).

• *After checking the views, meet me back here at Da Costa restaurant. The lane just next to its terrace leads to...*

Venetian Upper Fira

In addition to the native Greeks, people from Venice (whom locals call "Franks") have also left their mark on Santorini. While Venetians have always passed through as merchants, they took notice of this archipelago after the Fourth Crusade (early 13th century)—when Byzantium was conquered and its sprawling empire collapsed, opening the door to foreign influence. San-torini was ideally located  at a crossroads of the sea trade between the heart of Europe and the Middle East. Venetians also appreciated the protection its steep cliffs provided: Any would-be invader would need to stage an essentially vertical invasion. Venice fortified the island with a chain of five fortresses, including one in Imerovigli, steeply uphill from here; one in Oia; and one perched along the saddle of land to the south, just above Akrotiri. The name "Santorini" (which locals still don't entirely embrace) comes from the long-gone Venetian church of Santa Irini.

Venetian influence persists here to this day. While only a small percentage of locals are Catholic, the Catholic Church—in many ways the descendant of those original Venetian overlords—still owns lots of property. In general, beige and blocky Upper Fira—above this path—is Catholic, while the blue-and-white warren of cave houses in Lower Fira is Orthodox (including the huge, squat, blinding-white dome of the Greek Orthodox Cathedral, which you can see across the caldera).

Savor this view once more, then head up the lane next to Da Costa restaurant, hiking up the steps past the Art of the Loom gallery (which makes fancy underpants). The stairs dead-end at the red-painted (but usually closed) doorway of the Church of the Immaculate Conception—one of many Catholic churches built in this area in the late 18th and early 19th centuries.

Turn right and follow the cobbled path to the well-marked **Cathedral of St. John the Baptist.** This was built in 1823, heav-

ily damaged (like much of Santorini) by the 1956 earthquake, and reopened in 1975. Step through the gate into the courtyard, and continue inside the church itself (open long hours daily). While firmly Catholic, architecturally this feels like an eclectic hybrid of Catholic and Orthodox—with muted colors, a big chandelier, and Moorish-style arches flanking the main altar. Remember the details, which you can compare to the interior of the Orthodox Cathedral later on this walk.

Back outside, retrace your steps to the cobbled lane, where you'll turn right and head downhill, toward town. A few steps down, the wide cobbled street on your left leads to yet another Catholic institution—the **Dominican Monastery**—and good views back on the cathedral's dome and steeple. A complex of Catholic buildings sprawl from here uphill, all the way to the next town, Firostefani.

A few more steps down, displayed next to the door on the left (marked *Art and Iron Studio*), is a gnarled vine, twisted into a circular basket shape. This is how Santorini vintners cultivate their wine, to maximize retention of moisture. This door opens into a sweet little courtyard garden.

Finally, just below that—at the base of the stepped lane—is the entrance to the **Megaro Gyzi Museum,** which fills the mansion of a local parishioner who willed this property to the Church (described later, under "Sights in Fira").

• *Just below the museum, turn right onto Fira's...*

"Main Lane" (Erythrou Stavrou Street)

Locals ignore street names, but they think of this drag as the "Main Lane" of their little burg. ("Main Street," which carries car traffic, is lower down—we'll end our walk there.) One of the town's top shopping gauntlets, this lane is lined with all manner of tacky souvenir stands, posters and postcards, linens, natural sponges, seashells, and a surprising abundance of "fish pedicure" places.

Walk down the Main Lane. After about a block, on the square on the right (near the cable car station where we began), is the entrance to the **Archaeological Museum of Thira.** Its dusty cases are crammed with sparsely described jugs, statues, and other artifacts from ancient Thira. However, this is by far the less interesting of Santorini's two archaeological museums; skip it and save your energy for the excellent Museum of Prehistoric Thira, which has far older and more interesting Minoan pieces from Akrotiri, and is right at the end of this walk.

Continuing past the museum on Main Lane, keep straight at the fork. You'll pass **Sophia's** jewelry shop, one of many in Santorini that displays the local jewelry: Finely detailed and inspired by Byzantine pieces, they feature intricate beading and filigree. Greek Orthodox priests wear simple golden cuffs for important worship services, but bishops' cuffs are more elaborately detailed—offering inspiration for some of these frilly designs. Do a little window shopping and appreciate the fine craftsmanship.

Just past Sophia's is one of two entrances to the **Diporto** ("two doors") shop, which sells local products and offers tastings of Santorini's wines in the hope you'll buy a bottle (for more on local wines, see the "Santorini Wines" sidebar).

Carry along the narrow Main Lane. After a long block, on your left is the entrance to **The White Door Theater,** which puts on a fun "village Greek wedding" folk show each night (described later, under "Nightlife in Fira"). Just past that on the left, the same people run the classy **W.D. Concept Store,** with souvenirs that feel more modern and distinctively stylish than the norm. The next block has two recommended restaurants (both also on the left): **Dionysos** (with its big terrace), then **Nikolas** (a classic taverna).

• *Soon the Main Lane dead-ends at the stairs to a taverna. Turn right here and walk up the blue-painted steps. This street hits a T-intersection with the street called...*

"Gold Street"

Before we head left down Santorini's most touristy strip, take a few steps to the right. Signs point downhill to the Old Port. Notice that each of the steps from here on down is painted with a number—it's exactly 588 steps to the water. If you have strong knees, returning to your cruise-ship tender down these stairs could be more appealing than joining the lo-o-o-ong line for the cable car that snakes  through the streets of Fira shortly before call time. For now, you could head down to step #568 for some nice views over town.

From the top of the stairs, with the caldera to your back, turn right, take a deep breath, and plunge down tourist-crammed Gold

Street. There was a time when the majority of vendors along here actually did specialize in golden jewelry. But many of the storefronts have been taken over by tacky souvenirs, ice-cream parlors, resort wear, and other, less genteel goods.

Just after Classico, on the right, peer down into the ruins of a traditional Santorini cave house that collapsed after the 1956 earthquake. Rainwater was collected in the terrace out front, and the cave part of the home is under your feet. For more on this traditional style of architecture, see "Santorini's Cave Houses," later.

• *Make short work of this strip, until you pop out at the wide-open and gorgeous viewpoint I like to call...*

"Orthodox Cathedral Terrace"

This is where Fira opens up and really lets you breathe in some grand vistas. Lining the white wall, a half-dozen floating doorways

lead down steep staircases to hotels and restaurants with big views. (For a better-value meal, without the views, The Ouzerie restaurant—one of the best in town—is just before the cathedral, set back from the square on the left.)

Step up to the white wall and look down over the labyrinth of cave houses that are draped over the cliffs here. The lanes connecting these houses are far less crowded than the ones we've braved so far, and come with smashing views—they're a delight to explore. Many of these are hotels, but some turn their breakfast terraces into cafés; exploring this area to find your favorite perch for a cup of coffee is a fun activity (I particularly like the **Cori Rigas Art Café,** along the lower cliffside lane). The whole area is anchored, at the top of the hill, by the big, boxy Hotel Atlantis, which feels like it's keeping the steep warren of lanes from simply sliding down into the caldera. The steep lanes around the far side of the Atlantis are even quieter—it's surprisingly easy to escape most of the tourist crush.

The main feature of this terrace is the looming **Orthodox Cathedral of Candelmas** (Panagia Ypapantis). This modern cathedral, which caps Fira like a white crown, has a grandly painted interior that offers a beautiful taste of the Greek Orthodox faith (free entry, open long hours daily; for more on the features of a Greek Orthodox church, see page 74). Stepping inside, appreciate the typical Greek-cross floor plan (with four equal-length arms). Flanking the entry aisle are framed icons, which some visitors reverently kiss as they enter. Farther in is the grand, golden chandelier, with a giant ostrich egg dangling from its base. Representing the body of the Church, the egg is a common symbol in Orthodox churches. The writing on the chandelier is not Greek, but Cyrillic—this was a gift from the Russian patriarch (like the pope) to commemorate Russia's links to Santorini through the trade of a local wine used for Communion. Directly below the chandelier is a double-headed Byzantine eagle. Beyond that is the wooden iconostasis, with shimmering icons of saints. Looking up, notice the balcony overhead. Traditionally, women would worship there, while men stood on the main floor. But today, everyone fills the main hall, women on the left, men on the right. You can step through the side door into the tranquil, fenced courtyard that surrounds the cathedral, with the grave of a local bishop.

• *You could finish your walk here if you're in a rush or want to explore the meandering terraces below. Or stick with me to get a glimpse of workaday Fira and the town's top museum.*

Back outside, walk to the far end of the cathedral, and hook left between it and Hotel Atlantis. Heading downhill, you'll run into the back of the wavy-roofed Museum of Prehistoric Thira—the town's top sight. But to get inside, you'll have to circle around to the gate on its lower side: First jog right, then hook left, to walk along...

Fira's Main Street (25 Martou)

While it's not much to look at, this drag is the main artery of Fira—where the fantasyland at the cusp of the caldera meets the real world of humble island Greece.

Walk along Main Street, watching on your left for the gate to enter the excellent **Museum of Prehistoric Thira,** with a wonderful collection of artifacts (ceramics, frescoes, and a tiny golden ibex) from the Minoan-era settlement at Akrotiri. If you visit one museum on Santorini, make it this one (described later).

Now let's get practical: Across the street from the museum gate is the town's main taxi stand, where cabs fan out to the distant corners of the island. Nearby is a public WC. And around the corner is the bus station.

With the museum to your back, turn left and continue one more block—passing some recommended cheap eats, Mama's Place and Lucky's Souvlaki—to where the traffic-free zone begins. This is Fira's **"Main Square,"** crammed with tourist services that cater not to high-roller Gold Street shoppers, but to mere mortals and budget backpackers. You'll find lots of cheap-and-cheery eateries, ice-cream stands, takeaway coffee, greasy souvlaki, and more. This is a good place to regroup, refresh, and stock up before continuing your explorations of Santorini.

• *Our orientation walk is finished. To reach other parts of the island, backtrack one block to the taxi stand and bus station. Or, rent a car, scooter, or ATV at one of the rental places lining Main Street just past Main Square. To head toward the Old Port for a cruise tender, turn left up the street at the end of Main Square to return to the start of Gold Street with those 588 steps (the cable car is about a 10-minute walk to the right, along Main Lane).*

Sights in Fira

OLD TOWN

▲Megaro Gyzi Museum

Hiding in the alleys behind the Catholic cathedral, this modest local history museum celebrates Santorini life. It fills the 18th-century home of a prominent local resident, who willed it to the Catholic Church.

Cost and Hours: €3, Mon-Sat 10:00-16:00—may close later in peak season, closed Sun and Nov-April, tel. 22860-23077, www.gyzimegaron.gr.

Visiting the Museum: On the right as you enter, look for the map illustrating how the island has grown and shrunk with volcanic eruptions across the eons. Also in this main hall are evocative etchings of traditional Santorini lifestyles, and copies of old documents—some in Greek, others in Italian, still others in Arabic, emphasizing Santorini's status as a crossroads of civilizations.

In the room to the left, find the 1870 clipping from a London newspaper article about "Santorin," and, next to it, an engraving of a smoldering islet in the caldera. Nearby are photographs of the town from the early to mid–20th century (including scenes before and after the devastating 1956 earthquake), and samples of the various types of volcanic rock found on the island (some embedded with flash-fossilized palms and pistachio leaves).

Upstairs, you'll find a humble painting gallery with still-lifes and landscapes.

▲▲Museum of Prehistoric Thira

While no competition for Greece's top archaeological exhibits, this little museum is Santorini's best, presenting items found in the prehistoric city buried under ash near Akrotiri. A visit is particularly worthwhile if you plan to see the excavated ruins of that city at the southern end of the island (described under "More Sights on Santorini," later), but interesting to anyone. That settlement was the largest city outside Crete in the Minoan-era world, dating back to the earliest documented civilization in the Aegean (third to second millennium B.C.)—impossibly ancient, even to the ancients. The people who lived here fled before Santorini blew its top (likely around 1630 B.C.—see sidebar on page 438), leaving behind intriguing artifacts of a civilization that disappeared from the earth not long after. Most of those artifacts have been moved off-site, either to this museum or to the biggies in Athens. Everything in this manageable museum is described in English and well-presented in modern, air-conditioned comfort.

Cost and Hours: €6, covered by €14 combo-ticket; Mon, Wed, and Fri 8:00-15:00, Thu and Sat-Sun 8:00-20:00, Tue 12:00-20:00; Nov-March Wed-Mon 8:00-15:00, closed Tue; entrance across from taxi stand on the main drag, tel. 22860-23217, www.culture.gr.

Visiting the Museum: Enter the gate below the museum, head up the stairs to buy your ticket in the freestanding white building, then hook left to the entrance. Inside, everything is displayed in one big room, which you'll visit counterclockwise.

Turning right from the entrance (in section C), look for the Early Cycladic figures and vessels, dating from 2700-2300 B.C. The stiff figurines, with their arms crossed, perplex archaeologists, who speculate that they might represent the Mother Goddess worshipped here.

Next (section D), the model of the Akrotiri site puts the items in context. Most of the museum's pieces date from the Late Cycladic Period (mid-17th century B.C.), when Akrotiri peaked just before its residents fled the erupting volcano. Although they took valuable items (such as jewelry) with them, they left behind easily replaceable everyday objects and, of course, immovable items such as wall frescoes. These left-behind items form the core of the collection.

Section D1 displays an intriguing assortment: Primitive cooking pots, clay ovens, and barbeque grills, along with bronze

vases, daggers, tongs, and fishing hooks, offer clues to the Aegean lifestyle. The Thirans were traders rather than warriors, so many items reflect their relatively comfortable lifestyle, connection with the wider world, and consumer society. One plaster cast shows the shape left by a (now-deteriorated) three-legged wooden table that could have passed for Baroque from the 17th century A.D.—but it's from the 17th century B.C.

In section D2, each of the three large containers is marked

differently to suggest its contents—for example, a vessel that held water was decorated with reeds (aquatic plants). In the nearby case, the stack of metal weights illustrates the evolution of standardization during early trading.

The museum's highlights are the vibrantly colorful, two-dimensional **wall frescoes.** Local artists likely executed these wall

paintings, but their naturalistic style was surely influenced by the wider Minoan culture. In keeping with the style of Crete (the home of the Minoans), men appear brown, and the women, white. (If you've been to the National Archaeological Museum in Athens, you might recognize this style of fresco from that museum's collection, which includes wall paintings of antelopes, swallows, and young men boxing, all from this same Akrotiri site.

The wall frescoes from the House of the Ladies (section D3.5) show exquisitely dressed women. In one, an older woman leans over and appears to be touching the arm of another (now-missing) woman and holding a dress in her right hand.

Across the hall (section D7.2), you'll see a fragment of another wall fresco showing blue monkeys. Because monkeys are not indigenous to Greece, these images offer more evidence that the Cycladic and Minoan people traveled far and wide, and interacted with exotic cultures.

Along the wall between these two frescoes, a (brown) man holds fish—quite a catch.

Between these frescoes, the **vessels** (such as beautiful vases decorated with dolphins and lilies—near the frescoes from the

House of the Ladies) give us a glimpse of everyday life back then. Look for the ritual vessel shaped like a boar's head.

In the final display case (near the exit) is an exquisite miniature **golden ibex**—one of the few items of great value that was left behind by fleeing islanders. Notice the delicate artistry on the skinny, twisted horns.

OUTSIDE OF TOWN
Folklore Museum of Santorini

With bits and pieces left over from a bygone era, this museum gives visitors a sense of how Santorini sustained itself before tourism.

The highlight is a restored 19th-century cave house decorated with items from that period (furniture, pots, utensils, and even a toilet). It's especially interesting if you happen to be staying in a renovated cave house. You'll also find various workshops (including those of a carpenter, shoemaker, and blacksmith), a *canava* (wine cellar), and a small chapel—a modern example of those people built in their homes so they could pray for the safe return of family members who went off to sea for months or years.

Cost and Hours: €3, daily 10:00-14:00, closed Nov-March, tel. 22860-22792, www.santorinisfolkmuseum.com. If the place isn't busy (and it rarely is), ask whoever's manning it for a tour, which brings everything to life.

Getting There: It's a 10-minute walk from the center of Fira, on the northern (Oia) end of town: Find the road to Oia (one block east of 25 Martou) and follow it past several ATV/scooter rental outfits and a launderette or two; after the road bends left, it's a few more minutes (look for *MUSEUM* sign on right).

▲▲▲Hike to Oia

With a few hours to spare, you can venture out on one of Greece's most scenic hikes. While the main road connecting Fira to Oia is drab and dusty, a wonderful cliff-top trail links the two towns, offering fantastic views most of the way. It's about 5 miles (plan on at least 4 hours one-way), quite strenuous (with lots of ups and downs), and offers little or no shade in hot weather—so don't attempt it unless you're in good shape and have the right gear (good shoes, water, food, sun protection). Get an early start. You can catch a bus or taxi back to Fira when you're done.

From Fira, head north through the adjoining villages of Firostefani (where you can see the church, described next) and cliff-capping Imerovigli, then continue along the lip of the caldera. You'll briefly walk along the shoulder of a busy, narrow road, along the skinny spine of the island, with Aegean views on both sides. Then you'll hike steeply up, up, up and over the bluff, then down into Oia. (Donkeys are standing by for the steepest part of the climb, for those who'd rather catch a lift.)

▲▲Agios Theodori Church in Firostefani

This church—a steep 20-minute uphill hike from the center of Fira, on the trail to Oia, in the village of Firostefani—is quintessential Santorini: With a vivid blue dome, bright-yellow bell tower, and breathtaking caldera backdrop, it's perennially ready for its close-up. This is the only classic Santorini dome where you can snap a photo of the church with only water behind it—no other buildings or townscapes—making it a magnet for photographers. Inside is a precious icon of the Virgin Mary, bought here from Russia in 1570.

Nightlife in Fira

Folk Theater
White Door Theater puts on a faux Greek wedding in an open-air courtyard, with traditional music and dance and, of course, plate breaking. The audience, acting as guests at the wedding, is invited to participate. While this sounds tacky, it goes beyond the "Zorba the Greek" clichés. The program is thoughtfully researched, well-presented, and rooted in a deep respect for authentic Greek village customs. The organizers explain that, while every other major event in Greek village life (holidays, funerals) were religious and more introspective, a traditional wedding was the one time people could cut loose and fully enjoy themselves (€49 includes tapas dinner and wine, runs May-Oct nightly at 21:00, 2 hours, tel. 22860-21770, www.whitedoorsantorini.com).

Outdoor Cinema
In summer, **Volkan on the Rocks Café** often shows crowd-pleasing classics (*Mamma Mia!*, *My Big Fat Greek Wedding*, and so on) on a small outdoor screen perched over the caldera (€10, June-Oct most nights at 21:00 but subject to change—call ahead before making the trip, tel. 22860-28360, www.volkanontherocks.com).

Nightclubs
Fira is busy after hours. A popular venue is **Kira Thira Jazz Bar**, with good music and an artsy vibe (closed Mon-Tue). For a hard-partying nightclub—open late and packed with young people—**Casablanca Soul** is a classic (open nightly from 21:00). Both are buried deep in the town center.

Sleeping in Fira

Fira is the handier home base, but some prefer romantic Oia. All the accommodations I list have air-conditioning. Note that rates on this popular island skyrocket from July through September. While sticker-shock is epidemic here, keep in mind that the spectacular views are one of the main reasons you came. Therefore, splurging on a caldera view is, in a sense, a good value at just about any price.

SANTORINI

PLACES WITH CALDERA VIEWS

These accommodations all feature fantastic views and have peaceful terraces where you can watch the sunset. Most of these places spill down the cliffs from town and involve lots of stairs and steep climbs. To avoid so much climbing, try Kamares Apartments (a couple of minutes south of the Old Town, with parking right out front and a few stairs once you enter) or Villa Renos (some stairs, but fewer than most). Note that taxis can only take you to the top of the hill; you'll have to walk from there.

$$$$ Villa Renos, just below the Orthodox Cathedral, has nine well-appointed rooms. It's traditional (rather than trendy) and well-kept, with a small swimming pool at the bottom of the complex. It's well-run by Vassilis Matekas, who used to live in Rhode Island (great homemade breakfast that changes every day, tel. 22860-22369, www.villarenos.gr, hrenos@otenet.gr).

$$$$ Kamares Apartments surround a dreamy oasis of white-on-white stucco, with seven rooms, most with their own hot tub (some inside the room, some outside). The service is warm and attentive. At the very south end of town, it's sheltered from some of central Fira's nightlife noise, and also has handy parking right in front—a rarity for places with a view (family rooms available, tel. 22680-28110, www.kamares-apartments.gr, info@kamares-apartments.gr).

$$$$ Scirocco Apartments, run by a Greek-German couple (Eleftherios and Anja Sirigos and right-hand man Arthur), rents 17 straightforward, old-fashioned, but reasonably priced rooms for the location, some of them "cave houses" burrowed right into the cliffside. All rooms have sinks and are stocked with basic dishware, while some have bigger kitchenettes; all enjoy either a private or shared terrace and the swimming pool on the lowest level (breakfast extra, closed Nov-March, located facing the caldera below the Orthodox Cathedral, tel. 22860-22855, www.scirocco-santorini.com, info@scirocco-santorini.com). For drivers, they also rent seven rooms in the countryside on the far side of the island.

CHEAPER OPTIONS WITHOUT CALDERA VIEWS

If you're willing to give something up—view, luxury, and/or in-town convenience—you'll pay lower rates. But also lower your expectations: On Santorini, €100 buys a lot less comfort than it does in Athens.

Island Cuisine in a Desert

Santorini has an unusual approach to cuisine, dictated (like all facets of life here) by its volcanic geology. Most produce on the island is never watered...which is even more surprising when you think that Santorini—and the neighboring island of Anafi—are the only places in Europe technically classified as having a desert climate. But the island's very steep cliffs trap passing clouds, so on most mornings there's a fine layer of dew covering the ground—just enough to keep plants growing. Residents claim that this approach, along with the volcanic soil, makes their produce taste particularly sweet. Santorini specialties include grapes, tomatoes, eggplant, and cucumbers.

You'll find the predictable Greek classics on most menus, but also look for some local dishes. A Santorinian salad uses the island's cherry tomatoes and cucumbers; a popular starter is *tomatokeftedes*—deep-fried tomato croquettes. *Fava* is a chickpea spread similar to hummus. Because the main settlements of Santorini are perched on the tops of cliffs—with challenging access to the sea—fish isn't as integral to the cuisine as on other islands and is quite expensive. If you want fresh seafood, it's best to descend from the cliffsides and dine by the water, such as in Akrotiri in the south or on Ammoudi Bay in the north.

Close to Town: $$ Galatia Villas is calm and out of the way of Fira's stifling crowds, with 10 tasteful rooms—four larger studios and six doubles—plus a small swimming pool. Technically in Kontorhori, the next village over (around the corner from the Folklore Museum), it's about a 10-minute walk to Fira's action along a busy road (tel. 22860-24524, www.galatiavillas.gr, info@galatiavillas.gr).

In Town: $$ Villa Roussa offers 12 basic, worn budget rooms tucked in a dreary modern building overlooking a parking lot, behind the taxi stand and bus station. Some rooms have balconies, but not caldera views—which are a short walk away, over the ridge (no breakfast, tel. 22860-23220, www.villaroussa.gr, villaroussa@gmail.com, Peter Pelekanos).

Eating in Fira

You'll pay dearly to dine with a caldera view. I've focused my listings on simpler tavernas with great food at better prices, but less-thrilling vistas. Takeout fast-food options (grabbing a souvlaki to eat on a stool or to go) help keep costs down. Drivers note: One of my favorite places to eat on the island is **Metaxi Mas,** about a 15-minute drive into the countryside; for details, see page 471.

WITH A CALDERA VIEW

Santorini specializes in pricey restaurants with terraces facing the caldera—especially popular around sunset (reserve ahead). You'll basically pay double, and likely compromise on quality, to eat with a caldera view—but for a memorable meal, it could still be worth it. Many Fira caldera-view restaurants are interchangeable, but the ones noted below distinguish themselves in one way or another.

Below the Orthodox Cathedral: $$$$ Naoussa is a family-friendly place that churns out big plates of sloppy Greek cooking, served on its cozy and unpretentious terrace. While pricey, it's near the bottom end of this price range, and more affordable than other caldera-view eateries (daily 12:00-24:00, tucked below the big and boxy Atlantis Hotel, tel. 22860-24869, http://naoussa.restaurant).

Near the Cable Car: $$$$ Argo, also along the cliffs, serves traditional Greek food specializing in fish, at predictably high prices. While quite expensive, its quality is relatively reliable. Reserve ahead for the upper deck, with the best caldera views (daily 12:00-24:00, along the donkey path just below Gold Street, tel. 22860-22594, www.argo-restaurant-santorini.com).

Microbrews at the Top of Town, above the Catholic Cathedral: Some of the most sweeping views over Santorini can be found from the high-altitude trail toward Oia, about a five-minute hike up past the Catholic Cathedral. At the crest of the trail, just under the orange cultural center, **$$$ Volkan on the Rocks Café** is an inviting, low-key spot. They produce their own craft beer (five varieties, "filtered with volcanic rocks"), as well as pricey tropical cocktails and basic light bites and bar snacks. Come for the views, not the food (daily 9:00-24:00, tel. 22860-28360, www. volkanontherocks.com).

Cocktails with a View: Palia Kameni Cocktail Bar (ΠΑΛΙΑ ΚΑΜΕΝΗ), with an elaborately decorated "floating doorway" just in front of the Orthodox Cathedral, has cascading terraces with magnificent caldera views, a sophisticated vibe, and a tempting menu of good—if extremely expensive—cocktails (no food, daily 8:00-late, reserve a few weeks ahead for sunset table, tel. 22860-22430, www.paliakameni.com).

IN THE OLD TOWN

The Old Town streets teem with better-value eateries...still expensive by Greek standards, but far more affordable than caldera-view spots.

$$$ The Ouzerie (Το Ουζερι) is a big, popular, finely oiled machine of a restaurant churning out good traditional food with efficient service at the top of a shopping mall smack in the center. Their outside tables come with distant sea views—albeit ones looking east, rather than into the caldera. That means it doesn't work well at sunset (unless you're trying to avoid the crowds), but it's great for lunch or after dark. Try some of their local specialties, such as meatballs in an ouzo sauce and the *tomatokeftedes* starter—fried tomatoes with onions and herbs. They also have several vegetarian options (daily 11:00-24:00, head up the stairs next to Orthodox Cathedral, tel. 22860-21566).

$$$ Dionysos is another good choice, popular for its vast terrace (which faces the back of the island, rather than the caldera) and its good traditional food. While the service can be mixed, it's worth considering when you want to dine al fresco and The Ouzerie is packed (daily 12:00-23:30, tel. 22860-23845).

$$$ Nikolas oozes a family-run taverna vibe, with one big room crammed with tables overseen by a shrine-like photo of the namesake patriarch. Today his granddaughter Eleni runs the place, and while it's not quite what it used to be, they keep things traditional: stick-to-your-ribs Greek classics, specializing in casseroles and other oven-baked meals. There's no outdoor seating, but this is a good choice in bad weather or after sunset. It can get crowded—book ahead or be prepared to wait (daily 12:00-22:00, tel. 22860-36422).

$$$ Mama's House, with a nondescript interior and a breezy covered terrace a few steps down from the main road near the taxi stand, is popular with homesick Americans at breakfast time, here for their omelets and pancakes. At other times, they serve a solid menu of unpretentious Greek fare. The namesake materfamilias still takes orders, though these days she has help (daily 8:00-24:00, tel. 22860-21577).

$ Souvlaki: The local favorites for souvlaki are the hole-in-the-wall **Lucky's,** the glitzy **Obelix** for its sizable menu (summer only), and **Nick the Grill** for its handy people-watching location right on the main square.

Fira Connections

From Fira by Bus to: Oia (2-3/hour, 25 minutes), **Athinios/New Port** (nearly hourly—coordinated to meet boats, 20 minutes; for boat connections from Athinios, see "Santorini Connections" at the end of this chapter), **airport** (roughly hourly—coordinated to meet most flights, 15 minutes), **Kamari** and its nearby beaches (2-3/hour, 10 minutes), **Akrotiri** with its archaeological site and nearby red-sand beach (1-2/hour, 30 minutes), and **Perissa** with its black-sand beaches and access to the Ancient Thira archaeological site (2-3/hour, 30 minutes). A ride to virtually anywhere on the island costs about €2-3. Check schedules at the kiosk at the downhill edge of the lot, and buy tickets from the driver. Bus information: tel. 22860-25404, www.ktel-santorini.gr.

Oia

Oia (pronounced EE-ah, not OY-ah; sometimes spelled "Ia" in English) is the classic, too-pretty-to-be-true place you imagine

when someone says "Greek islands." This idyllic ensemble of whitewashed houses and blue domes is delicately draped over a steep slope at the top of a cliff. And in their wisdom, the locals have positioned their town just right for enjoying a sunset over the caldera. On a blue-sky day, there's no better place in Greece to go on a photo safari. Shoot the classic, blue-domed postcard views, but also wander around to find your own angle on the town. If you can't snap a postcard-quality photo here, it's time to retire your camera.

Oia wasn't always this alluring. In fact, half a century ago it was in ruins—devastated by an earthquake on July 9, 1956. When rebuilding, natives seized the opportunity to make their town even more picture-perfect than before—and it paid off. Though far from undiscovered, Oia is the kind of place that you don't mind sharing with boatloads of tourists. And if you break away from its main streets, you can find narrow, winding lanes that take you far from the crowds. This becomes more difficult at sunset, when what feels like every tourist on Santorini jams its tight streets (for strategies, see "Santorini Sunsets" sidebar, earlier). On the other hand, Oia is a delight in the early morning (before around 11:00)—before cruise excursions make their way to the town.

GETTING THERE

From Fira (the island's transport hub), it's about 7.5 miles north to Oia. You can take the bus (see "Fira Connections," earlier) or a taxi (€25 one-way), hike (several hours, see "Hike to Oia," earlier), or drive (see next).

Route Tips for Drivers: In normal traffic, it's about a 25-minute drive from Fira to Oia. The most scenic—and congested—route heads straight north out of Fira, passing the villages of Firostefani (consider pulling over and walking a few minutes for the classic Firostefani church view—see page 453) and Imerovigli, then driving along the spine of the island to Oia. However, they are widening what's intended to be a new main road, lower down and closer

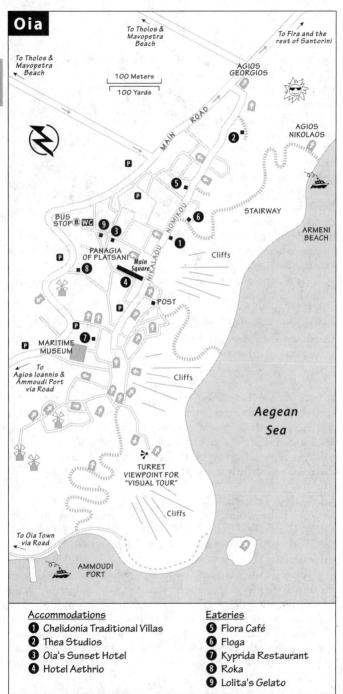

Oia

To Tholos & Mavopetra Beach

To Fira and the rest of Santorini

AGIOS GEORGIOS

To Tholos & Mavopetra Beach

AGIOS NIKOLAOS

100 Meters

100 Yards

MAIN ROAD

STAIRWAY

ARMENI BEACH

BUS STOP **B** **WC**

NIKOLAOU NOMIKOU

PANAGIA OF PLATSANI

Main Square

Cliffs

P

POST

MARITIME MUSEUM

To Agios Ioannis & Ammoudi Port via Road

Cliffs

Aegean Sea

TURRET VIEWPOINT FOR "VISUAL TOUR"

Cliffs

To Oia Town via Road

AMMOUDI PORT

SANTORINI

Accommodations
1 Chelidonia Traditional Villas
2 Thea Studios
3 Oia's Sunset Hotel
4 Hotel Aethrio

Eateries
5 Flora Café
6 Floga
7 Kyprida Restaurant
8 Roka
9 Lolita's Gelato

to the island's east coast, which will likely become the primary way to reach Oia (reducing traffic on the narrow road up top).

If you're coming on the upper road, as you approach Oia, you'll be routed down a long, one-way detour along the back side of the island, and then back up again, popping out just below the main part of town. A few parking lots are in this area, but they're often full. First, try turning right toward the port of Ammoudi; while you're still in Oia (before descending to the port), keep an eye out for parking lots that allow quick access to the scenic tip of town. If you find nothing available, go back the way you came, and continue along the one-way main road (past where you entered town) toward Fira, keeping a close eye out for additional parking lots. But don't go too far, or you'll have to loop all the way around again. (If you're here for sunset and want to enable a quick escape, it can make sense to park at the Fira end of town regardless—increasing walking but reducing traffic jams to leave town.) Some scattered spaces may be free, but most lots charge a small fee—carefully check for signs before leaving your car.

Orientation to Oia

Oia lines up along its cliff. The main pedestrian drag, which traces the rim of the cliff, is called Nikolaou Nomikou. Oia's steep seaward side is smothered with accommodations and restaurants, while the flat landward side is more functional. The town is effectively traffic-free except for the main road, which runs along the back of town, passing the town bus stop and parking lots. From here, it's a few short, nondescript blocks toward the cliff and its million-dollar views.

Sights in Oia

▲▲▲Visual Tour of Oia

You can see most of Oia with a sweep of the head from a prime vantage point: its ruined castle, at the very tip of town. Make your way there and follow this visual tour for an orientation to this picturesque little burg.

• *With your back to the water, face the homes and domes of Oia, and think of its history.*

Oia's Skyline: While today it's a posh resort, in its heyday Oia was the island's most prosperous town—located at the point where arriving ships first reached Santorini. Scan the distinctive townscape: The large, boxy buildings at the top of town were the homes of the wealthy sea captains (one of which is now a museum—see later). And the humble, whitewashed cave houses on the slopes

Santorini's Cave Houses

On Santorini, you'll see a unique type of building...and maybe even sleep in one: the cave house (*yposkafa*). In addition to serving as residences or hotels, these structures house churches, *cavanas* (wine-pressing rooms), and other establishments.

Cave houses were originally dug into the soft volcanic rock by poor workers who couldn't afford to build a freestanding house. High on the cliffs, they also provided security against invaders. The top of the cave is a rounded arch, rather than flat, to provide more durability in case of earthquakes. People would live and cook near the cave's front, and sleep in the back. Often the house includes a small aboveground structure; after the Venetians began to fortify the island in the 13th century—providing more safety to islanders—these became more common.

Between the inner and outer walls is a layer of pumice insulation—lighter than other types of stone, and very effective for keeping the interiors warm in winter and cool in summer. These days, new construction looks similar but uses a synthetic Styrofoam instead of pumice. A thinner layer of Styrofoam is needed, allowing them to carve out larger interiors without violating building codes by raising the roof.

For the trim (thresholds and windowsills), look for a porous, reddish, volcanic rock; while this is often plastered over and painted, it looks sharp in its natural state.

And why all the whitewash? For one thing, white reflects (rather than absorbs) the powerful heat of the sun. White is

the color of the mineral lime mixed with water, which makes a good antiseptic (islanders used it to paint their houses, so it would naturally disinfect the rainwater that was collected on rooftops). Later, white evolved into an aesthetic choice...

and a patriotic one: During the 400-year Ottoman occupation, Greeks were not allowed to fly their blue-and-white flag. But here in Oia—with its white houses, blue domes, blue sea and sky, and white clouds—the whole village was one big defiant banner for Greece. The blue-and-white color scheme also resembles the "evil eye," believed to fend off bad spirits.

below housed their crew, stevedores, and other laborers. These people couldn't afford to build a big, fancy house...so they dug one (see the sidebar). While the cave houses were once the poorest dwellings in town, today only millionaires can afford to own them (and virtually all of them are rented out as very pricey accommodations). The few residents who live in Oia can't afford to have a view. Most "locals" live in humble villages a 10- to 20-minute drive from the caldera.

By the way, much of the Oia you see today dates back only about 60 years. Santorini is famous for its 17th-century-B.C. erup-

tion. But a much more recent disaster also did its part to shape the island: In the middle of the night in July 1956, a 7.7-magnitude earthquake struck the nearby island of Amorgos, followed by a tsunami. Two-thirds of the island's buildings collapsed, forcing locals to rebuild. Oia was particularly hard-hit. Today, some locals reason that perhaps this was a blessing in disguise, as it jolted notoriously conservative Santorini out of its old-fashioned ways, setting the groundwork for the tourist onslaught that was to come.

• *You're standing on the site of...*

Oia's "Castle": This stubby tower is all that remains of the Castle of Agios Nikolaos—one of the original five fortresses that the occupying Venetians built to defend against pirate invasions. The complex still belongs to the Catholic Church, who have decided to keep it a ruin. And, with its 360-degree views, it's the prime location for watching the sunset. (If you'd like to do that, you'll need to stake out a space here well before—an hour or more—and defend it jealously.) So, why is Oia so famous for its sunset? In 1982, Daryl Hannah and Peter Gallagher frolicked here in the romantic comedy *Summer Lovers,* featuring idyllic Oia (then a ghost town) and its glorious sunset. While virtually nobody remembers the movie, the buzz it created around Oia's sunset has taken on a life of its own. (For more sunset tips, see the "Santorini Sunsets" sidebar.)

• *Nearby, about 250 steps lead steeply down (immediately below town) to the port of...*

Ammoudi: Historically, this was one of the island's main ports. Despite its desolate landscape, Santorini produced valuable exports that helped make it wealthy—most notably the sweet wine Vinsanto, which was used for Communion in Orthodox churches in Russia and southeastern Europe. In exchange, locals imported wood (on this virtually unforested island, timber was a major status symbol), barrels, kerosene, and

wheat and rye for the wealthy (the poor ate barley). Goods would be loaded onto donkeys to be hauled to or from the port. Imagine the steady trade—Greek grapes for Russian wood—that kept this remote island tethered to the outside world for centuries, right up until the Bolshevik Revolution of the early 20th century shut down Russian Orthodox churches and shot down Santorini's main source of export revenue. To compensate, Santorini's traders shifted to extracting and exporting pumice, a desirable building material. This remained a big export until the 1980s; you can see an (ugly) quarry at the right end of Thirasia, across the caldera; another abandoned one is just south of Fira.

• *Now that you're oriented, enjoy...*

The Rest of Oia: There's not much to see or do here, other than enjoy the commanding views. Near the castle, notice several **windmills**—taking advantage of the predictably blustery Cycladic winds. As you explore—particularly in the part of town toward Fira—you'll notice you're walking on paving stones made of **marble,** which is not indigenous to a volcanic island. The marble came to Santorini in the form of ballast, weighing down too-light ships returning from Russia after delivering their heavy loads of Vinsanto. If you're determined to do some sightseeing, dip into the Naval Maritime Museum, described next.

Naval Maritime Museum

Every Greek island seems to have its own maritime museum, and Oia hosts Santorini's. With two floors of old nautical objects and basic English labels, the collection includes roomfuls of old ship paintings, letters and documents, model ships, and well-endowed mastheads. It's the only museum in town, but it's nothing to jump ship for, unless you're a sailor or need a place to get out of the sun.

Cost and Hours: €3, Wed-Mon 10:00-14:00 & 17:00-20:00,

until 19:00 in shoulder season, closed Tue and Nov-March, well-signposted a block off the main cliff-top drag, tel. 22860-71156.

Sleeping in Oia

WITH A CALDERA VIEW

Several places rent out appealing "cave houses" just down from the main cliff-side road. They range from smaller rooms or studios for two people, to larger units sleeping four or more. Though expensive, a cave-house stay is an unforgettable experience.

$$$$ At **Chelidonia Traditional Villas,** friendly Greek-Austrian couple Triantaphyllos and Erika Pitsikali rent 13 traditional apartments surrounded by burgeoning bougainvillea and burrowed into the cliff face right in the heart of town. Triantaphyllos grew up in one of these houses, bought the others from his grandparents and cousins, and renovated them himself, retaining as much as he could of the original (large) footprint. Promising "panorama and privacy," this place lets you be a temporary troglodyte (includes breakfast, tel. 22860-71287, www.chelidonia.com, erika@chelidonia.com).

$$$$ **Thea Studios** offers the same caldera views as more expensive places but with fewer frills (no swimming pool or hot tub, no breakfast, etc.). The eight rooms, though basic, are clean, pleasant, a decent size, and come with kitchenettes (family loft apartment available, closed Nov-March, guests have access to pool at nearby Lioyerma Pool Bar, mobile 694-462-2333, www.theasantorini.com, info@theasantorini.com, managed by Markos and Torun).

IN TOWN

It's certainly cheaper to sleep in the town center, a short walk from caldera views—but in this pricey village, you're still paying dearly for basic lodgings.

$$$$ **Oia's Sunset Hotel,** on a busy little lane at the back of town (near the bus stop), is a tight little compound with 15 relatively well-priced apartments sharing a swimming pool. While a bit loosely run, it's one of the more affordable and reliable options in town (breakfast extra, minimal soundproofing, tel. 22860-71420, www.oiasunset.com, info@oiasunset.com).

$$$ **Hotel Aethrio** is a lovely little complex tucked deep in town (no caldera views). It feels like its own little village, with three entrances, 19 rooms scattered through several buildings, a swimming pool, a sunset deck, and even its own little church. While somewhat spartan for this swanky town, it's well-located and reasonably priced, and the grounds are inviting (tel. 22860-71420, www.aethrio.gr, info@aethrio.gr).

Eating in Oia

Oia must be the most expensive place to dine in all of Greece. Places with no view are plenty pricey—and ones with a view are even more so. Reservations at any place are wise for dinner; there's a big rush just before the sunset (for caldera-view places) and immediately after the sunset (for non-caldera view places).

FACING THE CALDERA

The cliffside places are pretty interchangeable, but if you can't make up your mind, consider one of these (but skip the hard-to-miss Kastro restaurant, with disappointing food at terrible prices).

$$ Flora Café is an affordable alternative to the budget-busting places along the cliff, with a straightforward menu of pizzas, pastas, salads, and meat dishes. Set along the main drag (at the Fira end of town), it's essentially a classy snack bar with a pleasantly casual setting and friendly service (daily 9:00-24:00, tel. 22860-71424, www.flora-santorini.com, Flora).

$$$$ Floga is a scenic splurge dishing up traditional Greek food with a modern spin. It's a few steps below the main drag at the Fira end of town, with dramatic caldera views—albeit not of the sunset (daily specials, daily 8:00-24:00, tel. 22860-71152, www.floga-oia.com).

BURIED IN TOWN, WITH DISTANT SEA VIEWS

$$$ Kyprida Restaurant, serving traditional Cypriot cuisine, is a rare reasonably priced option in Oia. It's set a couple of blocks back from the cliff edge, but its top terrace still has a fine sunset view (daily 12:00-24:00, live music on Wed nights and also Sat in summer, closed off-season, tel. 22860-71979, www.kyprida.gr).

$$$ Roka (ρόκα) is a humble little *kafeneio/ouzeri* (coffee-and-ouzo taverna serving traditional dishes), tucked deep in the heart of town. It has seating on the colorful courtyard, a cozy interior, and a terrace with views over the back of the island (daily 13:00-23:30, tel. 22860-71896, www.roka.gr).

Ice Cream: Facing the bus-stop bustle, **Lolita's Gelato** has a loyal following for pricey, top-end ice cream (daily 10:30-22:00, tel. 22860-71279).

More Sights on Santorini

Santorini has many worthwhile sights outside Fira and Oia, doable by bus or taxi but best by car. These include a string of beaches along its eastern side, two major archaeological sites, a lighthouse on a bluff, wineries, and boat trips around the caldera. A day or two on Santorini with a car is a delight.

▲▲BOAT TRIPS IN THE CALDERA

A variety of boat trips are designed to take tourists out into the caldera for stunning views back on the village-topped cliffs. Many of these sail from the Old Port below Fira, some depart from Ammoudi below Oia, and some can pick you up at your hotel.

One popular option takes you out to the active volcanic islets in the middle of the caldera: the crater on **Nea Kameni,** where you can hike up to the crater (exciting if you've never climbed around a lava field before); and **Palea Kameni,** known mostly for its shallow, muddy, tepid "hot" springs that's loaded with bobbing tourists. While this sounds intriguing, for most, the highlight is simply the views—not the activities on the islands themselves. Some boat trips also include a visit to **Thirasia,** the sleepy island across the caldera from Thira (with not much to see once on land). Sunset is, quite deservedly, a popular time to do these trips; cruises know where to position their passengers to be sure to see the sun swallowed up by the Aegean.

You have a variety of options for doing these trips. The basic choice is a crowded **tour boat,** which charges anywhere from €18 for a 2.5-hour tour to Nea Kameni, to €35 for a five-hour sunset tour including a drink. Travel agencies all over Santorini advertise basically interchangeable options. Just drop into one, peruse your options, and book.

For something more exclusive and expensive, **catamaran cruises** are a worthwhile spurge (book ahead; these typically include a transfer from your hotel to the boat). You'll pay much more (€100-150/person for similar itineraries to those described above), but enjoy a far more relaxed and exclusive experience—with unlimited drinks and only a couple dozen people on  a small, sail-masted catamaran...plenty of room to spread out and relax. I had a memorable evening out on the sunset cruise with

Caldera Yachting, which included pick-up and drop off at my hotel, an excellent dinner, a top-notch and attentive crew, opportunities to swim from the catamaran, and enough caldera views to fill up my camera, all for €150 per person (www.calderayachting.gr).

BEACHES

Beaches aren't Santorini's forte. Because most towns (including Fira and Oia) cap cliffs high above the water, it's a hassle to reach an inviting spot for a dip—and they're not quite as idyllic as beaches on other islands (such as Mykonos). Perhaps the most satisfying way to go for a swim is from a boat tour in the caldera; many of these drop anchor and invite passengers to dive in from the boat deck.

If you're spending time in Oia, the easiest option is to hike or drive steeply down to the pint-sized port of **Ammoudi,** at the base of the cliffs immediately below the pinnacle of town. This is a busy working port with a few fish restaurants and just enough opportunities to get into the water. Drivers be warned that the road tethering Ammoudi to Oia is tight and extremely congested; parking is limited, so you'll likely have to squeeze in along the side of the road and hike partway. Another little cove—called **Armeni**—is just around the corner, facing the caldera below Oia, and accessible only by a very steep hike (or by yacht).

By car or bus, you can reach some beaches with unusual volcanic compositions. Two black-sand beaches flank the steep mountain, capped by Ancient Thira, at the southeastern corner of the island: near **Kamari** (tidy and more upscale-feeling) and **Perissa** (more popular with backpackers). While pleasant, these are less exotic than they sound—the black "sand" is quite coarse, and the general vibe is a typical Greek-island beach.  While these beaches look close together as the crow flies, they're separated by a mountain—it's a half-hour drive, challenging three-hour hike, or 15-minute taxi-boat ride between them.

Along the southern arc of the island, there are some famous volcanically colorful beaches near Akrotiri (facing away from the caldera). The **White Beach,** in front of a backdrop of chalky cliffs, is accessible exclusively by boat. The **Red Beach,** given its distinctive color by iron deposits, can be reached by a quite treacherous hike over loose rocks and around the bluff (from the bay near the Akrotiri archaeological site, described later). Locals warn not to underestimate the danger of this hike, which is susceptible to rockslides. As this is quite close to the Akrotiri site, it's a good add-on for hardy hikers.

▲WINERIES

Santorini, one of Greece's most high-profile wine producers, has a dozen or so wineries open to the public. If visiting during the harvest (around mid-Aug), you may even find a winery that lets you stomp some grapes. While you'll pay for tastings, and bottles are quite expensive (typically starting around €20), it's fascinating to learn about the way wine is cultivated here (see the sidebar). These places are all within about a 10-minute drive of each other, in the island's interior, roughly on the way from Fira to Kamari, Perissa, or the airport. For a meal in the area, don't miss the excellent Metaxi Mas, listed at the end of this section. See the Santorini Island map for locations.

Santo is the best-known option, just up the road from the New Port, on the road between Fira and Akrotiri. It's a cooperative working with all the island's wineries—the biggest operation like this in the Cyclades. Established in 1947, it produces 500,000 bottles a year, 70 percent of which are consumed in Greece. Despite the cruise-ship tour crowds that descend on this place (it can be mobbed), Santo offers a good opportunity to taste Santorini's wine while enjoying great views (if coming for sunset, call ahead to reserve a scenic table). Tastings are pricey, but serious—giving you a substantial sampling of Santorini's wines (€25/6 tastes with light food pairings, €26/12 tastes focused on just the wine, daily 9:00-22:00, July-Aug until 23:00, shorter hours off-season and closed on Mon Dec-Feb). They also offer 25-minute tours of their production facility (€9/person, 25 minutes, call in the morning at 9:30 to check English tour schedule, does not include any tastings; tel. 22860-22596, www.santowines.gr).

Venetsanos, more boutique and rustic, is just a five-minute drive away and enjoys even grander views. The founder, George Venetsanos, was a real pioneer when he built this winery in 1947, using a system of interconnected equipment to turn grapes into wine, then flowing the final product from fermentation tanks through a series of pipes that ran down the hillside and straight into barrels on ships docked at the port. To see some of the original equipment and walk through the winery's tunnels, request a tour (€3, 10-15 minutes). Or you can pay €10 for five tastings, served to you either on the terrace with gorgeous caldera views or in the tasting room. It's best to call ahead and tell them you're coming (daily 10:00-21:00, tel. 22860-21100, www.venetsanoswinery.com).

Koutsoyannopoulos is another well-established winery, which also operates a "Cave Wine Museum." The included audio-guide tells the history of the winery (which dates back to 1880),

Santorini Wines

While Greece isn't particularly acclaimed for its wines, Santorini's are well-respected. The discovery of ancient grape seeds at Akrotiri indicates that the winemaking tradition here dates back more than 3,500 years. Wine would be mixed with collected rainwater to disinfect it, making it safer to drink. Historically, the wealthier the family, the sweeter their wine; peasants basically drank vinegar. Today, the most common local grapes are Assyrtiko, one of the best Greek varietals; they produce a dry white wine with minerality and acidity.

The growing vines are twisted into a round basket shape called *ampelies,* with the grapes tucked inside to protect them from the strong sunlight and fierce winds. The shape also helps retain moisture from nighttime fog on this otherwise arid isle. The pumice in the ground absorbs liquid from the atmosphere, then distributes it to the vines' roots. All of this means that, even though it can go months here without rain, local grapes typically don't require additional irrigation. Connoisseurs say that the terroir created by Santorini's unique conditions gives the wine a special flavor.

The most famous, and most expensive, Santorini-grown wine is Vinsanto (sweet dessert wine made from a blend of sun-dried grapes). Santorini's export of Vinsanto to Eastern Orthodox churches (especially in Russia), to use for the Eucharist, was historically one of its most lucrative exports. Also respected is Nykteri, a dry white wine produced in a single day (the name means "night work"). Several shops in Fira or Oia offer wine tasting, or you can visit one of the wineries on the island (I've listed a few).

explains how grapes have been grown, transferred, and crushed through the years, and discusses the challenges facing wine producers on this hot, dry island. With its cheesy sets and fake figures, the museum is a bit old-school, though it is interesting to see the equipment that was used back in the day. Allow about an hour for the full experience (€9.50, includes audioguide and four tastings, daily 9:00-19:00, off-season until 16:00, last entry one hour before closing, tel. 22860-31322, www.santoriniwinemuseum.com).

Argyros, in the valley just outside of Kamari, lacks grand caldera views but makes up for it with its sleek, picturesque estate, tucked amid rolling vineyards. You can sample their wines in the modern tasting room (€8/5 wines), or call ahead to arrange a tour of the vineyards and production line (€15, includes a tasting of three whites and two Vinsantos). While classy, Argyros has less pretense and feels a bit younger, fresher, and more personal than the others listed here (Mon-Sat 8:00-19:30, Sun 10:00-18:00, tel. 22860-31489, www.estate-argyros.com).

Beer Tasting: If your tastes skew to hops rather than grapes, stop in at **Santorini Brewing Company.** In their small production facility, they offer tastes of the three beers they brew on-site (plus occasional seasonal variations), and sell bottles to go. Their beers are also sold all over the island. As this is an easy walk down the road from Argyros, groups with a mix of beer and wine lovers can divide and conquer (Mon-Sat 11:00-17:00, shorter hours Oct-April, closed Sun year-round, in Mesa Gonia about 1.5 miles out of Kamari, tel. 22860-30268, www.donkey.gr).

Near Oia: For people staying in Oia, **Sigales** is a good nearby winery (tel. 22860-71644, www.sigalas-wine.com).

Eating near the Wineries: My favorite countryside eatery on Santorini—well worth a special trip—is **$$$ Metaxi Mas** (Μεταξύ Μας), in the village of Exo Gonia, less than a 10-minute drive from most recommended wineries. Park in the big lot by the town church, then hike over the ridge into town, and you'll spot it on your right. They have ample outdoor seating, a relaxed vibe, and top-quality traditional Santorini and Greek cuisine prepared with modern techniques. Foodies love it—reserve ahead. Their outdoor terrace—across the street—comes with big views over the island and sea, but lacks shade. If going for lunch, note its unusually late opening time (daily 13:30-24:00, tel. 22860-31323, www.santorini-metaximas.gr).

ANCIENT SITES

If you're hitting multiple archaeological sites on the island, invest in the great-value €14 combo-ticket, which covers Akrotiri, Ancient Thira, and the Museum of Prehistoric Thira in Fira. Both Akrotiri and Ancient Thira have a history of unexpected closures, so carefully confirm in town that they're open before you set out.

▲Akrotiri Archaeological Site

Just before Santorini's massive c. 1630 B.C. eruption, its inhabitants fled the island, leaving behind a city that was soon buried (and preserved) in ash—much like Pompeii, but 1,700 years earlier. (Consider this: The Minoan-era civilization that lived here was as ancient to the Romans as the Romans are to us; many scholars think this may have been what started the legend of Atlantis.) That city, near the modern-day town of Akrotiri, is still being dug up, with more than 30 buildings now excavated and viewable in a well-designed structure that makes it easy to explore the ruins. Keep in mind that only 3 percent of the site has been unearthed—this city was huge. Ramps let you climb around and through the streets of the prehistoric city, where careful observers can pick out sidewalks, underground sewage systems, and some ceramic vases left behind. However, the most interesting items discovered here—wonderful wall frescoes, fancy furniture, painted ceramics—are on display elsewhere, mainly at Fira's Museum of Prehistoric Thira (see "Sights in Fira," earlier) and the National Archaeological Museum in Athens.

Cost and Hours: €12, €6 off-season, covered by €14 combo-ticket, Fri-Wed 8:00-19:00, Thu until 15:00, one-hour guided tours-€10, private guide-€60, tel. 22860-81939, www.culture.gr.

Getting There: Without a car, Akrotiri is reachable by frequent buses from Fira (2/hour, 30 minutes, around €2) or taxi (€25).

Eating: For some of the freshest seafood on the island, try **$$$ The Dolphins** on Akrotiri Beach, a delightful family-run fish tavern with sheltered tables on a pier and more seating along the water (daily 12:00-23:00, turn left out the Akrotiri ruins and walk down into the village, tel. 22860-81151; mom and sons run the place, dad fishes).

Nearby: The treacherous trail to the famous **Red Beach** is near Akrotiri (described earlier). The **lighthouse** at Faros, at the southwest tip of the island, has amazing views (also a good place to watch the sunset at certain times of year).

Ancient Thira

Dramatically situated on a mountaintop between Perissa and Kamari, this site dates from a more recent civilization. It was settled post-volcano by Dorians from Sparta, likely in the ninth century B.C., and continued to thrive through the Hellenistic, Roman, and Byzantine periods. This place is less distinctive than the Akrotiri site and is only worth a visit by archaeology completists. If you've toured other Greek ruins from this era—in Athens, Delphi, Olympia, Epidavros, and so on—you'll see nothing new here. You can reach the Ancient Thira site from Kamari, which has regular bus excursions.

Cost and Hours: €4, covered by €14 combo-ticket, Tue-Sun 8:00-15:00, closed Mon, tel. 22860-22217, www.culture.gr.

Getting There: Besides driving or taxi, you can take a bus to Kamari, then either walk 30 minutes or catch an hourly minibus from the TI in that town. Hardy hikers can also huff up from Perissa on a very twisty serpentine path.

Santorini Connections

The New Port (Athinios) is a 20-minute bus ride from Fira, and buses can be very crowded in summer—allow enough time to make your connection. For ferry tips, see the Practicalities chapter; for office locations in Fira, see page 443.

By Boat from the New Port: Santorini is connected daily to **Piraeus** in Athens (slow boat: 1/day year-round, 8 hours, on Blue Star; fast boat: generally 2/day April-Oct, 5 hours), **Mykonos** (generally 2-4/day April-mid-Oct, 3 hours), and other Cycladic Islands, as well as to **Crete** (1-2/day April-Oct, 2.5 hours). The fast routes are all operated by Hellenic Seaways (www.hellenicseaways.gr) or SeaJets (www.seajets.gr).

GREEK HISTORY & MYTHOLOGY

Our lives today would be quite different if it weren't for a few thousand Greeks who lived in the small city of Athens about 450 years before Jesus was born. Democracy, theater, literature, mathematics, science, philosophy, and art all flourished in Athens during its 50-year "Golden Age"—a cultural boom time that set the tone for the rest of Western history to follow.

Greece's history since Classical times may be less familiar to most visitors, but it's fascinating nonetheless. From pagan to Christian to Muslim, to the freedom-fighters of the 19th century and the refugees of the 20th and 21st centuries, Greece today is the product of many different peoples, religions, and cultures.

THE PRE-GREEK WORLD:
THE MINOANS (2000-1450 B.C.)

The incredible civilization that we now call Classical Greece didn't just pop out of nowhere. Cursed with rocky soil, isolated by a rugged landscape, and scattered by invasions, the Greeks took centuries to unify. The civilization of Golden Age Greece was built on the advances of earlier civilizations: Minoans, Mycenaeans, Dorians, and Ionians—the stew of peoples that eventually cooked up what became Greece.

A safe, isolated location on the island of Crete, combined with impressive business savvy, enabled the Minoans to dominate the pre-Greek world. Unlike most early peoples, they were traders, not fighters. With a large merchant fleet, they exported wine, olive oil, pottery, and well-crafted jewelry, then returned home with the wealth of the Mediterranean.

Today we know the Minoans by the colorful frescoes they left behind on the walls of prosperous, unfortified homes and palaces. Surviving frescoes show happy people engaged in everyday life:

Ancient Greek World

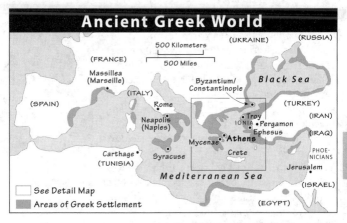

(UKRAINE) (RUSSIA)

500 Kilometers
500 Miles

(FRANCE)

Massillea
(Marseille)

(SPAIN)

(ITALY)

Byzantium/
Constantinople

Black Sea

Rome

Neapolis
(Naples)

Troy
IONIA • Pergamon
Ephesus

(TURKEY)

(IRAN)

(IRAQ)

Mycenae • Athens

Crete

Carthage •
(TUNISIA)

Syracuse

Mediterranean Sea

PHOE-
NICIANS

Jerusalem
•

(ISRAEL)

(EGYPT)

☐ See Detail Map
▨ Areas of Greek Settlement

GREEK HISTORY

ladies harvesting saffron, athletes leaping over bulls, and charming landscapes with animals.

The later Greeks would inherit the Minoans' business skills, social equality, love of art for art's sake, and faith in rational thought over brute military strength. Some scholars hail the Minoans as the first truly "European" civilization.

Between about 1450 and 1150 B.C., the Minoan civilization suddenly collapsed, and no one knows why (volcano? invasions?). Physically and economically weakened, they were easily overrun and absorbed by a tribe of warlike people from the mainland—the Mycenaeans.

Minoan-Era Sights
- Frescoes from Akrotiri on the island of Santorini—in the National Archaeological Museum in Athens, and the Museum of Prehistoric Thira on Santorini

MYCENAE (1600-1100 B.C.)
After the fall of the Minoans, the Greek mainland was dominated by the Mycenaeans (my-seh-NEE-uhns), a fusion of local tribes concentrated in the city of Mycenae (my-SEE-nee). Culturally, they were the anti-Minoans—warriors not traders, chieftains not bureaucrats. Their ruins at the capital of Mycenae (about two hours by bus southwest of Athens, or a half-hour's drive north of Nafplio) tell the story. Buildings are fortress-like, the city has thick defen-

sive walls, and statues are stiff and crude. Early Greeks called Mycenaean architecture "cyclopean," because they believed that only giants could have built with such colossal blocks. Mycenaean kings were elaborately buried in cemeteries and tombs built like subterranean stone igloos, loaded with jewels, swords, and precious objects that fill museums today.

The Mycenaeans dominated Greece during the era of the legends of the Trojan War. Whether there's any historical truth to the legends, Mycenae has become associated with the tales of Agamemnon, Clytemnestra, and the invasion of Troy.

Around 1100 B.C., the Mycenaeans—like the Minoans before them—mysteriously disappeared, plunging Greece into its next, "dark," phase.

Mycenaean Sights

- The citadel at Mycenae, with its Lion Gate, Grave Circle A, palace, and *tholos* tombs
- Mask of Agamemnon and other artifacts at the National Archaeological Museum in Athens
- Dendra Panoply, a 15th-century B.C. suit of bronze armor in the Nafplio Archaeological Museum

THE GREEK DARK AGES (1200-700 B.C.)

Whatever the reason, once-powerful Mycenaean cities became deserted, writing was lost, roads crumbled, trade decreased, and ban-

dits preyed on helpless villagers. Dark Age graves contain little gold, jewelry, or fine pottery. Divided by mountains into pockets of isolated, semi-barbaric, warring tribes, the Greeks took centuries to unify and get their civilization back on track.

It was during this time that legends passed down over generations were eventually compiled (in the ninth century B.C.) by a blind, talented, perhaps nonexistent man that tradition calls Homer. His long poem, the *Iliad*, describes the battles and struggles of the early Greeks (perhaps the Mycenaeans) as they conquered Troy. The *Odyssey* tells of the weary soldiers' long, torturous trip back home. The Greeks saw these epics as perfect metaphors for their own struggles to unify and build a stable homeland. The stories helped shape a collective self-image.

It was also during this time that Delphi, which was believed

Heart of Greek Ancient World

MACEDONIA

Byzantium•

To Italy

Mt. Olympus ▲

THRACE

•Troy

ASIA MINOR

Corcyra (Corfu)

Thermo-•pylae

Aegean Sea

•Pergamon

Delphi•

•Marathon

IONIA

Mycenae•

•Thebes

•Ephesus

Olympia•

•Argos•

•**Athens**

Nafplio•

•Epidavros

←Delos

To Persia

ARCADIA

•Sparta

Ionian Sea

•Santorini (Thira)

Rhodes

Sea of Crete

Knossos•

CRETE

To Egypt↘

Mediterranean   Sea

to be the center of the world, emerged as an important place where leaders would go to find answers and gain (divine?) inspiration.

Dark Age Sights

• The Kastalian Spring and omphalos monuments at Delphi

ARCHAIC PERIOD (700-480 B.C.)

Tradition holds that in 776 B.C., Greek-speaking people from all over the mainland and islands halted their wars and gathered in Olympia to compete in the first Olympic Games. Bound by a common language and religion, Greece's scattered tribes began settling down.

Living on islands and in valleys, the Greek-speaking people were divided by geography from their neighbors. They naturally formed governments around a single city (or polis) rather than as a unified empire. Petty warfare between city-states was practically a sport.

Slowly, the city-states unified, making alliances with one another, establish-

ing colonies in what is now Italy and France, and absorbing culture from the more sophisticated Egyptians (style of statues) and Phoenicians (alphabet). Scarcely two centuries later, Greece would be an integrated community and the center of the civilized world.

Statues from Archaic times are crude, as stiff as the rock they're carved from. Rather than individuals, they are generic people: called either kore (girl) or kouros (boy). With perfectly round heads, symmetrical pecs, and a navel in the center, these sturdy statues reflect the order and stability the troubled Greeks were striving for.

By the sixth century B.C., Greece's many small city-states had coalesced around two power centers: oppressive, no-frills, and militaristic Sparta; and its polar opposite, the democratic, luxury-loving, and business-friendly Athens.

Archaic Sights
- Dipylon Vase (National Archaeological Museum in Athens) and other geometric vases in various museums
- Kouros and kore statues (National Archaeological Museum in Athens, Acropolis Museum in Athens, Archaeological Museum in Delphi)
- The Olympic Stadium and Temple of Hera in Olympia
- *Sphinx of Naxos* (Archaeological Museum in Delphi)
- *Lions of the Naxians* statues on the island of Delos

PRE-GOLDEN AGE: THE RISE OF ATHENS AND THE PERSIAN WARS (480-450 B.C.)

In 490 B.C., an enormous army of Persians under King Darius I swept into Greece to punish the city of Athens, which had dared to challenge his authority over Greek-speaking Ionia (in today's western Turkey). A few thousand plucky Athenians raced to head off the Persians in a crucial bottleneck valley, at the Battle of Marathon. Though outnumbered three to one, the crafty Greeks lined up and made a wall of shields (a phalanx) and pushed  the Persians back. An excited Greek soldier ran the 26.2 miles from the city of Marathon to Athens, gasped the good news...and died.

In 480 B.C., Persia attacked again. This time all of Greece put aside its petty differences to fight the common enemy as an alliance of city-states. King Leonidas of Sparta and his 300 Spartans made an Alamo-like last stand at Thermopylae that delayed the invasion. Meanwhile, Athenians abandoned their city and fled, leaving

Athens (and much of the lower mainland) to be looted. But the Athenians rallied to win a crucial naval victory at the Battle of Salamis, followed by a land victory at the Battle of Plataea, driving out the Persians.

Athens was hailed as Greece's protector and policeman, and the various city-states cemented their alliance (the Delian League) by pooling their defense funds, with Athens as the caretaker. Athens signed a 30-year peace treaty with Sparta...and the Golden Age began.

Pre-Golden Age Sights

- Severe-style statues, such as the *Artemision Bronze* (Athens' National Archaeological Museum) and *Bronze Charioteer* (Delphi)
- Olympia's Temple of Zeus and the bronze helmet of Miltiades

GOLDEN AGE ATHENS (450-400 B.C.)

Historians generally call Greece's cultural flowering the "Classical Period" (approximately 500-323 B.C.), with the choice cut being the

two-generation span (450-400 B.C.) called the "Golden Age." After the Persian War, the Athenians set about rebuilding their city (with funds from the Delian League). Grand public buildings and temples were decorated with painting and sculpture. Ancient Athens was a typical city-state, with a population of at least 100,000 gathered around its acropolis ("high town"), which was the religious center and fort of last defense. Below was the agora, or marketplace, the economic and social center. Blessed with a harbor and good farmland, Athens prospered, exporting cash crops (wine and olive oil, pottery and other crafts) to neighboring cities and importing the best craftsmen, thinkers, and souvlaki. Amphitheaters hosted drama, music, and poetry festivals. The marketplace bustled with goods from all over the Mediterranean. Upwardly mobile Greeks flocked to Athens. The incredible advances in art, architecture, politics, science, and philosophy set the pace for all of Western civilization to follow. And all this from a Greek town smaller than Muncie, Indiana.

Athens' leader, a charismatic nobleman named Pericles, set out to democratize Athens. As with many city-states, Athens' government had morphed from rule by king, to a council of nobles, to rule by "tyrants" in troubled times, and finally to rule by the people. In Golden Age Athens, every landowning man had a vote in the As-

Greek Mythology

The following were the stars among a large cast of characters—gods, beasts, and heroes—who scampered through the Greek mindscape, mingled with mortals, and inspired so much classical art and literature.

The Gods

The major Greek gods (the Olympians) lived atop Mount Olympus, presided over by Zeus, king of the gods (and father of many of them). Each god had a distinct personality, unique set of talents, and area of responsibility over the affairs of the world (they specialized). Though they were immortal and super-powerful, these gods were not remote, idealized deities; instead, like characters in a celestial soap opera, they displayed the full range of human foibles: petty jealousies, destructive passions, broken hearts, and god-sized temper tantrums. They also regularly interacted with humans—falling in love with them, seducing them, toying with them, and punishing them. The Romans were so impressed by the Greek lineup of immortals that they borrowed them, but gave them new names (shown in parentheses below).

Zeus (Jupiter): Papa Zeus liked the ladies, and often turned himself into some earthly form (a bull, a cloud, or a swan) to hustle unsuspecting mortal females. Statues depict him wearing a beard and sometimes carrying a spear. He is also symbolized by a thunderbolt or an eagle.

Hera (Juno): The beautiful queen of the gods was the long-suffering wife of philandering Zeus. She was also—whether ironically or fittingly—the goddess of marriage.

Hades (Pluto): The king of the underworld and lord of the dead is depicted as sad, with a staff.

Poseidon (Neptune): The god of the sea, he was also responsible for earthquakes, earning him the nickname "Earth Shaker." He is often shown holding a trident.

Apollo: The ruler of the Sun, he drives the Sun's flaming chariot across the sky each day, and represents light and truth. He is also the god of music and poetry.

Hermes (Mercury): The messenger of the gods sports a helmet and shoes with wings. He delivers a lot of flowers in his current incarnation as a corporate logo.

Ares (Mars): The god of war (and Aphrodite's boyfriend), he dresses for battle and carries a spear.

Dionysus (Bacchus): The god of wine and college frats holds grapes and wears a toga and a laurel wreath.

Athena (Minerva): The virginal goddess of wisdom was born from the head of Zeus, and is depicted carrying a spear. Athens is named for her and the Parthenon was built in her honor.

Artemis (Diana): The goddess of the moon and hunting, she was the twin sister of Apollo. She carries a bow and arrow.

Aphrodite (Venus): The goddess of love and beauty, she was born of the sea. This good-looking lady was married to the crippled god Hephaistos, but was two-timing him with Ares.

Eros (Cupid): The god of desire is depicted as a young man or a baby with wings, wielding a bow and arrows.

Hestia (Vesta): Modestly dressed veiled goddess of the home and hearth, she oversaw domestic life.

Hephaistos (Vulcan): Poor cuckolded Hephaistos was lame and ugly, but useful. Blacksmith to the gods, he was the god of the forge, fire, and craftsmen.

Demeter (Ceres): Goddess of the seasons, the harvest, and fertility, she is shown holding a tuft of grain.

The Beasts

Pan (Faun): Happy Pan, with a body that's half man (on top) and half goat, was the god of shepherds and played a flute.

Centaur: This race of creatures, human on top and horse below, was said to be wise.

Satyr: Like Pan, satyrs were top-half man, bottom-half goat. And they were horny.

Griffin: With the head and wings of an eagle and the body of a lion, griffins were formidable.

Harpy: Creatures with the head of a woman and the body of a bird, harpies were known for stealing.

Medusa: With writhing snakes instead of hair, she had a face that turned people to stone. She was slain by Perseus.

Pegasus: The winged horse was the son of Poseidon and Medusa.

Cyclops: A race of one-eyed giants, they were known for their immense strength.

Minotaur: This beast with the head of a bull lived in the labyrinth at Knossos, the palace on Crete.

The Heroes

Hercules: This son of Zeus was born to a mortal woman. The strongest man in the world performed many feats of strength and tested negative for steroids. To make Hercules atone for killing his family in a fit of madness, the gods forced him to perform Twelve Labors, which included slaying various fierce beasts and doing other chores. He often wore a lion's skin.

Amazons: A race of powerful female warriors. Classical art often depicts them doing battle with the Greeks.

Prometheus: He defied the gods, stealing fire from them and giving it to humans. As punishment, he was chained to a rock, where an eagle feasted daily on his innards.

Jason: He sailed with his Argonauts in search of the Golden Fleece.

Perseus: He killed Medusa and rescued Andromeda from a serpent.

Theseus: He killed the Minotaur in the labyrinth on Crete.

Trojan War Heroes: This gang of greats includes Achilles, Ajax, Hector, Paris, Agamemnon, and the gorgeous Helen of Troy.

sembly of citizens. It was a direct democracy (not a representative democracy, where you elect others to serve), in which every man was expected to fill his duties of voting, community projects, and military service. Of course, Athens' "democracy" excluded women, slaves, freed slaves, and anyone not born in Athens.

Perhaps the greatest Greek invention was the very idea that nature is orderly and man is good—a rational creature who can solve problems. Their concept of the "Golden Mean" reveals the value they placed in balance, order, and harmony in art and in life. At school, both the mind and the body were trained.

Philosophers debated many of the questions that still occupy the human mind. Socrates questioned traditional, superstitious beliefs. His motto, "Know thyself," epitomizes Greek curiosity about who we are and what we know for sure. Branded a threat to Athens' youth, Socrates willingly obeyed a court order to drink poison rather than compromise his ideals. His follower Plato wrote down many of Socrates' words. Plato taught that the physical world is only a pale reflection of true reality (the way a shadow on the wall is a poor version of the 3-D, full-color world we see). The greater reality is the unseen mathematical orderliness that underlies the fleeting physical world. Plato's pupil Aristotle, an avid biologist, emphasized study of the physical world rather than the intangible one. Both Plato and Aristotle founded schools that would attract Europe's great minds for centuries. And their ideas would resurface much later, after Europe experienced a resurgence of humanism and critical thought.

Greeks worshipped a pantheon of gods, viewed as supernatural humans (with human emotions) who controlled the forces of nature. Greek temples housed a statue of a god or goddess. Because the people worshipped outside, the temple exterior was the important part and the interior was small and simple. Generally, only priests were allowed to go inside, where they'd present your offering to the god's statue in the hope that the god would grant your wish.

Most temples had similar features. They were rectangular, surrounded by rows of columns, and topped by slanted roofs. Rather than single-piece columns, the Greeks usually built them of stacked slices of stone (drums), each with a plug to keep it in line. Columns sat on a base, and were topped with a capital. The triangle-shaped roof formed a gable—typically filled with statues—called the pediment. A typical pediment might feature a sculpted gang of gods doing their divine mischief. Beneath the pediment was a line of carved reliefs called metopes. Under the eaves, a set of sculpted low-relief panels—called the frieze—decorated one or more sides of the building.

Classical art is known for its symmetry, harmony, and simplicity. It shows the Greeks' love of rationality, order, and balance. Greek art of this era featured the human body in all its naked

A Who's Who of Classical Age Greeks

Socrates (c. 469-399 B.C.) questioned the status quo, angered authorities, and calmly accepted his own death rather than change his teachings.

Plato (c. 424-348 B.C.) was Socrates' follower (and note taker), and focused on elucidating nonmaterial, timeless mathematical ideas.

Aristotle (c. 384-322 B.C.) was Plato's follower and championed the empirical sciences, emphasizing the importance of the physical world as a means of knowledge.

Pericles (c. 495-429 B.C.) was a charismatic nobleman who promoted democracy.

Pythagoras (c. 580-500 B.C.) gave us $a^2 + b^2 = c^2$.

Euclid (c. 335-270 B.C.) laid out geometry as we know it.

Diogenes (c. 412-323 B.C.) lived homeless in the Agora, turning from materialism to concentrate on ethical living.

Aristophanes (c. 446-386 B.C.), **Sophocles** (c. 496-406 B.C.), and **Euripides** (c. 480-406 B.C.) wrote comedies and tragedies that are still performed today.

Hippocrates (c. 460-370 B.C.) made medicine a hard science. He rejected superstition and considered disease a result of natural—rather than supernatural—causes.

Pheidias (c. 480-430 B.C.) designed the statuary of the Parthenon and several monumental statues.

Praxiteles (c. 400-330 B.C.) sculpted lifelike yet beautiful human figures.

GREEK HISTORY

splendor. The anatomy is accurate, and the poses are relaxed and natural. Greek sculptors learned to capture people in motion, and to show them from different angles, not just face-on. The classic Greek pose—called *contrapposto,* Italian for "counter-poise"—has a person resting weight on one leg while the other leg is relaxed or moving slightly. This pose captures a balance between timeless stability and fleeting motion that the Greeks found beautiful. It's also a balance between down-to-earth humans (with human flaws and quirks) and the idealized perfection of a Greek god.

Golden Age Sights

- The Acropolis in Athens, with the Parthenon, Erechtheion, Propylaea, Temple of Athena Nike, and Theater of Dionysus
- The Agora, Athens' main square—crossed by the Panathenaic Way and frequented by all the Golden Age greats

Greek Columns

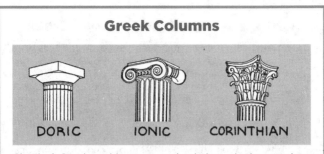

Classical Greek architecture evolved through three orders: Doric (strong-looking columns topped with simple and stocky capitals), Ionic (thinner columns with rolled capitals), and Corinthian (even thinner columns with leafy, ornate capitals). As a memory aid, remember that the orders gain syllables as they evolve: Doric, Ionic, Corinthian. The differences between the three orders point to how the Greek outlook mirrored its developing culture: Having mastered the ability to show balance and harmony in its finest Doric temples (the Parthenon being the cream of the crop), the Corinthian order caught on as architects began to prefer a more elegant look. The Corinthian order, developed to look good from all sides (Ionic columns didn't work well on corners), and to give temple interiors a foresty look, could only have come from the Hellenistic era, when Greek tastemakers preferred their art and architecture ornate and lavish.

- Temple of Hephaistos, in the Agora
- Panathenaic Stadium in Athens
- Sanctuary of Apollo at Delphi
- Workshop of Pheidias at Olympia
- Museum of Cycladic Art in Athens (top-floor exhibit)

LATE CLASSICAL PERIOD: THE DECLINE OF ATHENS (400-323 B.C.)

Many Greek city-states came to resent the tribute money they were obliged to send to Athens, supposedly to protect them from an invasion that never came. Rallying behind Sparta, they ganged up on Athens. The Peloponnesian War, lasting a generation, toppled Athens (404 B.C.), drained Greece, and ended the Golden Age. Still more wars followed, including struggles between Sparta and Thebes. In 338 B.C., Athens, Sparta, and all the rest

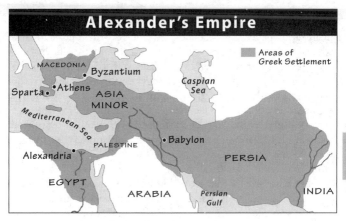

Alexander's Empire

Areas of Greek Settlement

MACEDONIA
Byzantium
Caspian Sea
Sparta
Athens
ASIA MINOR
Mediterranean Sea
PALESTINE
Babylon
Alexandria
PERSIA
EGYPT
ARABIA
Persian Gulf
INDIA

GREEK HISTORY

of the city-states were conquered by powerful Greek-speaking invaders from the north: the Macedonians.

Late Classical Sights
- Bronze statue of a youth at Athens' National Archaeological Museum
- *Statue of Hermes,* perhaps by Praxiteles, in Olympia

HELLENISM (323-100 B.C.)
"Hellenism," from the Greek word for "Greek," refers to the era when Greece's political importance declined but Greek culture was spread through the Mediterranean and Asia by Alexander the Great.

After King Philip of Macedonia conquered Greece, he was succeeded by his 20-year-old son, Alexander (356-323 B.C.). Alexander had been tutored by the Greek philosopher Aristotle, who got the future king hooked on Greek culture. According to legend, Alexander went to bed each night with two things under his pillow: a dagger and a copy of the *Iliad.* Alexander loved Greek high culture, but was also pragmatic about the importance of military power.

In 334 B.C., Alexander and a well-trained army of 40,000 headed east. Their busy itinerary included conquering today's Turkey, Palestine, Egypt (where he was declared a living god), Iraq, and Iran, and moving into India. Alexander was a daring general, a benevolent conqueror, and a good administrator. As he conquered,

he founded new cities on the Greek model, spread the Greek language, and opened Greek schools. After eight years on the road, an exhausted Alexander died at the age of 32, but by then he had created the largest empire ever. (What have you accomplished lately?)

Hellenistic art reflects the changes in Greek society. Rather than noble idealized gods, the Hellenistic artists gave us real people with real emotions, shown warts-and-all. Some are candid snapshots of everyday life, like a boy stooped over to pull a thorn from his foot. Others show people in extreme moments as they struggle to overcome life's obstacles. We see the thrill of victory and the agony of defeat. Arms flail, muscles strain, eyes bulge. Clothes and hair are whipped by the wind. Figures are frozen in motion, in wild, unbalanced poses that dramatize their inner thoughts.

For two centuries much of the Mediterranean and Asia—the entire known civilized world—was dominated by Greek rulers and Greek culture.

Hellenistic Sights
- Stoa of Attalos, in Athens' Agora, built by a Grecophile from Pergamon
- *Artemision Jockey, Fighting Gaul,* and other statues in Athens' National Archaeological Museum
- Head of Alexander the Great in Athens' Acropolis Museum
- Theater (and sanctuary) of Epidavros
- Philippeion temple in Olympia

ROMAN GREECE (146 B.C.-A.D. 476)
At the same time that Alexander was conquering the East, a new superpower was rising in the West: Rome. Eventually, Rome's legions conquered Greece (146 B.C.) and the Hellenized Mediterranean (31 B.C.). Culturally, however, the Greeks conquered the Romans.

Roman governors ruled cosmopolitan Greek-speaking cities, adopting the Greek gods, art styles, and fashions. Greek-style temple facades, with their columns and pediments, were pasted on the front of (Roman-arch) temples as a veneer of sophistication. Greek statues dotted Roman villas and public buildings. Pretentious Romans sprinkled their Latin conversation with Greek phrases as they enjoyed the plays of Sophocles and Aristophanes. Many a Greek slave was more cultured than his master, reduced to the role of warning his boss not to wear a plaid toga with polka-dot sandals.

Athens was a major city in the cosmopolitan Roman world. Paul—a Jewish Christian with Roman citizenship—came to Athens (A.D. 49) to spread the Christian message from atop Mars Hill. The Bible makes it clear (Acts 17) that the sophisticated Athenians were not impressed.

Athens, with its prestigious monuments, was well-preserved under the Romans, but as Rome began to collapse, it became less able to protect and provide for Greece. In A.D. 267, Athens suffered a horrendous invasion by barbarian Herulians, who left much of the city in ashes. Other barbarian invasions followed.

In A.D. 476, even the city of Rome fell to invaders. As Christianity established itself, Greece's pagan sanctuaries were closed. For a thousand years Athens had carried the torch of pagan and secular learning. But in A.D. 529, the Christian/Roman/Byzantine Emperor Justinian closed Athens' famous schools of philosophy... and the "ancient" world came to an end.

Greek culture would live on, resurfacing throughout Western history and eventually influencing medieval Christians, Renaissance sculptors, and Neoclassical architects, including the ones who designed Washington, DC in the Greek style.

Roman Sights
- Roman Forum (and Tower of the Winds) in Athens
- Temple of Olympian Zeus and Arch of Hadrian in Athens
- Odeon of Agrippa and Statue of Hadrian, in Athens' Agora
- Hadrian's Library (near Monastiraki) in Athens
- Temple of Roma and Monument of Agrippa, on the Acropolis in Athens
- Odeon of Herodes Atticus (built by a wealthy ethnic-Greek/Roman-citizen) in Athens
- Mars Hill (the rock where the Christian Apostle Paul preached to the pagans) in Athens
- Nymphaeum in Olympia
- Many Greek buildings and artworks that were renovated in Roman times

BYZANTINE GREECE (A.D. 323-1453)
With the fall of Rome in Western Europe, Greece came under the sway of the Byzantine Empire—namely, the eastern half of the ancient Roman Empire that *didn't* "fall" in A.D. 476. Byzantium remained Christian and enlightened for another thousand years, with Greek (not Latin) as the common language. The empire's capital was Constantinople (modern Istanbul), founded in A.D. 330 by Roman Emperor Constantine to help manage the fading Roman

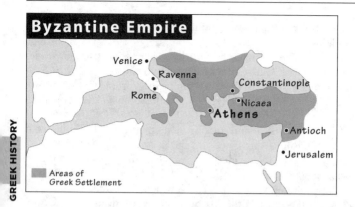

Byzantine Empire

Venice

Ravenna

Rome

Constantinople

Nicaea

Athens

Antioch

Jerusalem

Areas of
Greek Settlement

Empire. For the next thousand years, Greece's cultural orientation would face east.

Though ostensibly protected by the Byzantine emperor in Constantinople, Greece suffered several centuries of invasions (A.D. 600-900) by various Slavic barbarians. The Orthodox Church served as a rallying point, and the invaders were eventually driven out or assimilated.

After A.D. 1000, Greece's economic prosperity returned—farms produced, the population grew, and cities engaged in trade—and Athens entered a second, more modest, Golden Age (c. 1000-1200). Greece reconnected with the rest of Western Europe during the Crusades, when Western soldiers traveled through Greek ports on their way to Jerusalem. This revived East–West trade, which was brokered by Venetian merchants who were granted trading rights to establish ports in Greek territory.

This Golden Age is when many of Athens' venerable Orthodox churches were built. Christian pilgrims from across the Byzantine Empire flocked to Athens to visit the famous church housed within the (still-intact) Parthenon. Byzantine mosaics, featuring realistic plants, animals, and people, were exported to the West.

The Byzantine Empire—and, by extension, Greece—was weakened by the disastrous Fourth Crusade (1204), in which greedy Crusaders looted their fellow Christian city of Constantinople. Following this, Western Crusaders occupied and ruled many parts of Greece, including Athens, and Byzantine Christians battled Crusading Christians at Monemvasia. Meanwhile, the Ottomans were whittling away at the empire's fringes. In 1453, Constantinople fell to the Ottoman Turks.

Byzantine-Era Sights

- Athens' old Orthodox churches, including the Church of Kapnikarea (on Ermou street), Agios Eleftherios (next to the cathedral), and Holy Apostles (in the Agora)
- Byzantine and Christian Museum in Athens
- Icons of the Eastern Orthodox Church
- Monemvasia fortress
- Churches and palaces at Mystras

ISLAMIC/OTTOMAN GREECE (1453-1821)

Under the Ottomans, Greece was ruled by Islamic Turks from their capital of Constantinople. Like many other temples-turned-churches, Athens' Parthenon (still intact) became a mosque, and a minaret was built alongside it.

Greek Christians had several choices for surviving the new regime. Some converted to Islam and learned Turkish, while others faked their conversion and remained closet Christians. Some moved to the boonies, outside the reach of Ottoman administrators. Many of Greece's best and brightest headed to Western Europe, helping to ignite the Renaissance (which revived the Classical achievements of ancient Athens). Most Greeks just stayed put, paid the "Christian tax," and lived in peace alongside the Ottomans. The Ottomans were (relatively) benevolent rulers, and the Greek language and Orthodox Christianity both survived.

Greece found itself between the powerful Ottomans and powerful merchants of Venice. This made Greece a center for East–West trade, but also a battleground. Venetian traders (backed by their military) occupied and fortified a number of Greek seaports in order to carry on trade throughout the Ottoman Empire. In 1687, the Venetians attacked Ottoman-controlled Athens. The Ottomans hunkered down on the Acropolis, storing their gunpowder in the Parthenon. A Venetian cannonball hit the Parthenon, destroying it and creating the ruin we see today. Venetian looters plundered the rubble and carried off statues as souvenirs.

Ottoman-Era Sights

- Benaki Museum of Islamic Art in Athens
- The Tzami, a former mosque on Monastiraki Square in Athens
- Venetian fortresses (including those in Nafplio) established in Byzantine times

GREEK INDEPENDENCE AND NEOCLASSICISM (1800s)

After centuries of neglect, Greece's Classical heritage was rediscovered, both by the Greeks and by the rest of Europe. Neoclassicism was all the rage in Europe, where the ancient Greek style was used to decorate homes, and create paintings and statues. In 1801-1805, the British Lord Elgin plundered half of the Parthenon's statues and reliefs, carrying them home for Londoners to marvel at.

Greeks rediscovered a sense of their national heritage, and envisioned a day when they could rule themselves as a modern democracy. In 1821, the Greeks rose up against rule from Constantinople. It started with pockets of resistance by guerrilla Klepht warriors from the mountains, escalating into large-scale massacres on both sides. The Greeks' struggle became a cause célèbre in Europe, attracting Romantic liberals from England and France to take up arms. The poet Lord Byron died (of a fever) near the Gulf of Patra while fighting for Greece.

At one point the rebels gained control of the Peloponnese and declared Greek independence. The Greeks even sank the flagship of the Ottoman fleet in 1822, earning international respect for their nascent rebellion. But tribal rivalries prevented the Greeks from preserving their gains. With Egyptian reinforcements, the Ottomans successfully invaded the Peloponnese and captured several cities. An Egyptian army in Europe was too much to take for Britain, France, and Russia, who intervened with their navies and saved Greek independence.

By 1829, the Greeks had their freedom, a constitution, and—for the first time—a unified state of "Greece," based in Nafplio. But after its first president, Ioannis Kapodistrias, was assassinated in 1831, the budding democracy was forced by Europe's crowned heads to accept a monarch: 17-year-old King Otto from Bavaria (crowned in 1832). In 1834, historic Athens was chosen as the new capital, despite the fact that it was then a humble village of a few thousand inhabitants.

Over the next century, Greece achieved a constitution (or *syntagma*, celebrated by Syntagma Square in Athens, as well as Nafplio and many other cities) and steered the monarchy toward modern democracy. Athens was rebuilt in the Neoclassical style. Greek engineers (along with foreigners) built the Corinth Canal. The Greek nation expanded, as Greek-speaking territories were captured from the Ottomans or ceded to Greece by European powers. In 1896, Greece celebrated its revival by hosting the first modern Olympic Games.

19th-Century Neoclassical Sights

- Syntagma Square, Parliament, and the evzone at the Tomb of the Unknown Soldier, in Athens
- National Garden in Athens
- Patriotic paintings in the Nafplio Annex of the National Gallery
- Zappeion exhibition hall in Athens
- Athens' Panathenaic Stadium (ancient stadium renovated for the first modern Olympics in 1896)
- Cathedral in Athens
- Museum of Greek Folk Art (17th-19th century) in Athens
- Corinth Canal

20TH CENTURY

Two world wars and the Greek Civil War caused great turmoil in Greece. During World War I, Greece remained uncommitted until the final years, when it joined the Allies (Britain, France, Italy, Russia, and the US) against Germany.

World War I scrambled the balance of power in the Balkans. Greece was given control of parts of western Turkey, where many ethnic Greeks lived. The Turks, having thrown out their Ottoman rulers, now rose up to evict the Greeks, sparking the Greco-Turkish War (1919-1922) and massacres on both sides. To settle the conflict, a million ethnic Greeks living in Turkish lands were shipped to Greece, while Greece sent hundreds of thousands of its ethnic Turks to Turkey. In 1923, hordes of desperate refugees poured into Athens, and the population doubled overnight. Many later immigrated to the US, Canada, and Australia. Today there are more than a million Greek Americans living in the US.

In World War II Greece sided firmly with the Allies, heroically repulsing Mussolini's 1940 invasion. But Adolf Hitler finished the job, invading and occupying Greece for four brutal years of repression and hunger.

Making the situation worse, the Greek Resistance movement (battling the Nazis) was itself divided. It broke out into a full-fledged civil war (1944-1949) between Western-backed patriots and Marxist patriots.

World War II and the Greek Civil War left Greece with hundreds of thousands dead, desperately poor, and bitterly divided. Thanks to America's Marshall Plan (and tourism), the economy recovered in the 1950s and '60s, and Greece joined the NATO alliance. Along with modernization came some of Europe's worst pollution, which eroded the ancient monuments.

Politically, Greece would remain split between the extreme right (the ruling monarchy, military, and the rich) and the extreme left (communists, students, and workers), without much room in the middle. The repressive royalist regime was backed heavily by the United States, which made Greece the first battleground in the Cold War (the Truman Doctrine). By the 1960s, when the rest of Europe was undergoing rapid social change, the Greek government was still trying to control its society with arrests and assassinations. When the royalists began losing control, a CIA-backed coup put the military in charge (1967-1974). They outlawed everything from long hair and miniskirts to Socrates and the theme song from *Zorba the Greek* (because its composer was accused of being a communist).

For Greece, 1974 was a watershed year. In the midst of political turmoil, Turkey invaded the Greek-friendly island of Cyprus (sparking yet more decades of bad blood between Turkey and Greece). The surprise attack caught the Greek military junta off guard, and they resigned in disgrace. A new government was elected with a new constitution. Guided by two strong (sometimes antagonistic) leaders—Andreas Papandreou and Constantine Karamanlis—Greece inched slowly from right-wing repression toward open democracy. Greece in the 1970s and '80s would suffer more than its share of assassinations and terrorist acts. But the economy grew, and Greece joined the European Union (1981) and adopted the euro (2002).

20th-Century Sights

- National War Museum in Athens
- Central Market in Athens
- Greek flag atop the Acropolis in Athens (reminder of resistance leaders who flew it there during the Nazi occupation in World War II)

GREECE TODAY

After adopting the euro, the Greek economy boomed. EU subsidies flowed in for major infrastructure projects, such as highways and high-speed rail. As host of the 2004 Summer Olympics,

Athens cleaned up its city and installed a new airport and Metro. But the worldwide recession that started in 2008 hit Greece hard. Suddenly, international investors dumped Greek bonds, since the national debt was larger than the country's gross domestic product. In 2010, Greece received an unprecedented €110 billion bailout from the EU and the International Monetary Fund—and then needed an even bigger rescue package—€130 billion—just two years later. A third bailout—worth up to €86 billion—was approved in 2015. The bailouts required severe economic reforms, sending the economy into recession and pushing the unemployment rate over 25 percent.

The already volatile political scene became even more stirred up as Greeks argued about how to grapple with their financial crisis. Financial markets and European leaders feared a Greek exit from the euro, which could have caused a breakup of the currency. But the current leader, Alexis Tspiras (from the left-wing Syriza party), has made the Greek debt crisis a top priority and  says he's committed to keeping Greece in the EU.

Greece is seriously hampered by widespread governmental corruption and a bloated (indeed, "Byzantine") bureaucratic system that's tangled itself in red tape. Recent administrations have had some success with attempts to combat the corruption, but few Greeks are optimistic that the bureaucracy is headed toward efficiency.

Immigration is another hotly debated topic. People are divided over how the nation can and should accommodate the thousands of economic and political refugees who arrive here, both legally and illegally. Alarmingly, this has bolstered support for far-right, brazenly racist extremists. Greeks also argue among themselves about the nation's high military spending, the draft, and excessive privileges for the Greek Orthodox church. Meanwhile, relations with Turkey—its next-door neighbor across the Aegean pond—remain strained.

On my last visit, however, I was happily surprised by how tourism had rebounded vigorously, with hotels filling to capacity. Throughout the recent upheaval, most Greeks maintained a sunny outlook—and it appears that their optimism was not misplaced. By no means is Greece out of the economic woods, but things don't seem as dire. And, considering that the Greek language and culture have survived for more than two millennia—despite being conquered by Romans, Turks, and Nazis—there's good reason to feel confident that they'll overcome the latest turmoil, too.

Greece Today Sights
- Ermou street pedestrian zone in Athens
- Renovated Monastiraki Square in Athens
- Acropolis Museum in Athens
- Athens' Metro and airport
- 2004 Olympic Games sights, including new stadium, in Athens

To learn more about Greek history, consider Europe 101: History and Art for the Traveler, *by Rick Steves and Gene Openshaw (available at www.ricksteves.com).*

PRACTICALITIES

This chapter covers the practical skills of European travel: how to get tourist information, pay for purchases, sightsee efficiently, find good-value accommodations, eat affordably but well, use technology wisely, and get between destinations smoothly. To round out your knowledge, check out "Resources from Rick Steves." For more information on these topics, see www.ricksteves.com/travel-tips.

Tourist Information

The Greek **national tourist office** has a helpful website with lots of information and downloadable maps and brochures (www.visitgreece.gr). Other good websites include www.culture.gr (Greek Ministry of Culture, with information on major archaeological sites and museums), www.thisisathens.org (City of Athens Convention and Visitors Bureau), and www.athensguide.com (guide to Athens by travel writer Matt Barrett).

In Greece, tourist offices are often marked *EOT* (for the Greek phrase "Greek Tourism Organization"). Unfortunately, budget cuts have forced many towns to close their TIs. The offices that are still open can usually give you a free map, a few local tips, and some assistance with bus connections. In general, though, your hotelier may end up being your best source of information.

Travel Tips

Emergency and Medical Help: In Greece, dial 112 for English-speaking help for any emergency or 171 or 1571 for the Tourist Police.

The **Tourist Police** serves as a contact point between tourists and other branches of the police and is also responsible for handling problems such as disputes with hotels, restaurants, and other tourist services (available 24 hours daily; Athens office located south of the Acropolis in Koukaki at Veikou 43, office tel. 210-920-0724).

If you get sick, do as the locals do and go to a pharmacist for advice. Or ask at your hotel for help—they'll know the nearest medical and emergency services.

Theft or Loss: To replace a passport, you'll need to go in person to an embassy (see page 545). If your credit and debit cards disappear, cancel and replace them (see "Damage Control for Lost Cards" on page 501). File a police report, either on the spot or within a day or two; you'll need it to submit an insurance claim for lost or stolen rail passes or travel gear, and it can help with replacing your passport or credit and debit cards. For more information, see www.ricksteves.com/help.

Borders: If you enter Greece from most European countries (those that are part of Europe's open-borders Schengen Agreement), you won't need to go through customs. But if you arrive on a direct flight from the US, or from the neighboring countries of Turkey, Macedonia, Albania, or Bulgaria (which aren't part of the EU pact), you'll have to clear customs.

Time Zones: Greece, which is one hour ahead of most of continental Europe, is generally seven/ten hours ahead of the East/West Coasts of the US. The exceptions are the beginning and end of Daylight Saving Time: Europe "springs forward" the last Sunday in March (two weeks after most of North America) and "falls back" the last Sunday in October (one week before North America). For a handy online time converter, try www.timeanddate.com/worldclock.

Business Hours: Most shops catering to tourists are open long hours daily. In Athens stores are generally open weekdays from 9:00 to 20:00. Afternoon breaks are common, and some places close early a few nights a week.

Saturdays are virtually weekdays, with earlier closing hours. Sundays have the same pros and cons as they do for travelers in the US: Sightseeing attractions are generally open, while shops and banks are closed, public transportation options are fewer, and there's no rush hour. Friday and Saturday evenings are lively; Sunday evenings are quiet.

Watt's Up? Europe's electrical system is 220 volts, instead of North America's 110 volts. Most newer electronics (such as laptops, battery chargers, and hair dryers) convert automatically, so you won't need a converter, but you will need an adapter plug with two round prongs, sold inexpensively at travel stores in the US. Avoid bringing older appliances that don't automatically convert voltage; instead, buy a cheap replacement locally. Low-cost hair dryers and other small appliances are sold at Public stores (ask your hotelier for the closest branch; there's a hard-to-miss location on Syntagma Square).

Bathroom Etiquette: There's a reason every bathroom in Greece has a small wastebasket next to the toilet—bad plumbing. Don't flush toilet paper; use the wastebasket instead.

Discounts: Discounts for sights are generally not listed in this book. However, many sights offer discounts to youths (up to age 18), students or teachers (with proper identification cards, www.isic.org), families, seniors (loosely defined as retirees or those willing to call themselves seniors), and groups of 10 or more. Always ask. Some discounts are available only for EU citizens.

Online Translation Tips: Google's Chrome browser instantly translates websites. You can also paste text or the URL of a foreign website into the translation window at Translate.google.com. The Google Translate app converts spoken English into most European languages (and vice versa) and can also translate text it "reads" with your smartphone's camera.

Money

Here's my basic strategy for using money in Europe:
- Upon arrival, head for a cash machine (ATM) at the airport and load up on local currency, using a debit card with low international transaction fees.
- Withdraw large amounts at each transaction (to limit fees) and keep your cash safe in a money belt.
- Pay for most items with cash.
- Pay for larger purchases with a credit card with low (or no) international fees.

PLASTIC VERSUS CASH

Although credit cards are widely accepted in Europe, day-to-day spending is generally more cash-based than in the US, and cash is highly preferable in Greece. I find cash is the easiest—and sometimes only—way to pay for cheap food, bus fare, taxis, tips, and

---

Exchange Rate

1 euro (€) = about $1.20

To convert prices in euros to dollars, add about 20 percent: €20=about $24, €50=about $60. (Check www.oanda.com for the latest exchange rates.) Just like the dollar, one euro (€) is broken down into 100 cents. Coins range from €0.01 to €2, and bills from €5 to €200 (bills over €50 are rarely used; €500 bills are being phased out).

---

local guides. Some businesses (especially smaller ones, such as B&Bs and mom-and-pop cafés and shops) may charge you extra for using a credit card—or might not accept credit cards at all. Having cash on hand helps you out of a jam if your card randomly doesn't work.

I use my credit card to book and pay for hotel reservations, to buy advance tickets for events or sights, and to cover major expenses (such as car rentals or plane tickets). It can also be smart to use plastic near the end of your trip, to avoid another visit to the ATM.

WHAT TO BRING

I pack the following and keep it all safe in my money belt.

Debit Card: Use this at ATMs to withdraw local cash.

Credit Card: Use this to pay for larger items (at hotels, larger shops and restaurants, travel agencies, car-rental agencies, and so on).

Backup Card: Some travelers carry a third card (debit or credit; ideally from a different bank), in case one gets lost, demagnetized, eaten by a temperamental machine, or simply doesn't work.

US Dollars: I carry $100-200 US as a backup. While you won't use it for day-to-day purchases, American cash in your money belt comes in handy for emergencies, such as if your ATM card stops working.

What NOT to Bring: Resist the urge to buy **euros** before your trip or you'll pay the price in bad stateside exchange rates. Wait until you arrive to withdraw money. I've yet to see a European airport that didn't have plenty of ATMs.

BEFORE YOU GO

Use this pretrip checklist.

Know your cards. Debit cards from any major US bank will work in any standard European bank's ATM (ideally, use a debit card with a Visa or MasterCard logo). As for credit cards, Visa and MasterCard are universal, American Express is less common, and Discover is unknown in Europe.

Most credit and debit cards have chips that authenticate and secure transactions. Europeans insert their chip cards into the payment machine slot, then enter a PIN. With a US card, you provide a signature instead of a PIN number to verify your identity.

Any American card, whether with a chip or an old-fashioned magnetic stripe, will work at Europe's hotels, restaurants, and shops. For self-service payment machines, you may need a PIN number. I've been inconvenienced a few times by self-service payment machines in Europe that wouldn't accept my card, but it's never caused me serious trouble.

If you're concerned, ask if your bank offers a true chip-and-PIN card. Cards with low fees and chip-and-PIN technology include those from Andrews Federal Credit Union (www.andrewsfcu.org) and the State Department Federal Credit Union (www.sdfcu.org).

Report your travel dates. Let your bank know that you'll be using your debit and credit cards in Europe, and when and where you're headed.

Know your PIN. Make sure you know the numeric, four-digit PIN for each of your cards, both debit and credit. Request it if you don't have one and allow time to receive the information by mail.

Adjust your ATM withdrawal limit. Find out how much you can take out daily and ask for a higher daily withdrawal limit if you want to get more cash at once. Note that European ATMs will withdraw funds only from checking accounts; you're unlikely to have access to your savings account.

Ask about fees. For any purchase or withdrawal made with a card, you may be charged a currency conversion fee (1-3 percent), a Visa or MasterCard international transaction fee (1 percent), and—for debit cards—a $2-5 transaction fee each time you use a foreign ATM (some US banks partner with European banks, allowing you to use those ATMs with no fees—ask).

If you're getting a bad deal, consider getting a new debit or credit card. Reputable no-fee cards include those from Capital One, as well as Charles Schwab debit cards. Most credit unions and some airline loyalty cards have low-to-no international transaction fees.

IN EUROPE
Using Cash Machines

European cash machines have English-language instructions and work just like they do at home—except they spit out local currency instead of dollars, calculated at the day's standard bank-to-bank rate.

In most places, ATMs are easy to locate—in Greece, they are surprisingly labeled *ATM* in the Greek alphabet. When possible, withdraw cash from a bank-run ATM located just outside that bank. Ideally use it during the bank's opening hours; if your card is munched by the machine, you can go inside for help.

If your debit card doesn't work, try a lower amount—your request may have exceeded your withdrawal limit or the ATM's limit. If you still have a problem, try a different ATM or come back later—your bank's network may be temporarily down.

Avoid "independent" ATMs, such as Travelex, Euronet, Moneybox, Cardpoint, and Cashzone. These have high fees, can be less secure than a bank ATM, and may try to trick users with "dynamic currency conversion" (see below).

Exchanging Cash

Avoid exchanging money in Europe; it's a big rip-off. In a pinch you can always find exchange desks at major train stations or airports—convenient but with crummy rates. Banks in some countries may not exchange money unless you have an account with them.

Using Credit Cards

European cards use chip-and-PIN technology, while most cards issued in the US use a chip-and-signature system. But most European card readers can automatically generate a receipt for you to sign, just as you would at home. If a cashier is present, you should have no problems. Some card readers will instead prompt you to enter your PIN (so it's important to know the code for each of your cards).

At self-service payment machines (transit-ticket kiosks, parking, etc.), results are mixed, as US chip-and-signature cards aren't configured for unattended transactions. If your card won't work, look for a cashier who can process your card manually—or pay in cash.

Drivers Beware: Be aware of potential problems using a credit card to fill up at an unattended gas station, enter a parking garage, or exit a toll road. Carry cash and be prepared to move on to the next gas station if necessary. When approaching a toll plaza, use the "cash" lane.

Dynamic Currency Conversion

Some European merchants and hoteliers cheerfully charge you for converting your purchase price into dollars. If it's offered, refuse this "service" (called dynamic currency conversion, or DCC). You'll pay extra for the expensive convenience of seeing your charge in dollars. Some ATMs also offer DCC, often in confusing or misleading terms. If an ATM offers to "lock in" or "guarantee" your conversion rate, choose "proceed without conversion." Other prompts might state, "You can be charged in dollars: Press YES for dollars, NO for euros." Always choose the local currency.

Security Tips

Pickpockets target tourists. To safeguard your cash, wear a money belt—a pouch with a strap that you buckle around your waist like a belt and tuck under your clothes. Keep your cash, credit cards, and passport secure in your money belt, and carry only a day's spending money in your front pocket or wallet.

Before inserting your card into an ATM, inspect the front. If anything looks crooked, loose, or damaged, it could be a sign of a card-skimming device. When entering your PIN, carefully block people's view of the keypad.

Don't use a debit card for purchases. Because a debit card pulls funds directly from your bank account, potential charges incurred by a thief will stay on your account while the fraudulent use is investigated by your bank.

To access your accounts online while traveling, be sure to use a secure connection (see page 527).

Damage Control for Lost Cards

If you lose your credit or debit card, report the loss immediately to the respective global customer-assistance centers. Call these 24-hour US numbers collect: Visa (tel. 303/967-1096), MasterCard (tel. 636/722-7111), and American Express (tel. 336/393-1111). In Greece, to make a collect call to the US, dial 00-800-1311. Press zero or stay on the line for an English-speaking operator. European toll-free numbers (listed by country) can be found at the websites for Visa and MasterCard.

You'll need to provide the primary cardholder's identification-verification details (such as birth date, mother's maiden name, or Social Security number). You can generally receive a temporary card within two or three business days in Europe (see www.ricksteves.com/help for more).

If you report your loss within two days, you typically won't be responsible for unauthorized transactions on your account, although many banks charge a liability fee of $50.

TIPPING

Tipping in Greece isn't as automatic and generous as it is in the US. For special service, tips are appreciated, but not expected. As in the US, the proper amount depends on your resources, tipping philosophy, and the circumstances, but some general guidelines apply.

Restaurants: At Greek restaurants that have waitstaff, locals generally round up their bill after a good meal (usually about 10 percent). For more on tipping in restaurants, see "Eating," later.

Taxis: For a typical ride, round up your fare a bit (for instance, if the fare is €4.50, pay €5). If the cabbie hauls your bags and zips you to the airport to help you catch your flight, you might want to

PRACTICALITIES

toss in a little more. But if you feel like you're being driven in circles or otherwise ripped off, skip the tip.

Services: In general, if someone in the service industry does a super job for you, a small tip of a euro or two is appropriate...but not required. If you're not sure whether (or how much) to tip for a service, ask a local for advice.

GETTING A VAT REFUND

Wrapped into the purchase price of your Greek souvenirs is a Value-Added Tax (VAT) of about 24 percent. You're entitled to get most of that tax back if you purchase more than €120 (about $145) worth of goods at a store that participates in the VAT-refund scheme. Typically, you must ring up the minimum at a single retailer—you can't add up your purchases from various shops to reach the required amount. (If the store ships the goods to your US home, VAT is not assessed on your purchase.) Getting your refund is straightforward...and worthwhile if you spend a significant amount on souvenirs.

Get the paperwork. Have the merchant completely fill out the necessary refund document, called a "Tax-Free Shopping Cheque." You'll have to present your passport. Get the paperwork done before you leave the store to ensure you'll have everything you need (including your original sales receipt).

Get your stamp at the border or airport. Process your VAT document at your last stop in the European Union (such as at the airport) with the customs agent who deals with VAT refunds. Arrive an additional hour before you need to check in to allow time to find the customs office—and to stand in line. Some customs desks are positioned before airport security; confirm the location before going through security.

It's best to keep your purchases in your carry-on. If they're too large or dangerous to carry on (such as knives), pack them in your checked bags and alert the check-in agent. You'll be sent (with your tagged bag) to a customs desk outside security; someone will examine your bag, stamp your paperwork, and put your bag on the belt. You're not supposed to use your purchased goods before you leave. If you show up at customs wearing your new Greek sandals, officials might look the other way—or deny you a refund.

Collect your refund. Many merchants work with a service that has offices at major airports, ports, or border crossings. These services, which extract their own fee (usually around 4 percent), can refund your money immediately in cash or credit your card (within two billing cycles). Other refund services may require you to mail the documents from home, or more quickly, from your point of departure (using an envelope you've prepared in advance or one that's been provided by the merchant). You'll then have to wait—it can take months.

CUSTOMS FOR AMERICAN SHOPPERS

You can take home $800 worth of items per person duty-free, once every 31 days. Many processed and packaged foods are allowed, including vacuum-packed cheeses, dried herbs, jams, baked goods, candy, chocolate, oil, vinegar, mustard, and honey. Fresh fruits and vegetables and most meats are not allowed, with exceptions for some canned items. As for alcohol, you can bring home one liter duty-free (it can be packed securely in your checked luggage, along with any other liquid-containing items).

To bring alcohol (or liquid-packed foods) in your carry-on bag on your flight home, buy it at a duty-free shop at the airport. You'll increase your odds of getting it onto a connecting flight if it's packaged in a "STEB"—a secure, tamper-evident bag. But stay away from liquids in opaque, ceramic, or metallic containers, which usually cannot be successfully screened (STEB or no STEB).

For details on allowable goods, customs rules, and duty rates, visit http://help.cbp.gov.

Sightseeing

Sightseeing can be hard work. Use these tips to make your visits to Greece's finest sights meaningful, fun, efficient, and painless.

MAPS AND NAVIGATION TOOLS

A good map is essential for efficient navigation while sightseeing. The maps in this book are concise and simple, designed to help you locate recommended destinations, sights, and local TIs, where you can pick up more in-depth maps. Maps with even more detail are sold at newsstands and bookstores.

You can also use a mapping app on your mobile device. Be aware that pulling up maps or looking up turn-by-turn walking directions on the fly requires an Internet connection: To use this feature, it's smart to get an international data plan (see page 524). With Google Maps or City Maps 2Go, it's possible to download a map while online, then go offline and navigate without incurring data-roaming charges, though you can't search for an address or get real-time walking directions. A handful of other apps—including Apple Maps, OffMaps, and Navfree—also allow you to use maps offline.

PLAN AHEAD

Set up an itinerary that allows you to fit in all your must-see sights. For a one-stop look at opening hours in Athens, see the "Athens at a Glance" sidebar in the Sights in Athens chapter. Because these times can vary, it's best to confirm the latest by checking with the TI or your hotelier.

Don't put off visiting a must-see sight—you never know when a place will close unexpectedly for a holiday, strike, or restoration. Many museums are closed or have reduced hours at least a few days a year, especially on holidays such as Christmas, New Year's, and Labor Day (May 1). A list of holidays is on page 545; check online for possible museum closures during your trip.

Most of Greece's ancient sites and archaeological museums are operated by the government. In general, hours at sights are longer during peak season (April-October) and on weekends, and shorter on weekdays and in the off-season. The timing of this seasonal switch can be unannounced and differs between sights. Year-round, if things are slow, places may close early with no advance notice. It's smart to arrive well in advance of listed closing times and to hit your must-see sights in the morning, especially if traveling outside of summer.

The Ministry of Greek Culture website (www.culture.gr) purports to list the latest hours for virtually all of the major sights—including Athens' Acropolis, Ancient Agora, Acropolis Museum, and the National Archaeological Museum, plus the attractions at Delphi, Olympia, Epidavros, and Mycenae—but you'll get more reliable, up-to-date information by asking your hotelier or calling the sights directly.

Going at the right time helps avoid crowds. This book offers tips on the best times to see specific sights. Try visiting popular sights very early or very late. Evening visits are usually peaceful, with fewer crowds.

If you plan to hire a local guide, reserve ahead by email. Popular guides can get booked up.

All museums and archaeological sites run by the Ministry of Greek Culture, including the Acropolis, are free on national holidays and every first Sunday from November through March. Children under 18 always get in free to these sights.

Study up. To get the most out of the self-guided tours and sight descriptions in this book, read them before you visit. The Acropolis is much more entertaining if you've polished up on Doric architecture the night before.

AT SIGHTS

Most of Greece's artifacts have been plunked into glass cases labeled with little more than title and date. Sights run by the Greek Ministry of Culture provide a free information pamphlet, though usually only by request.

More than most destinations in Europe, Greece demands (and

rewards) any effort you make to really understand its treasures. If you read up on Greek history and art, the artifacts come to life; without this background, visiting Greece's museums can quickly become an unforgiving slog past stiff statues and endless ceramic vases.

It can also help to put your imagination into overdrive. As you stroll Athens' Ancient Agora, mentally clad the other tourists in robes. Approach the temple at Delphi as if you were about to learn your fate from an oracle; enter the stadium at Olympia ready to race its length in front of a huge crowd. At museums, imagine being the archaeologist who unearthed the intact glass vessels, intricate golden necklaces, and vases inscribed with the faces of people who lived four millennia ago.

Many major ancient sites have both an archaeological site and a museum for the artifacts and models. You can choose between visiting the museum first (to mentally reconstruct the ruins before seeing them) or the site first (to get the lay of the ancient land before seeing the items found there). In most cases, I prefer to see the site first, then the museum. However, crowds and weather can also help determine your plan. If it's a blistering hot afternoon, tour the air-conditioned museum first, then hit the ruins in the cool of evening (if opening hours allow). Or, if rain clouds are on the horizon, do the archaeological site first, then duck into the museum when the rain hits.

Here's what you can typically expect:

Entering: Be warned that you may not be allowed to enter if you arrive less than 30 to 60 minutes before closing time. And guards start ushering people out well before the actual closing time, so don't save the best for last.

Many sights have a security check, where you must open your bag or send it through a metal detector. Allow extra time for these lines in your planning. Some sights require you to check daypacks and coats. (If you'd rather not check your daypack, try carrying it tucked under your arm like a purse as you enter.)

Etiquette and Photography at Ancient Sites: Archaeological sites are meticulously monitored; you're sure to hear the tweets of many whistles aimed at visitors who've crossed a barrier or climbed on a ruin.

If an attraction's photo policy isn't clearly posted, ask a guard. Generally, taking photos without a flash or tripod is allowed. Some sights ban selfie sticks; others ban photos altogether. The Greeks take their ancient artifacts very seriously. Posing with ancient statues—or even standing next to them for a photo—is strictly forbidden.

Temporary Exhibits: Museums may show special exhibits in addition to their permanent collection. An extra fee, which may not be optional, might be assessed for these shows.

Expect Changes: Artwork can be on tour, on loan, out sick, or shifted at the whim of the curator. Pick up a floor plan as you enter, and ask museum staff if you can't find a particular item.

Audioguides and Apps: In Greece, audioguides are rare, but good guidebooks are available. And I've produced free download-able audio tours for my Athens City Walk, the Acropolis, Ancient Agora, and National Archaeological Museum; look for the 🎧 sym-bol in this book. For more on my audio tours, see page 9.

You can usually hire a live local guide at the entrance to major ancient sites or museums at a reasonable cost (prices are soft and negotiable; save money by splitting the guide fee with other travel-ers). I list recommended guides in the "Helpful Hints" section of many chapters. Two notable exceptions are Olympia, where guides are sparse, and the Acropolis, where the loitering guides are gener-ally of poor quality.

Services: Important sights may have a reasonably priced on-site café or cafeteria (usually a handy place to rejuvenate during a long visit). The WCs at sights are free and generally clean.

Before Leaving: At the gift shop, scan the postcard rack or thumb through a guidebook to be sure that you haven't overlooked something that you'd like to see.

Every sight or museum offers more than what is covered in this book. Use the information in this book as an introduction—not the final word.

Sleeping

I favor hotels and restaurants that are handy to your sightseeing activities. Rather than list accommodations scattered throughout a city, I choose places in my favorite neighborhoods. My recom-mendations run the gamut, from dorm beds to fancy rooms with all the comforts. In this book, the price for a double room ranges from about $50 (very simple, toilet and shower down the hall) to $500 (maximum plumbing and more), with most clustering around $95-145. Athens is a bit more expensive, while the Peloponnese is cheaper. Greek islands (especially Mykonos and Santorini) have the highest rates by far.

Extensive and opinionated listings of good-value rooms are a major feature of this book's Sleeping sections. I like places that are clean, central, relatively quiet at night, reasonably priced, friendly, small enough to have a hands-on owner and a stable staff, and run with a respect for Greek traditions. I'm more impressed by a con-venient location and a fun-loving philosophy than flat-screen TVs and a pricey laundry service. Most places I recommend fall short

PRACTICALITIES

Sleep Code

Hotels are classified based on the average price of a standard double room with breakfast in high season.

$$$$	**Splurge:** Most rooms over €150
$$$	**Pricier:** €100-150
$$	**Moderate:** €50-100
$	**Budget:** €25-50
¢	**Backpacker:** Under €25
RS%	**Rick Steves discount**

Unless otherwise noted, credit cards are accepted, hotel staff speak basic English, and free Wi-Fi is available. Comparison-shop by checking prices at several hotels (on each hotel's own website, on a booking site, or by email). For the best deal, *book directly with the hotel.* Ask for a discount if paying in cash; if the listing includes **RS%**, request a Rick Steves discount.

of perfection. But if I can find a place with most of these features, it's a keeper.

Book your accommodations as soon as your itinerary is set, especially if you want to stay at one of my top listings or if you'll be traveling during busy times (roughly Easter through October). See page 545 for a list of major holidays and festivals in Greece; for tips on making reservations, see the sidebar, later.

Some people make reservations as they travel, calling hotels a few days to a week before their arrival. If you anticipate crowds (worst on weekdays at business destinations and weekends at tourist locales) on the day you want to check in, call hotels at about 9:00 or 10:00, when the receptionist knows who'll be checking out and which rooms will be available. Some apps—such as HotelTonight.com—specialize in last-minute rooms, often at business-class hotels in big cities. If you encounter a language barrier, ask the fluent receptionist at your current hotel to call for you.

RATES AND DEALS

I've categorized my recommended accommodations based on price, indicated with a dollar-sign rating (see sidebar). The price ranges suggest an estimated cost for a one-night stay in a standard double room with a private toilet and shower in high season, include breakfast, and assume you're booking directly with the hotel (not through a booking site, which extracts a commission). Room prices can fluctuate significantly with demand and amenities (size, views, room class, and so on), but relative price categories remain constant. Taxes, which can vary from place to place, are generally insignificant (a dollar or two per person, per night). And keep in mind that some hotels in Greece, especially smaller places, may require payment in cash.

Room rates are especially volatile at larger hotels that use "dynamic pricing" to set rates. Prices can skyrocket during festivals and conventions, while business hotels can have deep discounts on weekends when demand plummets. Of the many hotels I recommend, it's difficult to say which will be the best value on a given day—until you do your homework.

Once your dates are set, check the specific price for your preferred stay at several hotels. You can do this either by comparing prices on Hotels.com or Booking.com, or by checking the hotels' own websites. To get the best deal, contact my family-run hotels directly by phone or email. When you go direct, the owner avoids the 20 percent commission, giving them wiggle room to offer you a discount, a nicer room, or free breakfast if it's not already included (see sidebar). If you prefer to book online or are considering a hotel chain, it's to your advantage to use the hotel's website.

Some hotels offer a discount to those who pay cash or stay longer than three nights. To cut costs further, try asking for a cheaper room (for example, with a shared bathroom or no window) or offer to skip breakfast (if included).

Additionally, some accommodations offer a special discount for Rick Steves readers, indicated in this guidebook by the abbreviation **"RS%."** Discounts vary: Ask for details when you reserve. Generally, to qualify, you must book direct (that is, not through a booking site), mention this book when you reserve, show this book upon arrival, and sometimes pay cash or stay a certain number of nights. In some cases, you may need to enter a discount code (which I've provided in the listing) in the booking form on the hotel's website. Rick Steves discounts apply to readers with ebooks as well as printed books. Understandably, discounts do not apply to promotional rates.

TYPES OF ACCOMMODATIONS
Hotels

You'll usually see the word "hotel," but you might also see the traditional Greek word *Xenonas* (ΞΕΝΩΝΑΣ/Ξενώνασ). In some places, especially Nafplio, small hotels are called *pensions.*

A "twin" room has two single beds; a "double" has one double bed. If you'll take either, let the hotel know, or you might be needlessly turned away. Some hotels can add an extra bed (for a small charge) to turn a double into a triple; some offer larger rooms for four or more people (I call these "family rooms" in the listings). If there's space for an extra cot, they'll cram it in for you. In general, a triple room is cheaper than the cost of a double and a single. Three or four people can economize by requesting one big room.

Hotels vs. Booking Websites vs. Consumers

In the last decade it's become almost impossible for independent-minded, family-run hotels to survive without playing the game as dictated by the big players in the online booking world. Priceline's Booking.com and Expedia's Hotels.com take roughly 80 percent of this business. Hoteliers note that without this online presence, "We become almost invisible." Online booking services demand about 20 percent in commission. And in order to be listed, a hotel must promise that its website does not undercut the price on the third-party's website. Without that restriction, hoteliers could say, "Sure, sell our rooms for whatever markup you like, and we'll continue to offer a fair rate to travelers who come to us directly"—but that's not allowed.

Here's the work-around: For independent and family-run hotels, book directly by email or phone, in which case hotel owners are free to give you whatever price they like. Research the price online, and then ask for a room without the commission mark-up. You could ask them to split the difference—the hotel charges you 10 percent less but pockets 10 percent more. Or you can ask for a free breakfast (if not included) or free upgrade.

If you do book online, be sure to use the hotel's website (you'll likely pay the same price as via a booking site, but your money goes to the hotel, not agency commissions).

As consumers, remember: Whenever you book with an online booking service, you're adding a needless middleman who takes roughly 20 percent. If you'd like to support small, family-run hotels whose world is more difficult than ever, book direct.

An "en suite" room has a bathroom (toilet and shower/tub) attached to the room; a room with a "private bathroom" can mean that the bathroom is all yours, but it's across the hall. If you want your own bathroom inside the room, request "en suite." If money's tight, ask about a room with a shared bathroom. You'll almost always have a sink in your room, and as more rooms go en suite, the hallway bathroom is shared with fewer guests. Most bathrooms come with just a shower (if you want a bathtub, ask for one when you reserve).

Arrival and Check-In: Hotel elevators are becoming more common, though some older buildings still lack them. You may have to climb a flight of stairs to reach the elevator (if so, you can ask the front desk for help carrying your bags up). Elevators are typically very small—pack light, or you may need to send your bags up without you.

Making Hotel Reservations

Reserve your rooms as soon as you've pinned down your travel dates. For busy national holidays, it's wise to reserve far in advance (see page 545).

Requesting a Reservation: For family-run hotels, it's generally cheaper to book your room directly via email or a phone call. For business-class hotels, or if you'd rather book online, reserve directly through the hotel's official website (not a booking agency's site). For complicated requests, send an email. Almost all of my recommended hotels take reservations in English.

Here's what the hotelier wants to know:

- type(s) of rooms you need and size of your party
- number of nights you'll stay
- your arrival and departure dates, written European-style as day/month/year (for example, 18/06/19 or 18 June 2019)
- special requests (such as en suite bathroom vs. down the hall, cheapest room, twin beds vs. double bed, quiet room)
- applicable discounts (such as a Rick Steves reader discount, cash discount, or promotional rate)

Confirming a Reservation: Most places will request a credit-card number to hold your room. If you're using an online reservation form, look for the *https* or a lock icon at the top of your browser. If you book direct, you can email, call, or fax this information.

Canceling a Reservation: If you must cancel, it's courteous—and smart—to do so with as much notice as possible, especially

---

When you check in, the receptionist will normally ask for your passport and keep it for anywhere from a couple of minutes to a couple of hours. The EU requires that hotels collect your name, nationality, and ID number. Relax. Americans are notorious for making this chore more difficult than it needs to be.

If you suspect that night noise will be a problem (if, for instance, your room is over a noisy café), ask for a quieter room in the back or on an upper floor.

If you're arriving in the morning, your room probably won't be ready. Check your bag safely at the hotel and dive right into sightseeing.

In Your Room: More pillows and blankets are usually in the closet or available on request. Towels and linens aren't always replaced every day. Hang your towel up to dry.

All over Greece, including Athens, most bathrooms have

PRACTICALITIES

From: rick@ricksteves.com
Sent: Today
To: info@hotelcentral.com
Subject: Reservation request for 19-22 July

Dear Hotel Central,

I would like to stay at your hotel. Please let me know if you have a room available and the price for:
• 2 people
• Double bed and en suite bathroom in a quiet room
• Arriving 19 July, departing 22 July (3 nights)

Thank you!
Rick Steves

for smaller family-run places. Cancellation policies can be strict; read the fine print or ask about these before you book. Internet deals may require prepayment, with no cancellation refunds.

Reconfirming a Reservation: Always call or email to reconfirm your room reservation a few days in advance. For *dhomatia* (privately rented rooms) or very small hotels, I call again on my day of arrival to tell my host what time to expect me (especially important if arriving late—after 17:00).

Phoning: For tips on calling hotels overseas, see page 524.

ancient plumbing that clogs easily. You may see signs requesting that you discard toilet paper in the bathroom wastebasket. This may seem unusual, but it keeps the sewer system working and prevents you from getting cozy with your hotel janitor.

Most hotel rooms have a TV, telephone, and free Wi-Fi (although in old buildings with thick walls, the Wi-Fi signal doesn't always make it to the rooms; sometimes it's only available in the lobby). There's often a guest computer with Internet access in the lobby. Simpler places rarely have a room phone, but often have free Wi-Fi.

If visiting areas with mosquitoes (such as Kardamyli and Monemvasia), avoid opening your windows, especially at night. If your hotel lacks air-conditioning, request a fan. Many hotels furnish a small plug-in bulb that helps keep the bloodsuckers at bay. If not already plugged into the electric socket, it may be on a table or nightstand. Some may have a separate scented packet that you have to unwrap and insert into the device.

Hotels in Greece are required by law to be nonsmoking, but

enforcement is spotty. Hoteliers are obsessive about eliminating any odors, but if your room smells like the Marlboro man slept there, ask to be moved.

To guard against theft in your room, keep valuables out of sight. Some rooms come with a safe, and other hotels have safes at the front desk. I've never bothered using one and in a lifetime of travel, I've never had anything stolen from my room.

Breakfast and Meals: A satisfying Greek breakfast with cheese, ham, yogurt, fresh bread, honey, jam, fruit, juice, and coffee or tea is standard and is sometimes included in hotel prices. More expensive hotels also tend to serve eggs and cereal.

Checking Out: While it's customary to pay for your room upon departure, it can be a good idea to settle your bill the day before, when you're not in a hurry and while the manager's in. That way you'll have time to discuss and address any points of contention.

Hotelier Help: Hoteliers can be a good source of advice. Most know their city well, and can assist you with everything from public transit and airport connections to finding a good restaurant, the nearest launderette, or a late-night pharmacy.

Hotel Hassles: Even at the best places, mechanical breakdowns occur: Sinks leak, hot water turns cold, toilets may gurgle or smell, the Wi-Fi goes out, or the air-conditioning dies when you need it most. Report your concerns clearly and calmly at the front desk. For more complicated problems, don't expect instant results. Above all, keep a positive attitude. Remember, you're on vacation. If your hotel is a disappointment, spend more time out enjoying the place you came to see.

Dhomatia (Rooms)

Rooms in private homes (similar to B&Bs, called *dhomatia/ ΔΩΜΑΤΙΑ/δωμάτια* in Greece) offer double the cultural intimacy for a good deal less than most hotel rooms. You'll usually have air-conditioning, your own bathroom, and a minifridge, but expect simple, stripped-down rooms, and little or nothing in the way of a public lounge. Hosts generally speak English and are interesting conversationalists. Your stay probably won't include breakfast, but you'll have access to a kitchen.

Local TIs may have lists of *dhomatia* and can book a room for you, but you'll save money by booking directly with the *dhomatia* listed in this book.

Short-Term Rentals

A short-term rental—whether an apartment, house, or room in a local's home—is an increasingly popular alternative, especially if you plan to settle in one location for several nights. For stays longer

The Good and Bad of Online Reviews

User-generated review sites and apps such as Yelp, Booking. com, and TripAdvisor can give you a consensus of opinions about everything from hotels and restaurants to sights and nightlife. If you scan reviews of a hotel and see several complaints about noise or a rotten location, it tells you something important that you'd never learn from the hotel's own website.

But as a guidebook writer, my sense is that there is a big difference between the uncurated information on a review site and a guidebook. A user-generated review is based on the experience of one person, who likely stayed at one hotel in a given city and ate at a few restaurants there (and who doesn't have much of a basis for comparison). A guidebook is the work of a trained researcher who, year after year, visits many alternatives to assess their relative value. I recently checked out some top-rated user-reviewed hotel and restaurant listings in various towns; when stacked up against their competitors, some were gems, while just as many were duds.

Both types of information have their place, and in many ways, they're complementary. If something is well-reviewed in a guidebook, and also gets good ratings on one of these sites, it's likely a winner.

than a few days, you can usually find a rental that's comparable to—and cheaper than—a hotel room with similar amenities. Plus, you'll get a behind-the-scenes peek into how locals live.

Many places require a minimum-night stay, and compared to hotels, rentals usually have less-flexible cancellation policies. And you're generally on your own: There's no hotel reception desk, breakfast, or daily cleaning service.

Finding Accommodations: Aggregator websites such as Airbnb, FlipKey, Booking.com, and the HomeAway family of sites (HomeAway, VRBO, and VacationRentals) let you browse properties and correspond directly with European property owners or managers. If you prefer to work from a curated list of accommodations, consider using a rental agency such as InterhomeUSA.com or RentaVilla.com. Agency-represented apartments typically cost more, but this method often offers more help and safeguards than booking direct.

Before you commit, be clear on the details, location, and amenities. I like to virtually "explore" the neighborhood using the Street View feature on Google Maps. Also consider the proximity to public transportation, and how well-connected the property is with the rest of the city. Ask about amenities (elevator, air-conditioning, laundry, Wi-Fi, parking, etc.). Reviews from previous guests can help identify trouble spots.

Keep Cool

If you're visiting Greece in the summer, the extra expense of an air-conditioned room can be money well spent, particularly in the south. Most hotel rooms with air-conditioners come with a control stick (like a TV remote; the hotel may require a deposit) that generally has similar symbols and features: fan icon (click to toggle through wind power, from light to gale); louver icon (choose steady airflow or waves); snowflake and sunshine icons (cold air or heat, depending on season); clock ("O" setting: run X hours before turning off; "I" setting: wait X hours to start); and the temperature control (20 degrees Celsius is comfortable; also see the thermometer diagram on page 552). When you leave your room for the day, turning off the air-conditioning is good form.

Think about the kind of experience you want: Just a key and an affordable bed...or a chance to get to know a local? There are typically two kinds of hosts: those who want minimal interaction with their guests, and hosts who are friendly and may want to interact with you. Read the promotional text and online reviews to help shape your decision.

Apartments and Rental Houses: If you're staying somewhere for four nights or longer, it's worth considering an apartment or rental house (shorter stays aren't worth the hassle of arranging key pickup, buying groceries, etc.). Apartment or house rentals can be especially cost-effective for groups and families. European apartments, like hotel rooms, tend to be small by US standards. But they often come with laundry machines and small, equipped kitchens, making it easier and cheaper to dine in. If you make good use of the kitchen (and Europe's great produce markets), you'll save on your meal budget.

Private and Shared Rooms: Renting a room in someone's home is a good option for those traveling alone, as you're more likely to find true single rooms—with just one single bed, and a price to match. Beds range from air-mattress-in-living-room basic to plush-B&B-suite posh. Some places allow you to book for a single night; if staying for several nights, you can buy groceries just as you would in a rental house. While you can't expect your host to also be your tour guide—or even to provide you with much info— some may be interested in getting to know the travelers who come through their home.

Other Options: Swapping homes with a local works for people with an appealing place to offer, and who can live with the idea of having strangers in their home (don't assume that where you live is not interesting to Europeans). A good place to start is

HomeExchange. To sleep for free, Couchsurfing.com is a vaga-bond's alternative to Airbnb. It lists millions of outgoing members, who host fellow "surfers" in their homes.

Confirming and Paying: Many places require you to pay the entire balance before your trip. It's easiest and safest to pay through the site where you found the listing. Be wary of owners who want to take your transaction offline to avoid fees; this gives you no re-course if things go awry. Never agree to wire money (a key indica-tor of a fraudulent transaction).

Hostels

A hostel provides cheap dorm beds where you sleep alongside strangers for about $25 per night. Travelers of any age are welcome if they don't mind dorm-style accommodations. Most hostels offer kitchen facilities, guest computers, Wi-Fi, and a self-service laun-dry. Hostels almost always provide bedding, but the towel's up to you (though you can usually rent one for a small fee). Family and private rooms are often available.

Independent hostels tend to be easygoing, colorful, and in-formal (no membership required; www.hostelworld.com). You may pay slightly less by booking directly with the hostel. **Official hos-tels** are part of Hostelling International (HI) and share an online booking site (www.hihostels.com). HI hostels typically require that you either have a membership card or pay extra per night.

Eating

Greek food is simple...and simply delicious. Unlike the French or the Italians, who are forever experi-menting to perfect an in-tricate cuisine, the Greeks found an easy formula and stick with it—and it rarely misses. The four Greek food groups are olives (and

olive oil), salty feta cheese, ripe tomatoes, and crispy phyllo dough. Virtually every dish you'll have here is built on a foundation of these four tasty building blocks.

When restaurant-hunting, choose a spot filled with locals, not the place with the big neon signs boasting, "We Speak English and Accept Credit Cards." Venturing even a block or two off the main drag leads to higher-quality food for a better price.

PRACTICALITIES

> ## Restaurant Price Code
>
> I've assigned each eatery a price category, based on the aver-
> age cost of a typical main course. Drinks, desserts, and splurge
> items (steak and seafood) can raise the price considerably.
>
> **$$$$**   **Splurge:** Most main courses over €15
> **$$$**   **Pricier:** €10-15
> **$$**   **Moderate:** €5-10
> **$**   **Budget:** Under €5
>
> In Greece, souvlaki and other takeaway food is **$;** a basic café
> or sit-down restaurant is **$$;** a casual but more upscale res-
> taurant is **$$$;** and a swanky splurge is **$$$$.**

RESTAURANT PRICING

I've categorized my recommended eateries based on price, indicated with a dollar-sign rating (see sidebar). The price ranges suggest the average price of a typical main course—but not necessar-
ily a complete meal. Sticking to souvlaki will save you plenty over
ordering meat and fish dishes. Obviously, expensive items (steak,
seafood, etc.), fine wine, appetizers, and dessert can significantly
increase your final bill.

The categories also indicate a place's personality:

Budget eateries include street food, takeaway, order-at-the-
counter shops, basic cafeterias, and bakeries selling pies and sandwiches.

Moderate eateries are nice (but not fancy) sit-down restaurants, ideal for a straightforward, fill-the-tank meal. Most of my
listings fall in this category—great for a good taste of local cuisine
on a budget.

Pricier eateries are a notch up, with more attention paid to
the setting, service, and cuisine. These are ideal for a memorable
meal that doesn't break the bank. This category often includes affordable "destination" or "foodie" restaurants. And **splurge** eateries are dress-up-for-a-special-occasion-swanky—typically with an
elegant setting, polished service, pricey and intricate cuisine, and
an expansive (and expensive) wine list.

To assign price ranges for restaurants in Greece, these price
points were my rule of thumb: **$$$$**—most salads and starters
over €8, main dishes over €15; **$$$**—most salads and starters €5-8,
main dishes €10-15; **$$**—most salads and starters under €5, main
dishes under €10; **$**—meals under €5. I haven't categorized places
where you might snack, graze, or assemble a picnic: supermarkets,
delis, ice cream stands, cafés or bars specializing in drinks, chocolate shops, and so on.

DINING TIPS

Greeks like to eat late: Dine at 18:00, and you'll be surrounded by other tourists; stick around until 21:00, and they'll all have been replaced by locals. Especially in cities, popular restaurants tend to stay open until midnight or even past that.

Restaurant hours can be informal. While the opening times I've listed are reasonably reliable, closing times often depend on how busy a place is—if you arrive too late on a slow day, you may find the place shuttered.

Smoking is banned in enclosed spaces, such as restaurants and bars. As a result, many smokers occupy outdoor tables—often that's where you'll want to sit too. Despite the law, many bars and some restaurants allow smoking inside, too.

Types of Restaurants

In addition to the traditional Greek restaurant *(estiatorio)*, you'll also encounter these places:

Taverna: Common, rustic neighborhood restaurant with a smaller menu, slinging Greek favorites. These tend to be cheaper, to cater to locals' budgets.

Mezedopolio: Eatery specializing in small plates/appetizers/ *mezedes.*

Ouzerie: Bar that makes ouzo, often selling high-quality *mezedes*—or even meals—to go along with it.

If you're looking for fast food, in addition to the usual international chains (McDonald's and Starbucks), there are some Greek versions. Grigoris Coffee Right is the local version of Starbucks, and Goody's is the Greek take on McDonald's. Everest is open 24/7, selling sandwiches and savory pies to go.

Ordering and Paying

When you sit down at a restaurant, you'll likely be asked if you want a basket of (generally fresh, good) bread, often with your napkins and flatware tucked inside. You'll pay a bread and cover charge of about €0.50-1 (usually noted clearly on the menu).

Menus are usually written in both Greek and English. Many tavernas will have a display case showing what they've been cooking for the day, and it's perfectly acceptable to ask for a look and point to the dish you want. This is a good way to make some friends, sample a variety of dishes, get what you want (or at least know what you're getting), and have a truly memorable meal. Be brave.

Greece has many local specialties. At least once, seek out and eat or drink the notorious "gross" specialties: ouzo, eggplant, fish eggs, octopus, and so on. You've heard references to them all your life—now's your chance to actually experience what everyone's talking about. *Kali orexi! (Bon appétit!)*

PRACTICALITIES

A small dessert (that you didn't order) may appear at the end of your restaurant meal—often a tiny pastry, candied fruit, or shot of grappa. It's included in the price of your meal. You are welcome to linger as late as you want—don't feel pressured to eat quickly and turn over the table.

Tipping: Tipping is an issue only at restaurants that have table service. If you order your food at a counter, don't tip. At Greek restaurants that have waitstaff, service is generally included, although it's common to round up the bill after a good meal (about 10 percent; so, for an €18.50 meal, pay €20). It's considered bad form to leave a single euro, though; if a bill is €10, leave a €2 tip.

GREEK CUISINE

Although the Greeks don't like to admit it, their cuisine has a lot in common with Turkish food, including many of the same dishes. (This is partly because they share a similar climate, and partly because Greece was part of the Ottoman Empire for nearly 400 years.) Some names—such as moussaka—come directly from Turkish. You'll find traces of Italian influences as well, such as *pastitsio*, the "Greek lasagna."

My favorite fast, cheap, and filling Greek snack is souvlaki pita, a tasty shish kebab wrapped in flat bread. Souvlaki stands are all over Greece (see sidebar on page 186). On the islands, eat fresh seafood. Don't miss the creamy yogurt with honey. Feta cheese salads and flaky nut-and-honey baklava are two other tasty treats. Dunk your bread into *tzatziki* (TZAHT-zee-kee), the ubiquitous and refreshing cucumber-and-yogurt dip. (Tourists often call it *tzitziki*, which sounds like the Greek word for crickets—a mispronunciation which endlessly amuses local waiters.)

In the early 20th century, chef Nikolaos Tselementes learned international cooking techniques and used them to revolutionize Greek cuisine—codifying many recipes you'll still find all over the country. It was Tselementes who introduced non-Greek elements like béchamel sauce to local cooking, in beloved recipes such as moussaka and *pastitsio*. To this day, Greeks call a cookbook—and anyone who's really adept at using it—a "Tselementes."

Here are more flavors to seek out during your time in Greece.

Olives

As you'll quickly gather when you pass endless tranquil olive groves on your drive through the countryside, olives are a major staple of Greek food—both the olives themselves and the oil they produce. Connoisseurs can distinguish as many varieties of olives as there are grapes for wine, but they fall into two general categories: those for eating and those for making oil.

Greeks are justifiably proud of their olive oil: Their country is the third-largest producer in the European Union, and they consume more olive oil per capita than any other Mediterranean nation—almost seven gallons per person a year. Locals say that the taste is shaped both by the variety and the terrain where the olives are grown. Olive oils from the Peloponnese, for example, are supposed to be robust with grassy or herbaceous overtones. Pay attention, and you'll notice the differences as you travel. Common, edible Greek olives include the following:

Amfissa: Found in both black and green varieties, grown near Delphi. These are rounder and mellower than other varieties.

Halkithiki: Large, green olives from northern Greece, often stuffed with pimento, sun-dried tomato, feta cheese, or other delicacies.

Kalamata: Purple and almond-shaped, the best-known variety. These come from the southern Peloponnese and are cured in a red-wine vinegar brine.

Throubes: Black, wrinkled olives, usually from the island of Thassos, that stay on the tree until fully ripe. Dry-cured, they have an intense, salty taste and chewy texture.

Tsakistes: Green olives grown mainly in Attica (near Athens) that are cracked with a mallet or cut with a knife before being steeped in water and then brine. After curing, they are marinated in garlic and lemon wedges or herbs.

Cheese

Feta: Protected by EU regulations, it's made with sheep's milk, although up to 30 percent of goat's milk can be added (but never cow's milk). Feta comes in many variations—some are soft, moist, and rather mild; others are sour, hard, and crumbly (it depends on how much goat milk is used, and how—and how long—it's aged).

Graviera: A hard cheese usually made in Crete from sheep's milk, it tastes sweet and nutty, almost like a fine Swiss cheese.

Kasseri: The most popular Greek cheese after feta, it's a mild, yellow cheese made from either sheep's or goat's milk.

Pies

Flaky phyllo-dough pastries (*pita*, not to be confused with pita bread) are another staple of Greek cuisine. These can be ordered as a starter in a restaurant or purchased from a bakery for a tasty bite on the run. They can be made out of just about anything, but the most common are *spanakopita* (spinach), *tiropita* (cheese), *kreatopita* (beef or pork), *meletzanitopita* (eggplant), and *bougatsa* (with a sweet cream filling).

Salads and Starters *(Mezedes)*

Mezedes (meh-ZEH-dehs), known internationally as *meze*, are a great way to sample several tasty Greek dishes. This "small plates" approach is common and easy—instead of ordering a starter and a main dish per person, get two or three starters and one main dish to split.

Almost anything in Greece can be served as a small-plate "starter" (including several items listed in other sections here—olives, cheeses, and main dishes), but these are most common:

Bekri meze: Literally "drunkard's snack"—chunks of chicken, pork, or beef cooked slowly with wine, cloves, cinnamon, bay leaves, and olive oil.

Dolmathes: Stuffed grape (or cabbage) leaves filled with either meat or rice and served hot or cold.

Gigantes (also **Gigantes plaki**): "Giant" lima beans oven-baked until tender in a mix of tomato, peppers, dill, other herbs, and sometimes sausage or pork.

Greek salad (a.k.a. *horiatiki*, "village" salad): Ripe tomatoes chopped up just so, rich feta cheese (usually in a long, thick slab that you break apart), olives, and onions, all drenched with olive oil. You'll find yourself eating this combination again and again—yet somehow, it never gets old. It's sometimes topped with rusk (or "Cretan rusk")—crunchy, dry croutons made of rustic barley bread.

Keftedes: Small meatballs, often seasoned with mint, onion, parsley, and sometimes ouzo.

Melitzanosalata: Cooked eggplant with the consistency of mashed potatoes, usually well-seasoned and delicious.

Pantzarosalata: Beet salad dressed with olive oil and vinegar.

Papoutsaki: Eggplant "slippers" filled with ground beef and cheese.

Roasted red peppers: Soft and flavorful, often drizzled with olive oil.

Saganaki: Cooked cheese, often breaded, sometimes grilled and sometimes fried, occasionally flambéed.

Soutzoukakia: Meatballs with spicy tomato sauce.

Taramosalata: Smoky, pink, fish-roe mixture with the consistency of mashed potatoes, used as a dip for bread or vegetables.

Tirokafteri: Feta cheese that's been softened and mixed with white pepper to give it some kick, served either as a spread or stuffed inside roasted red peppers.

Tzatziki: A pungent and thick sauce of yogurt, cucumber, and garlic. It seems like a condiment but is often ordered as a starter, then eaten as a salad or used to complement other foods.

Soups

Summertime visitors might be disappointed not to find much soup on the menu (including *avgolemono*, the delicious egg, lemon, and rice soup). Soup is considered a winter dish and is almost impossible to find in warm weather. If available, Greek chicken soup *(kotosoupa)* is very tasty. *Kremithosoupa* is the Greek version of French onion soup, and *kakavia* or *psarosoupa* is a famous fish soup often compared to bouillabaisse.

Main Dishes
Here are some popular meat and seafood dishes you'll likely see.

Meats
Arnaki kleftiko: Slow-cooked lamb, usually wrapped in phyllo dough or parchment paper. Legend says it was created by bandits who needed to cook without the telltale signs of smoke or fire. (Baked fish, and other meats, may also be served *kleftiko*.)

Gyro: Literally "turn," a gyro is not a type of meat but a way of preparing it—stacked on a metal skewer and vertically slow-roasted on a rotisserie, then shaved off in slices. In Greece it's usually made from chicken or pork, and often served wrapped in a pita, making a handy to-go sandwich.

Moussaka: A classic casserole with layers of minced meat, eggplant, and potatoes and a topping of cheesy béchamel sauce or egg custard.

Pastitsio: A layered baked dish called the "Greek lasagna." Ground meat is sandwiched between two layers of pasta with an egg-custard or béchamel topping.

Souvlaki: Pork or lamb cooked on a skewer, often wrapped in pita bread (and sometimes topped with fries); also can be served on a platter with rice.

Stifado: Beef stew with onions, tomatoes, and spices such as cinnamon and cloves. It was traditionally made with rabbit *(kouneli)*.

Fish and Seafood
Barbounia: Red mullet that is usually grilled or fried and is always expensive. These small fish are bony, but the flesh melts in your mouth.

Gavros: An appetizer similar to anchovies. Squeeze lemon luxuriously all over them, and eat everything but the wispy little tails.

Htapothi: Octopus, often marinated and grilled, then drizzled with olive oil and lemon juice.

Psari plaki: Fish baked in the oven with tomatoes and onions.

Sweets
Baklava: Phyllo dough layered with nuts and honey.

Ekmek: A cake made of thin phyllo fibers soaked in honey, then topped with custard and a layer of whipped cream.

Karydopita: Honey-walnut cake made without flour.

Kataifi: Thin fibers of phyllo (like shredded wheat) layered with nuts and honey.

Loukoumades: The Greek doughnut, soaked in honey or sugar syrup.

Meli pita: Honey-cheese pie, traditionally served at Easter.

DRINKS

Wine: There are two basic types of Greek wines—*retsina* (resin-flavored, rarely served) and nonresinated wines.

Retsina **wine,** a post-WWII rotgut with a notorious resin flavor, has long been famous as the working man's Greek wine. It makes you want to sling a patch over one eye and say, "Arghh." The first glass is like drinking wood. The third glass is dangerous: It starts to taste good. If you drink any more, you'll smell like it the entire next day. Why resin? Way back when, Greek winemakers used pine resin to seal the amphoras that held the wine, protecting the wine from the air. Discovering that they liked the taste, the winemakers began adding resin to the wine itself.

If pine sap is not your cup of tea, there are plenty of **nonresinated wine options.** With its new generation of winemakers (many of them trained abroad), Greece is receiving more recognition for its wines. More than 300 native varietals are now grown in Greece's wine regions. About two-thirds of the wine produced in Greece is white. The best known are Savatiano (the most widely grown grape used for *retsina* and other wines), Assyrtiko (a crisp white mostly from Santorini), and Moschofilero (a dry white from the Peloponnese). Red wines include Agiorgitiko (a medium red also from the Peloponnese; one carries the name "Blood of Hercules") and Xynomavro (an intense red from Naoussa in Macedonia). Greeks also grow cabernet sauvignon, merlot, chardonnay, and other familiar varieties. And Santorini bottles the sweet, luxurious, expensive dessert wine called Vinsanto.

Here are a few wine terms that you may find useful: *inos* (οίνος—term for "wine" printed on bottles), *krasi* (spoken term for "wine"), *ktima* (winery or estate), *inopolio* (wine bar), *lefko* (white), *erithro* or *kokkino* (red), *xiro* (dry), *agouro* (young), *me poli soma* (full-bodied), *epitrapezio* (table wine), and O.P.A.P. (an indication of quality that tells you the wine came from one of Greece's designated wine regions).

Beer: Greeks are proud of their few local brands, including Alpha, Fix, Vergina, and Mythos.

Spirits: Beyond wine and beer, consider special Greek spirits. Cloudy, anise-flavored **ouzo,** supposedly invented by monks on Mount Athos, is worth a try even if you don't like the taste (black licorice). Similar to its Mediterranean cousins, French *pastis* and

Turkish *raki,* ouzo turns from clear to milky white when you add ice or water (don't drink it straight). Greeks drink it both as an aperitif and with food. I like to sip it slowly in the early evening while sharing several *mezedes* with my travel partner. Some of the best-selling brands are Ouzo 12, Plomari Ouzo, and Sans Rival Ouzo.

Even better is **tsipouro.** Similar to Italian grappa, this brandy is distilled from leftover grape skins; it is sometimes flavored with anise. Stronger and purer than ouzo, it's best drunk with water on the rocks. Some of the best are Barbayanni, Tsilili, and Adolo.

Metaxa is to be savored after dinner. This rich, sweet, golden-colored liqueur has a brandy base blended with aged wine and a "secret" herbal mixture.

If you're traveling on the Peloponnese, try **Tentura,** a regional liqueur flavored with cloves, nutmeg, cinnamon, and citrus. It packs a spicy kick.

Coffee: All over Greece, Starbucks-style coffeehouses have invaded Main Street. But, while most modern Greeks drink espresso, you can still seek out traditional **Greek coffee** (similar to Turkish coffee). This unfiltered brew is prepared in a small copper pot called a *briki* or an *ibrik,* and usually served with a glass of water and a chunk of candy called *loukoumi.* While most of the world calls this candy "Turkish delight," locals boast that it was actually invented by Greek pastry chefs, then spread throughout the Ottoman Empire—so their name, "Greek delight," is more fitting.

In summer, cafés are filled with Greeks sipping **iced coffee** drinks. *Freddo cappuccino* (iced cappuccino) is the drink of choice, with a thick, creamy layer of milk on top, whipped with a special blender. You can also usually find a *frappé* (iced Nescafé; order it black or white—with milk), *freddo espresso* (iced espresso, no milk), and *freddo mokka.*

When ordering coffee, the barista will usually ask how much sugar you want in it. (They may say, "How much sugar? Normal?") You can order your coffee *pikro/sketos* (bitter/plain), *metrio* (semi-sweet—the default choice), or *gliko* (sweet).

Don't ask for a "regular coffee," as almost nobody will understand what you mean.

Water: Water is served in bottles. It's very cheap (even in otherwise expensive areas) and rarely carbonated.

Staying Connected

One of the most common questions I hear from travelers is, "How can I stay connected in Europe?" The short answer is: more easily and cheaply than you might think.

The simplest solution is to bring your own device—mobile

PRACTICALITIES

How to Dial

International Calls

Whether phoning from a US landline or mobile phone, or from a number in another European country, here's how to make an international call. I've used one of my recommended Athens hotels as an example (tel. 210-324-9737).

Initial Zero: Drop the initial zero from international phone numbers—except when calling Italy.

Mobile Tip: If using a mobile phone, the "+" sign can replace the international access code (for a "+" sign, press and hold "0").

US/Canada to Europe

Dial 011 (US/Canada international access code), country code (30 for Greece), and phone number.

▶ To call the Athens hotel from home, dial 011-30-210-324-9737.

Country to Country Within Europe

Dial 00 (Europe international access code), country code, and phone number.

▶ To call the Athens hotel from Turkey, dial 00-30-210-324-9737.

Europe to the US/Canada

Dial 00, country code (1 for US/Canada), and phone number.

▶ To call from Europe to my office in Edmonds, Washington, dial 00-1-425-771-8303.

Domestic Calls

To call within Greece (from one Greek landline or mobile phone to another), simply dial the phone number.

▶ To call the Athens hotel from Delphi, dial 210-324-9737.

phone, tablet, or laptop—and use it just as you would at home (following the tips below, such as connecting to free Wi-Fi whenever possible). Another option is to buy a European SIM card for your mobile phone—either your US phone or one you buy in Europe. Or you can use European landlines and computers to connect. Each of these options is described next, and more details are at www.ricksteves.com/phoning. For a very practical one-hour talk covering tech issues for travelers, see www.ricksteves.com/mobile-travel-skills.

USING A MOBILE PHONE IN EUROPE

Here are some budget tips and options.

Sign up for an international plan. To stay connected at a lower cost, sign up for an international service plan through your carrier. Most providers offer a simple bundle that includes calling,

More Dialing Tips
Toll-Free Calls: International rates apply to US toll-free numbers dialed from Greece—they're not free.

More Phoning Help: See www.howtocallabroad.com.

European Country Codes			
Austria	43	Ireland & N. Ireland	353 / 44
Belgium	32	Italy	39
Bosnia-Herzegovina	387	Latvia	371
Croatia	385	Montenegro	382
Czech Republic	420	Morocco	212
Denmark	45	Netherlands	31
Estonia	372	Norway	47
Finland	358	Poland	48
France	33	Portugal	351
Germany	49	Russia	7
Gibraltar	350	Slovakia	421
Great Britain	44	Slovenia	386
Greece	30	Spain	34
Hungary	36	Sweden	46
Iceland	354	Switzerland	41
		Turkey	90

PRACTICALITIES

messaging, and data. Your normal plan may already include international coverage (T-Mobile's does).

Before your trip, call your provider or check online to confirm that your phone will work in Europe, and research your provider's international rates. Activate the plan a day or two before you leave, then remember to cancel it when your trip's over.

Use free Wi-Fi whenever possible. Unless you have an unlimited-data plan, you're best off saving most of your online tasks for Wi-Fi. You can access the Internet, send texts, and even make voice calls over Wi-Fi.

Most accommodations in Europe offer free Wi-Fi, but some—especially expensive hotels—charge a fee. Many cafés (including Starbucks and McDonald's) have free hotspots for customers; look for signs offering it and ask for the Wi-Fi password when you buy something. You'll also often find Wi-Fi at TIs, city squares, major museums, public-transit hubs, airports, and aboard trains and buses.

Minimize the use of your cellular network. Even with an international data plan, wait until you're on Wi-Fi to Skype, download apps, stream videos, or do other megabyte-greedy tasks. Using a navigation app such as Google Maps over a cellular network can take lots of data, so do this sparingly or use it offline.

Limit automatic updates. By default, your device constantly checks for a data connection and updates apps. It's smart to disable these features so your apps will only update when you're on Wi-Fi, and to change your device's email settings from "auto-retrieve" to "manual" (or from "push" to "fetch").

When you need to get online but can't find Wi-Fi, simply turn on your cellular network just long enough for the task at hand. When you're done, avoid further charges by manually turning off data roaming or cellular data (either works) in your device's Settings menu. Another way to make sure you're not accidentally using data roaming is to put your device in "airplane" mode (which also disables phone calls and texts), and then turn your Wi-Fi back on as needed.

It's also a good idea to keep track of your data usage. On your device's menu, look for "cellular data usage" or "mobile data" and reset the counter at the start of your trip.

Use Wi-Fi calling and messaging apps. Skype, Viber, FaceTime, and Google+ Hangouts are great for making free or low-cost voice and video calls over Wi-Fi. With an app installed on your phone, tablet, or laptop, you can log on to a Wi-Fi network and contact friends or family members who use the same service. If you buy credit in advance, with some of these services you can call any mobile phone or landline worldwide for just pennies per minute.

Many of these apps also allow you to send messages over Wi-Fi to any other person using that app. Be aware that some apps, such as Apple's iMessage, will use the cellular network if Wi-Fi isn't available: To avoid this possibility, turn off the "Send as SMS" feature.

USING A EUROPEAN SIM CARD

With a European SIM card, you get a European mobile number and access to cheaper rates than you'll get through your US carrier. This option works well for those who want to make a lot of voice calls or needing faster connection speeds than their US carrier provides. Fit the SIM card into a cheap phone you buy in Europe (about $40 from phone shops anywhere), or swap out the SIM card in an "unlocked" US phone (check with your carrier about unlocking it).

SIM cards are sold at mobile-phone shops, department-store

Tips on Internet Security

Make sure that your device is running the latest versions of its operating system, security software, and apps. Next, ensure that your device and key programs (like email) are password- or passcode-protected. On the road, use only secure, password-protected Wi-Fi hotspots. Ask the hotel or café staff for the specific name of their Wi-Fi network, and make sure you log on to that exact one.

If you must access your financial info online, use a banking app rather than accessing your account via a browser. A cellular connection is more secure than Wi-Fi. Avoid logging onto personal finance sites on a public computer.

Never share your credit-card number (or any other sensitive information) online unless you know that the site is secure. A secure site displays a little padlock icon, and the URL begins with *https* (instead of the usual *http*).

electronics counters, some newsstands, and vending machines. Costing about $5-10, they usually include prepaid calling/messaging credit, with no contract and no commitment. Expect to pay $20-40 more for a SIM card with a gigabyte of data. If you travel with this card to other countries in the European Union, there may be extra roaming fees.

I like to buy SIM cards at a phone shop where there's a clerk to help explain the options. I've used the Germanos (ΓΕΡΜΑΜΟΣ) electronics stores, whose staff speak English, to buy a SIM card and help me switch my US mobile phone to a Greek number. They're all over Greece, including at the Athens airport. The Greek phone company is known by its initials: OTE. Certain brands—including Lebara and Lycamobile, both of which are available in multiple European countries—are reliable and especially economical. Ask the clerk to help you insert your SIM card, set it up, and show you how to use it. In some countries, you'll be required to register the SIM card with your passport as an antiterrorism measure (which may mean you can't use the phone for the first hour or two).

Find out how to check your credit balance. When you run out of credit, you can top it up at newsstands, tobacco shops, mobile-phone stores, or many other businesses (look for your SIM card's logo in the window), or online.

PUBLIC PHONES AND COMPUTERS

It's possible to travel in Europe without a mobile device. You can make calls from your hotel (or the increasingly rare public phone), and check email or browse websites using public computers.

Most **hotels** charge a fee for placing calls—ask for rates before you dial. You can use a prepaid international phone card (available at post offices, newsstands, street kiosks, tobacco shops, and train stations) to call out from your hotel. Dial the toll-free access number, enter the card's PIN code, then dial the number.

You'll see **public pay phones** in a few post offices and train stations. The phones generally come with multilingual instructions; most don't take coins but instead require insertable phone cards (*Telekarta*, THΛEKAPTA, sold at post offices, newsstands, etc.). With the exception of Great Britain, each European country has its own insertable phone card—so your Greek card won't work in a Turkish phone.

Most hotels have **public computers** in their lobbies for guests to use; otherwise you may find them at Internet cafés and public libraries (ask your hotelier or the TI for the nearest location). On a European keyboard, use the "Alt Gr" key to the right of the space bar to insert the extra symbol that appears on some keys. If you can't locate a special character (such as @), simply copy and paste it from a Web page.

MAIL

You can mail one package per day to yourself worth up to $200 duty-free from Europe to the US (mark it "personal purchases"). If you're sending a gift to someone, mark it "unsolicited gift." For details, visit www.cbp.gov and search for "Know Before You Go."

The Greek postal service works fine, but for quick transatlantic delivery (in either direction), consider a service such as DHL (www.dhl.com). Get stamps for postcards and letters at the neighborhood post office, newsstands within fancy hotels, and some minimarts and card shops.

Transportation

To connect the destinations in this book, you'll either drive, take a bus or boat, or fly (train service is minimal).

For touring around the mainland, your best options are car or bus. A **rental car** allows you to come and go on your own schedule, and make a beeline between destinations. Outside of congested Athens, roads are uncrowded, and parking is often free. However, driving in Greece can be stressful, as Greek drivers tackle the roads with a kind of anything-goes, Wild West abandon. And it's more expensive than the bus. But if you're a confident driver, the convenience of driving in Greece trumps the hassles of bus transport.

Greece's network of public **buses** is affordable and will get you most anywhere you want to go. Unfortunately, it's not user-friendly. Particularly outside of Athens, the frequency can be sparse and schedules are hard to nail down. You'd need to allow plenty of

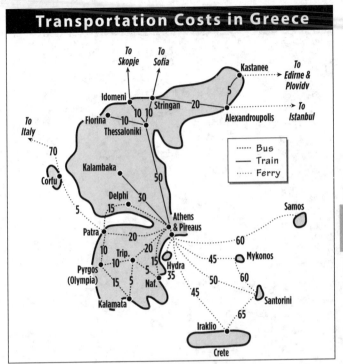

Transportation Costs in Greece

To Skopje

To Sofia

Kastanee

To Edirne & Plovidv

Idomeni

Stringan 20

10 10

Florina 10

Thessaloniki

To Italy

70

Kalambaka

Corfu

5

Delphi 30

15

Athens & Pireaus

Patra

20

Trip.

10

10

Pyrgos (Olympia)

15 5

Kalamata

50

Alexandroupolis

To Istanbul

Samos

60

45 Mykonos

20

15

Hydra

5

Naf.

35

50

60

45

Santorini

65

Iraklio

Crete

····· Bus
—— Train
······ Ferry

PRACTICALITIES

time, expect delays, and pack lots of patience to visit all of my recommended destinations.

BUSES

Greek buses are cheap, and the fleet is clean, modern, and air-conditioned, but the bus system can be frustrating. Athens has decent
bus service to popular destinations such as Delphi, Nafplio, and the
port town of Piraeus, but smaller destinations on the Peloponnese
are connected by only one or two buses a day.

All buses are run by a central company (KTEL, or ΚΤΕΛ in
Greek), but the local offices don't cooperate with each other—each
one sets its own schedules, and they often don't coordinate well.
Specific bus schedules can be very difficult to pin down, even for
buses leaving from the town you're in. (Forget about getting bus
schedules for other Greek towns.) Local TIs, where they exist, are
unlikely to have the information you need. Don't hesitate to ask
your hotelier for help—they're used to it.

KTEL has no helpful website or information office for the entire Greek bus system, but there is a list of local phone numbers
and websites at www.ktelbus.com (you'll need to know the name
of the province where you are traveling). The KTEL Athens site

Public Transportation in Greece

To Igoumenitsa

Delphi

Antirrio

Rio

Ag. Nikolaos

Aigio

Gulf of Corinth

To Corfu & Italy

Patra

Diakofto

Vouraikos Gorge

COG RAILWAY

Kalavryta

Killini

PELOPONNESE
(PELOPONNISOS)

Pyrgos

Olympia

Katakolo

Tripoli

Sparta

Kalamata

Messenian Gulf

Kardamyli

Ionian Sea

Gythio

Areopoli

MANI PENINSULA

Laconian Gulf

Vathia

10 Kilometers

10 Miles

----- Rail
- - - Bus
.... Boat

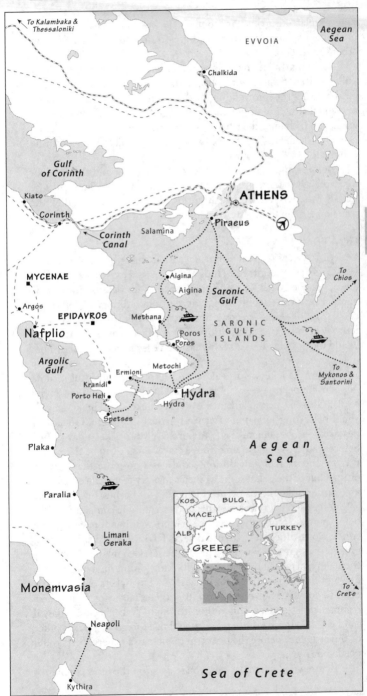

PRACTICALITIES

To Kalambaka &
Thessaloniki

*Aegean
Sea*

EVVOIA

Chalkida

*Gulf
of Corinth*

Kiato

Corinth

*Corinth
Canal*

ATHENS

Piraeus

Salamina

MYCENAE

Aigina

Argos

Aigina

*Saronic
Gulf*

EPIDAVROS

Methana

SARONIC
GULF
ISLANDS

Nafplio

Poros
Poros

*Argolic
Gulf*

Ermioni

Metochi

To Chios

Kranidi

Porto Heli

Hydra

Hydra

To
Mykonos &
Santorini

Spetses

Plaka

*Aegean
Sea*

Paralia

Limani
Geraka

KOS.   BULG.

MACE.

ALB.

TURKEY

GREECE

Monemvasia

Neapoli

To
Crete

Kythira

Sea of Crete

(www.ktelattikis.gr) is hard to navigate, but Matt Barrett's website has schedules for long-distance buses from and to Athens (www.athensguide.com).

Particularly on the Peloponnese, where your journeys likely will require a transfer (or multiple transfers), you frequently won't be able to get the information for the full route from the bus station at your starting point. For example, to go from Nafplio to Monemvasia, you'll change at Tripoli, then Sparta. The Nafplio bus station can give you details for the leg to Tripoli, but can't tell you anything about the rest of the journey.

Before you get on a bus, ask the ticket seller and the conductor explicitly if there are transfers—they might not volunteer these details otherwise. Then pay attention (and maybe even follow the route on a map) to be sure you don't miss your change.

BOATS

Greece has been a great seafaring nation since the days of Odysseus. Today the country's islands are connected to Athens' port (Piraeus, see the Athens Connections chapter for details) and to one another by a variety of ferries, ranging from hulking, slow-moving car ferries to sleek, speedy catamarans. While the decentralized ferry system isn't as straightforward or efficient as many travelers would like it to be, it's still fairly fast and easy to get around by boat in Greece.

Buying Tickets: In peak season (especially July-Aug), some popular connections—such as Piraeus-Hydra—can sell out early; book at least a week in advance. Advance tickets also make sense if you'll be setting sail soon after your arrival in Greece. Outside of peak season, it's generally safe to purchase your ticket a day or two before your crossing. Buying from a travel agency can be the easiest way to understand your options, and costs no more than buying online, but beware that some agencies may try to upsell you. Ferries are comfortable; there's no need to spring for business-class seats.

Greek ferry services are operated by multiple companies without a central information service. Good websites for researching connections include www.danae.gr/ferries-Greece.asp, www.greekferries.gr, and www.gtp.gr. Some ferry companies post only their current schedule—if you're looking online in January, you may not find sailing times for June. If you buy tickets online, you'll need to convert your reservation into an actual ticket. Some ferry companies let you do this online through Web check-in (they'll send you an eticket). Otherwise, you'll need to go to a ticket office or travel agency before the boat trip to pick up a paper ticket (you'll need your passport).

Before you buy, make sure you're clear on the ferry company's

Ferry Companies in Greece

Hellenic Seaways	Tel. 210-419-9000	www.hellenicseaways.gr
Blue Star Ferries	Tel. 210-891-9800	www.bluestarferries.com
ANEK Lines	Tel. 210-419-7470	www.anek.gr
Aegean Speed	Tel. 210-969-0950	www.aegeanspeedlines.gr
NEL Lines	Tel. 281-034-6185	www.ferries.gr/nel
SeaJets	Tel. 210-412-1001	www.seajets.gr
Minoan Lines	Tel. 210-414-5700	www.minoan.gr
Kallisti Ferries	Tel. 210-422-2972	www.ferries.gr/kallisti-ferries

PRACTICALITIES

refund and exchange policies. Since schedules can flex with demand, confirm your sailing time a day ahead.

Possible Delays or Cancellations: Smaller high-speed ferries (such as the Hellenic Seaways' "Flying Cat" and SeaJet's Super-Jet or SeaJet2) can be affected by high winds and other inclement weather. Larger ferries, such as the Hellenic Seaways Highspeed, SeaJet Champion Jet, and the Blue Star ferries are slower, more stable, and less likely to be canceled. In general, cancellations are rare but possible in summer, and more common off-season. If a sailing is canceled, the ferry company will contact you to rebook (for this reason, it's essential to provide a telephone number when you book). Usually you can go later that same day, but it's possible (though rare) to get stranded overnight. Even if the sea is rough, the ships may still run—but the ride can be very rocky. If you're prone to seasickness, be prepared.

Boarding the Ferry: If a place has several ports (such as Mykonos), make sure you know which port your boat leaves from. While ferry companies tell passengers to be at the dock 30 minutes before the boat leaves, most locals amble over to the dock about 10 minutes ahead. The sole advantage to turning up early is the chance to grab a better seat, which only makes a difference if your ferry has open seating, such as the Blue Star ferries (although even if there are assigned seats, they're often ignored). Don't be surprised if boats aren't on time—soak up some sun at the dock while you wait.

On the Ferry: Greece's ferries are very relaxing and can be a lot cheaper than flying, though they take longer. On big, slow-moving car ferries, you can sit outside and watch the islands slide by—but on the fast boats you'll be sitting inside, peering through saltwater-spattered windows.

Bigger ferries move slowly but can run in almost any weather. While the number of cars allowed onboard is limited, they can accommodate about 1,000-2,000 walk-on passengers, and tend to cost less. The smallest, fastest ferries are typically catamarans carrying only about 300-400 passengers, so they are more likely to sell out. While small boats are time-efficient, they have to slow down (or sometimes can't run at all) in bad weather. On some islands, such as Mykonos, bigger ferries arrive at a different point (usually farther from the main town) than the smaller boats (which may drop you right in the town center).

You may be able to stow your luggage on a rack on the boarding level of your boat; otherwise you'll haul it up several flights of stairs to the passenger decks. Ferries of all sizes typically are equipped with WCs and charging outlets; many offer Wi-Fi (usually for a fee and with spotty service). You can buy food and drinks on most boats. It's not too expensive, but it's usually not top quality, either. Bring your own snacks or a picnic instead.

RENTING A CAR

If you're renting a car in Greece, bring your driver's license. You're also technically required to have an International Driving Permit—an official translation of your driver's license (sold at your local AAA office for $20 plus the cost of two passport-type photos; see www.aaa.com). While that's the letter of the law, I generally rent cars without having this permit. How this is enforced varies from country to country: Get advice from your car-rental company.

Rental companies require you to be at least 21 years old and to have held your license for one year. Drivers under the age of 25 may incur a young-driver surcharge, and some rental companies do not rent to anyone 75 or older. If you're considered too young or old, look into leasing (covered later), which has less-stringent age restrictions.

Research car rentals before you go. It's cheaper to arrange most car rentals from the US. Consider several companies to compare rates.

Most of the major US rental agencies (including Avis, Budget, Enterprise, Hertz, and Thrifty) have offices throughout Europe. Also consider the two major Europe-based agencies, Europcar and Sixt. For a friendly local car-rental company in Athens, consider Swift/Escape (see page 213; www.greektravel.com/swift). It can be cheaper to use a consolidator, such as Auto Europe/Kemwel (www.autoeurope.com—or the sometimes cheaper www.autoeurope.eu), which compares rates at several companies to get you the best deal—but because you're working with a middleman, it's especially important to ask in advance about add-on fees and restrictions.

Always read the fine print or query the agent carefully for add-on charges—such as one-way drop-off fees, airport surcharges, or mandatory insurance policies—that aren't included in the "total price."

For the best deal, rent by the week with unlimited mileage. To save money on fuel, request a diesel car. I normally rent the smallest, least-expensive model with a stick shift (generally cheaper than an automatic). Almost all rentals are manual by default, so if you need an automatic, request one in advance; be aware that these cars are usually larger models (not as maneuverable on narrow winding roads). Because of the size of Greek roads (and Greek parking spaces), it's a good idea to rent a small vehicle.

Figure on paying roughly $250 for a one-week rental. Allow extra for supplemental insurance, fuel, tolls, and parking. For trips of three weeks or more, leasing can save you money on insurance and taxes. Be warned that international trips—say, picking up in Athens and dropping in Istanbul—while efficient, can be expensive if the company assesses a drop-off fee for crossing a border.

As a rule, always tell your car-rental company up front exactly which countries you'll be entering. Some companies levy extra insurance fees for trips taken in certain countries with certain types of cars (such as BMWs, Mercedes, and convertibles). Double-check with your rental agent that you have all the documentation you need before you drive off (especially if you're crossing borders into non-Schengen countries, such as Turkey, where you might need to present proof of insurance

Picking Up Your Car: Compare pickup costs (downtown can be less expensive than the airport) and explore drop-off options. Always check the hours of the location you choose: Many rental offices close from midday Saturday until Monday morning and, in smaller towns, at lunchtime.

When selecting a location, don't trust the agency's description of "downtown" or "city center." In some cases, a "downtown" branch can be on the outskirts of the city—a long, costly taxi ride from the center. Before choosing, plug the addresses into a mapping website. You may find that the "train station" location is handier. Returning a car at a big-city train station or downtown agency can be tricky; get precise details on the car drop-off location and hours, and allow ample time to find it.

When you pick up the rental car, check it thoroughly and make sure any damage is noted on your rental agreement. Rental agencies in Europe tend to charge for even minor damage, so be sure to mark everything. In Greece, your rental car is likely to come pre-scratched and dented for you (which is actually a plus, in that you're unlikely to get hassled for tiny dings in the vicinity of pre-existing ones). Find out how your car's gearshift, lights, turn signals, wipers, radio, and fuel cap function, and know what kind of fuel the

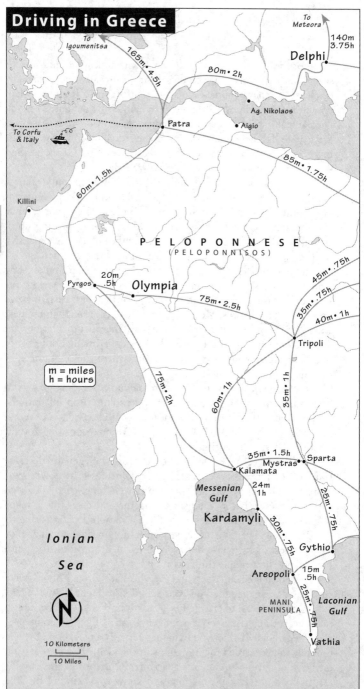

Driving in Greece

To Igoumenitsa

165m • 4.5h

To Meteora

140m
3.75h

Delphi

80m • 2h

Ag. Nikolaos

Patra

Aigio

To Corfu
& Italy

85m • 1.75h

60m • 1.5h

Killini

P E L O P O N N E S E
(PELOPONNISOS)

20m
.5h

Pyrgos

Olympia

75m • 2.5h

45m • .75h

35m • .75h

40m • 1h

m = miles
h = hours

Tripoli

75m • 2h

60m • 1h

35m • 1h

35m • 1.5h

Sparta

Mystras

Kalamata

*Messenian
Gulf*

24m
1h

25m
• .75h

Kardamyli

30m • .75h

Gythio

Ionian

Areopoli

15m
.5h

Sea

MANI
PENINSULA

25m
• .75h

*Laconian
Gulf*

N

10 Kilometers

10 Miles

Vathia

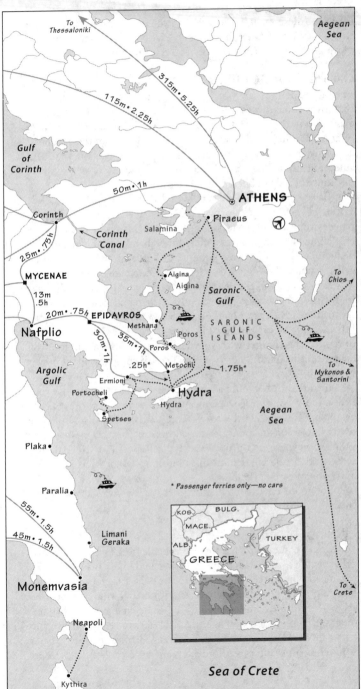

Aegean
Sea

To
Thessaloniki

315m • 5.25h

115m • 2.25h

Gulf
of
Corinth

50m • 1h

ATHENS

Corinth

Piraeus

Salamina

Corinth
Canal

25m • .75h

To
Chios

MYCENAE

Aigina

13m
.5h

Aigina

Saronic
Gulf

20m • .75h **EPIDAVROS**

Methana

SARONIC
GULF
ISLANDS

Nafplio

30m • 1h

35m • 1h

Poros

Poros

.25h*

Metochi

1.75h*

To
Mykonos &
Santorini

Argolic
Gulf

Ermioni

Hydra

Portocheli

Hydra

Spetses

Aegean
Sea

Plaka •

Paralia •

* Passenger ferries only—no cars

KOS.

BULG.

55m • 1.5h

MACE.

TURKEY

45m • 1.5h

Limani
Geraka

ALB.

GREECE

Monemvasia

Neapoli

To
Crete

Kythira

Sea of Crete

car takes (diesel vs. unleaded). When you return the car, make sure the agent verifies its condition with you. Some drivers take pictures of the returned vehicle as proof of its condition.

Car Insurance Options

When you rent a car, you are liable for a very high deductible, sometimes equal to the entire value of the car. Limit your financial risk with one of these options: Buy Collision Damage Waiver (CDW) coverage with a low or zero deductible from the car-rental company, get coverage through your credit card (free, if your card automatically includes zero-deductible coverage), or get collision insurance as part of a larger travel-insurance policy.

Basic **CDW** includes a very high deductible (typically $1,000-1,500), costs $15-30 a day (figure roughly 30-40 percent extra) and reduces your liability, but does not eliminate it. When you reserve or pick up the car, you'll be offered the chance to "buy down" the deductible to zero (for an additional $10-30/day; this is sometimes called "super CDW" or "zero-deductible coverage").

If you opt for **credit-card coverage,** you'll technically have to decline all coverage offered by the car-rental company, which means they can place a hold on your card (which can be up to the full value of the car). In case of damage, it can be time-consuming to resolve the charges with your credit-card company. Before you decide on this option, quiz your credit-card company about how it works.

If you're already purchasing a **travel-insurance policy** for your trip, adding collision coverage can be an economical option. For example, Travel Guard (www.travelguard.com) sells affordable renter's collision insurance as an add-on to its other policies; it's valid everywhere in Europe except the Republic of Ireland, and some Italian car-rental companies refuse to honor it, as it doesn't cover you in case of theft.

For more on car-rental insurance, see www.ricksteves.com/cdw.

Leasing

For trips of three weeks or more, consider leasing (which automatically includes zero-deductible collision and theft insurance). By technically buying and then selling back the car, you save lots of money on tax and insurance. Leasing provides you a brand-new car with unlimited mileage and a 24-hour emergency assistance program. You can lease for as little as 21 days to as long as five and a half months. Car leases must be arranged from the US. One of many companies offering affordable lease packages is Auto Europe.

Navigation Options

If you'll be navigating using your phone or a GPS unit from home, remember to bring a car charger and device mount.

Your Mobile Device: The mapping app on your mobile phone works fine for navigation in Europe, but for real-time turn-by-turn directions and traffic updates, you'll generally need Internet access. And driving all day while online can be very expensive. Helpful exceptions are Google Maps, Here WeGo, and Navmii, which provide turn-by-turn voice directions and recalibrate even when they're offline.

Download your map before you head out—it's smart to select a large region. Then turn off your cellular connection so you're not charged for data roaming. Call up the map, enter your destination, and you're on your way. View maps in standard view (not satellite view) to limit data demands.

GPS Devices: If you prefer the convenience of a dedicated GPS unit, consider renting one with your car ($10-30/day). These units offer real-time turn-by-turn directions and traffic without the data requirements of an app. Note that the unit may only come loaded with maps for its home country; if you need additional maps, ask. Also make sure your device's language is set to English before you drive off.

A less-expensive option is to bring a GPS device from home. Be aware that you'll need to buy and download European maps before your trip.

Maps and Atlases: Even when navigating primarily with a mobile app or GPS, I always make it a point to have a paper map. It's invaluable for getting the big picture, understanding alternate routes, and filling in when my phone runs out of juice. The free maps you get from your car-rental company usually don't have enough detail. It's smart to buy a better map before you go, or pick one up at a European gas station, bookshop, newsstand, or tourist shop (the Road Editions maps are tops).

DRIVING IN GREECE

Statistically, Greece is one of the most dangerous European countries to drive in. Traffic regulations that are severely enforced back home are treated as mere suggestions here. Even at major intersections in large towns, you might not see stop signs or traffic lights; drivers simply help each other figure out who goes next. And yet, like so many seemingly chaotic things in Greece, somehow it works quite smoothly. Still...drive defensively. Greeks won't hesitate to pass you, if they feel you're going too slowly.

Road Rules: The speed limit, almost never posted, can be hard to ascertain on backcountry roads. Generally, speed limits in Greece are as follows: city—50 km/hour; open roads—90 km/hour; di-

PRACTICALITIES

vided highways—110 km/hour, superhighways—130 km/hour. Making matters even more confusing, half of all Greek drivers seem to go double the speed limit, while the others go half the limit. On country roads and highways, the lanes are often a car-and-a-half wide, with wide shoulders, so passing is common—even when there's oncoming traffic in the other lane. Do as Greek drivers do on two-lane roads with wide shoulders—straddle the shoulder if someone wants to pass you.

Don't drink and drive: The legal alcohol limit is lower in Greece than in the US. Be aware of typical European road rules; for example, many countries require

STOP AND LEARN THESE ROAD SIGNS

Speed Limit (km/hr)	Yield	No Passing	End of No Passing Zone
One Way	Intersection	Main Road	Expressway
Danger	No Entry	Cars Prohibited	All Vehicles Prohibited
No Through Road	Restrictions No Longer Apply	Yield to Oncoming Traffic	No Stopping
Parking	No Parking	Customs or Toll Road	Peace

headlights to be turned on at all times, and nearly all forbid using a mobile phone without a hands-free headset. In Europe, you're not allowed to turn right on a red light, unless a sign or signal specifically authorizes it, and on expressways it's illegal to pass drivers on the right. Ask your car-rental company about these rules, or check the US State Department website (www.travel.state.gov, search for your country in the "Learn about your destination" box, then click "Travel and Transportation").

Road Signs: Because road numbers can be confusing and inconsistent, navigate by city names. Know the names of major cities en route to your destination. Often the signs will point only to the next major town, even if your final destination is a big city. Almost all road signs are in Greek and in English, but you should also know the name of your destination using the Greek alphabet—road sign transliteration can be confusing. Most Greek town names can be spelled a number of different ways in the Latin alphabet—don't be too worried about exact spelling, especially at the ends of town names.

Tolls: Special highways called *Ethniki Odos* (National Road) have tolls, which vary and usually must be paid in cash. This includes the road between Athens and the Peloponnese and part of the stretch between Athens and Delphi.

Fuel: Gasoline (*venzini*, βενζίνη) prices are around $6.50 a gallon for regular unleaded—labeled *95*, less for diesel, which is around $5 per gallon (*ntizel*, ντίζελ). Self-service gas stations are rare. Tell the attendant how much you want to spend and use cash. He's just there to pump gas, so don't expect him to wash your windshield or check your tires.

Parking and Safety: Choose parking places carefully. You'll rarely pay for parking, and parking laws are enforced only sporadically. If you're not certain, ask at your hotel (or ask another local) whether your space is legit. Keep your valuables in your hotel room, or, if you're between destinations, covered in your trunk. Leave nothing worth stealing in the car, especially overnight. If your car's a hatchback, take the trunk cover off at night so thieves can look in without breaking in. Try to make your car look locally owned by hiding the "tourist-owned" rental-company decals and putting a local newspaper in your front or back window. While you should avoid parking lots with twinkly asphalt, thieves break car windows anywhere, even at stoplights.

Drive carefully. If you're involved in an accident, expect a monumental headache—you will be blamed. Small towns come with speed traps.

TAXIS AND UBER

Most European taxis are reliable and cheap. In many cities, couples can travel short distances by cab for little more than two bus or subway tickets. Taxis can be your best option for getting to the airport for an early morning flight or to connect two far-flung destinations. If you like ride-booking services like Uber, these apps usually work in Europe just like they do in the US: You request a car on your mobile device (connected to Wi-Fi or a data plan), and the fare is automatically charged to your credit card. For more about taxis in Athens, see page 35.

FLIGHTS

The best comparison search engine for both international and intra-European flights is Kayak.com. An alternative is Google Flights, which has an easy-to-use system to track prices. For inexpensive flights within Europe, try Skyscanner.com.

Flying to Europe: Start looking for international flights about four to six months before your trip, especially for peak-season travel. Off-season tickets can usually be purchased a month or so in advance. Depending on your itinerary, it can be efficient to fly into one city and out of another. If your flight requires a connection in Europe, see our hints on navigating Europe's top hub airports at www.ricksteves.com/hub-airports.

Flying Within Europe: If you're considering a drive or bus ride that's more than five hours long, a flight may save you both time and money. When comparing your options, factor in the time it takes to get to the airport and how early you'll need to arrive to check in.

Well-known cheapo airlines include EasyJet and Ryanair. For flights within mainland Greece and to the Greek islands, the country's main carriers are **Olympic** (www.olympicair.com), **Aegean Airlines** (www.aegeanair.com), **Astra Airlines** (www.astra-airlines.gr), and **Sky Express** (www.skyexpress.gr). But be aware of the potential drawbacks of flying with a discount airline: nonrefundable and nonchangeable tickets, minimal or nonexistent customer service, and stingy baggage allowances with steep over-age fees. If you're traveling with lots of luggage, a cheap flight can quickly become a bad deal. To avoid unpleasant surprises, read the small print before you book.

These days you can also fly within Europe on major airlines affordably—and without all the aggressive restrictions—for around $100 a flight.

Flying to the US and Canada: Because security is extra tight for flights to the US, be sure to give yourself plenty of time at the airport. It's also important to charge your electronic devices before you board because security checks may require you to turn them on (see www.tsa.gov for the latest rules).

Resources from Rick Steves

Begin your trip at www.ricksteves.com: My mobile-friendly website is *the* place to explore Europe. You'll find thousands of fun articles, videos, photos, and radio interviews organized by country; a wealth of money-saving tips for planning your dream trip; monthly travel news dispatches; a video library of my travel talks; my travel blog; and my latest guidebook updates (www.ricksteves.com/update).

Our **Travel Forum** is an immense yet well-groomed collection of message boards where our travel-savvy community answers questions and shares their personal travel experiences—and our well-traveled staff chime in when they can be helpful (www.ricksteves.com/forums).

Our **online Travel Store** offers travel bags and accessories that I've designed specifically to help you travel smarter and lighter. These include my popular carry-on bags (which I live out of four months a year), money belts, totes, toiletries kits, adapters, other accessories, and a wide selection of guidebooks and planning maps (www.ricksteves.com/shop).

Choosing the right **rail pass** for your trip—amid hundreds of options—can drive you nutty. Our website will help you find the perfect fit for your itinerary and your budget: We offer easy, one-stop shopping for rail passes, seat reservations, and point-to-point tickets (www.ricksteves.com/rail).

Small Group Tours: Want to travel with greater efficiency and less stress? We offer more than 40 itineraries and have over 900 departures annually reaching the best destinations in this book... and beyond. We offer a 14-day tour of Athens and the Heart of Greece. You'll enjoy great guides, a fun bunch of travel partners (with small groups of 24 to 28 travelers), and plenty of room to spread out in a big, comfy bus when touring between towns. You'll find European adventures to fit every vacation length. For all the details, and to get our Tour Catalog, visit www.ricksteves.com/tours or call us at 425/608-4217.

Books: *Rick Steves Greece: Athens & the Peloponnese* is one of many books in my series on European travel, which includes country guidebooks, city guidebooks (Rome, Florence, Paris, London, etc.), Snapshot guidebooks (excerpted chapters from my country guides), Pocket guidebooks (full-color little books on big cities, including Athens), "Best Of" guidebooks (condensed country guides in a full-color, easy-to-scan format), and my budget-travel skills handbook, *Rick Steves Europe Through the Back Door.* Most of my titles are available as ebooks.

My phrase books—for Italian, French, German, Spanish, and Portuguese—are practical and budget-oriented. My other books include *Europe 101* (a crash course on art and history designed for travelers); *Mediterranean Cruise Ports* and *Northern European Cruise Ports* (how to make the most of your time in port); and *Travel as a Political Act* (a travelogue sprinkled with tips for bringing home a global perspective). A more complete list of my titles appears near the end of this book.

TV Shows: My public television series, *Rick Steves' Europe,* covers Europe from top to bottom with over 100 half-hour episodes, and we're working on new shows every year. To watch full episodes online for free, see www.ricksteves.com/tv.

Travel Talks on Video: You can raise your travel I.Q. with video versions of our popular classes (including my talks on travel skills, packing smart, European art for travelers, travel as a political act, and individual talks covering most European countries), see www.ricksteves.com/travel-talks.

Radio: My weekly public radio show, *Travel with Rick Steves*, features interviews with travel experts from around the world. It airs on 400 public radio stations across the US, and you can also listen to it as a podcast on iTunes, iHeartRadio, Stitcher, Tune In, and other platforms. A complete archive of programs (over 400 in all) is available at www.soundcloud.com/rick-steves.

Audio Tours on My Free App: I've also produced dozens of free, self-guided audio tours of the top sights in Europe, including sights in Athens. My audio tours and other audio content are available for free through my **Rick Steves Audio Europe app,** an extensive online library organized into handy geographic playlists. For more on my app, see page 9.

APPENDIX

Useful Contacts

Emergency Needs
Police, Fire, and Ambulance: 112 (Europe-wide in English)
Tourist Police: Tel. 171 or 1571 (English-speaking)
US Embassy in Athens: Tel. 210-720-2414, after-hours emergency tel. 210-729-4444; consular section open Mon-Fri 8:30-17:00, closed Sat-Sun and last Wed of month; Vasilissis Sophias 91, Metro: Megaro Moussikis, http://gr.usembassy.gov
Canadian Embassy in Athens: Tel. 210-727-3400, for after-hours emergency help call Canada collect at tel. 1-613-996-8885; open Mon-Fri 8:30-16:30, closed Sat-Sun; Ethnikis Antistaseos 48, www.canadainternational.gc.ca/greece-grece.

Holidays and Festivals

This list includes selected festivals, plus national holidays observed throughout Greece. Many sights and banks close on national holidays—keep this in mind when planning your itinerary. Before planning a trip around a festival, verify the dates with the festival website, the Greek tourist office (www.visitgreece.gr), or my "Upcoming Holidays and Festivals in Greece" web page (www.ricksteves.com/europe/greece/festivals).

Jan 1	New Year's Day
Jan 6	Epiphany
Mid-Jan-March	Carnival season (Apokreo), famous in Patra, peaks on the last Sunday before Lent
Late Feb-Early March	"Clean Monday" (Kathari Deftera), the first day of Lent in the Orthodox church
March 25	Greek Independence Day
April	Orthodox Good Friday-Easter Monday: April 26-29 in 2019; April 17-20 in 2020
May 1	Labor Day
June	Miaoulia Festival, Hydra (falls on the weekend closest to June 21)
June	Nafplio Festival, classical music
June-Aug	Athens & Epidavros Festival (music, opera, dance, and theater at the Odeon of Herodes Atticus beneath the Acropolis in Athens; drama and music at the Theater of Epidavros; www.greekfestival.gr/en)
July-Aug	Ancient Olympia International Festival (music, dance, and theater at the site of the ancient Olympics)
Aug 15	Assumption
Sept	Athens International Film Festival
Oct 28	Ohi Day (anniversary of the "No"; commemorates rejection of Mussolini's WWII ultimatum)
Dec 25-26	Christmas and "Second Day" of Christmas

Books and Films

To learn more about Greece past and present, check out a few of these books and films.

NONFICTION

Alexander the Great (Paul Anthony Cartledge, 2004). Alexander's legacy comes to life in this engaging history.

Apology (Plato, 390 B.C.). This is a classic for a reason, opening up a window into the Greek mind and soul.

The Cambridge Illustrated History of Ancient Greece (Paul Anthony Cartledge, 1997). Offered in large format, Cartledge's history is packed with gorgeous illustrations.

Colossus of Maroussi (Henry Miller, 1941). Miller tells a sometimes-graphic account of his down-and-out sojourn in Greece in the late 1930s.

A Concise History of Greece (Richard Clogg, 1986). For an overview of the 18th century to modern times, this history is surprisingly succinct.

Dinner with Persephone (Patricia Storace, 1996). This book is more than a memoir about living in Athens—it's one writer's critical look at modern Greek culture and family life.

Eleni (Nicholas Gage, 1983). Gage tells the riveting account of his quest to uncover the truth behind his mother's assassination during Greece's civil war.

The Greeks (H. D. F. Kitto, 1951). Considered the standard text on ancient Greece by a leading scholar, this decades-old work is still quite accessible.

The Greek Way (Edith Hamilton, 1930). Hamilton introduces the world of ancient Greece to the 20th century.

Inside Hitler's Greece (Mark Mazower, 1993). This shocking account of the Nazi occupation of Greece details the background for the country's civil war.

Lives (Plutarch, 100 A.D.). Written at the start of the second century, *Lives* is an epic attempt to chronicle the ancient world through biography.

Mani: Travels in the Southern Peloponnese (Patrick Leigh Fermor, 1958). This is the definitive book on the "forgotten" side of the peninsula.

Mediterranean in the Ancient World (Fernand Braudel, 1972). Braudel gives a marvelous overview of the ancient Mediterranean.

Mythology (Edith Hamilton, 1942). Along with *The Greek Way,* this is a must-read tome on classic myths and cultures.

The Nature of Alexander (Mary Renault, 1975). This biography from a famous novelist provides insight on Alexander the Great.

The Parthenon Enigma (Joan Breton Connelly, 2014). Connelly uses the temple's dramatic frieze—depicting, she says, human sacrifice—to go deep into the history of the Acropolis.

Persian Fire (Tom Holland, 2005). Holland offers an excellent history of the fifth-century B.C. Persian conflict.

Republic (Plato, 380 B.C.). In this classic, Plato captures the words of Socrates from Golden Age times.

Sailing the Wine-Dark Sea: Why the Greeks Matter (Thomas Cahill, 2003). Cahill astutely probes the relevance of ancient Greek culture to today's world.

The Spartans (Paul Anthony Cartledge, 2002). This history chronicles the rise and fall of the Spartan warriors.

The Summer of My Greek Taverna (Tom Stone, 2002). An American expat recounts his experiences in Greece while running a bar on the island of Patmos.

A Traveller's History of Greece (Timothy Boatswain and Colin Nicolson, 1990). This compact, well-written account covers the earliest times to the present.

FICTION

Corelli's Mandolin (Louis de Bernières, 1993). This novel about ill-fated lovers on a war-torn Greek island was made into a 2001 film starring Nicolas Cage and Penélope Cruz.

Deeper Shade of Blue (Paul Johnston, 2002). Detective Alex Mavros leaves Athens for the island of Trigono to find a missing woman.

Fire from Heaven (Mary Renault, 1969). The most renowned author of historical novels about Greece offers the dramatic story of Alexander the Great.

Gates of Fire (Steven Pressfield, 1998). Pressfield re-creates the Battle of Thermopylae, where 300 Spartans held back the Persian army—for a while.

The Iliad/The Odyssey (Homer, 850 B.C.). This classic epic follows the hero Odysseus through the Trojan War and his return home.

The King Must Die (Mary Renault, 1958). Renault reimagines the Theseus legend in this exciting tale.

The Last Temptation of Christ (Nikos Kazantzakis, 1953). Kazantzakis' literary reinterpretation of the Gospels is hailed internationally as a masterpiece.

Little Infamies (Panos Karnezis, 1903). This fine collection of short stories looks at the lives of Greek villagers with magical realism.

The Magus (John Fowles, 1965). An Englishman plays psychological games with a wealthy recluse on a Greek island.

Middlesex (Jeffrey Eugenides, 2002). An American author of Greek descent explores the Greek immigrant experience in the US, as well as sexual identity.

Stealing Athena (Karen Essex, 2008). The Parthenon plays a pivotal role in the lives of Pericles' mistress, Aspasia, and Lord Elgin's wife, Mary.

Uncle Petros and Goldbach's Conjecture (Apostolos Doxiadis, 1992). A Greek genius is obsessed with trying to prove one of mathematics' great theories.

The Walled Orchard (Tom Holt, 1990). Amusing and well-researched, this novel is the pseudo-autobiography of comic playwright Eupolis.

Zorba the Greek (Nikos Kazantzakis, 1946). A wily old rogue teaches life's lessons to a withdrawn intellectual.

TV AND FILM

300 (2006). Based on a graphic novel, this is a highly fictional and stylized account of the Battle of Thermopylae.

300: Rise of an Empire (2014). Also based on a graphic novel, this movie tells the tale of the final naval battle of Salamis after Thermopylae.

Alexander (2004). Colin Farrell plays the military genius who conquered the known world.

Boy on a Dolphin (1957). A beautiful sponge diver on Hydra, played by Sophia Loren, becomes aware of her cultural heritage.

Clash of the Titans (1981). Featuring an all-star cast including Laurence Olivier, Claire Bloom, and Maggie Smith, this adaptation of the Perseus myth is a classic.

The Guns of Navarone (1961). A team of English commandos tries to take out a WWII German artillery battery.

Mamma Mia! (2008). Filmed in the mainland region of Pelion and on the islands of Skiathos and Skopelos, this musical uses ABBA songs to tell the story of a young woman trying to find her father.

My Big Fat Greek Wedding (2002). Hilarity ensues when a Greek-American woman tries to plan her wedding while contending with her large and boisterous family (also a 2016 sequel, *My Big Fat Greek Wedding 2*).

My Family and Other Animals (2005). This film follows the adventures of an English family relocated to Greece in 1939.

My Life in Ruins (2009). This romantic comedy stars Nia Vardalos as a struggling tour guide leading her group of misfit tourists.

Never on Sunday (1960). Melina Mercouri stars as a Greek prostitute who is pursued by an American scholar with classical ideals.

Secrets of the Parthenon (2008). This NOVA episode, available on www.pbs.org, documents the restoration of the Parthenon.

Stella (1955). A young Greek woman must decide between falling in love and retaining her freedom.

The Trojan Women (1971). Euripides' classic tragedy of Troy's female aristocracy in chains features Katharine Hepburn, Vanessa Redgrave, and Irene Pappas.

Troy (2004). Brad Pitt stars as the petulant warrior Achilles in this adaptation of Homer's epic.

Z (1969). This thriller follows the assassination of a crusading politician—and the rise of the Greek junta—in the 1960s.

BOOKS AND FILMS FOR KIDS

Ancient Civilizations: Greece (Eva Bargallo I Chaves, 2004). Kids can brush up on ancient Greece, including history, art, government, and mythology.

Ancient Greece! 40 Hands-On Activities to Experience This Wondrous Age (Avery Hart and Paul Mantell, 1999). With this book, learn how to make traditional foods, build a model temple, and put on a play.

Greece (Changing Face of...) (Tasmin Osler, 2003). This nonfiction book weaves first-person accounts from modern Greeks with a summary of today's challenges.

Greece in Spectacular Cross-Section (Stephen Biesty, 2006). Kids and grown-ups alike will enjoy these cut-away diagrams re-creating ancient sites.

Hercules (1997). This animated Disney film is loosely based on the hero of Greek legend, Hercules, son of Zeus.

If I Were a Kid in Ancient Greece (Cricket Media, 2012). Kids can put themselves in the sandals of a young Grecian in this fun series.

Percy Jackson and the Olympians (Rick Riordan, 2005). A young boy learns that he is the son of a Greek god in this clever and amusing young adult series. Two *Percy Jackson* films bring the books to life (2010 and 2013).

The Random House Book of Greek Myths (Joan D. Vinge, 1999). Greek gods and goddesses are highlighted in this illustrated primer on Greek mythology.

This Is Greece (Miroslav Sasek, 1966). Reissued in 2009, Sasek's classic picture book captures the essence of ancient and modern Greece.

Conversions and Climate

Numbers and Stumblers

- Europeans write a few of their numbers differently than we do. 1 = 1, 4 = 4, 7 = 7.
- In Europe, dates appear as day/month/year, so Christmas 2019 is 25/12/19.
- Commas are decimal points and decimals are commas. A dollar and a half is $1,50, one thousand is 1.000, and there are 5.280 feet in a mile.
- When counting with fingers, start with your thumb. If you hold up your first finger to request one item, you'll probably get two.
- What Americans call the second floor of a building is the first floor in Europe.
- On escalators and moving sidewalks, Europeans keep the left "lane" open for passing. Keep to the right.

Metric Conversions

A kilogram is 2.2 pounds, and l liter is about a quart, or almost four to a gallon. A kilometer is six-tenths of a mile. I figure kilometers to miles by cutting them in half and adding back 10 percent of the original (120 km: 60 + 12 = 72 miles, 300 km: 150 + 30 = 180 miles).

1 foot = 0.3 meter	1 square yard = 0.8 square meter
1 yard = 0.9 meter	1 square mile = 2.6 square kilometers
1 mile = 1.6 kilometers	1 ounce = 28 grams
1 centimeter = 0.4 inch	1 quart = 0.95 liter
1 meter = 39.4 inches	1 kilogram = 2.2 pounds
1 kilometer = 0.62 mile	32°F = 0°C

Clothing Sizes

When shopping for clothing, use these US-to-European comparisons as general guidelines (but note that no conversion is perfect).

Women: For pants and dresses, add 30 in Greece (US 10 = Greece 40). For blouses and sweaters, add 8 for most of Europe (US 32 = European 40). For shoes, add 30-31 (US 7 = European 37/38).

Men: For shirts, multiply by 2 and add about 8 (US 15 = European 38). For jackets and suits, add 10. For shoes, add 32-34.

Children: Clothing is sized by height—in centimeters (2.5 inches = 1 cm), so a US size 8 roughly equates to 132-140. For shoes up to size 13, add 16-18, and for sizes 1 and up, add 30-32.

APPENDIX

Athens' Climate

First line, average daily high; second line, average daily low; third line, average days without rain. For more detailed weather statistics for destinations in this book (as well as the rest of the world), check www.wunderground.com.

J	F	M	A	M	J	J	A	S	O	N	D
56°	57°	60°	66°	75°	83°	88°	88°	82°	73°	66°	59°
44°	45°	47°	53°	60°	68°	73°	72°	67°	59°	53°	48°
24	22	26	27	28	28	30	30	28	27	24	24

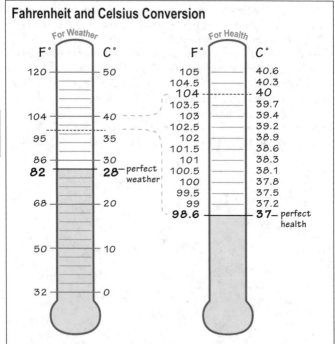

Fahrenheit and Celsius Conversion

Europe takes its temperature using the Celsius scale, while we opt for Fahrenheit. For a rough conversion from Celsius to Fahrenheit, double the number and add 30. For weather, remember that 28°C is 82°F—perfect. For health, 37°C is just right. At a launderette, 30°C is cold, 40°C is warm (usually the default setting), 60°C is hot, and 95°C is boiling. Your air-conditioner should be set at about 20°C.

Packing Checklist

Whether you're traveling for five days or five weeks, you won't need more than this. Pack light to enjoy the sweet freedom of true mobility.

Clothing

- ❑ 5 shirts: long- & short-sleeve
- ❑ 2 pairs pants (or skirts/capris)
- ❑ 1 pair shorts
- ❑ 5 pairs underwear & socks
- ❑ 1 pair walking shoes
- ❑ Sweater or warm layer
- ❑ Rainproof jacket with hood
- ❑ Tie, scarf, belt, and/or hat
- ❑ Swimsuit
- ❑ Sleepwear/loungewear

Money

- ❑ Debit card(s)
- ❑ Credit card(s)
- ❑ Hard cash (US $100-200)
- ❑ Money belt

Documents

- ❑ Passport
- ❑ Tickets & confirmations: flights, hotels, trains, rail pass, car rental, sight entries
- ❑ Driver's license
- ❑ Student ID, hostel card, etc.
- ❑ Photocopies of important documents
- ❑ Insurance details
- ❑ Guidebooks & maps

Toiletries Kit

- ❑ Basics: soap, shampoo, toothbrush, toothpaste, floss, deodorant, sunscreen, brush/comb, etc.
- ❑ Medicines & vitamins
- ❑ First-aid kit
- ❑ Glasses/contacts/sunglasses
- ❑ Sewing kit
- ❑ Packet of tissues (for WC)
- ❑ Earplugs

Electronics

- ❑ Mobile phone
- ❑ Camera & related gear
- ❑ Tablet/ebook reader/laptop
- ❑ Headphones/earbuds
- ❑ Chargers & batteries
- ❑ Phone car charger & mount (or GPS device)
- ❑ Plug adapters

Miscellaneous

- ❑ Daypack
- ❑ Sealable plastic baggies
- ❑ Laundry supplies: soap, laundry bag, clothesline, spot remover
- ❑ Small umbrella
- ❑ Travel alarm/watch
- ❑ Notepad & pen
- ❑ Journal

Optional Extras

- ❑ Second pair of shoes (flip-flops, sandals, tennis shoes, boots)
- ❑ Travel hairdryer
- ❑ Picnic supplies
- ❑ Water bottle
- ❑ Fold-up tote bag
- ❑ Small flashlight
- ❑ Mini binoculars
- ❑ Small towel or washcloth
- ❑ Inflatable pillow/neck rest
- ❑ Tiny lock
- ❑ Address list (to mail postcards)
- ❑ Extra passport photos

Greek Survival Phrases

Knowing a few phrases of Greek can help if you're traveling off the beaten path. Just learning the pleasantries (such as please and thank you) will improve your connections with locals, even in the bigger cities.

Because Greek words can be transliterated differently in English, I've also included the Greek spellings. Note that in Greek, a semicolon is used the same way we use a question mark.

English	Greek	Pronunciation
Hello. (formal)	Gia sas. Γειά σας.	yah sahs
Hi. / Bye. (informal)	Gia. Γειά.	yah
Good morning.	Kali mera. Καλή μέρα.	kah-lee meh-rah
Good afternoon.	Kali spera. Καλή σπέρα.	kah-lee speh-rah
Do you speak English?	Milate anglika? Μιλάτε αγγλικά;	mee-lah-teh ahn-glee-kah
Yes. / No.	Ne. / Ohi. Ναι. / Όχι.	neh / oh-hee
I understand.	Katalaveno Καταλαβαίνω.	kah-tah-lah-veh-noh
I (don't) understand.	(Den) katalaveno. (Δεν) καταλαβαίνω.	(dehn) kah-tah-lah-veh-noh
Please. (Also: You're welcome.)	Parakalo. Παρακαλώ.	pah-rah-kah-loh
Thank you (very much).	Efharisto (poli). Ευχαριστώ (πολύ).	ehf-hah-ree-stoh (poh-lee)
Excuse me. (Also: I'm sorry.)	Sygnomi. Συγνώμη.	seeg-noh-mee
(No) problem.	(Kanena) problima. (Κανένα) πρόβλημα.	(kah-neh-nah) prohv-lee-mah
Good.	Orea. Ωραία.	oh-reh-ah
Goodbye.	Antio. Αντίο.	ahd-yoh (think "adieu")
Good night.	Kali nikta. Καλή νύχτα.	kah-lee neek-tah
one / two	ena / dio ένα / δύο	eh-nah / dee-oh
three / four	tria / tessera τρία /τέσσερα	tree-ah / teh-seh-rah
five / six	pente / exi πέντε / έξι	pehn-deh / ehk-see
seven / eight	efta / ohto εφτά / οχτώ	ehf-tah / oh-toh
nine / ten	ennia / deka εννιά / δέκα	ehn-yah / deh-kah
hundred / thousand	ekato / hilia εκατό / χίλια	eh-kah-toh / heel-yah
How much?	Poso kani? Πόσο κάνει;	poh-soh kah-nee
euro	evro ευρώ	ev-roh
Write it?	Grapsete to? Γράψετε το;	grahp-seh-teh toh

English	Greek	Pronunciation
Is it free?	Ine dorean? Είναι δωρεάν;	ee-neh doh-ree-**ahn**
Is it included?	Perilamvanete? Περιλαμβάνεται;	peh-ree-lahm-**vah**-neh-teh

Where can I find /
   buy...?
	Pou boro na vro /
	   agoraso...?
	Που μπορώ να βρω /
	   αγοράσω...;
		poo boh-**roh** nah vroh /
		ah-goh-**rah**-soh

I'd like /
   We'd like...
	Tha ithela /
	   Tha thelame...
	Θα ήθελα /
	   Θα θέλαμε...
		thah **ee**-theh-lah /
		thah **theh**-lah-meh

...a room.	...ena dhomatio. ...ένα δωμάτιο.	**eh**-nah doh-**mah**-tee-oh

...a ticket
   to ___.
	...ena isitirio
	   gia ___.
	...ένα εισιτήριο
	   για ___.
		eh-nah ee-see-**tee**-ree-oh
		yah ___

Is it possible?	Ginete? Γίνεται;	**yee**-neh-teh
Where is...?	Pou ine...? Που είναι...;	poo **ee**-neh

...the bus station	...o stathmos ton
	   leoforion
	...ο σταθμός των
	   λεωφορίων
		oh **stahth**-mohs tohn
		leh-oh-foh-**ree**-ohn

...the train station	...o stathmos tou trenou ...ο σταθμός του τρένου	oh **stahth**-mohs too **treh**-noo

...the tourist
   information
   office
	...to grafeio
	   enimerosis
	   touriston
	...το γραφείο
	   ενημέρωσης
	   τουριστών
		too grah-**fee**-oh
		eh-nee-**meh**-roh-sis
		too-ree-**stohn**

toilet	toualeta τουαλέτα	twah-**leh**-tah
men / women	andres / gynekes άντρες / γυναικες	**ahn**-drehs / yee-**neh**-kehs
left / right	dexia / aristera δεξιά / αριστερά	dehk-see-**ah** / ah-ree-steh-**rah**
straight	efthia ευθεία	ehf-**thee**-ah
At what time...	Ti ora... Τι ώρα...	tee **oh**-rah
...does this open / close?	...anigete / klinete? ...ανοίγετε / κλείνετε;	ah-**nee**-yeh-teh / **klee**-neh-teh
Just a moment.	Ena lepto. Ένα λεπτό.	**eh**-nah lep-**toh**

now / soon /
   later
	tora / se ligo /
	   argotera
	τώρα / σε λίγο / αργότερα
		toh-rah / seh **lee**-goh /
		ar-**goh**-teh-rah

today / tomorrow	simera / avrio σήμερα / αύριο	**see**-meh-rah / **ahv**-ree-oh

In a Greek Restaurant

English	Greek	Pronunciation
I'd like to reserve...	*Tha ithela na kliso...* Θα ήθελα να κλείσω...	thah **ee**-theh-lah nah **klee**-soh
We'd like to reserve...	*Tha thelame na klisoume...* Θα θέλαμε να κλείσουμε...	thah **theh**-lah-meh nah **klee**-soo-meh
...a table for one / two.	*...ena trapezi gia enan / dio.* ...ένα τραπέζι για έναν / δύο.	**eh**-nah trah-**peh**-zee yah **eh**-nahn / **dee**-oh.
non-smoking	*mi kapnizon* μη καπνίζων	mee kahp-**nee**-zohn
Is this table free?	*Ine eleftero afto to trapezi?* Είναι ελεύθερο αυτό το τραπέζι;	**ee**-neh eh-**lef**-teh-roh ahf-**toh** toh trah-**peh**-zee
The menu (in English), please.	*Ton katalogo (sta anglika) parakalo.* Τον κατάλογο (στα αγγλικά) παρακαλώ.	tohn kah-**tah**-loh-goh (stah ahn-glee-**kah**) pah-rah-kah-**loh**
service (not) included	*to servis (den) perilamvanete* το σέρβις (δεν) περιλαμβάνεται	toh **sehr**-vees (dehn) peh-ree-lahm-**vah**-neh-teh
cover charge	*kouver* κουβέρ	koo-**vehr**
"to go"	*gia exo* για έξω	yah **ehk**-soh
with / without	*me / horis* με / χωρίς	meh / hoh-**rees**
and / or	*ke / i* και / ή	keh / ee
fixed-price meal	*menu* μενού	meh-**noo**
specialty of the house	*i specialite tou magaziou* η σπεσιαλιτέ του μαγαζιού	ee speh-see-ah-lee-**teh** too mah-gah-zee-**oo**
half-portion	*misi merida* μισή μερίδα	mee-**see** meh-**ree**-dah
daily special	*to piato tis meras* το πιάτο της μέρας	toh pee-**ah**-toh tees meh-rahs
appetizers	*proto piato* πρώτο πιάτο	**proh**-toh pee-**ah**-toh
bread	*psomi* ψωμί	psoh-**mee**
cheese	*tiri* τυρί	tee-**ree**
sandwich	*sandwich or toast* σάντουιτς, τόστ	"sandwich," "toast"
soup	*soupa* σούπα	**soo**-pah
salad	*salata* σαλάτα	sah-**lah**-tah
meat	*kreas* κρέας	**kray**-ahs

English	Greek	Pronunciation
poultry / chicken	*poulerika / kotopoulo* πουλερικα / κοτόπουλο	poo-leh-ree-**kah** / koh-**toh**-poo-loh
fish / seafood	*psari / psarika* ψάρι / ψαρικά	**psah**-ree / psah-ree-**kah**
shellfish	*thalassina* θαλασσινά	thah-lah-see-**nah**
fruit	*frouta* φρούτα	**froo**-tah
vegetables	*lahanika* λαχανικά	lah-hah-nee-**kah**
dessert	*gliko* γλυκό	lee-**koh**
(tap) water	*nero (tis vrisis)* νερο (της βρύσης)	neh-**roh** (tees **vree**-sees)
mineral water	*metalliko nero* μεταλλικό νερό	meh-tah-lee-**koh** neh-**roh**
milk	*gala* γάλα	**gah**-lah
(orange) juice	*himos (portokali)* χυμός (πορτοκάλι)	hee-**mohs** (por-toh-**kah**-lee)
coffee	*kafes* καφές	kah-**fehs**
tea	*tsai* τσάι	**chah**-ee
wine	*krasi* κρασί	krah-**see**
wine (printed on label)	*inos* οίνος	**ee**-nohs
red / white	*kokkino / aspro* κόκκινο / άσπρο	**koh**-kee-noh / **ah**-sproh

sweet / dry /
   semi-dry
	gliko / ksiro /
	   imixiro
	γλυκό / ξηρό /
	   ημίξηρο
		lee-**koh** / ksee-**roh** /
		   ee-**meek**-see-roh

glass / bottle	*potiri / boukali* ποτήρι /μπουκάλι	poh-**tee**-ree / boo-**kah**-lee
beer	*bira* μπύρα	**bee**-rah
Here you are. (when given food)	*Oriste.* Ορίστε.	oh-**ree**-steh
Enjoy your meal!	*Kali orexi!* Καλή όρεξη!	kah-**lee oh**-rehk-see
(To your) health! (like "Cheers!")	*(Stin i) gia mas!* (Στην υ) γειά μας!	(stee nee) yah mahs
Another.	*Allo ena.* Άλλο ένα.	**ah**-loh **eh**-nah

Bill, please.	*Ton logariasmo*
	   parakalo.
	Τον λογαριασμό
	   παρακαλώ.
		tohn loh-gah-ree-ahs-**moh**
		   pah-rah-kah-**loh**

tip	*bourbouar* μπουρμπουάρ	boor-boo-**ar**
Very good!	*Poli oreo!* Πολύ ωραίο!	poh-**lee** oh-**ray**-oh
Delicious!	*Poli nostimo!* Πολύ νόστιμο!	poh-**lee nohs**-tee-moh

INDEX

INDEX

MAP INDEX

Explore Europe

At ricksteves.com you can browse through thousands of articles, videos, photos and radio interviews, plus find a wealth of money-saving travel tips for planning your dream trip. And with our mobile-friendly website, you can easily access all this great travel information anywhere you go.

TV Shows

Preview the places you'll visit by watching entire half-hour episodes of Rick Steves' Europe (choose from all 100 shows) on-demand, for free.

your travel dreams into affordable reality

Radio Interviews

Enjoy ready access to Rick's vast library of radio interviews covering travel

tips and cultural insights that relate specifically to your Europe travel plans.

Travel Forums

Learn, ask, share! Our online community of savvy travelers is a great resource

for first-time travelers to Europe, as well as seasoned pros. You'll find forums on each country, plus travel tips and restaurant/hotel reviews. You can even ask one of our well-traveled staff to chime in with an opinion.

Travel News

Subscribe to our free Travel News e-newsletter, and get monthly updates from Rick on what's happening in Europe.

Rick's Free Travel App

Get your FREE **Rick Steves Audio Europe**™ app to enjoy…

- Dozens of self-guided tours of Europe's top museums, sights and historic walks
- Hundreds of tracks filled with cultural insights and sightseeing tips from Rick's radio interviews
- All organized into handy geographic playlists
- For Apple and Android

With Rick whispering in your ear, Europe gets even better.

Find out more at ricksteves.com

Gear up for your next adventure at ricksteves.com

Light Luggage

Pack light and right with Rick Steves' affordable, custom-designed rolling carry-on bags, backpacks, day packs and shoulder bags.

Accessories

From packing cubes to moneybelts and beyond, Rick has personally selected the travel goodies that will help your trip go smoother.

Save time and energy

This guidebook is your independent-travel toolkit. But for all it delivers, it's still up to you to devote the time and energy it takes to manage the preparation and logistics that are essential for a happy trip. If that's a hassle, there's a solution.

Rick Steves Tours

A Rick Steves tour takes you to Europe's most interesting places with great